D1035260

CORDED WARE AND GLOBULAR AMPHORAE NORTH-EAST OF THE CARPATHIANS

Published with the assistance of the
Gulbenkian Foundation

CORDED WARE AND GLOBULAR AMPHORAE NORTH-EAST OF THE CARPATHIANS

TADEUSZ SULIMIRSKI

UNIVERSITY OF LONDON
THE ATHLONE PRESS
1968

Published by
THE ATHLONE PRESS
UNIVERSITY OF LONDON
at 2 Gower Street, London WC1
Distributed by Constable & Co Ltd
12 *Orange Street, London,* WC2

U.S.A.
Oxford University Press Inc.
New York

Canada
Oxford University Press
Toronto

485 11091 1

Printed in Great Britain by
WESTERN PRINTING SERVICES LTD
BRISTOL

For my wife, Olga, in token of my deep gratitude for her help in many excavations, for her unfailing devotion, understanding and encouragement over many years without which this book could never have been written.

Preface

Topics connected with the Corded Ware assemblage are among the most widely discussed in archaeological literature dealing with the Late Neolithic in Europe. Many controversial views have been expressed with regard to the origin of the assemblage, its chronology and relation to other coeval cultures, in particular to the East European Ochre-graves, and its role in the formation of the Middle Bronze Age cultures of Europe, etc. Questions as to the origin and the home of the earliest Indo-Europeans have also been linked with and involved in its discussion. Another group of Late Neolithic remains about which there are similar controversies is the Globular Amphora culture, especially its eastern branch. Not only is its origin disputable, but also its character, its extent, and its role in the prehistoric past of the territories in which its remains were found have been very differently interpreted.

One important reason for this state of affairs seems to be the poor knowledge of the archaeological remains within the territory concerned, which extends east of the rivers Vistula and San, and of the Carpathians, as far as the Dnieper in the east, and south of the Pripet Marshes down to the Black Sea coast (Map 1). From time immemorial countless successions of expanding peoples have crossed this territory from east to west or from west to east. Central and West European cultures met there and overlapped with those of the eastern and south-eastern part of the continent. The importance of this area for the study of the prehistoric past of wider parts of Europe has been recognized by many archaeologists.

A large number of remains of the Corded Ware assemblage and of the Globular Amphorae were found within the territory described above in which both were intrusive. They overlapped there, partly with each other, but mainly with the remains of other local cultures of a different type, both of Central European parentage (e.g. the Funnel Beakers) and of East European origin (e.g. the Tripolye culture). This circumstance, combined with the wide distribution of the two intrusive cultures within and outside our area, gives a unique opportunity for the study of their equation with the various Central and East European cultures, and consequently for a proper correlation of the chronological scheme established for the Neolithic and Early Bronze Ages of Central Europe with that current in Eastern Europe for the same periods.

I have been engaged in the study of these topics for over thirty years. In this connection I visited (before the last war) all the main museums and archaeological collections of the territory concerned and of the neighbouring areas, including the U.S.S.R. However, my study is based mainly on excavations made by my collaborators and colleagues and by myself of nearly 150 barrow-graves, of several cemeteries, slab-cist graves, and settlements, etc. in the Sub-Carpathian area, West Podolia, and West Volhynia, which at that time were part of pre-war South-East Poland, and have now since the war been incorporated into the Ukraine.

Only a few short preliminary reports on these works and a few articles dealing with some special problems involved have so far appeared. I had intended to publish the results of my studies, with full reports on the excavations, in a series of three volumes. The first of these, dealing with the Middle Bronze Age Komarów culture, was already at the printers; unfortunately, two of its typescripts perished during the war. The second volume was devoted to the Corded Ware of the territory mentioned above; the work was well advanced before the war. The theme of the third intended volume was the eastern branch of the Globular Amphora culture; the relevant material was for the most part in hand.

During my recent journeys to Poland, especially to Cracow, and to Lviv (Lwów) I was able to recover most of my pre-war notes, records, drawings, and photographs of the material, which safely survived the war, and these form the foundation of the present work. They have been supplemented by the results of post-war investigations in the area, as far as these have been published. The discussions which I have had with colleagues, archaeologists working on similar problems, were very useful; particularly valuable were their communications regarding the relevant archaeological material to a great extent unpublished hitherto, which is in museums and other institutions in the U.S.S.R. and in Poland, and which they showed me always willingly and with great kindness.

The main object of the present work is the study of the relative chronology of the remains of the several Corded Ware groups and of the Globular Amphorae found within the huge territory described above (Map 1), extending east of the Vistula as far as the Dnieper, with a view to establishing the consecutive stages in their development and their position in the wider chronological framework embracing all the cultures of the area. I consider this to be of fundamental importance for any further study and proper understanding of all the changes in the evolution of the various cultures in the specified territory, as well as of the social and economic development of the peoples concerned. Accordingly the relations between the groups one with the other have been examined and likewise those with other contemporary cultures, inside and outside the area under review. Less attention has been given to a detailed description of the remains in question—unless they were important for the purposes above—and likewise to social, economic, etc. conditions, which have been discussed only on occasion.

The first three chapters are devoted to a detailed study of the western barrow-graves, in particular to the Sub-Carpathian culture. This was the best investigated of all groups of Corded Ware in the area under review and was the object of many years of study by me. I was able to establish a number of consecutive stages in its development and how they corresponded with other groups and cultures of the neighbouring territories. The results of this research provide the basis for the chronological division of other related groups of Corded Ware, and consequently for the establishment of their position in a wider chronological framework.

In the following two chapters, IV and V, various groups of the Globular Amphorae and its derived cultures, with their evolution, are discussed, and their gradual merging into the local groups is revealed. It seems that in the light of these results the theories which place the origin of the Globular Amphorae somewhere within our area must be definitely abandoned.

Two subsequent chapters, VI and VII, deal with the eastern barrow-graves, including the Ochre-graves, the Middle Dnieper, and the Usatovo cultures. Their relations with one another, with the Central European Corded Ware assemblage and with the local cultures are examined and their chronology is also discussed.

Chapter VIII contains a short synopsis of the results obtained and which have been summarized in the Chronological Scheme (Table 21). A number of wider issues are then briefly reviewed in the light of this, mainly concerning the Corded Ware, Ochre-graves, Globular Amphorae, and the Tripolye culture. The last chapter is devoted to a concise survey of the Bronze Age cultures deriving from those of the earlier periods dealt with in the preceding chapters, and it is given because there was definitely no break in evolution; the Middle Bronze Age cultures represent evidently only a new stage in the development of the earlier cultures.

The second part of the volume consists of a description of the actual archaeological material from the territory under review, namely the graves of all groups of the Corded Ware complex and of their successive cultures, and the graves attributable to the Globular Amphora culture and its derivatives. All relevant excavation reports hitherto unpublished are included.

The first section of Part II is devoted entirely to the cemetery of Komarów, the largest barrow-grave cemetery investigated completely, and to the study of its conditions and of the relative chronology of its graves.

In the second and third sections are described well over two hundred barrow-graves investigated within the western division of our territory; about one-third of these (including those of the Middle Bronze Age Komarów culture) were excavated by myself and my associates. Most of these graves, except the last-named, had already been described, mainly in local periodicals in Polish, sometimes in larger publications, which are now for the most part out of print or hardly accessible.

In including a description of Bronze Age graves it has been taken into account that barrow-graves attributable to the various groups of the Corded Ware assemblage often appear in cemeteries together with graves of the Komarów or Trzciniec cultures. There, they sometimes formed small tightly knit groups and were evidently the burial place of a single family or clan. To describe them in different publications according to their chronological classification would not seem, therefore, a proper method of dealing with them. The actual position of barrow-graves of different ages within such small groups was likewise of importance for the study of their relative chronology, which applies especially to the poorly furnished burials. This has been well demonstrated by the conditions in the cemetery of Komarów.

In the fourth section, barrow-graves of the eastern division of the territory under review are listed and the relevant literature quoted. The steppe Ochre-graves did not form part of the Corded Ware assemblage which is our main concern here, and the other two, the Middle Dnieper and the Usatovo cultures, were hybrid groups, Corded Ware being only one of the contributors in their formation. Most of the graves listed here have been described or dealt with in relatively recent publications, mainly in Russian or Ukrainian but also in West European languages, and these are in the main accessible to the scholars concerned.

The fifth section provides a short description of all graves attributable to the Globular Amphora culture and its derivatives from the territory under review and from Romania. Potsherds of the culture found in settlements and sites of other cultures are also included. The final section consists of various supplementary lists of sites.

Ukrainian, not Russian, names have been used for sites in the Ukraine, unless these were published in books and papers exclusively in Russian. Polish names have been used for the sites within the former Polish territory which were quoted or described in pre-war publications, or were investigated by my associates and myself and were on my pre-war lists. In transliterating Ukrainian and Russian names the common Slavonic signs have been applied: š to denote the sound 'sh', and č for 'tch'.

Numbers in the text after references to sites are those under which they have been described in the second part of the work. A list of abbreviations applied in the footnotes is given on p. xxiii.

This book was completed by the end of 1962. The literature accessible in London up to the end of 1964 dealing with the topics discussed has, however, been taken into account and the text has been brought up to date as far as practicable.

ACKNOWLEDGEMENTS

I BEGAN my investigations, which have resulted in the present volume, through the encouragement of the late Dr Leon Kozłowski, who was my professor at the University of Lwów, and whom I always remember with great respect and affection. I am greatly indebted to many of my friends, former students, colleagues, and many other persons, and to several institutions, for their help and co-operation without which I should not have been able to proceed with and complete my work. This applies first to those who helped me during my pre-war investigations and excavations, in particular to Dr Marcjan Smiszko, then Assistant at the University of Lwów, now Director of the Institute of Social Sciences of the Ukrainian Academy there; the late Dr Jan Bryk; Dr Józef Grabowski, then Director of the Museum in Stanisławów; Dr Rudolf Jamka, now Professor at the University of Cracow; the late Dr Volodymir Kobilnyk, Sambor; Dr J. Pasternak, then Director of the Ševčenko Museum, Lwów; the late Jan Fitzke, M.A., then Keeper of the Museum at Łuck; to my former students at both the University of Lwów and the Yagiellonian University in Cracow, in particular to Mrs I. Siwek-Wróbel, now in Canada; the late Misses J. Vogel, M.A., and A. Kimmel; Dr Kazimierz Żurowski, now Professor at the University of Poznań; Dr Adolf Nasz, now Professor at the University of Wrocław; Messrs Blajda, Stanisław Oczko, Zygmunt Walenta, K. Wardzała, and many others; to all the excavators, whose names I do not remember, on whose devotion, care, and skill the success of the work and proper results often depended. I am likewise very grateful to all those who offered me their help and hospitality during excavations in various parts of the country, to those landowners, teachers, etc., and their families, of whom I can only remember the names of a few: Messrs Bohusiewicz, Podhajczyki; Włodzimierz Czaykowski, Pietniczany-Sarniki; Baron J. Horoch, Gwoździec Stary; Tomasz Horodyski, Komarów; Dr S. Iszkowski, Rokitno; Henryk Janko, Hoszany; Włodzimierz Konopacki, Lisieczyńce; Kowalczewski, Daszawa; Count Stanisław Krasicki, Stratyn; Henryk Lessig, Zaborol; Jan Pawlikowski, Kniażyce; Bronisław Skibniewski, Stojańce; Kazimierz Wielowieyski, Olejowa-Korolówka; Count Roman Zaleski, Krasów.

I was able to undertake my excavations thanks to the funds provided by several institutions: the Polish Academy (Polska Akademia Umiejętności), Cracow; 'Fundusz Bezrobocia' (the Unemployment Fund) in various parts of the country; the Museums in Stanisławów and Łuck; by the Polish National Culture Fund (Fundusz Kultury Narodowej) which likewise sponsored my two-month study in 1934 of the archaeological collections in nineteen towns of the U.S.S.R., mainly in the Ukraine, and enabled me also to visit archaeological museums in Romania, Hungary, and Czechoslovakia.

I owe much to Professor R. Jamka, the late Dr Tadeusz Reyman, Director of the Archaeological Museum in Cracow, Dr Maria Trzepacz-Cabalska, Mrs Jadwiga Zakrzewska, Mrs Renata Michalska-Rogozińska, and to other members of the staff of the Museum for the care which they took in saving my notes and reports from destruction during the war and in preserving them afterwards.

For their willingness to show me unpublished archaeological material from post-war excavations, and for providing me with information, during my recent visits to Poland and the U.S.S.R., I am very grateful particularly to Dr Jan Kowalczyk and Mr Jerzy Głosik, M.A., both of the State Archaeological Museum (Państwowe Muzeum Archeologiczne), Warsaw; Professor Aleksander Gardawski, of the University of Lublin; Dr Jan Gurba, Lublin; to Messrs Dr Jan Machnik, and Jan Gromnicki, M.A., both in Cracow; to Professor M. I. Artamonov, then Director of the Hermitage Museum, Leningrad and B. A. Latynin, Keeper of the Neolithic Department there; V. M. Raushenbakh, Deputy Director of the Historical Museum, Moscow; to the scholars working at the Archaeological Institute of the Academy of the U.S.S.R. in Moscow, in particular to Messrs Iu. V. Kukharenko, I. I. Artemenko, V. S. Titov, and Mrs E. K. Černyš; S. N. Bibikov, Director of the Archaeological Institute of the Ukrainian Academy in Kiev; to the scholars working at that Institute, in particular Messrs V. M. Danylenko, M. L. Makarevych, M. Shmaglii, D. I. Telegin, A. I. Terenozhkin, I. N. Zakharuk, and Mrs O. G. Šapošnikova; Misses T. G. Movša and T. F. Zaliska of the Historical Museum in Kiev; Dr M. Smiško, Director of the Institute of Social Sciences in Lviv; Mr I. K. Sviešnikov of the same Institute; and to the personnel of the Archaeological Section of the Historical Museum in Lviv.

I have also to express my thanks for their very kind help and advice to Professor C. F. C. Hawkes of the University of Oxford, and especially to Professor W. F. Grimes, Director of the University of London Institute of Archaeology, for reading my typescript, and to friends and colleagues there, in particular to Professor J. D. Evans, Mr E. Pyddoke, Miss J. du Plat Taylor, Miss G. C. Talbot, Dr I. W. Cornwall, Dr F. R. Hodson, Mr H. M. Stewart, Mrs M. Hunt, to the late Mr M. B. Cookson, and Mrs V. M. Conlon; further to Miss B. J. Kirkpatrick, Librarian of the Royal Anthropological Institute, to Mr J. Hopkins, Librarian of the Society of Antiquaries of London, and to Dr M. Danilewicz, Librarian and Director of the Polish Library, London. I am also indebted to Miss M. Jefferson, Mr D. J. Welsh, B.A., and Mr N. H. MacMichael, for correcting and improving my English text, to Dr J. Mękarska, and to my sons Karol and Jerzy for their help in preparing the illustrative material.

The financial assistance, for which I am very grateful, received from the *Seven Pillars of Wisdom* Trust (Professor A. W. Lawrence), and in particular the grant from the Calouste Gulbenkian Foundation, were essential for the resumption of my work in London and its conclusion in the present volume. Special grants received from the Foundation, and also from the Pilgrim Trust Fund of the British Academy, the University of London Central Research Fund, the Gordon Childe Fund, the Polish Research Centre, London, and the Polish University College Association Ltd, enabled me in recent years to undertake visits to archaeological collections in several towns in Poland, Czechoslovakia, Hungary, Romania, Yugoslavia, the U.S.S.R., and to study the East European collections in the museums in Paris, Lyons, and Berlin.

T.S.

Contents

PART II

DESCRIPTION OF GRAVES AND REPORTS ON EXCAVATIONS

TABLES

LIST OF TABLES

List of Maps

List of Plans

LIST OF PLANS

List of Figures

B. Narodyči (no. 229) – decorated tulip-shaped pots and a bowl, from barrow-graves of the cemetery I (after I. Levyckyj).

34. Bronze ornaments found in barrow-graves of the Middle Bronze Age.
   1–7. Skurcze (no. 158) – bronze armlet with overlapping terminals, small spiral ring, oval armlet, two spiral bracelets and two flint arrow-heads.
   8. Unijew-Werników (no. 187) – bracelet with spiral terminals from a flat grave.
   9, 10. Kamionka Strumiłowa – spiral bronze armlet and bronze dagger with four rivet holes, found together (hoard or grave?).
   11, 12. Barh (no. 192) – spiral bronze armlet and bronze necklace with spiral terminals, from a barrow-grave.

35. Various stone and metal weapons or implements of the Bronze Age.
   1. Kiev – flanged bronze axe (Czartoryski Museum, Cracow).
   2. Ukraine – palstave of North-West European type (Choynowski collection of the Polish Army Museum in Warsaw, no. 32531–18805).
   3. Ukraine – winged celt of Bohemian type (Choynowski collection, as above, no. 32876).
   4. Ukraine – palstave of Lusatian type (Choynowski collection, as above, no. 32530–18804).
   5. Przewodów, district of Sokal – palstave of North-West European type (before the War at the Dzieduszycki Museum, Lwów).
   6. Darabani, Bessarabia -- copper (or bronze) shaft-hole axe found in the Tripolyan settlement on the Dniester (before the War in the possession of Mr M. Abrojevici, Cernauţi).
   7, 12. Horodenka (no. 102) – bronze socketed axe and flint dagger of type II, found in a barrow-grave (before the War at the Dzieduszycki Museum, Lwów).
   8, 9. Komarów – copper shaft-hole axe and copper (or bronze?) knife, found in the 19th c. on the site of the settlement investigated subsequently in 1935 (at the Historical Museum Lviv, no. 1639).
   10. Sapohów, district of Stanisławów – copper shaft-hole axe (State Archaeological Museum, Warsaw).
   11. Avramovka near Dniepropetrovsk – winged bronze celt of Lusatian type (before the War at the Archaeological Museum, Dniepropetrovsk, no. 9).
   13. Komarów 48 – stone battle-axe (b–6).
   14. Radzimin IV–1878 (no. 155) – small diorite battle-axe.
   15. Komarów 20 – small stone battle-axe (f-3).
   16. Krasów IV (no. 67) – whetstone or unperforated hammer (g-3).

List of Plates

1. Views of a few burials in barrow-graves.
   1. Ozimina II (no. 53). The almost completely decayed skeleton.
   2. Płaucza Wielka (no. 75). Skeleton of grave I, with legs contracted (Plate 6:22).
   3. Balice XVI (no. 1). Skeleton in an extended position, a flint dagger in its right hand (Plate 11:2), stone battle-axe in the left hand (Plate 10:10) and mace-head near its right shoulder (Plate 10:9) (after A. Chizzola).
   4. Rusiłów (no. 84). Crouched skeleton on its right side, a stone slab behind it (Plate 8:1) (after J. Bryk).
   5. Rokitno 3 (no. 82). Crouched skeleton on its left side.

2. A few burials with mutilated skeletons in barrow-graves.
   1, 2. Buhłow II (no. 194). Two views of the dismembered skeleton in grave 2, the skull displaced, the single-lugged mug among the bones (Plate 9:6, 10, 11).
   3. Buhłow I. Dismembered skeleton of grave 'a'.
   4. Komarów 38 (no. 47) Grave-goods indicating the site of the burial (Fig. 13:8, Fig. 15:12, Fig. 16:10).

3. Pottery of the Przemyśl group of barrow-graves.
   1. Koropuż (no. 17). Grave-goods: Thuringian amphora (a) of type I; flint knife (b); bone disc (g); cord-decorated potsherd (d); a few sherds typical of the Funnel Beaker ware (c, e, f, h).
   2, 6. Balice VII (no. 1). Small pedestalled dish and a Miechów amphora.
   3–5. Brusno (no. 2). Bowl, small amphora and Miechów amphora.

4. Thuringian amphorae and a few other vessels from Sub-Carpathian barrow-graves.
   1. Kołokolin IV (no. 66) – 'a', type I.
   2. Balice XV (no. 1) – type IIC.
   3. Załuże (no. 167) – dark double-handled vessel.
   4. Lisieczyńce (no. 203) – type I.
   5. Krasów II (no. 67) – type I.
   6. Ostapie 3 (no. 213) – double-handled vase.
   7. Zaborol (no. 188) – a variety of Miechów amphora.
   8. Nowosiółka Jaruzelskich III (no. 212) – debased Thuringian amphora of type IIa.
   9. Nowosiółka Jaruzelskich II – debased Thuringian amphora of type IIa.

5. Thuringian amphorae from Sub-Carpathian barrow-graves.
   1. Stratyn 2 (no. 87) – type IIa.
   2. Nowosiółki Liskie (no. 73) – special type.
   3. Ubynie (no. 90) – type IIa.
   4. Kulczyce Szlacheckie II (no. 49) – type IIa.
   5. Stratyn I (no. 87) – debased type IIa.
   6. Wiktorów VIII (no. 57) – debased type IIC.
   7. Siwki I–1878 (no. 157) – type IIC.
   8. Rokitno 2 (no. 82) – debased type IIC.
   9. Rokitno 6 – type IIa.
   10, 11. Małoszynka-Surmaczówka (no. 21), – two specimens of debased type IIa.

6. Beakers, bowls and cups from the Sub-Carpathian barrow-graves.
   1, 9, 20. Kołokolin I (no. 66) – cord-decorated beaker (M) undecorated beaker (N), and damaged bowl (L).

2. Nowosiółki (Przemyśl) (no. 25) – cord-decorated beaker.
3, 15, 16. Łotatniki 2 (no. 50) – beaker (b), handled bowl (a), wide deep bowl (c).
4. Komarów 39 (no. 47) – wide beaker or bowl (a).
5. Ostapie 5 (no. 213) – beaker.
6. Siwki I–1878 (no. 157) – beaker.
7, 8. Nowosiółki Liskie (no. 73) – pot and beaker.
10. Ostapie 3 – undecorated cup.
11. Balice XVI (no. 1) – wide bowl.
12. Kulczyce Szlacheckie III (no. 49) – beaker (H).
13, 14, 18. Siedliska B (no. 30) – two small cups and beaker.
17. Ostapie 6 (no. 213) – vessel from grave 2.
19. Kołokolin III (no. 66) – 'Złota' cup (k–1) from grave 1.
21. Morawsko (no. 24) – large beaker.
22. Płaucza Wielka (no. 75) – handled jug from grave 1.
23. Dziedziłów (no. 62) – cord-decorated 'Złota' handled cup.
24. Balice IV – cord-decorated 'Złota' handled cup.

7. Various vessels from Sub-Carpathian barrow-graves.
1. Rohatyn (no. 81) – handled cup of Mad'arovce type.
2. Jaktorów II (no. 63) – cord-decorated handled cup (after J. Pasternak).
3. Jaktorów IV – cord-decorated handled cup (after J. Pasternak).
4. Kołpiec 9 (no. 46) – cord-decorated basin.
5. Kołokolin III (no. 66) – damaged bowl (b) from grave 2.
6, 7. Kołokolin II – bowl (c) and beaker (a).
8. Kołpiec 8 – bowl (c-1).
9. Kołpiec 10 – bowl.
10. Miżyniec (no. 22) – collared flask.
11–13. Sobiecin (no. 33) – amphora, handled beaker and handled vase.

8. Grave-goods of a few Sub Carpathian barrow-graves.
1. Rusiłów (no. 84) – broken dagger, 'Irish' gold ear-pendant repaired and provided with a bronze ring, flint knives, stone battle-axe and flint arrow-heads.
2. Kołpiec 5 (no. 46) – faience beads, some segmented, double handled cup and flint axe.
3. Ostapie 1 (no. 213) – objects from grave 3 : flint arrow-head and flint blade; from grave 2: boar tusk; from secondary grave 1: decorated pot, cup, base of a larger vessel, single-lugged mug and two points made of roe antler.
4. Kaczanówka IV (no. 198) – two cups and stone battle-axe.

9. Various grave-goods from Sub-Carpathian barrow-graves.
1, 2. Chorostków I (no. 195) – handled mug and amber disc.
3. Nowa Sieniawa (no. 592) – single-lugged mug.
4–5, 9. Gwoździec Stary II (no. 101) – bronze ear-pendant (s), single-lugged mug (k), dark coloured vessel (h).
7, 8. Kaczanówka III (no. 198) single-lugged mug and potsherd.
6, 10, 11. Buhłow II (no. 194) – single-lugged mug (d), two silver rings and seven bone beads (e, f), all from grave 2.
12, 13. Ostapie 4 (no. 213) – bronze ornament and single-lugged mug.
14. Okniany I (no. 106) – single-lugged mug (a).
Flint arrow-heads from:
15. Komarów 20 (no. 47) – f-1.
16. Komarów 34 – s.
17, 23, 24, 26. Komarów 39 – f.
18. Komarów 21 – b.
19, 22. Kołokolin VII (no. 66) – B,C.
20, 21, 30. Okniany II (no. 106).
25. Kołokolin I – g.
27. Komarów 37 – g.
28, 29. Komarów settlement – g.

10. 'Showy' stone battle-axes from Sub-Carpathian barrow-graves.
1. Kołokolin IV (no. 66) – 'Baltic type' (b).
2. Morawsko (no. 24) – type 'A'.
3. Kołokolin III, grave 1 – knob-shaped butt, blade reconstructed (i).
4. Gwoździec Stary I (no. 101) – (a).
5. Kołokolin V – 'Baltic type' (d).
6, 7. Myszyn (no. 104) – type 'B-1' (c), and type 'H–E3' (e).
8. Łotatniki II (no. 50) – 'shoe-last type' (d) made of yellow slate.
9, 10. Balice XVI (no. 1) – mace head, and axe of 'Fatyanovo type'.
11. Zdołbunów (no. 168) – 'Sofiivka type' (after Отчет Арх.комм. 1918).

11. Daggers found in western barrow-graves.
1. Ostrożec (no. 150) – flint, type III.
2. Balice XVI (no. 1) – flint, type I.
3. Balice VI – flint, type I.
4. Kavsko 3 (no. 45) – flint, type II.
5. Kołpiec 4 (no. 46) – flint, (c), type II.
6. Załuże (no. 167) – flint, type II.
7. Ostapie 2 (no. 213) – flint knife or dagger of type II.
8. Korytne (no. 146) – flint, type II.
9. Zdołbunów (no. 168) – flint, type III.
10. Balice XIX (no. 1) – flint, type I.
11, 12. Ostapie 5 (no. 213) – two bone points, or daggers.
13, 14. Rokitno 6 (no. 82) – two horn points.
15, 16. Ostapie 6 – bone point found in the halved female skull, and a point made of antler found near the male skeleton.
17. Ostrów (no. 128) – flint, type II.

12. Amphorae of the Eastern Globular Amphora culture, of the earliest stage.
1, 2. Ulwówek III (no. 398) – Kuyavian type.
3. Międzyrzec (no. 435) – globular type.
4, 5. Horodnica on the Zbrucz (no. 494) – Kuyavian type, and a bone object.
6. Uwisła 1 (no. 518) – Kuyavian type with fish-scale decoration.
7. Hlubičok (no. 492) – globular type.

13. Vessels mainly of the western groups of the Eastern Globular Amphora culture.
1–4, 6. Mikołajów (no. 423) – two undecorated amphorae, decorated Kuyavian type and 2 small amphorae and a bowl.
5. Wola Gródecka (no. 399) – bowl decorated in 'Złota' style.
7. Białokrynica (no. 427) – cord-decorated small globular type.
8–10. Tworyczów (no. 397) – Kuyavian type; undecorated amphora; decorated bowl (after S. Nosek).
11. Kykova (no. 455) – spheric, double-lugged bowl, decorated.

14. Vessels mainly of the eastern groups of the Eastern Globular Amphora culture.
1, 5–7. Suyemtsi 1 (no. 459) – Kuyavian amphora, two globular amphorae and a double-lugged undecorated flat-based amphora.

2. Suyemtsi 2 – amphora.
3. Aneta (no. 452) – debased Kuyavian amphora.
4. Skolobiv (no. 475) – four-lugged decorated amphora with a high neck.
8. Vinnitsa (environments) (no. 465) – double-lugged, decorated beaker, (a debased globular amphora).
9. Koszyłowce 2 (no. 501) – handled mug.
10. Beremiany 2 (no. 484) – handled jar, cord-decorated.
11. Tartaki (no. 464) – debased Kuyavian amphora.
12. Łosiatyn (no. 250–564) – double-lugged globular amphora with a flat base from a barrow-grave of the Middle Dnieper culture.

15. Vessels mainly of the Podolian group of the Eastern Globular Amphora culture.
1–4. Ułaszkowce (no. 516) – Kuyavian amphora, two bowls and globular amphora.
5. Kykova (455) – small double-lugged globular amphora.
6. Voytsekhivka I (no. 460) – debased globular amphora, decorated (after I. Lewyckyj).
7, 8. Słobódka Koszyłowiecka (no. 513) – small globular amphora, and a Kuyavian amphora, both richly decorated and provided with a lid.
9, 10. Velyka Mukša (no. 519) – Kuyavian amphora and the lower part of a pedestalled vessel.
11. Dublany (no. 419) – flint dagger.
12. Skolobiv (no. 475) – small double-lugged globular amphora.

16. Vessels of periods I and II of the Komarów culture.
Period I:
1, 7, 8, 10. Komarów 8 (no. 47) – tulip-shaped beaker (b), small cup or bowl (c-3), goblet (c-1), handled cup (e).
2, 6. Komarów 6 – tulip-shaped beaker, decorated (e), and small cup (i-1).
3, 12. Komarów 34 – beaker (IV) and cylindrical cup (VI) from grave B.
4, 11, 14. Komarów 21 – handled cup (1-a), undecorated cup (a-4), and another handled cup (a-2).
5, 9, 13. Komarów 9 – tulip-shaped cup (a-2), decorated (a-3) and undecorated bowls (a-1).
Period II:
15, 16. Okniany II (no. 106) – decorated bowl (d or v), and another one provided with two perforated lugs (e).
17. Putiatyńce (no. 79) – bowl with vertically perforated protuberance.
18, 20. Komarów 10 – bowls, undecorated (c-2) and decorated (d-2).
19. Czyżyków I (no. 60) – deep bowl (N).

17. Vessels of period II of the Komarów culture.
1, 4, 10. Komarów 11 – decorated bowl (a–1), handled cup (p–3) and another decorated bowl (a–2).
2. Bukówna III (no. 97) – decorated bowl (d).
3, 6. Sarniki IV (no. 86) – two bowls (j, i).
5. Komarów 36 – decorated bowl (b).
7. Daszawa II (no. 42) – double-lugged bowl.
8. Komarów 46 – decorated bowl (F).
9, 11. Okniany II (no. 106) – handled cup (i), double-handled vase (h).
12. Czyżyków I (no. 60) – undecorated bowl.
13. Komarów 28 – double-handled vase (j).

18. Vessels of period II of the Komarów culture.
1, 11. Sarniki IV (no. 86) tulip-shaped pot (h) and beaker (n).
2. Czyżyków I (no. 60) – decorated tulip-shaped beaker.
3, 5, 7, 8, 16. Komarów 10 – tulip-shaped pots and beakers (d-1-bis, a-1, c-1, f) and small cup (a-2).
4, 6, 15, 17. Okniany II (no. 106) – two tulip-shaped pots (f, b), deep bowl (d or v) and a small cup (x).
9, 13. Komarów 46 – tulip-shaped cup (g) and flowerpot-shaped cup (E).
10. Komarów 23 – tulip-shaped pot (c-1).
12. Bukówna III (no. 97) – decorated cup (j).
14. Komarów 27 – tulip-shaped pot (c).
18. Komarów 11 – small cup (p-1).
19. Komarów 36 – clepsydra-shaped cup (a).

19. Vessels of period III of the Komarów culture.
1. Bukówna VI (no. 97) – handled cup.
2, 3. Stopczatów (no. 111) – handled bowl and handled cup (i), from grave A.
4. Komarów 48 – tulip-shaped pot (b-5).
5. Wolica 1 (no. 91) – handled cup (1).
6–8, 12. Wolica 4 – handled cup (j), handled bowl (g), decorated beaker (c), and decorated cup (f).
9, 11. Krasów III (no. 67) small cup (A-3) and handled cup (b).
10. Wolica 3 – handled jug (D).
13. Krasów IV – bowl (g-2).
14. Bukówna IV (no. 97) – bowl (F).

20. Vessels of period III of the Komarów culture.
1, 6, 9, 12. Stopczatów (no. 111) – tulip-shaped pot (a), small bowl (g-1), cup (g-2) and another small bowl (i-4).
2. Bukówna VI (no. 97) – tulip-shaped beaker (a).
3, 13. Wolica 1 (no. 91) – tulip-shaped beaker (j) and four-lugged bowl (i).
4. Wolica 4 – tulip-shaped pot (d).
5, 7, 11. Bukówna IV – bowl (G), cup (C) and decorated bowl (D).
8, 10. Krasów III (no. 67) – two bowls (A-2, A-1).

21. Vessels of periods III and IV of the Komarów culture.
Period III:
1–7. Komarów 45 – two bowls (g-3, g-7), handled cup (g-4), single-lugged mug (g-4), tulip-shaped pot (g-8), handled bowl (g-1) and deep dish or bowl (g-2).
8–11. Komarów 13 – handled cup (b), small bowl (a), and a cup with a lid (e, d).
Period IV:
12–16. Komarów 33 – tulip-shaped pot (I) *in situ*, three amber beads and two glass beads (a), handled cup (III), small bowl (XI) and another handled cup (II).

22. Vessels mainly of period IV of the Komarów-Biały Potok culture.
1, 2. Dubno (no. 170) – beaker and double-handled vase of Noua type.
3, 4. Kulczyce Szlacheckie (no. 49) – wide bowl (dish) and handled cup from the settlement.
5. Semenów (no. 216) – bowl from a barrow-grave.
6. Uwisła 2 (no. 518) – large vase.
7, 8. Podgórzany (no. 594) – tulip-shaped pot and double-handled vase of Noua type (after W. Demetrykiewicz).

23. Pottery from Volhynian Bronze Age barrow-graves, except no. 6.
1. Siwki III–1878 (no. 157) – decorated bowl.
2. Korytne II (no. 146) – double-handled vase.
3–5. Staryki (Sternia ?) (no. 160) – beaker, stone battle-axe and handled cup.
6. Rakowa I (no. 28) – tulip-shaped pot (I-1, 2).

Abbreviations

Acta AASH	*Acta Archaeologicae Academiae Scientiarum Hungaricae*, Budapest
Acta AC	*Acta Archaeologica Carpathica*, Cracow.
Arch.Hung.	*Archaeologia Hungarica*, Budapest
Arch.P.	*Archeologia Polski*, Warszawa
Arch.R.	*Archeologické rozhledy*, Praha
AUMCS	*Annales Universitatis Mariae Curie-Skłodowska*, Lublin
ESA	*Eurasia Septentrionalis Antiqua*, Helsinki
FAP	*Fontes Archaeologicae Poznanienses*, Poznań
IKC	*Ilustrowany Kurier Codzienny*, Kraków
Liverpool AAA	*Liverpool Annals of Archaeology and Anthropology*
Mat.Arch.	*Materiały Archeologiczne*, Kraków
Mat.St.	*Materiały Starożytne*, Warszawa
MCA	*Materiale şi Cercetări Arheologice*, Bucureşti
PMMAE	*Prace i Materiały Muzeum Archeologicznego i Etnograficznego w Łodzi*, Seria Archeologiczna, Łódź.
PPS	*Proceedings of the Prehistoric Society*, Cambridge
Prague Symposium	*L'Europe à la fin de l'âge de la pierre*, Praha 1961
Prz.A.	*Przegląd Archeologiczny*, Poznań
Rapportes des archéologues de l'URSS	*VI Congrès International des Sciences Préhistoriques et Protohistoriques, Les rapports et les informations des archéologues de l'URSS*, Moscou 1962
SCIV	*Studii şi Cercetări de Istorie Veche*, Bucureşti
SMYA	*Suomen Muinaismuitso Yhdistyken Aikakauskirkja*, Helsinki.
Spr.Arch.	*Sprawozdania Archeologiczne*, Wrocław-Kraków.
Spr.PAU	*Sprawozdania z czynności i posiedzeń Polskiej Akademii Umiejętności*, Kraków
Spr.PMA	*Sprawozdania Państwowego Muzeum Archeologicznego*, Warszawa.
W.A.	*Wiadomości Archeologiczne*, Warszawa
ZOW	*Z Otchłani Wieków*, Poznań, Wrocław
ZWAK	*Zbiór Wiadomości do Antropologii Krajowej*, Kraków.

Арх.Пам.	Археологічні Пам'ятки УРСР, Kiev
Artamonov Volume	Исследования по Археологии СССР, Leningrad 1961 (University of Leningrad edition)
Ксиаан	Краткие Сообщения Института Археологии Ак. Наук СССР, Moscow
Ксиак	Краткие Сообщения Института Археологии, Kiev
Ксиимк	Краткие Сообщения Института Истории Материальной Культуры, Moscow-Leningrad
Мдапв	Матеріали і Дослідження з Археології Прикарпаття і Волині, Kiev.
Миа	Материалы и Исследования по Археологии СССР, Moscow-Leningrad
Миаюз	Материалы и Исследования по Археологии Югозапада СССР и Румынской Народной Республики, Kishinev
Сов.Арх.	Советская Археология, Moscow.

PART I

Archaeological Investigations

CHAPTER I

Western Barrow Graves

GEOGRAPHICAL SETTING
(Map I)

THE TERRITORY we are concerned with lies on the border of Central and East Europe and belongs in part to each of these. Throughout the book it will for convenience be referred to as the Territory. It is not a homogeneous region, being divided into a number of smaller regions mostly with somewhat vaguely defined boundaries. Its easternmost part, extending along the western side of the Middle Dnieper south of Kiev and westwards quite near to the Boh (Southern Bug),[1] is called the 'Kiev country'—'Kyivščyna'. This borders in the south on the steppe belt north of the Black Sea shore, called 'Pričernomorie' (the land near the Black Sea) in Soviet archaeological literature; it bore the expressive name 'Dzikie Pola' (Wild Fields) when, up to the end of the eighteenth century, it lay on the confines of the Polish kingdom. Podolia extends west of the Kiev country, up to the Dniester, and beyond that river up to the Pruth lies Bessarabia. Podolia falls into two quite distinct parts, namely 'Southern Podolia' in the south-east bordering on the steppe belt further south, and 'West Podolia', the true Podolia; the western division of the latter lay within Poland's pre-war boundaries. Podolia is a hedgeless, mostly treeless, and for a large stretch waterless plateau. It is dissected by many parallel deep, canyon-like abrupt valleys, the slopes of which are frequently wooded. Present and also prehistoric settlements are concentrated mostly in these valleys or on their edge.[2]

South of Podolia, on the Carpathian bend west of Bessarabia, is the small region of Bucovina. The large strip of land north of Podolia, south of Polesie (the region of the Pripet Marshes), is Volhynia. It spreads east of the Bug nearly up to the Dnieper north of Kiev. It can be subdivided into West and East Volhynia; the former was almost entirely within the limits of pre-war Poland.

West Podolia and West Volhynia form a transitional area which shows many features typical of Central Europe; in this respect West Volhynia is much more Central European than West Podolia. The areas extending west of these countries indisputably belong to Central Europe. West of Volhynia, west of the Bug, is the Lublin plateau with its western boundaries on the Vistula. The region south of the above, and east of the San up to Podolia, we shall call here the 'Sub-Carpathian' area. Besides the proper Sub-Carpathian belt south of the Dniester, it also includes the hilly country north-west of Lwów and the hilly country of a different character south of that city, called 'Opole', which borders on West Podolia.

Boundaries between all the above areas and regions are seldom marked by distinct geographical features, though one of these is the southern boundary of West Volhynia, formed by the northern edge of the Podolian plateau. Seen from the Volhynian side, it has an appearance of a mountain ridge rising suddenly to a height of about 180 metres (approximately 550 feet) above the adjacent plain, its height gradually diminishing towards the north-east. There are considerably greater differences between these regions in geological structure, type of soil, climate, and above all vegetation which is the outcome of all these factors. These were the main elements which caused the division of the Territory in the units mentioned above.

The Carpathian Mountains form the western boundary of the Territory and the southern boundary in its western part. Several passes render their crossing relatively easy, and archaeological evidence shows that contact between the regions on both sides of the mountains has been maintained almost uninterruptedly from the most remote past. The western passes linked the Sub-Carpathian area with East Slovakia while those further east stimulated connections between West Podolia and Transilvania.

The Territory is intersected by a dense network of large

[1] 'Boh' is the Ukrainian name of that river which has also been adopted in Polish. This name appears on most nineteenth and early twentieth-century British maps. Lately its Russian name, 'Bug', has been introduced which, however, is confusing as this is the proper name of the Polish river, a tributary of the Vistula, at present forming a long section of the frontier between Poland and the U.S.S.R. To avoid mistakes, the Russians call the latter the 'Western' and the former the 'Southern Bug'. A much simpler method is to use its original name, the 'Boh'.

[2] For more detailed study, I refer to works devoted especially to these topics. A most valuable review of these conditions is the atlas: E. Romer (ed.), *Atlas Polski* (*Atlas von Polon, Atlas de la Pologne*), Warszawa-Kraków, 1916. It contains comprehensive commentaries in French, German, and Polish, by eminent Polish authorities on the subject, attached to a large series of special maps. The commentaries are by: Prof. E. Romer (geography, climate); Prof. W. Szafer (vegetation); Prof. A. Jakubski (fauna), etc. They deal with all the lands of pre-partition Poland (eighteenth century), including the whole territory with which we are concerned here. Various geographic manuals may also be consulted, particularly the chapters devoted to Poland and Russia: e.g., M. R. Shackleton, *Europe, A Regional Geography*, 6th ed., London 1958; P. Vidal de la Blanche et L. Gallois (ed.), *Geographie Universelle*, vol. IV, *Europe Central* (by Emm. de Martonne), Paris 1931, pp. 642 ff., and vol. v, *Russie* (by P. Camena d'Almeida), Paris 1932, pp. 34 ff., 144 ff., etc. I also recommend an excellent comprehensive exposition of these conditions (in East Europe in general): R. M. Fleming, 'An Outline of Some Factors in the Development of Russia, with Special Reference to European Russia', in *Studies in Regional Consciousness and Environment* (essays presented to H. J. Fleure), London 1930.

rivers and their tributaries. In the north, they flow over wide plains; in the south, especially in Podolia, they have formed deep valleys which mostly run parallel to each other. Two main rivers, the Dniester and the Boh, and a number of smaller ones in the south, and also several larger tributaries of the Dnieper, lie entirely within the boundaries of our area, as do the sources and upper courses of a number of others. But the following circumstances are of the utmost importance: first, the main European watershed between the Black Sea and the Baltic Sea runs across the north-western part of the Territory; secondly, the sources of the main rivers of the two above systems, or of their important tributaries, lie very close to each other and passage from one of these river systems to the other meets with no obstacle whatever. A glance at the map (Map 1) reveals how the valleys of the Boh and Dniester cut across the plateau to reach the advanced outposts of the river network of the other side of the watershed. This position played a great role in the promotion of traffic along these natural routes.

Almost the entire country has a considerable covering of loess; only East Volhynia and strips of West Volhynia and of the Sub-Carpathian area have a sandy covering with typical sand dunes. The subsoil is not identical throughout the entire territory. The Lublin region west of the Bug and West Volhynia has a subsoil of chalk, and the plateau of Podolia has developed on limestone bedrock. The subsoil of the entire east, including East Volhynia, is granite.

Far more important for our study are the soils[3] which varied to some degree from one region to another, more in response to conditions of climate and vegetation than to the geological substratum. Most of the Territory is covered by extremely fertile black-earth *chernozem*, in some areas only a little over one foot deep, but in others several feet deep; it varies in colour from dark grey, nearly black, to brownish grey. The chernozem soils have resulted from the long occupation of the area by steppe vegetation. They are formed under climatic conditions of high evaporation with consequent desiccation of the soil during summer, and long freezing of the soil in winter. Increased rainfall, or change in its seasonal distribution, causes 'degradation' of the chernozem: the black earth begins to lose its organic components and takes on an increasingly brown colour.[4]

Investigations of prehistoric sites in the western part of the Territory have revealed that originally chernozem extended over a much wider area. This relates in particular to the loess country of the Lublin plateau where the process of degradation resulted in its almost complete disappearance. It once also extended over the whole Sub-Carpathian area proper and the adjoining regions, as shown by archaeological evidence.[5]

A relatively large region in the north-west of our area has poor, sandy soil, as mentioned previously. The whole northern part of Volhynia and the country on the Dnieper north of Kiev are also sandy.

VEGETATION AND CLIMATE

Vegetation in various parts of the Territory shows considerable diversity, which is the outcome of both local soil and climate. The three vegetation zones usually distinguished for the southern part of East Europe,[6] the mixed coniferous and deciduous forest zone in the north, the forest steppe, or park steppe, zone in the middle, and the steppe zone in the south, are noticeable mainly in the eastern division of our area, although there is an absence of abrupt transition and conditions vary from one place to another inside these zones.

Volhynia and the country north of Kiev belong to the mixed forest zone. There is a distinct difference between their vegetation and that of Polesia further north, which belongs to the same zone. Polesia is covered with extensive woods on damp and swampy ground, whereas in Volhynia and further east up to the Dnieper, a different plant system grows on much drier land which is covered with loess in many parts of the country, chiefly in West Volhynia. In areas which were never under the quaternary ice cover, relics of archaic floral elements have survived.

The southern limit of the vegetation proper to Volhynia is formed by the northern edge of the Podolian plateau in the west. This is not only a very characteristic landmark but also a very sharp boundary between two large vegetational and faunal provinces, and also between the mixed forest zone and the forest steppe. Further east no such well-marked geographic boundary is visible. The southern border of the Volhynian vegetation, and of the mixed forest zone in general, has been established along the southern reach of the pine forests; it coincides roughly with the northern limit of loess cover in that part of our Territory.

The forest steppe zone embraces the Kiev country south of that city and Podolia. This is a large area, poor in woods, which cover less than 10 per cent of its surface. Small oak woods and other warmth-loving trees grow here in river valleys, while wide prairies, the steppe, now mostly under cultivation, extend between. Only the southern part of West Podolia and also the region near Uman are somewhat more densely afforested. It is of interest to note that this part of West Podolia is separated from Volhynia by a salient of the area poor in forests which encroaches here from the east up to the western limit of Podolia.

The true treeless steppe, which has insufficient rainfall for tree growth, extends over a broad belt along the shore of the Black Sea. Its northern boundary with the forest steppe zone runs north-eastwards from the Dniester, in the region north of Tiraspol, to the Boh somewhere near Pervomaisk and the Dnieper somewhere near Kremenchug, and then further north-east towards Poltava.

A series of smaller vegetation regions have been distinguished especially in the western division of the Territory, and our interest will concentrate in the first instance on this part of the country. The vegetation of all the provinces and

[3] I. W. Cornwall, *Soil for the Archaeologist*, London 1958; Z. Weyberg, 'Uwagi o gleboznawstwie jako nauce ogólno-przyrodniczej' ('Observations on soil study as a branch of Natural Science'), *Kosmos*, vol. LVI, series B, Lwów 1931.

[4] N. Florow, 'Ueber die Degradierung des Tschernosioms in den Waldsteppen', *Annuarul ist. geologic al Romaniei*, vol. XI, Bucharest 1925; W. L. Kubina, *The Soils of Europe*, Madrid 1953, pp. 192 ff. on steppe soils.

[5] For more details in this respect see T. Sulimirski, 'Climate and Population', *Baltic Countries*, vol. 1, Toruń 1935, pp. 1 ff.; and also its reprint in the Baltic Pocket Library, Toruń 1935, pp. 14 ff.

[6] Shackleton (op. cit., note 2), p. 432, fig. 142.

smaller regions has undergone several transformations in the past, concurrently with the climatic changes. It seems, however, that the continuance of these vegetation areas was not much affected by alterations in the composition of their plant associations. This is suggested by the results of the study of the archaeological material of the areas in question. Investigations have revealed that boundaries of smaller local cultures, or of their branches, particularly in the western part of the Territory, coincide almost exactly with those of the vegetation regions mentioned above. This is a good illustration of the dependence of prehistoric communities on the natural conditions in the areas in which they lived.

There is insufficient data at present for any detailed reconstruction of the vegetation of the areas under review during all the subsequent periods of their prehistoric past. In a few instances, however, archaeological evidence gives important hints of the conditions which prevailed in the periods concerned. The fossil chernozem found under the protective cover of large Neolithic and Bronze Age barrows clearly must have been formed in a period during which the Sub-Carpathian area was grassland. The woodlands in which most barrow-graves are found at present, and which contributed to their preservation, encroached upon this region only after the mounds were erected. In time prairies came to extend over the Lublin plateau too; fossil remains of chernozem-like soils and actual survivals of both black earth and steppe vegetation indicate that they had then reached deep into Central Europe.[7]

The climate of the eastern division of the Territory is continental, with severe winters and hot summers. However, the fact that winter isotherms run from north-west to south-east indicates that even the easternmost parts of our area are sufficiently affected by the warming influence of the Atlantic Ocean. The course of the summer isotherms, dependent mainly on latitude, is different, in that it runs west–east.

The yearly rainfall does not show any marked differences over the whole Territory, except in the steppe belt in the south, where it is notably low. Nevertheless, the seasonal distribution of rainfall varies considerably from region to region, and in this respect the contrast between Podolia and the Kiev area on the one hand, and the regions situated further north and west on the other, is remarkable.

Disparity between the summer and winter temperature, the duration of snow cover and ice-bound rivers, diversity in seasonal distribution of rainfall, etc., were the chief factors in the formation of the vegetation regions and their subdivisions.

Their importance in this respect is decidedly greater than that of the geological substratum.

Climate is not a constant factor. It underwent several transformations in the post-glacial era. These have been dealt with by me in an article devoted to these topics,[8] and their impact on settlement discussed.

BARROW-GRAVES

Burial mounds were very characteristic of the entire steppe and forest steppe countries of Eastern Europe; thousands have been recorded in the vast territory which extends east of the Carpathians to the Urals and the Caucasus. They have always aroused great interest, and hundreds were more or less methodically excavated though many others were spoiled by treasure-hunters or amateurs. A very large number of the barrow-graves have been ploughed up and destroyed.

Barrow-graves excavated in the Territory date from various periods, from the Neolithic to the fifteenth century of our era. The latter were found mainly in the steppe country (Map VIII). The oldest barrow-graves, of the Neolithic and the Bronze Age, were not uniform, and four main distinct groups forming four large provinces have been distinguished; each of these falls into smaller regions. The so-called 'Ochre-graves' (marked V–VI on Map VIII) were characteristic of the steppe country on the Lower Dnieper. The Usatovo culture belonged to another one, extending over the Ukrainian steppe country west of the latter (marked IV on Map IX). The black-earth region in the forest steppe zone between the Dnieper and the Boh was the home of the Middle Dnieper culture (marked II on Map VIII); finally, in the Sub-Carpathian region further west and in its adjoining areas, the 'Sub-Carpathian barrow-grave' culture had developed (marked I on Map VIII; see Map IV).

We shall discuss here topics relating to all groups of barrow-graves mentioned above. But special attention will be paid to the Sub-Carpathian culture. I made a close study of these barrow-graves before the war, and for this purpose carried out numerous excavations, either alone or with colleagues and students. Many more mounds were investigated previously. The determination of the stages in the development of the culture, its chronology, the associations and contacts with other contemporary cultures, etc., may, therefore, be more easily studied there. They are essential for obtaining a true picture of the wider relations which prevailed in the whole Territory in the Neolithic and Bronze Ages, and the results obtained may serve as a proper basis for the establishment of a chronological framework suitable for all the cultures concerned.

SUB-CARPATHIAN BARROW-GRAVES
(Map II)

Barrow-graves within this region date from various periods. Most were of the Neolithic or Early Bronze Age, but a considerable number date from the Middle and Late Bronze Age (Map XI); mounds dating from later periods were less frequent, being found in restricted areas. The oldest ones were clearly associated with the Corded Ware assemblage. They were first studied by L. Kozłowski,[9] who regarded them as the latest phase of the 'Bug Neolithic' culture and dated them at the very end of the Neolithic. J. Kostrzewski[10] treats

[7] K. Bertsch, 'Klima, Pflanzendecke und Besiedlung Mitteleuropas in vor- und frühgeschichtlicher Zeit nach den Ergebnissen der pollenanalytischen Forschung', *XVIII Bericht d. röm.-germ. Kommission,* 1929, p. 64.

[8] T. Sulimirski, 'The Climate of the Ukraine During the Neolithic and the Bronze Age', *Archeologia,* vol. XII, Warszawa 1961, pp. 1 ff.

[9] L. Kozłowski, *Młodsza epoka kamienna w Polsce (neolit),* Lwów 1924, pp. 102 ff., Pl. XXVII.

[10] J. Kostrzewski, 'Od mezolitu do okresu wędrówek ludów, *Prehistoria Ziem Polskich,* Kraków 1939–48, pp. 181 ff. Recently, the westernmost barrows of the region which remained within the boundaries of post-war Poland, have been dealt with by J. Machnik, *Studia nad kulturą ceramiki sznurowej w Małopolsce,* Wrocław-Warszawa-Kraków 1966, pp. 144 ff., 161 ff., etc. This important study of the Corded Ware culture of Southern Poland, in which also a number of leading types of vessels from several Sub-Carpathian barrow-graves have been discussed, could not have been here taken into account. However, the final results of this work, including

them as a separate, local group of the Corded Ware culture. In 1930–9 my associates and I investigated nearly two hundred more mounds situated in various parts of the country, including sixty mounds of the large cemetery at Komarów, described in the second part of this book. Our excavations brought to light new types of these remains.

TABLE 1. The number of barrow-graves excavated dating from the Neolithic and the Bronze Age arranged according to their geographical diffusion (1962)

Group	Total of mounds investigated		Neolithic and Early Bronze Age		Middle and Late Bronze Age	
	sites	mounds	sites	mounds	sites	mounds
Przemyśl	37	77	35	65	3	9
Sub-Carpathian	20	70	17	48	6	9
Komarów	1	65	1	27	1	26
Lwów-Opole	36	73	28	47	10	21
Horodenka Group	20	+42	15	22	6	18
Total of the Barrow-Grave culture	114	+327	96	209	26	83
Lublin-Bug	23	+34	19	19	3	15
West Volhynian	32	+85	25	29	13	40
West Podolian	32	+58	20	35	10	20
Total	87	+177	64	83	26	75
Grand Total	201	+504	160	292	52	158

Note: The number of sites and mounds in horizontal lines do not add up as in many sites mounds occurred of both chronological groups, and no particulars or insufficient data are available for establishing the date of more than 50 barrow-graves reckoned up in the left column.

Table 1 gives the number of barrow-graves investigated up to 1962 within the Sub-Carpathian area and its adjoining regions, dating from the Neolithic and the Bronze Age, including those of the first stage of the Early Iron Age (Hallstatt C period) (Maps II, XI). They form a series of smaller territorial groups which are quoted there and the number of mounds allocated to each of these is also given. The majority, over 327 mounds from 114 sites, extended over the whole Sub-Carpathian area and the adjoining region to the north (the Lwów-Opole group), and about 180 mounds from about 90 sites were investigated in other parts of the country. The main difference between the former and the latter groups lies in the fact that the Sub-Carpathian barrow-graves were the only remains of the Neolithic and the Bronze Age found within the territory of their extent, whereas in other parts of the area under review different cultures—coeval with the barrow-graves—were also in existence.

It is important to note that mounds with grave goods characteristic of the Neolithic and Early Bronze Age, named the 'Barrow-grave culture', and those typical of its subsequent 'Komarów culture'[11] of the Middle and Late Bronze Age, frequently occur together in common cemeteries, and many graves because of the poverty of goods are not attributable to either of these cultures. This is why the description of all barrow-graves in the second part of this volume has been given jointly, without regard to their date. There was evidently continuity in settlement and development between the two periods, the Komarów culture being the successor but also the descendant of the Barrow-grave culture. This is well illustrated by the results obtained at Komarów.

MOUNDS

The barrow-graves were situated mostly on the top of hills, ridges, or on other elevations; they were rarely found on lower ground. Occasionally, and mainly in the earlier period, they appeared in isolation, single, but more usually in small groups of two to five mounds; in later periods they usually formed larger concentrations, i.e., cemeteries, particularly in the Sub-Carpathian area (Plans 1–6). The cemetery at Komarów near Halicz (Plan 1) contained over seventy mounds scattered over more than two and a half kilometres along a wide ridge of the north extent of the lowest range of the Carpathians; this concentration was prolonged at both ends by mounds situated on the territory of the neighbouring villages, thus including well over one hundred mounds in all, of which at least eighty were investigated. A similar concentration, but smaller in size, was found at Daszawa (no. 41) and in many other Sub-Carpathian villages. Similar large cemeteries, extending a long distance along the ridges of the Carpathian hills, have been reported from the other side of the Carpathians, in East Slovakia;[12] they can be equated with our latest barrow-graves.

Mounds greatly varied in size. Some were up to three to four metres high, and up to thirty metres in diameter, though usually they were smaller, one metre high and ten to twenty metres in diameter, and several were only thirty to forty centimetres high. Those situated in the forests were better preserved than those in arable fields; the latter were mostly much ploughed up, sometimes nearly completely, and their graves were often ruined or destroyed, in particular when the burial had been laid on the ancient surface of the ground, and not in a shaft. The very small number of barrow-graves recorded on the Sub-Carpathian hills west of the San, up to Cracow, is due mainly to the fact that they lie for the most part on the soils which have been cultivated for centuries and were completely ploughed up. Battle-axes, flint axes, potsherds, rarely human bones, etc., sometimes found on elevated sites in this region, now constitute the only traces of ancient barrow-graves, although they are often not even recognized as such. The process of rapid disappearance of medium and small mounds on clearings has often been recorded by archaeological literature.

The size of the mounds cannot be taken as an indication of the age of the barrow-grave. The earliest were usually very large, but sometimes the later ones were also large, being raised over a secondary burial in a smaller mound dating from an earlier period.

Burials were laid either in a shaft, or on the ancient surface. The former were found mainly in the earlier period, whereas characteristic of later periods were burials in shallow holes or ground-graves. However, shafts were sometimes found in late

the proposed chronology of the relative finds, do not differ in any vital point from those presented by me.

[11] T. Sulimirski, 'Das Hügelgräberfeld in Komarów und die Kultur von Komarów', *Bulletin International de l'Academie Polonaise*, Cracovie 1936, pp. 172 ff.; Kostrzewski (op. cit., note 10), pp. 214 ff.

[12] V. Budinský-Krička, *Slovenské deiny*, vol. I, Bratislava 1937, p. 64.

periods also. A shaft-grave with a niche (Siennów; Plan 9:3) was unique: it calls to mind similar graves furnished with Corded Ware pottery found in the settlements of the Funnel Beaker culture on the Cracow-Sandomierz loess plateau[13] and also the 'Catacomb' graves of the Ukrainian steppe country east of the Dnieper.

The floor of the shaft-graves was usually covered with planks, and a layer of planks often lay over the burial also, in the middle of the shaft or covering the shaft at the ancient level. The lining of the sides of the shaft was not recorded. A layer of planks was also laid on the ancient ground in burials uncovered on the ancient surface; in a few cases planks formed a kind of a platform over the surface of the ground, or covered a much larger area around the burial. Some timber construction or a kind of coffin had presumably covered these burials, but this has never been ascertained in our mounds. Only in West Podolia and in a few cases in Volhynia and on the Bug, exclusively in the areas influenced by the Globular Amphorae, stone constructions, slab-cists, were uncovered in the mounds (Map v). In the same area cairns raised over the grave were also found in a few early Bronze Age barrow-graves, and in those of the Scythian period. Here, too, stone rings built around the main grave were recorded. Table 2 includes all barrow-graves in which stone constructions were uncovered.

TABLE 2. Stone construction under the mound

Group	Neolithic and Early Bronze Age		Later periods	
	sites	mounds	sites	mounds
		Slab-cists		
Lublin-Bug	1	1	1	1
West Volhynian			2	2
West Podolian	2	2	1	1
Horodenka	2	2		
Scythian type (W. Pod.)			1	1
		Cairns & Pavements (c & p)		
West Podolian	4	6 c(1 p)	1	7 c & p
Sub-Carpathian			3	7 p
Scythian type:				
Horodenka			2	6 c & p
			3	4 c
			1	1 p
West Podolian			5	7 c & p
			10	12 c
			1	1 p
		Stone rings (Plan 45)		
Sub-Carpathian			1	1
Horodenka			1	1
West Podolian	3	5	2	3
Scythian type:				
Horodenka			2	4
West Podolian			5	9

Note: Two barrow-graves at Komarów (nos. 14, 20), both of the Komarów culture, had special constructions.

In a few mounds remains of some wooden construction built close to the grave were noticed. They were mostly burned away, leaving only slight traces. Charred remains of a small hut uncovered at Koropuż were of particular interest (Plan 8:1). It was built on the ancient surface of interlaced timber logs and had a hearth in the centre. Its plan and construction are reminiscent of modern huts of Carpathian herdsmen (known as *koliba*). The hut evidently burned away during the funeral, and only its lowest logs, considerably charred, survived. The hut may have been built as a mortuary, but more likely it was the hut originally inhabited by the person buried close to it. It should be emphasized that no traces of any settlement were found around the barrow-grave.

Traces of a similar hut, or of a kind of funeral construction, were uncovered also under the mound of Klimkowce (Plan 44:1) in North Podolia. It was built of timber, its floor a little sunk in the ground: it perished in a conflagration, and no details of its construction could be established. Somewhat similar huts, or funeral constructions, were found at Stojańce (Plan 8:2) and in a few mounds at Komarów (16, 30, 39) (Plans 13:1, 16:3, 19:1). Barrow-graves from Kavsko (no. 45) may also be included in this list.

In the barrow-graves at Kavsko the usual Neolithic grave goods were excavated, but a number of objects were also found which seem to have formed part of some household. To the latter belonged flint flakes and waste, nodules, cores, small flint implements, also quern-stones either entire or in fragments, flint insets of some composite implements made of wood or bone, probably sickles, etc. On the other hand, no skeletons were found in these mounds, hence they have been regarded by their investigator[14] as remains of a settlement and their sepulchral nature denied, in spite of the fact that in one of these a cremation burial was uncovered. However, the assemblage of undamaged grave goods, their character, number, types, etc., correspond entirely with those from hundreds of barrow-graves investigated in the Territory; the same applies to the construction of the mounds, hearths under their cover, etc. Their skeletons have decayed, but this was the case in scores of mounds of the same area. The household objects found in the mounds may only suggest that the burials were placed on the sites of temporary encampments inhabited by herdsmen subsequently buried there, as was probably the case at Koropuż. Of importance in this connection is the fact that vessels excavated in these mounds differed from each other and were not of the same age. They ranged from the final Neolithic to the Middle Bronze Age, thus giving the time-span in which the site was used as a burial ground. Household objects, saddle-querns in particular, were not an unusual occurrence; such objects were frequently found in barrow-graves of North-Western Europe of the Overgrave period.[15]

The earth of which the mound was raised was invariably taken from the immediate vicinity of that mound. This was very clear in many cases, e.g. the barrow-grave at Gwoździec Stary II (Plan 40). By taking the earth in a wide radius round the centre on which was the grave, what appeared to be a

[13] Kostrzewski (op. cit., note 10), pp. 175 f., fig. 5.

[14] К. В. Бернякович, Роботи прикарпатської археологічної експедиції в 1956–7 pp. Археологічні роботи музею в 1925–1957, Lviv 1959, pp. 29 ff.

[15] K. W. Struve, *Die Einzelgrabkultur in Schleswig-Holstein und ihre kontinentalen Beziehungen*, Neumünster 1955, p. 66.

deliberate elevation arose in the centre. Thus a number of writers have not understood the nature of this elevation and have erroneously stated that a broad platform of earth was first of all raised on the grave site, on which the body was placed, after which a mound was raised over the grave. In sandy areas, e.g. Brzezinki IV, no. 3 (Plan 9:2), the central portion was usually surrounded by a narrow trench. This was of course the traces of a palisade or some such construction, intended to protect the mound from collapse.

Fairly well-preserved fossil humus, usually dark in colour and sometimes black was occasionally found under the mound of the barrow-graves, mainly of those larger in size. The kernel of the mound at the bottom inside the grave was of this same black or dark colour. Both the humus and the lower part of the mound which consisted of humus gathered round the grave were protected by the upper layers from the process of degradation of its organic contents. The upper layers, closer to the surface, were increasingly lighter in colour and degradate.

The dark kernel of non-degradate fossil humus and the mound raised upon it, always occurring inside the centre of the mound only, has sometimes been the source of erroneous hypotheses to the effect that this dark earth was deliberately brought from a considerable distance for raising the mound. Earth of this kind is not found at present in the near vicinity of the barrow-graves, except in Podolia where the chernozem has not undergone degradation.

The fact that the mound was raised of earth from the immediate vicinity has sometimes made it difficult to distinguish the earth of the mound from the earth on which the mound was raised. Very frequently, only the hearth and various small remains apparently scattered on the ancient surface enable us to establish the ancient level. These facts were not always taken into consideration in reports on the excavations, and the yellow subsoil was regarded as the ancient level: I have endeavoured to correct these obvious oversights as far as possible in my description of the barrow-graves which will be found in the second part of the book.

The grave shaft was sometimes difficult to discern, particularly if it was shallow and did not penetrate to the virgin subsoil. This also applied in sandy areas, where the walls of the shaft had collapsed into the grave shaft and its original outlines had been lost.

BURIALS

Mounds usually contained a single burial, but in many two or more contemporary graves, or double graves, were uncovered, mostly with a male and female skeleton, sometimes also that of a child, rarely of another adult. However, the establishment of the proper number of burials in each mound has been greatly handicapped by the circumstance that often no skeletons at all were found under the mound or even in the grave shaft. This was particularly the case in the Sub-Carpathian area, but also on sandy soils, where the bones had completely decayed owing to the acidity of the soil. In some graves only very slight traces of the skeleton could be discerned (e.g. Plate 1:1).

These circumstances resulted in mistaken views as to these barrow-graves on the part of a number of authors. Thus W. Demetrykiewicz[16] and M. Roska,[17] and recently K. V. Bernyakovyč,[18] having found no human bones, but, as well as the usual grave goods, traces of funeral fires, scattered potsherds, flints, etc., on the ancient surface under the mound, considered the barrow-graves investigated by them as remains of ancient settlements, or dwellings. Barrow-grave II at Stebnik (no. 55) excavated by me, was definitely not a dwelling but a sepulchral monument. The same evidently applies to barrow-grave I situated close to it, which M. Roska wrongly considered to be remains of a settlement.

In many instances the sole indication of the number of burials under the mound were the grave shafts uncovered, even the very shallow ones, their size, the position and the distance between the grave goods and between their groups, etc. (e.g. Plate 2:4). The distance between the grave goods forming a group may also suggest the position of the skeleton, crouched or extended, its orientation, etc.

The study of all the above data has shown that at least 15 per cent of Neolithic and Early Bronze Age barrow-graves in our area, and about 30 per cent of those of the Middle and Late Bronze Age, contained more than one contemporary burial. Considerably fewer barrow-graves yielded secondary burials. Only eight barrow-graves of this type in five sites were dated as of Neolithic and Early Bronze Age, and nine in three sites as later periods. In some of these the time lag between the original grave and the secondary burial was of relatively short duration, which suggests that such mounds were probably a tribal burial ground. The number of such graves was probably greater, but owing to the circumstances mentioned above no precise data could be collected in this respect. In some cases the old barrow-graves were used in a much later period, and the original grave destroyed or damaged. In the Lwów-Opole group in a few instances burials of the Lipica culture of the first centuries A.D. were placed in ancient mounds.[19]

Our knowledge of the burial ritual has been greatly restricted because of the decomposition of skeletons in a very large number of barrow-graves, particularly in the Sub-Carpathian area. However, as far as records are available, a crouched position of the skeletons was most common (Plate 1); men usually lay on their right side, women on their left. The crouched position was common not only during the Neolithic, but also in the developed Bronze Age and even in the Scythian barrow-graves.[20] In earlier graves the corpse lay slightly bent, as for sleep, whereas later their position was flexed, seldom contracted, and in some cases the position of the skeleton implies that the corpse must have been wrapped, or strongly bound. In the north-western group, skeletons lay mostly on their backs, in an extended position, which may be due to the influence of the neighbouring Funnel Beaker culture. Occasionally, this position was found also in later graves

[16] W. Demetrykiewicz, 'Kurhany w Przemyskiem i Drohobyckiem', *Materiały antropologiczno-archeologiczne i etnograficzne*, vol. II, Kraków 1898, pp. 124 ff.

[17] M. Roska, 'Glanement des antiquités de l'époque préhistorique en Galicie', *Dolgozatok-Traveau x*,vol. IX, Kolozsvar 1918, pp. 25 ff.

[18] Берняковнч (op. cit., note 14).

[19] M. Śmiszko, 'Stanowisko wczesnorzymskie w Kołokolinie pow.rohatyński', *W.A.*, vol. XIII, 1935, pp. 160 f.

[20] Sulimirski (op. cit., note 11).

in Podolia. Male heads were mostly to the west, or north-west, seldom to the north, women always in the opposite direction.

In a number of graves (listed in Table 3), mainly in the Sub-Carpathian area, ochre was found, but it was never as richly strewn as in the steppe barrow-graves east of the Dnieper which have been called 'ochre-graves' as a result. Usually only a few small lumps of ochre lay near the skull, or on the site where it is supposed to have lain, in cases where the skeleton has decayed completely. This custom survived to the Middle Bronze Age (Komarów culture).

TABLE 3. Graves in which ochre was found

Neolithic & Early Bronze Age graves	Graves of the Middle & Late Bronze Age
Kołpiec II, V, VI, VII (no. 46)	Komarów 36
Komarów 18, 35, 53, 58 (no. 47)	Luka Vrublivetska 1 (no. 205)
Koropuż (no. 17)	Radzimin II-1876 (no. 155)
Kryłos 1 (no. 48)	
Ozimina II (no. 53)	
Zawadyńce (no. 222)	
Kulczyce I, II, III, IV (no. 49)	

In barrow-grave 13 at Komarów loose fired clay was used instead of ochre.

A very common practice was human offerings. Fifteen to twenty per cent of Neolithic and early Bronze Age mounds of all groups, except the north-western, contained two contemporary burials, and often three, and the ratio of such mounds grew to 20–30 per cent during the later periods. In some cemeteries, e.g. at Luka Vrublivetska (no. 205), all mounds contained at least two, up to seven burials. Normally the wife had to follow her deceased husband. The couple were sometimes buried together in a single grave, but more often in separate graves, the female grave being placed either near the feet of the male, or on the ancient surface close to the shaft in which her husband lay, or on the periphery of the area covered by the mound. In mounds with stone rings, the female grave lay usually close to the circle, on its inner side. Bone or antler points, sometimes flint arrow-heads found in female graves in the chest or womb, indicate that the woman has been killed over the grave. The female skeleton in barrow-grave 6 at Ostapie (no. 213) had its skull halved from top to bottom, apparently by a bronze sword or a large dagger.

In a number of graves uncommon practices have been revealed (Plate 2). At Balice XVIII (no. 1) a loose human skull was found in the grave, and at Buhłów II (Plan 43:2) and Szepel (no. 161) the skull was missing. At Klimkowce (Plan 44:1) and Siwki III-1878 (no. 157) bones lay displaced in no natural order. In several instances the mutilation of corpses has been recorded: at Orzechowce (no. 26) the skull was cut off and lay 60cm higher than the skeleton; at Rusiłów (no. 85) (Plate 1:4) the male skeleton had both feet missing and one leg had been placed behind the skeleton. In both Buhłów I and II (Plan 43:1, 2; Plate 2:1–3) (female skeleton) the legs were torn out of the corpse and laid along the skeleton, as was the case with one of the four skeletons at Boratyn Wielki 1938 (no. 139); the skull of the female skeleton Buhłów II was cut off and lay in a special hole dug for it. At Rokitno 6 (Plan 35:4) an additional human leg lay on the skeleton of the main burial. Finally, at Radzimin I-1876 (no. 155) one skeleton lay face downwards. There were probably more graves with similar practices, but these were not noticed because of the decomposition of the skeletons.

Dismembering of the corpse was a widespread practice in Northern Europe, at the very end of the Neolithic and in the Early Bronze Age. It is recorded in the Radial Pottery culture, in the Funnel Beaker group of the Lublin area, in the Złota culture,[21] and also further west, in Greater Poland[22] and Thuringia.[23] It was also practised in the Strzyżów culture in West Volhynia (Torczyn).

Fire must have played an essential role in the funeral ritual, particularly in the Sub-Carpathian area. Fires were probably lit during the funeral as is indicated by the remains of hearths found on the ancient surface under the mound. Sometimes the grave itself, its shallow pit, or its area on the ancient surface of the ground, was fired before the corpse was laid on it. Where no fires were lit, at least lumps of charcoal were thrown in the grave and/or over the whole area subsequently covered by the mound. Charcoal was also frequently found in the mound.

Firing of the grave was sometimes done after the corpse had been laid in it. This resulted in the bones, although only slightly calcined, resisting the process of decomposition and remaining in their original place. They were left untouched with the remains of the pyre lit over the burial and were covered by the mound and the remains. Intentional cremation was less frequent. In such cases, the remains of the pyre were shovelled together with calcined bones and heaped in the centre of the grave, or in a corner of the grave shaft. Cremation outside the grave has been noticed only in graves of the developed Bronze Age and in later periods, and the same applies to burials in urns.

Cremation burials have been found in early barrow-graves, mainly in the Sub-Carpathian group. Their number here increased in later periods, but on the other hand they were not noticed then in the north-western group. In Podolia cremation was not practised in the earlier periods; it spread here later and was most common during the Scythian period. Table 4 shows the number of cremation graves in each group and their ratio.

An occurrence restricted to West Volhynian barrow-graves near Ostróg on the Horyn—rolls of clay laid across the burials—was noted in a number of Neolithic graves there. Outside this region, similar rolls were recorded in a single barrow-grave, Kuźminczyk II (no. 201) in the northern part of Podolia.

In a few graves animal bones were excavated; they were obviously remains either of food offered to the dead for their journey or of funeral feasts. The original number of such graves must have been much greater, but the bones had undoubtedly decayed and disappeared as the human skeletons

[21] Z. Krzak, 'Cmentarzysko kultury złockiej na stanowisku "Grodzisko II" we wsi Złota, pow.Sandomierz', *Arch.P.*, vol. II, 1958, p. 364.

[22] M. Kowiańska-Paszykowa, *FAP*, vol. VII, 1957, pp. 116 ff. Several graves with dismembered skeletons were quoted and discussed in my *Polska przedhistoryczna*, part II, London 1957–9, pp. 344 ff.

[23] K. W. Struve (op. cit., note 15), p. 76.

TABLE 4. Cremation burials

Group	Neolithic & Early Bronze Age			Later periods		
	mounds	crema-tions	%	mounds	crema-tions	%
Lublin-Bug	7	1	15	2	–	–
Przemyśl	40	6	15	6	–	–
Sub-Carpathian	66	13	20	38	9	22
Lwów-Opole	39	3	8	18	6	33
Horodenka	17	1	6	14	2	14
Scythian graves	–	–	–	18	9	50
Jointly	–	–	–	32	11	33
West Podolian	26	–	–	9	1	11
Scythian	–	–	–	31	5	17
Jointly	–	–	–	40	6	15
West Volhynian	26	1	4	31	2	6·5

did in so many graves. In some instances an entire skeleton of an animal was found, e.g. that of a sheep at Lisieczyńce (Plan 43:3), or a skeleton of a dog at Zakłodzie (no. 136). At Komarów 37 (Plan 20) and Klimkowce (Plan 44:1), large heaps of calcined animal bones were uncovered; unfortunately, the bones were not identified before the outbreak of the war. This practice survived to the Middle Bronze Age in our area, as is indicated by the barrow-grave 16 at Bukówna (no. 97) in which skeletons of two young horses lay in the centre of the mound. This burial calls to mind the so-called 'animal-graves' excavated in Kuyavia,[24] and in other parts of Poland, which were evidently offerings to supernatural forces; in our case, the horses seem rather to have been offerings to a person buried under one of the neighbouring mounds.

GRAVE GOODS

The usual grave goods consisted of pottery, weapons, and personal ornaments; the only implements deposited were flint and later iron knives, flint scrapers, perforators, bone awls, points, etc. In Table 5 are listed barrow-graves in which grave goods were excavated. They are divided into two main chronological groups, and their regional distribution is also indicated. There are some slight differences in the number of vessels and other goods found in coeval graves in various parts of the country.

It is of interest to note that in earlier graves weapons were very frequent: they were found in 59 per cent of barrow-graves of this period, whereas during the later period they were excavated only in 11 per cent of barrow-graves, or 16 per cent if the Scythian graves are included. On the other hand, the number of vessels deposited in the graves increased considerably in the later period: only 6 per cent of earlier

TABLE 5. The number of barrow-graves in which the main grave goods were found

Groups of barrow-graves:	No. of mounds	No. of mounds with vessels	Pottery: No. of vessels 1	2	3	4	5–10	11–27	No. of mounds with weapons	Mounds with a single weapon	Weapons: axes	battle-axes	spear-heads	arrow-heads	Ornaments Amulets	Metal objects
Neolithic and Early Bronze Age																
Lublin-Bug	7	3	1	1	1	–	–	–	5	3	3	3	1	–	2	1
Przemyśl	40	33	12	17	3	–	1	–	23	11	15	16	7	1	5	4
Sub-Carpathian	42	16	8	2	4	1	1	–	26	17	23	9	2	3	7	5
Komarów	24	13	7	5	–	–	1	–	24	8	10	7	1	2	–	–
Lwów-Opole	39	27	15	7	3	1	1	–	19	11	12	7	3	4	7	6
Horodenka	22	3	1	1	1	–	–	–	12	12	5	7	–	–	3	3
West Podolian	26	17	15	1	–	1	–	–	13	9	4	7	1	3	7	3
West Volhynian	26	11	9	2	–	–	–	–	9	7	5	3	3	–	2	–
Total	226	123	68	36	12	3	4	–	131	78	77	59	18	13	33	22
Bronze Age and Early Iron Age																
Lublin-Bug	2	1	1	–	–	–	–	–	–	–	–	–	–	–	–	–
Przemyśl	6	2	–	2	–	–	–	–	–	–	–	–	–	–	–	–
Sub-Carpathian	10	6	1	1	4	–	–	–	–	–	–	–	–	–	2	1
Komarów	28	25	7	4	1	4	7	2	6	4	1	2	1	3	4	4
Lwów-Opole	18	12	3	2	1	4	2	–	1	1	1	–	–	–	2	2
Horodenka	20	15	4	2	2	1	5	1	4	3	2	1	–	1	2	3
Scythian	18	7	6	–	–	1	–	–	2	1	1	1	–	2	2	3
West Podolian	9	7	3	3	1	–	–	–	1	1	1	–	–	–	2	2
Scythian	31	21	8	6	3	–	4	–	12	9	–	1	4	9	14	18
West Volhynian	31	21	7	2	1	–	1	–	2	2	–	–	–	2	4	4
Total	173	117	40	22	13	10	19	3	28	21	6	5	5	17	32	37

[24] L. Gabałówna, 'Pochówki bydlęce kultury amfor kulistych ze stanowiska 4 w Brześciu Kujawskim, w świetle podobnych znalezisk kultur środkowo-europejskich', *PMMAE*, no. 3, 1958, pp. 63 ff.; Sulimirski (op. cit., note 22), pp. 347 f., 352 ff.

graves in which pottery was found yielded four vessels or more, whereas this percentage in the later period was 32 per cent or 27·5 per cent if the Scythian graves are taken into consideration.

A custom very frequently recorded during both periods was that of destroying or at least damaging pottery and weapons laid in the grave. Many vessels were deliberately smashed: sometimes parts of a single vessel lay in two or more distinct places or its sherds were scattered over a larger area under the mound. This applies mainly to the kitchen ware and it seems that these were vessels used during the funeral feasts and then destroyed. But it also applies in particular to the Thuringian amphorae, a vessel characteristic of the earliest barrow-graves of our area, which were found smashed in eight graves with large parts missing (e.g. Fig. 9:1). Battle-axes, often damaged by fire, were excavated in at least twelve barrow-graves of all groups except Podolian and Volhynian, and broken-off parts of flint axes (rarely damaged by fire) were found in nine barrow-graves of the same region (e.g. Fig. 11:1). In five graves, i.e. 15 per cent of all graves in which flint arrow-heads were found, the tip of at least one specimen was broken off (e.g. Plate 8:1; Plate 9:16, 19, 23, 28), as was the tip of the flint dagger at Rusiłów (Plate 8:1). A list of all these graves is given in Table 6 below.

TABLE 6. List of Neolithic and Early Bronze Age burials in which smashed vessels and damaged weapons were excavated

Thuringian amphorae	*Other vessels*
1. Hartfeld (no. 10)	1. Boratyn Wielki (no. 139)
2. Kołokolin 1 (no. 66)	2. Kołokolin 3 (no. 66)
3. Komarów 5 (no. 47)	3. Kołokolin 4
4. Komarów 31	4. Ostapie 1 (no. 213)
5. Krasów 1 (no. 67)	5. Ostapie 6
6. Kulczyce 5 (no. 49)	6. Rokitno 3 (no. 83)
7. Płużne III (no. 153)	
8. Stratyn 1 (no. 87)	
Battle-axes	*Flint Axes*
1. Balice 1 (burned) (no. 1)	1. Kołokolin 1 (burned)
2. Balice 7 (burned)	2. Kołokolin 3 gr. 1
3. Gwoździec Stary (no. 101)	3. Kołokolin 4
4. Kołokolin 3 gr. 1 (no. 66)	4. Kołokolin 7
5. Kołokolin 4	5. Komarów 32
6. Komarów 39 (no. 47)	6. Komarów 39
7. Kryłos 7 (burned) (no. 48)	7. Kulczyce 3
8. Kulczyce 3 (burned) (no. 49)	8. Płużne III (no. 153)
9. Łotatniki 2 (no. 50)	9. Rokitno 6
10. Myszyn (no. 104)	
11. Płaucza Wielka (no. 75)	
12. Rokitno 2 (burned) (no. 83)	
13. Wiktorów 2 (burned) (no. 57)	
Arrow-heads	*Flint daggers*
1. Klimkowce (no. 199)	1. Rusiłów (no. 85)
2. Kołokolin 7 (no. 66)	
3. Komarów 39 (no. 47)	
4. Kulczyce 3 (no. 49)	
5. Rusiłów (no. 85)	

Similar practices were also recorded further west. The stone battle-axe from burial '35' of the 'eastern' barrow-grave at Rosiejów, district of Pińczów, north-west of Cracow, investigated by T. Reyman,[25] was burned and damaged, apparently having been thrown into the funeral pyre.

SUMMARY

The study of the barrow-graves of our area revealed that their construction was highly uniform. Only a number of West Podolian and West Volhynian mounds differed from others in that stone slab-cists and cairns, in some cases stone circles, were found under them, a feature not observed in other parts of the country; these appear solely within the areas which were affected by the influence of the Globular Amphora culture, topics to which we shall return later.

The funeral ritual, as reflected by the position of skeletons, their orientation, funeral fires, strewing with ochre, etc., was also very uniform within the whole Territory, particularly during the early periods. This also applies to the gradual changes which proceeded at about the same time and at the same rate nearly everywhere. However, well-marked differences existed in the grave goods, especially between those of the earlier periods and the later ones. They enable us to distinguish two different stages in the development of our barrow-graves, the earlier dating from the Neolithic and the Early Bronze Age and the later from the developed Bronze Age and Early Iron Age. These two main periods can be further divided into stages which will be discussed in the subsequent chapters.

Regional divergences, as well as chronological ones, can be distinguished in the type of grave goods and in their composition. Thus, seven local groups have been distinguished, and are quoted in the Tables. Differences between these groups were at first very slight and consisted mainly in a preference in some parts of the country for a particular type of vessel or other grave goods. They then increased gradually, but up to the end of the Early Bronze Age the entire Territory, all the groups, can be considered as forming one entity, one culture, the 'Barrow-grave culture'. This applies in particular to the Sub-Carpathian barrow-graves, the Horodenka and the Lwów-Opole groups, which formed a close-knit group; it survived into the succeeding period in the form of the Komarów culture.

The position was different during the developed Bronze Age and the Early Iron Age. There was no such uniformity of grave goods excavated in graves of different areas of that period. In some parts, particularly in the west, the custom of raising mounds over the burial seems to have been abandoned, but in the east the number of barrow-graves of that period increases. However, their grave goods differed in many respects from those of the central group, that of the Komarów culture, and many can be linked with the Trzciniec culture of Poland.

Burials of both periods were, on the whole, poorly furnished and in many graves no grave goods were found at all. Often only charcoal was strewn about, while odd potsherds and flint flakes were the only goods excavated. Richly furnished graves were an exception in the earlier periods; presumably many grave goods of the earlier period were of organic matter, and the food given to the dead was in wooden vessels or basketwork, which accounts for their disappearance owing to decay.

[25] T. Reyman, 'Dokumentaryczne wartości odkryć w kopcu wschodnim w Rosiejowie, w pow.pińczowskim', *Slavia Antiqua*, vol. 1, Poznań 1948, p. 75.

CHAPTER II

The Sub-Carpathian 'Barrow-grave' Culture

INTRODUCTORY REMARKS

In the preceding chapter, two main chronological groups of barrow-graves have been distinguished in the Sub-Carpathian area. The earlier one, of the Neolithic and the Early Bronze Age, formed the 'Barrow-grave culture', the core of which were mounds of the Sub-Carpathian proper and Lwów-Opole groups. The later barrow-graves, of the developed Bronze Age, belonged mainly to the Komarów culture or to its equivalent groups.

We shall devote our attention here to the 'Barrow-grave culture'. All grave goods found in these mounds will be dealt with, then an attempt will be made to establish successive phases in the development of the culture to which they belonged, and to relate them to the stages in the evolution of other coeval cultures of the Territory described in the preceding chapter.

POTTERY

As shown in Table 5 vessels were found in at least 123 mounds of the barrow-grave culture, fifty-six of which belonged to its central groups. This pottery was mostly typical of the Central European Corded Ware. Usually one, sometimes two, vessels were excavated in a single barrow-grave and only rarely was their number greater. They were mainly reddish in colour, made of tempered clay paste, insufficiently baked, brittle; most vessels were therefore found badly crushed and often could not be reconstructed. Their decoration consisted either of cord impressions or of incisions. Corded lines usually run round the neck and/or round the upper part of the body. Chevron ornament, zigzag lines, and similar patterns were also frequent. Many vessels, in particular of the later stages, were undecorated.

Vessels varied in size and shape, but almost all types characteristic of the Central European Corded Ware were represented: the 'Thuringian' amphorae and those of other types, beakers typical of the earlier period, and also single-lugged mugs (*Zapfenbecher*), handled cups, etc., pertaining to the later stage.

THURINGIAN AMPHORAE
(Plates 3:1, 4, 5; Figs. 9:1; 10:1)

These vessels were found in twenty-eight graves listed in Table 9. Some were cord-decorated or had incised ornament, others were undecorated, but all were unmistakably of the same type and characteristic of Central European Corded Ware (Map IX).

Thuringian amphorae have been dealt with recently by M. Buchvaldek[1] and U. Fischer,[2] both of whom distinguished earlier and later types in their respective countries, Bohemia and Thuringia. According to the stratigraphic evidence, Fischer divides them into two main groups which also mark two stages in the evolution of the Corded Ware culture of Thuringia and Saxony. To the earlier of these belonged amphorae of 'Schraplau' type, whereas during the second stage a few distinct variations evolved; they were reflected chiefly in the decorative style of the vessels, each of which was proper to a different region.

Buchvaldek discerns three successive stages in the evolution of the Bohemian 'Thuringian' amphorae. The earliest of these (type I) corresponded entirely with those of Fischer (Schraplau) type (Plates 3:1; 4:1, 4, 5; Fig. 9:1) and were one of the principal grave goods of the earliest 'common Central European Corded Ware horizon' (A-amphorae).[3]

During the second stage two slightly differing decorative styles evolved (types IIa and IIb), but many amphorae were already undecorated. Amphorae of the third stage departed a little from the standard type and were mainly undecorated.

Among Thuringian amphorae found in our graves the earlier and the later ones can also be clearly distinguished. Four from the central groups of our culture and one from North-west Podolia were of type I or of 'Schraplau' type, (Plates 3:1; 4:1, 4, 5; Fig. 9:1), all found in shaft-graves. To the same type a few amphorae from Złota near Sandomierz and one from Książnice Wielkie also belonged,[4] and that from Griščintsy on the Dnieper (Fig. 1:1).[5] The above vessels were evidently the earliest and belonged to the earliest 'common Central European Corded Ware horizon'. Two amphorae were found with another vessel: at Krasów I (Fig. 9:1, 3) with a wide-mouthed beaker decorated with horizontal fluting and an axe made of siliceous slate; at Koropuż (no. 17, Plate 3:1), with potsherds typical of the Funnel Beaker culture and with a decorated bone disc. Grave goods found with other amphorae of this type comprised: at Krasów

[1] M. Buchvaldek, 'Starši šnurová keramika v Čechách', *Arch.R.*, vol. IX, 1957, pp. 362 ff.

[2] U. Fischer, 'Mitteldeutschland und Schnurkeramik', *Jahresschrift f.Mitteldeutsche Vorgeschichte*, vol. 41–2, Halle 1958, pp. 254 ff.

[3] C. J. Becker, 'Die mittel-neolithischen Kulturen in Südskandinavien', *Acta Archaeologica*, vol. XXV, København 1955, pp. 114 ff. K. W. Struve, *Die Einzelgrabkultur in Schleswig-Holstein und ihre kontinentalen Beziehungen*, Neumünster 1955, pp. 117 ff. M. Buchvaldek (op. cit., note 1). Id. 'Z problematyki kultury ceramiki sznurowej w Europie', *Sprawozdania z posiedzeń Komisji PAN*, Kraków 1961, pp. 12 ff.

[4] L. Kozłowski, *Młodsza epoka kamienna w Polsce (neolit)*, Lwów 1924, Pl. XVI:3. T. Sulimirski, '"Thuringian" Amphorae', *PPS*, vol. XXI, 1955, Fig. 2:9. L. Kilian, 'Schnurkeramik und Ockergrabkultur', *SMYA*, vol. 59:2, 1957, Fig. 19:b. Z. Krzak, *Materiały do znajomości kultury złockiej*, Wrocław-Warszawa-Kraków 1961, Figs. 48a; 132:II, X; 133:d, e. J. Machnik, 'Groby kultury ceramiki sznurowej w Książnicach Wielkich', *Prace Komisji Archeologicznej Oddziału PAN w Krakowie*, no. 4, 1964, pp. 347 f., Pl. II:12.

[5] A. Äyräpää, 'Über die Streitaxtkulturen in Russland', *ESA*, vol. VIII, 1933, p. 124, Fig. 125. L. Kilian (op. cit., note 4), Fig. 6:b.

II a flint axe comparable to C. J. Becker's 'Bundsø-type',[6] proper to the Third Middle Neolithic period in Denmark; at Kołokolin 4 (no. 66) a battle-axe of an eastern type.

Amphorae of later types were more numerous. Eight were of Buchvaldek's type IIa, but that from Stratyn 2 (Plate 5:1) can be regarded as transitional to his type III. The amphorae from Rokitno 6 (Plate 5:9) was associated with three flint axes, two of which may be classed as Becker's 'Lindø-type', and one was more similar to his 'Valby-type'. The amphora from Kulczyce II (Plate 5:4) was found with an axe made of sandstone (Fig. 15:17). No grave goods, except flint knives, were found with the four remaining amphorae. A few specimens found in 'flat' graves at Vykhvatyntsi (Fig. 1:5, 8) on the Middle Dniester, on the steppe border in South Podolia,[7] may be included in this group, and also a few amphorae found in the western division of the steppe country, in the remains of the Usatovo culture at Usatovo itself (no. 366) and Ternovka[8] (no. 364).

No amphorae of type IIb were excavated in our mounds, but they appear further east. A single specimen was found as far as south-east Russia proper, in a barrow-grave at Rečitsa near Briansk (no. 277).[9] A few were found at Usatovo and Ternovka.[10] A somewhat debased amphora from layer II of the settlement of Mykhailivka on the Lower Dnieper[11] was seemingly of the same type (Fig. 6:1); cord-impressed decoration on the upper part of its body consisted of three horizontal girdles of shaded triangles and groups of vertical lines.

Of special interest are a few other amphorae from Vykhvatintsy, found in the same graves with specimens mentioned above (Fig. 1:4).[12] They were a painted ware, a kind of Tripolyan ware, modelled on Thuringian amphorae, provided with two lugs on the body. Their black-painted decoration, either simple, or elaborated in curving and straight lines, is reminiscent of that of the Thuringian amphorae, and may be compared with that found on specimens of Buchvaldek's type IIb.

Nor were any amphorae of Buchvaldek's type III found in the Sub-Carpathian area. However, an amphora with moulded ornament and four lugs on the body from the ochre-grave 22 at Valea Lupului in North Moldavia (Fig. 1:6)[13] closely resembles this type.

The most common amphorae of the Sub-Carpathian region (seven specimens) do not correspond with any of Buchvaldek's standard type. They call to mind his type IIb but differ from it in that their neck, not the upper part of the body, was decorated. We shall call them 'type IIc'. The zig-zag band in the decoration of one of these (Kołokolin 1, Fig. 10:1) links it with the amphorae of the 'Mansfeld' group in Thuringia, dated by Fischer as his second stage, and the ornament of the amphorae from Rokitno 2 (Plate 5:8) and Wiktorów VIII (Plate 5:6) corresponds to that of those of his 'Mansfeld Mixed group' (*Mansfelder Mischgruppe*) similarly dated as the second stage.[14] These agreements imply a late date for our amphorae of IIc type.

The amphora found in layer I of the settlement at Mykhailivka on the Lower Dnieper[15] was likewise of the above type (Fig. 6:2). It had a large spherical, undecorated body, a short cord-decorated cylindrical neck. It was found in sherds and as reconstructed it has no handles, but this fact does not preclude its originally having been provided with these.

Grave goods which accompanied them were fairly numerous and exhibit a greater variety than those associated with amphorae of type I. They were found twice with battle-axes, at Balice 15 of an eastern type (Fig. 13:2), at Rokitno 2 of a kind of Bundsø-type (Fig. 15:2); in the latter grave a perforated amber pendant was excavated (Fig. 19:21). Flint axes (found with three amphorae) were quadrangular in section, one of these (Kołokolin 1, no. 66) being very small. Only two amphorae were accompanied by vessels: at Siwki 1-1878 (no. 157) by a beaker proper to the Funnel Beaker culture; at Kołokolin 1 by three vessels, a cord-decorated beaker, an undecorated cup, and a bowl (Plate 6:1, 9, 20). The latter was similar to that from Brusno associated with an amphora of Miechów type (Plate 3:3–5) and a flint axe of Bundsø-type (Fig. 15:4). At Kołokolin 1 a flint arrow-head and sherds of Globular Amphora pottery were excavated (Plate 9: 25; Fig. 12:9).

The amphora from Nowosiółki Liskie (Plate 5:2) was of a particular type. It had a carinated body, and its cord decoration followed patterns proper to Thuringian amphorae of Buchvaldek's type I; the horizontal band on the body was raised and finger-tipped instead of being incised or cord impressed. However, its original shape may not have been carinated, at least not to the extent which appears from reconstruction done in the museum. The amphora was found with two beakers of uncommon types (Plate 6:7, 8); one calls to mind vessels excavated in barrow-graves of the Usatovo culture,[16] and the other, with its finger-tipped raised band around the rim, may be connected with the Funnel Beaker pottery. A flint dagger was also excavated in this barrow-grave.

Two 'degenerate' undecorated amphorae from Małoszynka (Plate 5:10, 11) and two similar from Nowosiółka Jaruzelskich II and III (Plate 4:8, 9) were apparently of a late date. That from Nowosiółka Jaruzelskich II was found with a battle-axe of *z*-2 type Glob-Struve's type K,[17] which points to a late date for these vessels.

Five amphorae were of an unknown type; four disin-

[6] C. J. Becker, 'Den Tyknakkede Flintökse', *Aarböger for Nordisk Oldkyndighed of Historie*, 1957.

[7] А. Е. Алихова, Выхватинский могильник, Ксиимк, no. XXVI, 1949, pp. 69 ff., Fig. 29:5, 6, 12.

[8] Т. С. Пассек, Периодизация трипольских поселений, МИА, no. 10, 1949, Figs. 97; 99:2.

[9] A. Äyräpää (op. cit., note 5), pp. 111 f., Fig. 108. L. Kilian (op. cit., note 4), Fig. 6:a.

[10] Op. cit. (note 8), Figs. 97; 99:3.

[11] О. Ф. Лагодовська, О. Г. Шапошникова, М. Л. Макаревич, Михайлівське поселення, Kiev 1962, Figs. 10, 30. О. Г. Шапошникова, КСИАК, no. 11, 1961, pp. 38 ff., Fig. 3.

[12] Op. cit. (note 7), Fig. 29:1. Т. С. Пассек, Ксиимк, no. 56, pp. 76 ff. M. Gimbutas, *The Prehistory of Eastern Europe*, part 1, Cambridge (Mass.) 1956, p. 106, Fig. 58:3.

[13] M. Dinu, *SCIV*, vol. VI, 1959, pp. 504 f., Fig. 4.

[14] Fischer (op. cit., note 2), Figs. 4:1; 5:3.

[15] See note 11, p. 41, Fig. 3.

[16] A. M. Tallgren, 'La Pontide préscythique', *ESA*, vol. II, 1926, p. 48, Fig. 37:6. Gimbutas (op. cit., note 12), pp. 85 ff., Figs. 47–9.

[17] Struve (op. cit., note 3), p. 24, Pl. I.

tegrated and their reconstruction was not practicable. Two of these, from Komarów 5 and 31, were each associated with a wide beaker (Fig. 9:2) which had a chevron decoration on the neck. A flint axe of the 'hybrid' type was also found with the former (Fig. 16:11). The amphora from Kulczyce v (no. 49) was excavated with a beaker of Struve's type I, but typical of M. Buchvaldek's IIa or IIb assemblage (Fig. 11:2). The amphora from Kulczyce III was evidently of a somewhat later age. Its grave assemblage comprised a baggy bowl, a 'simple' battle-axe of *x*-I type, halved and damaged by fire, a flint axe oval in section, and two arrow-heads with concave base (Plate 6:12; Fig. 16:14).

The latest was probably the undecorated amphora from Siedliska I (no. 30) presumably of IIc type. It was associated with five other vessels, among which were two undecorated beakers, a handled jug, a handled cup, and, in addition to a stone battle-axe, a mace head, and a flint axe, two metal objects were also excavated there: a copper or bronze open ring (or bracelet?) and a lead finger-ring.

'MIECHÓW' AMPHORAE
(Plate 3:5, 6)

In the north-western group amphorae of a different type were excavated; they were either cord-decorated (the neck and the upper part of the body) or undecorated, the latter being of a later date, as is indicated by the specimen from Balice VII (Plate 3:6) dated as Bronze Age period A-2 by its bronze grave goods. Amphorae of this type were provided with three or four small lugs under the neck, and some had a very narrow base.

Amphorae of this type, a list of which is given in Table 9, were a locally developed form, closely connected with similar vessels of the Cracow-Sandomierz group of Corded Ware,[18] hence the name which has been given them. Their closely related amphorae also appear in the Moravian group of Corded Ware.[19] The 'Miechów' amphorae of our area seem to be of a somewhat later date than those of the Thuringian type; they were coeval with the more evolved specimens of the latter, and were their complementary form in the northern part of the north-western group of our barrow-graves, where only one Thuringian amphora was found (Brzezinki IV, no. 3). In two instances our amphorae were found with bronze ornaments (Lublin-Sławinek, no. 131; Balice VII) which suggest a late date for this type.

The amphora from Zaborol I (Plate 4:7) may also be included in this list, although it deviates somewhat from the usual shape of these vessels. Similar amphorae found in a barrow-grave at Rosiejów north-east of Cracow,[20] point to its late date.

Of a different group were medium-sized amphora-like vessels with no lugs excavated in a few graves of the Przemyśl group. Some of these had the neck covered with horizontal cord-impressed lines (Brzezinki III), others (Łukawica K, no. 20) were undecorated; the late date of these vessels is suggested by a bronze dagger found with such an undecorated vase in a grave at Goszyce near Kielce attributed to the Mierzanowice culture.[21]

BEAKERS
(Figs. 9–11; Plates 6, 8, 9)

A score of vessels excavated in our graves may fall into the category of 'beakers', another main type of the 'common European Corded Ware horizon'. However, they were not typical of our culture and show a great variety of forms many of which greatly differed from those usually found in the assemblages of the Corded Ware further west.

Only a single beaker, from Kulczyce v (Fig. 11:2) was of Struve's[22] type I; it did not differ from those of Buchvaldek's assemblages IIa and IIb and being found with a Thuringian amphora may be regarded as one of the earliest beakers of our culture. The other beaker, from Ostapie 5 (Plate 6:5) with an elaborate cord decoration, differed from the above in that its neck widened upwards considerably which gave it a funnel shape. It was very similar to the beakers from Jackowica barrow-graves (no. 244) of the Middle Dnieper culture[23] in particular to the vessel from barrow-grave 48 (Fig. 4). It was excavated with a flint axe of Becker's Bundsø-type and two bone chisels or daggers (Plate 11:11, 12).

Another beaker of western type was that from Łukawica I (no. 20) which represents Struve's type 3, proper to the later stage of the Undergrave period in Jutland and North-West Germany. Two other cord-decorated beakers from Kołokolin I (Plate 6:1, 9) found with a type IIc Thuringian amphora, and from Nowosiółki (Przemyśl, Plate 6:2) differed from the above by their wide base and clumsy shape; they correspond well with beakers of the East Harz group of Corded Ware dated by Fischer[24] as his second stage.

A few beakers, both found on the western periphery of our culture, were of a type very common in the Cracow-Sandomierz Corded Ware,[25] usually called 'amphorae' there. They were large in size, had a nearly spherical body with a flat base and a well-marked everted neck covered with incised chevron ornament. One of these beakers (Morawsko, Plate 6:21) was found with an A-type battle-axe (Plate 10:2): another one (Brzezinki IV, no. 3) was associated with an undecorated four-lugged Thuringian amphora and a clumsy beaker (mug) the third specimen (Lublin-Sławinek, no. 131) was found with a Miechów amphora, a handled jug, and a small bronze earring. Closely related to those, but a little smaller in size, was the beaker from Łotatniki (Plate 6:3).

[18] Kozłowski (op. cit., note 4), Pl. XV:10. S. Zemełka, 'Groby kultury ceramiki promienistej i sznurowej w Zesławicach, pow.Kraków', *Mat. Arch.*, vol. I, 1959, pp. 81 ff., Pl. 1:3.

[19] M. Chleborád, *Pravěké hroby durinských skrčku na Bučovsku a v okoli*, Bučovice 1934, Pls. I:3; II:10; IV:9; V:2.

[20] T. Reyman, 'Dokumentaryczne wartości odkryć w kopcu wschodnim w Rosiejowie, w pow.pińczowskim', *Slavia Antiqua*, vol. I, Poznań 1948, Figs. 37, 41.

[21] S. Nosek, 'Zagadnienie Prasłowiańszczyzny w świetle prehistorii', *Światowit*, vol. XIX, 1948, p. 55, Fig. 16. J. Kostrzewski, 'Od mezolitu do okresu wędrówek ludów', *Prehistoria Ziem Polskich*, Kraków 1939–48, Pl. 62:16, 18.

[22] Struve (op. cit., note 3), pp. 42 f.

[23] A. Bydłowski, 'Mogiły w Nowosiółce', *Światowit*, vol. VI, 1906, p. 17, Pl. I:1. T. C. Пассек, К вопросу о среднеднепровской культуре, Ксиимк, no. XVI, 1947, pp. 34 ff., Figs. 10, 11. A. Häusler, 'Die kulturellen und wirtschaftlichen Beziehungen der Bevölkerungsgruppen Mittelrusslands am Ende der jüngeren Steinzeit', *Wissenschäftliche Zft d.Martin-Luther Universität*, vol. V/I, Halle 1955–6, pp. 69 ff., Pl. 2.

[24] Fischer (op. cit., note 2), Fig. 2.

[25] S. Nosek, *Zarys archeologii Małopolski*, Kraków 1956, Pl. XV. Id. (op. cit., note 21), Pl. XV:11 (found with bronze ornaments attributable to the Mierzanowice culture).

The most common in our graves were wide beakers often with a nearly spherical body, rounded base, their neck decorated in chevron patterns, or with rows of vertical incisions. They seem to have been in some way connected with those typical of the Cracow-Sandomierz group, mentioned above. This applies in particular to the beaker from Brzezinki found with an amphora of Miechów type; beakers of this type at Komarów 5 and 31 (Fig. 9:2) were associated with a late type of Thuringian amphora. These beakers show, however, close analogies to similar vessels of the Middle Dnieper culture,[26] and also some likeness to the beakers, or bowls, proper to the Dnieper-Desna and the Fatyanovo cultures of the forest zone of East Europe.[27] Perhaps the most marked eastern analogies are exhibited by the beaker from Kryłos VI (Fig. 11:1); it has a funnel-shaped neck, a spherical body, and a rounded base. The whole surface of the neck is adorned by very regular zigzag lines arranged in zones. A bronze torque found with this vessel implies its late date. These eastern connections are strengthened by the fact that in barrow-graves 38, 39 at Komarów (Plate 2:4; Fig. 11:4) beakers of the type in question were associated with battle-axes of eastern types (type *y*-1, *y*-2, Fig. 13:8).

A form which developed from eastern prototypes occurred as a few smaller beakers with a spherical body, and a round base. Those from Kołpiec 10 and Kulczyce III (Plates 7:9; 6:12), the latter somewhat clumsy, were adorned with cord impressions, whereas the specimen from Kołokolin II (Plate 7:7) had a chevron decoration on its cylindrical neck. The beaker from Kulczyce III was found with a Thuringian amphora. The beaker from Myszyn (Fig. 10:5) also belongs here, the upper part of which is missing; it was found with two battle-axes, types B-1 and H-E_3 (Plate 10:6, 7).

Finally a few small beakers, or mugs, should be mentioned here: Brzezinki IV (no. 3); Łukawica K (no. 20); Siedliska B (Plate 6:18); Wacowice (no. 56). They were clumsy, with a wide base, straight sides, the aperture smaller than the base. Their sides were covered with cord decoration consisting of horizontal lines and bunches of short slanting lines arranged in a few groups. They were found only in the western, Przemyśl group, and dated from a later stage of the development of our culture. They strikingly resemble in both shape and decoration the bowls characteristic of the Middle Dnieper culture. Their relation to these remains obscure.

Two barrow-graves yielded beakers typical of the Funnel Beaker culture, both found with Thuringian amphorae: at Siwki I-1878 of type IIC, at Nowosiółki Liskie with an amphora of a special type (Plate 6:6–8).

BOWLS
(Plates 6, 7; Fig. 12)

This was not a homogeneous group of vessels. Those from Balice XVI and Łotatniki 2 (Plate 6:11–16) with a flat base, straight sides widening upwards, were of a simple and long-lived type. Such bowls appear in Danubian II pottery in Bohemia,[28] but were also found in graves of the Wysocko culture of the Early Iron Age.[29]

The large, clumsy, undecorated bowls from Kołokolin II (Plate 7:6), Gwoździec Stary 2 (Plate 9:9) and Komarów 50 (Fig. 31:2) were of a type which was very popular in later periods up to the Early Iron Age. Some were decorated with incised grooves. Finally, a local Sub-Carpathian variety is represented by bowls from Kołpiec 8 and Kavsko 2 (Plate 7:8; Fig. 12:14). They were small in size, had a wide base, and very low sides slightly narrowed in the central part, covered with a cord ornament. They seem to be a form greatly influenced by, or deriving from, the small clumsy beakers found mainly further west in our Territory and dealt with in the preceding paragraph.

HANDLED CUPS, JUGS
(Figs. 10, 12; Plates 6, 7)

Handled vessels were typical of a later period of the culture with which we are concerned. The earliest of these were low, wide-mouthed, cord-decorated handled cups (e.g. Fig. 10:2). Several specimens of this type were excavated in barrow-graves and found in other assemblages in our region. Similar cups were also found in Corded Ware graves in the regions of Cracow and Sandomierz, in Upper Silesia, but also in Moravia and West Slovakia, where they were given the name of the 'Złota' handled cups;[30] in fact, however, they do not appear in the remains of the Złota culture.[31] They were dated there as the transitional stage from the 'Aeneolithic' to the Early Bronze Age (Reinecke's A-1). J. Machnik[32] calls them the 'Chłopice-Véselé type'. We shall deal with these cups again in the next chapter.

The handled bowl from Łotatniki 1 (Plate 6:15) corresponds to that excavated in grave 3 at Sobów near Tarnobrzeg[33] along with two boar tusks, each of which had two perforations at the broader end, and a necklace of small discoid beads made of mollusc shells. It belonged to the Early Bronze Age Mierzanowice culture.

Jugs appeared to be of a later date. That from Gwoździec Stary II (Fig. 10:6) found with an undecorated single-lugged mug and a large bronze (copper?) ear-pendant (Plate 9:4–6), closely resembles the handled, decorated cups of the Kisza-

[26] И. И. Артеменко, Среднеднепровская культура, Сов. Арх., 1962–3, pp. 12 ff., Figs. 2:3, 11; 3:1.

[27] Артеменко (op. cit., note 26), Fig. 2. Idem, Неолитические стоянки и курганы эпохи бронзы близ с. Ходосовичи гомельской обл. БССР, Памятники Каменного и Бронзового Веков Евразии, Moscow 1963, pp. 31 ff., Figs. 1, 10, 18, 26. Пассек (op. cit., note 23), Fig. 14. Äyräpää (op. cit., note 5), p. 110, Figs. 110, 114. Häusler (op. cit., note 23), Pl. 2:4; 7; 8.

[28] E.g., A. Stocký, *La Bohême préhistorique*, vol. I, Prague 1929, Pls. 37:8; 39; 118:19, etc. See also J. Żurowski, 'Neue Ergebnisse der neolithischen Forschung im südwestpolnischen Lössgebiet', *Prähistorische Zft*, vol. XXI, 1930, Fig. 16a.

[29] T. Sulimirski, *Kultura wysocka*, Kraków 1931, Pls. XVI:18; XVIII:10.

[30] Z. Trnačkova, 'Hrob z ozdobi šnurove keramiky v Hulině', *Arch.R.*, vol. XII, 1960, pp. 155 ff. B. Novotný, *Slovensko w mladšej dobe kamennej*, Bratislava 1958, pp. 50 ff. (or pp. 65 ff. of the German text), Pl. LXIV: 1, 2.

[31] Only one handled cup of the Złota-Grodzisko I cemetery, out of fourteen handled cups published by Z. Krzak (op. cit., note 4), was of 'Złota' or 'Chłopice-Véselé' type: Fig. 17:d. Those published by L. Kozłowski (op. cit., note 4), Pl. XVI:15, 17, and in Id. 'Epoka kamienna na wydmach wschodniej części Wyżyny Małopolskiej', *Archiwum Nauk Antropologicznych*, Warszawa-Lwów 1923, Pl. XXVII:1–6, were found on the south-western border of the territory occupied by that culture.

[32] J. Machnik, 'Uwagi o wczesnej fazie epoki brązu w dorzeczu górnej Wisły i Dniestru', *Sprawozdania Komisji PAN*, Kraków, VII–XII, 1960. Some of the vessels included in this group, in particular handled jugs, do not belong to this type. Id. *Studia nad kulturą ceramiki sznurowej w Małopolsce*, Wrocław-Warszawa-Kraków 1966, pp. 141 ff.

[33] Nosek (op. cit., note 21), p. 110, Pl. XVII.

postag culture in the Hungarian Plain,[34] dated as the very end of the Early Bronze Age. A cord-decorated jug—almost a replica of the 'Silesian' jugs proper to the Marszowice (Marschwitz) culture[35]—was excavated in our area in slab-cist grave 2 of the Globular Amphora culture at Beremiany 2 (Plate 14:10). Its late date is indicated by a very similar cord-decorated jug found at Prusy-Zastów near Cracow,[36] along with a bronze pendant of Irish type. The jug from Rypniów (Rzepniów) (no. 589) was found with a bronze ear-pendant of Stubło type, which will be dealt with later.

The second jug from the barrow-grave of our culture, was that excavated at Płaucza Wielka (Plate 6:22); it represents a type proper to the Oder and Marszowice (Marschwitz) type of Corded Ware in western Poland.[37] Finally, the jug from Lublin-Sławinek (no. 131) also belonged to a type well known in the Corded Ware of southern Poland.

Of interest was an undecorated handled cup from Kavsko 4 (no. 45) associated with an undecorated vase (Fig. 29: 1, 4). Both were Unetice types; similar handled cups found in Moravia[38] belonged to the Věteřov culture[39] transistory to the Middle Bronze Age. Finally, the undecorated handled cup from Rohatyn (Plate 7:1) should be mentioned. It represents a type proper to the Mad'arovce culture of Slovakia[40] of the advanced stage of the Early Bronze Age.

MUGS

Mugs were characteristic of late graves of our culture, and may be regarded as their principal vessel; they were typical of the Oder and Marszowice (Marschwitz) groups of Corded Ware in western Poland.[41] A few specimens were small in size, with a cylindrical body decorated by parallel cord-impressed lines around the upper part of the vessel (Balice XIV, no. 1; Klimkowce, Fig. 10:4; Kołokolin VII, Fig. 10:3; Kołpiec 9, no. 46; Kaczanówka 4, Plate 8:4). Most typical, however, were larger mugs with straight sides sometimes slightly widening upwards, with a flat lip, usually provided with an unperforated lug under the rim (*Zapfenbecher*). The late date of these vessels has been pointed out by L. Kilian,[42] who equates them with the Overgraves of Jutland; their late date is also indicated by metal objects associated with them: the decorated mug of this type at Buhłów 2 was found with two silver spiral rings (Plate 9:6, 10–11); at Gwoździec Stary II (Plate 9:4–5) and Ostapie 4 (Plate 9:12, 13), undecorated mugs of this type were found with bronze ornaments, that from the latter grave being of North Caucasian origin. It is worth noting in this connection that an undecorated, single-lugged mug strikingly similar to that from Ostapie 4, was excavated in a slab-cist grave at Koban in the Central Caucasian highland[43] along with an undecorated jug and some copper objects.

Single-lugged mugs were most frequent in the Podolian group. Only one specimen, in fact a single-lugged beaker, was found in the Sub-Carpathian group (Kołpiec 8, Fig. 11:3). They were also found in a few graves further east. A cord-decorated mug of this type was found at Nowa Sieniawa near Lityn (Plate 9:3),[44] and another in a barrow-grave at Krupol (no. 276),[45] over sixty kilometres east of Kiev, along with other vessels and a stone battle-axe.

Of importance is the fact that a mug of this type, but made and decorated in a manner proper to the Komarów culture, was excavated in barrow-grave 45 (of the Komarów culture) at Komarów itself (Plate 21:4). This fact also points to a late date for these vessels.

To the same group of vessels belong similarly shaped mugs provided, however, with a small loop-shaped handle. Such a specimen from Chorostków was found with a large perforated amber disc (Plate 9:1, 2), and another at Kavsko 6 (Fig. 12:11). A mug of this type, but larger in size and undecorated, was excavated in slab-cist grave 3 of the Globular Amphora culture at Koszyłowce (Plate 14:9), and a smaller one, undecorated, in barrow-grave 20 (Fig. 29:8) at Komarów which belonged to the Komarów culture. Mugs of this type were proper to the Cracow-Miechów Corded Ware[46] and also of the Wieselburg-Gata culture of the Hungarian Plain where they dated from Reinecke's period A-2, according to R. Pittioni.[47]

The two-lugged mug from grave 8 at Zakłodzie (no. 136), of a unique type in our culture, may also be included in this group of vessels.

CUPS

A relatively large number of small vessels can be classed as cups, although they do not form a homogeneous group. Some, e.g. that from grave 6 at Zakłodzie, had the shape of a drinking glass, other vessels, e.g. the cup from Kołokolin I or Ostapie 3 (Plate 6:9, 10), were tulip-shaped. They were mostly undecorated and, except a few, dated from a later stage of the Barrow-grave culture.

OTHER VESSELS

In several graves vessels were found which were unique in our group and often had no parallels in other groups of Corded

[34] A. Mozsolics, 'Der frühbronzezeitliche Urnenfriedhof von Kisapostag', *Arch. Hung.*, vol. XXVI, 1942, Figs. 1–3.

[35] Kostrzewski (op. cit., note 21), Pl. 57:1. Kozłowski (op. cit., note 4), Pl. VI:4. H. Seger, *Schlesiens Vorzeit in Schrift und Bild*, vol. NF VII, 1916, Figs. on p. 69. J. Filip, *Pravěké Československo*, Praha 1948, Pl. 14:9, 10.

[36] J. Bartys, 'Nowe stanowisko małopolskiej grupy ceramiki sznurowej', *Prz.A.*, vol. VI, 1937, Fig. 4.

[37] Kozłowski (op. cit., note 4), Pl. VI:1. J. Kostrzewski, *Wielkopolska w pradziejach*, 3rd ed., Warszawa-Wrocław 1955, p. 51, Fig. 95. Seger (op. cit., note 35), p. 67, Fig. 254.

[38] Filip (op. cit., note 35), P. 16:7. K. Tihelka, *Cezavy u Blučiny*, Brno 1957, Pl. 5:d.

[39] I. Pleinerová, 'Zur Datierung der jüngeren Aunjetitzer Kultur', *Chronologie Préhistorique de la Tchecoslovaquie*, Prague 1956, pp. 80 ff. K. Tihelka, 'On the Relations Between the Věteřov Type and the Unétice Culture in Moravia', in the same work, pp. 86 ff.

[40] J. Eisner, *Slovensko v pravěku*, Bratislava 1933, Pl. XXXII:8–13.

[41] R. Schroeder, *Die Nordgruppe der Oderschnurkeramik*, Berlin 1951, Pls. 18:1, 3; 22:5; 24:7, etc. Kozłowski, (op. cit. note 4), p. 66, Pl. XV:4. Nosek (op. cit., note 25), pl. XVI. Seger (op. cit., note 35), p. 67, Figs. 255, 275, etc.

[42] L. Kilian, 'Schnurkeramik und Ockergrabkultur', *SMYA*, vol. 59:2, 1957, p. 27.

[43] Е. И. Крупнов, Труды Г.И.М., vol. VIII, Moscow 1938, pp. 43 ff., Fig. 3.

[44] G. Ossowski, *ZWAK*, vol. XIII, 1889, p. 44, Fig. 3.

[45] Äyräpää (op. cit., note 5), p. 125, Fig. 127. В. Щербаківський, Камяна доба в Україні, Münich 1947, p. 47.

[46] Kozłowski (op. cit., note 4), Pl. XV:6. Nosek (op. cit., note 21), Pl. XVI.

[47] R. Pittioni, *Urgeschichte des österreichischen Raumes*, Wien 1954, p. 321.

Ware culture. Some, e.g. simple basins (Kołpiec 9, Plate 7:4), or miniature cups (Siedliska B, Plate 6:13, 14; Bolechowce) are of no particular importance for our purposes. There are, however, a few unique vessels which deserve some attention.

To the latter belongs the cord-decorated two-handled vase from Ostapie 5 (Plate 4:6). Two-handled vases of a similar type were found in the Jordanów (Jordansmühl) culture in Silesia[48] and were typical of the Bodrogkeresztur culture of the Hungarian Plain.[49] Vases of this type survived there to later periods, up to the Early Iron Age, and within our Territory were one of the characteristic vessels of the Komarów culture of the Middle Bronze Age. The vase from Ostapie was probably of a late date and had some connection with the trend which introduced vessels of this type into the Komarów culture.

The two-handled, black vessel from Załuże (Plate 4:3) has sometimes been regarded as a degenerate globular amphora, which seems erroneous. This was in fact a single-handled cup with an additional handle of a different shape affixed unsymmetrically on the vessel. It is a unique specimen.

Of particular interest was the small, black, undecorated bowl with two perforated lugs under the rim from Kołpiec 5 (Plate 8:2), found with faience beads, a flint knife and axe, and another small vessel of unknown type. Small, undecorated bowls of two lugs, similar to our specimen, were found in barrow-graves of the Corded Ware culture in East Slovakia.[50]

Finally, a high-footed dish from Balice VII should be mentioned (Plate 3:2). It was unique in our culture, and dates from the advanced stage of the Early Bronze Age, as is indicated by bronze objects found in the same grave. Similar vessels were common in Czechoslovakia, dating from the same period.[51] Pedestalled cups were sometimes found in the Komarów barrow-graves.

ALIEN POTTERY

A few barrow-graves yielded pottery typical of the Funnel Beaker culture. Sometimes (Miżyniec, Sobiecin, Plate 7:10–13) this was the only sepulchral pottery but in other graves (Nowosiółki Liskie, Siwki, Plate 6:6–8) pots proper to the Funnel Beaker pottery, or at least closely related to them, were found in association with vessels characteristic of the Corded Ware. Of particular interest, however, were two barrow-graves of the Przemyśl group (Koropuż, Stojańce); their burials were accompanied by Thuringian amphorae (Plate 3:1) but in both cases, remains of a hut were uncovered under the same mound close to the grave, in which pottery typical of the Funnel Beaker culture was found (Plate 3:1; Fig. 12:1, 2). The huts were indisputably of the same date and formed an entity with the respective graves, although it is still doubtful whether they were previously inhabited by the persons buried close to them, or were built solely as a kind of a mortuary hut.

Funnel Beaker pottery found in our western barrow-graves was apparently related to that found at Trzciniec in the north-western corner of the Territory of our concern;[52] the beaker from Siwki (Plate 6:6) has counterparts in the pottery from the settlement at Gródek Nadbużny[53] which belonged to the final stage of the Funnel Beaker culture.

A few potsherds of the Globular Amphora culture were excavated in barrow-graves I and V at Kołokolin (no. 66, Fig. 12:3, 9). However, the decoration of one of these, from Kołokolin V (Fig. 12:3), does not differ substantially from that proper to the Wiórek stage of the Funnel Beakers in Greater Poland.[54]

At Komarów, pottery of Tripolyan 'D-ware' type was excavated in at least two barrow-graves (nos. 2, 3) which presumably belonged to a late stage of their culture.

DECORATION

Most vessels, particularly those of the earlier stages, were decorated; their decoration did not differ in any respect from that proper to other Corded Ware groups in Central Europe and further west.[55] Common were single but mainly double lines round the neck of the vessel made by simple cord impressions, often repeated several times and forming several groups. A number of vessels had more complicated decorative patterns consisting of horizontal lines and wavy lines between them (Ostapie 1, Plate 6:5), or the lower part of the body had a 'radial' decoration of vertical lines tending towards the base (Jaktorów 2, Plate 7:2); the latter was clearly borrowed from the Złota culture. Thuringian amphorae had a more complicated ornament, on the origin of which I have commented in a special article.[56] Incised decoration also appears, often in the form of rows of short vertical incisions, but more often in the form of chevron patterns. Raised decoration was an exception met with almost exclusively in Podolia; it was more proper to a late phase in the development of the culture. Characteristic of the late phase were undecorated vessels of all types.

AXES

(Figs. 15, 16)

Nearly ninety axes were found in our barrow-graves, of which only about ten specimens were not of flint. Approximately half the total number of flint axes were made of the black, or black-and-grey variety, the 'Bug' or 'Volhynian' flint which was extracted from natural outcrops in the region on the Upper Bug and along the northern edge of the Podolian Plateau,[57] and also found in deep river valleys of West

[48] Seger (op. cit., note 35), Fig. 5–9.

[49] J. Hillebrand, 'Das Kupferzeitliche Gräberfeld von Pusztaistvánháza', *Arch. Hung.*, vol. 4, Budapest 1929. F. Tompa, '25 Jahre Urgeschichtsforschung in Ungarn, 1912–1936' *24/25 Bericht d.röm.-germ.Kommission*, Berlin 1937, pp. 51 ff., Pls. 18; 23; 28.

[50] Novotný (op. cit., note 30), pp. 51 f. (or p. 69 of the German text), Pl. LXIV:3.

[51] Filip (op. cit., note 35), Pl. 14:6, 8. B. Novotný, 'Slavonska kultura v Československu', *Slovenská Archeológia*, vol. III, 1955, pp. 5, 56 ff., Pls. I–III.

[52] A. Gardawski, 'Wyniki prac wykopaliskowych przeprowadzonych w 1952 r. w miejscowości Trzciniec, pow.Puławy', *W.A.*, vol. XX, 1954, pp. 380 ff., Pls. XXIX:c; XXXII:c, d.

[53] J. Kowalczyk, 'Osada kultury pucharów lejkowatych w miejsc. Gródek Nadbużny, pow.Hrubieszów, w świetle badań 1954 r'., *W.A.*, vol. XXIII, 1956, Pls. III:5; VI:5.

[54] K. Jażdżewski, 'Zusammenfassender Überblick über die Trichterbecher Kultur', *Praehistorische Zft*, vol. XXIII, 1932.

[55] Struve (op. cit., note 3), pp. 44 ff.

[56] Sulimirski (op. cit., note 4), pp. 34 ff.

[57] T. Sulimirski, 'Remarks Concerning the Distribution of Some

Podolia further south where, however, the grey colour predominated.

Less frequent (about 25 per cent) were axes made of the grey-white spotted variety called 'Rachów' or 'Świeciechów' flint after two villages on the right bank of the Vistula north of the junction of the San in which its deposits were exploited.[58] Axes and other implements made of this flint were found almost exclusively in barrow-graves of the north-western part of the Territory, but they sometimes extended along the Dniester far to the south-east (Kołokolin IV).

A few axes were made of a grey variety, of which the origin has not been established. Those made of a slightly banded flint, found mainly in the southern and western part of our area, seem to have originated from the western part of the Lublin Plateau. The axe made of banded flint from Kołokolin IV (a fragment, Fig. 17:4) must have been brought from the mine at Krzemionki near Opatów, about 250km (nearly 140 miles) away.

Seven axes were of siliceous slate, pale yellow in colour (Fig. 9:4). Of these, four were found near the western border of Podolia where adzes made of this raw material were very common in Tripolyan settlements; three other specimens were excavated in graves in the western part of the Territory. The axe from Kulczyce II (Fig. 15:17), made of sandstone, found with a Thuringian amphora of IIa type (Plate 5:4), seems to have been the dummy of a flint axe in a region where flint was not available.

All the above axes belonged to two main types, and were nearly equal in number; one type was quadrangular in section (Fig. 15), the other oval or lenticular (Fig. 16). Among the quadrangular, medium-sized were most numerous, but there were also many small, thick-butted axes similar to the Bundsø-type of Becker's scheme (Fig. 15:5, 7–9);[59] many of these axes, being broader in their upper part, bear more resemblance to his Blandebjerg-type. Less frequent were the axes comparable to Becker's Lindø- and Valby-types (Fig. 15:10, 11, 15, 16, 18–20). However, none of these types can serve as an indicator of the earlier or later date of the given graves, as is well exemplified by a Bundsø-type axe found at Balice VII, one of the latest graves of our culture.

Many axes do not correspond with any one type of Becker's scheme. These include in particular very small, thin, flat, thick-butted axes, well-polished all over their surface, reminiscent of copper axes on the model of which they were probably made (Fig. 16:20, 25, 26; Fig. 17:1, 2). Axes of this type were found mainly in Podolia, often in slab-cist graves under the mounds, which points to their connection with the Globular Amphora culture (Fig. 25); axes of this kind were proper to that culture. Outside the above area, they were found in a few barrow-graves situated either close to the western border of Podolia (Kołokolin IV, Rokitno I) or on the western border of the Territory (Siedliska), in both cases within reach of the influence of the Globular Amphora culture.

Oval or lenticular axes formed another large group (Fig. 16:1–6). In this group we may also include axes irregular in section, often with one side oval, the other rectangular, mostly thin-butted, the butt usually being narrow and semicircular (Fig. 16:7, 18). They were a hybrid form of the axes lenticular in section and those of the Bundsø-type. Similar axes were also found in the Funnel Beaker settlement at Ćmielów west of the Vistula.[60]

The geographical distribution of the two main types of axes is of interest. Those oval in section, with few exceptions, were at home mainly in the region south of the Dniester, and the same applies to the hybrid form. Axes of the Bundsø-type were also found mainly in the south but they reached further north than the oval ones. On the other hand, later axes, similar to Danish Lindø- and Valby-types were found chiefly in the central part of this territory, and only appeared exceptionally south of the Dniester.

Axes oval in section seem to be the earliest ones in the south. This was the territory previously inhabited by late Danubian I settlers, bearers of the linear pottery, whose stone axes were oval; this form was deeply rooted here and survived even up to the Scythian period.[61] Quadrangular axes seem to have appeared here at a little later date and then their hybridization took place.

BATTLE-AXES

(Plate 10; Figs. 13, 14)

Battle-axes, which are highly characteristic grave goods in many Corded Ware and Beaker cultures, were not of particular importance in our culture. A similar observation was made by Fischer[62] with regard to the Thuringian group of Corded Ware. Our battle-axes, well over sixty of which were found in the barrow-graves, varied greatly in size and shape. Only a few can be assigned to some of the North-West European types, as they were more closely related to the axes of the East European forest zone.

These axes may be divided into two main groups: the 'showy' (Plate 10) and the 'simple' axes (Figs. 13, 14). They are all listed in Tables 7 and 8. To the 'showy' type (Prunk-Äxte) belonged a few axes regarded by N. Åberg[63] as an eastern 'degenerate' variety of 'Jutland' axes; L. Kozłowski[64] called them the 'Baltic' type. They were somewhat large in size, slightly bent, quite slim, their upper part conic or cylindrical, the blade drooping. They were made of granite or of a greenish variety of stone, the surface thoroughly polished.

Several stray axes of this type were found within our Territory,[65] but only three in graves. The specimen from Morawsko (Plate 10:2) resembles Glob's type A, whereas the axe from Stare Sioło (no. 34) seems to be akin to his type B-1, as was that from Myszyn (Plate 10:6) of which only the upper part and the butt survived; similar axes were often found in Unetice assemblages in Silesia and Moravia. Another axe from Myszyn was similar to Glob's type E-3 (Plate 10:7).

Varieties of Flint in Poland', *Światowit*, vol. XXIII, 1960, pp. 299 ff., Fig. 4 (map).

[58] Ibid., pp. 286 ff., Fig. 2 (map).

[59] Becker (op. cit., note 6), p. 14, Fig. 5.

[60] Z. Podkowińska, 'Osada neolityczna na górze Gawroniec w Ćmielowie, pow.Opatów', *W.A.*, vol. XVII, Pl. XXXI:1, 2.

[61] T. Sulimirski, *Scytowie na zachodniem Podolu*, Lwów 1936, p. 22, Pl. IV:2g.

[62] Fischer (op. cit., note 2), p. 272.

[63] N. Åberg, *Das nordische Kulturgebiet in Mitteleuropa während der jüngeren Steinzeit*, Uppsala 1918, pp. 70 f., 260 f., Figs. 121–3.

[64] Kozłowski (op. cit., note 4), p. 78, Pl. XXI.

[65] Ibid., pp. 100 f., Pl. XXVI.

The variety of stone of which the above axes were made is not available within the Territory we are dealing with. They must have been brought from some region further north where many axes of similar types were found.[66] It is of interest to note that those found in our graves belonged to the second period of our culture.

TABLE 7. 'Showy' stone battle-axes found in Sub-Carpathian barrow-graves

A. 'Showy' axes	Glob's* and other types	
1. Morawsko (Plate 10:2)	A	
2. Myszyn (2nd specimen) (Plate 10:6)	B-1	
3. Stare Sioło	B-1	
4. Myszyn (1st specimen) (Plate 10:7)	H/E-3	
5. Gwoździec Stary 1 (blade) (Plate 10:4)	–	eastern?
6. Kołokolin III/I (damaged) (Plate 10:3)	–	'knob-hammer' type)
7. Łotatniki I (Plate 10:8)	–	'shoe-last' type
8. Łukawica	C-2	
9. Zdołbunów (Plate 10:11)	–	'Sofiivka' type

B. Fatyanovo-axes

(a) Found in barrow-graves

1. Balice XVI (Plate 10:10)	4. Kołokolin V ('Baltic' type (Plate 10:5))
2. Daszawa	5. Komarów 25
3. Kołokolin IV	6. Korytne
	7. Siedliska A

(b) Stray specimens found outside the territory defined by Äyräpää†

1. Bachory (Cieszanów-Lubaczów)	7. Halicz (L. Kozłowski, Neolit., Plate XXVI:7)
2. Bohorodczany	8. Sniatynka (Drohobycz)
3. Bucovina, location unknown	9. Stanin (Radziechów)
4. Czerniawka (Jaworów)	10. Ulicko (Rawa Ruska)
5. Dowhopole (Kosów)	11. Wiktorów (Stanisławów)
6. Dublany (Sambor)	12. Wołświn (Sokal)
	13. Lesko‡

* P. V. Glob, *Studier over den Jyske Enkeltgravskultur*, København 1945, p. 17.
† Äyräpää (op. cit., note 5), Fig. 35 (map).
‡ T. Aksamit, *Pradzieje Rzeszowszczyzny*, Rzeszów 1963, Fig. 8.

A number of 'showy' battle-axes found in our graves (Table 7) were of eastern types. The specimen from Kołokolin IV (Plate 10:1) was found with a Thuringian amphora of type I (Plate 4:1); the axe from Kołokolin V (Plate 10:5) was associated with Funnel Beaker pottery (Fig. 12:5). These facts imply that the above battle-axes belonged to the early period of our culture. They all have close counterparts in the Russian and Bielorussian forest zone.[67] Eastern connections are also shown by the battle-axe from Balice XVI (Plate 10:10),[68] which at the same time calls to mind Glob's type E-3.

[66] Ibid., pp. 78 f.
[67] Äyräpää (op. cit., note 5), p. 25, Figs. 8, 14.
[68] Ibid., p. 26, Figs. 12, 66.
[69] Ibid., Fig. 35 (map).
[70] Ibid., p. 25, e.g., Fig. 15.

Two axes were of the genuine Fatyanovo type, and originated from a destroyed barrow-grave at Daszawa (no. 41) and from Komarów 25. The latter was broken, and its lower part provided with a new shaft: it had been given the shape of a 'simple' type. These two and the specimen from Siedliska A (no. 30) were found outside the extent of Fatyanovo axes drawn by A. Äyräpää.[69] The latter axe and two other specimens correspond well with East Russian axes and other types included in the Fatyanovo type.[70] Table 7 gives the list of all Fatyanovo axes found in our area outside the territory mentioned above; they considerably enlarge its western and southern extent.

Fatyanovo battle-axes seem to have belonged to a later period of culture. This is indicated by the specimen from Komarów 25, and also by the bronze shaft-axe of Caucasian type from the hoard from Stubło. The Fatyanovo axes, with their drooping blade and bent shape were obviously modelled on these metal prototypes.

Two specimens which differed from each other belonged to the 'showy' axes. That from Kołokolin III/I (Plate 10:3) was of the 'knob-hammer' type, slightly bent, rectangular in section, with sharp edges. Its blade is missing. It must have been brought from Central Poland where axes, similar though round in section, are often found in the remains of the Funnel Beaker culture. An axe of this type was found in the settlement of the Funnel Beaker culture at Gródek Nadbużny[71] and a few stray specimens are recorded from various parts of the country outside the extent of this culture. The specimen from Kołokolin was found with two small cord-decorated handled cups (Fig. 10:2; Plate 6:19), a replica of which, at Czyżyków 2 (Fig. 12:10) was excavated with two bronze earrings (Fig. 19:12, 13); these vessels were typical of the second period of our culture. The other 'showy' axe was that from Gwoździec Stary I (Plate 10:4); only its lower part with the blade survived. The blade was slightly enlarged on both sides. A similar axe 'from Galicia' was published by N. Åberg[72] and an axe with a similarly widened blade from East Russia was published by A. Äyräpää.[73]

All other battle-axes found in our barrow-graves were of the 'simple' type, which corresponds roughly with Glob's type K, though it had many counterparts in various Central European groups and in Eastern Europe. Hundreds of such stray axes varying in size and shape were recorded in all parts of our territory; L. Kozłowski[74] mentioned only a few of the most characteristic.

The 'simple' battle-axes from our barrow-graves (listed in Table 8) can be divided into three main groups which we shall call type *x*, *y*, and *z*, to distinguish them from Glob's terminology. All but a few were markedly smaller in size than those of the 'showy' types.

Axes of type *x* (thirteen specimens, Fig. 13:1–7) were probably a degenerate or simplified version of the boat-axes of the 'Baltic' type. Four varieties of this type may be distinguished. Some (*x*-1) were relatively thin, slightly bent, and widened towards the slightly drooping blade, but a few had

[71] Kowalczyk (op. cit., note 53), pp. 23 ff., Pl. 1:9.
[72] Åberg (op. cit., note 63), p. 113, Fig. 218.
[73] Äyräpää (op. cit., note 5), p. 13, Fig. 5.
[74] Kozłowski (op. cit., note 4), pp. 77 ff., 100 ff.

the blade narrower than the butt. The largest specimen of this variety, from Rusiłów (Plate 8:1), calls to mind Glob's type B-3 or C-2. Another variety (*x*-2) was similar to these but thicker, of the same width from butt to blade. Battle-axes of variety *x*-3 were usually shorter but thicker, their upper part and the butt rounded, circular, but sometimes markedly thinning out, which marks already their variety *x*-4.

The second group, type *y* (Fig. 13:8–11; Fig. 14:1–3), is formed of axes (fourteen specimens) of the same size and very similar to those of type *x*. However, their upper part differs from that of the latter in narrowing markedly just over the shaft-hole, then thinning gradually towards the butt. They can be divided into five varieties which roughly correspond to those distinguished for type *x*, the difference being in the characteristic 'narrowing' of their upper part. Those of variety *y*-1 were relatively slim, widened towards the slightly drooping blade; axes of type *y*-2 did not much differ from those of type *x*-2, and the same applies to the two other varieties, *y*-3 and *y*-4, in respect of types *x*-3 and *x*-4. Axes of type *y* seem to be a simplified form of Fatyanovo axes and similar East European types.[75]

Axes of the third group, of type *z* (eleven specimens; Fig. 14:4–11), were the smallest in this series. Their characteristic feature was the position of the shaft-hole, which was very near the butt. In this they call to mind late copper or bronze axes; they were undoubtedly among the latest of all stone battle-axes of our area. Here also five distinct varieties can be distinguished. To the first of these (*z*-1 and *z*-2) axes may be included which do not much differ from those of type *x*-3 except for their much lower upper part. One axe (Kaczanówka 4, Plate 8:4) had a very small shaft-hole and the butt slightly higher, markedly narrowed upwards; it may be called variety *z*-5. Axes of type *z*-4 were definitely much narrower and gradually thinned out from the butt down towards the blade. On the other hand those of the variety *z*-3 were thick and rather clumsy, not unlike battle-axes of type *x*, but had the butt flat.

A few battle-axes of the 'simple' types remain unclassified; they were either very badly damaged, or only fragments survived and their type could not be specified.

Similar axes of the 'simple' type were also found in other regions of Central Europe and in Eastern Europe. Many were found at random within our territory. They were made of granite, diorite, serpentine, sandstone, etc. No special study has yet been devoted to them, while the geographical distribution of the different types and varieties, or the centres of their production have not been established. Axes made of granite must have originated from glaciation areas, and those of the greenish variety of stone (serpentine?) were probably products of workshops situated somewhere near Ovruch or in some parts of East Volhynia. Traces of a workshop of this kind were found at Moszczanica near Dubno in Volhynia.[76] Its site was marked by a large number of cones extracted when boring shaft-holes. Axes made of siliceous slate found mainly in graves close to the Carpathian foothills (Balice vi; Łotatniki i; Plate 10:8; Kołpiec 3) were obviously made somewhere in the southern part of this territory. It was the raw material of which axes and other larger implements were

TABLE 8. 'Simple' stone battle-axes found in Sub-Carpathian barrow-graves

A. TYPE X

Group 1
1. Balice xv, b(Fig. 13:2)
2. Kavsko 1 (no. 45)
3. Kryłos vi (Fig. 11:1a)
4. Kulczyce Szlacheckie iii (no. 49)
5. Piatyhorce (Ukraine) (no. 254)
6. Rusiłów (Plate 8:1d), Glob's type B-3 or C-2
7. Wiktórów ii (Fig. 13:1), b

Group 2
8. Czarna (no. 5)
9. Kavsko 2 (no. 45)
10. Klimkowce, a-1 (Fig. 13:3)
11. Okniany i, j-2 (Fig. 13:4)
12. Sarniki 1 (no. 86)
13. Popovtsy ii (Fig. 24:8) (slab-cist grave)

Group 3
14. Balice vi (Fig. 13:5)
15. Kołokolin iv, e (Fig. 13:6)
16. Stawki (no. 217)

Group 4
17. Okniany i, c (no. 106), j–1
18. Okniany i, d (Fig. 13:7)

B. TYPE Y

Group 1
1. Balice xvi (no. 1)
2. Komarów 38, b (Fig. 13:8)

Group 2
3. Komarów 39, d, edge missing
4. Komarów 50, e (Fig. 13:9)

Group 3
5. Kołpiec 3, a-5 (no. 46)
6. Komarów 44, g
7. Komarów 63, b
8. Okniany i (no. 106), c
9. Ostrów (Fig. 13:11)
10. Worwolińce (Fig. 13:10)

Group 4
11. Chocimierz (no. 99)
12. Kołokolin iii, grave iii, d (Fig. 14:1)
13. Wiktorów ii, f (Fig. 14:2)

Group 5
14. Niegowce (Fig. 14:3)

C. TYPE Z

Group 1
1. Klimkowce, grave 1, a-1 (Fig. 14:6)
2. Klimkowce, grave 2, b-1 (no. 199)
3. Płaucza Wielka, grave 2 (Fig. 14:4)
4. Siedliska B (Fig. 14:5), made of yellow slate
5. Zdolbitsa (no. 451, slabcist grave)

Group 2
6. Nowosiółka Jaruzelskich ii (Fig. 14:7)

Group 3
7. Capowce (Fig. 14:8)

Group 4
8. Hrubieszów (Fig. 14:9)
9. Sokal (Fig. 14:10)

Group 5
10. Kaczanówka iv, b (Fig. 14:11)

D. UNSPECIFIED

1. Balice i (no. 1)
2. Balice vii
3. Komarno (no. 14)
4. Komarów 40, t, missing
5. Myszyn (no. 104), second butt
6. Płaucza Wielka (no. 75), grave 1, half-damaged by fire
7. Rokitno 2 (no. 82), g, disintegrated

[75] Äyräpää (op. cit., note 5), Figs. 36–9, 66.

[76] A. Pawłowski, 'Wykopaliska moszczanickie', *Światowit*, vol. xvi, 1934–5.

made in many West Podolian settlements of the Tripolye culture.

Battle-axes of the 'simple' types were of a later date than those of the 'showy' types. They were only exceptionally found with Thuringian amphorae (of a late type, e.g. Balice xv; Plate 4:2, Fig. 13:2) and were usually associated with vessels typical of the later periods. The latest were battle-axes of type *z*, as is indicated by their association with assemblages dating from the latest period in the development of our culture.

The relationship between flint axes and battle-axes is of interest. It seems that flint axes were first to appear in barrow-graves, and battle-axes were introduced at a somewhat later date. Flint axes were found in ten graves which also yielded Thuringian amphorae, whereas battle-axes were found only in five such graves. On the other hand, battle-axes were often associated with cord-decorated mugs and with bronze objects, flint axes were very seldom excavated with bronze objects, and only once with a cord-decorated mug. More battle-axes (of the simple type) appeared in barrow-graves of a later date than in the earlier ones.

Apart from the two above series are two battle-axes which deserve mention. One of these, from Łotatniki I (Plate 10:8), was of the 'shoe-last' type, made of siliceous slate, and belonged to a type well known in Danubian cultures. Unperforated shoe-last celts, also made of siliceous slate, were frequently found in the remains of the West Podolian group of Tripolye culture. The specimen from Łotatniki seems to belong to an earlier stage of the barrow-graves culture. The other battle-axe, from Zdolbunov (Plate 10:11) found with a flint dagger, or spear-head, was of a type very characteristic of the Sofiivka culture in the Kiev country.[77] It forms an important link between the latter and our culture.

Finally, two mace-heads should be mentioned which differed from battle-axes of the simple type in that their edge was thick and blunt. The specimen from Balice XVI (Plate 10:9) made very thoroughly, resembles axes of type *y*-2, whereas the other, from Kawsko 2, was very clumsy and calls to mind those of type *x*-4. Both dated from a later stage.

CHISELS

Only one flint chisel was found, at Rokitno I (Fig. 16:28). It was of a type proper to the Globular Amphora culture (Fig. 25). Another chisel, from Łotatniki 2, the upper part of which is missing, was made of siliceous slate. At Ostapie 5 two bone points were found (Plate 11:11, 12): at least one of these was a narrow dagger, but the other may have been a chisel. All these remains dated from the later stage of the culture under review.

DAGGERS, SPEAR-HEADS (Plate 11)

Two slightly different three-riveted bronze daggers were found in our graves. The specimen from Sarniki I (Fig. 19:23), a little larger in size, was flat, and the other from Balice VII (Fig. 19:18), was rhomboid in section with a marked longitudinal rib. Both represent an Early Bronze Age type, that from Balice VII being of a little later date.

More numerous (eighteen specimens) were flint daggers, in which three main types can be distinguished. They all differed from Scandinavian flint daggers, and also from those found in graves of the Bell Beaker and Unetice cultures of Central Europe.

The first group includes three (Balice VI, XVI, XIX) wide relatively large specimens covered with a very fine retouch on both sides usually called 'sickles' or 'bent knives' (Plate 11:2, 3, 10). The position of the specimen in barrow-grave XVI at Balice (Plate 1:3) implies that they were used as daggers; they may also have been used as halberds, as is suggested by their shape. One specimen of this type was found at Komarów in a flat grave. Similar daggers ('sickles') were excavated in a few graves of the Strzyżów group of Corded Ware culture (e.g. Torczyn near Łuck,[78] or Raciborowice near Hrubieszów), all dating from the Early Bronze Age. Many stray daggers of this type were recorded in the whole area of our concern. They were also frequently found further west,[79] several being in graves of the Early Bronze Age cemetery at Mierzanowice.[80] Specimens from our territory were made of black Volhynian flint and were produced in special workshops, several of which were reported from the neighbourhood of Krzemieniec.[81]

The second group of flint daggers includes a series of larger or medium-size implements usually made of a large massive flake, sometimes of a large blade. They had a large base and a pointed end, and were trimmed on the edges, in particular near the pointed end. At least eight specimens of this type can be quoted (Kavsko 3, Komarów 17, Kołpiec IV, Korytno, Ostrów, Ostapie 2, Wacowice I, Załuże; Plate 11:4–8, 17), but probably many strong and relatively wide flint knives served the same purpose (e.g. from Wiktorów I and IV). The dagger from the slab-cist grave at Dublany (Plate 15:11) and that from the barrow-grave at Horodenka (Fig. 35:7, 12), found with a bronze socketed axe, belonged to the same series; the latter dated from the Middle Bronze Age.

Large tanged daggers formed the third and the latest group; they may have been used as spear-heads instead of daggers. They were well made, covered on both flat sides with a fine retouch and their shape clearly aimed at imitating daggers (or spear-heads?) of the Unetice culture made of bronze. Three specimens were found in our barrow graves (Ostrożec, no. 150; Rusiłów, Plate 8:1; Siekierzyńce 1876, no. 156) and similar ones were excavated in the cemetery of Torczyn near Łuck, referred to above;[82] one dagger of this type was found in a barrow-grave at Popówka near Vinnitsa (no. 257).[83] The dagger or spear-head from Zdolbunov (Plate 11:9) may also be included in this group; it was found with a stone battle-axe of Sofiivka type (Plate 10:11).

[77] Ю. М. Захарук, Софіївський тілопальний могильник, Арх. Пам., vol. IV, 1952, pp. 112 ff., Pl. I:5; 7. Gimbutas (op. cit., note 12), p. 109.

[78] J. Fitzke, 'Cmentarzysko kultury ceramiki sznurowej w Torczynie w pow.łuckim', *Spr.PAU*, vol. XLIII, 1938, pp. 26 f.

[79] Kozłowski (op. cit., note 4), pp. 85 ff., 181 f., Fig. 4, Pl. XXIII.

[80] K. Salewicz, 'Tymczasowe wyniki badan prehistorycznych w Mierzanowicach (pow.opatowski, woj.kieleckie)', *ZOW*, vol. XII, 1937, pp. 37 ff., Fig. 17.

[81] J. Bryk, *Kultury epoki kamiennej na wydmach zachodniej części południowego Wołynia*, Lwów 1928. М. Я. Рудинский, Дубно-кременецька палеолітична експедиція, Арх. Пам., vol. IV, 1952, pp. 143 f.

[82] See note 78. T. Sulimirski, *Polska przedhistoryczna*, part II, London 1957–9, Fig. 59.

[83] F. Pułaski, 'Kurhan popowiecki', *ZWAK*, vol. XVII, 1893, pp. 41 ff., Fig. 2.

Another spear-head (dagger?) very similar to that from Zdolbunov, was excavated in the Scythian barrow-grave at Horodnica, district of Kopyczyńce.[84] The two latter spear-heads were shorter than the others in this group, and clumsy.

No data are available regarding the type of the remaining four flint daggers, or spear-heads (Gdeszyce, no. 8; Nowosiółki Liskie, no. 73; Tomachów, no. 163; Wyrów, no. 92).

Flint daggers of the first and third groups above clearly dated from the Early Bronze Age, as is well indicated by the specimen from Rusiłów and the cemeteries at Torczyn, Raciborowice, and Mierzanowice. Daggers of the second group were probably of a little earlier date but likewise belonged to an advanced period in the development of the Barrow-grave culture.

In Thuringia, daggers (bone daggers) were typical of the second stage of the local Corded Ware culture.[85] In our barrow-graves at least three bone daggers were found (Orzechowce; Ostapie 5; Plate 11:11, 12) described in the reports concerned as 'bone chisels' or 'polishers'. In principle they correspond with flint daggers of the second group. A few large bone points (e.g. Ostapie 6, Rokitno 6; Plate 11:13–16) may likewise belong to this group.

Of interest is the geographical distribution of daggers. Flint daggers of types 1 and 3, also bone daggers, were found mainly in the northern part of our region, closer to the areas in which remains of the Globular Amphora culture were reported. Daggers of type 2 tend to concentrate more in the southern part of our territory.

FLINT ARROW-HEADS
(Plate 9:15–30)

Small triangular arrow-heads were excavated in at least sixteen barrow-graves. They were of the usual type, rather small in size, some very small, covered with a very fine retouch on their flat sides, the base usually being slightly concave, but some, evidently of a later date, had the base deeply hollowed. No tanged arrow-heads were found. A few specimens differed from the standard type: those from Płaucza Wielka (no. 75) were more elongated, as were a specimen from Ostapie 1/3 and another one from Komarów 39 (Plate 9:26). Triangular flakes, a little larger than the proper arrow-heads and usually thicker, found in a few graves (Komarów 37, Okniany 2, no. 106) were also used for the same purpose (Plate 9:21, 27).

Arrow-heads found in these graves were considerably smaller in size than similar specimens from Tripolyan settlements of period B/1 (e.g. from Niezwiska 1). They were a long-lived type; they appeared by the end of the early period of the Barrow-grave culture and were in a few instances associated with Thuringian amphorae of type IIc (Kołokolin 1, Kulczcye 3, Rokitno 2). They were, however, found mostly in graves of the later period in which single-lugged mugs and/or bronze objects were also excavated (Fig. 11:1; Plate 8:1). They were likewise found in a number of graves of the Komarów culture of the Middle Bronze Age. In Thuringian Corded Ware graves they appear only during the second stage.[86]

At Kavsko 2, 3, and 4, small flint trapezoid points were excavated; these represent a well-known mesolithic type of arrow-points, but Mr I. K. Sviešnikov has kindly informed me that they all had one corner of the blade highly polished, a fact which in his view indicates that they were not used as arrow-heads. They were probably flint insets of composite sickles, or some other implement, made of wood or bone (antler).

ORNAMENTS
(Fig. 19)

Metal ornaments were found in several graves. They were mainly of bronze, though some were of lead, silver, and gold. They may be classed in a few groups.

Most common were earrings and pendants which were used mainly as hair adornment as is emphasized by E. Zaharia,[87] who devoted a special study to such ornaments found in Romania. The small ring from Lublin-Sławinek, with overlapping terminals, represents the simplest and earliest form. Of a little later date were two small earrings (hair-rings) from Czyżyków 2 (Fig. 19:12, 13), which had one terminal flat and considerably widened, and which represent an early Unetice type. Similar earrings were also found in the flat graves of Poczapy (no. 92)[88] where they seem to have been late survivals of an early type. Similar specimens, though a little larger, were excavated in graves of the Strzyżów culture.

A more evolved form of this type were large pendants or temple ornaments, made of plain bronze wire with one terminal elongated, flattened, either oar or leaf shaped, often slightly hollowed along both sides of the central rib. Two varieties of these pendants were found within our territory: one had a relatively narrow terminal plate, the other a considerably wider one (once with two middle ribs: Chłopy: Fig. 19:10).

The narrower variety was proper to the Unetice culture in Silesia;[89] several specimens of this type were also excavated in the cemeteries of the Mierzanowice culture of the region of Sandomierz.[90] Pendants of this type were recorded in the remains of the Strzyżów culture in the environments of Hrubieszów.[91]

More common within our territory, were pendants with a wider terminal plate, some very wide, others narrower, but wider than those further west, all provided with a middle rib. Only one specimen of this type was found (badly damaged) in a barrow-grave at Gwoździec Stary 2 (Plate 9:4); others occurred in flat graves at Perediwanie and Rypniów (no. 589) and two at Chłopy near Rudki[92] in a peat-bog (probably an offering; Fig. 19:1–8, 10). More pendants of this type were found in West Volhynia: in slab-cist graves at

[84] Sulimirski (op. cit., note 61), p. 22, Pl. IX:9.

[85] Fischer (op. cit., note 2), p. 272.

[86] Fischer, loc. cit.

[87] E. Zaharia, 'Die Lockenringe von Sărăta-Monteoru und ihre typologischen und chronologischen Beziehungen', *Dacia*, vol. NS III, 1959, pp. 105 ff.

[88] Я. Пастернак, Перша бронзова доба в Галичині, Записки наук, т-ва ім. Шевченка, vol. CLII, Lviv 1933, pp. 64 f., Figs. 1, 5, 6.

[89] According to H. Seger note 35, and discussed by J. J. Butler, 'The Late Neolithic Gold Ornament from Bennekom', *Palaeohistoria*, vol. v, Groningen 1956, pp. 63 ff., Pls. VII, VIII.

[90] Salewicz (op. cit., note 80), p. 48, Fig. 14. Nosek (op. cit., note 21), pl. XV.

[91] Z. Ślusarski, 'Cmentarzysko kultury mierzanowickiej w miejscowości Skomorochy Małe, pow.Hrubieszów', *W.A.*, vol. XXIII, 1956, p. 100, Fig. 6.

[92] Sulimirski (op. cit., note 82), p. 229. Fig. 56.

Gródek district of Równe (no. 429) and Stadniki (no. 446) in the grave of the Strzyżów culture at Torczyn[93] and ten at Stubło. The latter formed part of a bronze hoard[94] and on their account the name of the 'Stubło' type was given to these ear-pendants. No ornaments of this type were found further east except a few somewhat different specimens from Kiev.[95]

Pendants very similar to those of the 'Stubło' type were found in a series of Slovakian cemeteries of the Nitra culture[96] which has been dated as Reinecke's Bronze Age period A-1. Our specimens, as is clearly indicated by the hoard from Stubło dealt with in Chapter V, apparently dated from the later stage of the Early Bronze Age, which can be equated with period A-2 of Reinecke's scheme. The Romanian specimens of a similar type were also of a later date. They were excavated in the cemeteries of the Monteoru culture and Zaharia[97] calls them type 'C'. According to stratigraphic evidence, they were of the second stage of the Monteoru culture, which corresponded with period B of the Bronze Age according to Reinecke.

Finally, the same group of ornaments included the gold basket pendant, or earring, from Rusiłów (Plate 8:1), presumably of Irish origin. Its late origin is shown by the flint spear-head, or dagger, of a type related to Scandinavian form v, and was a replica in flint of Unetice bronze daggers with a handle. A similar ear-pendant from Bennekom has been radiocarbon dated as 1590±130 B.C.[98] which places it in period A-2 of the Bronze Age.

Another type of earring, or temple ornament, were naprings. They were proper to the Central European Early Bronze Age. Naprings were found at Jaktorów I (Fig. 19:11), in the grave at Perediwanie (no. 109, Fig. 19:5–8), and also in the ruined graves at Poczapy (no. 191). E. Zaharia[99] considers the specimen from Perediwanie to be the earliest of this type in this part of Europe which seems unlikely. Specimens from the cemetery at Výčapy-Opatovce in Slovakia[100] represent a more primitive form which dated, as mentioned above, from period A-1. A napring nearly identical with the above was excavated in the settlement of the Funnel Beaker culture at Gródek Nadbużny.[101]

The two silver rings from Buhłów 2 (Plate 9:10) were of a type common in Early Bronze Age assemblages. They were the only silver objects found in our graves; another silver object of the same period found within our territory was the damaged bracelet from the late Tripolyan settlement at Koszyłowce (Obóz).

In a few graves (Balice VII, Fig. 19:22; Kryłos VI, Fig. 11:1; Siedliska I) finger-rings made of lead band were excavated. These graves belonged to a late period of the Barrow-grave culture.

Nothing can be said about the only (damaged) bronze torque found at Kryłos VI (Fig. 11:1). Such ornaments appear in Central Europe as early as the Early Bronze Age, in period A-1, and were found also in later assemblages. Bronze bracelets were excavated in four graves: Balice VII; Gdeszyce (no. 8); Wiktorów II (no. 57); Załukiew, but particulars are available only for those from Balice VII and Załukiew (Fig. 19:9, 17). Both were made of an undecorated bronze bar round in section, with thinner terminals. Bracelets of the same type formed part of the hoard of Stubło.

Bronze pins were excavated in three barrow-graves. That from Balice VII (Fig. 19:14) had its head missing, and that from Kryłos III was spiral-headed. Of interest is the knot-headed 'Cypriot' pin from Putiatyńce (Fig. 19:15) proper to the developed stage of the Unetice culture. A pin of the same type was found further east in the Tripolyan settlement of Sabatinovka I (Fig. 8),[102] and another one formed part of the bronze hoard from Kolodnoe in the Carpatho-Ukraine[103] dating from the 'end of the Middle Bronze Age', Reinecke's period B or C. Two 'Cypriot' pins were recently excavated at Gîrbovăț in Moldavia,[104] in a settlement of the early phase of the Noua culture. These finds suggest a rather late date for the 'Cypriot' pins found north and east of the Carpathians, and referred to above.

No beads made of metal were found in our graves. A few oblong beads from Peresopnytsia (no. 152) were of clay, and at Buhłów II, seven small bone beads were excavated (Plate 9:11). But the most important were twenty-eight faience beads of a necklace, some segmented, excavated at Kołpiec 5 (Plate 8:2). Faience beads, mostly single but several segmented, were found in five sites within the Territory, in graves of the Strzyżów group of the Corded Ware culture at Raciborowice, Skomorochy, Strzyżów, and Torczyn, and in a slab-cist grave at Stadniki (no. 446). A further five sites were recorded of the Mierzanowice culture west of the San and Vistula;[105] they were also reported from the settlement of Babino III on the Lower Dnieper near Nikopol and from several graves in the countries east of the Dnieper.[106] Undoubtedly, they were in some way connected with the Trojan (Troy VI) and Mycenean trade with Central Europe and dated from about the fifteenth century B.C. Their connection with the Mycenean trade is corroborated by a bone cheek-

[93] Ibid., p. 236, Fig. 59.

[94] W. Antoniewicz, 'Der in Stubło in Wolhynien aufgefundene Bronzeschatz', *ESA*, vol. IV, 1929, p. 140, Figs. 14–19. (See pp. 60 f.)

[95] Т. Г. Мовша, Медньіе украшения из Киева, Ксиимк, no. 70, 1957, pp. 94 ff., Fig. 36.

[96] *The Prehistory of Czechoslovakia*, National Museum, Prague 1958, p. 25, Pl. XIII. J. Neustupny and others, *Pravěk Československa*, Praha 1960, pp. 195 ff., Pl. 30. See also A. Točik, 'Zpráva o výskume v rokoch 1957–1959 na Zámečku v Nitrianskom Hrádku, okres Nové Zamký', *The Conference of the Czechoslovak Archaeologists at Libice*, 1960, pp. 19 ff.

[97] Zaharia (op. cit., note 87), pp. 121 ff., Fig. 10.

[98] Butler (op. cit., note 89), pp. 66 ff.

[99] Zaharia (op. cit., note 87), pp. 108, 131.

[100] See note 96.

[101] Unpublished; a photograph was kindly given me by Dr J. Kowalczyk.

[102] А. В. Добровольський, Перше сабатинівське поселення, Арх. Пам., vol. IV, 1952, pp. 78 ff., Pl. II:17.

[103] K. Bernjakovič, 'Bronzezeitliche Hortfunde vom rechten Ufergebiet des oberen Theisstales', *Slovenská Archeológia*, vol. VIII, 1960, p. 349, Pl. XIII:13.

[104] A. Florescu, 'Contribuții la conoașterea culturii Noua', *Arheologia Moldovei*, vol. II–III, Iași 1964, pp. 177 f., Fig. 22:2, 3. M. Petrescu-Dimbovița, 'Date noi relativ la discoperile de objecte de bronze de la sfîrșitul epocii bronzului si începutul Hallstatt-ului din Moldova', *Arheologia Moldovei*, vol. II–III, Iași 1964, p. 271, Fig. 7:4.

[105] T. Sulimirski, *Man*, vol. XLVIII, London 1948, p. 124.

[106] А. В. Добровольский, Поселение бронзового века Бабино III, Ксиак no. 7, 1957, p. 42. J. F. S. Stone and L. C. Thomas, 'The Use and Distribution of Faience in the Ancient East and Prehistoric Europe'. *PPS*, vol. XXII, 1956, pp. 53 ff. V. Moucha, 'Faience and Glassy Faience Beads in the Unětice Culture in Bohemia', *Epitymbion Roman Haken*, Prague 1958, pp. 44 ff.

piece ornamented in the characteristic 'Mycenean' decorative style, found at Bełz, about 45km south of Strzyżów, and of other sites of the group mentioned above.[107]

A few discoid or slightly rectangular pendants were found; all had a perforation in the centre. One of these, a decorated bone disc, was excavated at Koropuż together with a Thuringian amphora of type I (Plate 3:1; Fig. 19:19). A slightly rectangular amber pendant with a large perforation in the centre, from Rokitno 2, was associated with a Thuringian amphora of type IIC (Fig. 19:21; Plate 5:8), and one similar but made of fired clay, was excavated at Kołokolin VII (Fig. 19:20). Of a later date were large discoid amber pendants; they were associated mainly with the Globular Amphora culture which will be dealt with later; two specimens from our territory were found in remains of that culture. But a similar large amber pendant with a larger perforation in the centre and a smaller one near the edge, was excavated in the barrow-grave at Chorostków with a cord-decorated handled mug (Plate 9:1, 2). Also at Batowice near Cracow[108] a similar amber pendant was found with a cord-decorated handled mug of the same type as that above. The late date of these amber discs is indicated by finds in the western part of Poland, where they were associated with remains (graves and hoards) of the developed Unetice period,[109] e.g. Buczek (Buchholz),[110] Przysieka Polska.[111] The earlier amber ornaments, e.g. from Złota[112] were small plaques, oblong or quadrangular in shape, with perforations on their corners, or were small buttons with a V-perforation but no hole in the centre. Nothing is known about the amber object found in the barrow-grave of Zimno.

All pendants mentioned above were undoubtedly used as amulets, and this applies to the *Pectunculus* shell from Ostapie 2 (no. 213). Similar shells were found in the Werteba cave at Bilcze Złote among the remains of the Tripolye culture of period C-1. At Zawadyńce (no. 222) a bone amulet of unknown shape was found.

Boar tusks seem to have belonged to an advanced period of the Barrow-grave culture; they were found in four graves: Klimkowce (no. 109), Ostapie 1/2 (no. 213), Płaucza Wielka (no. 75), Siedliska B (no. 30), also in a few graves of the Strzyżów culture and in those of the Globular Amphora culture within our territory.

OTHER GRAVE GOODS

Two metal objects are of particular interest. One of these, from Ostapie 4 (Plate 9:12) has a cast decoration imitating a twisted cord, which points to its North Caucasian origin.[113] It was typical of the second stage of the North Caucasian culture which developed approximately from 1700 to 1400 B.C. The same direction is indicated by its chemical analysis. The other object, a round, slightly concave plaque from Ostapie 2 (no. 213) was made of bronze with a high tin content. It was undecorated but had a few holes on its circumference which suggest that this was a belt decoration (*Gürtel-Platte*). In North-West Europe plaques of this type appear by the end of the Early Bronze Age (period A-2), but were in use mainly in the subsequent periods.[114]

In a few instances objects were excavated which do not usually appear in graves, e.g. the clay whorls: Bolechowce (no. 39), Boratyn Wielki 1896 (no. 139), Komarów 50, Łukawica 1 (no. 20). A unique occurrence were two clay tubes from Komarów 39 (Fig. 12:8) probably dating from the second stage of our culture. Clay tubes of the same type (regarded as 'phalli') were found in a number of Cucuteni-Tripolye settlements in Moldavia[115] of the Cucuteni A (Tripolyan B-1) period; they were excavated in the settlement of the Lublin Painted pottery culture at Złota,[116] in the remains of Danubian II period at Brześć Kujawski,[117] and within our area in the settlements of the Funnel Beaker culture at Klementowice[118] and Gródek Nadbużny,[119] in this case regarded as loom-weights. Clay tubes of the same type, presumably connected with metallurgical work, were found in the Tirol[120] and also in a Late Bronze Age barrow-grave at Kalinovka near Stalingrad.[121]

In almost all our barrow-graves at least one though usually several small flint implements were excavated. A large group of these is formed by knives made of long blades, with well-trimmed edges (Fig. 12:4, 6; Plate 8:1, 3), but often with no trimming at all. Some may have been used as inlays of 'sickles'[122] or curved knives; others, particularly the longer ones, may have served as daggers. At Ostapie 1 (no. 213) a flint saw was excavated, a unique specimen in our graves. Various points were found, but by far the largest group was formed by flints of irregular shape representing no definite type of tools, the purpose of which is difficult to establish. In most barrows many flint chips and waste were also excavated, scattered over the entire ancient surface under the mound, and often originating from implements deliberately destroyed, axes in particular. A selection of various flint implements found in our barrow-graves is shown in Figs 17 and 18.

[107] T. Sulimirski (op. cit., note 82), pp. 170 f. Id., 'Barrow-grave 6 at Komarów', *University of London Institute of Archaeology Bulletin*, no. 4, 1964, pp. 178 ff. Id., 'Die thrako-kimmerische Periode in Südostpolen', *Wiener Prähistorische Zft*, vol. xxv, 1938, pp. 143 f., Fig. 7. I have erroneously considered the specimen to be a Thraco-Cimmerian type.

[108] Kozłowski (op. cit., note 4), p. 211, Pl. XV:13.

[109] Sulimirski (op. cit., note 82), p. 278, Figs. 72, 74.

[110] K. Kersten, *Die Funde der älteren Bronzezeit in Pommern*, Hamburg 1958, 7 Beiheft zum Atlas d.Urgeschichte, Pl. 56:577.

[111] A. Knapowska-Mikołajczykowa, 'Wczesny okres epoki brązu w Wielkopolsce, *FAP*, vol. VII, 1957, pp. 71 f., Fig. 83.

[112] Krzak (op. cit., note 4), p. 146, Figs. 12, 42, 97, 98, etc.

[113] В. И. Марковин, Культура племен северного Кавказа в эпоху бронзы, МИА, no. 93, 1960, p. 69.

[114] R. Hachmann, *Die frühe Bronzezeit im westlichen Ostseegebiet und ihre mittel- und südosteuropäische Beziehungen*, Hamburg 1957, pp. 57 f.

[115] V. Dumitrescu and others, *Hăbăşeşti*, Bucureşti 1954, p. 468, Fig. 50. R. Vulpe, *Izvoare, Săpăturile din 1936–1948*, Bucureşti 1957, p. 242, Fig. 241:1, 2, 4.

[116] Z. Podkowińska, 'Pierwsza charakterystyka stanowiska neolitycznego na polu Grodzisko I we wsi Złota, pow.Sandomierz', *W.A.*, vol. XIX, 1953, p. 17, Pls. XVIII:2; XX:1; XXI:2–4.

[117] K. Jażdżewski, *W.A.*, vol. XV, 1938, Pl. XXXV:5.

[118] J. Kowalczyk, 'Osada i cmentarzysko kultury pucharów lejkowatych w miejscowości Klementowice, pow.Puławy', *Mat.St.*, vol. II, 1957, Pl. C,A.

[119] Kowalczyk (op. cit., note 53), Pl. II:18.

[120] Pittioni (op. cit., note 47), Fig. 254.

[121] A. L. Mongait, *Archaeology in the U.S.S.R.*, Pelican Books, 1961, p. 137, Fig. 13.

[122] С. Н. Бибиков, Из истории каменных серпов на юго-востоке Европы, Сов. Арх., vol. 3, 1962, pp. 3 ff.

CHAPTER III

Stages in the Development and Chronology

THE ANALYTICAL TABLE

GRAVE GOODS excavated in Sub-Carpathian graves were not uniform, as has been shown in the preceding chapter. They reflect both regional and chronological differences. The Barrow-grave culture which they represent did not develop in isolation, and its relations with several coeval cultures are reflected in many ways. These are of importance for the establishment of the consecutive stages in the evolution of our culture and their relative chronology. Topics connected with the origin of the culture and its position in a wider chronological framework will be discussed later, against a background which will include all the related and coeval cultures within the Territory.

The few secondary burials uncovered in the Sub-Carpathian mounds dated mostly from much later periods, and there is no stratigraphic evidence available for the establishment of the successive stages in the evolution of the Barrow-grave culture. Accordingly, their institution has to be based on the chronology of grave goods, the relative position of which, and/or their date, have been settled outside the remains of our culture, or in some other areas. To these belong, first of all, metal objects and other imported wares, but also a number of vessels of particular types which represent forms proper to the Corded Ware widespread in many parts of Central and North-Western Europe.

Sixty-six barrow-graves are listed in Table 9 below, in which six of the most characteristic types of vessels were excavated; included in the list are also mounds in which at least one metal object was found. Furthermore, other grave goods found in these graves are quoted, and the regional groups to which the respective graves belonged are also indicated. The following vessels were singled out for the purpose: (a) Thuringian and (b) Miechów amphorae; (c) handled and (d) single-lugged mugs; (e) handled cups and (f) jugs. Beakers, although frequently found in our graves, were not taken into account as they were of various types.

A few conclusions can be drawn from the study of this graph. One is that the leading types of vessels never appear together in a single grave, except for one handled cup and two jugs, which in two graves (Siedliska I, Lublin-Sławinek) were found in association with a vessel of another leading type.

The second conclusion is that all barrow-graves fall into two main distinct groups: one embracing twenty-eight burials in which Thuringian amphorae were excavated; and another subdivided into a few smaller units, to which all other graves belonged. The distribution of these vessels, indicated in the last columns of Table 9, implies that Thuringian amphorae were found in all groups except the Lublin-Bug and Horodenka groups. On the other hand, the distribution of other leading vessels was different: each of these keeps markedly with some particular group. Thus Miechów amphorae were excavated almost exclusively in the western part of our area, handled cups chiefly in the Lwów-Opole group, and single-lugged mugs were found solely in the eastern regions.

The above circumstances lead to another conclusion, i.e. that the two main groups of barrow-graves mentioned represent two different stages in the development of our culture, the one with Thuringian amphorae being the earlier. This is indicated by the fact that Thuringian amphorae were characteristic of the early stage of the Corded Ware culture in the countries further west, and it is supported by the absence of metal objects in burials in which these vessels were found, except the one grave of Siedliska I. All other leading vessels were found in several instances either with bronze objects or with goods clearly of a late date.

Closer examination in the preceding chapter of the Thuringian amphorae has shown that they were all not of the same period, and that at least two stages in their evolution can be clearly distinguished. The study of grave goods of the other, 'non-Thuringian amphora', group leads to a similar conclusion: there also earlier and later assemblages are discernible in each of the sub-groups. The question then arises as to (1) whether we have to deal here with four subsequent stages in the evolution of the Barrow-grave culture, or (2) whether these hypothetical stages overlapped, the differences in grave goods being, at least partly, a parallel occurrence.

Study of Table 9 gives no answer to these questions. Barrow-graves of the Lwów-Opole region seem to form four groups there, but the fourth has been formed by graves in which no pottery and only bronze objects were found. In other regions the graves form either two or three groups. The solution of the problem may be found in the study of the circumstances prevailing in the few larger barrow-grave cemeteries which were almost entirely investigated.

LARGE CEMETERIES

One of the earliest cemeteries investigated was at Kołokolin (no. 66) (Plan 4:1) consisting of seven mounds, six of which were excavated. In one of these (no. IV), a Thuringian amphora of type I (Plate 4:1), in another (no. I), a Thuringian amphora of type IIC was found (Fig. 10:1). These two graves were undoubtedly of an early date and belonged to an early period of the development of the Barrow-grave culture. The remaining mounds were of a little later date, but they all belonged either to the early period or to the beginning of the subsequent one. The latest of all was probably barrow-

TABLE 9. Distribution of leading vessels and associated material

	Pottery									Weapons				Ornaments			Metal			Groups						
	Thuringian amphorae	Miechów amphorae	Jugs	Handled cups	Handled mugs	Single-lugged mugs	Funnel Beaker Pottery	Beakers	Various vessels	Axes	Battle-axes	Arrow-heads	Daggers, spearheads	Amber	Boar tusks	Pendants, etc.	Ornaments	Lead rings	Various objects	Lublin-Bug	Przemyśl	Sub-Carpathian	Lwów-Opole	Horodenka	West-Podolian	West-Volhynian
1. Lisieczyńce	*																								*	
2. Krasów 2	*									*													*			
3. Krasów 1	*							*	*	*													*			
4. Kołokolin IV	*						*		*	*	*												*			
5. Koropuż	*						*									*					*					
6. Stojańce	*						*														*					
7. Hartfeld	*																				*					
8. Siwki 1–1878	*						*	*																		*
9. Korytne I	*																									*
10. Płużne III	*									*																*
11. Nowosiółka Jar. 2	*										*														*	
12. Nowosiółka Jar. 3	*																								*	
13. Nowosiółki Liskie	*						*	*	*				*										*			
14. Kołokolin I	*						*	*	*	*		*											*			
15. Rokitno 2	*									*	*	*		*									*			
16. Rokitno 6	*									*													*			
17. Stratyn 1	*																						*			
18. Stratyn 2	*																						*			
19. Wiktorów 8	*																					*				
20. Kulczyce 5	*							*														*				
21. Kulczyce 2	*							*														*				
22. Komarów 31	*							*														*				
23. Komarów 5	*							*		*												*				
24. Kulczyce 3	*							*	*	*	*	*										*				
25. Komarno	*									*	*										*					
26. Balice 15	*										*										*					
27. Surmaczówka	*								*												*					
28. Siedliska 1	*		*	*					*	*	*						*	*			*					
29. Brzezinki I		*						*													*					
30. Lukawica K		*					*	*		*	*										*					
31. Brusno		*							*	*											*					
32. Balice VII		*							*	*	*	*	*				*	*			*					
33. Balice XVI		*							*	*	*		*								*					

Table 9—*continued*

	Pottery									Weapons				Ornaments			Metal			Groups						
	Thuringian amphorae	Miechów amphorae	Jugs	Handled cups	Handled mugs	Single-lugged mugs	Funnel Beaker Pottery	Beakers	Various vessels	Axes	Battle-axes	Arrow-heads	Daggers, spearheads	Amber	Boar tusks	Pendants, etc.	Ornaments	Lead rings	Various objects	Lublin-Bug	Przemyśl	Sub-Carpathian	Lwów-Opole	Horodenka	West-Podolian	West-Volhynian
34. Zaborol		*																								*
35. Sławinek-Lublin		*	*					*									*			*						
36. Płaucza Wielka			*								*	*			*								*			
37. Łotatniki I			*					*	*	*	*											*				
38. Kołpiec 3				*				*	*		*											*				
39. Balice IV				*																	*					
40. Dziedziłów				*																			*			
41. Jaktorów 2				*																			*			
42. Jaktorów 4				*																			*			
43. Czyżyków 2				*													*						*			
44. Kołokolin III/1				*					*	*	*												*			
45. Zawadyńce				*						*		*													*	
46. Chorostków					*									*											*	
47. Kavsko 6					*																	*				
48. Komarów 20					*				*		*	*										*				
49. Zakłodzie gr. 2						*														*						
50. Staryki 2						*																				*
51. Buhłów 2						*										*	*								*	
52. Klimkowce						*					*	*			*										*	
53. Ostapie 4						*													*						*	
54. Ostapie 1/sec.						*		*	*																*	
55. Kaczanówka 3						*																			*	
56. Okniany 2						*																		*		
57. Komarów 45						*		*	*													*				
58. Kryłos VI								*		*	*	*					*	*				*				
59. Kryłos 3									*								*					*				
60. Wiktorów 2										*	*						*					*				
61. Putiatyńce																	*						*			
62. Jaktorów 1																	*						*			
63. Sarniki 1											*		*						*				*			
64. Wyrów													*				*						*			
65. Rusiłow											*	*	*				*						*			
66. Ostapie 2									*							*	*								*	

grave III in which two cord-decorated handled cups of Chłopice-Vĕselé type were found.

The largest cemetery investigated was that at Komarów, which was of a later date than that above (Plan 1). It extended over a distance of about 2·5km on a ridge of the Carpathian foothills north of the village, and embraced sixty-nine mounds, including that called Kryłos VI (no. 48) which lay on the border of the adjoining village. Sixty-three of these mounds were excavated. Another four mounds, three of which were investigated, were situated on the southern slopes of the main ridge, on its elevated places.

Our investigations have shown that twenty-eight mounds on the ridge and one in a lower position were Neolithic or of the Early Bronze Age; another twenty-seven mounds on the ridge were of a later period, and belonged to the Bronze Age 'Komarów' culture, named after this cemetery. The chronology of the few remaining mounds could not be established. Investigations have also proved that there was no chronological gap between the earlier barrow-graves and those of the Komarów culture, the latter being a direct successor of the former.

Neolithic barrow-graves were very evenly distributed along the whole length of the ridge. They appear mostly singly and isolated, seldom in smaller groups, e.g. one group of two mounds, three of three, and one of four. The distance between the single mounds and/or the groups was 150–200m, only in three cases being a little over 100m. The two barrow-graves with Thuringian amphorae (nos. 5 and 31) lay nearly 1·3km apart, which suggests they were left by different tribal or family groups, to each of which a number of barrow-graves belonged. A closer study of these groups—which consisted chiefly of 'Komarów culture' graves—has been carried out in the report on excavation of the cemetery in the second part of this work (pp. 105 ff.)

The respective Neolithic and Early Bronze Age barrow-graves are listed in Table 10. They have been arranged according to their actual position on the ridge, roughly from west to east, and their main grave goods quoted. No significant differences existed between grave goods found in any of the mounds investigated. All, except barrow-grave Kryłos VI, were very poorly furnished, and they all seem to date from the same period. Only two mounds, those with Thuringian amphorae (nos. 5, 31), were probably of a little earlier date.

In a few graves, which belonged to the Komarów culture, were found vessels very similar to those typical of the late assemblages of the Barrow-grave culture. Thus in barrow-grave 20, an undecorated handled mug proper to the late stage of the Corded Ware was excavated with a very large vase characteristic of the Komarów culture (Fig. 29:7, 8). In barrow-grave 45, a single-lugged mug (*Zapfenbecher*, Plate 21:4) was excavated with vessels typical of the Komarów culture; this vessel was also made and decorated in a manner characteristic of the Komarów culture. The same applies to decorated cylindrical mugs (with no lugs) from barrow-graves 28 and 34 (Plate 16:12; Fig. 28:10, 11).

It should be emphasized that no such vessels were found in any of the graves of the Barrow-grave culture at Komarów. However, those mentioned above have no significance for dating purposes; they appear in graves of the second and third periods of the Komarów culture.

Barrow-graves from Balice (no. 1) seem on the whole to have been coeval with those of the Barrow-grave culture at Komarów. Unfortunately, there are insufficient particulars of the nineteen mounds excavated there. They lay in different parts of the village, but eight situated in the forest formed a close-knit group. However, there is no indication in the publication as to which of the mounds described belonged to the latter group.

The study of grave goods from Balice shows that mounds dated from two periods, one earlier and the other somewhat later. The earliest of all was probably barrow-grave XV, in which a Thuringian amphora of type IIC was excavated (Plate 4:2), and the latest was barrow-grave VII in which, besides an undecorated Miechów amphora (Plate 3:6), several bronze objects were found, i.e. several personal ornaments, a dagger and a lead ring (Fig. 19:14, 17, 18, 22). The latest graves of Balice dated from the latest period in the development of the Barrow-grave culture.

Of a similar date was also the cemetery of Kołpiec (no. 46; Plan 3:2). Barrow-graves were found there in three distinct sites. The largest group consisted of over ten mounds of which only eight survived; seven of these were investigated (nos. 2–8).

The latest of the above was barrow-grave 6 which yielded a large tulip-shaped vessel proper to the Komarów culture. Other mounds belonged to the Barrow-grave culture. One of the latest of these was barrow-grave 8 in which a wide cord-decorated bowl of a local type, a small unique beaker with a spheric body and rounded base provided with a kind of unperforated lug on its cylindrical neck (Fig. 11:3), and two other vessels were found. Barrow-grave 9 with its small straight-sided basin (Plate 7:4) was also late. Barrow-grave 3 was probably of a little earlier date; it yielded a handled cup, a bowl, a beaker, and a battle-axe. Of interest is barrow-grave 5 in which faience beads, including segmented specimens, and a small dark two-lugged bowl were excavated (Plate 8:2). The earliest in the cemetery was probably its largest mound 2. Lumps of ochre and a flint axe were found in its shaft-grave, and a completely crushed vessel lay on the periphery of the proper grave area. It does not seem, however, that the latter grave was very remote in time from other graves of the cemetery. The cemetery dated from a late period of the Barrow-grave culture.

Finally, another cemetery completely investigated was that at Kavsko (no. 45), consisting of six mounds. The excavation report is incomplete, but the study of grave goods published reveals that the cemetery was of a late date. It was typical of the latest stage of the Barrow-grave culture.

The latest in this cemetery was barrow-grave 5 with a cremation burial and vessels characteristic of the developed stage of the Komarów culture (Fig. 29:2, 5, 6). Of a little earlier date was mound 4 which yielded a bowl and a handled cup of Unetice type (Fig. 29:1, 4). Vessels found in other mounds represent types proper to the late stage of the Corded Ware culture, namely the handled cord-decorated mug from mound 6, and also low, wide cord-decorated bowls from mounds 1 and 2, especially the latter which was a replica of the bowl from Kołpiec 8 (Fig. 12:11, 14, 15).

The main grave goods of these cemeteries are listed in Table 11.

TABLE 10. Main grave goods of the early barrow-graves of the cemetery at Komarów arranged according to their position at the cemetery from west to east

No.	Mound No.	No. of burials	Cremation burial	No. of vessels	Thuring. amphora	Beaker	Bowl	Larger vessel	Cup	Odd potsherds	Axe	Battle-axe	Flint arrow-head	Flint knives	Remarks
1	59										*				
2	30									*					Timber logs
3	39	1				*					*	*	*	*	Two clay 'phalli'
4	42	1									*			*	Charred beam
5	40	1								*	*	*			
1	31	1		2	*	*				*					
2	18	1	*											*	Red ochre
3	16	1	*											*	Timber logs
4	17													*	Flint dagger?
5	63	1										*		*	
6	37									*	*			*	Destroyed by a secondary burial
7	38	1		1		*				*	*	*	*		Over it a second burial
8	52	1	*											*	
9	50		*	2			*	*							
10	32	3		2					*	*					Graves on two levels
11	53	2												*	Lumps of ochre
1	26									*					Timber logs
2	25	1		1		*				*		*		*	
3	24									*	*				Mound partly destroyed
4	5	1		2	*	*				*	*			*	
5	29			1		*				*					
6	44	1		1		*					*	*		*	
7	1													*	
8	2		*							*				*	
9	3									*					
1	65	1	*											*	
2	4			1		*								*	
3	VI	1		1		*					*	*	*	*	(Krylos) bronze torque, lead ring

TABLE 11. Main grave goods of three larger cemeteries

No.	Mound No.	No. of burials	No. of vessels	Thuring. amphorae	Miechów amphorae	Funnel B. pottery	Beakers	Bowls	Cups	Handled cups	Various vessels	Odd potsherds	Axes	Battle-axes	Mace-heads	Flint arrow-heads	Daggers	Flint knives	Metal ornaments	Faience beads	Pendants	Remarks
Kołokolin No. 66																						
1	4	2	2	I		*					1		*	*								
2	1	2	6	IIC		*	*	*	*		2		*			*		*				cremation burial
3	5	1	1			*			*				*					*				
4	2	1	2				*	*					*					*				
5	7	2	2						*		1		*			*					*	
6	3	3	3					*		*	1	*	*	*								one cremation burial
Balice No. 1																						
1	15		1	IIC										*								
2	1												*	*				*				
3	18												*					*				
4	14		1						*													
5	17		1							*												
6	4		1							*												
7	6													*			*	*				
8	19		1								1						*	*				
9	16		2		*			*					*	*	*		*	*				
10			2		*						1		*	*		*	*	*	*			
Kołpiec No. 46																						
1	2	1	1							*		*	*									ochre
2	4											*	*				*					
3	3		3				*	*		*				*				*				
4	5		2						*		1	*	*					*		*		ochre
5	7		2						*		1											ochre
6	8		5				*	*	*		2											
7	6		1								1											ochre, Komarów period
Kavsko No. 45																						
1	1	2?	1					*				*	3	*	*			*				
2	2		3					*			2	*	2	*				*				
3	3		1						*			*	*				*	*				
4	4		2					*		*		*						*				
5	5		3				*		*	*		*						*				Komarów period, cremation burial
6	6		1							*		*						*				

STAGES IN THE DEVELOPMENT AND CHRONOLOGY

STAGES IN EVOLUTION

The circumstances at the cemetery of Komarów, combined with those at other cemeteries reviewed in the preceding paragraph, suggest that the Barrow-grave culture passed through three main stages in its development. These stages were all marked by special 'horizons'. Thus the 'horizon of Thuringian amphorae' opens this evolution. The next, the 'horizon of the handled cups of Chłopice-Véselé type' indicates the beginning of the second period, and the 'horizon of single-lugged mugs' marks the beginning of the final stage.

The above evolution was a gradual process which proceeded at an uneven pace in various parts of the country; this resulted in some overlapping of the periods distinguished, well illustrated by the position at Komarów on the one hand, and at Kavsko and other sites on the other. In several instances, earlier types of grave goods survived to the subsequent period, and some leading vessels did not appear in graves of all groups of our culture. The dividing line between the periods cannot therefore be drawn precisely nor can all barrow-graves allotted them. The distinctive features of these periods can be defined only in very broad lines.

THE FIRST PERIOD

Graves of this period were almost exclusively in shafts, at least shallow ones. Cremation burials appear seldom, mainly by the end of this period, and human sacrifice (women) was an exception (Kołokolin IV, no. 66). A feature which seems to have been restricted to the western part of the country were huts, or special sepulchral constructions, uncovered under the mound close to the grave (Koropuż, Stojańce; Plan 8:1, 2).

The leading vessels were Thuringian amphorae of Schraplau type, or Buchvaldek's type I, sometimes accompanied by potsherds of the Funnel Beaker type. Beakers were seldom found, and were not uniform. Those from Kulczyce V (Fig. 11:2) and Lipie 2 represent evolved Central European Corded Ware types.

In eight graves flint axes were found, most of which were Becker's Bundsø-type, though some were oval. The only axe comparable to Lindø-type, from Kołokolin IV, probably originated from a secondary grave. Only one battle-axe was found, of the 'showy' type, typical of the eastern forest zone (Kołokolin IV). In other graves no weapons were excavated.

No personal ornaments nor metal objects were found in graves of the first period; the position in Bohemia with regard to the earliest assemblages, coeval with our graves, was similar.

Barrow-graves of the first period appear isolated, single, and very rarely in small groups of two or three mounds. Larger barrow-grave cemeteries dated exclusively from the more advanced periods (second and third) of the Barrow-grave culture or belonged to the Komarów culture.

The above development was probably the outcome of a change in the way of life of the bearers of the Barrow-grave culture. At first they seem to have led a nomad life within a larger area, but later they gradually took to a more sedentary life, or lived within a fixed and restricted district. This resulted in the formation of larger barrow-grave agglomerations, cemeteries, burial grounds in which eminent members of the local groups, or tribes, were buried and mounds raised over their graves. This is well illustrated at the cemetery of Komarów which was set up either at the very end of the first period, or more likely at the beginning of the second. The few earliest graves here lay quite apart, then around and/or in the neighbourhood of these later mounds were raised, and those of the Komarów culture were concentrated in a few very restricted sections of the cemetery. The same can be also observed in other larger cemeteries.

The early barrow-graves were confined mainly to the stretch of land which extended across the central part of our territory north of the Dniester, from the northern part of West Podolia westwards up to the San and beyond that river. Probably by the very end of the first period they had reached the eastern part of the Sub-Carpathian area (Komarów 5).

RELATIVE CHRONOLOGY

Connections with contemporary cultures reflected in the remains of the first period serve to establish its relative chronology. Thuringian amphorae are among these; they link our culture with the 'common Central European Corded Ware horizon'. The latter has been dated by Struve[1] as the developed Passage-grave period, Danish Middle Neolithic (MN II), but according to Becker[2] the earliest Undergraves of Jutland dated from MN III (Bundsø-period). Radiocarbon dating of the *Einzelgrab* culture in Lower Saxony[3] puts the date of the Corded Ware horizon to the time around 2200–2100 B.C.

In Bohemia, the Corded Ware appeared at the end of the local Middle Neolithic (equated with the turn of Danish MN II and MN III), and the date of the earliest Moravian Corded Ware[4] was similar.

A *terminus ante quem* for the appearance of the Thuringian amphorae is given by a number of cultures extending further south, within the Hungarian Plain and its bordering countries. Vessels representing evolved forms of Thuringian amphorae or reminiscent both in shape and decorative patterns of those of type I were found in flat graves with crouched skeletons and cremation burials of the Bell Beaker culture in Bohemia, Moravia, and Hungary,[5] but also further south, in the pottery of the Ljubljanske Barje (Laibacher Moor) and of the Vučedol cultures (Map IX).[6] Of the same derivation are urns typical of the Slavonian culture in the western part of the Hungarian Plain.[7] Vessels modelled on Thuringian

[1] K. W. Struve, *Die Einzelgrabkultur in Schleswig-Holstein und ihre kontinentalen Beziehungen*, Neumünster 1955, p. 117.

[2] C. J. Becker, 'Die mittel-neolithischen Kulturen in Südskandinavien', *Acta Archaeologica*, vol. XXV, København 1955, p. 114, Fig. 36.

[3] J. Pätzold, 'Dreischichtiger Grabhügel der Einzelgrabkultur bei Holzhausen, Gmd. Wildeshausen', *Nachrichten aus Niedersachsens Urgeschichte*, vol. 27, 1958, p. 13.

[4] M. Zápotocký, 'Příspěvký k poznam českeho středniho eneolitu', *Arch.R.*, vol. XII, 1960, pp. 724, 735, Fig. 278. F. Kalousek, *K otázce původu kultury se šňůrovou keramiku*, Brno 1947, pp. 9, 24. M. Buchvaldek, 'Přispevék k třidem šnůrove keramiky v Čechách', *Arch.R.*, vol. VII, 1955, p. 240.

[5] L. Hájek, 'Die Glockengräberkultur in Böhmen und Mähren: Šlapanice', *Inventoria Archaeologica—Československo*, no. 18/2/2, Bonn 1962.

[6] M. Wosinsky, *Die inkrustierte Keramik der Stein- und Bronzezeit*, Berlin 1904, Pls. LXIV, LXXXII:7–9, XCIX, etc. O. Menghin, *Urgeschichte der bildenden Kunst in Europa*, Wien 1925, p. 325, Fig. 5; p. 405, Fig. 6.

[7] V. G. Childe, *Prehistoric Migrations in Europe*, Oslo 1950, Fig. 113. B. Novotný, 'Slavonska kultura v Československu', *Slovenská Archeológia*, vol. III, 1955, pp. 5 ff.

amphorae were also found in the *Furchenstich* culture of Transilvania,[8] and their Mediterranean parallels have often been quoted.[9] The earliest of these were from Troy (cities II–V).

The advancing representatives of the Barrow-grave culture must have met their predecessors in the Sub-Carpathian area, the people of the Lublin Painted pottery culture (Map III), as is correctly pointed out by I. K. Svešnikov.[10] The cemetery of that culture investigated at Zvenyhorod (Dźwinogród) (no. 94) lay right in the centre of the extent of the Lwów-Opole group of the Barrow-grave culture; it dated from the Early Bronze Age, the period of many graves of the latter culture, although its grave goods do not reflect any contact between these two coeval groups. According to Svešnikov pottery typical of the Lublin Painted pottery culture was excavated in the settlement of the Funnel Beaker culture at Zimno in West Volhynia along with pottery characteristic of the Tripolye culture of Passek's period C. Finally, among potsherds excavated by M. Roska in the barrow-grave of Bolechowce (no. 39) one painted potsherd is said to have been found which Svešnikov ascribed to the Lublin Painted pottery culture. The frequency in which oval flint axes appeared in the Sub-Carpathian area, as well as axes made of the siliceous slate, is possibly the result of the adoption of traditions of the earlier inhabitants of the country.

There is ample evidence of contact with the Funnel Beaker culture which bordered on the Barrow-grave culture in the north-west from the San up to the Bug (Map IV), and the remains of both overlap here in many areas. The two south-easternmost fortified settlements of the Funnel Beakers (Grzybowice Małe, Winniki)[11] were set up in the territory of our culture, and Funnel Beaker potsherds were found still further south at Zalistsi on the Dniester (Map IV).[12] The red sandstone originating from the region of Trembowla (Tripolyan territory) found in the remains of the Funnel Beaker settlement at Gródek Nadbużny, must have been delivered across the country occupied by our culture.[13] The beaker from Siwki I-1878 (Plate 6:6) bears witness to the impact of the Funnel Beaker colonists in West Volhynia. But most affected by the latter were our barrow-graves in the north-western periphery, where not only potsherds (Stojańce, Koropuż; Plate 3:1; Fig. 12:1, 2), but also vessels typical of the Funnel Beaker culture appeared as the sole sepulchral pottery in a few graves (Miżyniec, Sobiecin; Plate 7:10–13). Here even the position of the corpse had been changed under its influence, from the traditional Corded Ware crouched position to the extended (Balice XVI; Plate 1:3).

Contact with the Funnel Beakers was not confined to the first period of our culture, but it also lasted during the subsequent one, while some graves quoted above date already from the later period. Connections between the Funnel Beakers and the Corded Ware groups of the early 'common European horizon' have been established in the loess country north of Cracow, and also in the countries further to the west; the impact of the Funnel Beakers on these has been emphasized, e.g. by Struve.[14]

Potsherds found in our earlier graves (Koropuż, Stojańce) were decorated in a manner characteristic of the 'Wiórek' period of K. Jażdżewski's 'eastern group'.[15] Flint axes of the early barrow-graves are comparable to the Bundsø-type axes of Danish MN III; they were obviously taken over from the Funnel Beakers and suggest a similar date, both for our barrow-graves and the Funnel Beaker group which affected them, equating them also with Danish early Undergraves. Axes found in barrow-graves of the second period were, to a large extent, of a type which corresponds with Danish Lindø-type proper to Danish MN IV, the period of the late Undergraves and Ground-graves. Funnel Beaker pottery found in our later barrow-graves (Miżyniec, Siwki I-1878) seems to derive from Jażdżewski's 'southern groups',[16] the Sandomierz group in the west and the Gródek Nadbużny group in the east. The latter in particular must have had steady intercourse with our culture.

A very important find was likewise a large jar from the Tripolyan settlement Kolomiščyna I (Map IX), dated by Passek as her period C-I.[17] This was typical Tripolyan ware the shape of which and the decorative patterns recall a Thuringian amphora although deprived of handles or lugs. This jar, modelled on a Thuringian amphora and obviously posterior to the Corded Ware horizon, gives the *terminus ante quem* for the appearance of the Thuringian amphorae in the region of Kiev. Of importance in this respect are also amphorae found in the settlement of Mykhailivka on the Lower Dnieper (Fig. 6; Map IX); their significance will be discussed in Chapter VII.

THE SECOND PERIOD

There was no fundamental difference between graves of the first period and those of the subsequent one. However, graves on ancient surface now prevailed, shaft-graves being found only rarely. Cremation burials were more frequent and chiefly in the Sub-Carpathian area. Human offerings also increased, being either double burials (man and woman) but graves contained sometimes three or four skeletons, the added ones being either child or adult.

The appearance, mainly by the end of this period, of stone constructions under the mound was significant: cairns and stone circles in the northern part of West Podolia: Nowosiółka Jaruzelskich (no. 212), Kaczanówka I (no. 198),

[8] H. Schroller, *Die Stein- und Kupferzeit Siebenbürgens*, Berlin 1933, pp. 31 ff., Pls. 26:2; 28:1.

[9] See my ' "Thuringian" Amphorae', *PPS*, vol. XXI, 1955, p. 114.

[10] И. К. Свешников, Могильник в селе Звенигород, львовской области, Ксиимк, no. 63, 1956, p. 66.

[11] M. Śmiszko, 'Odkrycia przedhistoryczne pod Lwowem', *Z Bliska i z Daleka*, vol. I, Lwów 1933. М. Ю. Смішко and М. А. Пелещишин, Поселення культури лійчастого посуду в с. Малі Грибовичі, Мдапв, vol. 4, 1962, pp. 26 ff.

[12] Я. Пастернак, Нові археологічні набутки музею Наук. тов. ім. Шевченка, Записки Наук. тов. ім. Шевченка, vol. CLIV, Lviv 1937.

[13] J. Kowalczyk, 'Osada kultury pucharów lejkowatych w miejsc. Gródek Nabużny, pow.Hrubieszów, w świetle badań 1954 r.,' *W.A.*, vol. XXIII, 1956, pp. 43 ff., Fig. 18 (map).

[14] J. Machnik, 'Groby kultury ceramiki sznurowej w Książnicach Wielkich pow.Kazimierza Wielka', *Prace Komisji Archeologicznej Oddziłu PAN*, no. 4, Kraków 1964, pp. 356 ff., on connections north of Cracow. Struve (op. cit., note 1), p. 116, on impact of Funnel Beakers.

[15] K. Jażdżewski, 'Zusammenfassender Überblick über die Trichterbecherkultur', *Prähistorische Zft.*, vol. XXIII, 1932, pp. 96 ff.

[16] Ibid., pp. 100 ff. Id., *Kultura pucharów lejkowatych w Polsce zachodniej i środkowej*, Poznań 1936, pp. 220 ff.

[17] Т. С. Пассек, Периодизация трипольских поселений, МИА, no. 10, Leningrad 1949, pp. 131 ff., Fig. 75:2.

Ostapie I (no. 213), and slab-cists further south, e.g. Beremiany 1827 (no. 96). No such constructions were found in other groups of our culture at that period (see Table 2), but a stone circle was reported in an East Slovakian barrow-grave.[18] Stone circles were found in Pomerania south of Danzig,[19] in the barrow-graves of the Usatovo culture on the Black Sea,[20] in the steppe barrow-graves further east[21] and in the Middle Bronze Age graves of the region of the Dnieper Rapids.[22] Slab-cist graves were a characteristic feature of the Globular Amphora culture; their appearance in barrow-graves within the Territory was obviously due to the influence emanating from this culture, which is well indicated by the geographical diffusion of these barrow-graves (Map v).

Pottery of the second period was not uniform and no other vessel had a distribution comparable to that of the Thuringian amphorae. The latter belonged exclusively to types IIa and IIc. Beakers were of two main forms: a few of western Corded Ware type (Kołokolin I, Nowosiółki-Przemyśl; Plate 6:1, 2), but mainly related to eastern beakers, wide with a rounded base and hemispheric body (e.g. Kryłos VI, Myszyn; Fig. 10:5; Fig. 11:1). Significant was the distribution of various types of vessels which appear in distinct parts of the country and mark the emergence of local groups quoted in Chapter I. Thus the Chłopice-Véselé handled cups were found mainly in the Lwów-Opole group, whereas the Miechów type amphorae were proper to the north-western group.

The frequency of weapons was approximately similar to that of the preceding period. However, battle-axes now outnumbered the flint axes, and the increased number of weapons found in graves was very suggestive. A single weapon was an exception, burials being usually furnished with several types, e.g. axe, battle-axe, sometimes a mace-head, dagger, or arrow-heads. A characteristic ritual developed, or was adopted under some external influence of damaging at least one weapon laid in the grave (see Table 6). This custom was first noticed in very late graves of the first period (Kołokolin 4), but during the second period it became very common. Often one of the several arrow-heads in a grave had its tip broken off (Komarów 39, Kulczyce 3), stone battle-axes were thrown in the funeral fire or broken, their blades missing (Kulczyce 3, Kołokolin 3, Wiktorów 2, Myszyn). In some graves the blade of the flint axe was missing (Rokitno 6, Kołokolin 3). It is of interest to note that this ritual was restricted mainly to the eastern part of our area without regard to the groups of the Barrow-grave culture distinguished.

A new type of weapon, besides arrow-heads, were flint daggers mainly of the second type, though also of the first, dealt with in the previous chapter. Bronze daggers also occur (Sarniki I, Balice 7) typical of the Early Bronze Age (Fig. 19:18, 23).

Objects of adornment (Fig. 19), never found in earlier graves, were now a common feature. Most frequent were small bronze rings and earrings (Lublin-Sławinek, Czyżyków 2, Kryłos 3, Wiktorów 2). In a few graves boar tusks (Ostapie I gr. 2) and perforated amber or clay pendants (Rokitno 2, Kołokolin 7) were excavated and at Kołpiec 5 faience beads, several being segmented, were found. Other bronze ornaments mainly of a somewhat larger size, the nap-ring (Jaktorów 2) and in particular bracelets (Balice 7, Gdeszyce), torque (Kryłos VI), and lead rings (Balice 7, Kryłos VI, Siedliska I) may have dated from the very end of this period, but possibly from the third one.

The area embraced by the Barrow-grave culture during the second period was considerably enlarged. It expanded northwards into the Lubaczów area north-east of the Lower San, and further north to Lublin. Further east, barrow-graves now appeared in the region on the Middle Bug, and throughout the whole Sub-Carpathian region south of the Dniester.

RELATIVE CHRONOLOGY

The appearance of Chłopice-Véselé handled cups marks a definite chronological horizon, the beginning of the second period of the Barrow-grave culture. They were found in several graves of the culture (Fig. 10:2:2; Plate 6:19, 23, 24; Plate 7:2, 3; Fig. 12:10) and in other graves and settlements east of the San (Chłopice district of Jarosław, Mokre district of Zamość, Strzyżów district of Hrubieszów, Ulwówek district of Sokal, etc.).

The cups were dealt with by Machnik[23] who, however, includes in this group handled jugs which represent a different type. The geographical distribution of these vessels includes Upper Silesia, Northern Moravia, Western Slovakia, the Cracow-Sandomierz country and part of the Lublin Plateau, not to mention our area. They were found, except for the specimens east of the San, almost exclusively within an area in which both Corded Ware and the late Baden culture (or the Radial pottery culture,[24] a late outpost of the latter north of the Carpathians) overlapped, and—still more important—in an area which was affected by the Bell Beakers. Machnik[25] is right in seeking their derivation from similar cups of the Bell Beaker culture, but it does not seem justified

[18] B. Novotný, *Počiatky výtvarneho prejavu na Slovensko*, Bratislava 1958, p. 122. Id. (op. cit., note 7), p. 52 (or p. 69 of the German text).

[19] L. Kozłowski, *Młodsza epoka kamienna w Polsce (neolit)*, Lwów 1924, p. 171.

[20] A. M. Tallgren, 'La Pontide préscythique', ESA, vol. II, 1926, p. 48, Fig. 37. M. Gimbutas, *The Prehistory of Eastern Europe*, part I, Cambridge (Mass.) 1956, pp. 85 ff., 108.

[21] E.g., Tallgren (note 10), pp. 50 ff. А. И. Тереножкин, Курган Сторожова могила, Археологія-Kiev, vol. v, 1951, pp. 183 ff., Figs. 1–9. Id., Ксиимк, no. XXXVII, 1951, pp. 117 ff.

[22] Нариси Стародавної Історії Української РСР, Kiev 1957, p. 99.

[23] J. Machnik, 'Uwagi o wczesnej fazie epoki brązu w dorzeczu górnej Wisły i Dniestru', *Sprawozdania Komisji PAN*, Kraków, VII–XIII, 1960. Id., 'Ze studiów nad kulturą ceramiki sznurowej w Karpatach polskich', *Acta AC*, vol. II, 1960, pp. 55 ff. Id., 'Uwagi o związkach i chronologii niektórych znalezisk kultury ceramiki sznurowej w Karpatach', *Acta AC*, vol. IV, 1962, pp. 91 ff. Id., *Studia nad kulturą ceramiki sznurowej w Małopolsce*, Wrocław-Warszawa-Kraków 1966, pp. 141 ff.

[24] Kozłowski (op. cit., note 19), pp. 58 ff., Pl. XIII. J. Żurowski, 'Neue Ergebnisse der neolithischen Forschung im südwestpolnischen Lössgebiet', *Praehistorische Zft.*, vol. XXI, 1930 Id., 'Problem kultury ceramiki promienistej', *W.A.*, 1933. The present position concerning the research relating to this culture has been summarized in my *Polska przedhistoryczna*, part II, London 1957–9, pp. 207 ff., Figs. 48 (map), 49. A number of sites have been recently reported from the neighbourhood of Racibórz in Upper Silesia: J. Gedingowa, 'Z prac wykopaliskowych na stanowisku neolitycznym 8 w Pietrowicach Wielkich, pow.Rabibórz', *Śląskie Sprawozdania Archeologiczne*, vol. III, Wrocław 1960, p. 6.

[25] J. Machnik, 'Kultura pucharów dzwonowatych a kultura ceramiki sznurowej w Małopolsce', *Sprawozdania Komisji PAN*, Kraków 1963, pp. 67 ff.

to consider them to be of a post-Złota period. The cups do not appear in the Złota burials (except for one or two specimens)[26] or in other assemblages within the Złota territory. They belonged to cultures which developed outside but parallel with that culture.

The spread of the Bell Beakers in Central Europe has been dated as *c.* 1800 B.C.,[27] and their final date in Bohemia has been estimated as *c.* 1700 B.C.[28] Graves of the Bell Beaker culture are reported from several sites in the southern part of Poland;[29] their date must have been approximately similar to that of the finds above. The appearance of the Chłopice-Véselé handled cups may, therefore, be equated with the Bell Beaker horizon, the time about 1800 B.C., and this was also the presumed date of the beginning of the second period of the Barrow-grave culture.

The second period runs parallel to a developed stage of the Cracow-Sandomierz group of Corded Ware, as is evidenced by the 'Miechów' amphorae (Plate 3:5, 6) proper to that group, found in a series of graves of the north-western group; and also by large beakers similar to those found in the region of Cracow (Morawsko, Plate 6:21; Lublin-Sławinek), battle-axes of western type, a bronze dagger (Sarniki 1, Fig. 19:23), and ornaments of Central European origin.

At the same time, however, contact with the countries to the north-east of the Territory was maintained, as is witnessed by Fatyanovo axes and 'simple' *y* axes of eastern type, found chiefly in the eastern part of our area. The same probably relates to vessels with a hemispheric body and rounded base (beakers and smaller bowls) found mainly south of the Dniester, which were possibly modelled on prototypes characteristic of the forest zone of Eastern Europe.

The impact of the Globular Amphora culture on our barrow-graves of the second period is evidenced by the adoption, mainly in the West Podolian group exposed to its strongest influence, of stone constructions in the burial mounds, slab-cists, and possibly cairns. On the other hand, however, the Globular Amphora culture, in particular its Podolian group, was exposed to the reciprocal influence of our culture, which resulted in the subsequent appearance in the sepulchral pottery of vessels typical of Corded Ware.

THE THIRD PERIOD

During this period the earlier unity of the Barrow-grave culture began to fade, and three distinct groups emerged within its extent instead.

Graves on the ancient surface were now almost the only type of burial. In Podolia stone constructions, adopted during the second period, were frequent and survived up to the Scythian period (see Table 2). Simple stone constructions, chiefly pavements, appear also later in the graves of the Komarów culture (Komarów 20, 45), this apparently being due to Podolian influence. Another phenomenon, restricted however to the north-eastern part of our area and recorded in a number of graves of the neighbouring Strzyżów culture in West Volhynia, was the dismembering and mutilation of the corpse (Buhłow 1, 2; Rusiłów; Plate 2:1–3; Plate 1:4). This ritual was taken over from the west, as is pointed out in Chapter I.

Transition to the new period was most clearly marked in the whole eastern part of our culture by the emergence there of new types of vessels. To these, first of all, belonged the single-lugged mugs (Fig. 10:4; Plate 8), exclusively found within that area and in the north, which mark a definite chronological horizon there. At that time in the eastern part of the Sub-Carpathian area south of the Dniester the earliest graves of the Komarów culture appeared. The western part of the Sub-Carpathian area and the north-western region were more conservative in keeping to ancient forms and patterns, and graves of the third period can therefore often hardly be distinguished from the earlier ones. But new forms had penetrated even there, as is exemplified by the beaker from Kołpiec 8 (Fig. 11:3); it had a spheric body and a long unperforated lug on its cylindrical neck, and was obviously related to the single-lugged mugs on which it was modelled. Typical of this period in this area were also low, clumsy cord-decorated bowls (Kavsko 2, Kołpiec 8) (Plate 7:8; Fig. 12:14) clumsy cord-decorated cups, or small beakers (Łukawica K, Siedliska B; Plate 6:18), also the undecorated amphora with no lugs or handles (Łukawica K), and the undecorated 'Unetice' cup from Kavsko 4 (Fig. 29:4).

Of interest was the double-handled vase from Ostapie 3 (Plate 4:6) which, in spite of its 'old-fashioned' cord decoration, represents a vessel typical of the developed Komarów culture. It must have dated from a period in which, in other parts of our area, the Komarów culture and its related groups had replaced the old Barrow-grave culture.

In spite of regional differences and lack of uniformity, pottery of the second period shows a marked tendency towards the abandonment of any decoration of vessels. Another common tendency was the almost complete disappearance of flint axes from the usual furniture of graves. The number of battle-axes also decreased, those found being solely of the simple *z* type. Instead, the number of daggers or spear-heads increased; daggers of the 'third group' all dated from this period. Flint arrow-heads did not differ from those of the preceding period.

Personal ornaments consisted of boar tusks (Klimkowce, Siedliska B), a large amber disc (Chorostków 1; Plate 9:2), and various metal ornaments. At Buhłów 2 (Plate 9:10) silver rings were found. Of interest were the Irish gold basket ear-pendant (Rusiłów, Plate 8:1) and the Caucasian 'cord-decorated' bronze ornament (Ostapie 4, Plate 9:12). A number of bronze personal ornaments quoted previously may have dated from this period, or from the end of the second period (Balice VII, Fig. 19:14, 17, 18, 22; Kryłos VI, Fig. 11:1; Siedliska 1). But definitely of this period was the bronze Cypriot wire-headed pin (Putiatyńce, Fig. 19:15), and also large bronze basket ear-pendants (or temple ornaments) of

[26] Z. Krzak, *Materiały do znajomości kultury złockiej*, Wrocław-Warszawa-Kraków 1961, pp. 160 ff.

[27] V. G. Childe, *The Dawn of European Civilisation*, 6th ed., 1957, p. 347.

[28] L. Hajek, 'Chronologie de la civilisation des gobelets campaniformes en Tchécoslovaquie', *Chronologie Préhistorique de la Tchecoslovaquie*, Prague 1956, p. 65.

[29] J. Żurowski, 'Pierwsze ślady kultury pucharów dzwonowatych w Polsce', *W.A.*, vol. XI, 1932, pp. 117 ff. J. Kostrzewski, 'Od mezolitu do okresu wędrówek ludów', *Prehistoria Ziem Polskich*, Kraków 1939–48, pp. 190 ff. S. Nosek, 'Zagadnienie Prasłowiańszczyzny w świetle prehistorii', *Światowit*, vol. XIX, 1948, pp. 88 ff.

Stubło type (Okniany 2, Perediwanie, Chłopy; Plate 9:4; Fig. 19:1–4, 10); similar pendants were also found in a number of graves of the Strzyżów culture in West Volhynia.

RELATIVE CHRONOLOGY

During the third period, this region separated, its south-west and the centre forming one cultural area, and the north and the east another. The Barrow-grave culture within the first of these areas kept to ancient forms and a few items or particular features of an evidently late character serve as an indication that the given assemblage belonged to the third period. Connections were maintained almost exclusively with the region of Cracow and the countries further south, Moravia and West Slovakia.

The position in the other area was different. There, graves of the third period were clearly distinguishable. Within that territory appeared the single-lugged mugs, the leading vessel of that period. They belonged to a large group of vessels typical of the late Corded Ware of Central Europe. Single-lugged mugs, and also handled mugs were found in late graves of the Cracow-Sandomierz group[30] where their late date is attested by their appearance, e.g. at Rosiejów,[31] in graves immediately preceding those of the Middle Bronze Age Trzciniec culture. They were also found in the assemblages of the Early Bronze Age Mierzanowice culture.[32] Single-lugged mugs of a somewhat different shape were typical of the Oder Corded Ware[33] and the 'flower-pot' beakers (Brzezinki III) belonging to the same group of vessels were characteristic of the Danish final Neolithic.[34]

The late date of these vessels has also been shown by the conditions in which they were found within our region. At Gwoździec Stary II (Plate 9:4–5, 9) the single-lugged mug was excavated in association with a large bronze ear-pendant of Stubło type and with a handled jug closely related to those of the Kisapostag culture of the Hungarian Plain,[35] dated as the last stage of the Early Bronze Age. At Komarów 45 a typical single-lugged mug decorated in a manner proper to the Komarów culture (Plate 21:4) was found in a grave of that culture, which also points to a late date for these vessels.

A number of types of grave goods bear witness to connections with distant countries. To these belonged the Irish gold basket ear-pendant from Rusiłów (Plate 8:1). Another object of Irish origin found in Poland was the gold basket ear-pendant of a somewhat different form, found in the bronze hoard from Wąsosz near Poznań,[36] dating from Reinecke's period A-2; of Irish type, although probably not Irish origin, was the bronze basket ear-pendant from Zastów near Cracow[37] found with a cord-decorated jug of Unetice type. North-western connections are indicated by the large discoid amber pendant from Chorostków 1, found with a handled mug. Such amber pendants were characteristic of the Globular Amphora culture in North Poland, and were found in Early Bronze Age assemblages in Western Poland.[38]

The bronze 'cord-decorated' ornament from Ostapie 4 (Plate 9:12) found with an undecorated single-lugged mug, was of North Caucasian origin;[39] according to A. M. Tallgren[40] graves in which similarly decorated bronze ornaments were found dated from the Middle Kuban period, 1700 to 1300 B.C.—recently called the second stage of the North Caucasian Culture, and dated 1700–1400 B.C.[41]

The bronze hoard from Stubło, district of Dubno in Volhynia,[42] also points to North Caucasian, Kuban, connections, as does the bronze hoard from Prelipcze in the Bucovina[43] which was of a little later date, in the early stage of the Middle Bronze Age. At least one Caucasian shaft-hole axe (battle-axe) formed part of the latter. The hoard from Stubło will be dealt with in Chapter V. One of its shaft-hole axes was of Caucasian origin,[44] and the other might have been likewise of East European origin. However, axes of the latter type were found also in the Hungarian Plain. Moulds for casting them were excavated there in layers dating from Reinecke's period B or C,[45] although Milojčić[46] dates them as period A-2.

The above axes were a long-lived type but of importance for our purpose is the fact that they were never reported in assemblages undisputably dated as period A-1 or even A-2 of the Central European Bronze Age. This circumstance implies a late date for the hoard from Stubło and also of the ear-

[30] Kozłowski (op. cit., note 19), Pl. XV:4, 6.

[31] T. Reyman, 'Dokumentaryczne wartości odkryć w kopcu wschodnim w Rosiejowie, w pow.pińczowskim', *Slavia Antiqua*, vol. I, 1948, pp. 79 f., Figs. 36, 47.

[32] K. Salewicz, 'Tymczasowe wyniki badań przedhistorycznych w Mierzanowicach (pow.opatowski, woj.kieleckie)', *ZOW*, vol. XII, 1937, pp. 39 ff. Nosek (op. cit., note 29), pp. 105 ff., Pls. XIII–XIX. Kostrzewski (op. cit., note 29), pp. 202 ff. T. Sulimirski, *Polska przedhistoryczna*, part II, London 1957–9, pp. 263 ff. J. Kowalczyk, 'Zagadnienie kultury mierzanowickiej zwanej także tomaszowską', *W.A.*, vol. XXVI, 1959, pp. 1 ff.

[33] Kozłowski (op. cit., note 19), Pl. VI:2, 6, 7.

[34] Struve (op. cit., note 1), pp. 42 f.

[35] A. Mozsolics, 'Der frühbronzezeitliche Urnenfriedhof von Kisapostag', *Arch. Hung.*, vol. XXVI, 1942, Figs. 2, 3, 8; Pl. IX.

[36] A. Knapowska-Mikołajczykowa, *FAP*, vol. VII, 1957, pp. 85 ff., Figs. 110–11.

[37] J. Bartys, 'Nowe stanowisko małopolskiej grupy ceramiki sznurowej', *Prz.A.*, vol. VI, 1937–9, pp. 96 ff., Fig. 4.

[38] Knapowska-Mikołajczykowa (op. cit., note 36), p. 71, Fig. 83. Sulimirski (op. cit., note 32), p. 278, Figs. 72, 74.

[39] Б. Е. Деген, Курганы в Кабардинском парке г. Нальчика, МИА, no. 3, 1941, pp. 258 ff., Figs. 35, 36. A. M. Tallgren, 'Zu der nordkaukasischen Bronzezeit', *ESA*, vol. VI, 1931, Figs. 21, 31–41.

[40] Tallgren (note 39), pp. 134 ff.

[41] В. И. Марковин, Культура племен северного Кавказа в эпоху бронзы, МИА, no. 93, 1960, p. 69.

[42] W. Antoniewicz, 'Der in Stubło in Wolhynien aufgefundene Bronzeschatz', *ESA*, vol. IV, 1929, pp. 145 f.

[43] J. Kostrzewski, 'Z badań nad osadnictwem wczesnej i środkowej epoki bronzowej na ziemiach polskich', *Prz.A*, vol. II, 1922–4, p. 217, Fig. 9 (wrongly indicated as from Babin). J. Hampel, *Magyarorszagi eredetü bronzleletek*, vol. III, Budapest 1896, Pl. CLXXIV:1–3. Tallgren (op. cit., note 20), p. 146, Fig. 100. T. Sulimirski, 'Einige rumänische Funde in polnischen Museen', *Revista de preistorie şi antichităţi naţionale*, vol. I, Bukarest 1937, p. 5 (off-print). Id., 'Barrow-grave 6 at Komarów', *Bulletin of the University of London Institute of Archaeology*, no. 4, 1964, pp. 171 ff. I. Nestor, 'Der Stand der Vorgeschichtsforschung in Rumänien', *22 Berich d.röm.germ.-Kommission*, 1932, pp. 128 f., Pl. 12:7.

[44] А. А. Иессен, Греческая колонизация северного причерноморья, Leningrad 1947, p. 23, n. 4. Id., К хронологии "больших кубанских курганов", Сов. Арх., vol. XII, 1950, p. 200, table (group IV). Id., К вопросу о древних связях северного Кавказа с западом, Ксиимк, no. XLVI, 1952, p. 48.

[45] D. Popescu, *Die frühe und mittlere Bronzezeit in Siebenbürgen*, Bucureşti 1944, pp. 64 f., Figs. 26, 27. R. Pittioni, *Urgeschichte des österreichischen Raumes*, Wien 1954, p. 354, Fig. 251. S. Foltiny, 'Bemerkungen zur Chronologie der Bronzezeit Ungarns', *Germania*, vol. 38, 1960, pp. 347 f.

[46] V. Milojčić, 'Zur Frage der Chronologie der frühen und mittleren Bronzezeit in Ostungarn', *Congrès Internat. des Sciences Préhist.*, Zürich 1950, p. 267.

pendants which formed part of it, called 'Stubło type' after this find. Ear-pendants very similar to these were excavated in a number of graves in West Slovakia, as pointed out previously: Točik[47] considers them to belong to period A-1, which cannot be applied to those found in our region. Our specimens were of a later date and cannot be placed earlier than the end of period A-2, or the beginning of period B. Romanian specimens[48] which did not much differ from ours dated from Reinecke's period B.

The third period of the Barrow-grave culture runs parallel to the Alpine Bronze Age period A-2, and to period I of the Northern Bronze Age, the beginning of which has been put at *c.* 1600 B.C., and the end at *c.* 1450 B.C.[49]

THE CHARACTER OF THE SUB-CARPATHIAN BARROW-GRAVES

Sub-Carpathian barrow-graves were not burial places for the entire population of that time. Only members of the ruling class, or even solely the rulers, local chiefs, etc., were buried in them. This is clearly indicated by the number of graves in the cemeteries. However, no contemporary settlements have been found attributable to the sub-Carpathian Barrow-grave culture.

As mentioned previously, the number of barrow-graves situated close to each other varied greatly, but small groups usually prevailed. Larger groups survived mainly in the areas in which they were protected by woods or forest cover. A number of such cemeteries were investigated and in some groups almost all the graves were excavated. The following cemeteries may be quoted:

(1) Komarów-Wiktorów-Medynia-Kryłos (Plan 1). This large agglomeration of over one hundred barrow-graves, extending over a narrow area nearly five kilometres long, cannot be considered as the burial ground of a single community. Several smaller groups of mounds have been distinguished which probably belonged to a single group or family. One of these, group C-c (mounds nos. 37, 38, 52, 63), consisted solely of 'Neolithic' graves plus two secondary burials of a much later date. They all dated from the second period of the Barrow-grave culture and the range of the graves was supposedly about 150 years (1750–1600 B.C.). Another group, F-a, consisted of eight mounds (nos. 19, 20, 21, 22, 23, 24, 27, 51); the earliest of these was the 'Neolithic' barrow-grave 19, probably from the turn of the second and third periods of the Barrow-grave culture, and all others were of periods I–II of the Komarów culture (*c.* 1600–1200 B.C.). The range of the graves of this group was about four hundred years.

(2) Kavsko (no. 45). Six mounds in one group were excavated. The earliest of these (no. 1) was probably of the turn between the second and third periods, and the latest (no. 5) was typical of the second period of the Komarów culture. The cemetery lasted from *c.* 1600 to *c.* 1250 B.C., about 350 years.

(3) Kołpiec (Plan 2:2). Only eight barrow-graves survived of a larger group; seven of these were excavated. The earliest was probably barrow-grave 2 from the end of the first period of the Barrow-grave culture, possibly *c.* 1800 B.C., and the latest was grave no. 6 with a vessel proper to the Komarów culture, dating probably from the very beginning of that culture, approximately 1400 B.C. This cemetery presumably lasted four hundred years.

(4) Balice-Nowosiółki (no. 1). Thirteen barrow-graves formed a single group, all of which were excavated. The earliest was barrow-grave XV, probably of the beginning of the second period of the Barrow-grave culture. The latest was barrow-grave VII with Unetice bronze objects. The date of this cemetery may cover the period from *c.* 1800 to *c.* 1400 B.C., or for about four hundred years.

(5) Kaczanówka-Nowosiółka Jaruzelskich (nos. 198, 212). Seven barrow-graves lying quite near each other were excavated. The earliest was probably barrow-grave 2 from Nowosiółka with its debased Thuringian amphora, which might date from *c.* 1700 B.C. The latest was probably the secondary grave in barrow-grave 4 at Kaczanówka with its undecorated mug, which probably dated from *c.* 1400 B.C. The range of the graves was about three hundred years.

(6) Ostapie (no. 213). Six mounds with eight burials, two of these secondary, were investigated. The earliest of these dates not earlier than *c.* 1500 B.C.; the latest, no. 6, with a skeleton, of which the head was slashed by a sword, cannot be dated earlier than the third period of the Bronze Age (Montelius), approximately 1200 B.C. This implies about three hundred years for the duration of this cemetery.

Table 12 shows the dates quoted above and the average period in which barrow-graves were probably erected.

TABLE 12. The range of graves in various cemeteries

Cemetery	Beginning	End	Duration years	No. of graves	Proportion of years per grave
Komarów C-c	1750	1600	150	4	37
Komarów F-a	1600	1200	400	8	50
Kavsko	1600	1250	350	6	58
Kołpiec	1800	1400	400	8?	50?
Balice	1800	1400	400	13	31
Kaczanówka	1700	1400	300	8	37
Ostapie	1500	1200	300	8	37

Datings in the table are tentative and subject to alteration, and the range of the respective graves may be modified accordingly. Nevertheless, the only conclusion which can be drawn from the figures—even if the range of the graves in a single cemetery is reduced by half—is that barrow-graves were not a common burial place for the whole population; they were burial places of selected persons only. The grave goods, the great amount of labour involved in raising the particularly large mounds of the earlier period, and above all, the relatively large time-lag between the date of the burials within a single cemetery, suggest that only outstanding persons, chiefs or rulers, were buried in those.

[47] A. Točik, 'Zpráva o vyskume v rokoch 1957–9 na Zámečku v Nitrianskom Hrádku, okres Nové Zamký', *The Conference of the Czechoslovak Archaeologists at Libice*, 1960, pp. 19 ff.

[48] E. Zaharia, 'Die Lockringe von Sărăta-Monteoru und ihre typologischen und chronologischen Beziehungen', *Dacia*, vol. NS III, 1959, pp. 105 ff.

[49] E. Lomborg, 'Donauländische Kulturbeziehungen und die relative Chronologie der frühen nordischen Bronzezeit, *Acta Archaeologica*, vol. XXX, København 1959, pp. 52 ff.

SUMMING UP

The main features characteristic of the three periods distinguished in the development of the Barrow-grave culture of the Sub-Carpathian region are summed up in Table 13. A review of the connections and equations with contemporaneous cultures in other parts of the country or in other territories is also given there. Table 14 shows the assignment of the more important barrow-graves to the periods established.

TABLE 13. Periods in the development of the Barrow-grave culture and their relative chronology

Date	Characteristic grave goods	Connections	Equations
	PERIOD I		
2200/2100 B.C.?	Thuringian amphora of type I (Schraplau)	Funnel Beakers Graves of pre-Złota culture at Złota (Corded Ware); Globular Amphorae at a later stage	Common European Corded Ware Horizon Danish MN; III Tripolyan period B-2–C-1
	PERIOD II		
1800 B.C.?	Thuringian amphorae of types IIA and IIC; Miechów type amphorae; Chłopice-Véselé handled cups	Late Funnel Beakers (Gródek Nadbużny); Globular Amphorae; Classic Złota culture	Bell Beaker Horizon Danish MN IV Eastern Globular Amphorae; Złota culture; Tripolyan period C-1; Fatyanovo culture; Vučedol-Laibach Slavonian culture; Reinecke Br. A-1
	PERIOD III		
1600 B.C.?	Single-lugged mugs; handled jugs; bronze ear-pendants of Stubło type	Late slab-cists (post Globular Amph.) Strzyżów culture; Mierzanowice culture; earliest Komarów graves	Tripolyan period C-1 (C-2) Oder Corded Ware Kisapostag Reinecke Br. A-2 and the beginning of B in some parts of the country; Irish and Caucasian connections Northern Br. Age I and partly II

TABLE 14. Chronological division of the main burials

Przemyśl Group	Sub-Carpathian	Lwów-Opole	Horodenka	Lublin-Bug	West-Volhynian	North-West Podolian
PERIOD I						
Koropuż Lipie 2 Miżyniec Stojańce Sobiecin	Bolechowce Kołpiec II Kulczyce 5	Kołokolin 4 Kołokolin 5 Krasów 1 Krasów 2			Siwki I-1878	Lisiczyńce
PERIOD II						
Balice 4 Balice 7 Balice 15 Balice 16 Brusno Brzezinki I Brzezinki IV Gdeszyce Nowosiółki Siedliska 1	Kavsko 1 Kołpiec V Komarów 5 Komarów 31 Komarów 39 Kryłos 3 Kryłos VI Kulczyce 2 Kulczyce 3 Łotatniki 2 Myszyn Wiktorów 2 Wiktorów 8	Czyżyków 2 Jaktorów 2 Jaktorów 4 Kołokolin 1 Kołokolin 2 Kołokolin 3 Kołokolin 7 Rokitno 2 Rokitno 3 Rokitno 6 Sarniki 1 Stratyn 1 Stratyn 2		Sławinek	Korytne I-1878 Płużne III	Kaczanówka 1 Nowosiółka Jar. 2 Nowosiółka Jar. 3 Ostapie 1
PERIOD III						
Balice 14 Brzezinki 3 Łukawica K Siedliska B	Kavsko 2 Kavsko 4 Kavsko 6 Kołpiec VIII Kołpiec IX Komarów 20 Komarów 28 Komarów 45	Płaucza Wka Putiatyńce Rusiłów	Gwoździec St. Okniany 2 Perediwanie	Guciów XIII Hrubieszów Sokal Zakłodzie (2)	Ostrożec Siekierzynce A-1876 Staryki A Zaborol Zdolbunov	Buhłów 2 Chorostków 1 Kaczanówka 3 Kaczanówka 4 Klimkowce Ostapie 1 (sec.) Ostapie 2 Ostapie 3 Ostapie 4

CHAPTER IV

Eastern Globular Amphorae

GENERAL
(Map v)

EASTERN and western branches of the well-known Central European culture, the Globular Amphora, have been distinguished and have been the subject of many papers. H. Priebe[1] produced a large work on the western variety but no similar work on the eastern branch of the culture has been published. The latter extended over a very large area east of the Oder, almost up to the Dnieper in the east and down to the central part of Moldavia in the south-east. At least four hundred sites of this culture have been recorded and these include over sixty settlements, the latter situated mostly in the northern part of Greater Poland.

Occupation of this vast area appears to have been very uneven, for there were several scattered groupings which were linked by odd graves in between, as shown in Map vi. Many of these groupings have been dealt with by various scholars. Thus the graves within the boundaries of pre-war Poland were dealt with by L. Kozłowski,[2] W. Antoniewicz,[3] and J. Kostrzewski;[4] North Polish sites were the theme of the work by W. La Baume,[5] and those in the Lublin region, excavated mostly since the war, were described by S. Nosek.[6] Globular Amphora graves (all slab-cist) in Volhynia were dealt with by I. Levitskyi,[7] also by T. S. Passek[8] and A. I. Briusov;[9] and Podolian ones recently by I. K. Svešnikov.[10] I have given a short summary of all these sites,[11] but in recent years a number of new sites, graves, and settlements have been recorded, and a new grouping in Romania (Moldavia) has emerged.[12]

The Globular Amphora culture played an important role in the development of almost all the cultures within the countries in which we are concerned, some of which were greatly affected by it. A summary and analysis of the whole eastern branch of this culture seems to be, therefore, urgently required. Our interest is restricted here, however, to the eastern groupings of the eastern branch. Only the most important topics connected with the groupings situated further west, and required for a better understanding of the development which proceeded within our area, will be briefly reviewed.

The eastern Globular Amphorae differed in many respects from the western ones. They were scattered over an enormous territory forming a series of local groups which have their own distinguishing features. In dealing with these groups it is always necessary to bear in mind the great distances which separate them (Map v). Thus the Kuyavian sites are some 200km from the East Prussian graves and even the nearest group, the Masovian on the Middle Vistula, is about 100km away. The route which must have been followed to connect the Masovian group with the southern part of its neighbouring Chełm-Hrubieszów group, along the Vistula and the Bug Rivers, involves a distance of about 350km, and another 450km must be added to reach the southern border of the Podolian group. This means that the Podolian and Kuyavian groups are separated by a total distance of nearly 800km. An even greater distance (some 850km) lies between the Kuyavian group and the most eastern graves of the Volhynian group, which is some 400km east of the Bug, and the Moldavian graves are about 200km south of the Podolian group, about 1000km from Kuyavia. The grave from Pekliuk in Bulgaria lay well over 500km south of the southernmost Moldavian slab-cist.

Each of the groups above developed in a different geographical environment and under different conditions. Each group of the Globular Amphora people was surrounded by a different set of existing cultures, which influenced local development from originally common patterns, in different ways. For this reason the eastern Globular Amphorae cannot be treated as a single, uniform cultural whole.

WESTERN GROUPS
(Map v, groups I–IV)

The largest and apparently the most important group was the Kuyavian (group I), which extended over the north-western part of Greater Poland and the adjoining part of Eastern Pomerania. Over forty settlements and over forty

[1] H. Priebe, 'Die Westgruppe der Kugelamphoren', *Jahreschrift f.d. Vorgeschichte sächsisch-thüring. Länder*, vol. XXVIII, Halle 1938.

[2] L. Kozłowski, 'Groby megalityczne na wschód od Odry', *Prace i Materiały antropologiczno-archeologiczne*, vol. II, Kraków 1921. Id., *Młodsza epoka kamienna w Polsce (neolit)*, Lwów 1924, pp. 93 ff.

[3] W. Antoniewicz, 'Z dziedziny archeologii Ziem Polski', *Światowit*, vol. XVII, 1938, p. 341. See the Note at the end of this Chapter.

[4] J. Kostrzewski, 'Od mezolitu do okresu wędrówek ludów', *Prehistoria Ziem Polskich*, Kraków 1939–48, pp. 147 ff., 155 ff.

[5] W. La Baume, 'Die jungsteinzeitliche Kugelamphoren Kultur in Ost- und Westpreussen', *Prussia*, vol. 35, Königsberg 1943, pp. 13 ff.

[6] S. Nosek, 'Kultura amfor kulistych na Lubelszczyźnie', *AUMCS*, vol. V F, 1950, pp. 55 ff.

[7] I. Левицький, Пам'ятки мегалітичної культури на Волині, Антропологія, vol. II, Kiev 1928, pp. 192 ff.

[8] Т. С. Пассек, Периодизация трипольских поселений, МИА, no. 10, 1949, pp. 219 ff.

[9] А. Я. Брюсов, Очерки по истории племен европейской части СССР в неолитическую эпоху, Moscow 1952, pp. 220 ff.

[10] І. К. Свешніков, Мегалітичні поховання на західному Поділлі, Lviv 1957.

[11] T. Sulimirski, *Polska przedhistoryczna*, part II, London 1957–9, pp. 271 ff.

[12] C. Matasa, 'Descoperiri arheologice in raionul Piatra Neamţ', *MCA*, vol. V, 1959, pp. 723 ff.

graves have been recorded. This group developed within the Funnel Beaker culture area and absorbed many elements of this culture, in particular its decorative patterns and a number of pot-forms, including the 'Kuyavian amphora' which evidently derived from similar vessels belonging to the Funnel Beaker culture. The use of amber beads and amulets appears also to be an adopted habit, amber being frequently found in local Funnel Beaker graves; the same applies to axes and other implements made of banded flint, which originated in the mines at Krzemionki near Opatów, about two hundred kilometres to the south-east. The influence of the Funnel Beaker culture is also to be inferred from the fact that a number of skeletons in Globular Amphora graves were buried in an extended position.

In the earlier literature, the large triangular megalithic Kuyavian graves were regarded as typical of the Kuyavian facies of the Globular Amphora culture; W. Chmielewski,[13] however, has shown that these structures were built by Funnel Beaker people during the preceding period; burials in the mounds attributable to the Globular Amphora culture have proved to be secondary interments.

Settlements, of which over forty are known, are indicated by a few potsherds found on the surface of sandy soils. In Kuyavia proper, on the fertile soils, pits and pit-dwellings attributable to the Globular Amphora culture have been found in long-established Neolithic settlements, inhabited first by Danubians and later by Funnel Beaker and Corded Ware peoples. A relatively small number of settlements attributable exclusively to the Globular Amphora culture have been recorded, e.g. at Tuczno and Chełmża.[14]

Twenty-two graves and three settlements in East Prussia (Map v, group II) represent a peripheral group dating mainly from a later stage of the culture. It had played no role in the development of Globular Amphora groups within the Territory. Of considerably greater importance in this respect are the Masovian graves on the Vistula, north-west of Warsaw (Map v, group III). Their pottery differs in some respects from that of the Kuyavian group, but it seems that the two groups developed simultaneously and parallel to each other.

The commonest vessels were globular amphorae, the Kuyavian variety being less frequently found. All the pottery is decorated with patterns either of stamp or cord impressions, but the really rich decorative motifs such as the rows of triangles which are typical of the Kuyavian pottery, were not met with there. Amber beads, pig jaws, and bones were included in the normal assembly of grave goods among which were also bone plaques (belt buckles) with carved decoration. A few graves in this group were evidently of a later date and marked a late stage in its development. Into this category fall the slab-cist graves at Grodkowo. Their pottery exhibits many decadent features both as regards shape and decoration. Flint axes are of Corded Ware type, as was a flint spear-head, a weapon characteristic of the later stage of the Corded Ware culture.

A number of graves scattered over a larger territory east of the Masovian group differed in no way from the latter, but two are worthy of special mention. The stone cist at Piątnica near Łomża,[15] close to the East Prussian group, contained seven burials, two of which were of children. Grave goods included four pots, one of which was a collared flask, typical of the Funnel Beaker culture, and also a stone battle-axe proper to the Corded Ware culture. The other grave, at Chojewo near Bielsk Podlaski,[16] was the easternmost of the whole group. It yielded sixteen vessels with the normal stamped decoration and a single one with cord decoration; with these pots were round, richly decorated lids similar to lids found in almost all the southern groups of the eastern Globular Amphora culture, and in the Złota culture.

Finally two more cist-graves should be mentioned, namely those found at Rębków-Parcele,[17] midway between the Masovian and Puławy groups. Their pottery is typical of the Globular Amphora culture, but the decoration displays many features of Złota pottery. One vessel in each grave had a swastika incised on the inside.

The Globular Amphora culture evidently contributed considerably to the formation of the Złota culture west of the Vistula near Sandomierz (Map v, group IV). However, it does not seem right, as some scholars do, to consider the Złota culture as its local branch.

THE PUŁAWY GROUP
(Map v, group v) (p. 190)

This was a small group of the Globular Amphora culture extending over a restricted area in the district of Puławy, on the fertile loess plateau east of the Vistula. Its graves were usually grouped in small cemeteries of two to five. They differed in construction from those of other groups; they consisted of shallow pits surrounded and covered by medium-sized slabs of quarried limestone. The floors of the graves were often cobbled. No cists were found. Graves constructed in the same way, excavated in the same area, were also associated with the local Nałęczów group of the Funnel Beaker culture; the main difference between them and those of the Globular Amphorae was that the skeletons were in a contracted position in the latter and extended in the former. Graves constructed in the same way have been also excavated in Kuyavia and were similarly associated there with the Globular Amphora culture, and in Złota.[18]

Human offerings were common.[19] Many graves contained more than one burial, sometimes as many as four, but all contemporary. In two graves with a single skeleton an additional human skull was excavated. Usually the largest part of the grave was reserved for the main, male skeleton, others, one of which was always female, were laid near by. In a grave at Klementowice (no. 373) a bone point was found among

[13] W. Chmielewski, *Zagadnienie grobowców kujawskich w świetle ostatnich badań*, Łódź 1952, pp. 34 ff.

[14] K. Jażdżewski, 'Osada grobów megalitycznych w Tucznie w pow. inowrocławskim w Wielkopolsce', *W. Demetrykiewicz Memorial Volume*, Poznań 1930.

[15] Z. Podkowińska, 'Grób skrzynkowy neolityczny w Poniatówce, pow.chełmski, woj.lubelskie', *Światowit*, vol. XVI, 1936, p. 94.

[16] Antoniewicz (op. cit., note 3), pp. 355 ff.

[17] Nosek (op. cit., note 6), pp. 91 ff.

[18] D. Rauhut, 'Grób kultury ceramiki sznurowej (grupa złocka) znaleziony na stanowisku Pole Grodzisko I we wsi Złota, pow.Sandomierz', *W.A.*, vol. XIX, 1935, pp. 52 ff. Z. Krzak, *Materiały do znajomości kultury złockiej*, Wrocław-Warszawa-Kraków 1961.

[19] J. Kowalczyk, 'Zagadnienie grobów zbiorowych w neolicie Polski', *W.A.*, vol. XXVIII, 1962, pp. 1 ff.

the bones of the subordinated skeleton; it was apparently used for killing the person buried. Animal bones and parts of animal skulls (cows, pigs) found in the graves were traces of funeral feasts. Of particular interest were graves in which entire skeletons of animals (Bovidae) were excavated; in two graves these lay beside the human skeleton, in the third they were in a special compound close to the main grave. In many cases traces of fires lit after the interment were visible and skeletons were often damaged by combustion. This partial cremation on the spot was characteristic of this branch exclusively, the practice never being met in other groups of the culture in our area, except for a single grave of the Dubno-Ostróg group (Mirohoszcza, no. 436).

Each grave contained between four and fifteen pots, and at least one had as many as four axes, the latter made almost exclusively of the banded variety of flint. Amber beads and boar tusks were less frequent, and exceptional were a lump of belemit, a bone ornament, a small plate of reddish-brown schist of foreign origin, and a decorated clay disc. Three flint arrow-heads came from one of the graves; two of these were rhomboid and represent a survival of the Mesolithic tradition.

Vessels were well made of a clay paste tempered with sand and were very brittle. Their surface was usually smoothed and decorated. 'Kuyavian' amphorae were the most important vessels whilst the large globular, or rather ovoid, amphorae with two lugs on the junction of the neck and shoulder were less frequent. However, similar, very small and usually spherical amphorae were one of the commonest types of vessel. Other types include wide bowls, beakers, and large usually undecorated pots. Decoration is by means of stamped or incised patterns, but cord impressions are also common. Patterns are closely related to those in the Kuyavian group, although no triangles appeared there. One small amphora (Klementowice A-I) bears fish-scale decoration. Except in the Podolian group, this form of decoration is rare in the eastern branch of the Globular Amphora culture; it was typical of the western Globular Amphorae.

The Puławy variety must have been developed by immigrants from Kuyavia, who assimilated the local Funnel Beaker people and adopted many elements of their culture. Amphorae with four lugs on the shoulder of the so-called 'Kuyavian' type were almost identical with those found in Kuyavia, and this applies to many other vessels.

Intimate connection with the Funnel Beaker culture is well marked in the Puławy group. Graves of both cultures were sometimes found here in common cemeteries. The large undecorated pots, or axes made of a banded variety of flint, from Globular Amphora graves did not differ from those of the Funnel Beaker burials. Both cultures were coeval, at least for a short period, although the Globular Amphorae went on longer. This has been revealed at Klementowice[20] where a pit in the settlement of the Funnel Beaker culture was overlaid and partly ruined by a grave (no. III) of the Globular Amphora culture. Similar sequence of the two cultures has been proved by the stratigraphic evidence in Kuyavia.[21]

That connections between the Puławy group and Złota culture were close is shown by the similarity of burial customs and grave construction, and also by the similarity of the accompanying axes which are of the banded flint obtained from the mines at Krzemionki not far from the centre of the Złota culture area. There is also some similarity of pottery and of the decorative patterns on it. The similarity of these two groups is due to their having common origins in (a) the southern Funnel Beaker, (b) the Danubian III (Lublin Painted pottery culture) substratum (Map III), (c) Corded Ware, and (d) the Globular Amphora culture. In the Złota culture it was the Corded Ware element which provided the strongest influence, whereas with the Puławy group it is the Globular Amphora element which shows most strongly.

The contribution of all these elements was not equal in both cultures. In the Złota culture the Danubian element in the form of the Radial pottery culture is well traceable, whereas in the Puławy group it was negligible.

Grave goods, pottery in particular, of the Puławy group were very homogeneous, but earlier and later assemblages are clearly discernible. The earlier ones were graves with vessels of a nearly genuine Kuyavian character (e.g. Klementowice A-I and B-I, Las Stocki G-I, nos. 373, 374), whereas those with Corded Ware, or with flint arrow-heads typical of the final Neolithic, were obviously of a later date (e.g. Las Stocki C-II, Stok A-I, nos. 374, 377).

The bearers of the Puławy group were probably cattle breeders like the bearers of the Funnel Beakers, with whom they must have been closely associated. In this respect a difference exists between this group and other groups of the eastern Globular Amphora culture in which only bones of pigs were excavated. Graves with human sacrifices, particularly those with servants buried with their masters, imply the existence of social differences.

The Puławy group was evidently coeval with the Złota culture and developed also during the period when Mierzanowice graves were being replaced by the Trzciniec culture of the Middle Bronze Age.[22]

THE HRUBIESZÓW GROUP
(Map V, group VI) (pp. 191 ff.)

Somewhat over twenty burials, mainly in slab-cists attributable to the Globular Amphora culture, have been found scattered over a broad belt of the area about 250 kilometres in length, along the western side of the Middle Bug and on the Upper Wieprz. They cannot really be regarded as a connected group.

Cists built of regular granite or limestone slabs (Plan 46:1) were found during field works or mechanical excavation and were seldom investigated afterwards; records rarely seem to have been made of the number of skeletons found or their other contents. In two cases it has been established that the grave contained two burials. A few graves have been uncovered with no stone constructions (Raciborowice no. 392), Stadarnia no. 393, Wytyczno no. 400).

Pottery found in graves seem to have been mostly destroyed by the casual discoverers, but so far as evidence does exist, the number of pots found in each grave was usually two or three but did not exceed five. They were all typical of the eastern

[20] J. Kowalczyk, 'Osada i cmentarzysko kultury pucharów lejkowatych w miejscowości Klementowice, pow.Puławy', *Mat.St.*, vol. II, 1957, pp. 175, 183 ff.

[21] Chmielewski (op. cit., note. 13), pp. 28 ff.

[22] A. Gardawski, 'Plemiona kultury trzcinieckiej w Polsce', *Mat.St.*, vol. V, 1959, pp. 102 ff.

longed to the descendants of the Lublin Painted pottery Globular Amphora culture, the Kuyavian amphorae being the leading vessel. However, vessels found in different graves exhibit marked differences; several were almost indistinguishable from those of the same type found in Globular Amphora graves in Kuyavia, whereas pots from other burials departed more or less from their prototype.

These differences were undoubtedly due to the different age of the graves concerned. Those burials which were accompanied by typical Kuyavian amphorae (Kryłów, Fig. 21:1; Ulwówek, Plate 12:1, 2; Zimno, possibly Branica Suchowolska II) were evidently the earliest. Pots decorated solely with cord impressions (Miedniki, Fig. 23:7), or the decorative patterns of which were often reminiscent of the Złota style (Wola Gródecka, Plate 13:5), mark burials of a later date.

Other grave goods were axes. Most typical were axes made of a creamy-white flint, and only specimens from two graves situated in the northern part of the whole group were of banded flint; the latter axes were never found further south although they have been found in that region during excavations of fortified settlements attributed to the Funnel Beaker culture. All axes like those further east (Fig. 25) were quadrangular in section and were thoroughly polished. No personal ornaments were found except boar tusks in two graves (Kryłów no. 387, Ulwówek no. 398).

Unlike the Puławy group, no traces of any fire lit in the cist-graves were reported, and no animal burials were found. In the grave at Ulwówek a pig jaw and a tooth were excavated.

Globular Amphorae obviously appear as intrusive along the Bug. Their wide but sparse distribution implies that their users were not native to the area. They had no proper settlements within it. A few potsherds typical of that culture found on the surface of sandy soils around Lublin and further south around Biłgoraj (nos. 402, 410) were evidently traces of temporary encampments; however, the same sites also often yielded potsherds of other cultures of the Funnel Beakers and Corded Ware, but their reciprocal relation has not been established. In the central area of our group potsherds typical of the Globular Amphora culture were excavated in a few settlements belonging to other cultures. They were found, for example, in the remains of the fortified settlement of the Funnel Beakers at Gródek Nadbużny (no. 403), and also in the remains of the settlement of the Strzyżów culture (late Corded Ware) at Strzyżów.

According to J. Kowalczyk[23] the settlement of the Funnel Beaker culture at Gródek Nadbużny and similar settlements in the same area (Map IV) were assaulted and destroyed by the invading Globular Amphora people. On the other hand, the stratigraphic evidence at Raciborowice (no. 392), where a grave of the Globular Amphorae was found under a hut of the Strzyżów group of Corded Ware, implies that the Globular Amphorae had preceded the latter culture. Another indicator of the chronology of the Hrubieszów group of Globular Amphorae is the debased Thuringian amphora from the above grave, which equates it with the second stage of the Barrow-grave culture. Of importance in this connection is also the barrow-grave from Hrubieszów (nos. 121, 573), in which a slab-cist grave was uncovered under the mound. Potsherds associated with this burial unfortunately perished, but its battle-axe of *z*-type (Fig. 14:9) equates it with the third period of the Barrow-grave culture.

The Chełm-Hrubieszów group of Globular Amphorae seems to have been of short duration being absorbed relatively soon by the surrounding Corded Ware culture. This is suggested by the above barrow-grave from Hrubieszów, but also by pottery from a number of slab-cist graves (Miedniki, Fig. 23:7; Poniatówka; Tworyczów, Plate 13:8, 9, 10; Wola Gródecka, Plate 13:5). The vessels only slightly departed from their prototypes, but their decoration reflects strong influence exercised by the Corded Ware. A further step in this direction led to the Chełm-Hrubieszów Globular Amphorae losing their independence and merging gradually in the surrounding Corded Ware culture.

THE LWÓW GROUP
(Map V, group VII) (p. 193)

Further south of the above group, a few scattered graves of the Globular Amphora culture were found which link the Chełm-Hrubieszów group with the Volhynian concentrations and the Podolian group.

The grave from Dźwinogród (no. 420) seems to have been the earliest of these; J. Kostrzewski[24] emphasizes that both in shape and in decoration its vessels did not differ in any respects from those of Kuyavia. The grave evidently could be equated with the earliest burials of the two groups of the Globular Amphora culture dealt with above. The same applies to the find from Mikołajów (no. 423, Plate 13:1–4, 6; Fig. 21:2), but the cord decoration of some of its vessels suggests a somewhat later date. Definitely of a later date was the grave from Dublany (no. 419) in which metal (gold or bronze?) finger-rings were found. The flint dagger (Plate 15:11) found in this grave also points to its late date, equating it with the second, perhaps even the third, period of the Barrow-grave culture.

The relation of these few Globular Amphora graves to the Barrow-grave culture within the territory of which they were found is conjectural. This area might possibly have been taken over by the advancing Globular Amphorae, but was soon recovered by the Barrow-grave culture. This would account for the small number of Globular Amphora burials and the circumstance that the connection between the west Podolian group of the Globular Amphora culture with the northern groups of that culture was severed very soon after the formation of the former.

A few potsherds and flints typical of the Globular Amphora culture found in two barrow-graves at Kołokolin (no. 66; Figs. 12:3, 9; 17:1, 2) and at Rokitno I (no. 82; Fig. 16:26, 28) imply a relatively early contact between the two cultures. The slab-cist grave found at Zaderewacz (no. 520), on the Carpathian foothills south of the Dniester, was the southernmost point reached by this group of the Globular Amphora people (Map V).

At Dzwinogrod (Zvenyhorod), where one of the slab-cist graves of our group was uncovered (no. 420), an Early Bronze Age cemetery was investigated (no. 94) which be-

[23] J. Kowalczyk, 'Prace badawcze w 1957 r. osady kultury pucharów lejkowatych w Gródku Nadbużnym, pow.Hrubieszów', *W.A.*, vol. XXIV, 1958, p. 319.

[24] Kostrzewski (op. cit., note 4), p. 151.

culture (Map III).[25] The reciprocal relation between these two different groups of remains of approximately the same age has not been established.

VOLHYNIAN GLOBULAR AMPHORAE

About forty Globular Amphora burials have been found in Volhynia. In the Soviet archaeological literature they are labelled as belonging to the 'Volhynian megalithic culture' as all the burials were made in slab-cists. A number of these graves were investigated by I. Lewyc'kyj[26] and were dealt with by several authors mentioned previously.[27]

Volhynian Globular Amphorae have usually been treated, erroneously, as a close-knit entity. In fact they formed three distinct groups (Map V), the burial ritual of which, and also grave-goods, exhibit more or less well-marked differences. The most western of these, which centred between the Styr and the Horyn, will be called here the 'Dubno-Ostróg group', and the name of the 'Sluch group' will be given to a few cist-graves found along the Sluch; the 'Zhitomir group' will include all cist-graves from the region on the Teterev and those further north near Ovruch.

THE DUBNO-OSTRÓG GROUP (Map V, group VIII) (pp. 194 f.)

This group extended over the area between the rivers Styr and Horyn; it consisted of over thirty cists found at twenty-five separate sites, only a few of which were investigated. They usually contained a single skeleton, but in one cist (Lachów, no. 432) two, and in another one three interments (Zdolbitsa, no. 451) were found. Skeletons, as far as evidence is available, were all in a contracted position. They were accompanied by one or two vessels, exceptionally by six (Lachów), but in several graves no pottery appeared. Flint axes were reported to have been found in several graves (Fig. 25:13, 14, 19); they were typical of the eastern Globular Amphorae. In each of two cist-graves (Młynów, no. 437, and Zdolbitsa, no. 451) a stone battle-axe and a flint spear-head (or dagger) were excavated. More numerous were bronze, or copper, ornaments found in four cists. They consisted of spiral earrings, or temple ornaments, and larger ear-pendants (hair decoration). The latter were all of the Stubło type with one end flattened.

There was no uniformity as regards pottery. Vessels from Lepesivka (no. 433, Fig. 22:3, 7), black in colour, were of a strikingly 'western' appearance, and their fish-scale ornament links them with the Middle German Globular Amphorae. This was obviously one of the earliest graves of this group. Fish-scale ornament was found also on sherds from the settlement at Nowyj Dwir near Równe (no. 555). No such ornament was recorded in any graves of our culture further east, but was found on sherds from a settlement at Sokal (no. 406) in the Chełm-Hrubieszów group, and also in the Puławy group on the Vistula; it was adopted by the Podolian group of Globular Amphorae.

The Kuyavian amphora excavated at Varkovytsia (no. 448, Fig. 22:1) suggests an early date for this grave also. Possibly of a little later date was the grave from Międzyrzec (no. 435, Plate 12:1) in which only globular amphorae were found, one of these having stamped ornament characteristic of eastern Globular Amphorae, and also three flint axes of western type (Fig. 25:13, 14, 19). Different and evidently of a late date was pottery from the grave at Lachów (no. 432, Fig. 23:3–5, 10, 11). Only two of its vessels were proper to the Globular Amphora culture: a small globular amphora provided with two small lugs on the base of the neck, which was stamp-decorated, and a similarly decorated bowl; both vessels deviated considerably from their prototypes however. No data are available with regard to vessels found in the other four graves of our group.

In spite of the very inadequate data available, it appears that the Dubno-Ostróg group underwent development similar to that of the Globular Amphora groups further west. Grave goods of the earliest burials did not differ substantially from those in the west and this applies especially to their pottery, Kuyavian amphorae in particular, and their stamped ornaments. But at the next stage a slackening of old traditions began, and the influence of the local Corded Ware group, and also of the Barrow-grave culture, was strongly marked.

The adoption of alien types of pottery and weapons (battle-axes) led to the gradual disappearance of the Globular Amphora culture in its original form. Only the slab-cist proved to be its strongest traditional element; it survived to the later period and marked the identity of this ancient group in spite of the loss of almost all of its other constituent elements. In the following period mounds were thrown up over slab-cists and thus resembled the burials of the Barrow-grave culture, or of its successive Middle Bronze Age culture (Radzimin, no. 155; Siekierzyńce, no. 156).

The final stage of the Dubno-Ostróg group is marked by the graves of Zdolbitsa and Stadniki (nos. 446, 451). Those from Zdolbitsa will be dealt with in the paragraph devoted to the Strzyżów culture in Chapter V. The grave from Stadniki was the most richly endowed burial of the whole group and may likewise be considered to belong already to the Strzyżów culture. No pottery was found in this grave, but there were a number of small tubular beads consisting of spirals of bronze wire, biconic bone beads, and a number of faience beads. There were also small spiral temple ornaments made of this bronze wire and large ear-pendants of the Stubło type. These grave-goods appertained to the late stage of the Early Bronze Age, and equated this grave with the last period of the Barrow-grave culture. Similar grave goods were also found in graves of the Strzyżów culture at Torczyn in the western part of West Volhynia. It is of interest to note that at Skurcze (no. 445), situated in the vicinity of the latter site, a slab-cist grave was uncovered which belonged to the following period. It

[25] T. Sulimirski, 'Notatki archeologiczne z Małopolski Wschodniej', *W.A.*, vol. XIV, 1937, pp. 189 ff. Id. (op. cit., note 11), pp. 221 ff. Z. Podkowińska, 'Pierwsza charakterystyka stanowiska eneolitycznego na polu Grodzisko I we wsi Złota pow.Sandomierz', *W.A.*, vol. XIX, 1953, pp. 1 ff. S. Nosek, 'Kultura wstęgowej ceramiki malowanej na Lubelszczyźnie', *Światowit*, vol. XXI, Warszawa 1956, pp. 125 ff. Id., 'Materiały do badań nad historią starożytną i wczesnośredniowieczną międzyrzecza Wisły i Bugu', *AUMCS*, vol. VI F, 1957, pp. 53 ff. И. К. Свешников, Культура линейно-ленточной керамики на территории верхнего Поднистровья и западной Волини, Сов. Арх., vol. XX, 1954, pp. 100 ff. Id., Могильник в селе Звенигород львовской области, КСИИМК, no. 63, 1956, pp. 57 ff.

[26] Op. cit., note 7.

[27] Op. cit., notes 3, 8, 9, and also M. Gimbutas, *The Prehistory of Eastern Europe*, part I, Cambridge (Mass.) 1956, pp. 142 ff.

yielded bronze rings, spiral armlets, and tanged flint arrowheads typical of the final stage of the Middle Bronze Age. No earlier slab-cist graves were found in that region although the impact of the Globular Amphora on the local Strzyżów group of Corded Ware was strongly marked, particularly on its pottery.

Finally, two sites should be mentioned (Nowyj Dwir and Staryj Mylsk, nos. 555, 558). Both, situated at a relatively small distance from each other, were settlements which yielded pottery typical of the Funnel Beaker culture (Fig. 20:4, 5) and also of the local Strzyżów group of Corded Ware. But as well as those above, potsherds proper to the Globular Amphora culture were also found in both sites (Fig. 21:6); unfortunately none of these sites was investigated and the reciprocal relation of the three types of pottery found here has not been established. However, the relatively small number of Globular Amphora potsherds suggest that the settlements belonged to the bearers of one of the other cultures mentioned above; the representatives of the Globular Amphora culture had evidently formed only a small fraction of their inhabitants.

THE SLUCH GROUP
(Map V, group IX) (pp. 195 ff.)

Eleven slab-cist graves were found in eight sites along the Sluch, and a few more in the northern part of East Podolia further south. They exhibit some distinct features of their own and deserve special treatment.

Graves on the Sluch were all granite or gneiss slab-cists, in one instance nearly oval in shape (Aneta, no. 452). They differed from those of the groups dealt with previously in that they all contained more than one skeleton. In the cists from Suyemtsi (no. 459) five, or alternatively seven, persons were buried; the large cist-grave at Voytsekhivka I (no. 460) contained skeletons of ten persons, all buried at one time. The main burial was that of an elderly man; he was accompanied by his two wives, each with their two small children, and near by lay skeletons of two adolescents, whilst a serf or slave lay in a special annexe at the entrance to the cist.

Anthropological study has shown that all skulls found in the cists were dolichocephalic, except that of the slave from Voytsekhivka I which was brachycephalic.

The cist from Kykova (no. 455) contained cremation burials in urns of a man and of at least two members of his family cremated outside the grave; the grave Voytsekhivka 2 was also a cremation burial. In the cists of the Zhitomir group situated further east, similar cremation was very common, whereas it was never found in graves of the Globular Amphora culture further west, except in those of the Puławy group, where, however, it was of a different type.

Graves were richly furnished but grave goods differed to some extent from those of the western groups of our culture. At least three, though more usually six to nine vessels were excavated in a single cist. Two flint axes, but on one occasion three and five (Voytsèkhivka I), were found in one cist; they were all quadrangular in section (Fig. 25:2), made of the local Volhynian variety of flint in a technique proper to the 'Bug' industry. No extremely well-polished flat, trapezoid flint axes characteristic of the eastern Globular Amphorae of the regions further to the west were recorded in these graves. A very common feature were flint chips: in some cases (Kykova, Suyemtsi II), they originated from polished axes chipped into small pieces and strewn over the floor of the cist. Once a stone battle-axe (Suyemtsi I, Fig. 24:10) was found. Personal ornaments were rare; they included amber beads (Aneta), tubular bone pendants (Voytsekhivka, Suyemtsi II), and pendants made of boar-tusks (Voytsekhivka, Suyemtsi II).

An unusual occurrence for the Globular Amphora culture were lumps of ochre found in almost all graves; all the skeletons at Voytsekhivka I were strewn with ochre, as was even the floor of the cist of Kykova with its cremation burials. Charcoal was found on the floor under the male skeleton of Aneta. Pig bones were excavated in all graves, and at Aneta the entire skeleton of a pig lay in the cist.

The most common vessels were amphorae of three main types, the Kuyavian variety (Plate 14:1–3; Fig. 22:8, 11), the large ovoid amphorae (Plate 15:6; Fig. 22:4), and the smaller ones more or less globular in shape (Plate 14:5, 6; Plate 15:5). They all show a basic similarity to their corresponding types of the western groups of the eastern Globular Amphora culture, but at the same time they exhibit several features of their own. This applies in particular to those of the Kuyavian type which differed considerably from their prototype in both shape and ornament. Their decorative patterns, although usually stamped in the western manner and seldom cord-impressed, include motifs unknown to the western pottery of the Globular Amphora culture. The same, but to a lesser degree, applies to the decoration of the two other types of amphora. The large ovoid amphorae from Voytsekhivka I were closely related to those of the Masovian group,[28] but their shape was somewhat debased (Plate 15:6). Many ovoid amphorae were undecorated and cord-impressed decorative patterns of some of these (Kykova, Fig. 22:4) call to mind those characteristic of the lugged, or handled, mugs of the Oder Corded Ware. Some ovoid amphorae were provided with four lugs instead of two. A special type consisted of two-lugged amphorae akin to those of the ovoid type, the lugs of which were, however, fixed on the shoulder, not the base of the neck; they were usually undecorated (Plate 14:7). Such amphorae, sometimes with four lugs, were typical of the pottery of the whole Zhitomir group, being found in graves situated further east. They seem to represent a local blend of the Kuyavian and the ovoid (globular) types. Another local feature were amphorae of all types provided with vertically perforated lugs (Aneta, Voytsekhivka I). It is of interest to note that the amphora from Suyemtsi II was painted, which, according to Passek[29] implies an influence exercised by the Tripolye culture. The small globular amphorae from Suyemtsi II were provided with decorated lids (Fig. 21:4), a feature met with in the Podolian and Zhitomir groups, and in some Masovian graves,[30] but not in graves of the Hrubieszów concentration.

Vessels of other types were seldom found. In two graves (Kykova, Suyemtsi II) bowls were excavated (Plate 13:11),

[28] L. Sawicki, 'Groby megalityczne w Potyrach w pow.płońskim', *W.A.*, vol. V, 1920, Figs. 24, 25. E. Stołyhwowa, *Światowit*, vol. XIII, 1929, Figs. 1, 2.

[29] Пассек (op. cit., note 8), p. 223.

[30] Antoniewicz (op. cit., note 3), pp. 355 ff., 382.

and in two (Voytsekhivka I, Staryi Myropil) beakers were found (Fig. 21:5). The beaker from Staryi-Myropil was cord decorated.

A closer study of pottery of the Sluch group, of its decorative patterns and of other grave goods suggests that here, as in the more westerly groups, earlier and later graves are distinguishable. However, no early graves were found here comparable to the earliest ones in the region of Hrubieszów or in the Dubno-Ostróg group.

In spite of their amphorae with vertically perforated lugs, the cists from Aneta and Voytsekhivka I probably belonged to the earlier graves of the Sluch region. The cist from Suyemtsi I with a stone battle-axe, and Suyemtsi II with cord-decorated vessels, seem to have been of a little later date as was that from Myropil with the beaker decorated in a manner typical of the late Corded Ware. The cremation burial from Kykova was obviously of a late date.

Cord decoration, battle-axes, and ochre-sprinkled corpses are all evidence of the strong influence which the surrounding Corded Ware peoples (Map VI) exerted on the local Globular Amphora culture. This was a short-lived community which soon disappeared. In the Middle Bronze Age, the Voytsekhivka culture[31] developed within its region, a culture of Corded Ware parentage which shows no links with its predecessor, except for a few decorative motifs in its pottery[32] (Fig. 33:B).

It seems that the bearers of the Sluch group migrated southwards. A few graves on the Upper Boh in the north-western part of Podolia (the Boh group, Map VI, marked XI), and a slab-cist grave further south on the Middle Dniester (Zahnitkova, no. 466) were evidently a southern extension of the Sluch group. The decoration of their vessels (Vinnitsa, no. 465, Plate 14:8) and vertically perforated lugs of the amphora from Nowa Sieniawa (no. 462, Fig. 22:1) point to this parentage. They also show the route by which the bearers of the Sluch group had reached Moldavia and contributed to the formation there of the Moldavian branch of the Globular Amphora culture (Map V, group XIII), which exhibits many elements characteristic of the Volhynian group.

THE ZHITOMIR GROUP
(Map V, group X) (pp. 197 ff.)

At least fifteen sites with slab-cist graves of the Globular Amphora culture were recorded east of the Sluch, within a relatively extensive area north of the Teterev, up to the Ovruch. They were the most eastern graves of that culture, which we shall call the Zhitomir group. Unfortunately, a description of only two of these graves has been published (Skolobiv, no. 475; Vysoke, no. 478), and only very vague reports exist concerning all other slab-cists.

Graves of the Zhitomir group differed from those of the more westerly groups in that about half of them, as far as records exist, contained cremation burials in urns, some times without urns, the calcined bones being heaped near the vessels; cremation always took place outside the grave. In this peripheral group cists of an unusual shape were also found: a cist nearly oval in plan from Aneta was mentioned in the preceding paragraph; the cist from Skolobiv was oval in plan and was provided with a kind of short passage, or porch, at the eastern narrow side, possibly marking the entrance to the cist.

A number of cists seem to have contained a single burial (Vysoke), but in others more cremations were found (Zhitomir, no. 481). The same probably applies to the cists with inhumation burials. According to the schematic plan published by S. Hamtchenko, presumably of a slab-cist from Zhitomir, four persons were buried there at one time: a man in a sitting position accompanied by his two wives and a slave, all in a contracted position.

Very little information exists concerning the grave goods. A characteristic feature, at least of the graves described, was the large number of vessels: at Vysoke (no. 478) four amphorae and a small dish were found as well as the urn with a lid; the cist with cremation from Zhitomir contained seven vessels including urns according to the schematic plan by Hamtchenko, and another cist from Zhitomir with inhumation burials was, according to a similar plan, furnished with nine vessels. The cist from Skolobiv (no. 475) probably had nineteen vessels, including two urns, most of which were more or less damaged, six being reduced to small sherds by the casual discoverers (Plates 14:4, 15:12; Figs. 21:7, 22:5, 6).

However, not more than twelve vessels found in all cists of the Zhitomir group have been published, including that from Mininy (no. 473) wrongly considered by A. Äyräpää[33] to have been found in a catacomb grave near Kkarkov. The study of this pottery, despite its scarcity, shows that it did not differ substantially from that of the Sluch sub-group but that the shapes of vessels were still more debased. Amphorae used as cinerary urns were provided with a lid. The Kuyavian amphorae are well recognizable among vessels published, although those from Vysoke or Mininy (Fig. 22:10) differed considerably from their western prototypes in shape and especially in decoration, which was cord impressed. A very characteristic decorative motif of pottery from Vysoke (Fig. 22:9), and also from Mininy, were cord-impressed concentric semicircles placed round the shoulder of the vessel, or round its neck. This motif, which had already appeared on some globular amphorae of the Dubno-Ostróg group (Międzyrzec, Plate 12:3), seems to have derived from rows of concentric triangles, a motif typical of the Kuyavian decorative style of the Globular Amphora culture.

Debased Kuyavian amphorae (Fig. 22:5), but no large ovoid amphorae similar to those from Voytsekhivka, were found here; however one large amphora from Skolobiv (Plate 14:4) was of the 'hybrid' type provided with four lugs; it was stamp-decorated. The small globular, or spherical, amphorae from Skolobiv (Plate 15:12; Fig. 22:6) were provided with two lugs on the base of the neck, or with unperforated lugs on the shoulder, and were decorated in a manner similar to those above. The decoration of the two-lugged bowl from Skolobiv (Fig. 21:7) was of the same kind. Another type of

[31] О. Лагодовська, Войцехівський могильник бронзової доби на Волині, Археологія-Kiev, vol. II, 1948, pp. 62 ff. О. Ф. Лагодовська, Ю. М. Захарук, Нові дослідження войцехівського могильника, Арх. Пам., vol. VI, 1956, pp. 69 ff.

[32] І. Левицький, Стація в ур. Піщаному біля Народич, Антропологія, vol. IV, Kiev 1931, p. 230, Fig. 38:6, 7.

[33] A. Äyräpää, 'Über die Streitaxtkulturen in Russland', *ESA*, vol. VIII, 1933, p. 120, Fig. 118. Пассек (op. cit., note 8), pp. 220 ff.

vessel which seems to have been common here were shallow, hemispheric bowls or dishes (Vysoke, Zhitomir).

Other grave goods, very frequently found, were the flint knives and axes present in almost all graves. The number of axes in a single grave varied from one to thirteen (Skolobiv); it is of interest to note that one of the latter was chipped into pieces which were strewn over the floor of the cist, a custom also recorded in the graves of the Sluch sub-group. A tanged flint arrow-head was found in the cist at Skolobiv. Two cists (Davydivka, no. 468; Volodarske-Horoški, no. 477) yielded stone battle-axes, and the only personal ornaments found in this group were amber discs and beads excavated in two graves (Skolobiv, Vyševyči, no. 479).

The archaeological material—fragmentary though it is—indicates very clearly a late date for the establishment of the Zhitomir group. Pottery—Kuyavian amphorae in particular (Fig. 22:5), differing considerably from their prototypes—and the entirely cord-impressed ornament (Vysoke, Mininy) and its motifs equate the Zhitomir graves with those of the later stages of the more westerly groups of the Globular Amphora culture. The grave from Skolobiv with its exclusively stamp-decorated vessels, in a style closely related to that of the earlier stages in the west, was not of an early date either. The debased shape of its vessels, the oval plan of the cist, and above all the tanged flint arrow-head, imply a late date for this cist, and its cremation burials support this assumption.

The Zhitomir group was very strongly affected by the local group of Corded Ware and the Gorodsk culture (Map VI), as emphasized by Passek.[34] The influence of these is reflected in the pottery and also in the flint industry found in cist-graves. Cremation burial, common in this whole group including the Sluch sub-group, was presumably adopted from the neighbouring Sofiivka culture[35] which extended over the region around Kiev (Map VI).

The Zhitomir group of the Globular Amphora culture was a short-lived community as was the group on the Sluch. It dissolved relatively early and merged with the surrounding cultures. Rows of concentric semicircles, a very characteristic decorative motif proper to our group of Globular Amphorae, which appear on some vessels of the subsequent, Voytsekhivka, culture of the Middle Bronze Age (Fig. 33:B)[36] were the last vestiges of the ancient culture.

NORTHERN AND NORTH-EASTERN SITES (Map V)

No graves attributable to the Globular Amphora culture have been found further east of the Zhitomir group. The globular amphora excavated in the barrow-grave at Łosiatyn near Vasylkov (nos. 250–564, Plate 14:12), south-west of Kiev, cannot be regarded as belonging to our culture; the barrow-grave formed part of the Middle Dnieper culture and had no stone construction under the mound. It is only a witness of contact between these two cultures.

Potsherds typical of the Globular Amphora culture, but no graves, were found, however, on the northern border of the Territory, along the Pripet in Polesia (nos. 554, 560, 561) and also at Černin on the eastern bank of the Dnieper north of Kiev (no. 547), in a site attributable to the local branch of the Dnieper-Elbe (Dnieper-Donetz) culture. The presence of the Globular Amphora people in the region of Kiev is likewise attested by the deep incised zigzag ornament found on a series of Tripolyan vessels of period C-I (nos. 565, 566). Recently a number of Globular Amphora potsherds have been found in several sites in the region on the Upper Dnieper (nos. 553, 557). In a series of sites on the Upper Volga potsherds were excavated the comb-stamped decorative patterns of which were typical of the Globular Amphora culture (parallel rows of short vertical incisions and horizontal zigzag lines). These motifs appear also on a number of vessels of the cemetery at Balanovo on the Middle Volga; a small, partly damaged, amphora from this cemetery, similarly decorated, represents a vessel characteristic of the Globular Amphora culture.[37]

SOUTH-EASTERNMOST GRAVES (pp. 199, 206 f.)

A few slab-cist graves were uncovered further south in the Ukraine, in the region of Uman and Smyela, on the northern steppe border (nos. 482, 483). Since nothing is known of their grave goods their derivation, whether from the Zhitomir or the Sluch group (by the way down the Boh or along the Dnieper: Kanev, no. 599), cannot be established. A few potsherds typical of the Globular Amphora culture found at Seredni Stog II (no. 556) and flint chisel from Kamenka (no. 550), both in the region of the Dnieper Rapids, suggest the Globular Amphora parentage for the slab-cists of that region which were common there during the developed Bronze Age (nos. 558–591).

No genuine Globular Amphora pottery or other remains were found, so far, in the western division of the Ukrainian steppe country within the area of the Usatovo culture, although Äyräpää[38] maintains that pottery of the latter culture was influenced by the Globular Amphorae. However, several slab-cist graves have been recorded in the mounds of that culture and in barrow-graves in the steppe further east (Map V).

THE PODOLIAN GROUP (Map V, group XII) (pp. 199 ff.)

This was the largest of the eastern groups of the Globular Amphora culture which markedly differed from the East Volhynian branches. Thirty-eight slab-cist graves from thirty-one sites have been recorded here so far, exclusive of those found under mounds in the peripheries of this area which were attributed to the Barrow-grave culture and dealt with previously. The custom of depositing the dead in slab-cists survived there into the subsequent periods: it was current in the Biały Potok branch of the Middle Bronze Age Komarów culture (Map XI), the heir and successor of the Podolian Globular Amphora culture (Plan 46:2, 3) and also in later periods.

Cists were built of large limestone or sandstone slabs.

[34] Пассек (op. cit., note 8), pp. 219 ff., 223.

[35] Gimbutas (op. cit., note 27), pp. 109 f., and the literature quoted there.

[36] Op. cit., note 32.

[37] О. Н. Бадер, Балановский Могильник, Moscov 1963, figs. 63, 91, 141. See also figs. 142:1, 2 and 164, and pp. 254 f.

[38] Äyräpää (op. cit., note 33), p. 157.

Usually one slab-cist grave was found in each site, and only in a few cases were two slab-cists reported to be found near each other (Latacz, no. 503; Popovtsy, no. 509; Beremiany, no. 489; Uwisła, no. 518; Zastawie, no. 522); however, some of these additional graves dated from the Middle Bronze Age (Biały Potok group, Plan 46:2). A larger number of slab-cist graves, up to three or four, or cemeteries, were recorded merely from the Middle Bronze Age and later periods.

Neolithic and Early Bronze Age slab-cists contained a single skeleton: of seventeen cists the particulars of which in this respect are known, not more than three contained two skeletons, five contained three, and one is said to have contained six or seven bodies (Zastawie 2). It is of interest to note that male skulls found in these graves were almost all dolichocephalic, whereas those of women were either brachycephalic or intermediate. Mostly adults were buried in cists; skeletons of a child were reported twice (Hlubičok, no. 492; Podhajczyki Justynowe, no. 508). Skeletons always lay in a contracted position; their orientation varied; heads to north (Hlubičok), to east (Popovtsy), to south-east and south-west (Uwisła), or were orientated south–north (Velyka Mukša, no. 519) and west–east (Zastawie; Zawadyńce, no. 523).

Grave goods had usually greatly suffered, being destroyed either completely, or at least partly, by the casual discoverers; this especially applies to pottery. Out of thirty-eight slab-cists under review, information is available concerning their grave goods in respect of only twenty-eight. Study reveals that those graves fell into three distinct groups, the grave goods of which, particularly pottery, differed markedly. They denote three successive periods in the development of the group. Table 15 shows the allotment of the respective graves to these periods.

Usually from one to four vessels were found in cists of the Podolian group, and only exceptionally (Słobódka Koszyłowiecka, no. 513) were five vessels plus two lids excavated. Most typical were large amphorae of Kuyavian type provided with four lugs on the shoulder. A few of these vessels, which must be considered as being the earliest marking the first period (e.g. Horodnica-Kopyczyńce, Zastawie, Plate 12:4) did not differ in any respects from similar vessels in Kuyavia, being of the same shape, black in colour, and decorated in the same manner. This has been already emphasized by J. Kostrzewski.[39]

The specific West Podolian Globular Amphora pottery, which denotes the second period, had a special character of its own. L. Kozłowski[40] points to many features, especially to its decorative patterns consisting of rows of lines, rows, or triangles made by small semicircular incisions, the 'fish-scale' motifs, small squares, etc., often filled in with white paste (Plate 15) which were not found in the Kuyavian group; however, they were characteristic of western (German) Globular Amphorae. Amphorae of Kuyavian type were usually smaller in size, and more globular in shape, with flat bases (Plate 15:1, 8, 9; Fig. 23:9); they were of very fine texture, very well fired, brownish or reddish in colour, the surfaces smoothed, frequently polished. They show unmistakable influence of the experienced local potters of the Tripolye culture. Their decoration consisted almost exclusively of fish-scale patterns or small squares, usually filled in with white paste.

Globular amphorae of invariably small size (Plate 15:7) were another typical vessel. They were made and decorated in the same manner as the larger 'Kuyavian' type amphorae. Ovoid amphorae, very frequent in the Volhynian groups, were an exception here (Kociubińce, Fig. 23:8). Other types of vessels included deep bowls sometimes provided with wide horizontally perforated lugs under the rim, decorated in the same manner as amphorae (Plate 15:2, 3). A unique type was a pedestalled bowl from Velyka Mukša (Plate 15:10) of which only the hollow stand has survived, decorated in the usual manner. The Słobódka Koszyłowiecka amphorae were provided with lids (Plate 15:7, 8). They were flat with a broad rim, and their surface was richly decorated with incised patterns consisting of white incrusted nail and semi-circular impressions.

Well-polished flint axes were found in most graves, usually two or three together, once (Velyka Mukša) as many as four. They were quadrangular in section, usually trapezoidal in shape, very well polished all over their surface with the apparent aim of imitating flat copper or bronze axes (Fig. 25). Their size varied. Some (Velyka Mukša, Fig. 25:1) were up to 20cm long, but in other graves (Czarnokońce, Fig. 25:7) much smaller specimens were found 7·5cm long. They were mostly made of a whitish or 'milky' variety of flint, some of local Podolian origin, but many were evidently of alien origin, most probably brought from the north-west (Mecklenburg, Rugen) where such raw material is available. In a few graves (Ułaszkowce, Fig. 25:18; Kociubińce) axes were made of the local black, 'Volhynian' variety with the technique proper to the 'Bug' industry. Besides axes, flint chisels also were found in a few graves (Fig. 25:8, 18). They were nearly square in section, and were made from the same raw material and in the same manner as the flint axes.

Other grave goods were seldom found. However they include belt buckles made of bone plaques, decorated with incised geometric patterns (Czarnokońce, Uwisła, Fig. 24: 11, 12); similar belt buckles were found in a slab-cist grave at Kosewo in the Masovian group,[41] and were excavated recently in slab-cist graves in Romania dealt with below. In one cist (Kociubińce) a perforated amber disc was found (Fig. 24:5), typical of the Globular Amphora culture of the north-western part of Poland. A similar perforated amber disc was also found, allegedly in a grave at Kadyivtsi near Kamenetz Podolskii;[42] it was undoubtedly connected with our group of the Globular Amphora culture.

A smaller number of graves can be assigned to the next, third stage. The burial ritual displayed in these graves did not differ in any respect from that proper to the earlier periods, but a change in grave goods is well marked. It provides evidence of the influence on the Podolian group of Globular Amphorae of the neighbouring Sub-Carpathian Barrow-grave culture and of other groups of the Corded

[39] Kostrzewski (op. cit., note 4), p. 151.

[40] Kozłowski (op. cit., note 2, 1924), p. 95.

[41] Antoniewicz (op. cit., note 3), Fig. 10. For similar specimens found in the cemetery of Balanovo on the Middle Volga, see note 37.

[42] Before the Second World War in the Museum at Kamenets Podolskii.

Ware complex. This change was, however, a gradual process and there was no break between the two phases of the Podolian cist-graves. They both evidently belonged to the same group of people who still kept to its traditional burial ritual and customs, in spite of adopting their neighbours' pottery. The late Podolian slab-cists cannot be just attributed to the Corded Ware culture.[43]

The beginning of the change was marked by the appearance of debased amphorae (Fig. 18:6) and of cord-impressed decoration on vessels of the well-known types proper to the Globular Amphora culture (Hlubičok, Plate 12:7). In other instances (Beremiany 2, Koszyłowce 2), vessels typical of the late phase of the Corded Ware assemblage (single-lugged mug, handled jar, Plate 14:9, 10) were found with vessels bearing fish-scale decoration characteristic of the Podolian Globular Amphorae. A further development led to the complate disappearance of ancient types of vessels and of the fish-scale ornament, and to their replacement by Corded Ware types (Popovstsy, Fig. 23:2). A similar change took place in respect of other grave goods: flint axes and chisels proper to the Globular Amphora culture gave way to the battle-axes and flint knives typical of the Corded Ware graves (Koszyłowce, Latacz, Fig. 24:1–4, 6–9). The only ornament found in graves of the later group was already made of bronze (Ładyczyn, no. 504). The burial ritual and the slab-cists proved to be the most conservative elements which indicate the identity of the Podolian group during the early and later stages in its development.

Potsherds with a fish-scale ornament, typical of the Globular Amphora culture, were excavated in the well-known Tripolyan settlement of Koszyłowce (Fig. 21:3). They equate the second, the 'classic' stage of the Podolian group of Globular Amphorae with period C-1 of the West Podolian branch of the Tripolye culture. The later stage of the culture under review with its pottery of later Corded Ware type was coeval with the late period of the Barrow-grave culture. A few graves with pottery typical of the Kuyavian and West Polish Globular Amphora culture were apparently the earliest of the Podolian slab-cists; they—with the axes made of 'milky' flint and the amber discs—point to the north-western origin of the Podolian group of Globular Amphorae. Another element, besides the Kuyavian branch, that must have contributed to its establishment, was most probably the German branch of the Globular Amphorae. This is shown in particular by the fish-scale ornament very characteristic of the German branch but absent in the Kuyavian group. The Masovian group which contributed to the formation of the Volhynian groups of the Globular Amphora culture had no bearing on the Podolian group.

The descendants of the bearers of the Podolian group of Globular Amphorae survived to the Middle Bronze Age, although the ancient pottery, and even other characteristic grave goods, completely disappear from the inventories of the later graves. During the Middle Bronze Age a gradual evolution into the Biały Potok branch of the Komarów culture took place (Map XII), parallel to a similar evolution of the ancient Barrow-grave culture in the neighbouring areas. The identity of the old group is again indicated by the burial ritual and the slab-cist form of grave which was the most conservative link with the past (Plan 46:2, 3).

ROMANIAN GLOBULAR AMPHORAE
(Map V, group XIII) (pp. 205 f.)

Over a dozen slab-cist graves of the Globular Amphora culture were uncovered in nine sites in Moldavia, Romania. They do not form a close geographical unit, being scattered along the river Siret over a distance of about 160 kilometres. A few of these were found in the north, near Suceava-Fălticeni, and others in the south in the region of Piatra-Neamţ and Negreşti.

Particulars are available of a few slab-cist graves only, most graves having been completely ruined by their casual discoverers. Slab-cist 2 of Dolheşti Mari (no. 527) contained two skeletons, of a man and his wife; they lay on their backs, their legs contracted, in a position proper to the Yamna barrow-graves of the Ukrainian steppe country. The decorated belt-buckles found in this grave were of the same type as those from Podolian (Czarnokońce, Uwisła, Fig. 24:11, 12) and Masovian slab-cists, which have been referred to in the preceding paragraph.[44] One of the six vessels from this grave was a somewhat debased amphora of Kuyavian type provided with four lugs on the shoulder (Fig. 23:12), its cord-impressed ornament consisted of concentric semicircles. Another amphora, with two lugs on the shoulder, had several rows of vertical short, deep incisions and a double zigzag band around the neck, characteristic of the Masovian and Volhynian branches of the Globular Amphorae but never met with in the Podolian group. A small, slightly debased double-lugged globular amphora likewise links the grave with the Volhynian (Sluch-Boh) graves by both its shape and its ornament of groups of horizontal cord-impressed lines and girdles of concentric semicircles round the neck and the body (Fig. 23:13).

The 'Kuyavian' amphora from slab-cist grave 2 at Piatra-Neamţ (no. 530), a site situated some 70km south of the former, also had a similar cord-decorated ornament of rows of concentric semicircles. However, another amphora from this grave had fish-scale decoration on its short neck, the whole vessel being covered with horizontal rows of short, shallow incisions. One of its accompanying bowls, provided with lugs, was likewise decorated with fish-scale patterns, mainly triangles, as were a few sherds from two or more vessels found in this grave. This decoration links the grave with the Podolian group, as fish-scale ornament does not appear in the East Volhynian groups.

Of particular interest was the animal grave uncovered at Dolheşti Mari in the immediate vicinity of the two slab-cists. Near the head of the animal (Cervidae or Bovidae) stood a vessel proper to the Globular Amphora culture. Such burials, apparently offerings, were not found in the Globular Amphora groups east of the Vistula; they were, however, very

[43] І. К. Свешніков, Підсумки дослідження культур бронзової доби Прикарпаття і західного Поділля, Lviv 1958, p. 18. See also Ю. Н. Захарук, Погребення в каменных гробницах около с. Поповцев, тернопольской области, КСИАК, no. 8, 1959, p. 132.

[44] Op. cit., note 3.

characteristic of the Kuyavian Globular Amphora culture[45] and were adopted also by the Złota culture.[46]

The fact that the second slab-cist at Dolheşti Mari was uncovered under a layer attributable to the 'Gorodsk' culture is of importance chronologically and for the establishment of the relative chronology of the various cultures which developed within the Territory. The implications connected with the above fact and other related topics will be discussed in the next chapter.

Traces of a Globular Amphora penetration further south, into Transilvania, are clearly discernible. A. Prox[47] is of the opinion that Globular Amphora pottery, along with that of the Funnel Beakers, belonged to the 'essential stock' of Schneckenberg pottery of stage A. But undoubtedly connected with the arrival of the bearers of the Globular Amphorae, or their immediate descendants, were Transilvanian slab-cist graves placed in stage B of the Schneckenberg culture. In their construction and their burial ritual, they do not differ from those of the Globular Amphora culture; their pottery, although not of the type belonging to that culture, was adorned by girdles of concentric semicircles and triangles,[48] motifs met on several vessels of the Moldavian and East Volhynian branches of the culture (Fig. 22:13). Another link with the Globular Amphora culture are bone belt-buckles found in these slab-cist graves.[49]

The grave from Pekliuk, near Sofia (no. 546), nearly 200km south of the Transilvanian slab-cists, is the southernmost grave of the Globular Amphora culture so far known. The shape of the vessel in the grave and of its lid (Fig. 23:1), which considerably departed from that of the genuine globular amphorae, suggest its late date.

[45] L. Gabałówna, 'Pochówki bydlęce kultury amfor kulistych ze stanowiska 4 w Brześciu Kujawskim, w świetle podobnych znalezisk kultur środkowo-europejskich', *PMMAE*, no. 3, 1958, pp. 63 ff., 183 ff.

[46] Ibid. See also Sulimirski (op. cit., note 11), pp. 352 ff.

[47] A. Prox, *Die Schneckenbergkultur*, Kronstadt 1941, pp. 88 ff.

[48] Ibid., pp. 70 ff., Pls. IV; XVI:9; XVIII:8; XXVI; XXVIII.

[49] Ibid., Pl. XXVII. V. Moucha, *Arch.R.*, vol. X, 1958, pp. 62 ff.

Note. The recently published, important work by T. Wiślański, *Kultura amfor kulistych w Polsce północno-zachodniej* (Globular Amphora Culture in North-Western Poland, with a summary in English), Wrocław-Warszawa-Kraków 1966, could not have been taken into account here. Nearly 450 graves, settlements and occupation sites have been listed and described in that area, which according to the author was original of the culture. The results of this study are in agreement with the views expressed in the present work.

CHAPTER V

Eastern Globular Amphorae and the Local Cultures

GENERAL CONSIDERATIONS

THE SURVEY in the preceding chapter of the remains of the Globular Amphora culture east of the Vistula (Map V) revealed the existence of a series of its groups within the territory with which we are concerned. At first sight, their remains seem to exhibit remarkable uniformity, in spite of the distances which separate them. Their basic shapes, the incised and stamped ornament and its pattern relate them to the Kuyavian group of that culture, although the fish-scale decoration, characteristic of the Podolian group, connects the latter rather with the Western Globular Amphora culture, west of the Oder. Other grave goods, in particular the very well-polished flat axes, usually rhomboid in shape, made of greyish varieties of flint, often of the 'milky' flint of Mecklenburg or Rugen origin, amber discs, decorated bone belt-buckles, etc., also contribute greatly to the basic uniformity of all these groups.

However, closer study of all the remains reveals that this astonishing uniformity over a very extensive area is confined almost entirely to a relatively small number of graves which can be regarded as the earliest. Such graves were found only in the Chełm-Hrubieszów (Kryłów, no. 387; Ulwówek, no. 398) and the Dubno-Ostróg groups (Varkovytsia, no. 448), and in the northern part of West Podolia (Dźwinogrod, no. 420; Horodnica-Kopyczyńce, no. 494); they do not occur either further east or south. Grave goods from these slab-cist graves (pottery, flint axes, etc.) do not seem to differ in any respect from those in Kuyavia and Masovia.

Much more numerous were slab-cist graves, evidently of a somewhat later date, which show to varying degrees how the influence of the surrounding indigenous cultures resulted in the gradual disintegration of this uniformity and in the formation of local variants of the Globular Amphora culture. Their grave goods deviate considerably from the common patterns although in type and the decorative style of pottery they exhibit characteristic features of the original Globular Amphorae. These graves mark the second stage in the development of the eastern Globular Amphora culture in which the local groups quoted in the preceding chapter were formed. It is of interest to note that slab-cist graves with remains typical of the second stage were found within an area larger than that covered by the graves of the first category: they extended over the whole of West Podolia, Moldavia, and Volhynia, where no earlier Globular Amphorae reached. This seems to imply that during the second period a further expansion of the Globular Amphora culture took place.

In most areas the development of local groups of the Globular Amphora culture did not go beyond this point. A further stage was disintegration which appears to have been fastest within the Hrubieszów group. It soon disappeared, merging into the Strzyżów culture, a local branch of the Corded Ware, following a process similar to that which took place in the Sandomierz area (west of the Vistula) where the Globular Amphorae contributed to the formation of the Złota culture.

A different development occurred in West Podolia and in the Dubno-Ostróg group, where another, the third stage of the culture can be distinguished. The traditional Globular Amphorae pottery and other grave goods were replaced by those typical of the Corded Ware. Accordingly, some authors[1] consider these graves to belong to the Corded Ware culture: but this appears incorrect. The old groups evidently survived by adapting themselves to new conditions. The grave form, slab-cist, and the burial ritual, all very important elements of the old culture, bear witness to the identity of the groups which is also confirmed by the geographical distribution of the late graves covering the same areas as previously. Important, in this respect, are a few slab-cist graves in which vessels decorated in fish-scale patterns were found together with those typical of the Corded Ware (Beremiany 2, no. 484; Koszyłowce 2, no. 501).

The replacement of the traditional grave goods by new forms took place under the pressure from the neighbouring and surrounding Barrow-grave culture and other groups of Corded Ware (Map VI). It should be noted, however, that only late types of Corded Ware have been found in slab-cists: the early types (Thuringian amphorae, beakers) were never found in them. Similar factors were also responsible for a further change in the grave goods of the West Podolian slab-cist graves which mark the fourth stage in their development. At that period pottery appeared in graves very similar to that of the Komarów culture, the Middle and Late Bronze Age successor of the Barrow-grave culture. The identity of these late West Podolian slab-cist grave groups, to which the name 'Biały Potok group' has been given, is shown by their grave form and the territory within which they were found, the same as that of their ancestral Globular Amphorae (Map XI). Outside West Podolia, a similar development seems to have taken place only in Transilvania; at Moreşti[2] in a slab-cist

[1] I. K. Свешніков, Підсумки дослідження культур бронзової доби Прикарпаття і західного Поділля, Lviv 1959, p. 18. Ю. Н. Захарук, Погребення в каменных гробницах около с. Поповцев, тернопольской области, КСИАК, no. 8, 1959, p. 132.

[2] K. Horedt, 'Santierul arheologic Moreşti', *SCIV*, vol. VI, 1955, p. 658, Figs. 10, 16.

grave with a contracted skeleton (no. 92) pottery was found, corresponding with that of the Biały Potok graves. Different, however, was the position in East Volhynia. There, the slab-cist grave, one of the most characteristic features of the eastern Globular Amphorae, disappeared, but some decorative patterns belonging to the Zhitomir group appear on pottery of the local Voytsekhivka culture of the Middle Bronze Age (Fig. 33:B).[3]

ORIGIN

In the territories east of the Vistula, the people of the eastern Globular Amphora culture were not the indigenous population. The very small number of graves in relation to the territory they cover, and the fact that no real settlements of the Amphora people have been found there, are cogent arguments in favour of this assumption. Pottery was almost without exception a sepulchral pottery; the few Globular Amphora potsherds found in settlements were an alien element in sites settled by peoples with existing local cultures of a different origin.

The Globular Amphora culture was evidently intrusive within the region under review which it entered from the north-west. Any theories which suggest its eastern origin must be dismissed; they receive no support whatever from the archaeological material.

A. I. Briusov,[4] in dealing with the remains of the East Volhynian groups, expressed the opinion that they did not belong to the Central European Globular Amphora culture but constituted an independent, different 'Volhynian megalithic culture'. He maintains that the difference in the shape and decoration of vessels of the Volhynian culture and those of the Central European Globular Amphorae was of much greater significance than their similarity; he firmly rejects the idea of the 'megalithic culture' in Volhynia being evidence of a foreign western invasion, the Central European Globular Amphorae being of a somewhat later date than their counterparts in Volhynia. He concludes that the Volhynian culture developed locally; there is not enough archaeological material to prove the actual existence of parallels to the Central European Globular Amphorae.

Similar ideas were expressed by Gimbutas.[5] The Globular Amphora culture was considered by her to be a hybrid culture consisting of elements of local Neolithic cultures and brought by these from the eastern steppes by an intrusive culture. This last is supposed to derive from the late Yamna (pit-grave) culture of the steppe country east of the Dnieper, the bearers of which, in their western drive, overran the territory held previously by the Danubians and the Funnel Beaker people.

A closer study of the archaeological material of our territory in which, according to the above views the Globular Amphora culture is supposed to have originated (Map v), shows that this culture appeared there as a definitely formed complex on the verge of disintegration. Nothing can be found in its remains to suggest that this was a newly formed culture, an expanding culture which subsequently began its western drive to the Elbe forming a whole series of vigorous local branches on the way.

No Yamna elements are discernible in the remains of the Volhynian group of the Globular Amphorae, which is the easternmost and the nearest to the Yamna territory, thus supposedly the first to have been formed. Graves of the two cultures were absolutely different; the few barrow-graves in which slab-cists were uncovered were found without exception further west, in the areas in which the Globular Amphora culture bordered on the Barrow-grave culture; they are apparently the evidence of reciprocal relations between the two different but coeval cultures.

Slab-cists did not evolve locally either in Volhynia or in Podolia and did not aim at imitating houselike structures. This was simply a technical development, a simpler and easier method of building grave-chambers instead of using boulders and large pebbles for this purpose. Regular slab-cists were found exclusively in areas in which suitable raw material was available for their construction; no genuine slab-cists appear in Kuyavia where no such material was at hand. Volhynian slab-cists could not have derived from the south of the Ukraine where such graves were of a later date. The construction of the Caucasian slab-cists was different and they were provided with a porthole (*Seelenloch*) never found in Volhynian slab-cists or those of other groups. On the other hand, cists built of large boulders were proper to the Kuyavian branch of the Funnel Beaker culture, and the stratigraphic evidence there[6] shows that this type of grave was subsequently adopted by the local Globular Amphora culture of the succeeding period.

The origin of the eastern branch of the Globular Amphora culture must be sought somewhere in Kuyavia or in Pomerania. This is suggested by the relatively large number of settlements and other sites on sand-dunes there (Map v).[7] From this original centre it had expanded south-eastwards which is shown by: (a) their geographical diffusion, clearly indicating the route by which they proceeded in their south-eastern drive; (b) grave form: cists built of large boulders (no slabs were available) were typical of the Kuyavian graves of the preceding Funnel Beaker culture; (c) grave goods, in particular amber and axes made of 'milky' flint of north-western origin, also pottery almost identical with that of Kuyavia, or Masovia, found exclusively in graves not very remote from these regions; (d) the anthropological study of skulls which reveals that they were all of Nordic type except the skull of the slave from the grave at Voytsekhivka and women of the Podolian group who were of a brachycephalic stock, the southernmost Moldavian graves being the only ones to reveal hybridization of the Nordic type with some local brachycephalic elements; and (e) the fact that no precursory elements of the Globular Amphora culture can be found either in Volhynia or Podolia.

[3] І. Левицький, Стація в ур. Піщаному біля Народич, Антропологія, vol. iv, Kiev 1930, p. 230, Fig. 38:6, 7.

[4] А. Я. Брюсов, Очерки по истории племен европейской части СССР в неолитическую эпоху, Moscow 1952, pp. 224 ff.

[5] M. Gimbutas, *The Prehistory of Eastern Europe*, part I, Cambridge (Mass.) 1956, pp. 140 ff.

[6] W. Chmielewski, *Zagadnienie grobowców kujawskich w świetle ostatnich badań*, Łódź 1952, pp. 35, 57.

[7] T. Sulimirski, *Polska przedhistoryczna*, part II, London 1957–9, pp. 276 ff. T. Wiślański, 'Uwagi o pochodzeniu tzw. amfor kulistych', *Sprawozdania Komisji PAN*, Kraków, VII–XII 1963, pp. 356 ff. Id., 'Próba wyświetlenia genezy tzw. kultury amfor kulistych', *Arch.P.*, vol. viii–2, 1963, pp. 222 ff. See also the Note on p. 48.

THE CHARACTER OF THE BEARERS

The bearers of the Globular Amphora culture are usually regarded as hunters and swineherds engaging in casual robbery and trade.[8] The character of their graves and grave goods, combined with a relatively small number of burials scattered over a very wide area, imply however that they were primarily warriors who forcibly entered areas which were already inhabited. They must have met several alien peoples in their eastern drive. They most probably imposed their rule over the regions in which they settled, marked by the eastern groups of the Globular Amphora culture, but they had obviously not exterminated the indigenous population. Their position as members of a ruling, or upper, class is indicated in particular by slab-cists in which slaves or serfs were buried together with their master, and above all by the different racial stock to which the serfs belonged, the representatives of the subdued population.

The very small number of graves of the Globular Amphorae in each region described suggest that their bearers were not numerous. They must have lived in the settlements of the conquered indigenous population, as is indicated by the almost complete lack in these regions of settlements attributable to the Globular Amphora culture. Potsherds typical of that culture found in the remains of the settlements of the Strzyżów culture, or of the Funnel Beakers in the northern part of the country we are dealing with (Nowyj Dwir, Sokal, Staryj Mylsk, Strzyżów, etc.), or in those of the Tripolye culture in Podolia (Koszyłowce), support this assumption.

The distribution of the eastern groups of the Globular Amphora culture along the waterways leading from the Baltic coast south-eastwards towards the Black Sea suggests that the amber trade played some part in the activities of their bearers. Another field of their activity seems to have been the setting up of flint workshops specializing in the making of very fine 'sickles', 'bent knives', daggers, etc., and trade and distribution of these over wider areas. The geographical distribution of these flint implements largely includes the areas of the eastern groups of the Globular Amphora culture (e.g. the large hoard found at Kyslytske near Vapnyarka no. 726, and also other hoards listed on p. 210), although such objects were only exceptionally found in their graves. It seems very likely that the (poor) local Volhynian copper ores were exploited at that time; they lay within the territory of the Dubno-Ostróg group. Slab-cist graves from the Transilvanian metalliferous region seem to show that the Globular Amphora people, or their immediate descendants, intended to secure control of copper and possibly of gold mines.

RELATIONS WITH THE FUNNEL BEAKERS

The influence of the indigenous population on the newcomers of the Globular Amphora culture was considerable and very soon apparent on the remains of the latter; it was obviously responsible for the differences which developed between the various groups of the eastern Globular Amphorae. The local cultures or groups which chiefly affected the Globular Amphorae were the Funnel Beakers, the Tripolye culture, and Corded Ware. Relations with these cultures will be discussed here, starting with the Funnel Beakers.

The stratigraphic evidence in grave I of cemetery B at Klementowice[9] of the Puławy group (Map v, group v), the westernmost of our Globular Amphora sites, reveals that the Funnel Beakers of the Nałęczów group preceded the Globular Amphorae there, although at a later stage both must have coexisted within that area, at least for a short period. The particular burial ritual, different grave construction, and the somewhat differing pottery which distinguish the Puławy group from other groups of our Globular Amphorae were the outcome of the influence of the Funnel Beakers.

The impact of the latter culture on the Globular Amphora groups further east is also clear. It is of interest to note that pottery of all groups of the latter in the northern part of our area, within the reach of the actual remains of the Funnel Beakers, or at least within reach of their influence, was decorated with deep incised or stamped patterns which ultimately derived from the ornament of the Funnel Beaker culture. On the other hand, the fish-scale patterns, alien to the latter culture but proper to the Globular Amphorae west of the Oder, were characteristic of the Podolian group of Globular Amphorae, a group which had developed outside the territory affected by the Funnel Beakers.

In the regions on the Middle Bug and between the Styr and the Horyn, the Globular Amphorae (the Chełm-Hrubieszów and Dubno-Ostróg groups, Map v, groups VI, VIII) undoubtedly succeeded the Funnel Beakers. No remains of the Globular Amphora culture here were ever found with those of the Funnel Beakers which might have implied they were contemporaneous. The site of Staryj Mylsk (no. 558), where pottery of the two cultures was found together with Corded Ware, has not been investigated; all potsherds were found there on the surface of the soil.

J. Kowalczyk[10] emphasizes that the fortified settlement of the Funnel Beakers at Gródek Nadbużny was destroyed by some savage aggressors. The stratigraphic evidence shows that the Globular Amphora culture was next in succession in this site. Accordingly, he connects the destruction of this settlement, and of other similar settlements of the Funnel Beaker culture on the Middle Bug and further south, with the invading Globular Amphora people. The relative position of the Globular Amphora culture in that area based on stratigraphic evidence is shown in Table 16 (p. 57).

RELATIONS WITH CORDED WARE ASSEMBLAGE

The eastern Globular Amphorae were in close contact with several groups of the Corded Ware complex and their reciprocal relations with each of these need special treatment.

The contact between these two complexes occurred first of all in the region of Puławy, as indicated by the appearance of cord decoration on the vessels typical of the Globular Amphorae and by similar occurrences. In that part of the country, especially in its southern division close to the border of the Barrow-grave culture, many sites with cord-decorated pottery were found on sand-dunes (Map VI), but neither their character nor date have been established. J. Machnik[11] attributes them to the Chłopice-Veselé horizon, which

[8] V. G. Childe, *The Dawn of European Civilization*, 5th ed., 1950, p. 191.
[9] J. Kowalczyk, *Mat.St.*, vol. II, 1957, pp. 175, 183 ff.
[10] J. Kowalczyk, *W.A.*, vol. XXIV, 1958, p. 319.
[11] J. Machnik, 'Archeologiczne badania powierzchniowe na niektórych

equates them with the second period of the Barrow-grave culture. The reciprocal relations between these remains and the advancing Globular Amphorae are ambiguous.

The impact of Corded Ware on the Globular Amphora culture was not as strong there as it was on the other side of the Vistula, in the Sandomierz region where, under similar conditions, the Złota culture was formed. The Puławy group retained its character of a branch of the Globular Amphora culture, whereas in the Złota culture the elements of the Corded Ware were dominant. Very instructive in this respect is the pottery of the slab-cist graves at Rębków-Parcele[12] situated north of the Puławy group. The cord-impressed ornament of their vessels (typical of the Globular Amphorae) bears the unmistakable character of the Złota decorative style. The Złota culture was evidently coeval with the Puławy group. This is also indicated by flint axes which were made of the banded variety; no axes made of banded flint were found in any of the more easterly groups of our culture.

Relations were close between the Globular Amphora culture and Corded Ware in the region on the Middle Bug, and also further east in Volhynia (Maps v and vi). They were to a considerable extent responsible for the formation of the Strzyżów culture, and in East Volhynia both cultures contributed to the formation of the Gorodsk culture. Potsherds of the Globular Amphora culture were found together with corded ware of the Dnieper-Desna type at Černyn (no. 547) close to the eastern bank of the Dnieper north of Kiev; S. S. Berezanska[13] equates them with the Middle Dnieper culture and the Yamna-Catacomb culture of the steppe country, and thinks that they followed the Sofiivka culture.[14] This does not seem right. The Sofiivka cemeteries were contemporary with the Volhynian Globular Amphorae; the cremation ritual characteristic of the Zhitomir group of the latter culture (Map v, group x) was likewise practised by its neighbouring Sofiivka culture (Map vi). Potsherds typical of the Globular Amphora culture were found also still further east, in the region north of Gomel (nos. 549, 553, 557, 600).

Contact between the Globular Amphora culture and the neighbouring barrow-grave groups is reflected in the remains of both cultures. Here may be mentioned potsherds of the Globular Amphora culture found in barrow-graves I and v at Kołokolin (no. 66, Fig. 12:3, 9) or slab-cists uncovered under the mounds of the northern part of West Podolia and in West Volhynia (see Map vi, Table 2, p. 7), or the barrow-grave of the Middle Dnieper culture at Łosiatyn (no. 250), which yielded a typical globular amphora (Plate 14:12) but had no slab-cist grave. On the other hand, the influence of the Corded Ware assemblage on the Globular Amphorae of the Chełm-Hrubieszów group, and also of the East Volhynian and Podolian branches, resulted in the abandonment of the pottery and weapons proper to the Globular Amphora culture and the adoption of grave goods typical of Corded Ware burials. Consequently, some authors[15] regard these late slab-cist graves, which mark the third period in the development of the Globular Amphora culture, as forming part of the Corded Ware assemblage.

The approximate date at which in the crucial region on the Middle Bug (the Hrubieszów group, Map v, group vi) these two cultures came into contact with each other is given by the grave from Raciborowice (no. 392). An undecorated amphora of a debased Thuringian type was found with a Kuyavian amphora typical of the second stage of the Globular Amphora culture. The grave equates the latter stage with the second period of the Barrow-grave culture. An earlier date, the end of the first period of the Sub-Carpathian barrow graves, is suggested for this contact by the Thuringian amphorae found in the barrow-graves at Kołokolin, mentioned above, which also yielded potsherds of the Globular Amphora culture (Fig. 12:3, 9).

No actual remains of the Globular Amphora culture and no traces of its influence have been found in the Ukrainian forest zone and the steppe country before the early Corded Ware. This fact implies that the early Corded Ware (the Thuringian amphorae) in the Ukraine had preceded the southern drive of the Globular Amphora people.

A similar position existed further south in Transilvania, where the prior appearance of the early Corded Ware has been likewise attested. Vessels of 'Thuringian amphora' type dated there from stage A of the Schneckenberg culture, whereas slab-cist graves and decorative motifs of pottery, deriving from the eastern Globular Amphorae (Fig. 22:13) belonged to its stage B.[16] The conditions recorded at Dolheşti Mari (no. 527) suggest a close association of the Moldavian Globular Amphora with the late Corded Ware assemblage of Gorodsk type.

RELATIONS WITH THE TRIPOLYE CULTURE

The slab-cist from Biały Potok (no. 485),[17] dug into the remains of a late Tripolyan hut, is of no significance for the establishment of the date of the Globular Amphora culture in West Podolia. In this grave no grave goods were found, and the green spot on the skull, implying the presence of a decomposed metal (copper or bronze) object points to its late date. The burial might have belonged to the Middle Bronze Age Komarów-Biały Potok culture.

Of importance, however, for the study of the reciprocal relations of the Globular Amphorae with the Tripolye culture are potsherds of the former excavated in the late Tripolyan settlement at Koszyłowce in West Podolia (no. 552, Fig. 21:3), which equate the culture with Tripolyan period C-1. The same equation is given by the deep incised

schyłkowo-neolitycznych i wczesnobrązowych stanowiskach w Małopolsce', *Sprawozdania Komisji PAN*, Kraków, I–VI 1964, pp. 14 ff.

[12] S. Nosek, 'Kultura amfor kulistych na Lubelszczyźnie', *AUMCS*, vol. v F, 1950, p. 91, Figs. 16–35. Id., 'Materiały do badań nad historią starożytną i wczesnośredniowieczną międzyrzecza Wisły i Bugu', *AUMCS*, vol. vi F, 1957, pp. 234 f., Figs. 9–14.

[13] С. С. Березанська, Археологія-Kiev, vol. xii, 1961, p. 104, Fig. 2:3.

[14] Ю. М. Захарук, Софіївський тілопальний могильник, Арх. Пам., vol. iv, 1952, pp. 112 ff. В. М. Даниленко, М. Л. Макаревич, Червонохутірський могильник мідного віку з трупоспаленням, Арх. Пам., vol. vi, 1956, pp. 92 ff. В. И. Канивец, Могильник епохи міді біля Чернина на Київщині, Арх. Пам., vol. vii, 1956, pp. 99 ff.

[15] Op. cit., note 43 in Chapter IV.

[16] A. Prox, *Die Schneckenbergkultur*, Kronstadt 1941, Pls. ii:4; iv; xvi:7; xviii:2.

[17] J. Kostrzewski, 'Groby eneolityczne ze skuczonymi szkieletami w Białym Potoku', *Prz.A.*, vol. iii, 1925–7, pp. 9 ff.

decorative motifs characteristic of the Globular Amphorae applied to a series of Tripolyan vessels of period C-1, especially at the settlement of Kolomiščyna 1 (nos. 565, 566).[18]

The evidence available shows that during the Tripolyan period C-1 the people of the Globular Amphorae entered some regions inhabited by the Tripolyans, particularly West Podolia (Map VII). They imposed their rule over them but did not exterminate the indigenous population. They do not seem to have interfered much in the development of other branches of the Tripolye culture further east, the Uman and the Kiev groups. They seem, however, to have proceeded from Podolia and Volhynia southwards to Moldavia and possibly also along the Dniester towards the Black Sea coast (the Usatovo culture, Map VI).

Some time after the conquest a significant influx of Corded Ware people is noticeable in West Podolia; settlements have been recorded there in which almost exclusively Corded Ware of Volhynian Gorodsk type was found (e.g., Koszyłowce-Tovdry, Kasperowce-Lipniki).[19] In North Moldavia, Corded Ware of Gorodsk type appeared a little later, in the sites of late Tripolyan culture (e.g. Horodiştea).[20] They seem to have been colonies set up by newcomers from the north. This development was followed by a decline of the local potters' craft, as is witnessed by the early Komarów pottery ('D' ware). Soon, however, a reaction took place which resulted in the revival of the old elements and potters' craft; it marks the beginning of a new period, that of the Komarów-Biały Potok of the Middle Bronze Age. The West Podolian slab-cist graves with Corded Ware, characteristic of the third period of the Globular Amphora culture, belonged to the time when the influence exercised by late Corded Ware culture was at its height.

CHRONOLOGY

The Globular Amphora culture proper was not long-lived; not more than three to four generations (up to about two hundred years) can be allocated to its existence, including the third, 'Corded Ware' stage. The various groups were not established at the same time: those in the west (Puławy and possibly the Hrubieszów groups) were probably set up by the end of the Neolithic, early in the second millennium B.C., those further south and east during the early stage of the Early Bronze Age (Reinecke's A-1).

The large bronze napring from the settlement of the Funnel Beaker culture at Gródek Nadbużny,[21] destroyed supposedly by the invading Globular Amphora people, seems to place their arrival there in the Early Bronze Age (period A-1); however, a vessel evidently of Globular Amphora derivation found in a pit in the settlement of the Funnel Beakers at Zimno near Włodzimierz Wołyński[22] implies at least a temporary coexistence of the two cultures involved. The vessel was an undecorated amphora with two small lugs on the junction of the neck and the body, covered with a lid belonging to the Tripolye culture. The Thuringian amphora in the grave at Raciborowice equates the Gródek Nadbużny branch with the second period of the Barrow-grave culture. The East Volhynian branches, as well as the Podolian group, were set up at a somewhat later date than the Hrubieszów branch; they can be equated with the Tripolyan period C-1 and the settlement of Seredni Stog II. By the very end of this period the Moldavian group was formed, mainly by Volhynian immigrants, partly by those from West Podolia. Transilvania was reached in the second stage of the Schneckenberg culture which can be equated with the third stage of the Globular Amphora culture.

During the second stage of the Early Bronze Age (Reinecke A-2) the Globular Amphora culture had gradually lost its identity and disappeared. Its development during the subsequent period, the Middle Bronze Age, can only be followed in West Podolia. By that time, the slab-cists remained as one element of the ancient culture; pottery and other grave goods were very similar to those of the Komarów culture. The name of the Biały Potok group has been given to these Bronze Age graves in West Podolia (Map XI).

In Table 15 is shown the regional and chronological division of the remains of the Globular Amphora culture and some of its coeval cultures quoted.

WESTERN SITES OF CORDED WARE

In its south-eastern drive, the Globular Amphora culture met with several groups of the Corded Ware assemblage (Map VI). Their reciprocal relations were different in various parts of the territory involved, but ultimately the Globular Amphorae succumbed almost everywhere to the local Corded Ware groups. This has led some authors to suppose that the Globular Amphorae were forebears of the Corded Ware assemblage.[23]

The Globular Amphora culture never entered the territory of the Sub-Carpathian barrow-graves (Map II). It seems that the sandy soils east of the Vistula, in the area between that of the Puławy group of the Globular Amphorae and the territory occupied by the Sub-Carpathian barrow-graves further south, were likewise unaffected by that culture (Map VI). Well over thirty sites attributable to the Corded Ware were recorded there;[24] they were mainly traces of temporary encampments and only a few were settlements. Isolated graves and inhumation cemeteries were also uncovered in that region including a few isolated barrow-graves which were closely related to those of the Sub-Carpathian culture (e.g. Sławinek-Lublin, no. 131).

Very little of the archaeological material in question has been published, but the available data suggests a late date for most of these remains.[25] Only one 'boat-axe' was found in a grave (Trójnia).[26] The beakers from Dratów and Klemen-

[18] Т. С. Пассек, Периодизация трипольских поселений, МИА, no. 10, Moscow–Leningrad 1949, pp. 222 f., Fig. 76:3, 6.

[19] Pottery from site Kasperowce I (Lipniki) and IX, at the Natur-Historisches Museum, Vienna (nos. 49722–53, 49848–51); for Koszyłowce, see В. Кравец, КСИАК, no. 4, 1955, p. 135.

[20] H. Dumitrescu, 'La station préhistorique de Horodiştea sur le Pruth', *Dacia*, vol. IX–X, 1941–7, pp. 127 ff.

[21] J. Kowalczyk, *W.A.*, vol. XXIV, 1957, p. 49. Dr J. Kowalczyk has kindly given me a photograph of this pendant.

[22] Ю. М. Захарук, МДАПВ, vol. 2, 1959, p. 63, Fig. 5.

[23] J. E. Forssander, *Die schwedische Bootaxtkultur und ihre kontinentaleuropäischen Voraussetzungen*, Lund 1933, pp. 172 ff. Gimbutas (op. cit., note 5), pp. 150 ff.

[24] Nosek (op. cit., note 12: 1957), pp. 245 ff. J. Machnik and J. Potocki, *Spr.Arch.*, vol. V, 1959, p. 255. J. Machnik, *Spr.Arch.*, vol. VII, 1959, pp. 69 ff.

[25] Machnik (op. cit., note 11).

[26] L. Gajewski, *ZOW*, vol. XX, 1951, p. 67.

TABLE 15. Chronological division of graves (slab-cists) of the Globular Amphora culture and its successive cultures, inclusive in the Biały Potok group

Periods	Chełm-Hrubieszów group	Lwów group	Dubno-Ostróg group	Sluch group	Easternmost group	West Podolian group	Romania and Bulgaria	Equates with
I	Kryłów Poniatówka Tworyczów Ulwówek 3	Dzwinogród Mikołajów	Lepesivka Varkov-ytsia	Voytse-khivka 1		Czarne Wody Horodnica Zbr. Uwisła 1 Zastawie 1, 2		Advanced stage of the Barrow-grave period I
II	Branica Such. Miedniki Raciborowice Stadarnia Strzyżów Wola Gró-decka Wytyczno		Gródek-Równe 1960 Międzyrzec Mokre Nowomalin	Aneta Kykova Staryi Myropil Suyemtsi 1,2 Nowa Sieniawa Tartaki Vinnytsia	Fasova Mininy Skolobiv Vysoke	Chorostków Czarnokońce Hlubičok Kociubińce Kolubaivtsi Słobódka Kosz. Strilče Ułaszkowce Velyka Mukša Zawadyńce	*Moldavia* Dolheşti Mari Graniceşti *Bulgaria* Pekliuk	Barrow-graves period II Tripolyan period C-1 Złota culture
III	(Torczyn) Strzyżów culture	Dublany Łany	Biało-krynica Gródek-Równe Lachów Młynów Stadniki Zdolbitsa		Davydivka Volodarske-Horoški Vyševyči	Beremiany 2 Koszyłowce 2, 3 Latacz 1 Ładyczyn Niżniow Popovtsy 1, 2 Rożniów	*Moldavia* Gîrceni *Transilvania* Zeiden	Barrow-graves period III Tripolyan period C-2(D)
IV Biały Potok group			Skurcze		*Dnieper Rapids* Fedorivka Osokorivka Balka	Beremiany 3 Biały Potok Czernelica Horodenka Horodnica Hor. Nagórzanka Ruzdwiany Semenów Trembowla Zieleńcze Żeżawa	*Transilvania* Moreşti	Periods II and III of the Komarów culture Noua culture
V						Ivanye Zolote Uwisła 2		Period IV of the Komarów culture

sów[27] have been attributed to the Mierzanowice culture of the Early Bronze Age; the late date of this group is furthermore indicated by copper (or bronze) objects and a horse burial (the cemetery of Krzewica)[28] and it is supported by the furniture of the few barrow-graves of the region (Sławinek, no. 131; Zakłodzie, no. 136). These cemeteries, settlements and other sites can be equated with the second and third periods of the Barrow-grave culture.

The relationship to the Funnel Beaker culture, the remains of which were found in the same area (Map IV), has not so far been established, nor that with the Globular Amphorae, the territory of which extended further north and north-east (Map V). Close connections linked our remains with the Przemyśl group of the Sub-Carpathian barrow-graves (Map II) and later with the Corded Ware culture of the regions west of the Vistula. The group seemingly played the role of an intermediary between the latter culture and the Strzyżów culture further east, which will be discussed below.

The origin of the group is obscure, as no remains are known which could be considered as its ancestor. These may possibly be found in deeper layers of the local peat-bogs, as in East Prussia.[29] Its final date is given by pottery of the Trzciniec culture of the Middle Bronze Age which was sometimes associated with cord-decorated pottery in a number of sites of our region.

EASTERN SITES OF CORDED WARE

About one hundred and fifty sites, settlements, barrow-graves, 'flat' cemeteries and graves of the Corded Ware culture have been recorded in the territory extending over the fertile soils

[27] Nosek (op. cit., note 12: 1957), pp. 258, 262, Pl. XX:1.
[28] J. Gurba, *Prz.A.*, vol. XII, p. 18.
[29] H. Gross, 'Ergebnisse der moorgeologischen Untersuchungen der vorgeschichtlichen Dörfer im Zedmar-Bruch', *Nachrichtenblatt f. deutsche Vorzeit*, vol. 14, 1938.

of the eastern part of the Lublin Plateau and West Volhynia as far as the Horyn (Goryn), and over sandy soils south and north of this area (Map VI). To these many more sites (over sixty west of the Bug) may be added, usually attributed to the Corded Ware culture which, however, yielded only flints but no pottery.[30]

The remains above were not of the same date, and they represent at least two stages in the development of the culture. There were also marked regional differences. Sites on the northern sandy soils differed from those in the fertile loess country; the latter formed two well-distinguishable groups, the western and eastern groups. It is important to note that both groups extended over the area which corresponded almost exactly with that covered by the Hrubieszów and the Dubno-Ostróg groups of the Globular Amphora culture.

Not much can be said about the northern sites. They mostly consist of a number of potsherds found mainly on sand-dunes, and do not differ from those on the sandy soils of the Lublin area west of the river Wieprz, dealt with in the preceding section. They were evidently traces of temporary encampments of small migratory groups of hunters. The only grave recorded in this region (Chotivel, no. 117) was undoubtedly of an earlier stage; it yielded a 'Thuringian' amphora of type IIC, which equates the grave with the second stage of the Sub-Carpathian Barrow-grave culture. To a later stage of the local development belonged the only site excavated in that region (Majdan Mokwinski, no. 653). Its pottery, a grey sand-gritted ware, was to some extent similar to that of the Strzyżów culture, but was likewise closely related to that of the Gorodsk culture dealt with in the subsequent chapter. There were several handled, cord-decorated, amphorae of Strzyżów type showing the influence of the Globular Amphora culture, and also handled cups calling to mind those of the Chłopice-Véselé type. The hut could be equated with the third period of the Barrow-grave culture.

The northern sites extended over the territory which, in the preceding period, was in the possession of a culture of which comb-decorated ware was characteristic. This pottery differed considerably from the 'pit-comb' (or 'pit-marked') pottery[31] of the forest zone of Eastern Europe. It has often been referred to as the 'Pre-Finnish' culture,[32] and lately various names have been given to this group: the 'Baltic Neolithic,'[33] the 'Masovian culture',[34] the 'Dnieper-Elbe culture'.[35]

Sites with pottery typical of the 'Masovian', or 'Dnieper-Elbe' culture have been recorded within the wide stretch of land west of the Dnieper up to the Elbe. They are confined exclusively to the sandy soils, and their position was usually close to the ancient lakes, nowadays moors or peat-bogs. The bearers of the culture must have been hunters and fishers with no permanent settlements.

This was a long-lived culture, and Gardawski[36] distinguishes two stages in its development. The early date of the first stage of the Dnieper-Elbe culture is shown by the stratigraphic position of its remains in some of the peat-bogs investigated in distant regions. They were found under the peat layer at Kwaczała, near Cracow,[37] and in East Prussia.[38] The early stratigraphic position of the culture was revealed at Lasek, near Poznań,[39] and Kamionka Nadbużna east of Warsaw.[40] The relatively small number of early sites recorded is due to the remains being covered with peat, or existing in fossil, buried occupation-layers, and so not easily found or exposed. Later sites of the second stage, traces of which lie on the surface of sand-dunes exposed by the action of winds, are more likely to be noticed.

Masovian pottery definitely differs from that of the Danubian type and must have been of a different origin; its close links with that of the valley of the Dnieper have been pointed out.[41] It seems to have been related to that of the so-called 'Southern Bug' culture of the Early Neolithic of the region between Vinnitsa and Pervomaisk in the Ukraine, and might have ultimately derived from the Criş pottery of Romania. The culture extended over the territory which previously, during the Mesolithic, belonged to the eastern branch of the Tardenoisian culture, and it evidently developed locally out of the Tardenoisian substratum.[42] This is also well illustrated by the overwhelmingly microlithic character of its flint industry. During its long lifetime, it was in contact with several coeval cultures, in particular with the Funnel Beakers and Globular Amphorae.[43] It seems to have been parental to the Corded Ware assemblage.

THE STRZYŻÓW CULTURE (pp. 157 ff.)

Typical of the western section of the loess country was the Strzyżów culture,[44] named after a settlement on the Bug (no. 621). The type of settlement of the culture was very close to that of the cultures which had preceded it, i.e., the Lublin Painted pottery culture and the Funnel Beakers (Maps III and IV). Pit-dwellings occur here, although huts built on the surface predominate. The people led a sedentary life and were engaged in agriculture and animal husbandry.

The fully developed Strzyżów culture was proper to a later stage in the local development. To an earlier phase belonged

[30] J. Gurba, 'Neolithic Settlements on the Lublin Loess Uppland', *AUMCS*, vol. XV B, 1960, pp. 222 f.

[31] Gimbutas (op. cit., note 5), pp. 207 ff.

[32] J. Kostrzewski, 'The North-Eurasiatic Pottery in Poland', *Palaeologia*, vol. III, Kyoto 1954, p. 195.

[33] L. Kozłowski, *Młodsza epoka kamienna w Polsce (neolit)*), Lwów 1924, pp. 70 ff., Pl. XX.

[34] T. Sulimirski, *Polska przedhistoryczna*, part I, London 1955, pp. 123 ff.

[35] A. Gardawski, 'Zagadnienie kultury "ceramiki grzebykowej" w Polsce', *W.A.*, vol. XXV, 1958, pp. 287 ff.

[36] Ibid., pp. 290 ff.

[37] T. Sulimirski, 'Climate and Population', *Baltic Countries*, vol. I, Toruń 1935, pp. 1 ff., and also its reprint in the Baltic Pocket Library, Toruń 1935, pp. 14 ff.

[38] H. Gross, op. cit., note 29.

[39] Investigated by J. Kostrzewski, *Prz.A.*, vol. IV, 1928, pp. 2 f.

[40] Gardawski (op. cit., note 35), p. 289.

[41] G. Rosenberg, *Kulturströmungen in Europa zur Steinzeit*, Kopenhagen 1931. Gardawski (op. cit., note 35), p. 309.

[42] A. Formozow, 'Mezolityczne i neolityczne obszary kulturowo-etniczne europejskiej części ZSRR', *PMMAE*, no. 5, 1960, pp. 16 ff. Д. Я. Телегін, Неолітичні поселення лісостепнового лівобережжя і полісся України, Археологія, vol. XI, Kiev 1957, pp. 70 ff.

[43] Gardawski (op. cit., note 35), p. 305.

[44] Sulimirski (op. cit., note 7), pp. 233 ff. A. Gardawski, 'Plemiona kultury trzcinieckiej w Polsce', *Mat.St.*, vol. V, 1959, pp. 118 ff. J. Głosik, 'Osada kultury ceramiki sznurowej w Strzyżowie, pow.Hrubieszów, w świetle badań w latach 1935–7 i 39', *Mat.St.*, vol. VII, 1961, pp. 154 ff. Ю. М. Захарук, Нове джерело до вивчення культур шнурової кераміки на Волині, Мдапв, vol. 3, 1961, pp. 22 ff.

pottery characteristic of Corded Ware of areas further west. A large number of potsherds typical of the Cracow-Sandomierz Corded Ware[45] were found round the graves of the Strzyżów culture at Gródek Nadbużny (no. 602), while potsherds of ordinary Corded Ware constituted some 5 per cent of the pottery excavated in the Strzyżów settlement (no. 621).[46] To the earlier stage likewise belonged handled cups of Chłopice-Véselé type found in some settlements and graves in the region. The transition between the two stages must have been a gradual process, as indicated by graves and cemeteries of the culture, a few of which were investigated.

The graves were of two kinds. Those found within the area of the settlements were presumably of the older phase. The dead buried in these were in larger pits and in a contracted position. The grave from Walentynów (no. 627), which contained three highly characteristic vessels, also derived undoubtedly from the older phase.

The other type of burial occurred in the cemeteries outside the area of the settlement: they include a larger number of graves, that at Torczyn (no. 623) consisting of nineteen. The skeletons were almost invariably crouched, although the burials at Gródek Nadbużny (no. 602) were lying in an extended position, as in graves of the Funnel Beaker culture. The cemetery at Skomorochy Małe (no. 617) differed from others in that the graves were lined with stones and covered with a layer of stones in the manner of the Nałęczów group of the Funnel Beaker culture and the later Puławy group of the Globular Amphora culture. A fairly large number of the graves were provided with various kinds of personal ornaments, and weapons were occasionally found: however, there was a remarkably small amount of pottery, the Skomorochy Małe cemetery (no. 617) containing none at all. The grave goods from these cemeteries show that they derive from the later developmental phase of the Strzyżów culture.

The most common ornaments were various beads and pendants of mollusc shells, bone, and faience. Four graves investigated at Skomorochy contained a total of 286 beads made of *Spondylus* shells and eighteen of faience. Perforated boar tusks were also found in all the cemeteries. Bronze (copper) ear or hair pendants of the Stubło type were common. One of these, from Torczyn, had three longitudinal ribs instead of one.

Weapons were found in only a few graves. Finely made flint daggers (possibly spear-heads) from the Torczyn cemetery belong to the third type distinguished by us in discussing the flint daggers excavated in the burials of the Barrow-grave culture (Chapter II). Flint arrow-heads, triangular and with a concave base, occurred in all the cemeteries investigated. A copper shaft-hole axe, of the type known in Slovakia, was found in one of the destroyed Skomorochy graves.

Pottery typical of the Strzyżów culture differed from that found in sand-dunes or in barrow-graves, and from that of all other groups of Corded Ware in both their make and shapes, while the decorative patterns were distinctive too.[47] It was a gritted ware, insufficiently baked so that it was brittle. The vessels usually had very broad and flat bases (Fig. 2), were wide-mouthed, and their rims were invariably thickened in a highly characteristic manner, often being provided with one or more lugs, either plain or vertically perforated. The upper part of the vessels was usually decorated, while the lower part, undecorated, bore traces of heavy wiping with straw or dry grass; the latter connect this pottery with the ware of the Masovian (Dnieper-Elbe) culture. The decoration consists of horizontal lines placed close together and impressed with cord, sometimes being enclosed by short vertical rows: wavy triangular lines also occur, as well as oblique lines or cross-hatching, etc.

Several basic types of vessels can be distinguished, some evidently modelled on those of the Globular Amphora culture, others which can be derived from the Corded Ware. Most frequent and typical were clumsy, deep-bottomed amphorae with two lugs (Fig. 2). These vessels are quite clearly associated with the ovoid amphorae known in the Globular Amphora culture, and undoubtedly derive from them. Another type of vessels, also deriving from the Globular Amphora culture, consists of amphorae with four lugs or warts on the shoulder; these are a clumsy and variant form of the Kuyavian amphorae, a similarity mainly due to their much broader base and wide mouth. Even the decoration of these vessels is clearly reminiscent of the typical decoration of the Kuyavian prototypes (Gródek Nadbużny grave 1/2, Torczyn). In addition to the above, somewhat different amphorae occurred in a few graves, e.g. that at Oborowiec (no. 614).

A second large group consisted of the vessels belonging to forms typical of a late stage of the Corded Ware culture, e.g. handled cups and basins, but commonest among these were the beakers (Fig. 2). These had flat, wide bottoms, and wide mouths, and were very much heavier and more clumsy than the typical beakers of the Corded Ware of Central Europe. Many had spherical bodies. They were usually cord-decorated, although undecorated beakers also occurred, and some had decorated bottoms as well as decoration on the upper part (Raciborowice). Sometimes and particularly in the case of the smaller beakers, the rims were very thick and had two or four warts, often perforated vertically (Krasnystaw, no. 608, Fig. 2), thus being reminiscent of the lugged mugs typical of the late Corded Ware. Late types of Corded Ware were provided by the cups with straight walls widening upwards, usually decorated with horizontal cord lines under the rim and having one or more warts under the rim, often vertically perforated. Some cups had large handles instead of lugs.

The larger spherical vessels (Strzyżów, Zawisznia),[48] sometimes provided with warts under the rim, and also the wide hemispherical bowls with two lugs under the rim, have no corresponding specimens in the Corded Ware, and are evidently a local form proper to the culture. The vessel with two small lugs under the rim from Walentynów (no. 627) also belonged to this group; it is clearly reminiscent of the typical vessels of the Lublin Painted pottery culture within the same

[45] J. Kowalczyk, 'Zagadnienie kultury mierzanowickiej zwanej także tomaszowską', *W.A.*, vol. XXVI, 1959, p. 4.

[46] Głosik (op. cit., note 44), pp. 150 f.

[47] Ibid., p. 150.

[48] Kozłowski (op. cit., note 33), pp. 195, 198, Pl. XXVI:16; XXXI:7. Nosek (op. cit., note 12: 1957), p. 250. Sulimirski (op. cit., note 7), p. 234. Fig. 57.

area. It was accompanied by vessels the shape and decoration of which were characteristic of the fully developed Strzyżów culture.

CHRONOLOGY AND ORIGIN

The relative chronological position of the Strzyżów culture is indicated by the stratigraphic evidence of a number of sites, shown in Table 16.[49] It followed the Funnel Beakers and the Globular Amphorae, but preceded the Trzciniec culture of the Middle Bronze Age.

TABLE 16. Stratigraphic sequence of early cultures within the Strzyżów territory (after I. M. Zakharuk)

Culture	SITES			
	Raciborowice	Gródek Nadbużny	Zimno	Stavok
Trzciniec				–o–
Strzyżów	–o–	–o–		–o–
Globular Amphorae	–o–			
Funnel Beakers and Tripolye		–o–	–o–	
Lublin Painted Pottery			–o–	

Bronze personal ornaments (sometimes made of copper, which does not preclude their date), particularly earrings and pendants, faience beads and other imported objects, provide a basis for establishing the chronology of the Strzyżów culture and its links with other contemporary cultures. The handled cups of Chłopice-Véselé type, bone pins with perforated heads (Strzyżów), graves which yielded copper shaft-hole axe and ear-pendants with one end flattened and widened (Skomorochy Małe), belonged to the older phase, the formative period of the culture. These finds can be associated with the Alpine Bronze Age A-1; they equated with the second period of the Sub-Carpathian barrow-graves. Most settlements and cemeteries belonged, however, to the subsequent period, that of the fully developed Strzyżów culture. A number of specific grave goods, bronze ear-pendants of 'Stubło' type (see p. 22), flint daggers or spear-heads (Torczyn), faience beads, some of these segmented (Skomorochy Małe, Raciborowice, Strzyżów, Torczyn) equate the period with the third stage of the Sub-Carpathian barrow-graves, with period A-2, probably B also, of the Alpine sequence.

There is a divergence of opinion as to the origin of the Strzyżów culture. Some authors[50] hold that it arose on the Bug as an already crystallized foreign element clearly separate from other cultures in the area: they derive it from the Upper Vistula. Others[51] emphasize that its finds only occur within the extent of the Neolithic cultures, particularly of the Funnel Beakers; the centre of the Strzyżów culture was on the Bug: 'Strzyżów' characteristics decrease and finally disappear the further east one goes. Finally, some[52] held that the Strzyżów culture is clearly separate from other groups of Corded Ware; it includes characteristics of various cultures of the Early Bronze Age, such as the Złota, Mierzanowice, and Iwno cultures, and corresponds to them in the area it occupied.

Examination of the geographical extent of the Strzyżów culture (Map VI) shows that it covered the area previously occupied by the Lublin Painted pottery culture (Map III) and then by the Gródek Nadbużny group of the Funnel Beakers (Map IV). It may well be that some survivals of the Lublin Painted pottery culture entered into the Strzyżów culture. Pottery of the former type was found in the Strzyżów settlement in a large number of pits along with pottery of the Strzyżów culture, while the double-lugged vase from Walentynów was a late survival of vessels characteristic of the ancient culture. Outside the area of the Strzyżów culture, small centres of the Lublin Painted pottery culture survived into the Early Bronze Age (Zvenyhorod no. 94).[53]

The appearance of the Corded Ware of the Strzyżów type in settlements of the Funnel Beaker culture implies that some close connection must have existed between these two cultures. The bearers of both cultures followed the same way of life. In a few cases, it has been difficult to know to which culture the graves investigated should be attributed: this applied particularly to the five graves at Gródek Nadbużny, all of which were very similar and yielded no grave goods: two have been attributed to the Funnel Beaker culture, and the other three to the Strzyżów culture. It seems highly probable that the bearers of the Strzyżów culture were, at least in part, descendants of the local group (i.e. the Gródek Nadbużny group) of the Funnel Beaker folk who had intermingled with some other racial elements. However, there is a remarkably small quantity of elements of the Funnel Beakers in the pottery of the Strzyżów culture. Only in the Oborowiec grave[54] was an amphora typical of the Funnel Beakers found, along with two amphorae proper to the Corded Ware.

The Strzyżów culture was very closely linked with the Globular Amphora culture. In its western section it occurs in an area which was affected by the Hrubieszów group of the latter, although the people of the Globular Amphorae never had a firm grip on the country, as has been attested further east, in the region of Dubno and Równe (Map V).

The stratigraphic evidence at Raciborowice shows that the Globular Amphora preceded the Strzyżów culture. On the other hand, the Strzyżów pottery is clearly connected with pottery of the Globular Amphora. The Strzyżów amphorae (Fig. 2) represent a debased form of globular amphora, a vessel which is typical of the culture of that name. This also applies to other vessels which are a debased form of Kuyavian amphora, decorated with an ornament linked to the ornament proper to these vessels. It is typical that Sviešnikov[55] relates both amphorae from the Torczyn graves (one ovoid, the other similar to the Kuyavian) directly to the Globular Amphora culture, not to the Strzyżów culture,

[49] Ю. Н. Захарук, Вопросы хронологии культур энеолита и ранней бронзы Прикарпатья и Волыни, КСИАК, no. 12, 1962, p. 50, Fig. 3.

[50] Kowalczyk (op. cit., note 45), p. 5.

[51] Głosik (op. cit., note 44), p. 155.

[52] Gardawski (op. cit., note 44), p. 119.

[53] И. К. Свешников, Могильник в селе Звенигород львовской области, Ксиимк, no. 63, 1956.

[54] (no. 614). Nosek (op. cit., note 12: 1957), pp. 235 f., Pl. XII:3; XIII.

[55] І. К. Свешніков, Мегалітичні поховання на західному Поділлі, Lviv 1957, pp. 21 f. (no. 623.)

since both these vessels are still closer to their prototypes. A link with the Globular Amphora culture is provided by the graves of cattle (Strzyżów), as at Złota, and by the dog burial (Strzyżów); a handled, cord-decorated cup of the Chłopice-Véselé type was found in the latter with an ovoid amphora very close to those typical of the Globular Amphora culture.

The link between the Strzyżów culture and the Globular Amphora culture applied to the Hrubieszów group of the latter. When this group was referred to in the previous chapter, it was emphasized that this group was short-lived. The small number of its graves, the absence of any burials which might be equated with later graves of the Podolian or East Volhynian groups, and the occurrence of marked elements of the Globular Amphora culture within the range of the Strzyżów culture, all indicate that we are concerned here with a process similar to that which occurred in the Sandomierz region. The intrusive Globular Amphora culture, which most probably originated from the Masovian group near Płock, became one of the essential elements which contributed to the emergence of the Strzyżów culture on the Middle Bug. Here, as in the Sandomierz region, the Globular Amphora culture was unable to impress its own character on the newly emerging culture. Hence the Strzyżów culture, as did the Złota culture further west, retained the character of a local group of the Corded Ware assemblage.

Corded Ware was the basic element which formed the Strzyżów culture. However, the fact that no pottery characteristic of the early stage of this culture has been found within the range of the Strzyżów culture is of importance, although such pottery has been found in barrow-graves of the southern part of Western Volhynia and in the neighbourhood of Lwów, situated south of the Strzyżów culture. The only Thuringian amphora (Raciborowice) was of a late type, as were the few beakers.

Some writers emphasize the link between the Strzyżów pottery and the Strzyżów culture as a whole, with pottery of the Cracow-Sandomierz Corded Ware. Pottery similar to that of the latter group was actually found in the settlement of Gródek Nadbużny, being attributable to the early, formative period of the culture. But it seems highly unlikely that this distant group took part in the formation of the Strzyżów culture. In other settlements (Strzyżów) the early cord-decorated pottery was of the common type similar to that found on sand-dunes in the area north of the Strzyżów territory. Some local groups, which bordered on the Strzyżów area to the north, were undoubtedly among the formative elements of that culture.

A special problem is presented by the Raciborowice grave of the Globular Amphora culture (no. 392), already referred to and which yielded the Thuringian amphora of a late type; it indicates that the contact between these two cultures occurred on the Middle Bug before the formation of the Strzyżów culture. However, vessels of this type were known to the people of the sandy soils in the north (Chotivel, no. 117), and this territory formed part of the original area of these vessels.[56] Thuringian amphorae were likewise characteristic of the early stage of the Sub-Carpathian Barrow-graves and have been discussed in Chapter II.

[56] T. Sulimirski, '"Thuringian" Amphorae', *PPS*, vol. XXXI; 1955, pp. 108 ff.

Several barrow-graves were found within the territory of the Strzyżów culture (Map II). They suggest that the Sub-Carpathian Barrow-grave culture either penetrated into this territory or that the custom of raising mounds over the graves of outstanding persons was adopted by a local population influenced by their southern neighbours. Unfortunately, the barrow-graves in the Strzyżów territory were not investigated systematically, and we have no knowledge of the pottery found in them: the battle-axes, flint axes, and other grave goods which have been preserved suggest that the earliest of them date from the second period of the Barrow-grave culture, for they were more or less contemporary with the advancing Globular Amphora culture. This dating is supported by the slab-cist in the Hrubieszów barrow-grave (no. 121). The Sub-Carpathian Barrow-grave culture was undoubtedly one of the contributors to the formation of the Strzyżów culture.

Finally, the contribution in this respect of the Masovian (Dnieper-Elbe) culture must also be taken for granted (Map III). Gardawski[57] emphasizes the very strong links which connected the Strzyżów culture with the latter. The technique used for making vessels was the same in both cultures, both had the same method of brushing the outside of vessels with dry straw or grass, while the clay paste was tempered with a large admixture of thickly crushed pebbles. Both cultures used twisted cord to ornament vessels, and the decoration frequently covered the entire vessel, as well as its bottom; some types of vessels in both are very similar, though this may be the result of independent borrowing from other cultures. The Dnieper-Elbe culture is not, however, supposed to be a local element, since its sites are only known in regions situated further north, on sandy soils, whereas their sites do not occur in the fertile loess country of the East Lublin plateau and/or in West Volhynia.

The later stages of the Strzyżów culture have not been fully explained. It probably lasted only to the beginning of the Middle Bronze Age, and its place was probably occupied by the Trzciniec culture. This is indicated by pottery typical of the Trzciniec culture found in a few pits in the Strzyżów settlement, often mingled with pottery of the Strzyżów culture. A few barrow-graves with pottery of a Trzciniec-Komarów character appear within the Strzyżów territory (Map II). On the other hand, Gardawski[58] claims that there is no evidence of direct links between the pottery of the Strzyżów culture and that of the Trzciniec type. He bases this statement on study of the Trzciniec pottery from other areas, and it may well be that closer study of the Trzciniec-type pottery from the Strzyżów culture area will reveal links between them.

THE EASTERN SECTION (pp. 169 ff.)

A somewhat different development took place in the eastern division of the Strzyżów culture, within the area dominated by the Dubno-Ostróg group of the Globular Amphora culture. Several settlements have been investigated there in recent years, and the stratigraphic evidence in one of these (Zoziv, no. 669) shows that the Strzyżów culture was pre-

[57] Gardawski (op. cit., note 35), p. 316. Id. (op. cit., note 44), p. 127.
[58] Id. (op. cit., note 44), p. 119.

ceded by the Zdovbytsia (Zdolbitsa) culture, another local group of the Corded Ware assemblage.[59]

The Strzyżów culture was a late arrival in this area. The transition was a gradual process; Svešnikov[60] emphasizes that for a time both cultures coexisted in the country before the final replacement of the Zdovbytsia culture by the latter one. In several settlements, huts of both cultures were uncovered side by side (Čudvy, Karayevyči, Zoziv, nos. 647, 651, 669).

Huts of the Zdovbytsia culture were semi-pit-dwellings, oblong or rectangular in plan, with an open hearth at one corner. Typical of the culture were large amphorae with a bulging body, provided with two large handles on the neck. Vessels were decorated mostly by cord-impressed horizontal lines in a manner typical of the Corded Ware cultures, which differed from the style of the Strzyżów pottery. Rows of small triangular stamp impressions and short slanting incisions were also frequent. In each dwelling many flint implements were found, knives, chisels, axes, and also bone awls and points, sometimes small copper ornaments and pins.

The Zdovbytsia culture seems to have been formed during the formative period of the Strzyżów culture further west, and equates with the second period of the Sub-Carpathian barrow-graves (Alpine Bronze Age A-1). It continued to the subsequent period and seems to have been replaced by the Strzyżów culture at a time not earlier than the middle of the Strzyżów period in the west (Alpine Bronze Age A-2).

Many graves of the culture have been uncovered. Skeletons lay in a crouched position in shallow shafts with no lining and with no mounds over the grave. Only a few barrow-graves have been recorded within the limits of the group, all of a late date corresponding with the third stage of the Sub-Carpathian barrow-graves, or of the Middle Bronze Age. Pottery, mainly handled cups, was found in a few graves only, and the attribution of the burials to the two subsequent cultures often meets with difficulties. The most common grave goods were necklaces made of tubular animal bones and perforated animal teeth. In a few graves flint daggers, arrow-heads, stone battle-axes, and copper ornaments (a small ring, an ear-pendant made of flattened wire), and once a bone pin, were found.

The slab-cist graves of the culture (Lipa, no. 175; Zdovbytsia, no. 451) are of special interest. They raise the question of the reciprocal relationship between the Zdovbytsia-Strzyżów culture and the Globular Amphorae, both of which at the same time developed within the same territory.

Potsherds of the Globular Amphora culture were found in settlements of Corded Ware (Nowyj Dwir, no. 555, Fig. 21:6), although they formed only a very small proportion of the bulk of cord-decorated pottery. The few graves of the Globular Amphorae, scattered over a large region imply that, as in West Podolia, persons buried in them did not belong to the indigenous population; they were most probably their conquerors and rulers. It seems likely that Corded Ware (the Strzyżów culture) represents the local population which ultimately absorbed their rulers. The latter, under the influence of the surrounding population, changed their culture and gradually adopted that of their subject people. The slab-cist graves from Zdovbytsia (no. 451) are a good example of such a process. They were obviously burials of the descendants of the Globular Amphora people.

The slab-cists above mentioned evidently occupied an intermediate position between the Globular Amphorae and the Strzyżów culture. Their grave goods connect them and equate them with late cemeteries of the latter culture, whereas slab-cists and the burial ritual were characteristic of the Globular Amphora culture. They correspond with the third stage of that culture in West Podolia. The graves must be attributed, however, to the Strzyżów culture, owing to their association with the settlement of that culture. Huts of the latter lay at a distance of only 14m from the nearest grave.

The Zdovbytsia culture had no roots in the country. Its predecessor was a late survival of the Lublin Painted pottery culture, but the easternmost outposts of the Funnel Beaker culture also reached the area. It seems that elements similar to those which contributed to the formation of the Strzyżów culture further west have taken part in the formation of the Zdovbytsia culture. The terminal date of the Strzyżów culture, or rather of its eastern branch successive to the Zdovbytsia culture, cannot be established yet. At Kostyanets[61] (no. 653) corded ware was found in a settlement of the Trzciniec culture (wrongly considered to be of the 'Komarów' culture), dating from the Middle Bronze Age, but the reciprocal relation, chronological and otherwise, between the different types of pottery of this settlement remains unclear.

FLINT WORKSHOPS

When dealing with the Globular Amphora culture, and the Corded Ware group of the area east of the Styr, the flint workshops must also be considered (nos. 681–721, pp. 209 f.).

It has been emphasized previously that the very fine flint daggers or spear-heads, 'sickles', 'crooked knives', 'saws', sometimes also flint axes, etc., were products of well-trained and experienced artisans who worked in workshops specializing in making single types of these weapons or implements. A considerable number of such workshops have been discovered[62] along the northern edge of the high Podolian plateau, in sites where black 'Volhynian' flint of excellent quality was easily available from natural outcrops. They were mostly situated in the regions south and east of Dubno, and north and west of Krzemieniec, within the territory of the Dubno-Ostróg group of the Globular Amphora culture. A few similar workshops, which dated approximately from the same period, were recorded in East Volhynia, and many more have been found along the Teterev and its tributary, the Usha. They all lay within the territory of the Zhitomir group of the Globular Amphorae.

[59] І. К. Свешніков, Памятки культур шнурової кераміки в басейні р. Устя, Мдапв, vol. 4, 1962, pp. 44 ff.

[60] Ibid., p. 53.

[61] І. К. Свешников, Розкопки в с. Костянці на полі Лиственщина, Арх. Пам., vol. IV, 1952, p. 131, Pl. I:9, 10.

[62] В. Б. Антонович, Труды XI археол. сьезда, 1899, Moscow 1901, vol. I, p. 142. В. Данилевич, Археологічна минувщина Київщини, Kiev 1925, pp. 21 ff. М. Я. Рудинський, Дубно-кременецька палеолітична експедиція, Арх. Пам., vol. IV, 1952, p. 144. J. Bryk, *Kultury epoki kamiennej na wydmach zachodniej części południowego Wołynia*, Lwów 1928. B. Janusz, *Zabytki przedhistoryczne Galicyi Wschodniej*, Lwów 1918, pp. 82 ff., 158 ff., 206 ff., 278 ff., 292.

The name of the 'Bug flint industry' has been given by L. Kozłowski[63] to the products of these workshops, and this has been generally accepted. A special flint technique was employed in the working of these objects which, according to this author, derived from the 'Baltic flint industry' proper to the regions situated further north, up to the Baltic; the latter industry was in turn closely related to that of the Scandinavian and North-West European late Stone Age. Other scholars[64] also emphasize that the Bug flint industry was closely related to that of North-Western Europe, and this fact seems undeniable.

The beginning of the Bug flint industry has been dated by L. Kozłowski as the second period of the Neolithic (according to Montelius). In fact, no flints worked in the Bug technique, nor typical of that industry, have been found in the remains either of the Lublin Painted pottery culture or of the early Tripolyan culture.[65] The earliest appear in the settlements of the Funnel Beakers.

The above fact suggests that the roots of the Bug flint technique lay somewhere west of our territory, probably in the northern part of Central Europe or in North-Western Europe. Once introduced in our area by the newcomers of the Funnel Beaker culture, it began an independent development here, fostered by the profusion of the local flint of excellent quality. However, it is only after the establishment of special workshops that the finest products of this industry began to appear, being then distributed over a very wide area.

It is highly probable that the industrial exploitation of the flint deposits and the establishment of the workshops did not start until after the arrival of the Globular Amphorae. No flint workshops are datable as prior to the appearance of the Globular Amphora culture in this region; this was the district in which several slab-cist graves of the Dubno-Ostróg group of that culture were found (Map v). The bearers of this culture seem to have been closely associated with trade in flint in our area[66] while employing local artisans of a different stock and culture in their workshops. Their connection with the appearance of flint axes and other flint implements in Moldavia has been pointed out by A. Florescu.[67]

The above conclusions are also supported by a study of the pottery. Investigations of a number of workshops have revealed that Corded Ware was found rarely there; occasionally pottery attributable to the Middle Bronze Age 'Komarów' culture appeared, but the bulk of pottery was of a type which L. Kozłowski[68] and J. Bryk[69] considered to belong to the 'Bug culture' and they connected it with the 'comb pottery' of the Baltic area. M. Ia. Rudynskyi[70] dated this pottery as of later periods, that is, the Late Bronze Age and Early Iron Age. Pottery of the same type was also found in a series of sites in this area unconnected with the workshops. No earlier pottery was found in the region concerned.

A closer study of the above pottery reveals that in its structure, its raised decoration, and some other features, it corresponds to some extent with the Funnel Beakers; its incised decorative patterns call to mind those typical of the Globular Amphora culture. This pottery was also related to that of the Wysocko culture of the Late Bronze Age and Early Iron Age. All these circumstances indicate that the flint workshops were set up in the Early Bronze Age; they must have existed for a considerable span of time, most probably up to the Early Iron Age.

It is difficult to establish who the artisans were who worked in the workshops. It has been already mentioned that no pottery was found in this region which could be dated as the early part of the Neolithic. It seems therefore that during that period the country was either peopled by some tribes who still followed the mesolithic way of life and traditions, or was uninhabited. The climatic conditions of the Early Neolithic, with its hot and dry climate, were evidently not favourable for vegetation on sandy soils and made them inhospitable. Only during the later part of the Neolithic did some tribes advance here from the north; their pottery suggests that they must have been affected by the Funnel Beaker agriculturalists whose small groups advanced eastwards nearly up to the Horyn.

Finally, stone battle-axes of 'Fatyanovo' type should be mentioned. These axes were probably manufactured mainly somewhere near Ovruch, in the area where serpentine is available, of the stone variety of which they were almost exclusively made. They were also made in some other parts of the country, in particular in the region of Dubno, e.g. at Mała Moszczanica[71] where cones produced during the manufacture of stone shaft-hole axes were found in larger quantities. Such workshops seem to have been of an earlier date than those specializing in the manufacture of flint artifacts. They all lay likewise within the territory occupied by the eastern Globular Amphorae, the Dubno-Ostróg, and the Zhitomir groups respectively.

THE HOARD FROM STUBŁO

Some attention should be given to the bronze hoard from Stubło in Volhynia, already mentioned in Chapter IV, found in the area of the Dubno-Ostróg group of the Globular Amphora culture. It was dealt with by W. Antoniewicz,[72] who pointed to its connections with the bronze industry of the Hungarian Plain and Transilvania and considered it to be of Danubo-Carpathian origin. He dated it as the Unetice period, the Early Bronze Age. It is attributable to the late stage of the Globular Amphora culture.

The hoard consisted of two bronze shaft-hole axes, several bracelets, ten ear-pendants of 'Stubło' type, and of three other ornaments, made of thin bronze plaque or sheet (no. 745).

Bronze ornaments corresponding to those which formed part of the hoard have been found in several sites within the western part of the Territory. The pendants of 'Stubło' type,

[63] Kozłowski (op. cit., note 33), pp. 82 ff.

[64] М. Я. Рудинський, Деякі підсумки та ближчі завдання палетнологічних вивчень у межах УСРР, Антропологія, vol. iv, Kiev 1930, pp. 176 f.

[65] А. Флореску, К вопросу о кремневых топорах в Молдове, *Dacia*, vol. NS iii, Bucureşti 1959, p. 94.

[66] Topics connected with the trade in flint were discussed by me in a separate article: T. Sulimirski, 'Remarks Concerning the Distribution of Some Varieties of Flint in Poland', *Światowit*, vol. xxiii, 1960, pp. 299 ff.

[67] Op. cit., note 65, pp. 95 ff.

[68] Kozłowski (op. cit., note 32), p. 93.

[69] Bryk (op. cit., note 62), pp. 48 ff., Pl. ix.

[70] Рудинський (op. cit., note 62), pp. 143 f.

[71] A. Pawłowski, 'Wykopaliska moszczanickie', *Światowit*, vol. xvi, 1934–5, pp. 175 ff.

[72] W. Antoniewicz, 'Der in Stubło in Wolhynien aufgefundene Bronzeschatz', *ESA*, vol. iv, 1929, pp. 135 ff., Figs. 1–19.

with one end widened, have been already dealt with in Chapter II (Fig. 19:1–4, 10). Volhynian specimens were excavated in two slab-cist graves (Gródek-Równe, no. 429, Stadniki, no. 446) and in the flat cemetery of the Strzyżów culture at Torczyn (no. 623). They seem to be of West Slovakian origin or modelled on West Slovakian prototypes. The bracelets, all tapering towards the terminals, represent a common Unetice type. Specimens of exactly the same type were excavated in barrow-graves Balice VII (no. 1, Fig. 19:17) and Załukiew (no. 58, Fig. 19:9).

Shaft-hole axes forming part of the hoard differ from each other. One of these represents a very common type widespread over the whole of the southern part of East Europe, from the Urals and the Caucasus up to the Carpathians, during the middle of the second millennium B.C.[73] Moulds for casting them were also found there, but likewise on the other side of the Carpathians, in the eastern part of the Hungarian Plain; one of the latter found in Stratum XIII at Pecica, and another one at Toszeg B-II, were nearly identical with that from Stubło; both dated as Reinecke's Bronze Age period A-2, or even period B or C.[74]

Similar axes were found in our area at Komarów (Fig. 35:8) and at Słoboda Rungurska near Kołomyja[75] close to the approaches to a convenient Carpathian pass, about eighty kilometres south-east of Komarów. Another specimen was found by the late C. Ambrojevici in the remains of the Tripolyan settlement at Darabani on the Dniester near Hotin (Fig. 35:6); this site lies about one hundred kilometres east of the former. A mould for casting such axes is said to have been found on the other (northern) side of the Dniester, near Kamenets Podolskii.[76]

The other axe of the Stubło hoard, with a drooping, curved blade, has no counterparts on the other side of the Carpathians. Antoniewicz pointed out its similarity to the Fatyanovo stone battle-axes, and A. Yessen[77] regarded this axe as being most probably of Caucasian origin. Bronze axes of a similar type, although not identical, were common in the pre-Koban period in the central part of the Caucasian highland, and specimens from the cemeteries from Faskau and Kumbulta have been dated by M. Gimbutas[78] as about 1400 B.C. E. I. Krupnov[79] dates these cemeteries as the 'second half of the second millennium B.C.', i.e. about 1400–1200 B.C. Very similar axes found in the North-Western Caucasus were dated by Yessen[80] as the end of the second millennium B.C.

The axe from Stubło was not the only specimen of Caucasian origin or type found within our area. Another was the bronze ornament with cast 'corded' ornament (Plate 9:13) excavated in barrow-grave 4 at Ostapie (no. 213) in the northern part of West Podolia, about 120 kilometres south of Stubło; it was dealt with in Chapter II. It is of interest to note that the gold ear-pendant, probably of Irish origin (Plate 8:1) from a barrow-grave at Rusiłów (no. 84) was found at the same distance of 120 kilometres from Stubło to the south-west, as at Ostapie to the south-east. These finds imply that our area had commercial connections at that time with very distant countries both to the east and west.

The hoard from Stubło dated from the final stage of the early Bronze Age within our area. The two barrow-graves mentioned above belonged to the third period of the Barrow-grave culture. All ear-pendants of Stubło type (Fig. 19:1–4, 10) were found either in barrow-graves of the third period of their culture (Gwoździec Stary II, no. 101), or in late slab-cist graves (Stadniki, no. 446, Gródek-Równe, no. 429) in which no more pottery was excavated typical of the Globular Amphora culture. The late date of the grave of the Strzyżów culture at Torczyn, in which Stubło ear-pendants were found, is indicated by the associated flint spear-heads or daggers. The axe of the 'Hungaro-East-European' type, places the Stubło hoard in Reinecke's Bronze Age period A-2 or even period B, and the other axe of Caucasian origin confirms this date.

A few more stray bronze objects found north of the Carpathians, dating from the Early Bronze Age, deserve mention (pp. 210 f., nos. 733–744). One of these was a flanged bronze axe found on a sand-dune at Chilczyce near Złoczów (Fig. 19:16). Kozłowski[81] points out that similar specimens were found in the Hungarian Plain in hoards, also dating from later periods. Two small slightly flanged bronze axes, similar to each other, nearly rectangular in shape, were found at Severynivtsi near Kemenets Podolskii[82] and at Mamajestie in the Bucovina[83] respectively; both were probably connected with the Tripolye culture. Another axe (of copper?), probably of the early stage of the Early Bronze Age, was found at Bussowo near Chełm, within the area of the Hrubieszów group of the Globular Amphora culture. S. Nosek[84] attributed it to the Mierzanowice culture. It was very similar to a series of axes from Greater Poland[85] and seems to have been brought into our area from North-Western Poland.

Finally, the shaft-hole copper axe from Sapohów, district of Stanisławów, should be mentioned (Fig. 35:10), from a village situated close to that of Komarów. The axe was erroneously published by Antoniewicz[86] as originating from Komarów. It was presumably of Transilvanian origin and may be dated as the Early Bronze Age.

[73] M. Gimbutas, 'Middle Ural Sites and the Chronology of Northern Eurasia', *PPS*, vol. XXIV, 1958, pp. 125 f., Fig. 4.

[74] V. Milojčić, 'Zur Frage der Chronologie der frühen und mittleren Bronzezeit in Ostungarn., *Congrès Internat. de Sciences Préhistoriques*, Zürich 1950, pp. 268 ff., Figs. 24:4; 32:15. R. Pittioni, *Urgeschichte des österreichischen Raumes*, Wien 1954, p. 354, Fig. 251. S. Foltiny, 'Bemerkungen zur Chronologie der Bronzezeit Ungarns', *Germania*, vol. 38, 1960, p. 347.

[75] M. Much, *Die Kupferzeit in Europa*, 2nd ed., Jena 1893, p. 45, Figs. 40, 41.

[76] A. M. Tallgren, 'La Pontide préscythique', *ESA*, vol. II, 1926, p. 354, Fig. 251.

[77] А. А. Йессен, Греческая колонизация северного Причерноморья, Leningrad 1947, p. 23, n. 4.

[78] M. Gimbutas, 'Borodino, Seima and their Contemporaries', *PPS*, vol. XXII, 1956, p. 148, Figs. 2:2, 9, 13.

[79] Е. И. Крупнов, Материалы по археологии Северной Осетии докобанского периода, МИА, no. 23, 1953, pp. 43 ff., Fig. 27.

[80] А. А. Йессен, Прикубанский очаг металлургии и металлообработки в конце медно-бронзового века, МИА, no. 23, 1953, pp. 84 f., Figs. 8, 9.

[81] L. Kozłowski, *Wczesna, starsza i środkowa epoka bronzu w Polsce*, Lwów 1928, p. 37.

[82] Before the Second World War in the Museum at Kamenets Podolskii.

[83] Natur-Historisches Museum, Vienna, no. 36866.

[84] Nosek (op. cit., note 12: 1957), p. 256, Pl. XX:7.

[85] A. Knapowska-Mikołajczykowa, 'Wczesny okres epoki brązu w Wielkopolsce', *FAP*, vol. VII, 1957, Figs. 1, 15, 61g, 73, 78.

[86] W. Antoniewicz, *Archeologia Polski*, Warszawa 1928, Pl. XIV. The axe is at the State Archaeological Museum in Warsaw.

CHAPTER VI

North Ukrainian Cultures

THE GORODSK CULTURE
(Map VII) (pp. 211 f.)

NEOLITHIC and Early Bronze Age remains in the territory east of the Strzyżów culture and east of the Sluch, have been considered to be Tripolyan by many authors, in particular by T. S. Passek.[1] They form two distinct groups. Those in the western section of the area have usually been called the 'Gorodsk group' (Map VII), after the fortified settlement at Horodsk (Gorodsk in Russian) on the Teterev; sometimes the name 'Gorodsk-Kolodiazhne' or 'Gorodsk-Raiki' is used for the group. The eastern remains, from the neighbourhood of Kiev chiefly east of the Dnieper, consist of a few cremation cemeteries of Sofiivka type (Map VI) and of a number of settlements similar to those of Gorodsk type; the chief representative of the latter is the settlement at Evminka on the Desna, north-east of Kiev (Map VII). We shall call this group the 'Sofiivka-Evminka group'; the region where it appears lies entirely outside the Territory with which we are concerned.

At least twelve settlements have been attributed to the Gorodsk culture. They lie mainly on fertile loess soils within an area nearly 150 kilometres square extending north of the Upper Boh, east of the Sluch, and over the basin of the Upper Teterev and the Upper Ross. Only a single settlement, Pečora on the Middle Boh, is isolated about 100 kilometres south of the sites above named (nos. 746–756, 761).

Although the remains have often been dealt with, including detailed descriptions in archaeological publications,[2] nevertheless controversial opinions have been expressed as to their character. Some authors, e.g. Passek, consider that they belong to the Tripolye culture and represent the latest stage of its development, termed period C-2. Others, among whom are the investigators of the settlement at Gorodsk,[3] are of the opinion that it was a distinct culture evolved under a strong Tripolyan influence.

The question whether the above remains were 'Tripolyan' or formed part of a distinct 'Gorodsk' culture is of no particular importance for our study. In all sites the non-Tripolyan elements undeniably prevail over those typical of the Tripolye culture, and the further north the settlements lie the less they exhibit Tripolyan features. Huts of *ploščadka* type, characteristic of the Tripolye culture, appeared only on sites in the southern part of the Gorodsk territory, whereas huts further north were of a different type. Eighty to ninety per cent of the pottery in southern sites was non-Tripolyan,[4] but in the northernmost settlement, at Gorodsk itself,[5] Tripolyan painted ware formed only five per cent of the whole pottery excavated.

The Gorodsk group was evidently a hybrid. The remains may be regarded as Tripolyan, if the character of the settlements and the economy of their inhabitants are considered to be the decisive factors for their classification. But if pottery has to be the chief indicator in this respect, this was definitely a distinct culture although formed under a strong Tripolyan influence. However, for the sake of convenience we shall apply here the term of the 'Gorodsk culture' to these remains.

The Tripolye culture was one of the contributors in the formation of the Gorodsk culture. The other one was the local branch of the Corded Ware which will be dealt with later.

Controversial views have been expressed as to the chronology of the Gorodsk culture. Most authors following Passek consider the remains to be characteristic of the latest Tripolyan period C-2. But in discussing these topics one has always to bear in mind that the remains of the Gorodsk type extend over an area within which no other Tripolyan remains whatever have been found: Tripolyan settlements of the alleged preceding period C-1 lay exclusively outside that area (Map VII). There is no Tripolyan substratum out of which the Gorodsk or C-2 type remains could have evolved locally, and there are no signs of such an evolution in the areas over which extend remains of type C-1. Neither is there any stratigraphical evidence implying the chronological succession of remains of type C-2 to those of type C-1. In the stratified settlement at Pečora on the Boh,[6] remains of Gorodsk (or C-2) type lay immediately over those considered to belong to period A or B-1.

On the other hand, ample evidence exists supporting the equation of the Gorodsk culture with the Tripolyan remains

[1] Т. С. Пассек, Периодизация трипольских поселений, МИА, no. 10, 1949, pp. 157 ff. Id., 'Problème de l'Enéolithique du Sud-Ouest de l'Europe orientale', *L'Europe à la fin de l'age de la pierre*, Praha 1961, pp. 152 ff.

[2] Id., 1949. Е. Ф. Лагодовска, Войцеховское позднетрипольское поселение, Ксиак, no. 3, 1954, pp. 86 ff. Id., Пізнотрипільське поселення у с. Сандраках, Арх. Пам., vol. VI, 1956, pp. 118 ff. О. Ф. Лагодовська and Ю. Захарук, Нові дослідження войцехівського могильника, Арх. Пам., vol. VI, 1956, p. 70. П. Курінний, Раєцька могила на Бардичівщині, Коротке звідомлення за 1926 р, Kiev 1927, pp. 71 ff. М. Л. Макаревич, Трипільське поселення біля с. Паволочі, Арх. Пам., vol. IV, 1952, pp. 96 ff. М. М. Шмаглій, Кераміка поселень городського типу, Археологія Kiev, vol. XIII, 1961, pp. 20 ff. Ю. М. Захарук, Пізньотрипільське поселення у верхів'ях р. Случі, Арх. Пам., vol. VI, 1956, pp. 130 ff.

[3] Є. Ю. Кричевський, Поселення в Городську (1937), Трипільська культура, vol. I, Kiev 1940, pp. 383 ff. В. П. Петров, Поселення в Городську (1936), Трипільська культура, vol. I, Kiev 1940, pp. 339 ff.

[4] Шмаглій (op. cit., note 2), pp. 23 ff.

[5] Works cited in note 3.

[6] К. К. Черныш, Многослойны памятник у с. Печоры на Южном Буже, Археологический сборник, no. 1, Leningrad 1959, pp. 166 ff.

characteristic of period C-1. Similarities in the shape and in the decorative patterns of the Gorodsk pottery with those characteristic of Tripolyan C-1 and even B-2 ware have been emphasized although unreasonably interpreted as of a posterior date.[7] Divergences in the decorative style which differentiate the Gorodsk painted ware from that of the genuine Tripolyan ware of period C-1 have no chronological significance. They represent (a) either a local development of the culture of the expanding Tripolyan settlers of period B-2 or early C-1 who found themselves in a different environment; or (b) they mark an evolution of the culture of the local population under the influence, possibly with a small admixture, of the neighbouring Tripolyans of the above periods.

Connections with several coeval western cultures are explicitly confirmed: those with the Funnel Beakers of the Gródek Nadbużny group by painted ware akin to that of Gorodsk type found in the settlements of the latter group (Map IV) and by clay models of stone shaft-hole axes with a nearly spherical butt excavated at Troyaniv and Novo-Čortorya;[8] similar clay models were found in the settlements of Gródek Nadbużny, Zimno and Grzybowice Małe.[9] Knee-shaped lugs on a series of large amphorae[10] were characteristic of the Lublin Painted pottery culture. Of special interest are amphorae (Kolodiazhne, Novo-Čortorya[11]) which have a short cylindrical neck and a large body provided with two lugs; they are strikingly reminiscent of the Thuringian amphorae and undoubtedly modelled on them, although none was decorated; they equate the Gorodsk culture with the second stage of the Sub-Carpathian barrow-graves. Likewise of importance are potsherds characteristic of the Globular Amphora culture found among the remains of the Gorodsk culture (Gorodsk, Voytsekhivka[12]) and a double-lugged beaker at Troyaniv;[13] slab-cist graves were uncovered at Voytsekhivka and Kolodiazhne (nos. 460, 453), but they mostly appear west and north of the Gorodsk territory. Both cultures only slightly overlapped in the border areas (Maps V and VII).

EAST VOLHYNIAN-POLESIAN CORDED WARE

The bulk of the Gorodsk pottery consisted of cord-decorated ware which implies a considerable, if not decisive, share of Corded Ware assemblage in the formation of the culture. Several features distinguish this pottery from that of kindred groups, e.g. of the Strzyżów culture or the common Central European Corded Ware. Related to it, although differing in many respects, was the cord-decorated pottery of the Usatovo culture which will be dealt with in Chapter 7. Furthermore, an almost identical cord-decorated ware was found in a number of late Tripolyan settlements in West Podolia (Fig. 5)[14] and Moldavia;[15] it must have been left by some East Volhynian (Gorodsk) immigrants (nos. 757–763).

Corded ware of the same or of a closely related type was likewise found further north in sites on the sandy soils of East Volhynia, Polesia and also north of the Pripet, in Byelorussia (Map VII). The reconstruction of the mostly fragmentary pots found there was seldom practicable but the clue to the identity of this pottery is given by the very distinctive feature of its decorative style represented by semicircular, crescent-like, or 'horse-shoe', impressions made with plaited-cord stamps. This ornament does not appear on Western or Central European corded ware, but was common in the Gorodsk and Usatovo cultures. These decorative patterns were found within the whole territory described above, up to the source of the Dnieper in the north-east,[16] or in sites along the whole course of the Pripet[17] in the west. This geographical distribution implies the northern derivation of the above decorative patterns and, by implication, the northern derivation of the Gorodsk corded ware itself.

All the sites above, including those on East Volhynian sandy soils north of the settlements of Gorodsk type, e.g. the site at Kalenske on the Mostva,[18] cannot be considered to be 'late Tripolyan' or to belong to the Gorodsk culture. No Tripolyan features appear in their remains and both habitat and economy of the people were different from those of the inhabitants of the Gorodsk settlements. They are attributable to the Baltic-Byelorussian Corded Ware described by A. Äyräpää;[19] they lie within the blank area marked on the maps by V. G. Childe of his period III.[20] But this was also the territory of the Masovian, or Dnieper-Elbe culture of the preceding period dealt with in Chapter V (Map III); the firm association of the cord-decorated pottery with Masovian ware in the sites of this area suggests the Masovian parentage of Corded Ware.

In the southern portion of the above territory another type of late Neolithic and Early Bronze Age remains was also found, the Zhitomir group of Globular Amphorae (Map V). These, namely slab-cist graves, were confined to the fertile loess patches scattered over the country, but potsherds typical of the Globular Amphorae were found in a number of sites of the Corded Ware, particularly along the Pripet (nos. 554, 560, 561).[21] They imply close connections between the two cultures, though to which of them is to be given the priority of appearance in the country under review remains questionable.

[7] Пассек (op. cit., note 1: 1949), pp. 161 ff. Id., Ксиимк, no. XIV, 1947, pp. 153 ff. Шмаглій (op. cit., note 2), pp. 35 ff.

[8] Захарук (op. cit., note 2), p. 133. Troyaniv: at the Archaeological Institute of the Ukrainian Academy in Kiev.

[9] Захарук, loc. cit., note 8. М. Ю. Смішко and М. А. Пелещишин, Поселення культури лійчастого посуду в с. Малі Грибовиці, Мдапв, vol. 4, 1962, pp. 35, 41 ff., Pl. IV:17, 18.

[10] Ibid. (1962), Pl. I:6. Макаревич (op. cit., note 2), Pl. I:1. Кричевський (op. cit., note 3), Fig. 156. Шмаглій (op. cit., note 2), Pl. I:6.

[11] Пассек (op. cit., note 1: 1949), Fig. 88:8. Захарук (op. cit., note 2), Pl. I:7.

[12] Лагодовська and Захарук (op. cit., note 2), p. 70. Кричевський (op. cit., note 3), p. 401, Fig. 98.

[13] At the Archaeological Institute of the Ukrainian Academy in Kiev.

[14] E.g. Kasperowce near Zaleszczyki, Lipniki site. Pottery at the Natur-Historisches Museum, Vienna, nos. 49722–65; 49848–51.

[15] E.g. at Horodiştea on the Pruth: H. Dumitrescu, *Dacia*, vol. IX–X, 1945, pp. 127 ff.

[16] E.g. Mokhov near the junction of the Sozha with the Dnieper: И. И. Артеменко, Ксиимк, no. 78, 1960, p. 39, Fig. 11:11.

[17] Ю. В. Кухаренко, Первобыные памятники на территории Полесья, Археология СССР (Б 1–18), Moscow 1962, Pls. IV:1, 4, 8, 10; V:4, 11.

[18] І. Ф. Левицький, Арх. Пам., vol. IV, 1952, pp. 70 ff.

[19] A. Äyräpää, 'Die Streitaxtkulturen in Russland, *EAS*, vol. VIII, 1933, pp. 109 ff.

[20] V. G. Childe, 'The Dawn of European Civilisation', 5th ed., London 1950, p. 343, Map III.

[21] Кухаренко (op. cit., note 17), Pls. IV:2; V:6, 7; VI:6.

No stratigraphical evidence is available in this respect. Conditions in the East Prussian peat-bogs[22] point to the early date of Corded Ware which there preceded the Globular Amphorae. The position in a few other sites investigated in our area seems to suggest a similar chronological sequence.

Three superimposed occupation layers have been distinguished in the peat-bog site on the River Mostva at Kalenske near Korosten (no. 597) in East Volhynia mentioned above. The earliest was mesolithic. The next one yielded comb-pricked pottery and was considered to be typical of the 'Dnieper-Desna' culture by D. I. Telegin,[23] and was included in the Dnieper-Elbe culture by A. Gardawski.[24] Pottery found in the lower part of the upper layer (layer 3) is considered to be similar to that of the Gorodsk culture and a few sherds call to mind Tripolyan kitchen ware characteristic of period C-1. Pottery found in the upper part of this layer already exhibits features characteristic of the Trzciniec culture of the Middle Bronze Age; also excavated there were flat-bottomed pots the whole surface of which was decorated. Their ornament, consisting of horizontal rows of alternating oblique, deep stamped strokes and a zigzag line made by the same stamp, ran around the middle of the body;[25] the latter motif, the stamp, and the manner in which the ornament was executed was characteristic of the Globular Amphora culture.

At Piščane-Narodyči (no. 567), a site north of the former, two cremation cemeteries on a sand-dune were investigated. Urns of cemetery I were a typical Trzciniec ware of the Middle Bronze Age (Fig. 33:8); the decorative patterns of a few of these vessels include motifs very characteristic of the Volhynian branch of the Globular Amphorae and were evidently either borrowed or inherited from that culture,[26] which points to its relatively late date. Cemetery II was of an earlier date. There a flanged bronze celt was found with potsherds having plaited-cord impressions proper either to the Gorodsk culture, or to the Corded Ware of the sites north of it;[27] no features proper to the Globular Amphora culture were found there.

Connections with the Strzyżów culture are reflected in the western part of the Corded Ware group under review, and in particular in the pottery of the sites at Polesia in the southern part of Chwojanka and Majdan Mokwinski north-east of Kostopol (nos. 646, 654)[28] dealt with in the preceding chapter. Pottery was to some extent similar to that of the Strzyżów culture, but as pointed out by E. G. Kričevskii,[29] it was likewise closely related to that of the Gorodsk culture; crescent-like impressions made by plaited cord and 'horseshoe' patterns connect it with the latter and the whole Corded Ware group discussed in this paragraph.

THE EVMINKA-SOFIIVKA GROUP
(Maps VI, VII)

Settlements similar to those of the Gorodsk culture were also found further east,[30] mainly east of the Dnieper, outside the territory of our concern; only a few sites, in Kiev and in the close vicinity of that city, lay west of the river. The settlements of Kirillovskaya and Syrets in Kiev and at Evminka on the Desna, about forty kilometres north-east of Kiev, are among the best known, and the settlement at Lukaši, about fifty kilometres east of Kiev, was the easternmost of the group. All sites lay on sandy soils.

The bulk of the pottery found in these settlements was a local ware, and only a fraction of it, about 5 to 10 per cent of the total excavated, was a kind of Tripolyan painted or kitchen ware. In a few cases huts of Tripolyan *ploščadka* type were uncovered. Tripolyan features enabled the scholars concerned to attribute the sites to the Tripolye culture; the sites are considered to represent the latest stage in its development of period C-2, similar to the Gorodsk culture with which they equated.

However, as in the Gorodsk group, there is no stratigraphical evidence for the late date of the remains above. Settlements of Evminka type extended over an area within which no earlier Tripolyan remains were found. In discussing these remains both Passek and Kričevskii[31] admitted their close resemblance to, and connections with, the pottery characteristic of Tripolyan settlements south of Kiev of period C-1 and even B-2; the settlements of the Evminka group evidently could be equated with these. Their position is shown in Table 17.

Non-Tripolyan pottery of Evminka settlements, being connected with pottery of the local culture of the preceding period, differs from that of the Gorodsk group. The Evminka group must have been formed under the impact of the Tripolye culture in similar conditions to those which affected the Gorodsk culture; the different background resulted in the difference between the two similar and kindred groups. Connections with the Catacomb culture, unknown in the Gorodsk group, have been emphasized, but here no elements of the Globular Amphora culture seem to appear. Exceptions were a few Globular Amphora potsherds found in the northernmost settlement of the group, at Černyn on the eastern bank of the Dnieper (no. 547) (Map V).[32]

In the same group may be included cremation cemeteries found within the territory of the Evminka settlements. They have been called of the 'Sofiivka' type, after a cemetery investigated in the vicinity of Kiev.[33] Two of the three cemeteries of this type known so far, lay on sandy soils east of the Dnieper.

[22] H. Gross, 'Ergebnisse der moorgeologischen Untersuchungen der vorgeschichtlichen Dörfer im Zedmar-Bruch', *Nachrichtenblatt f. deutsche Vorzeit*, vol. 14, Leipzig 1938.

[23] Д. Я. Телегін, Неолітичні поселення лісостепового лівобережжя і полісся України, Археологія-Kiev, vol. XI, 1957, pp. 70 ff.

[24] A. Gardawski, 'Zagadnienie kultury "ceramiki grzebykowej" w Polsce', *W.A.*, vol. XXV, 1958, pp. 287 ff.

[25] Левицький (op. cit., note 18), Fig. 2.

[26] I. Левицький, Стація в ур. Пішаному біля Народич, Антропологія, vol. IV, Kiev 1930, pp. 191 ff., 227 ff., Fig. 38:6, 7.

[27] Ibid., pp. 231 ff., Fig. 39.

[28] T. Sulimirski, 'O poleskiej praojczyźnie Słowian', *ZOW*, vol. XIV, 1939, pp. 33 ff. Id., *Polska przedhistoryczna*, part II, London 1957–9, pp. 241 f., Fig. 61.

[29] Е. Ю. Кричевский, Ксиикм, no. 3, 1940, p. 12.

[30] Пассек (op. cit., note 1: 1949), pp. 177 ff. Ю. М. Захарук, Поселення софіївського типу в околицях Києва, Арх. Пам., vol. VI, 1956, pp. 111 ff.

[31] Works cited in note 7.

[32] С. С. Березанська, Археологія-Kiev, vol. XII, 1961, pp. 102 ff., Fig. 2:3.

[33] Ю. М. Захарук, Софіївський тілопальний могильних, Арх. Пам., vol. IV, 1952, pp. 112 ff. I. М. Самойловський, Арх. Пам., vol. IV, 1952, p. 121. В. М. Даниленко and М. Л. Макаревич,

TABLE 17. Correlation of North Ukrainian cultures

	Tripolyan sites C-1			Gorodsk culture								North Volhynian Corded Ware			Evminka and Sofiivka groups				
	Khalepye B	Kolomiščyna I	Stena	Voytsekhivka	Kolodiazhne	Novo-Čortorya	Troyaniv	Gorodsk	Pavoloč	Sandraki	Pečora	Mostva upper layer	Majdan Mokwiński	Pripet-Polesie sites	Evminka	Lukaši	Sofiivka	Červonyi Khutor	Černyn
Tripolyan B-2 elements					×											×			
Tripolyan C-1 elements	×	×	×	×	×		×	×		×		×			×	×			
Thuringian amphora elements		×			×	×											×	×	×
Copper objects	×			×			×										×	×	×
Globular Amphora sherds or ornament	×	×		×				×				×							
Amphorae with knee-shaped lugs			×			×	×	×	×										
Funnel Beaker elements (clay shaft-hole axes)						×	×												
Masovian pottery						×		×						×					
Crescent-like or horse-shoe decorative patterns								×			×		×	×			×		

Pottery in the Sofiivka cemeteries, including the urns, was a kind of Tripolyan ware and was either undecorated or had a cord-impressed ornament. The cemeteries have been attributed to the Tripolye culture and dated to period C-2. Copper (or bronze) weapons, especially daggers, and ornaments—including a blue glass bead found in the cemetery of Sofiivka[34]—equate the group with the Alpine Bronze Age A-1 and A-2, the middle of the second millennium B.C.

Of interest for our study are a number of urns which were evidently modelled on the Thuringian amphorae; some of these are nearly replicas of type IIa (Fig. 1:7, 9).[35] The group seems to have developed parallel to the end of the second and the third periods of the Sub-Carpathian Barrow-graves.

THE MIDDLE DNIEPER CULTURE
(Map x) pp. 183 ff.)

Another group of Late Neolithic and Early Bronze Age remains, which must be discussed here, are barrow-graves found in the black-earth (chernozem) region bordering to the south-east on the territory of the Gorodsk culture. In the earlier archaeological literature the terms 'Jackowica group'[36] or 'Kiev group of Corded Ware'[37] have been applied to this group of remains, but the name 'Middle Dnieper culture' proposed by Passek[38] has now been generally accepted.

There is no general agreement as to the extent, chronology, or origin of the 'Middle Dnieper culture'. According to Passek, it consisted of three groups of remains. Two of these, the 'Stretovka' and 'Gatnoe' groups, were formed of barrow-graves extending over the black-earth area south-west of Kiev in the forest steppe zone. They are looked upon as two consecutive stages in the development of the culture. Sites of the third group, called the Dnieper-Desna group, over eighty of which have been recorded, so far,[39] were scattered over a wide territory north of Kiev, mainly in Byelorussia,

Червонохутірський могильник мідного віку з трупоспаленням, Арх. Пам., vol. VI, 1956, pp. 92 ff. В. І. Канівець, Могильник епохи міді біля с. Чернина на Київщині, Арх. Пам., vol. VIII, 1956, pp. 99 ff. M. Gimbutas, *The Prehistory of Eastern Europe*, part I, Cambridge (Mass.), 1956, pp. 109 ff., Fig. 61.

[34] Т. Б. Попова, Племена катакомбной культуры, Труды ГИМ, no. 24, Moscow 1955, p. 129, n. 1.

[35] Захарук (op note cit., 33), Pl. III:2, 6. Канівець (op. cit., note 33), Pl. II:9, 11, 12.

[36] J. Borkovśkyj, 'Šnurová keramika na Ukrajině', *Obzor Praehistorický*, vol. IX, Praha 1930–1, pp. 70 ff.

[37] Äyräpää (op. cit., note 19), pp. 129 ff.

[38] Т. С. Пассек, К вопросу о среднеднепровской культуре, Ксиимк, no. XVI, 1947, pp. 34 ff.

[39] И. И. Артеменко, Среднеднепровская культура, Сов. Арх., vol. 1963–2, pp. 12 ff., Fig. 1 (map).

along the Upper Dnieper and its tributaries, especially the Sozh north of Gomel.

The Dnieper-Desna group consisted chiefly of settlements (encampments) and of a number of 'flat' graves. A few barrow-graves were recorded, mostly on the Desna, on the border of the forest steppe zone (the black-earth region); in one of these, at Rečitsa, near Briansk,[40] a genuine 'Thuringian' amphora was excavated. A group of barrow-graves were also investigated near Gomel;[41] they were all of a relatively late date and can be equated partly with the second, but mainly with the third period of the Sub-Carpathian Barrow-grave culture. Bronze (copper) shaft-hole axes of 'Hungarian' or Caucasian origin, double-spiral pendants, a socketed bronze spear-head and faience beads excavated in these burials put their date after 1500 B.C.

Remains of the Dnieper-Desna group, which lay outside the Territory, will not be discussed. These sites lay all within the forest zone, the area with an ecological environment very different from that in which barrow-graves of the Middle Dnieper culture were found. There is also a marked difference in the shape and in other particulars of vessels between the remains of the Dnieper-Desna sites on the one hand and those of the Kiev group and of the loess country east of the Desna on the other. It does not seem justifiable, therefore, to combine all these remains into a single cultural unit. The Dnieper-Desna group formed an independent culture different from the Middle Dnieper culture of the country south and south-west of Kiev.[42]

Neither does there seem to be any justification for including in the Middle Dnieper culture a few settlement-sites in the region of the Dnieper Rapids, situated in the steppe zone at a distance of over 250km from the nearest barrow-grave cemetery of the Kiev group, as Briusov[43] has proposed. Inspection of the distribution map of the culture, as drawn by Briusov, illustrates how artificial such a conception is.

The term 'Middle Dnieper culture' will be applied here only to the barrow-graves of the black-earth region south-west of Kiev. All Neolithic and Bronze Age barrow-graves investigated within that area have been included here, in addition to those termed of the 'Kiev' or the 'Stretovka-Gatnoe' group which consisted of a number of selected graves only. A few settlements situated exclusively in the valley of the Dnieper, in the vicinity of Kiev and further south, have also been attributed to the culture.

Not enough particulars are available regarding most of the mounds of the Middle Dnieper culture investigated. Barrow-graves usually appear in small groups of a few mounds, but in some regions, in particular in the semi-steppe on the watershed between the Dnieper and the Boh, they formed larger cemeteries. In this respect cemeteries at Jackowica (no. 244) (recently renamed Dolinka) and in its vicinity are of particular interest.[44] A large number of mounds were excavated there which are of importance for the study of the relative chronology of the culture under review.

At Jackowica about two hundred barrow-graves were counted inside an area of about 1,500 hectares. They lay in the flat steppe cut by a shallow valley. Mounds were mostly small and low, scattered in groups usually of three barrows in one; some were of a larger size. Forty-four mounds situated on one side of the valley were investigated; eleven of these were of the advanced Scythian period, the other thirty-three were pre-Scythian. Their grave goods displayed a considerable chronological and typological variety which shows that there was a long span of time during which the cemetery was in continuous use. That this cemetery belonged to the same community during the whole period of its existence is indicated by the lack of chronological gaps in its use, and also by the appearance—in a few cases—of grave goods of an early type in graves which indisputably belonged to a later stage.

Two barrow-grave cemeteries were recorded at Nowosiółka (no. 253), the neighbouring village to Jackowica. One of these lay in a flat field, ancient steppe; it extended over an area of about twenty-five hectares, and consisted of three large and twenty smaller mounds all of which were investigated. All were of the Scythian period except barrow-grave 19 which was of an earlier date. The other cemetery, consisting of fifteen mounds, lay on an elevated area close to the River Tykicz, a tributary of the Siniukha (basin of the Boh); the date of these mounds, all of which were investigated, ranged from the Late Neolithic (or Early Bronze Age) up to the Early Iron Age.

Burials in barrow-graves lay mostly on the ancient surface. Shafts were typical of the latest, the 'pre-Scythian' stage, but were also recorded in the earliest burials. Skeletons lay in a crouched position, heads to the west, but very occasionally mainly in the late graves, to the south. In a few earliest graves (according to stratigraphic evidence),[45] skeletons lay on their backs with legs crouched, a position characteristic of the Yamna culture of the steppe country. The extended position on the back was found only in late burials, including secondary burials in earlier mounds. Only one dismembered or mutilated skeleton has been noticed, at Stanisławka (no. 263). Its head was cut off and slightly displaced.

No elaborate stone structures similar to those found in the steppe graves further south were recorded in our mounds, and no settlements were found in our area which can be attributed to the Middle Dnieper culture.

GRAVE GOODS

Graves were poorly furnished, and about 10 per cent of their total number yielded no grave goods whatever. Most frequent was pottery, found in fifty-six graves (two-thirds of the total); in thirty-five of these it was the only furniture; only fourteen graves had grave goods not accompanied by pottery. Usually,

[40] Äyräpää (op. cit., note 19), Fig. 108. Пассек (op. cit., note 38), Fig. 14:4.

[41] И. И. Артеменко, Неолитические стоянки и курганы эпохи бронзы близ с. Ходосовичи гомельской обл. БССР, Памятники каменного и бронзового веков Евразии, Moscow 1963, pp. 31–87.

[42] A. Häusler, 'Die kulturellen und wirtschaftlichen Beziehungen der Bevölkerungsgruppen Mittelrusslands am Ende der jüngeren Steinzeit', *Wissenschaftliche Zft d. Martin-Luther Universität*, no. 5–1, Halle 1955, p. 79.

[43] А. Я. Брюсов, Очерки по истории племен европейской части СССР в неолитическую эпоху, Moscow 1952, pp. 215 ff., Figs. 58, 59. Id., *Geschichte der neolithischen Stämme im europäischen Teil der UdSSR*, Berlin 1957, pp. 252 ff., Fig. 59. See also: L. Kilian, 'Schnurkeramik und Ockergrabkultur', *SMYA*, vol. 59:2, 1957, pp. 21 f., Fig. 5.

[44] A. Bydłowski, *Światowit*, vol. v, 1904, pp. 59 ff.; vol. vi, 1905, pp. 1 ff. Some of the descriptions have been repeated by Häusler (op. cit., note 42), pp. 70 ff.

[45] И. И. Артеменко, О памятниках раннего этапа среднеднепровской культуры, Ксиаан, no. 93, 1963, pp. 38 ff.

as was the case in thirty-four mounds, a single vessel was found in a barrow-grave, but sometimes there were two or three. Only once were seven vessels excavated in a single burial, and in another case five.

The standard vessel was a deep bowl with a wide, slightly rounded, usually decorated base; we shall call this the 'Middle Dnieper type'. Each was provided with a small circular depression right in the centre of the base. Walls were mostly cylindrical or slightly narrowing upwards, seldom widening, covered with a rich ornament. A wide furrow around the middle of the vessel divided this into two parts. The characteristic ornament consisted of rows of slanting alternating incisions, chevron patterns, or shaded triangles arranged in zonal bands combined with horizontal grooves and punctures. The lower part of the vessel often had groups of vertical grooves combined with chevron patterns and punctures, and a few specimens had the body undecorated.

The Middle Dnieper bowls were found in eighteen graves (at twelve sites). One vessel of the same type and another very similar were found further north, at Evminka on the Desna.[46] Three vessels of exactly the same type and decorated in the same manner were found far outside our group, at Kerch in the Crimea (Fig. 3),[47] at a distance of over six hundred kilometres from our region; their connection with our culture remains obscure. The Middle Dnieper bowls, which were of an unusual shape, were possibly modelled on some metal prototype. The only vessels which are to some extent reminiscent of them are the clumsy beakers, or mugs, with a wide base, typical of the Przemyśl group of Sub-Carpathian barrow-graves (Plate 6:18).

Of a different type were a few wide beakers, or bowls, characteristic of the Dnieper-Desna group found in our graves.[48] A few other vessels were a hybrid form combining features proper to the beakers and those of the genuine Middle Dnieper bowls.[49]

Another common vessel, in particular at Jackowica (seven specimens out of eleven found in our group) were ovoid beakers with a pointed or a very small rounded base and a short, mostly funnel-shaped neck.[50] The neck and the upper part of the body were decorated by horizontal grooves, seldom cord-impressed, sometimes with rows of short incisions or chevron patterns; some had a single or double zigzag line around the vessel, and a few were undecorated, or had the surface brushed with a comb-like instrument.

The beakers evidently derived from the vessels with a pointed base typical of the Yamna and Catacomb cultures on the Lower Dnieper discussed in the subsequent chapter (Fig. 5). The high neck, which distinguishes the specimens of the Middle Dnieper culture from those of the steppe country further south, is evidence of western influence for they tend to resemble Central European Corded Ware beakers.

A few beakers in this class were hybrids, especially the specimens from Jackowica (Fig. 4),[51] which had particularly high necks. Their specific analogy is represented by the beaker from Ostapie 5 in West Podolia (Plate 6:5) dealt with in Chapter II. The decorative patterns of the beakers from Jackowica and Stretivka are characteristic of the Oder Corded Ware. Western analogies seem to equate the respective graves with the late stage of the Sub-Carpathian barrow-graves.

Several vessels were of types characteristic of Central European Corded Ware. A genuine 'Thuringian' amphora, of Buchvaldek's type 1, was excavated at Griščintsy (no. 242)[52] on the Dnieper (Fig. 1:1). This was not the easternmost specimen of this type: the 'Thuringian' amphora from Rečitsa (no. 277) near Briansk[53] was found in a barrow-grave included by Passek in the Desna-Dnieper group, at a distance of over four hundred kilometres north-east of Griščintsy. A large vessel which both in shape and decoration calls to mind a Thuringian amphora, but is deprived of its characteristic horizontally perforated lugs, was found in the Tripolyan settlement of Kolomiščyna 1 of period C-1;[54] it equates the two genuine 'Thuringian' amphorae above with period C-1 of the Tripolyan development.

Of a later date was a genuine late Corded Ware type, the single-lugged mug from Krupol (no. 276), found in a barrow-grave east of the Dnieper,[55] wrongly stated by some authors to have come from Grečaniki (no. 275).[56] It was associated with a cord-decorated pot and a wide bowl with a slightly carinated body and a nearly cylindrical neck. This shows marked connection with the early Srubna pottery of the region of Voronezh dated by Krivtsova-Grakova[57] to the beginning of the second half of the second millennium B.C.

Two more vessels represent western types. One of these is the globular amphora from a barrow-grave at Łosiatyn (no. 250, Plate 14:12). Its shape and decoration link it with the earliest vessels of this type in the Sluch group of the Globular Amphora culture dealt with in Chapter IV. No other grave goods were found in this grave but the characteristic 'Yamna' position of its skeleton suggests that the burial belonged to a relatively early stage of the Middle Dnieper culture. The other vessel which may be connected with the Globular

[46] Ю. М. Захарук, Археологія-Kiev, vol. VI, 1952, pp. 126 ff., Figs. 1, 2. Häusler (op. cit., note 42), Pls. III:1; IV:2.

[47] At the Archaeological Museum, Cracow, nos. 3164, 3165, 3166.

[48] Пассек (op. cit., note 38), Figs. 10:1, 2; 12:1, 2. Häusler (op. cit., note 42), Pl. 2:1–1, 2.

[49] Bydłowski (op. cit., note 44), Pl. II:4. Пассек (op. cit., note 38), Figs. 10:5, 7; 11:9. Häusler (op. cit., note 42), Pl. 2:1–5, 7; 2:2–9

[50] Bydłowski (op. cit., note 44), Fig. 12; Pls. I:2, 3; II:1, 3; III:1; V. Äyräpää (op. cit., note 19), Fig. 132. J. Głosik, *Arch.R.*, vol. IX, 1957, p. 662, Fig. 273:2, erroneously published as from Nowosiółka in West Podolia. Пассек (op. cit., note 38), Figs. 11:6, 8; 12:3. Häusler (op. cit., note 42), Pl. 2:2–6, 8. Kilian (op. cit., note 43), Fig. 11.

[51] Bydłowski (op. cit., note 44), Pl. VI:1. Пассек (op. cit., note 38), Figs. 10:4, 6; 11:1; 12:6. Häusler (op. cit., note 42,) Pl. 2:1–4, 5; 2:2–1. Kilian (op. cit., note 43), Figs. 8:a, d; 11:3.

[52] Äyräpää (op. cit., note 19), Fig. 215. Пассек (op. cit., note 38), Fig. 10:3. Häusler (op. cit., note 42), Pl. 2:1–4. Kilian (op. cit., note 43), Fig. 6:b.

[53] Äyräpää (op. cit., note 19), Fig. 108. Пассек (op. cit., note 38), Fig. 14:4. Häusler (op. cit., note 42), Pl. 2:2–4; Kilian (op. cit., note 43), Fig. 6:a.

[54] Op. cit., note 1 (1949), Figs. 67:3; 75. Kilian (op. cit., note 43), Fig. 6:c.

[55] V. Schtscherbakiwskyj, Кам'яна доба в Україні (*Die Steinzeit in der Ukraine*), München 1947, p. 47. Häusler (op. cit., note 42), p. 76. Kilian (op. cit., note 43), Fig. 10:a.

[56] Äyräpää (op. cit., note 19), Fig. 127. Пассек (op. cit., note 38), Fig. 14:3; the drawing shows two lugs whereas the vessel had only one lug.

[57] A. M. Tallgren, 'La Pontide préscythique', *ESA*, vol. II, 1926, Figs. 46:1; 70. A. O. Кривцова-Гракова, Степное Поволжье и Причерноморье в эпоху поздней бронзы, МИА, no. 46, 1955, pp. 87 ff., Fig. 17.

Amphora culture is the richly decorated vase from Yankovitsi 7 (no. 270).[58] Its late date is indicated by its shape, in which it has departed considerably from its prototype; its decoration was already proper to the Middle Dnieper culture. The amber bead from Gatnoe must also be connected with the Globular Amphorae.

Only a few more vessels deserve mentioning: the cord-decorated Tripolyan type vessel from Grečaniki (no. 275) on the eastern side of the Dnieper, associated with a stone battle-axe;[59] and two pots, or beakers, of Srubna type.[60] A series of vessels of various types and shapes from the barrow-graves at Jackowica (no. 244)[61] exhibit a marked similarity to the pottery of Early Iron Age cultures, the Wysocko[62] and Biluhrudivka[63] cultures, and one vessel with a hole cut in its side[64] seems to represent a type proper to the Milograd culture of East Volhynia and Polesia.[65] Significant is a complete dearth of vessels of the Middle Bronze Age Trzciniec or Komarów types, or at least reminiscent of these.

Battle-axes were found in ten graves (eight sites). They were mainly of the 'simple' type, only two being of the 'showy' class; one of the latter was found with a debased beaker covered with a zigzag ornament.[66] Eleven flint axes (seven sites) were mostly rectangular in section, but a few were lenticular. One of the flint axes was found accompanied by the Thuringian amphora (Griščintsy; Fig. 1:1). It is of interest to note that one specimen, rectangular in section, was made of the 'milky' variety of flint characteristic of the Globular Amphora culture;[67] it was found in barrow-grave 54 at Jackowica with a spear-head (or possibly dagger) made of the black Volhynian flint.

Single flint arrow-heads occurred in five graves and flint daggers (or spear-heads) in another four. One of the latter, found at Popówka (no. 257)[68] was of type III distinguished in the Sub-Carpathian barrow-graves. The two arrow-shaft straighteners from Yankovitsi 3 (no. 270)[69] equate the grave with the Catacomb culture east of the Dnieper.[70]

Personal ornaments were frequent and consisted of necklaces made of animal (usually wolf) fangs and tubular beads made of spiral bronze wire, or imitations of the latter made from thin tubular bone; boar tusks;[71] bronze or silver spiral rings and ear-pendants with flattened and hooked terminals bent inwards, proper to the Early Bronze Age.[72] At Gatnoe 5 (no. 241), an amber pendant was associated with a bronze disc. Another bronze disc with a perforation in the centre was found at Iwachny 72 (no. 243)[73] and in two other graves[74] perforated bone discs; one of the latter was associated with an iron object which disintegrated, and with a vessel of the 'flower-pot' type, both of which imply a late date for the grave. The late date of the perforated bone discs is likewise indicated by a similar bone specimen found in a Srubna period grave at Kut (no. 317),[75] in the steppe country within the reach of the Lower Dnieper group dealt with in the subsequent chapter.

A special problem is presented by two bone hammer-headed pins, typical of the Catacomb culture, but here seemingly of a later date. One of these, from Iwachny 72 (no. 243)[76] was associated with a decorated, perforated bronze disc, mentioned above, which Popova[77] regards as an imported Caucasian object; on the other hand, the disc closely resembles bone specimens the late date of which has been pointed out above. The other pin, from Nowosiółka 26 (no. 253) was found in a shaft near a skeleton in an extended position, proper to later periods, together with three bronze amulets typical of the early Scythian culture (Fig. 4).[78] Its strange association with objects of the Scythian period has been commented upon by E. Majewski[79] who accepts the accuracy of the excavation report. Accordingly, he considers this grave to be of the Scythian period, but his remarks have never been taken into account by those who dealt with the pin.[80] Furthermore, Majewski points out that in the centre of the mound of Iwachny 72, the other barrow-grave of our group in which a hammer-headed bone pin was found, sherds of a two-handled red-coloured amphora, most probably of Greek origin, were excavated; amphorae of the same type were often found in Scythian barrow-graves in that region. This circumstance seems also to support a late date for the hammer-headed pins excavated in our barrow-graves. They may have survived to a late period there, in an area situated away from the main currents of that time.

COMMENTS, CHRONOLOGY

The brief review above revealed connections of the Middle Dnieper culture with a number of cultures of different ages. They imply a long existence of the culture, and the differences in grave goods suggest several stages in its development.

The early date of the well-marked connections with the Yamna culture have often been pointed out,[81] and Artemenko[82] seems to be right in deriving the Middle Dnieper culture from the latter. Shaft graves, the 'Yamna position' of skeletons richly sprinkled with ochre, probably also the cus-

[58] Пассек (op. cit., note 38), Fig. 13:4. Häusler (op. cit., note 42), Pl. 2:3–4.

[59] Schtscherbakiwskyj (op. cit., note 55), p. 47.

[60] Bydłowski (op. cit., note 44), Fig. 39, Pl. IV:4. Kilian (op. cit., note 43), Fig. 8:i.

[61] Bydłowski (op. cit., note 44), Figs. 21, 24, 25, Pl. IV:3.

[62] T. Sulimirski, *Kultura wysocka*, Kraków 1931, Pls. X–XV.

[63] А. И. Тереножкин, Предскифский период на днепровском правобережье, Kiev 1961, Figs. 28 ff.

[64] Bydłowski (op. cit., note 44), Fig. 6.

[65] Ю. В. Кухаренко, Памятники железного века на территории Полесья, Археология СССР, Moscow 1961, pp. 9 ff., Pls. 1–4.

[66] Bydłowski (op. cit., note 44), Fig. 20, Pl. IV:2. Kilian (op. cit., note 43), Fig. 12.

[67] Bydłowski (op. cit., note 44), p. 19.

[68] F. Pułaski, *ZWAK*, vol. XVII, 1893, pp. 41 ff., Fig. 2.

[69] Пассек, (op. cit., note 38), Fig. 13:7, 8. Hausler (op. cit., note 42), Pls. 2:3–7, 8.

[70] Попова (op. cit., note 34), p. 169, Pl. VII.

[71] Samhorodek II; see B. Popowski, *ZWAK*, vol. VI, 1882, p. 15.

[72] Bydłowski (op. cit., note 44), pp. 3 f., 11, 21, Figs. 3, 5, 26, 27. Popowski (op. cit., note 71), p. 15. А. А. Спицын, Записки Имп. Русс. Археол., Общества, vol. XI, 1899, p. 115.

[73] Bydłowski (op. cit., note 44), pp. 26 f., Fig. 38.

[74] Ibid., Figs. 8, 19.

[75] Д. Т. Березовець, Арх. Пам., vol. IX, 1960, p. 77, Fig. 31:5.

[76] Loc. cit., note 73.

[77] Попова (op. cit., note 34), pp. 125 f.

[78] Bydłowski (op. cit., note 44), p. 5, Fig. 7, and also Figs. 50a, 67, 68.

[79] E. Majewski, *Światowit*, vol. VI, 1905, pp. 69 ff.

[80] V. Milojčić, 'Zur Zeitstellung der Hammerkopfnadeln', *Germania*, vol. 33, 1955; pp. 240 ff.

[81] J. E. Forssander, *Die schwedische Bootaxtkultur und ihre kontinentaleuropäischen Voraussetzungen*, Lund 1933, p. 171. Kilian (op. cit., note 43), pp. 20 ff.

[82] Артеменко (op. cit., note 39), pp. 33 ff.

tom itself of raising a mound over the grave, ovoid or spherical vessels with a rounded or pointed base, are among the elements evidently taken over from the Yamna culture (Map VII). Later, as emphasized by Popova,[83] connections with the Catacomb culture, or rather with its equivalent culture in the Lower Dnieper region, had developed. They are reflected in the shape of a number of vessels, in some decorative patterns of the pottery, and also in some other grave goods. The extent and the early date of the eastern elements suggest that they were the basic constituent component in the formation of the Middle Dnieper culture.

Very strong and important likewise was the impact of the Corded Ware assemblage. Thuringian amphorae of the early stage, and the single-lugged mugs, point to connections with the wide Central European Corded Ware culture; but these connections seem to have been of a little later date than those with the east. They resulted in the acquiring by the Middle Dnieper culture of a specific character which induced several authors, including Gorodtsov and Äyräpää[84] to look upon the culture as an eastern outpost of the Central European Corded Ware assemblage. Close contact was also maintained with other groups of the Corded Ware assemblage, the Gorodsk culture, or rather its preceding and ancestral group, and also with the Dnieper-Desna culture.[85]

Only a single vessel, the globular amphora from Łosiatyn (Plate 14:12), implies the contact with the Globular Amphora culture, the territory of which extended north of that of the Middle Dnieper culture.

Significant is the fact that no Komarów or Trzciniec elements were found in any graves within the territory of the Middle Dnieper culture, although remains of this type were excavated in a series of Middle Bronze Age barrow-graves further north, within the area occupied in the preceding period by the Globular Amphora culture.[86]

The Middle Dnieper barrow-graves extended partly over the territory of the Kiev group of the Tripolye culture. According to Passek[87] the Middle Dnieper culture is supposed to have been post-Tripolyan. However, several circumstances indicate that the culture equated with Tripolyan period C-1. Decorative patterns of some Tripolyan vessels, especially of the amphora from Kolomiščyna 1 modelled on a Thuringian amphora,[88] or the Tripolyan vessel from a barrow-grave at Grečaniki (no. 275)[89] are evidence which cannot be simply dismissed. Decorative patterns of some other vessels, likewise from Kolomiščyna 1, typical of the Globular Amphora culture,[90] equate the latter with Tripolyan period C-1, and by implication with the Middle Dnieper culture.

It has often been emphasized that the post-Tripolyan date of the Middle Dnieper barrow-graves is demonstrated by the fact that a number of these were raised over the Tripolyan remains. However, Artemenko[91] emphasizes that the few Tripolyan settlements over the debris of which Yamnaya barrow-graves were raised, belonged to period B-2. At Raiki (no. 232)[92] the barrow-grave in question was of the developed Bronze Age.

The distribution of the larger barrow-grave cemeteries, particularly in the neighbourhood of Jackowica, shows that they extended over a territory within which no Tripolyan settlements have so far been found.[93] It seems, therefore, that the two peoples, the Tripolyans and the people of the Middle Dnieper culture, lived side by side in neighbouring areas, the former closer to the streams, the latter rather in the steppe. In any case, their reciprocal relations need further investigation.

STAGES IN THE DEVELOPMENT

Two subsequent stages, the Stretivka and Gatnoe stages, named after the relative cemeteries, have been distinguished by Passek[94] in the development of the Middle Dnieper culture. A different allotment of barrow-graves has been recently proposed by Artemenko[95] who likewise distinguishes two stages in the evolution of the culture, called the 'early' and the 'late' stages, which he dated to 2400–2200/2100 B.C., and 2200/2100–1600 B.C. respectively. The present study based on wider connections of the Middle Dnieper culture, especially with the Sub-Carpathian barrow-graves and other Central European groups of the Corded Ware assemblage, reveals yet another division of these remains.

Graves with flint axes and battle-axes, but in particular those with skeletons in the 'Yamna' position strewn richly with ochre seem to be among the earliest. They can be equated with the Yamna graves of the steppe country. To the early period also the Thuringian amphora (Griščintsy, Fig. 1:1) and the globular amphora (Łosiatyn, Plate 14:12) belonged. A beaker, or bowl, with a pointed base cannot be considered as an indicator of the early date of the graves containing them. The ornament of some of these (Jackowica 41, 56; no. 244) equates them with the Catacomb period east of the Dnieper. But the beaker from Jackowica 48 (Fig. 4), decorated in a manner typical of the Oder Corded Ware, must be assigned to a later period, and the same applies to the similarly decorated beaker from Stretivka 1 (no. 264).

A bronze ear-pendant from Jackowica 60 equates it with the Unetice period (probably Reinecke's Bronze Age A-1) in Central Europe. Of a later date was the barrow-grave from Popówka (no. 257) with a flint dagger. The 'Srubna' decorated pot from Jackowica 65 implies the survival of our culture into the Srubna period (Late Bronze Age) in the steppe country east of the Dnieper. The survival even to the Early Iron Age (the so-called pre-Scythian period) is attested by pottery of Bilohrudivka and Wysocko type found in a few barrow-graves.

The late date of some of the graves and a long survival of

[83] Попова (op. cit., note 34), pp. 125 ff., and Borkovśkyj (op. cit., note 36), pp. 43 ff.

[84] В. Городцов, Бронзовый век на территории СССР, Большая Советская Энциклопедия, vol. VII, Moscow 1927, p. 616. Äyräpää (op. cit., note 19), pp. 123 ff.

[85] Äyräpää (op. cit., note 19), pp. 129 f.

[86] Op. cit., note 26, and Лагодовська and Захарук (op. cit., note 2).

[87] Op. cit., note 1 (1949), pp. 218 ff.

[88] Works cited in note 54.

[89] Loc. cit., note 59.

[90] Op. cit., note 1 (1949), pp. 222 f., Fig. 27:3, 6.

[91] Op. cit., note 39, pp. 30 ff.

[92] П. Курінний, Коротке Звідомлення за 1926 р., Kiev 1927, pp. 72 ff.

[93] Borkovśkyj (op. cit., note 36), p. 72.

[94] Loc. cit., note 38.

[95] Loc. cit., note 44, and op. cit., note 39, p. 31.

the Middle Dnieper culture is also indicated by the conditions in some of the cemeteries investigated. A good example in this respect is offered by the second cemetery of Nowosiółka (no. 253) consisting of fifteen mounds all of which were investigated. The plan of the cemetery has not been published, but Bydłowski[96] remarks that the continuity in use was well marked by grave goods found in the mounds: the earliest, 'Neolithic' according to him, lay nearer to the River Tykicz, and the further from the river the later was the date of the respective graves. Those on the northern limit of the group (cemetery) were already Scythian (eight in all). Only barrow-grave 10, which contained a contracted skeleton accompanied by a flint axe, can possibly be regarded as 'Neolithic'; all other graves dated either from the developed Bronze Age or the Early Iron Age. In barrow-grave 25 a large undecorated vessel with a pointed base was found; it was definitely of a late date. The bone hammer-headed pin from grave 26 found with the early-Scythian, or pre-Scythian bronze amulets mentioned previously (Fig. 4) must be included in the early Scythian period.

Similar conditions were reported also at Stretivka[97] (no. 264). The five barrow-graves excavated there ranged from the Neolithic or Early Bronze Age (barrow-grave 1 with a number of vessels and battle-axes, and barrow-grave 3 with a flint dagger), to the developed Bronze Age (barrow-graves 4 and 5) and the early Scythian period (barrow-grave 2).

Taking all the circumstances into account, the following chronological division of the Middle Dnieper culture is suggested:

Period I

Typical graves: Bielilovka, Griščintsy, Łosiatyn, probably Jackowica 29, 36, 46, 52, and possibly the primary burial in shaft of Stretivka 4 (nos. 238, 242, 250, 244, 264).

Connections: Late Yamna culture, the first stage of the Sub-Carpathian barrow-graves, the earliest East Volhynian Globular Amphorae, Tripolyan period C-1.

Period II

Typical graves: Jackowica 41, 44, 49, 50, 55, 56, 60, Medvin, Yankoviči 3, 5, 7, Stretivka 1, 3 (nos. 244, 251, 270, 264). The last must be considered as one of the latest graves of this period transitional to Period III. During this period features characteristic of the Middle Dnieper culture developed: bowls, decorative patterns, etc.

Connections: the second stage of the Sub-Carpathian barrow graves (presumably), late stage of the East Volhynian Globular Amphorae, the Catacomb culture, the Dnieper-Desna culture.

Period III

Typical graves: Jackowica 48, 61, 62, Krupol, Popówka, and for an advanced stage: Jackowica 65, Podwysokie 75 (nos. 244, 276, 257, 258).

Connections: the third stage of the Sub-Carpathian barrow-graves and by the end of the period with the Early Srubna culture.

Period IV

Here belong all late graves: Jackowica 38, 43, 45, 57, 58, 59, most graves from Nowosiółka and Iwachny 72 (nos. 244, 253, 243).

Connections: Bilohrudivka and Wysocko cultures, Volhynian barrow-graves of the Early Iron Age.

None of the cemeteries lasted throughout the existence of the culture. The relatively small number of graves distributed over a very long span of time suggest that only selected persons of a higher social position were buried in barrow-graves.

The Middle Dnieper culture seems to have been a very conservative group. This applies in particular to its western division represented, e.g., by the cemeteries of Jackowica and Nowosiółka, where we have to deal with an unexpected survival of ancient elements and types to a very late period. This conservatism seems to have been due to the isolated position of that region during the whole Bronze Age. The circumstances changed there only during the Early Iron Age and the Scythian period when new types of vessels and other grave goods replaced the survivals from the bygone periods.

The position of the Middle Dnieper culture in the wider framework of eastern European cultures has often been commented upon in archaeological literature. Häusler[98] and Kilian[99] are right in insisting that our culture extended over a border area between two different *Kulturkreise*, the eastern of the Ochre-graves, and the western of the Central European Corded Ware. Its grave goods reflect the presence of various different elements during the whole time of its existence. During the second period of the development of the culture the 'western' elements seem to have definitely prevailed and gave the culture a rather 'western' character.

None of the component parts, whether 'eastern' or 'western', seems to have originated in the country. Stratigraphical evidence[100] available in this respect reveals that the Yamna elements definitely preceded the arrival of the 'western' elements. The custom of raising a mound above the grave was definitely of an earlier date in the territories south and east of our area than in those to the west and north. Vases with a pointed base cannot be regarded as a chronological indicator, but they appeared in the country under review at a period which preceded the appearance there of remains proper to the Middle Dnieper culture; characteristic remains of the latter developed under western influence or simply originated from the Central European cultures.

[96] Loc. cit., note 44.
[97] Х. Вовк, Материяли українсько-русскої етнольогії, vol. III, Lviv 1900, pp. 1 ff.

[98] Op. cit., note 42, pp. 75 f.
[99] Op. cit., note 43, pp. 43 ff.
[100] Loc. cit., note 45.

CHAPTER VII

Steppe Cultures

OCHRE-GRAVES

THE NAME of 'Ochre-graves' was given to the Neolithic and Bronze Age barrow-graves of Eastern Europe on account of the reddish colour of the skeletons, from the corpses having been richly sprinkled with ochre. Many mounds contained secondary burials and the stratigraphic evidence enabled their investigators to distinguish their three chronological groups, for each of which a different type of grave was characteristic. Periods represented by these have been named by V. G. Childe,[1] from the corresponding Russian or Ukrainian terms, the 'Yamnaya' or 'Yamna', the 'Catacomb', and the 'Srubnaya' or 'Srubna' periods. We shall keep here to these terms, although some other authors apply an entirely English terminology.[2]

Recently, a new chronological division of the 'Ochre-graves' has been proposed by N. I. Merpert,[3] who splits the Yamna period into four stages, followed by the period for which the Catacomb graves were characteristic—at least in a part of the territory involved. He also distinguishes four main territorial groups of the culture of which only the westernmost, the 'Dnieper-Azov' group concerns us here. In his opinion, the easternmost groups, on the Eurasiatic border, were the first to appear and were followed by the successive groups further west, the 'Dnieper-Azov' group being the last one to be formed. Regarding the westernmost group, however, this scheme, and especially the chronology, need revision.[4]

Only barrow-graves of the steppe country on the Lower Dnieper east of the Ingul, the eastern tributary of the Boh, can be attributed to the 'Dnieper-Azov' group distinguished by Merpert (Map VIII). Different in many respects from these were graves in the steppe further west, to which the name of the 'Usatovo' group, or culture, has been given. Another group can be distinguished on the border of the proper steppe and the forest steppe zone, to which the provisional name of 'Cherkasi-Kirovograd-Uman' group can be applied. Barrow-graves of the black-earth region further north, called the 'Middle Dnieper culture', have been already dealt with in Chapter VI.

THE LOWER DNIEPER BARROW-GRAVES
(Map VIII, group VI) (pp. 187 f.)

A few hundred mounds in over thirty sites, and a few 'flat' cemeteries and settlements to which they belonged, were investigated in the steppe enclosed by the Dnieper bend.[5] In 1951–3, 53 barrow-graves were excavated in the district of Apostolovo alone,[6] each containing 3 to 40 secondary burials, jointly 305 burials, dating from various periods: 191 of these were 'ochre-graves' of the Bronze Age, mostly of the Srubna period (Late Bronze Age) and the least numerous were graves of the Yamna period.

Graves of the Yamna period of the area under review did not differ substantially from those of the steppes east of the Dnieper. They were usually shallow oval shafts in which a single skeleton lay on a litter of birch bark in a position which we shall call the 'Yamna position', namely on the back with legs slightly contracted, sometimes with the knees upwards. Heads were almost exclusively to the north-east, north, or east. Skeletons were richly sprinkled with ochre, but graves were poorly furnished; sometimes a single vessel was found and most burials had no equipment at all.

Burials of the subsequent 'Catacomb' period were chiefly secondary burials either in shafts or in the mound itself. Only a few genuine 'catacombs' were uncovered: shafts with a niche, or a chamber, dug under one of its longer sides in which the corpse was laid; 'catacombs' were exclusively secondary burials in the mounds of the preceding period.

Most graves do not allow a precise dating, but an indication of their late date (of the Catacomb period) is the increased number of grave goods, and also their kind; sometimes furniture was typical of the genuine Catacomb culture of the grassland east of the Dnieper. Another indication of the late date were double burials which were only found exceptionally in earlier graves, or mutilated and dismembered skeletons, skeletons deprived of their skulls, etc. Such practices were recorded in barrow-graves situated exclusively on the western border of our group, and were noted also further north, in the Cherkasi-Kirovograd-Uman group. They call to mind similar practices in a series of graves in Poland in the

[1] V. G. Childe, *The Dawn of European Civilisation*, e.g. 5th ed., 1950, pp. 153 ff. Id., *Prehistoric Migrations in Europe*, Oslo 1950, pp. 143 ff.

[2] M. Gimbutas, *The Prehistory of Eastern Europe*, part I, Cambridge (Mass.) 1956, pp. 71 ff. W. M. Thompson, transl. of A. L. Mongait, *Archaeology in the USSR*, Penguin Books, 1961, pp. 153 ff.

[3] N. I. Merpert, 'L'Énéolithique de la zone steppique de la partie européene de L'URSS', *Prague Symposium*, pp. 176 ff.

[4] M. Gimbutas, 'Notes on the Chronology and Expansion of the Pit-Grave Culture', *Prague Symposium*, pp. 193 ff.

[5] В. И. Гошкевич, Клады и древности херсонской губернiи, vol. I. Kherson 1903, pp. 97 ff. Д. Т. Березовець, Арх. Пам., vol. IV, 1960, pp. 39 ff.; vol. X, 1961, pp. 56 ff. Д. Т. Березовець, Е. Ф. Покровська, А. I. Фурманська, Арх. Пам. vol. IX, 1960, pp. 102 ff. Д. I. Бліфельд, Арх. Пам., vol. X, 1961, pp. 46 ff. Л. Д. Дмитров, Наукові записки, vol. II, Kiev 1946, pp. 55 ff. Б. Граков, Археологія-Kiev, vol. II, 1948, pp. 208 f. Id. Арх. Пам., vol. II, 1949, pp. 112 ff. В. А. Іллінська, Г. Т. Ковпаненко, Е. О. Петровська, Арх. Пам., vol. IX, 1960, pp. 127 ff. I. П. Костюченко, Арх. Пам., vol. IX, 1960, p. 88.

[6] Д. Т. Березовець, Ксиак, no. 4, 1955, pp. 81 ff.

region of Lublin, in West Podolia and West Volhynia, in the areas affected by the Globular Amphora culture, discussed in Chapter II, which, as mentioned there, were of the Early Bronze Age, the middle of the second millennium B.C.

A feature characteristic of the Catacomb period, as emphasized by O. G. Šapošnikova,[7] was a wide use of stones in the construction of graves. The grave shaft was often covered by stone slabs, whereas a timber cover was typical of the Yamna period, a stone cover being an exception. The entrance to the few catacombs found in our area was usually closed by a stone slab or by stones heaped at the entrance shaft.

Another familiar structure, met with already in the Yamna period, were stone rings around the grave, or around the original perimeter of the mound, called 'cromlechs' in Soviet archaeological literature. They consisted of large boulders, occasionally of slabs, and had sometimes an entrance gap. The smaller ones, up to 3·5m in diameter, were very common in the Neolithic pre-Yamna 'flat' cemeteries in the region of the Dnieper Rapids. They seem to have been adopted later by the builders of the barrow-graves. One of the earliest seems to have been the stone ring laid around the original, central grave of the Yamna period in barrow-grave 'Storozhovaya Mogila' near Staryi Kodak (no. 328);[8] it had an entrance gap. The original purpose of large enclosures was seemingly to protect the mound from erosion. Timber enclosures of this type, tight paling around the mound of sand, were found in several barrow-graves in Poland (Plan 9:2).[9] 'Cromlechs' of this type, often built of large stone slabs, were a feature characteristic of the Usatovo culture, and were also found further west, in West Podolia. Stratigraphic evidence at Slobodka Romanovka in Odessa (no. 361)[10] suggests their late appearance; they had probably developed out of the smaller stone rings of the Neolithic.

'Stelae' found in several graves deserve special mention. These were usually larger amorphous stones, seldom slabs, placed near the head or feet of the skeleton. In two instances slabs were given a crude anthropomorphic shape.[11] The stones were evidently Neolithic or Early Bronze Age representatives of the large group of remains of the Ukrainian steppe country, mainly of the Early Iron Age (the 'Cimmerian' and Scythian periods), which consisted of roughly carved anthropomorphic stelae, 'Menhir'-like stones sometimes covered with engraved geometric figures, double zigzag lines, etc.: here also belong the famous rock-engravings of the Kamennaya Mogila near Melitopol, north of the Sea of Azov, east of the territory with which we are concerned. These remains have often been discussed in archaeological literature, and opinions vary as to their meaning and origin. They were recently reviewed by Häusler,[12] who connects them with similar occurrences in the Mediterranean-Atlantic 'megalithic *Kulturkreis*', including the Caucasus and Thuringia, and concludes that the Ukrainian stelae and engravings were possibly the outcome of a western 'megalithic' current which reached the steppe country via Central Europe. In this context it is of interest to note that a clay plaque (an 'altar') in the shape of a crude anthropomorphic figure of the same type as some of the stone stelae mentioned above, with a similar zigzag ornament incised around the edges, was found in the Tripolyan settlement of the turn of B-2 and C-1 periods at Stena, in the Tomašpol district, province of Vinnitsa;[13] the site lay within the area affected by the Globular Amphora influence (see no. 726).

A few graves, exclusively secondary burials, were regular slab-cists; slab-cists were common in the Usatovo culture and are discussed later on in this chapter.

Our graves of the Catacomb period markedly differed from those of the genuine Catacomb culture of the steppe country further east. Popova[14] considers them to form the 'Lower Dnieper variation' of the Catacomb culture, whereas according to Klein[15] they constituted a different culture. The Catacomb period corresponded with the Early and Middle Bronze Age of Central Europe. The appearance of remains of the 'Srubna' type, which has been assigned to *c.* 1250 B.C. by both Popova and Krivtsova-Grakova[16] marks its end which coincided with the disappearance in the Ukraine of bronze objects typical of the Central European Middle Bronze Age; the famous hoard of Borodino[17] was among the latest remains of this type.

GRAVE GOODS

Well over seventy vessels were found in graves of the territory under review. The pots belonging to the Yamna period were of medium size and had a spherical body which narrowed towards a pointed or rounded base, and they were provided with a short, cylindrical neck (Fig. 7). They were seldom decorated, except with some simple stamped impressions or zigzag lines, and in a few cases with a simple cord ornament. However, vessels which did not differ in any respect from these were likewise found in later graves undeniably of the Catacomb period, e.g. in grave 6 of barrow 8 at Kut (no. 317)[18] where such a vessel was excavated together with a flat-based vase typical of the Catacomb period.

Vessels of the latter period were more diverse. As before there were very frequently spherical vessels with a pointed base which were now usually provided with an everted neck, and some had one or two perforated lugs on the body. Their decoration consisted of incised, or cord-impressed, shaded triangles, of double or triple zigzag lines, or of similar patterns. A feature considered to be characteristic of the Cata-

[7] О. Г. Шапошникова, Арх. Пам., vol. x, 1961, p. 3.

[8] А. И. Тереножкин, Ксиимк, no. xxxvii, 1951, p. 117. Id., Археологія-Kiev, vol. v, 1951, pp. 183 ff. See also Gimbutas (op. cit., note 2), p. 78.

[9] E.g. A. Dzieduszycka-Machnikowa, *Spr.Arch.*, vol. x, 1960, pp. 9 ff., Figs. 1, 2.

[10] A. M. Tallgren, 'La Pontide préscythique', *ESA*, vol. ii, 1926, p. 51, Fig. 37. Gimbutas (op. cit., note 2), pp. 85 ff.

[11] Г. Т. Титенко, Ксиак, no. 5, 1955, pp. 78 f., Fig. 1.

[12] A. Häusler, 'Die Felszeichnungen der Kamennaja Mogila bei Melitopol und die megalithischen Einflüsse in Südrussland', *Wissenschaftliche Zft. d. Martin Luther Universität*, vol. vii/2, Halle 1958, pp. 497 ff.

[13] М. Л. Макаревич, Ксиак, no. 10, 1960, pp. 23 ff., Fig. 5:1.

[14] Т. Б. Попова, Племена катакомбной культуры, Труды Гим, no. 24, Moscow 1955, pp. 68 ff.

[15] Л. С. Клейн, Сов. Арх., vol. 2, 1962, pp. 26 ff.

[16] О. А. Кривцова-Гракова, Степное Поволжье и Причерноморье в эпоху поздней бронзы, МИА, no. 46, 1955, pp. 110 ff.

[17] M. Gimbutas, 'Borodino, Seima and their Contemporaries', *PPS*, vol. xxii, 1956, pp. 143 ff. and the literature quoted there. T. Sulimirski, 'Barrow-grave 6 at Komarów', *University of London Institute of Archaeology Bulletin*, no. 4, 1964, pp. 175 ff.

[18] Д. Т. Березовець (op. cit., note 5: 1960), p. 85, Fig. 15.

comb period was the scratched surface of the vessels, done by smoothing it with a comb-like instrument. It was applied mainly to the vases with a pointed base, but flat-based pots were often treated in a similar way; this usage was noticeable, though not often, already in the Yamna period. It is important to note that the shell-gritted Tripolyan kitchen ware of periods B-2 and C-1 had the surface scratched in the same manner, and that some of the flat-based pots with the surface scratched, found in graves of the Catacomb period,[19] strikingly resembled the corresponding Tripolyan vessels.[20] These convergences equate the relative periods of the two cultures.

Flat-based vessels of various shape were in use in the Catacomb period; some of them correspond with those characteristic of the Catacomb culture of the Donetz region,[21] or with those of the Usatovo culture.[22]

Other grave goods, found almost exclusively in graves of the Catacomb period, were amulets and personal ornaments. They consisted of perforated wolf or fox fangs, bone beads, etc., usually forming necklaces. There were numbers of thin tubular specimens made of bird bones covered with an incised spiral groove, which imitate spiral beads made of a thin copper or bronze band or wire. They were sometimes accompanied by a bone (or antler) hammer-headed pin. These pins, typical of the Catacomb culture, dated from the beginning of the second millennium B.C.,[23] although some authors would prefer a higher date.[24]

Metal objects, excavated in six graves, included small spiral ear-pendants made of a thin, narrow silver or copper strip. In grave 13 of barrow grave 5 at Pervomaivka (no. 323)[25] a copper knife and awl were found; the grave is considered to be of the Yamna period, but a copper knife of the same type as that above, and an ovoid vessel, both found in the upper layer of the settlement of Mykhailivka (no. 333)[26] point to a later date for the grave, i.e. to the Catacomb period.

A few weapons were found in graves of the Catacomb period: three stone battle-axes (two of these in catacombs), triangular flint arrow-heads with a concave base (in two graves) and two flint spear-heads (in two graves). In double grave 11 of barrow-grave 5 at Marianske (no. 318)[27] arrow-heads were found stuck in the chest bones of the female skeleton and they evidently caused her death.

In a few graves of the Yamna period sheep (or goat) leg bones were excavated and sometimes a broken mollusc shell. In graves of the Catacomb period sheep (or goat) astragali or hooves were frequent, and sometimes a rib or shoulder blade of a cow was found; once a sheep skeleton deprived of its skull was uncovered. One or more Unio shells, often crushed, appeared in many graves.

Of special interest were the remains of a two-wheeled cart, an *arba* found in the secondary burial, supposedly of the Yamna period, excavated in barrow-grave 'Storozhovaya Mogila' in the region of the Dnieper Rapids (no. 328). It implies a nomadic way of life for the people of the Lower Dnieper group. As the cart was accompanied by no other grave goods the date of the grave is disputable. It has been dated by Terenozhkin[28] to the second half of the third millennium B.C., but Childe[29] remarks that 'this figure could be reduced by 500', which would bring its date down to the beginning of the second millennium B.C., the turn of the Yamna and Catacomb periods. A cart of the same type was also found east of the Dnieper, about 160 kilometres (100 miles) south of the former site, in a barrow-grave on the River Molochna north of Melitopol.[30] The solid wheels from the Netherlands,[31] dated by Carbon-14 to 2140–2010 B.C. suggest a similar date for the Ukrainian carts.

In this connection a clay model of a wheel should be mentioned; it was found in a barrow-grave of the Catacomb culture south of Kherson, on the sea-coast between the peninsula of Djelatch and Tendra (no. 327).[32]

SETTLEMENTS OF THE DNIEPER RAPIDS (Map IV)

Besides the barrow-graves, settlements and 'flat' cemeteries were found in the area under review; all were situated in the valley of the Lower Dnieper.

Neolithic remains characteristic of the region of the Dnieper Rapids belonged to a local group of a larger province which embraced the whole steppe country east of the Dnieper up to the Lower Donets and the Don; the Crimea also formed part of this province. The remains in the valley of the Dnieper lie outside the scope of our present study except for their reciprocal relations with the cultures of our area. They were briefly described by Gimbutas,[33] who also gave a summary of the topics involved in them.

The Late Neolithic of the Dnieper Rapids region has been divided into three stages called the 'Sobačky', 'Seredni Stog I', and 'Seredni Stog II',[34] after the respective sites with their typical remains (Table 18). Some authorities consider the latest of these to belong to the subsequent Copper Age. Characteristic of the Late Neolithic was the appearance of the comb-pricked pottery which seems to be due to the

[19] Д. І. Бліфельд (op. cit., note 5), Fig. 6.

[20] Т. С. Пассек, Периодизация трипольских поселений, МИА, no. 10, 1949, Fig. 56.

[21] Op. cit., note 14, Pl. II. Tallgren (op. cit., note 10), Figs. 39–45. Gimbutas (op. cit., note 2), Pl. 18.

[22] И. В. Фабрициус, Археологическая карта Причерноморья Украинской ССР, Kiev 1951, Pls. III; V:2, 3.

[23] Op. cit., note 14, pp. 119 ff., Figs. 28, 29, Pl. V.

[24] V. Milojčić, 'Zur Zeitstellung der Hammerkopfnadeln', *Germania*, vol. 33, 1955, pp. 240 ff.

[25] В. А. Іллінська, Г. Т. Ковпаненко, Е. О. Петровська (op. cit., note 5), Pls. II:9; III:12, 14, 15.

[26] Е. Ф. Лагодовская, Ксиак, no. 4, 1955, pp. 119 ff., Figs. 1, 8.

[27] Березовець, Покровська, Фурманська (op. cit., note 5), p. 123.

[28] See note 8.

[29] V. G. Childe, 'The Diffusion of Wheeled Vehicles', *Ethnographisch-archäologische Forschungen*, vol. 2, Berlin 1954, pp. 6 ff.

[30] А. И. Тереножкин, Роскопки курганов в долине р. Молочной в 1952 г., Ксиимк, no. 63, 1956, pp. 70 ff.

[31] J. D. van der Walls, *Prehistoric Disc Wheels in the Netherlands*, Groningen 1964; and also *Palaeohistoria*, vol. x, 1964.

[32] A. Bertrand, 'Tumulus de la Tauride', *Revue Archéologique*, vol. NS 25, Paris 1873, pp. 203 ff. Grave goods at present at the Musée St. Germain-en-Laye, nos. 18680–4.

[33] Gimbutas (op. cit., note 17), pp. 17 ff.

[34] В. М. Даниленко, До питання про ранній неоліт південної Надднiпрянщини, Археологія-Kiev, vol. III, 1950, pp. 121 f. А. В. Добровольський, Матеріали до археологічної карти дніпровського Надпоріжжя в межах запорізької області, Археологія-Kiev, vol. VII, 1952, pp. 78 ff. І. Г. Шовкопляс, Археологічні дослідження на Україні 1917–1957, Kiev 1957, pp. 60 ff.

arrival of a wave of northern settlers from the regions east of the Middle Dnieper. Telegin[35] connects them with the 'Dnieper-Donets' culture.

The final stage of the Dnieper Rapids Neolithic, the Seredni Stog II stage, is of special importance for our study. In several sites of this period were found potsherds belonging to a number of cultures which concern us. Thus Tripolyan pottery, evidently not earlier than B-2 or C-1, was excavated at Seredni Stog II, Strelča Skela, etc.[36] In the earlier reports it was called simply 'Tripolyan' or 'middle Tripolyan'; lately it has always been labelled 'Tripolyan B-1', although no Tripolyan B-1 sites were found east of West Podolia, as is shown below. Recently Telegin[37] says that the three Tripolyan potsherds found in the upper layer of Seredni Stog (Seredni Stog II) were 'late Tripolyan' (C-1); a clay vessel found in the double grave of site 8 at Igrin (Ihren) was likewise late Tripolyan. He also mentions three 'middle Tripolyan' potsherds from Piščiki considered by T. S. Passek to be of her period B-1, and concludes that sites of Seredni Stog II type yielded pottery of both middle and late Tripolyan periods.

TABLE 18. Sequence and synchronism of Neolithic Cultures in the Ukraine

West	North	West Podolia	Boh Region	Dnieper Rapids
Globular Amphorae	Globular Amphorae	Tripolyan C-1	Tripolyan C-1	Seredni Stog II
x—	—x—	—x—	—	—x
	Mostva II		x—	—x
Funnel Beakers				
x—	—	—x		
		Tripolyan B-2	Tripolyan B-2	
			x—	—x
Lublin Painted Pottery	Mostva I–Mykilska-Slobidka	Tripolyan B-1	Sabatynivka II	Seredni Stog I
	x—	—	—	—x
				Sobačky period
	x—	—	—	—x
			x—	—x

The appearance of cord-decorated pottery in Late Neolithic sites in the region of the Dnieper Rapids is noteworthy. Danilenko[38] is not right in asserting that it is earlier than the Corded Ware of Central Europe; its true position is discussed in Chapter VIII and also shown in Table 18 above. Potsherds characteristic of the Globular Amphora culture found at Seredni Stog II[39] show that the site corresponds with the advanced period of that culture, which is also in agreement with the statement by Äyräpää,[40] according to whom pottery of Seredni Stog II type was influenced by that of the Globular Amphorae (see pp. 206 ff.).

SETTLEMENTS ON THE LOWER DNIEPER

Eighteen settlements of the period in question are said to have been recorded in the valley of the Lower Dnieper.[41] The most important of these is that investigated at Mykhailivka (Mikhailovka in Russian) in which three superimposed layers of occupation were uncovered, each with somewhat different remains.[42] The site was on the right bank of the Dnieper, twenty-five metres above the level of the river. It lay at a distance of about sixty kilometres south-west of Nikopol (Map IX).

The settlement of Mykhailivka has often been mentioned in archaeological literature, and its stratigraphical evidence referred to for dating purposes and for establishing chronological schemes. A full publication of the results has appeared recently;[43] Mrs O. G. Šapošnikova was very kind in giving me information about the site during my week-long stay in Kiev in 1961, and she also kindly showed me the material in question.

Pottery of the lowest layer (Mykhailivka I) was a shell-gritted ware; vessels were flat-based, their surface dark-brownish, slightly polished, covered with comb-stamped or cord-impressed decorative patterns. Kitchen ware was of Tripolyan type, most probably of period B-2. No Tripolyan painted ware was excavated. Of importance for our study was a large amphora with a spherical body and a cord-decorated cylindrical neck (Fig. 6:2). It represents a 'Thuringian' amphora of type IIc described in Chapter II. It was found in sherds; as reconstructed, it has no handles though this does not preclude it from originally having been provided with these. The vessel equates the layer either with the second stage, or the very end of the first stage of the Sub-Carpathian barrow-graves.

According to the excavators, Mykhailivka I equates with Seredni Stog II of the Dnieper Rapids which, in turn, has been equated with Tripolyan period B-1. This has been done on the strength of a few Tripolyan potsherds found at Seredni Stog which in earlier reports[44] were quoted simply as 'Tripolyan' or 'middle Tripolyan'. But on the Middle Boh, in the Tripolyan area nearest to the site of Seredni Stog and other similar ones in the region of the Dnieper Rapids, only settlements of periods B-2 and C-1 have been recorded (Maps III and VII). The date of the settlement at Sabatynivka I con-

[35] Д. Я. Телегин, К вопросу о днепро-донецкой неолитической культуре, Сов. Арх., vol. 1961–4, pp. 34 ff.

[36] В. М. Даниленко (op. cit., note 34), pp. 121 ff. А. В. Добровольський, Арх. Пам., vol. VI, 1952, p. 79. Телегин (op. cit., note 35), p. 37.

[37] Телегин, loc. cit. (note 35).

[38] See note 34, p. 128.

[39] Т. Г. Мовша, О связях племен трипольской культуры со степными племенами медного века, Сов. Арх., vol. 2, 1961, p. 193, Fig. 7:5.

[40] A. Äyräpää, 'Über die Streitaxtkulturen in Russland', *ESA*, vol. VIII, 1933, p. 157.

[41] А. В. Добровольський, Арх. Пам., vol. IX, 1960, pp. 141 ff. В. Д. Рибалова, Арх. Пам., vol. IX, 1960, pp. 5 ff. М. І. Вязьмітіна, Арх. Пам., vol. X, 1961, pp. 64 ff. Шапошникова, loc. cit., note 7.

[42] Лагодовская (op. cit., note 26), pp. 119 ff. М. Л. Макаревич, Ксиак, no. 4, 1955, p. 122 ff. О. Г. Шапошникова, Ксиак, no. 4, 1955, pp. 124 ff.; no. 11, 1961, pp. 38 ff. Е. Ф. Лагодовская, М. Л. Макаревич, О. Г. Шапошникова, Ксиак, no. 5, 1955, pp. 13 ff.; no. 9, 1959, pp. 21 ff.

[43] О. Ф. Лагодовська, О. Г. Шапошникова, М. А. Макаревич, Михайлівське поселення, Kiev 1962.

[44] Добровольський (op. cit., note 41), pp. 80 f. Нариси стародавної історії Української РСРС, Kiev 1957, p. 46.

sidered to be of period B-I[45] is highly questionable, because of the 'Cypriot' bronze pin and clay vessel modelled on a Caucasian cauldron of the middle of the second millennium B.C.[46] which were found in the relative layer 'A' (Fig. 8).

In the next occupation layer, Mykhailivka II, two levels were distinguished with a slightly different content. The shell-gritted ware was still present there, but the bulk of pottery was made of sand-gritted clay paste. Of a new type were vessels with a pointed or rounded base and usually a high cylindrical, sometimes slightly everted neck. Their surface was often smoothed with a comb-like implement, similar to that applied to the vessels with a pointed base found in barrow-graves of the Catacomb period in the same area. The usual decoration confined mainly to the neck and shoulder consisted of cord-impressed or stamped patterns arranged in horizontal lines or zones. Only two metal objects, two small copper awls, were found in this layer.

Mykhailivka II has been equated with Seredni Stog II, as has Mykhailivka I. Merpert[47] is of the opinion that Mykhailivka II corresponds to his third stage of the Yamna culture. The proper position of this settlement within a wider chronological framework is indicated however, by the debased 'Thuringian' amphorae found in its occupation layer. One of these vessels (Fig. 6:1)[48] had a short undecorated neck and two lugs on the body; its cord-impressed decoration on the upper part of the body consisted of three horizontal girdles: two made of shaded triangles and the third of groups of short vertical lines. It calls to mind some of the Sub-Carpathian 'Thuringian' amphorae of the advanced stage and can be classed as of type IIb. It equates the layer with the end of period II or period III of the Sub-Carpathian barrow-grave culture.

The results of the investigation of barrow-grave 11 of Akkermen on the Molochna east of the Dnieper, are also of importance for the establishment of the relative date of Mykhailivka II. Pottery found in secondary burials of this barrow was closely related to that of Mykhailivka II, as has been pointed out by Terenozhkin[49] who also emphasizes that other grave goods from these graves place them close to the Catacomb period. The primary burial of this barrow was a slab-cist grave in a stone ring ('cromlech'). Slab-cists were characteristic of the Globular Amphorae, which, as shown previously, had reached eastwards as far as the Dnieper. It is interesting to note that according to Äyräpää,[50] the influence of the Globular Amphorae is reflected on pottery of the Seredni Stog II type on the Dnieper, which equates both cultures, and also both layers, I and II, of Mykhailivka with these.

Remains of the upper layer, Mykhailivka III, were evidently of a late date. Its pottery was made of a clay paste tempered with sand, and no shell-gritted ware appeared in it. Most common, as before, were vessels with a pointed or rounded base. Many were undecorated, but others had a rich ornament consisting of cord or stamped impressions, hatched triangles being one of the most common decorative patterns. Twenty-six copper objects were excavated: awls, knives, a flat axe, chisel. There were also stone battle-axes and many flint implements: arrow-heads of the triangular type, knives, etc., and above all, flint daggers with the surface entirely covered with a fine retouch, an imitation of metal archetypes.

According to Merpert, this layer corresponded to his fourth stage of the Yamna culture. However, 'late Tripolyan' ware found there[51] equates Mykhailivka III with the developed period of the Usatovo culture further west and with the Catacomb period of the steppe barrow-graves. All the metal and flint implements found in the layer point to the same date.

Another site of importance is the stratified settlement of Moliukhov-Bugor at Novoselitsa on the Tiasmin near Chigirin,[52] at a distance of a few kilometres from the Dnieper. It was situated on the border of the proper steppe and the forest steppe zone, outside the area of the Lower Dnieper group, already in that of the Cherkasi-Kirovograd-Uman group (Map III).

Three superimposed occupation layers were uncovered. In the lowest one, microlithic flints and a number of potsherds were found comparable to the pottery of site Mykilska Slobidka near Kiev (Map III);[53] it has been equated to site Ihrin (Igren) 8, layer D.[54] Typical of the next, the middle layer, were ovoid vessels with a high cylindrical or slightly everted neck; their lightly polished surface was decorated by cord or stamped impressions. Flat-based cord-decorated vessels closely resembling Tripolyan vessels were also found in this layer but no metal objects.

Common in the upper layer was a shell-gritted ware. Vessels were flat-based, mainly cord-decorated, but many had a stamped ornament. A fragment of a stone battle-axe and a number of vessels of Tripolyan C-I ware are of importance for dating purposes.

'FLAT' CEMETERIES OF THE DNIEPER VALLEY (p. 188)

Graves in the 'flat' cemeteries, like those in the mounds, were oval shafts and were likewise covered with one or more stone slabs. Once a genuine 'catacomb' was uncovered. Skeletons, sprinkled with ochre, lay in the 'Yamna position', but in later graves the crouched position was common. Heads were to the north or east, and in later graves to the west. Burials were poorly furnished, the grave goods usually consisting of a single vessel seldom accompanied by animal bones, or bone beads; once a small copper ear-pendant was found.

Stone constructions were very common. Stone circles, 'cromlechs' up to 6·5m in diameter, surrounding several graves were normal with the earlier graves, whereas smaller rings, up to 3·5m in diameter, usually enclosing a single grave, were of a slightly later date. Typical of the Late Bronze Age, of the 'Srubna period', were 'stone covers', stones in one or two layers laid over the shaft.

[45] Op. cit., note 20, p. 13, map, Fig. 1.

[46] А. В. Добровольський, Арх. Пам., vol. IV, 1952, pp. 82 ff., Fig. 2, Pl. II:17. Пассек (op. cit., note 20), pp. 50 ff. V. Dumitrescu, Berichten van de rijksdienst voor het oudheidkundig bodemonderzoek, no. 9, 1959, p. 44. See also C. F. C. Schaeffer, *Antiquity*, vol. XVII, 1943, pp. 183 ff., Fig. E.

[47] Merpert (op. cit., note 3), pp. 183 ff.

[48] The amphorae (Fig. 6:1, 2) were published in the work cited in note 43 as Figs. 5:1; 30.

[49] О. І. Тереножкін, Арх. Пам., vol. VIII, 1960, p. 9; also pp. 112 ff.

[50] Äyräpää, (loc. cit., note 40).

[51] Op. cit., note 43, p. 42, Fig. 4.

[52] В. Н. Даниленко, Ксиак, no. 8, 1959, pp. 13 ff.

[53] В. М. Даниленко, Арх. Пам., vol. VI, 1956, pp. 172 ff.

[54] Gimbutas (op. cit., note 2), pp. 18 ff.

Pottery found in the earliest graves, e.g. at Osokorivka (no. 336), was a dark shell-gritted ware with a slightly polished surface. According to Rybalova[55] it corresponded with that of the settlement of Mykhailivka I (the lowest layer) and was definitely different from that of the two upper layers (II and III) of that site; she also considers it to be related to the Tripolyan ware and equates it with site 8 at Ihrin (Igren),[56] but emphasizes at the same time that the burial ritual and similar occurrences connect the graves in question with the Yamna barrow-graves.

The graves of the Catacomb period in which the vessels did not differ from those excavated in the corresponding barrow-graves were most numerous. An uncommon type was a decorated bowl with a wide base, provided with a knob-like hilt;[57] a similar bowl was found in a barrow-grave of the region.[58] Undecorated bowls on three legs, similar to the pedestalled 'incense burners' of the Catacomb culture (without their inner partition) were excavated in a flat grave of our group, and also in the upper layer of the settlement at Mykhailivka;[59] no such vessels have so far been found in barrow-graves.

Likewise important for our study are a few settlements and 'flat' cemeteries situated further east, in the valley of the Dnieper near Dnepropetrovsk, although in fact they lay just on the border of the area with which we are concerned here and belonged to a *Kulturkreis* characteristic of the country further east.

The settlement and cemetery (106 graves) at Dereivka[60] were amongst these. Vessels with a pointed base found there and their decoration correspond with those of sites Ihren 8 and Seredni Stog II. More important was the cemetery at Mykilske (Nikolskoe in Russian, no. 334), situated at a distance of about twenty-five kilometres south of Dnepropetrovsk on the western bank of the river, on the edge of the plateau. Seventy-one burials were uncovered. Skeletons lay in an extended position on the back, heads to the west or south-west, like those at Mariupol [61] and similar Neolithic cemeteries of the region. Many graves, mainly of the earlier periods, yielded no grave goods whatever. Furniture of the later burials consisted almost exclusively of personal ornaments, a fact which again links this cemetery with that of Mariupol. Several were made of metal: copper rings, beads, and pendants; one pendant was made of a thin gold sheet. No complete pots were found but sherds of about sixty broken vessels of various types lay scattered over the area of the cemetery; they were obviously broken during the funeral feasts.

Pottery was quite uniform. Most common were beakers with a wide aperture and a narrow base, with a straightened rim. The whole outer surface of the vessels, including the flat base, was covered with a pricked stamped ornament. Decorative patterns consisted either of incised horizontal lines or of short slanting lines arranged in alternating horizontal zones.

Slightly overlapping burial pits enabled the excavator to establish four consecutive periods in the use of the cemetery. No grave goods were found in the burials of the two earliest pits; they are considered to have dated from the Neolithic. Flint dart-heads, knives made of boar-tusks, and several other features equate the next pit, Б, with the period of the Mariupol cemetery, and pottery which lay on the surface and in the filling of the pit connect it with the sites of Seredni Stog I type of the Dnieper Rapids[62] and with the Tripolye culture; period A[63] of the latter culture was meant by the excavator but it should properly be connected with period B-2. In the filling of the latest pit, A, a vessel with a pointed base was excavated which the excavator connects with the Yamna (ochre-grave) culture. Over the cemetery lay 'stone covers', a kind of loosely cobbled area, typical of burial places of the Middle and Late Bronze Age of the Dnieper valley.[64]

The cranial material from the cemetery was quite homogeneous[65] and has been classified as of the 'Cromagnon' racial type, similar to that from the cemetery at Mariupol and other Late Neolithic cemeteries of the region of the Dnieper Rapids.

In Table 19, the stratigraphical sequence is shown of the layers of the settlements and cemeteries and some other sites discussed in this chapter; their reciprocal connections and equations pointed out by the investigators concerned, have been taken into account.

BARROW-GRAVES OF THE STEPPE BORDER
(Map VIII, group III) (pp. 185 ff.)

Barrow-graves of the wide transitional belt between the proper steppe and the forest steppe zones were a northern extension of the Lower Dnieper group. As has been said, the provisional name of 'Cherkasi-Kirovograd-Uman group' can be given them, although they do not form a homogeneous unit. Many do not differ from the steppe burials of the Yamna period further south, and many of the later ones have been included by Popova[66] in her Middle Dnieper variation of the Catacomb culture, the centre of which lay east of the Dnieper. Some features link the group with the Middle Dnieper culture which bordered on them to the north, and also with barrow-graves of the countries further west and north.

Graves were mostly in shafts dug in the ancient ground or in mounds already existing. Burials on the ancient land surface were seldom found and no catacombs were uncovered. In a few cases graves were surrounded by stone rings or 'cromlechs'. That at Verbovka, district of Chigirin (no. 303), was of particular interest; its ring was formed by twenty-nine vertical slabs many of which bore incised ornament consist-

[55] See note 41, p. 13.
[56] Gimbutas (op. cit., note 2), pp. 18 ff.
[57] Шапошникова (op. cit., note 7), Pl. I:1, 2.
[58] Березовець (op. cit., note 5: 1960), Fig. 21:5.
[59] Op. cit., note 7, Pl. II:1, and note 26, p. 120, Figs. 3, 5.
[60] Д. Я. Телегин, Ксиак, no. 12, 1962, pp. 13 ff., and 94 ff., Fig. 2:7. A. Häusler, 'Die Grabsitten der mesolithischen und neolithischen Jäger- und Fischergruppen auf dem Gebiet der UdSSR', *Wissenschaftliche Zft. d.M.Luther Universität*, Halle, vol. XI/10, 1962, p. 1164.
[61] M. Makarenko, 'Neolithic Man on the Shores of the Sea of Azov', *ESA*, vol. IX, 1934, pp. 135 ff. Gimbutas (op. cit., note 2), pp. 48 ff. Häusler, (op. cit., note 60), pp. 1161 f., 1168 f.
[62] А. В. Добровольський, Археологія, vol. VII, Kiev 1952, pp. 78 ff.
[63] See note 20.
[64] Häusler (op. cit., note 60), p. 1169.
[65] Г. П. Зиневич, Ксиак, no. 11, 1961, pp. 27 ff.
[66] Op. cit., note 14, pp. 75 ff.

TABLE 19. Correlation and connections of layers of three stratified sites in the Ukraine

Western Equations	Tripolyan Sequence	Vykhvatyntsi	Novoselitsa (Moliukhov-Bugor)	Mykilske (Nikolskoe)	Osokorivka	Mykhailivka	Yamna Catacomb Cultures	Dnieper sites
				Stone covers		Stone covers		Stone covers
					Late graves	III Upper layer	Catacomb	
					x	x	x	
							Usatovo	
						x	x	
								Durna Skela
						x		x
						II Middle layer	Usatovo	
			Upper layer	Pit 'A'		x	x	
Sub-Carpath. stage II/III	C-1							
	x		x			x		
x		x				x	Yamna cult.	
				x		x	x	
Globular Amphorae			Middle layer					Seredni Stog II
x								x
								Seredni Stog II
						x		x
Sub-Carpath. stage I/II			Lower layer		Early graves	I Lower layer		
x		x				x		Ihren 8
			x		x			x
	B-2							Seredni Stog II
	x					x		x
		x			x	x		Mykliska Slob.
			x					x
				Pit 'B'				
	x			x				Seredni Stog I
				x				x

ing of geometric figures, rhombs, double zigzag lines, etc., and even of schematic human figures. According to Formozov this ornament corresponds with that of the Caucasian dolmens.[67] The late date (the Catacomb period) of the barrow-grave from Verbovka is indicated by bone beads found in it. At Suškivka (no. 301) the secondary burial was encircled by stone boulders which, however, did not form a regular ring.

Skeletons in early graves were either in the 'Yamna position', on the back with legs contracted, heads to north or east, or more often in a crouched position, heads to the west. It is interesting to note that in a barrow-grave at Kobrynowa (no. 285)[68] the skeleton of the primary burial in the central shaft lay in a contracted position, head to west, whereas skeletons in the 'Yamna position' were found exclusively in secondary burials; the late date (Catacomb period) of the latter was shown by their grave goods among which were tubular bone beads, and bone hammer-headed pins. A single corpse was usually found in each grave but sometimes double burials were uncovered. Human offerings have been recorded at an early date. Thus in the barrow-grave of Kobrynowa, mentioned above, two skeletons lay in a shaft which was coeval with the original burial in the central shaft; both skeletons lay parallel in an extended position facing downward, both sprinkled with ochre, but with no grave goods whatever. Mutilated or completely dismembered skeletons were found in a few cases and once there was an additional, loose, human skull.[69] These practices seem to appear only in graves of an advanced stage of the culture which equated with the Catacomb period in the country further south. Cremation was an exception. In barrow-grave 8 at Kolodiste (no. 287) several cremations in urns were found within an area enclosed by a stone ring, where also lay two skeletons, one contracted, the other in an extended

[67] A. M. Tallgren, *ESA*, vol. IX, 1934, pp. 1 ff.

[68] G. Ossowski, *ZWAK*, vol. XII, 1888, p. 62, Pl. IX:12.

[69] Ibid., p. 68, Pl. IX:14.

position on its back. Vessels, thirteen in all including urns, are considered 'Tripolyan' by some authors, but 'Hallstatt' by others. This barrow-grave, except one burial in which a vessel with a pointed base was found, and also barrow-grave 9 from Kolodiste (also having cremations) seem to have belonged either to the very end of the Catacomb period, or to have been coeval with the Srubna graves of the steppe country and equated with the Central European Late Bronze Age.

Grave goods most frequently took the form of pottery. Usually a single vessel was found in one grave, but occasionally there were two or more. They were mostly ovoid with a pointed or rounded base and like those of the steppe graves were normally provided with a short neck (Fig. 7). Most were undecorated, some had the surface brushed with a comb-like implement, others had a simple decoration on the upper part of the body mainly incised, seldom impressed. Flat-based vessels with a cord-impressed decoration were likewise found, but none of these belonged to the well-known types of Central European Corded Ware. In a few barrow-graves Tripolyan vessels were excavated (e.g. Rotmistrovka, no. 296).

Personal ornaments were of the same type as those of the steppe graves: amulets made of perforated boar-tusks or animal fangs, marble and bone beads, necklaces made of beads of thin tubular bird bones usually covered with an incised spiral ornament, an imitation of beads made of metal wire. In a few graves bone hammer-headed pins were excavated,[70] in others amber beads, an amber disc, clay whorls, and a clay pendant.

Metal objects, almost exclusively personal ornaments, were very rare: a bronze ear-pendant with ends flattened (Ryżanówka 5; no. 298); two bronze pins with large rhomboid heads of Borodino type (Gulay-Gorod 41, no. 283) found together with a bronze pendant and four tubular beads made of a thin bronze sheet; an armlet with spiral terminals and two loose spirals, originally part of a large brooch (Teklino 347, no. 302). The latter ornaments were of the same type as those found at Voytsekhivka (no. 236) in Bronze Age barrow-graves; they seem to place the grave in the Late Bronze Age. The pins from Gulay-Gorod were typical of the Middle Bronze Age, *c.* 1500–1300 B.C.[71] In addition, at Grečkovka (no. 282, barrow-grave 249) was found a bronze or copper object which disintegrated; a copper axe at Olšanka (no. 294);[72] and copper awls and a copper knife in a few more graves.

Weapons were an exception. Two stone-battle-axes, flint arrow-heads, and a flint dagger complete the list. Once a hoe made of antler was excavated and at Kobrynowa sheep hooves were found in a few graves.

Barrow-graves under review encroached partly on Tripolyan territory, and in a few instances mounds were raised over the debris of Tripolyan huts.[73] This circumstance has been taken as evidence of the chronological precedence of the Tripolye culture over that represented by the barrow-graves. But in fact, this does not preclude at least partial contemporaneity of the two cultures and some sort of symbiosis of the people concerned.

THE CEMETERY OF VYKHVATYNTSI (no. 371) (Map IX)

The Usatovo culture bordered on the ochre-graves to the west, but before discussing that culture, the cemetery at Vykhvatyntsi and topics connected with it should be considered.[74]

The site was situated on the Middle Dniester near Ribnitsa. The cemetery lay on the edge of the plateau over the river valley on its left side. Sixty-one graves were excavated, all inhumations, in quadrangular, seldom oval, shafts with no external sign. Many graves were covered with small limestone slabs; some were within circles of slabs laid in a vertical or horizontal position. Sometimes only a single stone was found, either over the burial, or placed near the skeleton. These constructions of the graves and burial practices were of the same kind as those met with in the flat cemeteries and some barrow-graves on the Lower Dnieper, described above.

Skeletons lay in a contracted position, heads almost exclusively to the east, north-east, or south-east. The 'Yamna' position has been noticed in a few instances, chiefly in children's graves. Child burials amounted to a half of the total number of graves; two-thirds of the remaining ones being male burials. Ochre lumps were found in a few graves but the skeletons, or parts of them, were seldom sprinkled with ochre.

Only a few graves had no furniture. The grave goods normally consisted of pottery and usually two to five vessels were found in a single grave; graves with eight or eleven were exceptional. Vessels were of two categories. The bulk were of a well-baked Tripolyan ware made of well-silted clay paste, their surface decorated in black-painted geometric patterns; a black- and red-painted ornament appears on a number of bowls. The other variety was of vessels made of a sand or shell-gritted clay paste decorated with an incised, but mostly cord-impressed, ornament.

The common vessels were wide-mouthed bowls, spheroid vases with a short neck, vases with two small perforated lugs on the shoulder and corresponding bowl-shaped lids with perforated lugs on the top (base), etc. The most important for our study were the 'Thuringian' amphorae, or vessels evidently modelled on these. Such specimens of the sand-gritted category were cord decorated and did not differ in any respect from those of type IIC of the Sub-Carpathian barrow-graves (Fig. 1:8). Specimens which belonged to the Tripolyan ware represent slightly debased Thuringian amphorae (Fig. 1:4); they had a black-painted ornament which either followed the patterns characteristic of these vessels or was more elaborate, the original patterns being nevertheless discernible.

Other grave goods consisted of beads and pendants made of bone, stone, or Unio shells, once an entire necklace of Unio shell, and once a pendant of boar tusks. Flint knives and other small flint implements and flint chips were com-

[70] Ibid., Pls. IX:6, 7; X:1, 2.
[71] See note 17.
[72] Op. cit., note 20, p. 202, Fig. 98:12.
[73] Kolodistoe XII, no. 287; Suškivka, no. 301; Volodymirivka, no. 304.
[74] Т. С. Пассек, Раннеземледельческие (трипольские) племена Поднестровья, МИА, no. 84, 1961, p. 175.

mon. Awls made of bone and clay whorls were found sometimes in female graves and in a number of graves there were clay figurines, the so-called 'idols'.

Two richly furnished graves deserve mentioning. The grave goods of one of these, no. 9, in which probably a chief was buried, consisted of a stone battle-axe (or mace-head), a flint knife and a bone dagger, 13–14cm long, incorrectly described as a 'bone idol' in the report. In the shaft-hole of the axe remains of its wooden hilt survived covered with a thin copper sheet and fixed with two copper wedges. Other objects found there were a hoe of antler, a copper awl, flint chips, and six vessels. Among the latter was a deep black- and red-painted bowl and a black-painted vase of 'Thuringian' type.

The other grave, no. 11, was likewise of an adult male buried in a contracted position, head to the east. Lumps of ochre were found near the feet and a small flat limestone slab near the head. Grave goods consisted of ten vessels of both categories, among which was a 'Thuringian' black-painted amphora, a boar tusk, part of a clay 'idol', and a bone dagger labelled as a 'polisher' in the report.

According to Passek the cemetery was in use for not more than three generations, and is regarded by her as typical of her period C-2, the final one of Tripolyan development. However, a closer study of grave goods and of the character of the graves points to an earlier date.

The cemetery of Vykhavtyntsi, and a similar one uncovered at Holerkani on the Dniester further north-west in Bessarabia, belonged to a local group, to the formation of which at least three distinct elements had contributed. One of these was the local branch of the Tripolye culture, as witnessed by its painted ware. The shapes of the vessels of this category often differ from those of the genuine Tripolyan ware and connect the group with the Gorodsk and Usatovo culture in the north and south respectively. But the study of its decorative patterns shows that similar ones were current in Tripolyan period B-2 for the monochrome black-painted pottery, e.g. at Volodymirivka; the characteristic 'late Tripolyan' black cross-hatching appears likewise among Tripolyan decorative patterns of period B-2 but not in period C-1.[75]

Another element must have been the steppe population who were closely related to the people of the settlements and 'flat' cemeteries in the region on the Lower Dnieper; this is suggested particularly by stone constructions ('cromlechs') found around many graves, by the 'Yamna position' of several skeletons and similar circumstances. But the leading element in the formation of the Vykhvatyntsi group must have been the Corded Ware people. This element is represented by the sand-gritted cord-decorated ware, the 'Thuringian' amphorae, and also by the richly furnished male graves.

The results of the anthropological study also point to a mixed, hybrid character of the group, although only eleven skulls were studied; all others being badly preserved, their study was not practicable. All male skulls were of the dolichocephalic Mediterranean type, whereas female skulls were mesocephalic, of a type proper to the Catacomb culture and the Srubna-Khvalinsk culture of the steppes east of the Dnieper.

Taking into account all this, the Vykhvatyntsi group should be equated with the later stage of the first, and the second period of the Sub-Carpathian barrow-graves, and also with the earliest graves of the cemetery of Osokorivka (no. 336) and the earliest (I) layer of the settlement of Mykhailivka, both in the region on the Lower Dnieper. Accordingly the group must be equated with the final stage of Tripolyan period B-2 and with period C-1. Its relative position is shown in Table 19.

THE USATOVO CULTURE
(Map VIII, group IV) (p. 189)

This name has been given to barrow-graves and settlements of the Early Bronze Age which yielded Tripolyan type painted vessels. They extended over the western portion of the Pontic steppe, west of the Ingul and the Bohl.[76] A few sites in Bessarabia, west of the Dniester, were also included in this culture, and the graves from Brăiliţa on the Lower Danube in Romania[77] are considered to be the south-westernmost finds of the culture, although their pottery differs from that of the genuine Usatovo sites.

According to Passek[78] the Usatovo group was an integral part of the Tripolye culture and represented the latest stage in its development termed period C-2 (γ-2). Her views have been contested by several authors[79] according to whom the remains in question had formed an independent unit of the barrow-grave assemblage, although strongly influenced by the Tripolye culture.

Barrow-graves of the Usatovo culture exhibit a great variety in many respects. 'Cromlechs', or stone rings, around the original perimeter of the mound, often built of vertical slabs, were very common. Sometimes two or three concentric rings were uncovered; on some slabs of the 'cromlechs' incised human or animal figures were found, and on some there were geometric patterns.

According to stratigraphic evidence in the Slobidka (Slobodka in Russian, no. 361) barrow-grave of Odessa, the earliest graves were in shafts of Yamna type. Later burials were often on the ancient land surface, but secondary interments were mostly in mounds. Slab-cist graves were relatively numerous, often looted soon after the funeral. Catacombs were rare.

The 'Yamna' position of the skeletons seems to have prevailed in graves of an earlier date, whereas later the crouched position was common. The usual eastern or northern orientation of heads seems to be due to the Yamna substratum of the Usatovo culture. Heads to the west, characteristic of Corded Ware culture, were found mainly in later graves.

At Usatovo (nos. 366, 370), besides two barrow-grave cemeteries, a 'flat' cemetery was uncovered. The burials were in shafts covered with a large stone slab, and skeletons

[75] E.g. Пассек (op. cit., note 20), Fig. 60 (Volodymirivka). Id., Ксиимк, no. 37, 1951, Fig. 29:2 (Polivaniv Yar). V. Dumitrescu, *Hăbăşeşti*, Bucureşti 1954, Pl. LXXXVI:2. Cross-hatching appears also on several painted vases of the Tripolyan settlement at Zhury on the Dniester.

[76] Пассек (op. cit., note 20), pp. 189 ff. See also: О. Ф. Лагодовська, Археологія, vol. VIII, Kiev 1953, pp. 95 ff., Fig. 2 (map).

[77] I. T. Dragomir, *MAC*, vol. V, 1959, pp. 671 ff., Fig. 7.

[78] Op. cit., note 20, p. 200; and also *L'Europe à la fin de l'âge de la pierre*, Praha 1961, pp. 154 f.

[79] T. Sulimirski, *PPS*, vol. XVI, 1950, pp. 42 ff. A. J. Brjussow, *Geschichte der neolithischen Stämme im europäischen Teil de UdSSR*, Berlin 1957. L. Kilian, 'Schnurkeramik und Ockergrabkultur', *SMYA*, vol. 59:2, 1957, pp. 37 ff. V. Dumitrescu (op. cit., note 46), pp. 36 ff. Лагодовська, loc. cit., note 76.

were almost exclusively in the crouched position. Grave goods did not differ from those found in barrow-graves but were less numerous, which, together with evidence of a less showy burial ritual, indicates that a poorer section of the Usatovo society was buried there.

A fortified settlement was uncovered at Usatovo. Houses, quadrangular in plan, were built of vertical slabs and blocks. Very large deposits of archaeological remains were excavated there, as well as potsherds, shells, etc. Bones were mainly of domesticated beasts, sixty per cent being those of sheep, and a lesser proportion those of cows.

Much has been written about the grave goods and other remains of the Usatovo culture, and about the close resemblance of its pottery to that of the Gorodsk (Horodsk) culture in East Volhynia, and the term 'Usatovo-Gorodsk' group has been coined on this account. Connections with Aegean countries and Anatolia during EM III and MM I periods have been pointed out; they are reflected, e.g. by silver-plated copper daggers.[80] But all this applies only to the material excavated at Usatovo, in the richly furnished graves and in the settlement. This was, however, a unique occurrence and no similarly furnished graves have been found in other parts of the Usatovo territory, which implies that the site of Usatovo must have held a special position. It was conveniently placed on a liman close to the Black Sea shore, near to the site of modern Odessa, and must have been an important centre of trading with overseas. Burials of the culture outside the centre at Usatovo were poorly furnished and in this respect they do not much differ from those of the Lower Dnieper group of ochre-graves.

Pots, usually one or two vessels but never more than four, were the commonest grave goods; other objects, chiefly personal ornaments, were seldom found. Pottery was of two types. One of these was a kind of Tripolyan ware, well made and fired, the surface smoothed, reddish in colour and covered with a black-painted ornament; it formed only eight per cent of pottery excavated in the settlement at Usatovo. It has been termed the γ-2 ware by Passek who wrongly considers it to be characteristic of her final period in Tripolyan sequence.

The bulk of Usatovo pottery, whether in graves or settlements, consisted of sand or shell-gritted ware, mostly cord decorated. Shaded triangles, bands, etc., were its usual decorative patterns, but characteristic of the Usatovo style were small semicircular, or semi-lunar impressions made with a twisted cord stamp, arranged in various figures. These patterns, as mentioned when discussing the northern Corded Ware, appear also in the Gorodsk group and further north, outside the reach of Tripolyan influence. 'Thuringian amphorae' found in a series of graves of the culture and also in the settlement of Usatovo[81] belong likewise to the same category; they were mostly of IIa and IIc types distinguished in the Sub-Carpathian Corded Ware.

Weapons were very scarce. Two stone battle-axes were evidently connected with north-western Corded Ware. Of interest was a specimen from Horozheno (no. 341) found in a barrow-grave attributable to a group transitional from the proper steppe ochre-graves to those of the Usatovo culture. It had an incised decoration related to the 'Mycenaean' ornament of the silver pin and spear-head from Borodino.[82] No flint axes were found in any grave. The few copper daggers and flat axes from Usatovo were seemingly of Anatolian origin. Outside Usatovo itself, only one (bronze) dagger with four rivet holes was found (Sukleia, no. 362);[83] it was seemingly of Central European origin, typical of Montelius II, of Reinecke's A-2 or B period of the Bronze Age.

Copper knives and awls were found outside Usatovo only in two or three graves. Personal ornaments, seldom found, consisted mainly of perforated animal teeth and discoid bone beads. The bone pin from Tiraspol (no. 365), with a flat perforated head, was an imitation of an Unetice bronze pin. Three small copper and silver pendants were found, one of these (Sukleia) together with the bronze dagger mentioned above.

ORIGIN, CHRONOLOGY

That the people of the Usatovo culture were not a homogeneous society is indicated by the diversity of grave structures, by the differences evident in their furniture and burial rites, by graves of servs and attendants situated close to those of their masters, etc. In the roots of this social stratification lies presumably the complex origin of the Usatovo population.

According to the views widely accepted in Soviet archaeological literature, two main factors contributed to the formation of the Usatovo culture. One of these was the local group of the Yamna culture, a branch of the large assemblage which extended over the steppes further east; the other was the Tripolye culture. The disagreements between scholars apply mainly to the importance attributed to the relative contributions of the cultures; accordingly the Usatovo culture has been assigned to one or the other of the above assemblages. But the two cultures above were not the only contributors; the role of some other elements was possibly of even greater importance. In discussing these topics the following points should be considered:

(*a*) The stratigraphic evidence offered by the barrow-grave of Slobidka in Odessa (no. 361)[84] implies the priority of Yamna graves over the Tripolyan element. The painted pottery was found there exclusively in secondary burials, in a catacomb grave and in a secondary slab-cist grave. The original grave and some of the earliest burials were of Yamna type with hardly any grave goods.

(*b*) The Usatovo painted ware was strikingly similar to that of the Vykhvatyntsi cemetery (no. 371) dealt with previously, and also to that of the Gorodsk group of Volhynia.[85] This points to the direction from which it reached the West Ukrainian steppe and suggests a later date for the Usatovo pottery.

[80] Лагодовська (op. cit., note 76), p. 99. М. Ф. Болтенко, Ксимк, no. XII, 1946, p. 164. G. Rosenberg, *Kulturströmungen in Europa zur Steinzeit*, Kopenhagen 1931, p. 15.

[81] Пассек (op. cit., note 20), Fig. 97. Gimbutas (op. cit., note 2), Fig. 60.

[82] See note 17.

[83] Tallgren (op. cit., note 10), Fig. 112:2. Op. cit., note 20, p. 195, Fig. 99:8, 11.

[84] Tallgren (op. cit., note 10), pp. 48 ff., Fig. 37. Gimbutas (op. cit., note 2), pp. 85 ff., Figs. 47–9.

[85] Gimbutas (op. cit., note 2), pp. 106 ff., Fig. 59 Пассек (op. cit., note 20), pp. 157 ff., Figs. 82–91, 96.

(*c*) Some of the decorative patterns of the Gorodsk and Usatovo painted ware call to mind those of the incised ornament of the Corded Ware, and this applies in particular to the pottery of the Vykhvatyntsi cemetery, which seems to be the earliest of the three. But other patterns closely resemble the monochrome black-painted ornament of Tripolyan ware of period B-2, e.g. that from Volodymirivka.[86] The presence of features characteristic of period B-2 in the remains of the Gorodsk group has been emphasized by scholars.[87] This circumstance implies that there must have been no great time lag between the remains of Vykhvatyntsi-Gorodsk-Usatovo type and Tripolyan period B-2.

(*d*) The geographical distribution of sites with the genuine 'Usatovo' painted ware is restricted to the valley of the Lower Dniester and to a short narrow strip of land along the sea shore further east. Tripolyan pottery found in barrow-graves of the steppe further east, the Lower Boh and even east of the Dnieper[88] has also been included in the Usatovo group. This pottery differs, however, from The 'Usatovo' painted ware both in the shape of its vessels and in their decorative style. It must have been of a different origin, although likewise Tripolyan, and was evidently due to the contact of the steppe population with the Tripolyans on the Middle Boh, on the steppe border. The 'Usatovo' pottery excavated in graves on the Lower Danube in Romania[89] also differs from the genuine Usatovo painted ware.

(*e*) No pottery typical of Passek's period C-2 (or γ-2), whether of the Corded or painted class, has been found in Tripolyan settlements south of Kiev or in the region on the Middle Boh, although the latter must have been in existence during the period in which the Usatovo culture flourished further south. The 'Cypriot' bronze pin and the clay vessel modelled on the Caucasian cauldron found at Sabatynivka I (Fig. 8) mentioned previously, offer good evidence of this, although the layer in which they were found is considered by Passek to belong to her period B-1.[90]

(*f*) Painted ware formed a relatively small fraction of pottery of the Usatovo culture, the bulk of which was a kind of Corded Ware, evidently of northern origin. Its early appearance in the steppe before the monochrome black-painted ware, is evident from the stratigraphical position of the 'Thuringian' amphorae (Fig. 6) in the settlement of Mykhailivka I; painted vessels from Vykhvatyntsi modelled on the Thuringian amphorae (Fig. 1:4, 5, 8) likewise point to the early date of the Corded Ware current.

(*g*) Slab-cist graves, common in the Usatovo culture, were known neither to the Yamna nor Tripolye and Corded Ware cultures; they were, however, typical of the Globular Amphorae. The character of these graves—burials of an alien ruling class over the local population—has been emphasized previously in this volume. A few isolated graves and other remains typical of the Volhynian branch of the Globular Amphorae found south of its proper area link the latter with the Usatovo culture (Map V). Äyräpää[91] points out that some of the Usatovo vessels derived from pottery of the Globular Amphora culture, and amber found at Usatovo also supports the idea of close connections between the two groups. The Globular Amphorae must be included in the list of contributors to the formation of the Usatovo culture, although they arrived somewhat later.

In summing all this up, we may conclude that:

1. The basic element in the development of the Usatovo culture were most probably the steppe pastoralists, the people of the early Yamna culture; their graves mark the first period in the Usatovo sequence, the beginning of which may be assigned to the late third millennium B.C. An admixture of the original inhabitants of the country of mesolithic ancestry, fishers and gatherers in the valley of the main rivers, cannot be ruled out.[92]

2. Next to appear were the early Corded Ware people who came there from the north, or north-west, along the Dniester. Their arrival marks the beginning of the second period of the Usatovo sequence of which the proper 'classic' Usatovo culture was typical. The cemetery of Vykhvatyntsi shows the way they had come. They were in some way connected with the people of the Sub-Carpathian barrow-graves and its related groups, and their remains equate with those of the late stage of the first or the second stage of the Sub-Carpathian group. They belonged to the same wave of Corded Ware which was responsible for the appearance of Corded Ware in the earliest layer of the Mykhailivka settlement, and also for the appearance of the 'Thuringian' amphorae in the cemeteries of the Sofiivka group around Kiev (Fig. 1:7, 9), and in the Tripolyan settlement of Kolomiščyna I, and likewise further east, near Briansk.

3. The third formative element at Usatovo was the Tripolye culture. On the Lower Boh and in the steppe further east, this was the influence of the Middle Boh (Uman) group of the culture which was responsible for the presence of Tripolyan pottery in the steppe barrow-graves. The position in the western portion of the steppe, on the Dniester, was different. Painted ware found there in the remains of the Usatovo culture, being closely related to that of the Vykhvatyntsi cemetery and of the Gorodsk group further north, seems to have been brought by the immigrants to the steppe, and its origin must be sought somewhere in East Podolia or South Volhynia.

4. The latest to arrive were the representatives of the Globular Amphora culture. It seems very likely that they were also responsible for the southern extension of the Gorodsk-Tripolyan elements, and that the development of commercial relations with the north (amber) and with the oversea countries (Anatolia) was due to their activity. The commercial, and possibly also political, centre of the culture was then established at Usatovo or somewhere near by. Connections with the Aegean countries, reflected in the archaeological material,[93] suggest the time *c.* 2000–1800 B.C. for the formation of the proper Usatovo culture which emerged then

86 Пассек (op. cit., note 20), Fig. 60, and also pp. 97 f.

87 See note 7 in Chapter VI.

88 Kolodiste, Olšanka, Serizlievka, Krivoy Rog, Zhyvotylivka north-east of Dnepropetrovsk (nos. 287, 294, 299, 316); see note 20.

89 I. T. Dragomir, 'Necropola Tumulară de la Brăilița', *MCA*, vol. V, 1951, pp. 671 ff., Fig. 7.

90 Op. cit., note 20, pp. 48 ff.

91 Äyräpää (op. cit., note 40), p. 121.

92 В. М. Даниленко, Археологія, vol. X, Kiev 1957, pp. 36 ff. Id., Ксиак, no. 12, 1962, pp. 23 ff.

93 See note 80.

as a blend of the elements mentioned above. This was the second, the 'classic' period of the Usatovo culture.

5. By the middle of the second millennium B.C. connections with Anatolia and the Aegean seem to have ceased and instead those with Central European countries, the Hungarian Plain in particular, had developed. This was the third period of the Usatovo development, a typical example of which was the barrow-grave of Sukleia (no. 362). The stratigraphic evidence of the barrow-grave at Odessa (no. 361) implies that graves of the Srubna type were already characteristic for the subsequent period. It has been established[94] that the Srubna culture had not reached the Lower Dnieper before the thirteenth century B.C. This was the approximate final date of the Usatovo culture.

[94] Op. cit., note 14, pp. 47 ff. O. A. Кривцова-Гракова (op. cit., note 16), pp. 110 ff.

CHAPTER VIII

Conclusions

OCHRE-GRAVES

THERE ARE a number of topics which could not be discussed within the restricted limits of smaller territorial units, some of which are of the utmost importance for the study of the prehistoric past of the whole of Central and Eastern Europe. We shall briefly review them here against the background discussed in the respective chapters.

Typical of the East European grassland during the Neolithic and the Bronze Age were the 'ochre-graves', the Yamna type being the earliest of these burials. According to Merpert,[1] the steppe on the Lower Volga and the Don was the original centre from which they expanded westwards and ultimately crossed the Dnieper. He distinguishes four stages in the development of the culture, the beginning of which is thought to have been early in the third millennium B.C.; the Dnieper is supposed to have been reached during the second stage of the Yamna period, in the second quarter of the third millennium B.C. Gimbutas[2] proposes *c.* 2400–2300 B.C. for the appearance of the Yamna culture on the Dnieper, which is in agreement with the date of 'ochre-graves' of Yamna type investigated at Baia Hamangia near the Danubian Delta in Romania, Carbon-14 dated as 2140±160 (Bln. 29) and 2580 B.C. (GrN. 1955).[3]

Graves of Yamna type, inhumations in shafts under mounds with hardly any grave goods, with skeletons on the back, the legs contracted, sprinkled with ochre, head to east or north, were found likewise in other parts of Romania.[4] They preceded the expansion of the Corded Ware, as shown by stratigraphic evidence at Gurbaneşti,[5] where corded ware appeared in the secondary burials in mounds the primary graves of which were of the Yamna type.

Ochre-graves under mounds, of Yamna type with no pottery, were excavated furthermore in the north-eastern corner of the Hungarian Plain, on the Upper Theiss,[6] where they dated to the very end of the Bodrogkeresztur period. All the above ochre-graves, whether in Romania or in Hungary, are considered to be of East European origin, and this, in turn, implies that the Yamna culture must have entered the Ukraine and crossed the Dnieper at a date not later than the Bodrogkeresztur period in the Hungarian Plain.

The expansion of the Yamna people into the Ukraine west of the Dnieper seems neither to have been a warlike expedition, nor to have resulted in a displacement of the former inhabitants of the areas affected. The climate of the Early Neolithic being very dry,[7] the early agriculturalists in the country under review kept exclusively to the river valleys, and the then inhospitable plains seem to have been avoided. It was only after the change to a more humid climate, the equivalent of the Atlantic phase in Western Europe, that the steppe, and also what was later the forest steppe, offered more opportunity for pastoral economy. The expansion of the nomad pastoralists of the Yamna culture seems to have taken place at a time when conditions considerably improved and thus the whole Ukrainian grassland was by degrees inhabited by the Yamna people.

In this context, I should like to draw attention to a very striking phenomenon revealed by the study of the geographical diffusion of the relevant cultures in the Ukraine.

Map VIII shows the diffusion of various groups of Neolithic and Early Bronze Age barrow-graves. They cover almost the whole forest steppe and steppe country west of the Dnieper and constitute a marked link between the eastern ochre-graves and the Sub-Carpathian Barrow-grave culture and similar groups further west. However, they leave a very noticeable gap in their distribution: no Neolithic and Early Bronze Age barrow-graves appear within the territory which extends north-east of the Middle Dniester up to the Boh and a little beyond that river, as marked on Map VIII. The importance of that fact is that this is precisely the area identical with the reach of the early Tripolyan settlements of A and B-I periods, shown in Map III.

The above coincidence does not seem fortuitous, and we may conjecture that the country which extended north of the early Tripolyans was grassland at that time and was in the possession of early pastoralists, possibly the bearers of an early group of ochre-graves or of some related group. They seem to have avoided the arid country further south where the early Tripolyans lived, exclusively in the river valleys. Because of the changing climatic conditions, which became more humid, the Tripolyans were able to cultivate the soil of the plains and to proceed further north. They ultimately settled over the whole forest steppe country, the chernozem area, as shown by

[1] N. I. Merpert, 'L'Énéolithique de la zone steppique de la partie européene de l'URSS', *Prague Symposium*, pp. 176 ff.

[2] M. Gimbutas, 'Notes on the Chronology and Expansions of the Pit-grave Culture', *Prague Symposium*, pp. 193 ff.

[3] G. Kohl, H. Quirra, 'Ausgrabungen und Funde', *Nachrichtenblatt f. Vor- und Frühgeschichte*, vol. 8/6, 1963, p. 286. J. C. Vogel, H. T. Waterbolk, *Radiocarbon*, vol. 5, 1963, p. 184.

[4] D. Berciu, 'Chronologie relative du Néolithique de Bas Danube à la lumière des nouvelles fouilles faites en Roumanie', *Prague Symposium*, pp. 117, 120 ff. V. Dumitrescu, 'The Date of Earliest Western Expansion of the Kurgan Tribes', *Dacia*, vol. NS VII, 1963, pp. 495 ff.

[5] D. V. Rosetti, 'Movilele funerale de la Gurbaneşti, *MCA*, vol. VI, 1959, pp. 791 ff.

[6] F. Köszegi, 'Contribution à la question de l'origine des tombes à ochre en Hongrie', *Archaeologiai Estesitö*, vol. 89, 1962, pp. 21 ff.

[7] T. Sulimirski, 'The Climate of the Ukraine During the Neolithic and the Bronze Age', *Archeologia*, vol. XII, Warszawa 1961, pp. 13 ff.

their remains of periods B-2 and C (Map VII). However, they had to share the land with the pastoralists who were there the earlier inhabitants of the country (Map VIII).

These presumed events imply a relatively early appearance of the Yamna or barrow-grave pastoralists in the Ukraine west of the Dnieper. But irrespective of the date of their appearance, upon entering new areas, the pastoralists must have met the local inhabitants of the river valleys, especially of the Dnieper Rapids region where the Yamna type of graves appear, and also further west near Mikhailivka, on the Boh, etc. That some sort of peaceful coexistence seems to have developed between the two populations is suggested by the appearance in the steppe graves of pottery related to that of their sedentary neighbours. No pottery was found in the earliest Yamna graves, their sepulchral vessels being probably made of some perishable organic matter, leather, bladders, basketry, etc. The diversity of pottery found in the steppe graves of a somewhat later date in various parts of their area, seems to be due to the different types of pottery made by various peoples with whom the pastoralists came into contact, and whose pottery they subsequently adopted. Consequently, pottery cannot always be looked upon as an identification mark of the early pastoralists, as it can in the case of more or less sedentary peoples.

The actual traces of early contact of the Yamna people with the inhabitants of the region of the Dnieper Rapids can be found in the remains of Seredni Stog II type, although the arrival of the pastoralists may be put rather to the preceding period, of Seredni Stog I. The contact with the Tripolyans had taken place mainly on the steppe border on the Middle Boh. Traces of this contact have likewise been attested right in the steppe country: in a barrow-grave at Krivoy Rog on the Ingulets (no. 316)[8] a vessel was found provided with two lugs under the rim, reminiscent of the Bodrogkeresztur beakers. The vessel, although made in the Tripolyan technique, was not of Tripolyan type and its position in the Tripolyan chronological scheme is difficult to establish.

The Yamna influx seems to have reached the Sub-Carpathian area. A number of barrow-graves there, either with no grave goods at all, or but poorly furnished, e.g. Kołpiec II (no. 46), were demonstrably of Yamna type, even though the position of the skeletons is unknown, faint traces of them having been found only in exceptional cases. The custom itself of raising a mound over the grave seems likewise to be of eastern origin and connected with the advance of the Yamna pastoralists. No prototype of the burial mounds can be found locally: they appear in the area suddenly as a well-established and constituted custom. The earliest Yamna burials in the steppe on the Lower Volga seem to have been the earliest known barrow-graves although their date has been perhaps estimated too high by Merpert.[9] The earliest West European barrow-graves were seemingly of a later date.

The expansion of the Yamna people cannot be identified with the spread of Corded Ware, for the latter formed a different grouping. The relations of the two assemblages with one another are discussed below.

CORDED WARE

The Corded Ware assemblage was one of the most important of the Late Neolithic in Europe. It consisted of a variety of cultures which in various degrees differed from each other and were not all of the same period. They fall into two main easily distinguishable categories. To one of these belongs the cord-decorated pottery found on sand-dunes within the Central European forest zone between the Dnieper and the Oder, and even to the Elbe; the sites there were traces of temporary encampments, and only seldom have remains of settlements of a more permanent character been noticed there (Map VI).

A few groupings of remains of a similar character but evidently of a later date were found outside the above territory, but close to its borders. Among these are the Strzyżów and the Gorodsk cultures in the south, and the Rzucewo culture[10] on the Baltic coast in the north. They were hybrid groups, and besides the Corded Ware element, other local cultures also took part in their formation.

The other category distinguishable in the Corded Ware assemblage were cultures consisting almost exclusively of sepulchral remains, with no settlements or encampments attributable to them. They kept to the territories outside that of the first category. In some areas, e.g. the Sub-Carpathian region (Map IV), a culture in this category was the only one of the period, in others it was found along with contemporary cultures of a different type and origin.

The so-called 'A-complex' consisting of an 'A-amphora', 'A-beaker' and 'A-battle-axe' is considered to be characteristic of the earliest stage of the second category;[11] it is supposed to have spread over large territories within a relatively short period and therefore to have formed a chronological horizon called the 'Common European Corded Ware Horizon'. The name of 'Battle-axe cultures' is usually given to this complex after its typical weapon.

According to recent archaeological research, the Battle-axe complex did not form such a uniform entity as has hitherto been accepted. Both Struve[12] and Fischer[13] emphasize that in north-western Europe, two distinct provinces of it can be distinguished: a northern province of the 'Single-graves', or the 'Beaker area', and the southern one, with its centre in Thuringia, the 'Amphora area'. The results of our study show that in the Sub-Carpathian region and in the neighbouring areas, the 'A-beakers' were very seldom found, being replaced mostly by beakers of a different type, and more often there are no beakers among grave goods. It seems, therefore, that 'A-beakers' appear mainly in the western groups of the Corded Ware assemblage, i.e. within the territory affected by

[8] О. Ф. Лагодовська, Пам'ятки усатівського типу, Археологія-Kiev, vol. VIII, 1953, p. 106, Fig. 3.

[9] Merpert, loc. cit., note 1.

[10] J. Żurek, 'Osada z młodszej epoki kamiennej w Rzucewie pow. wejherowski i kultura rzucewska', *FAP*, vol IV, 1953. L. Kilian, *Haffküstenkultur und Ursprung der Balten*, Bonn 1955.

[11] P. V. Glob, *Studier over den Jyske Enkeltgravskultur*, København 1945. K. W. Struve, *Die Einzelgrabkultur in Schleswig-Holstein und ihre kontinentalen Beziehungen*, Neumünster 1955, pp. 11 ff. C. J. Becker, *Die mittel-neolithischen Kulturen in Südskandinavien*, København 1955, pp. 114 ff. M. Buchvaldek, 'Z problematyki kultury ceramiki sznurowej w Europie', *Sprawozdania Komisji PAN*, Kraków 1961, pp. 12 ff.

[12] Struve (op. cit., note 11), pp. 98, 116 f.

[13] U. Fischer, 'Mitteldeutschland und die Schnurkeramik', *Jahresschrift f. mitteldeutsche Vorgeschichte*, vol. 41/42, Halle 1958, opp. 254, 290.

the Bell-beakers and being probably connected with these in some way.

Likewise battle-axes have not been found in graves of all the groups in question; the circumstances in the Sub-Carpathian area show that they were proper to an advanced stage of the culture and were preceded there by flint axes. The same has been reported in Thuringia[14] and in the Danish Under-graves, and noticed also on the Dnieper (Griščintsy, no. 242) and even further east (Rečitsa, no. 277). The burial ritual was fairly uniform, the skeletons being mostly in the crouched position, heads to the west, occasionally sprinkled with ochre. But here again a difference exists between areas in which 'flat' graves were typical and those where a mound was raised over the burial. Graves of the latter type occur only within a broad strip of land on the northern fringe of the loess soils of Central Europe, from the eastern grassland to Jutland, thus suggesting some connection of this custom with the relative practice of the steppe population, the people of the Yamna culture.

The facts above indicate that the Battle-axe Corded-ware complex must have consisted of a series of originally different elements. The element which really unified them was the cord-impressed decoration, and also a special type of vessel, the so-called 'Thuringian amphora' of Schraplau type. These vessels appear in almost all groups at their early stages. Those in their pure form, the 'A-amphorae', were probably all of approximately the same date and denote the 'Common European Corded Ware Horizon'. Those of the more developed or 'debased' forms, and also various local hybrid types, must be placed in periods, which followed the 'Horizon'. In our area, the latter applies to the amphorae from the cemetery at Vykhvatyntsi, of the Sofiivka group and the Usatovo culture, of the settlement at Mikhailivka, and also to the vessel from grave 22 at Valea Lupului[15] (Fig. 1:4–9). The latter, Buchvaldek type III, equates the grave, and the respective stage of Moldavian barrow-graves, with the third stage of the Sub-Carpathian Barrow-grave culture.

The relative date of the 'Horizon' within the Ukrainian chronological framework is given by the amphorae from Mykhailivka, and also by the Tripolyan vessels from Kolomiščyna I modelled on these amphorae. The 'Horizon' equated with the end of Tripolyan period B-2, or the turn of period B-2 to C-1.

THE ORIGIN OF CORDED WARE

The considerations above lead on to discussion of the origin of Corded Ware, which is a subject of the utmost importance for a proper understanding of development in the country under review.

The literature on this subject is very extensive; the main issue being whether it was of eastern or western origin. In a paper published over thirty years ago,[16] I was in favour of the eastern origin and held that the Yamna culture was an ancestor of the Central European barrow-graves and other groups of the Corded Ware/Battle-axe assemblage. Further study inclined me to change my opinion in this respect, and I think that the results of my research presented in this book, which have been attained by other authors as well,[17] fully support my views as expressed a few years ago,[18] in spite of the reservations since made by Kilian.[19]

I consider that the two categories of Corded Ware distinguished above originally formed one entity, their division and differences being the effect of their different development in different circumstances.

The light sandy soils of the Central European forest zone between the Dnieper and the Oder are most likely to have been the original home of the Corded Ware; the actual archaeological material found there on the surface of sand-dunes seems to represent a rather later stage in its development. Remains of the earlier stage should be sought in the deeper layers of the peat-bogs within that territory, as similarly they were found in East Prussian peat-bogs.[20] The early date of the Corded Ware has often been pointed out.[21]

The country where Corded Ware is conjectured to have originated was nearly identical with that of the Masovian (Dnieper-Elbe) culture, which was possibly its ancestor.[22] Corded Ware often appears on the same sites mixed with a microlithic flint industry and pottery of 'Masovian' type; seventy-five per cent of the Masovian sites in the north-western part of the Territory yielded sherds of Corded Ware as well. Gardawski[23] emphasizes the close contact which must have existed between the two cultures and is reflected in the shape and decoration of their vessels. From this centre the Corded Ware people seem to have expanded in small groups in various directions in search of better pastures for their cattle which the forest could no more provide owing to climatic deterioration. K. Bertsch[24] points out that the spread of the beech and the fir over Central Europe (at the end of the Neolithic and the Early Bronze Age) resulted in the formation of large impenetrable forests there, inhospitable to the human groups. Another cause may have been the rise in the level of ground water which in that area resulted in the formation of marshes and swamps.[25]

The hallmark of the expanding groups were the 'Thuringian' amphorae. Each of these vessels bears a striking resemblance to the others, either in shape or decoration or in both, in spite of the very distant countries in which they have

[14] Ibid., p. 272.

[15] M. Dinu, *MCA*, vol. VI, 1959, p. 206, Fig. 4.

[16] T. Sulimirski, 'Die schnurkeramischen Kulturen und das indoeuropäische Problem', *La Pologne au VIIe Congrès Intern. des Sc. Historiques*, Varsovie 1933.

[17] E.g. Struve (op. cit., note 11), pp. 116 ff. Glob (op. cit., note 11), pp. XII f. G. Mildenberger, *Studien zum mitteldeutschen Neolithikum*, Leipzig 1953, pp. 65 ff.

[18] T. Sulimirski, ' "Thuringian" Amphorae', *PPS*, vol. XXI, 1955, pp. 108 ff.

[19] L. Kilian, 'Schnurkeramik und Ockergrabkultur', *SMYA*, vol. 59:2, 1957, pp. 45 f.

[20] H. Gross, 'Ergebnisse d. moorgeologischen Untersuchungen d. vorgeschichtlichen Dörfer im Zedmar-Bruch', *Nachrichtenblatt f. deutsche Vorzeit*, vol. 14, 1938.

[21] Glob (op. cit., note 11), pp. 104 ff. Struve (op. cit., note 11), p. 117. F. K. Bicker, 'Bodenständige Kulturentwicklung in Mitteldeutschland von der Altsteinzeit bis zur Indogermanenzeit', *Mannus*, vol. 28, 1936, pp. 416 ff. G. Mildenberger, loc. cit., note 17.

[22] T. Sulimirski, *Polska przedhistoryczna*, part I, London 1955, pp. 155 f.

[23] A. Gardawski, 'Zagadnienie kultury "ceramiki grzebykowej" w Polsce', *W.A.*, vol. XXV, 1958.

[24] K. Bertsch, 'Klima, Pflanzendecke und Besiedlung Mitteleuropas in vor- und frühgeschichtlicher Zeit nach den Ergebnissen der pollenanalytischen Forschungen', *XVIII Bericht d.röm.-germ.Kommission*, 1929, p. 67.

[25] Sulimirski, loc. cit., note 7.

been found (Map IX).[26] They appear almost exclusively outside the area presumed to be their original country, within a territory extending over a distance of about 2,400 kilometres (*c.* 1,600 miles) from Jutland to the region near Kazan on the Middle Volga in East Russia (the Balanovo culture, Fig. 1:3).[27] They have likewise been found further south, in the Hungarian Plain, in the Ukraine, in Romania, and even in the Aegean countries, at a distance of *c.* 1,200 kilometres from their northern centre. Usually the further south they were the more their shape departed from the standard type. Several spheroid amphorae of the Fatyanovo culture of Central Russia may also be included here, although mostly they had no lugs on the body (Fig. 1:2).

'Thuringian' amphorae, though widely diffused, exhibit a surprising persistence in their basic shape and standard decorative patterns, which are always recognizable even if we have to deal with their most simplified version. The only conclusion which can be drawn from this fact is that the early specimens in all the distant countries were modelled independently on the same prototype made of some perishable organic material. We must admit that the vessels used by the original Corded Ware people were not only of pottery. The character of their sites on sandy soils indicates that they must have been a semi-nomadic population; they must have had vessels made of some organic material, of wood, leather, bladders, fabric, etc.

The prototype of the 'Thuringian' amphora must have been a wooden bowl with two, or four, carved lug-handles on its edge, to which a cover or lid, made probably of a soft substance, was fastened to prevent the liquid contents running out when carried; a wooden ring forming the neck prevented the outlet from shrinking. The joints of the horizontal bands, and the stiffening of the soft cover or its webbed decoration, was reproduced by vertical bands on their replicas in clay.

Once set in clay, the vessels followed each country's own line of evolution, began to be less thoroughly executed, their original decorative patterns being gradually abandoned, and often a variety of hybrid forms evolved, influenced by the local types of vessels. At the same time, the vessels important for the nomadic way of life lost their purpose in the new country, and in new conditions they acquired the character of sepulchral pottery. In accepting this thesis, we also dispose of the apparent difficulty that Thuringian amphorae (clay vessels) were only in exceptional cases found within the centre of the area of their distribution. There, they probably continued to be a vessel of everyday use made of the perishable material.

The territory above, presumably the birthplace of the 'Thuringian' amphorae and of the Corded Ware assemblage, is considered by Kilian[28] to be a secondary area, the first one to be taken over after the formation of the culture; their original country, that of the 'A-complex', he places in western Poland, East Germany (Thuringia and Saxony), and Jutland. A simple glance at Kilian's map (Map X), which indicates the order in which he claims the respective territories were occupied by the expanding Corded Ware, shows that the area regarded by me as the original one, marked IIa on the map, lies right in the centre of the distribution of Corded Ware, whereas all the other secondary areas (marked IIb, IIIa, b, c, d), including Kilian's so-called primary area I, are clustered around it. In view of this it seems more reasonable to regard rather the central area 'IIa'—not the peripheral area 'I'—as the original one.

This is also supported by other arguments. Thuringian 'A' amphorae of Schraplau type appear far outside the area marked 'I'. They have often been found in the Sub-Carpathian barrow-graves on the south-eastern periphery of the supposed secondary area 'IIa', and even further east on the Dnieper (Griščintsy, no. 242) in the area marked 'IIIc' (Fig. 1:1). The vessels from the cemetery at Vykhvatyntsi on the Middle Dnieper, and likewise those from barrow-graves at Balanovo on the Middle Volga (Fig. 1:2–5, 8), must have been modelled either on early Thuringian amphorae, or on their prototypes made of perishable material. These facts do not seem compatible with placing the cradle of the Thuringian amphorae in the west, but are consistent with the ideas outlined above.

Neither do chronological considerations support the western origin of the Thuringian amphorae and of the Corded Ware. Carbon-14 dating suggests *c.* 2200–2400 B.C. for the arrival of the 'beaker people' in Holland, the equivalent of the Thuringian Corded Ware.[29] The 'Thuringian' amphorae from Vykhvatyntsi, and also from the settlement of Mykhailivka (Fig. 6), equate with the turn of the Tripolyan periods B-2 to C-1, which must be placed at *c.* 2200 B.C. The coincidence of the dates above cannot be fortuitous, and this is comprehensible when the central region which roughly corresponds with L. Kilian's area IIa is accepted as the starting-point of the movements, the archaeological equivalent of which was the 'European Corded Ware Horizon'.

CORDED WARE AND OCHRE-GRAVES

Häusler[30] and Kilian[31] rightly emphasize that the Ochre-graves and Corded Ware assemblage had formed two distinct and independent *Kulturkreise*, the latter typical of Central Europe, the former characteristic of the East European grassland. According to both of them the two cultures had developed at approximately the same time and their territories overlapped in the black-earth area west of the Dnieper; the hybrid which resulted was the Middle Dnieper culture.

Our study has shown that the Yamna culture had reached

[26] Id., loc. cit., note 18.

[27] О. А. Кривцова-Гракова, Хронология памятников фатьяновской культуры, Ксиимк, no. XVII, 1947, pp. 33 f., Fig. 7. О. Н. Бадер, К вопросу о балановской культуре, Сов. Этнография, vol. I, 1950, pp. 59 ff. Id., Балановская культура, Сов. Арх., vol. 4, 1961, pp. 41 ff., Figs. 6, 9. Id., Балановский могильник, Moscow 1963, Figs. 125–30, 163. A. Häusler, 'Die kulturellen und wirtschaftlichen Beziehungen der Bevölkerungsgruppen Mittelrusslands am Ende der jüngeren Steinzeit', *Wissenschaftliche Zft d.M.Luther Universität*, vol. V–1, Halle 1955, pp. 90, 101 ff., Pl. 19.

[28] Kilian (op. cit., note 19), pp. 50 ff., Fig. 21 (map).

[29] W. van Zeist, 'Some Radio-Carbon Dates from the Raised Bog near Emmen', *Palaeohistoria*, vol. IV, Groningen 1955, pp. 113 ff. H. L. Thomas, 'The Significance of Radiocarbon Dating for the Bronze Age Chronology of Central Europe', *Bericht über d. V. Internat. Kongress f. Vor- und Frühgeschichte, Hamburg 1958*, Berlin 1961, p. 805. J. D. van der Waals, *Prehistoric Disc Wheels in the Netherlands*, Groningen 1964, pp. 22 ff., Fig. 6.

[30] Häusler (op. cit., note 27), pp. 73 ff.

[31] Kilian, loc. cit., note 19.

considerably further west, and that the contact between the two above assemblages took place along a much wider front. It occurred in the steppe between the Boh and the Dniester where the Usatovo culture was formed, and also in various parts of Romania down to the Danube near Bucharest. It seems very likely that both met and overlapped in the Sub-Carpathian area, and even further west, if the custom of raising mounds over the grave can be attributed to the Yamna influence or to its representatives there.

The stratigraphical evidence shows that the Yamna culture definitely preceded the Corded Ware elements within the southern part of the Territory. This is shown by the position of the relative graves in the mound of Slobidka in Odessa (no. 361) and confirmed by the barrow-graves at Gurbanești near Bucharest.[32] The priority of the Yamna elements in the Middle Dnieper culture seems to be evident, and the same seems to apply to the Sub-Carpathian barrow-graves.

The appearance of cord-impressed ornament on vessels characteristic of the local cultures outside the presumed original Corded Ware area, and also the appearance there of the Thuringian amphorae, took place—as shown by the stratigraphical evidence—after the spread of the Yamna culture. However, unlike the latter, the expansion of the Corded Ware resulted in considerable tribal displacements and disturbances within large regions of Central and also of Eastern Europe. Within the territory with which we are concerned, these movements affected the Lublin plateau, Volhynia, the Sub-Carpathian area and (partly) West Podolia, and also the western part of the Ukrainian grassland. The thinly scattered outposts of the Yamna culture in some of these regions were soon absorbed and a series of hybrid cultures evolved. The cord-decorated pottery of the Tripolye culture of period C-1 was likewise influenced by the outcome of this thrust.

The spread of the Corded Ware/Battle-axe assemblage also affected territories situated further east. The extent of this influence has been discussed by Äyräpää,[33] although much of what he maintained is now out of date. The Fatyanovo and Balanovo cultures of Central Russia proper,[34] and also the Catacomb culture of the grassland east of the Dnieper, were among the assemblages formed under the western impact.

In conclusion we may say that the Yamna culture was the main one of the Late Neolithic in the East European grassland. The influx into that territory of the Corded Ware, probably by the end of the third millennium B.C., resulted in the formation there of several hybrid cultures, to which other local cultures of a different character and origin also contributed.

THE INDO-EUROPEAN ENIGMA

Both the Yamna culture and particularly the Corded Ware assemblage (under the name of the 'Battle-axe cultures') have usually been considered to be the archaeological equivalent of the earliest Indo-Europeans. Some attention should, therefore, be given to this subject although I do not intend to engage here in too wide a discussion of the topic. A review of the various opinions concerning the attribution of the different archaeological cultures to the earliest Indo-Europeans has been given in the recent work by Bosch-Gimpera;[35] a good compendium which briefly states the present position of the problem from the archaeological point of view was published by Marstrander.[36]

Any discussion of the origin and the earliest home of the Indo-Europeans must have its starting-point in the results of linguistic studies and only these can serve as a proper basis for the search for their archaeological equivalent. Here again many controversial opinions exist; the position in this respect has been well summarized in two different papers quoted below.

According to Bender[37] from the study of words common to all Indo-European languages, supplemented by other considerations, it can be inferred that just before their separation the Indo-Europeans were still, at least partly, a more or less nomadic cattle-grazing people, probably widely spread geographically and inhabiting vast plains. He says that the balance of probability seems to lean towards the great plains of central and south-eastern Europe which roughly speaking embrace Poland, Lithuania, Ukraine, and Russia south and west of the Volga. Almost every condition is satisfied if we think of the Indo-Europeans as inhabiting some parts of this plain as late as 3000 or 2500 B.C., as being early differentiated linguistically into distinct groups and covering a vast territory, a pastoral people partially gone over to primitive agriculture but still nomadic enough to change their habitat freely under changing economic or political conditions. He is of the opinion that their dispersion was rather a gradual spreading and dividing which required a considerable period of time.

According to the above, the earliest home of the Indo-Europeans should be placed somewhere within the grassland of Eastern Europe, within the territory of the Yamna culture east of the Dnieper but also west of that river. The Central European forest zone, presumed to be the original territory of the Corded Ware, lies also within the area above-mentioned.

The same two areas are likewise claimed as early Indo-European by Brandenstein.[38] His study of the Indo-European languages has led him to consider the East European grassland as the original country of all the Indo-Europeans, who were then pastoralists. In fact, he places them in the steppe east of the Volga, roughly within the area considered by Merpert[39] to have been where the Yamna culture originated. The Central European forest zone, the home of the Corded Ware, is regarded by Brandenstein as a secondary centre of the Indo-Europeans, and one that belonged only to their western branch; he looks upon them as a people with some knowledge of agriculture.

The results of linguistic studies evidently favour the Yamna people as the representatives of the earliest Indo-Europeans, although the present state of archaeological research offers

[32] Rosetti, loc. cit., note 5.

[33] A. Äyräpää, 'Über die Streitaxtkulturen in Russland', *ESA*, vol. VIII, 1933.

[34] See note 27.

[35] P. Bosch-Gimpera, *El Problema Indoeuropeo*, Mexico 1960. Id., *Les Indo-Européens—Problèmes archéologiques*, Paris, 1961.

[36] S. Marstrander, 'The Original Home of the Indo-Europeans', *D. K. Norske Videnskabers Selskabs Forhandlinger*, vol. 30, 1957, no. 13, pp. 82 ff.

[37] H. H. Bender, *The Home of the Indo-Europeans*, Princeton 1922.

[38] W. Brandenstein, 'Die erste "Indogermanische" Wanderung', *Klotho*, vol. 2, Wien 1936.

[39] Merpert, loc. cit., note 1.

no decisive proof in this respect. Archaeological evidence shows that the Yamna culture extended over the whole of the East European steppe, reached the Romanian grassland and the Hungarian Plain in the west, and probably also the Sub-Carpathian area. It seems very likely that the custom of raising a mound over the grave, met with in the southern groups of the 'Corded Ware Horizon', was of eastern origin, brought into the heart of Europe by small groups of the expanding Yamna pastoralists. In this case, the Yamna culture may have been the archaeological equivalent of the earliest Indo-Europeans.

Linguistic data seems to go against the theory that the Corded Ware represented the earliest Indo-Europeans and that the Central European forest zone was their ancient home, though according to Brandenstein's thesis it may be looked upon as their secondary centre.

There is, however, still another possibility. The original Indo-Europeans may have emerged as the result of the intermingling of the peoples of both the Yamna and Corded Ware cultures. It may be that both have to be looked upon as their ancestors but neither of them as originally Indo-European. Each of these peoples may have contributed to the formation of a new entity, so that the linguistic, cultural, and other traditions belonging to each became to a great extent a common heritage.

The origin of the Indo-Europeans may also be put back to the Mesolithic,[40] and consequently, the Neolithic assemblages discussed above might both be considered as originally Indo-European.

THE TRIPOLYE CULTURE
(Maps III and IV)

The Tripolye culture was the most important assemblage in the territory with which we are concerned here; it occupied almost the whole of the central area (Map VII) and was very long-lived. However, its people were not the earliest agriculturalists there. The culture originated presumably in Moldavia[41] and in expanding north and north-eastwards it absorbed and assimilated its local predecessors, the small primitive agricultural communities in the valleys of the main rivers, the 'Danubians'[42] in West Podolia, the 'Boh' or 'Southern Bug' culture on the Middle Boh,[43] and some groups of the 'Comb-pricked pottery'[44] culture in the area south of Kiev. Against this background the various groups of the Tripolye culture were gradually formed, first—in period A according to Passek's scheme[45]—the West Podolian branch, then at an advanced stage of this period, the Uman group, and in period B-2 the Kiev group. The absolute date is difficult to establish for the beginning of Tripolyan evolution in West Podolia, but Carbon-14 dates of the Early Neolithic sites in the Balkans[46] seem to suggest the beginning of the fourth millennium. Last to appear, in period C-1, were the Gorodsk and the Evminka-Sofiivka groups, if they have to be included in the Tripolyan sequence. Probably at the same time was formed the Usatovo culture which was definitely non-Tripolyan, although ultimately it embraced many Tripolyan elements.

The development of the Tripolye culture had not proceeded uniformly within the whole of its territory. This was admitted by Passek for the late period in which she distinguishes two distinct decorative styles termed C and γ, each belonging to a different region. Our study revealed that the position in the 'middle Tripolyan period' was similar: pottery of style B-1 appears only in West Podolia, whereas that of style B-2 was mainly characteristic of the eastern part of the Tripolyan territory, where it succeeded a local variety of style 'A'. This sequence has been shown in Table 20 and in Tables 18–19, where also the respective equations with the neighbouring cultures are shown.

Major changes in the Tripolyan development occurred at the end of period B-1 and again at the turn of periods B-2 to C-1; the former were restricted to West Podolia (and also Moldavia), the latter affected the whole territory of the culture. They were brought about by external causes, probably by an influx of new settlers, or by movements of some uprooted tribes in those periods of widespread unrest.

Tripolyan kitchen-ware of period B-1 in West Podolia differs substantially from that in the succeeding periods there. The latter was a kind of comb-pricked ware, termed 'C-ware', and was closely related to the comb-pricked pottery of the northern part of the territory under review (the Dnieper-Donets culture).

Considerable changes have been recorded in the region east of the Dnieper at the very same time; the comb-pricked pottery was there replaced by the pit-comb ware proper to the Central Russian forest zone.[47] We may conjecture that this was in some way connected with the spread of C-ware over the Tripolyan territory; the people of the comb-pricked ware were driven southwards out of their original country. Carbon-14 dating of Hăbăşeşti[48] suggests the end of the fourth

[40] A. Briusov, 'Le problème indoeuropéen et la civilisation des haches de combat', *Rapports des archéologues de l'URSS*, pp. 10, 15.

[41] V. Dumitrescu, 'Origine et évolution de la civilisation de Cucuteni-Tripolye', *Archeologia*, vol. XIV, Warszawa 1963, pp. 1–40.

[42] E. Comşa, 'Betrachtungen über die Linearbandkeramik auf dem Gebiet der rumänischen Volksrepublik und der angrenzenden Länder', *Dacia*, vol. NS II, Bucureşti 1959, pp. 41 ff., Fig. 1 (map). И. К. Свешников, Культура линейно-ленточной керамики на территории верхнего Поднистовья и западной Волини, Сов. Арх., vol. XX, 1954, pp. 100 ff. Ю. Н. Захарук, О так называемой волынской группе культуры линейно-ленточной керамики, Сов. Арх., vol. XXIX–XXX, 1959, pp. 114 ff. R. Vulpe, *SCIV*, vol. VII, 1956, pp. 55 ff. T. Sulimirski, *Acta AC*, vol. II, 1960, pp. 123 ff., Fig. 2 (map). Е. К. Черныш, К истории населения энеолитического времени в среднем Приднестровье, МИА, no. 102, 1962, pp. 5 ff. 58 ff., Fig. 1 (map). E. Tchernych, 'Territoire orientale des tribus de la ceramique lineaire', *Rapports des archéologues de l'URSS*, 1962.

[43] Ф. А. Козубовський, Археологічні дослідження на територiї Богесу, 1930–1932 pp., Kiev 1933. В. М. Даниленко, Дослідження неолітичних пам'яток на Південному Бузі, Археологія-Kiev, vol. X, 1957, pp. 36 ff. Id., Археологія, vol. XI, Kiev 1957, p. 165. Id., Ксиак no. 9, 1959, pp. 5 ff. T. Passek, 'Relations entre l'Europe Occidentale et l'Europe Orientale à l'époque néolithique', *Rapports des archéologues de l'URSS*, 1962.

[44] Д. Я. Телегін, Неолітичні поселення лісостепового Лівобережжя і Полісся України, Археологія-Kiev, vol. XI, 1957, pp. 70 ff.

[45] Т. С. Пассек, Периодизация трипольских поселений, МИА, no. 10, 1949.

[46] J. Mellaart, 'Anatolia and the Balkans', *Antiquity*, vol. XXIV, 1960, pp. 270 ff. S. Piggott, 'Neolithic and Bronze Age in East Europe', *Antiquity*, vol. XXIV, 1960, pp. 286 ff.

[47] See note 44.

[48] V. Dumitrescu, 'La civilisation de Cucuteni', *Berichten v. d. rijksdienst voor h. oudheidkundig bodemonderzoek*, vol. 9, 1959, p. 48. Id. (op. cit., note 41), p. 34. Passek (op. cit., note 43), pp. 10, 15.

millennium B.C. for those events (the end of Tripolyan period B-1).

The Tripolyans managed to retain their identity, but it seems that the northern settlers who penetrated into their territory were responsible for the changes which then took place in the Tripolyan culture, especially with regard to their economy. In Podolia the river valleys were gradually abandoned and settlements were founded on the edge of the plateau. The large settlements like that of Volodymirivka, or Kolomiščyna I, with their large courts, or enclosures encircled by huts, point to the importance of animal husbandry.

The copper hoard from Horodnica on the Dniester[49] equates it with the Bodrogkeresztur culture of Hungary, usually dated *c.* 2000–1900 B.C.,[50] but recently to a few centuries earlier.[51] The axe-pike from Veremye, a site dated by Passek to period B-2 (although she assigns the axe itself to period C-1),[52] and seven flat copper axes (celts) found likewise in settlements of period B-2 (Veremye, Ščerbanovka, Tripolye)[53] equate Tripolyan period B-2 of the Kiev region with the Bodrogkeresztur culture. A similar copper axe, but of a more developed type, was found at Kolodiazhne, in a settlement attributed to the Gorodsk culture.[54]

It seems very likely that the Yamna pastoralists had also contributed—at least to some extent—to the changes above. It has already been pointed out that the geographical diffusion of early Tripolyan settlements on the one side (Map III) and of the Neolithic and Early Bronze Age barrow-graves in the Ukraine west of the Dnieper on the other (Map IX), is in favour of the early date of the spread of the Yamna pastoralists. The actual position of the remains of both the Tripolye culture and the barrow-graves is of importance for the study of their reciprocal relation in the areas where they overlap. We see that Tripolyan settlements kept mainly to the river valleys or their neighbourhood, and the plateau was not inhabited by them. Some parts of the country were possibly even avoided by them, e.g. the area west of Kiev where no Tripolyan settlements were found. On the other hand, the latter was the territory of the western division of the Middle Dnieper culture (the Jackowica group). In other regions barrow-graves appear mainly on watersheds, at a distance from the valleys inhabited by the indigenous agriculturalists.

It appears, therefore, that the people of the Tripolye culture lived side by side in the same country with those of the Yamna culture and the groups which succeeded it, although not exactly in the same areas, and that they did not interfere much in the life of each other. The circumstances that a few barrow-graves with Yamna burials were raised over the debris of Tripolyan huts (e.g. Khalepie, no. 246; or Volodymirivka, no. 304) does not disturb the picture. The huts in question were mostly of Tripolyan period B-2 and the settlements to which they belonged might have been already abandoned by their inhabitants.

Crucial finds for the establishment of the date of period C-1 were the copper objects, especially the three-riveted dagger found with a blue glass bead in Werteba Cave at Bilcze Złote, together with Tripolyan pottery considered to be of period C-2,[55] but in fact of period C-1. The dagger represents a type of Reinecke's period A-1 of the Bronze Age, and cannot be placed earlier than the early part of the second millennium B.C., even if Carbon-14 dating is applied.[56] It links our site with the Radial pottery culture of the region of Cracow where daggers of the same type were likewise excavated.[57] The blue bead from Werteba Cave was, however, of a little later date, Reinecke's period A-2.[58] A similar blue glass bead was found in a cremation-grave at Sofiivka.[59]

A similar date (around 1800 B.C. and later) for the Tripolyan period C-1 is suggested by striking agreements of some of the decorative patterns of Tripolyan painted pottery of γ-1 type[60] with the decorative style of the Mostiščarska culture of Laibacher Moor and Vučedol,[61] and also that of the Mondsee pottery.[62] The basic principles of their decoration, the zonal arrangements, encircled crosses, cross-decorated bases, etc., are similar if not identical, in spite of the different techniques in which the vessels were decorated in these distinct groups. Furthermore, Childe,[63] and before him J. L. Myres and M. Hoernes, drew attention to the remarkable parallels to Slavonian motives which occur in the Middle Bronze Age pottery of Cyprus. This noticeable coincidence applies equally to the decoration of a considerable portion of the pottery from Bilcze Złote, Cucuteni B, Stena, Šypentsi, etc.[64]

A knot-headed 'Cypriot' bronze pin and a clay cauldron were excavated in the Tripolyan settlement at Sabatynivka I on the Boh,[65] in layer 'A' supposed to be of period B-1 (Fig. 6).[66] However, pins of this type were common in the Szöreg group of East Hungary and in the Nitra culture of Slovakia, both of Reinecke's period A-1;[67] they were likewise found in

[49] T. Sulimirski, 'Copper Hoard from Horodnica on the Dniester', *Mitteilungen d. Anthropol. Gesellschaft in Wien*, vol. XCI, 1961, pp. 91 ff.

[50] V. Milojčić, *Chronologie der jüngeren Steinzeit Mittel- und Südosteuropas*, Berlin 1948, chronological diagram. E. Ehrich, *Relative Chronologies in Old World Archaeology*, Chicago 1954, pp. 108 ff., table 1. V. G. Childe, *The Dawn of European Civilisation*, 5th ed., London 1950, p. 331.

[51] Childe (op. cit., note 50: 6th ed., 1957), p. 346. A. Benac, 'Studien zur Stein- und Kupferzeit im nordwestlichen Balkan', *42 Bericht d. röm.-germ. Kommission*, 1961, p. 154.

[52] Op. cit., note 45, pp. 54 f., 130, Fig. 100:8. Sulimirski (op. cit., note 49), Pl. 2:7.

[53] Loc. cit., notes 45 and 52. Ф. Вовк, Антропологія, Kiev, vol. I, 1927, pp. 3 ff., Pl. III:4–6, Fig. 14 a–d.

[54] Пассек (op. cit., note 45), Fig. 89:12.

[55] T. Sulimirski, 'Tripolyan Notes', *PPS*, vol. XXX, 1964, pp. 59 ff.

[56] H. L. Thomas, 'The Significance of Radiocarbon Dating for the Bronze Age Chronology of Central Europe', *Bericht über d. V. Internation. Kongress f. Vor- und Frühgeschichte, Hamburg 1958*, Berlin 1961, pp. 806 f.

[57] J. Kostrzewski, 'Od mezolitu do wędrówek ludów', *Prehistoria Ziem Polskich*, Kraków 1939–48, pp. 158 ff., Pl. 53:12. T. Sulimirski, *Polska przedhistoryczna*, part II, London 1957–9, pp. 207 ff., Fig. 49. S. Buratyński, *ZOW*, vol. XXII, 1953, pp. 109 f.

[58] R. Pittioni, *Urgeschichte des österreichischen Raumes*, Wien 1954, p. 277.

[59] Т. Б. Попова, Племена катакомбной культуры, Труды Г.И.М., no. 24, Moscow 1955, p. 129, n. 1.

[60] Пассек (op. cit., note 45), fig. 62. М. Л. Макаревич, Ксиак, no. 10, 1960, pp. 23 ff., Fig. 2.

[61] S. Dimitrijević, *Opuscula Archaeologica*, vol. I, Zagreb 1956, Pls. I–XIV.

[62] L. Franz and J. Weninger, *Die Funde aus den prähistorischen Pfahlbauten im Mondsee*, Wien 1927, Pl. XXVI:7–9.

[63] V. G. Childe, *The Danube in Prehistory*, Oxford 1929, p. 212.

[64] See note 45.

[65] А. В. Добровольський, Арх. Пам., vol. IV, 1952, pp. 82 ff., Fig. 2, Pl. II:17. See also Dumitrescu (op. cit., note 48), p. 44.

[66] Пассек (op. cit., note 45), pp. 50 ff.

[67] V. Milojčić, 'Zur Frage der Chronologie der frühen und mittleren Bronzezeit in Ostungarn', *Congrès Internat. des Sciences Préhist. et Protohist.*,

the remains of the third phase of the Monteoru culture of the Middle Bronze Age in Romania,[68] and at a still later date, the end of the Middle Bronze Age, similar pins were found in graves of the Noua culture at Gîrbovăţ in Moldavia[69] and in the hoard of Kolodnoe in the Carpatho-Ukraine.[70] A 'Cypriot' pin was also excavated in one of the Sub-Carpathian barrow-graves (Fig. 19:15). The clay vessel from Sabatynivka was evidently modelled on a Caucasian cauldron of the middle of the second millennium B.C. A double-looped pot from the settlement at Hrenivske on the other side of the Southern Bug, opposite Sabatynivka, likewise represents a North Caucasian type. Several pots of this type occurred in the barrow-graves of the period *c.* 1700–1500 B.C. at Nalchik.[71] The objects above-mentioned imply that the settlement of Sabatynivka must have survived to the middle of the second millennium B.C.

The final date of the Tripolye culture as a whole has been variously estimated by different authors; I have devoted a special article to this subject.[72] In West Podolia, its final date is given by two bronze fibulae of Peschiera type found in the settlement of Nowosiółka Kostiukowa. The hut in which they were excavated yielded chiefly a black-polished post-Tripolyan pottery, but the presence in it of Tripolyan 'D' ware implies that the time of its existence was not very remote from the Tripolyan era proper. The 'D' pottery was typical of the final Tripolyan stage in West Podolia, and was likewise found in the Early Bronze Age settlement at Komarów. This was a sand-gritted or grog-gritted slipped ware, very soft, easily 'washed-off'; the edges of its sherds being rounded and deformed, the reconstruction of vessels was difficult. The reddish surface was never decorated. The chronology of the Peschiera fibulae is debatable; their conjectural date in Central Europe is *c.* 1300 B.C.[73]

Finally, a number of finds should be mentioned which reflect relations between the Tripolye culture and other cultures of the Territory, and are of importance for the establishment of the date of their contact. Tripolyan potsherds appear in several sites in the steppe country south of the reach of the culture, especially along the valley of the Dnieper. They were found in sites of Seredni Stog II type in the region of the rapids,[74] and in the settlement of Mykhailivka (Tables 17, 18, 20; Map III).[75]

Corded Ware appeared in the Ukraine at the turn of Tripolyan periods B-2 to C-1, earlier than is usually admitted. Its influence on the Tripolyan culture is witnessed by cord-impressed decorative patterns on kitchen-ware, but also by vessels modelled on Thuringian amphorae (Kolomiščyna I). The same applies to the painted decorative motifs of a series of vessels in West Podolia (Bilcze Złote, Koszyłowce)[76] which tie up Tripolyan period C-1 with the beginning of the second period of the Sub-Carpathian barrow-graves, as likewise do the two stone battle-axes from the Tripolyan settlement of period C-1 at Popudnia of the Uman group.[77] The position regarding the Vykhvatyntsi group on the Middle Dniester was similar; the Corded Ware evidently contributed much to the formation of the Gorodsk culture, irrespective of whether the latter is considered a branch of the Corded Ware or of the Tripolye culture. It belonged to period C-1, although following Passek, its decorative patterns may be called C-2.

The relations of the Tripolye culture and the Funnel Beakers within one another are of great importance for correlating the Central European chronology with the Tripolyan scheme (Tables 17, 18). Thus Tripolyan pottery was found in several settlements of the Funnel Beaker culture on the Bug (Map IV); on the other hand, vessels (usually Tripolyan painted ware) evidently modelled on the amphorae characteristic of the Funnel Beaker culture were found in a number of Tripolyan settlements in West Podolia (Bilcze Złote, Koszyłowce).[78] Their contact took place during a late period in the evolution of both: on the Tripolyan side this was Passek's period C-1, not period C-2 as is commonly suggested.[79] A few potsherds with a 'scale' decoration characteristic of the Globular Amphorae found in the Tripolyan settlement of period C-1 at Koszyłowce[80] equate this period with the second stage of the Eastern Globular Amphora culture (Tables 17, 18 and 20). The Gorodsk culture, which bordered on the territory within which remains of the Funnel Beakers were found, was to a lesser degree affected by this culture.

Connections with the Globular Amphora culture are likewise reflected in the decorative patterns of Tripolyan pottery of the Kiev group of period C-1 (Tables 17, 20).[81] Inversely, a few vessels from slab-cist graves of the Volhynian group of the Globular Amphora culture were painted red, which was evidently due to the influence of the Tripolye culture, seemingly through the medium of the Gorodsk culture.

In Table 20 the chronological sequence is shown of a series

Zürich 1950, Figs. 27, 28, 42. C. Chropovský, *Archaeologia Slovaca-Fontes*, vol. III, Bratislava 1960, p. 72.

68 Piggott (op. cit., note 46), p. 290.

69 A. Florescu, 'Contribuţii la cunoaşterea culturii Noua', *Arheologia Moldovei*, vol. II–III, Iaşi 1964, p. 177, Fig. 22.

70 K. Bernjakovič, 'Bronzezeitliche Hortfunde vom rechten Ufergebiet des oberen Theisstales', *Slovenská Archeológia*, vol. VIII–2, 1960, pp. 349 f., Pl. XI:13.

71 C. F. A. Schaeffer, *Antiquity*, vol. XVII, 1943, pp. 183 ff., Fig. E. М. Л. Макаревич, Арх. Пам., vol. IV, 1952, pp. 89 ff., Pl. I:21. Б. Е. Деген, Курганы в Кабардинском парке г. Нальчика. МИА, vol. III, 1941, pp. 213 ff., Pls. IV, VII, IX, etc.

72 T. Sulimirski, 'The Problem of the Survival of the Tripolye Culture', *PPS*, vol. XVI, 1950, pp. 42 ff. Id. (op. cit., note 55), pp. 56 ff.

73 V. G. Childe, 'The Final Bronze Age in the Near East and in Temperate Europe', *PPS*, vol. XIV, 1948, pp. 186 ff.

74 See note 36 in Chapter VII.

75 О. Г. Шапошникова, Ксиак, no. 11, 1961, pp. 38 ff., and the earlier reports quoted there. О. Ф. Лагодовська, О. Г. Шапошникова, М. Л. Макаревич, Михайлівське поселення, Kiev 1962.

76 K. Hadaczek, *Osada przemysłowa w Koszyłowcach*, Lwów 1914, Pl. V:14. Id., 'La colonie industrielle de Koszyłowce', *Album de fouilles*, Lwów 1914, Pl. XV:124, 127 etc.

77 M. Himner, 'Étude sur la civilisation prémycenienne dans le basin de la Mer Noir', *Światowit*, vol. XIV, 1930–1, Pl. XLI.

78 Hadaczek (op. cit., note 76: *Osada*), Pl. V:15 (note 76: *Album*); Pl. XVII:145–8. L. Kozłowski, *Zarys pradziejów Polski południowo-wschodniej*, Lwów 1939, Pl. X:7. W. Antoniewicz, 'Eneolityczne groby szkieletowe ze wsi Złota w pow.sandomierskim', *W.A.*, vol. IX, 1924–5, p. 239, Figs. 37–9. J. Kowalczyk, 'Die Trichterbecherkultur und Tripolye', *Prague Symposium*, p. 201.

79 K. Jażdżewski, *Arch.P.*, vol. II, 1958, pp. 283 f. Ю. М. Захарук, До питання про співвідношення і зв'язки між культурою лійчастого посуду та трипільською культурою, Мдапв, no. 2, 1959, pp. 61 ff.

80 Hadaczek (op. cit., note 76: *Album*), Pl. VII:46.

81 Пассек (op. cit., note 45), pp. 222 f., Fig. 76:3, 6. (See pp. 20 f.)

TABLE 20. Equation of a number of selected Tripolyan sites

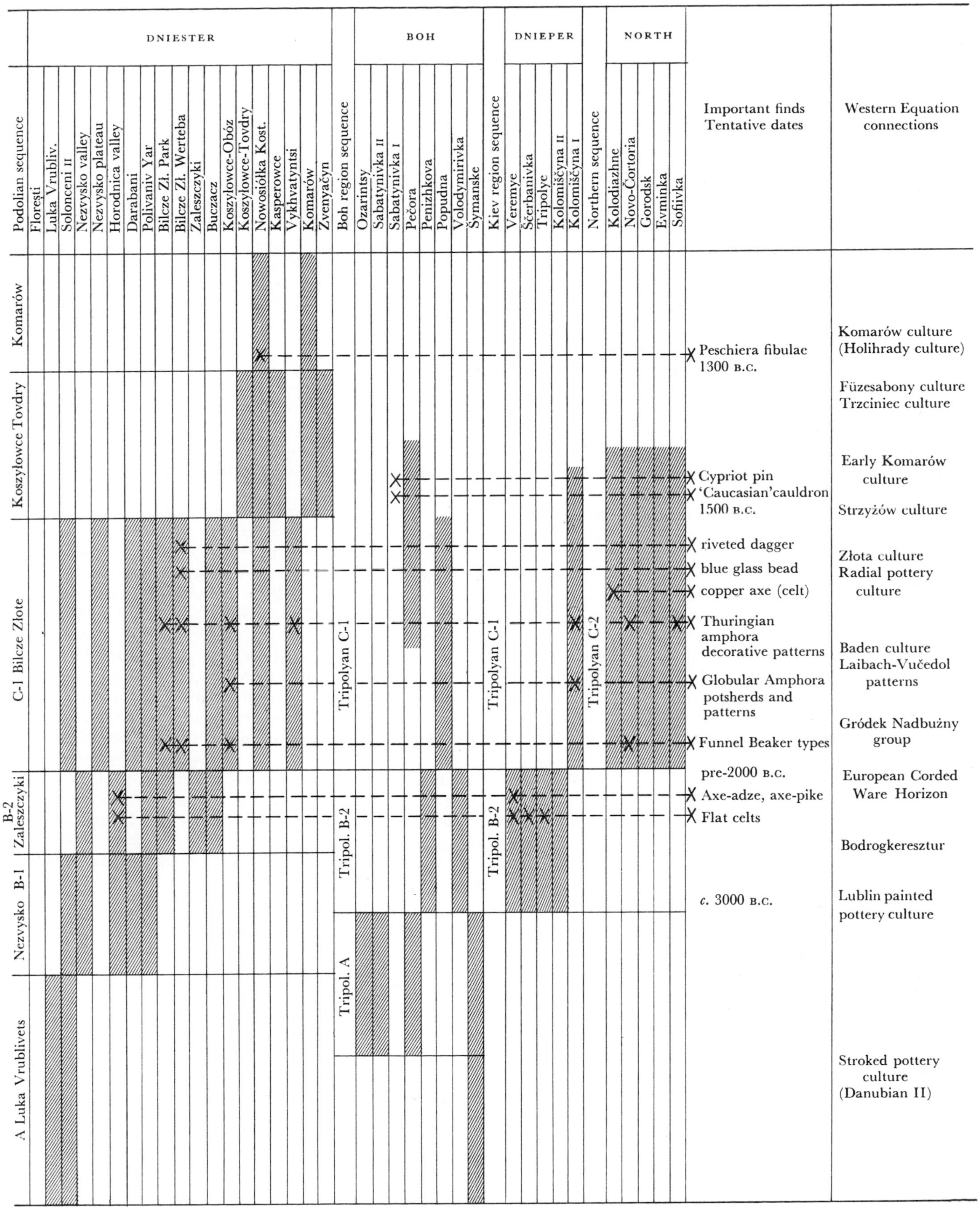

Podolian sequence (DNIESTER)	Boh region sequence (BOH)	Kiev region sequence (DNIEPER)	Northern sequence (NORTH)	Important finds / Tentative dates	Western Equation connections
Komarów				Peschiera fibulae 1300 B.C.	Komarów culture (Holihrady culture)
Koszyłowce Tovdry				Cypriot pin; 'Caucasian' cauldron; 1500 B.C.	Füzesabony culture; Trzciniec culture; Early Komarów culture; Strzyżów culture
C-1 Bilcze Złote	Tripolyan C-1	Tripolyan C-1	Tripolyan C-2	riveted dagger; blue glass bead; copper axe (celt); Thuringian amphora decorative patterns; Globular Amphora potsherds and patterns; Funnel Beaker types	Złota culture; Radial pottery culture; Baden culture; Laibach-Vučedol patterns; Gródek Nadbużny group
B-2 Zaleszczyki	Tripol. B-2	Tripol. B-2		pre-2000 B.C.; Axe-adze, axe-pike; Flat celts	European Corded Ware Horizon; Bodrogkeresztur
Nezvysko B-1				c. 3000 B.C.	Lublin painted pottery culture
A Luka Vrublivets	Tripol. A				Stroked pottery culture (Danubian II)

Sites — DNIESTER: Floreşti, Luka Vrubliv., Solonceni II, Nezvysko valley, Nezvysko plateau, Horodnica valley, Darabani, Polivaniv Yar, Bilcze Zł. Park, Bilcze Zł. Werteba, Zaleszczyki, Buczacz, Koszyłowce-Obóz, Koszyłowce-Tovdry, Nowosiółka Kost., Kasperowce, Vykhvatyntsi, Komarów, Zvenyačyn

BOH: Ozarintsy, Sabatynivka II, Sabatynivka I, Pečora, Penizhkova, Popudna, Volodymirivka, Šymanske

DNIEPER: Veremye, Ščerbanivka, Tripolye, Kolomiščyna II, Kolomiščyna I

NORTH: Kolodiazhne, Novo-Čortoria, Gorodsk, Evminka, Sofiivka

mainly of long-lived Tripolyan settlements in West Podolia; the leading finds, connections, and tentative dates are indicated. The scheme, and that presented in Table 21, differ considerably from that published by Passek in her recent paper.[82]

GLOBULAR AMPHORAE

The people of the Globular Amphorae had played a considerable role in the territory with which we are concerned. The origin of the culture, its division into consecutive stages, its relations with other cultures, etc., have been dealt with in Chapters IV and V. It was definitely an expanding culture which entered the area under review from the north-west; it formed several local groups which ranged themselves in a line from the Bug eastwards, across Volhynia to the Dnieper, and another one from the Bug southwards over West Podolia and Moldavia to Transilvania even reaching Bulgaria (no. 546).

The theory that the Corded Ware evolved out of the Globular Amphorae, and that this evolution took place somewhere within the Territory must be dismissed.[83] Our study has shown that the two cultures had no 'genetical' connection but were alien to each other; both extended over different regions which only slightly overlapped. The available evidence implies that the spread of the Globular Amphorae was subsequent to that of Corded Ware.

The people of the Globular Amphorae seem to have been armed conquerors who imposed their rule upon the subdued population of the countries they had entered. The Strzyżów culture (like the Złota culture west of the Vistula) owed its formation to the invading Globular Amphorae, although its basic element was the local Corded Ware group which retained its character. It seems that the formation of the Gorodsk culture was likewise considerably fostered by the Globular Amphorae, though here again the Corded Ware and Tripolyan elements were important in determining the character of the new culture. The expansion of the Gorodsk culture southwards and the appearance of settlements of its type in West Podolia (Koszyłowce-Tovdry, Kasperowce) (Fig. 5), and in Moldavia (Horodiştea) were possibly connected in some way with the pressure of the Globular Amphorae; perhaps they were even undertaken under their leadership. In this respect it is instructive that slab-cist graves of the latter culture and the southern remains of the Gorodsk type appear along the same track.

The population of the West Podolian branch of the Tripolye culture was undoubtedly subdued by the Globular Amphora people. This resulted in the growth of closer ties of this branch with the Central European cultures of the period, and consequently it developed somewhat differently from that of the other Tripolyan groups further east.

The Corded Ware current preceded that of the Globular Amphorae within the Territory. This is indicated by the circumstances at Vykhvatyntsi (no. 371) where the influence of the early Corded Ware (of the 'European Horizon') is clearly reflected in the sepulchral pottery whereas no Globular Amphora elements are noticeable. The same applies to the Sofiivka group of cremation cemeteries in which urns modelled on Thuringian amphorae are common (Fig. 1:7, 9), but no vessels appear modelled on pots belonging to the Globular Amphorae culture. The position further south in the steppe was similar, e.g. in the settlement of Mykhailivka where no traces of the Globular Amphorae were found either prior to, or contemporary with, the early Corded Ware current.

I have already emphasized that the Globular Amphora culture was not a long-lived group, and it can only be allowed to have existed in its proper form for three to four generations. In most areas of its extent, the culture soon succumbed to the influence of the surrounding Corded Ware groups. In some areas it merged with these (the Strzyżów culture), but sometimes (e.g. in West Podolia and in parts of Volhynia) the genuine Globular Amphora pottery was replaced in slab-cist graves by vessels typical of the late Corded Ware. In the latter groups, in spite of the acceptance of alien goods and pottery, the people of the culture retained their identity, as is shown by the burial ritual and the form of the grave.

CONCLUSION

The purpose of this work has not been to give a detailed description of all the cultures which during the Neolithic and the Early Bronze Age developed within the huge territory extending east of the Vistula to the Dnieper, and southwards to the Black Sea coast. The main effort has been directed—besides publishing the results of my own excavations—towards the establishment of stages in the development of the cultures of some importance within the area, the verification of their connections with one another, and the equation of them with cultures outside the territory involved, in order to work out a proper chronological scheme. The results of this study are given in Table 21 which also offers a tentative chronological framework for the Neolithic and the Early Bronze Age of the whole area under review.

The chronological positions assigned there to a number of cultures differ in many instances from those usually given them in standard works on Ukrainian and East European archaeology,[84] or in other publications. I am well aware that this scheme is subject to amendments and corrections. Nevertheless, it seems that changes and alterations in the accepted datings carried out here are for the most part well grounded, and that they will contribute considerably to a proper understanding of the turn of events in the periods concerned within the territory above, and of their consequences.

[82] Passek (op. cit., note 43), pp. 15 f.

[83] M. Gimbutas, *The Prehistory of Eastern Europe*, part I, Cambridge (Mass.) 1956, pp. 150 ff.

[84] Нариси стародавноï історiï Украïнскоï, PCP, Kiev 1957, pp. 36 ff. A. Ja. Brjussow, *Geschichte der neolithischen Stämme im europäischen Teil der UdSSR*, Berlin 1957. Очерки истории СССР. Первобытно-общинный строй, Moscow 1956. A. L. Mongait, *Archaeology in the U.S.S.R.* (transl. M. W. Thompson), London 1961, Pelican Books. Gimbutas, loc. cit., note 83.

Table 21. Chronological scheme showing the relative position of main cultures discussed in the volume

Approximate dates	Equations	Sub-Carpathian Barrow-graves	Eastern Globular Amphorae	Lublin Plateau and West Volhynia	East Volhynia	West Podolia	Bessarabia and Romania	Region on the Middle Boh	The Kiev region	Usatovo culture	Steppe west of the Dnieper	Dnieper Rapids region	Eastern Ochre graves
		Komarów period IV	Stage V		Voytsekhivka barrow-graves	Holihrady	Noua culture	Bilohrudivka	Bilohrudivka				
		Komarów III	Stage IV (Biały-Potok)	Lusatian culture									
		Komarów II											
1300 B.C.		Komarów I		Trzciniec culture	Mostva III	Period C-2				Srubna graves		Srubna graves	Srubna graves
Reinecke A-2	Mierzanowice Oder Corded Ware	Period III	Stage III	Strzyżów culture		(Koszyłowce-Tovdry)	Horodiștea	Pechora upper level		late Usatovo Catacomb graves	Mykhailivka III	Durna Skela	
Reinecke A-1	Złota culture	Period II	Stage II	Corded Ware	Gorodsk culture	Tripolyan period C-1 (Bilcze-Złote)	Cucuteni B Vykhvatyntsi	Tripolyan period C-1	Tripolyan C-1 Sofiivka group	Usatovo culture	Mykhailivka II		Catacomb culture
2000 B.C.		Period I	Stage I	Funnel Beaker							Mykhailivka I	Seredni Stog 2 Ihren 8	
	Corded Ware Horizon Bodrogkeresztur culture			Culture Lublin Painted Pottery	Mostva II	Tripolyan period B-2 (Zaleszczyki)	Yamna graves Cucuteni AB	Tripolyan period B-2	Tripolyan period B-2	Early Yamna graves			
												Seredni Stog 1	Yamna culture
												Sobačky	

CHAPTER IX

Postscript

FURTHER DEVELOPMENT

THE DEVELOPMENT of the cultures dealt with in the preceding chapters did not cease suddenly at the end of the Early Bronze Age, and it seems that some attention should be paid to their further evolution. This applies especially to cultures clearly deriving from those known in the preceding period, and whose transformation more or less marked, denoted only a new period in their evolution.

Thus the Trzciniec culture and its related groups in the northern part of the Territory evolved out of the Corded Ware. The Komarów culture in the south-west was simply a new stage in the evolution of the Sub-Carpathian barrow-graves and their associated groups; the disappearance of the Tripolye culture was only an apparent one and was caused probably by the changed decorative technique of its pottery.[1] There is, however, no room here for a wider discussion on these topics, and only the general trends in the development during the Middle Bronze Age will be briefly reviewed.

The most characteristic feature of this period was the supremacy of Central European cultures and influences within the whole Territory. The Trzciniec culture, which greatly affected the northern and eastern parts of the area under review was typical of the central part of Poland. In the south, in the area of the Komarów culture and its related groups, the influence of the Hungarian Plain was predominant; it reached and even crossed the Dnieper, as is indicated by a series of stray bronze objects and hoards of Koszider type, mainly of Hungarian derivation found there.[2] The expansion of the Srubna culture, which probably during the thirteenth century B.C. reached and crossed the Dnieper ended the preponderance of the Central European cultures in the eastern and southern part of the Territory. This was the end of the Middle Bronze Age, and the beginning of the Late Bronze Age in West Pontic lands.

THE TRZCINIEC CULTURE

The Trzciniec culture of Central Poland in the early stage of the Middle Bronze Age has been dealt with by Gardawski.[3] He distinguishes several territorial groups of the culture one of which, the 'Lublin' group, stretched exclusively across the Territory. Nearly ninety sites have been recorded, occurring mostly on sandy soils; as with Corded Ware, both types of pottery are often found on the same site. In the eastern part of the Lublin loess plateau and of West Volhynia, Trzciniec potsherds (usually a few specimens only) are occasionally found in settlements of the Strzyżów culture (Gródek Nadbużny,[4] Strzyżów[5]). Both cultures were at least partly coeval, one extending over the sandy soils (Trzciniec),[6] the other over the loess country. This conclusion is indicated also by the fact that the successor of the Strzyżów culture (e.g. at the settlement of that name) was the Lusatian, not the Trzciniec, culture.[7]

No Trzciniec settlements, or traces of encampments, were found in East Volhynia; here pottery of Trzciniec type was excavated in graves (Narodyči-Piščane, no. 229; Fig. 33:B; Voytsekhivka, no. 236) only. Closely related to the Trzciniec ware, and probably deriving from it, but definitely different, was pottery from a series of settlements in the region of Kiev and likewise further south, e.g., from Mošna on the Dnieper near Cherkasi, all erroneously considered to be of 'Komarów culture'.[8] Similar diffusion is also shown by bronze flanged axes at least some of which were presumably imported from the northern part of Central Europe[9] (Fig. 35:1). Tallgren[10] mentions that nearly fifty specimens were found, almost exclusively west of the Dnieper, chiefly in the northern part of the Ukraine; twenty-eight of these were found in Volhynia, several on the Dnieper around Kiev and further south, one specimen in the region of Chernigov and one even near Bryansk. He thinks that the axes, although a western type, were made mostly locally. They occurred at random except for a few, e.g., the damaged specimen from Narodyči which was found in the cremation burial 3 of cemetery II. The cemetery dated from a post-Trzciniec period, but in Poland, within the proper Trzciniec territory, these axes date from period II of the Bronze Age (Montelius), in which the Trzciniec culture has been placed.

[1] It was replaced by 'D' ware described in the preceding chapters. See also: T. Sulimirski, 'The Problem of the Survival of the Tripolye Culture', *PPS*, vol. XVI, 1950, pp. 42 ff.

[2] T. Sulimirski, 'Barrow-grave 6 at Komarów', *University of London Institute of Archaeology Bulletin*, no. 4, 1964, pp. 183 ff.

[3] A. Gardawski, 'Plemiona kultury trzcinieckiej w Polsce', *Mat.St.*, vol. V, 1959, pp. 7 ff., Pls. I–LXXVI.

[4] J. Głosik, *Arch.R.*, vol. IX, 1957, pp. 660 ff. Id., *W.A.*, vol. XXV, 1958, pp. 160 ff., 382 ff. Id., *Spr.Arch.*, vol. VI, 1959, pp. 23 ff.; vol. IX, 1960, pp. 81 ff. J. Kowalczyk, *W.A.*, vol. XXIV, 1957, pp. 49, 303.

[5] Z. Podkowińska, *ZOW*, vol. XI, 1936, pp. 72 ff. Id., *Arch.P.*, vol. V, 1960. J. Gurba, *AUMCS*, vol. V F, pp. 159 ff. S. Nosek, *AUMCS*, vol. VI F, pp. 248 ff. J. Głosik, *Mat.St.*, vol. VII, 1961, pp. 112 ff.

[6] Gardawski, loc. cit., note 3.

[7] Podkowińska (op. cit., note 5: 1960), pp. 39 ff.

[8] В. А. Ильинская, Поселение комаровской культуры у с. Мошны, Ксиак, no. 10, 1960, pp. 48 ff.

[9] A. M. Tallgren, 'La Pontide préscythique', *ESA*, vol. II, 1926, p. 178, Figs. 101:8–10; 103:1. О. Ф. Лагодовська, Археологія-Kiev, vol. IX, 1954, p. 133, Pl. III:3. І. Ф. Левицький, Антропологія, vol. IV, Kiev 1948, pp. 230 ff., В. Д. Рыбалова, О связях правобережной лесостепной Украины с центральной Европой в эпоху бронзы и раннего железа, Исследования по археологии СССР, Leningrad 1961, Figs. 3; 6:6. А. И. Тереножкин, Срепное Поднепровье в начале железного века, Сов. Арх., vol. 2, 1957, Fig. 6:1.

[10] Tallgren (op. cit., note 9), p. 178.

POSTSCRIPT

Pottery related to the Trzciniec culture and characteristic of the Sosnitsa culture also appears east of the Dnieper along the Seim up to Putivl,[11] and vessels strikingly similar both in shape and decoration to those of the Trzciniec culture, were found in a few Srubna graves along the Russo-Ukrainian border.[12] I have already commented on this theme.[13] A beaker with an incised decoration on the neck, almost indistinguishable from the genuine Trzciniec beakers, was excavated in barrow-grave III at Lysa Hora near Lubni.[14]

All these occurrences were evidently the outcome of a Trzciniec penetration, although the nature of this penetration and its extent cannot be established at present. It is worth remembering in this context that early Koban bronzes include a number of personal ornaments[15] which are strikingly reminiscent of Central European types of period II of the Bronze Age (Montelius); these concordances cannot have been fortuitous.

THE LUSATIAN CULTURE

Following the Trzciniec culture in the area west of the Bug was the Lusatian culture, over sixty sites of which have been recorded. Its 'eastern' group[16] covered the country east of the Wieprz, and crossed the Bug.

According to generally accepted views,[17] the eastern branches of the Lusatian culture evolved out of the Trzciniec culture. However, this assumption meets with some difficulty when applied to our area: in the eastern part of the Lublin loess plateau almost no Trzciniec remains were found, and the Strzyżów culture was succeeded there immediately by the Lusatian culture.

Only a few Lusatian cemeteries were found east of the Bug, but the impact of this culture on its neighbouring groups to the south-east was considerable. It contributed to the forma-

TABLE 22. Stray early Lusatian bronze objects and hoards found east of the Bug

Site	Reference
A. HOARDS	
1. *Czechy* district of Brody Winged palstave, several bracelets and rings, a sickle of Hungarian type	I. Siwkówna, 'Skarb brązowy z Czech, pow. Brody', *Przegl. Archeol.*, VI, 1937–9, pp. 239 ff., figs. 1–9.
2. *Kamionka Strumiłowa* A large, four-riveted dagger and a large, wide armband	Fig. 34:9, 10. L. Kozłowski, *Wczesna, starsza i środkowa epoka bronzu w Polsce*, Lwów 1928, pl. XIII:19, 20.
B. PALSTAVES (North-west European types)	
3. *Przewodów* district of Sokal	Fig. 35:5. Kozłowski, as above, pl. XIII:21
4. *Ukraine* Two specimens	Fig. 35:2, 4. Before the war in the Chojnowski Collection of the Army Museum, Warsaw (nos. 32531–18805; 32530–18804).
C. WINGED AXES	
5. *Abramovka* district of Dniepropetrovsk. Two specimens, part of a large hoard of the Late Bronze Age	Fig. 35:11. Tallgren (op. cit., note 9), p. 160.
6. *Chernigov* One specimen	Sulimirski (op. cit., note 19, p. 44, pl. XII:5; see also: Terenozhkin (op. cit., note 9), fig. 6:3; and Rybalova (op. cit., note 9), fig. 2:1.
7. *District of Kanev* Winged palstave of 'Bohemian' type	Tallgren (op. cit., note 9), fig. 101:11; Terenozhkin (op. cit., note 9), fig. 6:2.
8. *Region of Kanev* One specimen	Tallgren, as above, p. 178.
9. *Middle Dnieper region* (Cherkasi?) One specimen	Rybalova (op. cit., note 9), fig. 2:2.
10. *Ukraine* Two winged axes of 'Bohemian' type	Fig. 35:3. Before the war in the Chojnowski Collection of the Army Museum, Warsaw, nos. 32876 and 44458–7008.
D. ORNAMENTS	
11. *District of Ovruch* Heavy armring with spiral terminals	Sulimirski (op. cit., note 19), p. 44, pl. XII:3.

tion of the Wysocko culture;[18] a relatively large series of bronze objects evidently of either Lusatian origin or forming part of the Lusatian current (winged celts, palstaves, socketed axes, pins, etc.), found in East Volhynia and along the Dnieper, illustrate the extent of Lusatian penetration, whether connected with trade in metal or otherwise (Fig. 35). The earliest of these are listed in Table 22.

[11] В. А. Іллінська, Нові дані про пам'ятки доби бронзи в лівобережному лісостепу, Археологія-Kiev, vol. x, 1957, pp. 50 ff. С. С. Березанська, Пам'ятки періоду середної бронзи на Десні та Сеймі, Археологія-Kiev, vol. XI, 1957, pp. 70 ff. Id., Културы средней бронзы в левобережном полесье Украины, Ксиак, no. 10, 1960, pp. 41 ff., Fig. 3.

[12] E.g. Tallgren (op. cit., note 9), p. 70, Fig. 47.

[13] T. Sulimirski, 'The Cimmerian Problem', *University of London Institute of Archaeology Bulletin*, no. 2, 1959, pp. 57 ff.

[14] Before the Second World War in the museum at Poltava. L. Kilian, 'Schnurkeramik und Ockergrabkultur', *SMYA*, vol. 59:2, 1957, p. 27, Fig. 10:a.

[15] See e.g. R. Virchow, *Das Gräberfeld von Koban im Lande der Osseten, Kaukasus*, Berlin 1883, Pl. IV:17; XI:5, etc. C. F. Schaeffer, *Stratigraphie Comparée et Chronologie de l'Asie Occidentale, III–II mill.*, London 1948, Pl. 303:10, etc.

[16] Gardawski (op. cit., note 3), p. 140. J. Głosik, 'Z problematyki kultury łużyckiej na wschód od środkowej Wisły', *Arch.R.*, vol. IX, 1957, pp. 698 ff. Id., 'Cmentarzysko ciałopalne kultury łużyckiej z IV okresu epoki brązu w Topornicy, pow.Zamość', *Mat.St.*, vol. III, 1958, pp. 155 ff. T. Węgrzynowicz, 'Cmentarzysko kultury łużyckiej w Młyniskach, dawniej pow.Włodzimierz Wołyński', *W.A.*, vol. XXIX, 1963, pp. 9 ff.

[17] Summarized by Głosik, op. cit., note 16 (1957).

[18] T. Sulimirski, *Kultura wysocka*, Kraków 1931. J. Dąbrowski, 'Materiały ze Strzyżowa, pow.Hrubicszów, a niektóre powiązania ziem Polski Wschodniej i Ukrainy w późnej epoce brązu', *Mat.St.*, vol. VIII, 1962, pp. 7 ff.

In an article I published nearly twenty-five years ago,[19] I discussed the eastern expansion, or penetration, of the Lusatian culture which seems to be undeniable,[20] although, as pointed out by Terenozhkin,[21] I erred in quoting a number of vessels which exhibit Wysocko, not Lusatian, parallels. This penetration very clearly followed the path of the preceding Trzciniec expansion, but unlike it did not cross the Dnieper; however, it reached the Black Sea.

OTHER CULTURES

The Wysocko culture,[22] of which nearly sixty sites have been recorded, was characteristic mainly of sandy soils east of the Bug. It was presumably formed late in the Late Bronze Age (end of period IV, Montelius): it developed chiefly during the Early Iron Age (Hallstatt C, D). Its principal vessels were the tulip-shaped pots some of which had a finger-tip decoration around the body, or raised band (finger-tipped) around the neck, and/or a row of small perforations under the rim. Similar vessels were also typical of the Trzciniec culture, although differently decorated. The latter, as convincingly shown by Gardawski,[23] evolved from funnel beakers, the leading vessels of the culture of that name. The tulip-shaped vessels of the Wysocko culture may have derived from similar Trzciniec vessels.

We have, however, also to reckon with an ancient local tradition going back to the final Neolithic or the Early Bronze Age. It has been pointed out in Chapter V that what is known as 'Bug' pottery of the flint workshops exhibits marked connections with the eastern Funnel Beakers; the flint workshops appear mainly within the northern part of the Wysocko territory, and the tulip-shaped pots from earliest Wysocko graves are hardly distinguishable from similar vessels of the 'Bug' pottery.

Presumably of a similar origin were the tulip-shaped pots found in the Bronze Age settlements in East Volhynia of the 'Bilohrudivka' or rather 'pre-Bilohrudivka' type.[24] They were the leading vessel there, just as in the Bilohrudivka culture proper of the Late Bronze Age of the Ukraine west of the Dnieper, and its successor of the Early Iron Age, the Chornolis culture.[25] Rybalova[26] rightly sees the West Volhynian roots of the Bilohrudivka culture, as against Terenozhkin,[27] according to whom this culture spread in the opposite direction. The north-western origin (West Volhynian) of the Bilohrudivka culture and its related groups is suggested also by the fact that they extended over the areas more or less affected by the Trzciniec culture; the Lusatian bronzes and its local derivatives were likewise found almost exclusively within the same region.

NORTHERN BARROW-GRAVES
(Map XI) (pp. 155 ff.)

A group of remains of the later periods which should also be mentioned were barrow-graves. They followed those of the Early Bronze Age, but covered a much wider territory than their predecessors, nearly the whole of the northern part of the Territory. The character of these graves as burials of the more important members of the society does not seem to have changed.

Barrow-graves were not uniform throughout the whole area. Those in the west yielded pottery typical of the Central Polish Trzciniec culture (Dominikanówka, no. 118; Guciów, no. 120); on the Middle Bug no mounds were found attributable to the Middle and Late Bronze Age, whereas such graves were quite common further east, in the eastern part of West Volhynia and in East Volhynia.

TABLE 23. Chronological Scheme of Northern Barrow-graves

Periods	North-west	West Volhynia
I Barrow-grave culture	Łukawica I	Siwki I-1878
II	Brusno Brzezinki I Lipie Lublin-Sławinek	Korytne I-1878 (Nadyszen) Płużne III
III & I Komarów	Brzezinki III Guciów XIII Hrubieszów Łukawica K Sokal Zakłodzie gr.2	Ostrożec Siekierzyńce A-1876 Staryki A Zaborol neolithic Zdolbunov
II Komarów	Guciów I–XII	Narodyči-Piščane Radzimin IV-1878 Siwki III-1878
III Komarów		Dubno Radzimin II-1876 Staryki B Voytsekhivka I-1 Voytsekhivka 9-1949 Zaborol 4
IV Komarów (Table 14, see p. 37)		Radzimin I-1878 Siekerzynce C-1886 Zaborol F Zaborol G

There they succeeded not only the few Neolithic and Early Bronze Age barrow-graves but also replaced the slab-cists of

[19] T. Sulimirski, 'Zagadnienie ekspansji kultury łużyckiej na Ukrainę', *W.A.*, vol. XIV, 1936, pp. 40 ff.

[20] Рыбалова (op. cit., note 9), pp. 80 ff. Тереножкин (op. cit., note 9), pp. 57 ff. Id., Предскифский период на днепровском правобережье, Kiev 1961, pp. 133, 198 ff., Fig. 114 (map). Pottery, strikingly similar to the genuine Lusatian ware of the 'eastern' group and differing definitely from that proper to the region on the Black Sea, was before the Second World War in the museum at Kherson. It was found on sand-dunes near Khutor Perrotè, Rodenskoe, etc. near Kherson, south of the Dnieper.

[21] А. И. Тереножкин, Лужицка культура и культуры среднего Поднепровья, Ксиимк, no. 67, 1957, pp. 3 ff.

[22] Sulimirski, loc. cit., note 18. Id., 'Ergebnisse archäologischer Forschungen im Dorfe Wysocko, Kr.Brody, Südostpolen', *Bulletin Internationale de l'Académie Polonaise*, Cracovie 1930, pp. 115 ff. М. Ю. Брайчевський, Пам'ятки скіфської епохи на волино-подільському ирпкордонні, Арх. Пам., vol. IV, 1952, pp. 152 ff. В. И. Канивец, Вопросы хронологии высоцкой культуры, Ксиак, no. 4, 1955, pp. 94 ff. Dąbrowski (op. cit., note 18), pp. 28 ff. Z. Bukowski, 'W sprawie genezy i rozwoju grupy wysockiej kultury łużyckiej', *Archeologia Polski*, vol. XI, 1966, pp. 28–106.

[23] Gardawski (op. cit., note 3), pp. 113 f., Pl. LXVI.

[24] О. Ф. Лагодовська, Поселення часу пізньої бронзи в с. Сандраки, Археологія-Kiev, vol. IX, 1954, pp. 133 ff.

[25] Тереножкин (op. cit., note 20: 10961), pp. 6 ff.

[26] See note 9, pp. 94 ff.

[27] Тереножкин (op. cit., note 9: 1957), pp. 14 ff.; id. (op. cit., note 20: 1961), pp. 198 ff., Fig. 115 (map).

the local groups of the Globular Amphora culture. Their pottery and other grave-goods reflect strong influence by the Trzciniec culture (e.g. Zaborol 4, no. 166; Narodyči-Piščane, no. 229) and that of the Komarów culture is marked in later graves (Siwki III, no. 157; Radzimin II-1876, no. 155; Voytsekhivka, no. 236; Plates 23, 24; Fig. 33). The earliest graves of this type can be equated with the second period of the Komarów culture; in the third period, vessels typical of the Romanian Noua culture[28] appear (Dubno, no. 170; Voytsekhivka, no. 236; Plate 22:1, 2).

In East Volhynian barrow-graves of the Early Iron Age pottery was found consisting of mainly undecorated vessels, ovoid in shape with a rounded, rarely flat, base (Plate 24:13–17). Such pottery was also found in a series of graves at Zaborol (no. 166) in West Volhynia (Plate 23:7, 8) which constituted the westernmost outpost of this group of remains. The name 'Hremyače-Pidhirtsi' culture, or type, has been given in Soviet archaeological literature to this group after a site in the village of Kurbativka near Zhitomir (no. 226) and another near Kiev;[29] this group was closely related to the Milograd culture proper to the region on the Upper Dnieper in Byelorussia[30] dated as the period from the sixth century B.C. onwards. Our group seems to be of a little earlier date.

THE KOMARÓW CULTURE
(Map XI)

Considerably less expansive was the other, the southern, or rather south-western group of cultures, which developed under a strong influence of the Hungarian Plain.

The latest stage in the development of the Sub-Carpathian barrow-grave culture witnessed several changes in grave goods, particularly in the pottery, and the number of cremations increased. The name of the Komarów culture has been given to these remains.[31] There was no break in the settlement of the country, but a small change in the geographical extent of the remains of the latter culture took place. No mounds with grave goods typical of the Komarów culture were found in the north-western area of the preceding Barrow-grave culture, whereas several Komarów graves appeared further east on the Dniester and south of the river, within the Horodenka group, where only a few barrow-graves typical of the earlier culture were recorded.

It should be mentioned that in recent Soviet archaeological literature the term 'Komarów culture' has been greatly expanded to embrace all Middle Bronze Age graves (mainly barrow-graves) and settlements found in Volhynia, West Podolia and further east in the Ukraine nearly up to the Dnieper.[32] All these remains show some features in common (in particular their pottery) with the Komarów culture proper, but they never formed a close-knit entity with these. They were evidently connected with the Trzciniec culture, and their vague similarity to the Komarów pottery rests on the basic resemblance, and to some extent on the common origin, of the Komarów and Trzciniec cultures. The term 'Komarów culture' has been applied here solely to the original group of barrow-graves in the Sub-Carpathian area, and its closely related groups.

The Komarów culture, nearly twenty sites of which have so far been recorded, evolved out of the preceding Barrow-grave culture following the trend that was responsible for the formation of the Tumulus culture of the Middle Bronze Age in Bohemia and in the Alpine regions. In its development four stages may be distinguished. The typological study of the remains and their parallels in other cultures were on the basis of this division. It has been confirmed by the study of the position of the relative graves within smaller groups in the cemetery of Komarów, as pointed out in the description of the latter in Part II of the present work. A somewhat different division of the Komarów development has been proposed by Svešnikov and A. Vulpe.[33]

To the earliest stage belonged only a few graves at Komarów and Kavsko 4 (Plate 16; Fig. 29:1, 4), among which were the two most richly furnished, nos. 6 and 8 (Fig. 26:1–9). The large vase from grave 20, associated with an undecorated handled tankard (Fig. 29:7, 8), equates the period with the Salka cemeteries in Slovakia dated to the Alpine Bronze Age periods B-2 and C.[34] Grave 6 has been dealt with by the present author in a special article;[35] it yielded a flat-headed bronze pin of the Borodino type,[36] and a bronze dagger typical of the early stage of the Srubna culture of the steppe on the Volga.[37] The grave was most probably of the thirteenth century B.C., and gives the date of the first period of the Komarów culture.

Pottery typical of the second stage of the Komarów development is shown in Plate 16:15–20; Plates 17, 18; Figs. 27, 28, 29:2, 5, 6. The surface of the vessels was covered with a thin layer of reddish-brown slip and the decorative patterns were incised. One of the most popular types of vessel was a tulip-shaped pot which points to strong influence from the

[28] *SCIV*, vol. III, 1952, pp. 19 ff.; vol. IV, 1953, pp. 415 ff., etc. M. Петреску-Дымбовица, К вопросу о гальштатской культуре в Молдове, Миаюз, 1960, pp. 151 ff. A. Florescu, 'Contribuţii la cunoaşterea culturii Noua', *Arheologia Moldovei*, vol. II–III, Iaşi 1964. D. Popescu, 'Einige Bemerkungen zur Bronzezeit Siebenbürgens', *Acta AASH*, vol. VII, 1956, pp. 317 ff.

[29] В. М. Даниленко, Дослідження пам'яток підгірського та бобрицького типів на Київщині в 1950 р., Арх. Пам., vol. VI, 1956, pp. 5 ff.

[30] О. Н. Мельниковска, Памятники раннего железного века верхнего Поднепровья, Ксиак, no. 7, 1957, pp. 46 ff. Id., Древнейшие городища южной Белоруссии, Ксиимк, no. 70, 1957, pp. 28 ff. Ю. В. Кухаренко, Памятники железного века на территории Полесья, Археология СССР, no. Д 1–29, Moscow 1961, pp. 9 ff.

[31] T. Sulimirski, 'Das Hügelgräberfeld in Komarów und die Kultur von Komarów', *Bulletin International de l'Académie Polonaise, Cracovie*, 1936, pp. 172 ff.

[32] See notes 8 and 9.

[33] І. К. Свєшніков, Підсумки дослідження культур бронзової доби Прикарпаття і західного Поділля, Lviv 1958, pp. 21 ff. Id., К вопросу о сходстве и различии тщцинецкой и комаровской культур. Новое в советской археодогии, МИА, vol. 130, 1965, pp. 86–92. A. Vulpe, К вопросу о периодизации бронзового века в Молдове, *Dacia*, vol. NS v, 1961, pp. 105 ff. Id., 'Săpăturile de la Costişa', *MCA*, vol. VIII, 1962, pp. 309 ff.

[34] A. Točik, 'Die Gräberfelder der Karpathenländischen Hügelgräberkultur', *Fontes Archaeologici Pragenses*, vol. 7, Prague 1964, p. 54, Pls. XI, XVIII, etc.

[35] Sulimirski, loc. cit., note 2.

[36] Tallgren (op. cit., note 9), pp. 129 ff. О. А. Кривцова-Гракова, Бессарабский клад, Moscow 1949. M. Gimbutas, 'Borodino, Seima and Their Contemporaries', *PPS*, vol. XXII, 1956, pp. 143 ff.

[37] О. А. Кривцова-Гракова, Степное Поволжье и Причерноморье в эпоху поздней бронзы, МИА, no. 46, 1955, pp. 110 ff., 162.

Trzciniec culture; such vessels were the standard type of that culture, as mentioned above. Other types of vessels reflect a strong influence by the Middle Bronze Age cultures of the Hungarian Plain of period III (Mozsolics).[38] Very characteristic were handled cups and double-handled vases with oblique fluting which equate this stage with the Čaka culture in Slovakia, the Alpine Bronze Age period D,[39] the twelfth century B.C. Similar double-handled vases, and also tulip-shaped pots (urns) were excavated in a number of Lusatian cremation cemeteries in the Sub-Carpathian area, west of the Komarów territory.[40] They belonged to the 'early stage' of the culture, the third and fourth periods of the Polish Bronze Age. Bronze personal ornaments found in graves of this period also represent types current on the other side of the Carpathians (Fig. 26: 10–15).

Close ties with the Hungarian Plain, which lasted during the whole of the Bronze Age, are likewise reflected by stray bronze objects and hoards found within the area of the Komarów culture and its related Biały Potok group in West Podolia;[41] they give our region the character of a 'Hungarian' Bronze Age province.

During the third period of the Komarów culture, which may be equated with period IV of the Hungarian Bronze Age (Mozsolics), and also with period IV of the Polish Bronze Age (Montelius), a few changes took place which are reflected mainly in the pottery (Fig. 29:7, 8; Fig. 30; Plates 19, 20, 21:1–11). An increase in the impact of the Lusatian culture can be observed on the latter, while Lusatian types of bronze objects appear alongside those of 'Hungarian' types. At that time the Lusatian culture had reached the region on the Bug, and north-east of the Komarów territory the Wysocko culture began to emerge.[42]

The very large number of bronze hoards, especially of bronze swords[43] dating from this period and found in our area, was highly significant. They imply unsettled times which finally resulted in considerable changes, characteristic of the fourth and final period of the Komarów culture.

The fourth, the latest period of the Komarów culture, can be equated with the Early Iron Age (Hallstatt B–C). Connections with the Hungarian Plain were severed; grave goods, especially pottery, found in some burials (Komarów 33, Plate 21:12–16) point to southern (Transilvanian and Moldavian) links. In the western section of the culture (Horodyszcze I, no. 43) the old type of pottery survived and only iron objects indicate the late date of the graves concerned (Fig. 31:1, 3–6).

Table 24 shows the distribution of the graves into the relative periods, and a similar division has been carried out of the illustrative material.

The remains of the Komarów culture consisted almost exclusively of graves, as was the case with the Barrow-grave culture, and only a few settlements have been recorded. Oen

TABLE 24. Graves typical of the four subsequent stages of the Komarów culture

Period I	Komarów 6, 8, 9, 20, 21, 27, 34 (primary) Kavsko 4 Kołpiec 6	1200 B.C.
Period II	Komarów 7, 10, 11, 12, 23, 28, 36, 46, 55 Bukówna III Czyżyków I Daszawa II Kavsko 5 Okniany II Ostapie 6 Putiatyńce b Sarniki IV	1000 B.C.
Period III	Komarów 13, 14, 15, 19, 45, 48 Bukówna IV, VI Krasów 3, 4, 5 Stopczatów Wolica I, III, IV	800 B.C.
Period IV	Komarów 33 (secondary, 34 (secondary), 43, 47 Horodyszcze I Rakowa I	

of these, of the early stage of the culture, was that at Komarów, described in Part II of the present volume. Another, dating from the Late Bronze Age (probably period IV of the Bronze Age) was uncovered at Kulczyce Szlacheckie (no. 49, Plate 22:3–4); it may be attributed to the third stage of the Komarów culture. Strong Lusatian influence is reflected in its pottery. Pit-dwellings, chaff found in the clay plaster, bones of domesticated animals, pigs in particular, and similar evidence imply that the inhabitants of the settlement were a sedentary population engaged in, or at least acquainted with, agriculture. The settlement at Zatoka near Gródek Jagielloński[44] might have also belonged here.

No remains attributable to the Komarów culture (or its descendant culture) dating from a period parallel to the Scythian period in West Podolia, have been found so far in the Sub-Carpathian area.

WEST PODOLIA

(Map XI) (pp. 171 ff.)

No barrow-graves with pottery of Komarów type were found in West Podolia, except that at Semenów (no. 216, Plate 22:5). A few barrow-graves dating from the Late Bronze Age lay further east, on the Dniester (Barh, no. 192; Nenia, no. 211) their bronze ornaments showing close connection with contemporary barrow-graves in Volhynia (Table 23).

Proper to West Podolia during the Middle and Late Bronze Age were the so-called Biały Potok graves.[45] They

[38] A. Mozsolics, 'Archäologische Beiträge zur Geschichte der grossen Wanderung', *Acta AASH*, vol. 8, 1957, pp. 119 ff. Id., 'Der Goldfund von Kengyel', *Acta AASH*, vol. 9, 1959, pp. 253 ff.

[39] A. Točik, A. Paulík, 'Výskum mohyly v Čake v rokoch 1950–1951', *Slovenska Archeológia*, vol. VIII–1, Bratislava 1960, pp. 59 ff., Fig. 24, Pl. VI:5. See also T. G. E. Powell, 'The Inception of the Final Bronze Age in Middle Europe', *PPS*, vol. XXIX, 1963, pp. 217 ff., Fig. 5.

[40] M. Gedl, *Spr.Arch.*, vol. IX, 1960, pp. 87 f., Figs. 4, 5.

[41] For the Middle Bronze Age see Sulimirski, loc. cit., note 2; for the Late Bronze Age and Early Iron Age see K. Żurowski, 'Zabytki brązowe młodszej epoki brązu i wczesnego okresu żelaza górnego dorzecza Dniestru', *Prz.A.*, vol. VIII, 1949, pp. 155 ff.

[42] Głosik, loc. cit., note 16. On the Wysocko culture, see note 22.

[43] W. Antoniewicz, 'Miecze bronzowe znalezione w Galicji', *Prz.A.*, vol. I, 1919, pp. 28 ff.; vol. II, 1922, pp. 1 ff.

[44] I. К. Свешніков, Арх. Пам., vol. II, 1949, p. 212.

[45] J. Kostrzewski, 'Groby eneolityczne z skurczonymi szkieletami w Białym Potoku', *Prz.A.*, vol. III, 1925–7, pp. 9 ff., Pl. IV. Id., 'Od mezolitu

were mainly slab-cists and a number of 'flat' graves which yielded pottery, and in a few cases also bronze ornaments, either typical of the Komarów culture or closely related to it (Fig. 32, Plate 22). The structure of the slab-cists and the burial ritual displayed by the graves did not differ from those characteristic of the local group of the Globular Amphora culture (Plan 46:2, 3). The people of the Biały Potok group were evidently the descendants of the latter who in the course of time changed their culture and adapted themselves to the new currents and conditions. The Biały Potok group of graves must be included in the Podolian Globular Amphora sequence as its latest link.

The development of the Biały Potok group of graves runs parallel with that of the Komarów culture, but began in period II of the latter; thus only three periods (A, B, C) may be distinguished in its development (Tables 15, 25).

Pottery of period B reflects a strong influence of the Noua culture (Plate 22:8). Cemeteries of the latter culture appeared close to the southern border of the group (Ostrivets, no. 507). The Noua culture has been dated in Romania to the period eleventh to ninth century B.C.[46] Recently, however, Florescu[47] proposes a much higher date, from the fourteenth to the twelfth century B.C. In our area, finds of the Noua type were definitely of a later date, of period B. They possibly denote an influx of some Noua tribes from the south, displaced by the push of the Srubna culture. Elements of the latter culture have been noticed in the Noua remains in Moldavia. During period C, the Wysocko culture began to encroach on the territory of the group in the north, as indicated by the slab-cist grave from Rakówkąt,[48] the bronze inventory of which was typical of that culture.

East of the Biały Potok group, in the eastern part of West Podolia, and also along the Dniester, a series of barrow-graves of the Early Iron Age (Hallstatt B and C) have been excavated (Myszków, no. 210; Uście Biskupie, no, 219; Fig. 32:5, 6; Luka Vrublivetska, no. 205; Mervintsy, no. 206; see Table 25). Some of the barrow-graves—many of them excavated by myself (Beremiany, Bilcze Złote, Szydłowce)—previously dated by me to the Scythian period (Hallstatt D)[49] belonged also to this group of remains.

In Table 25, the tentative chronological scheme is given of the Biały Potok graves and their equation with other cultures.

THE HOLIHRADY CULTURE

Within the territory of the Biały Potok group, and also further east in the region of the late barrow-graves mentioned above, nearly fifty Late Bronze Age and Early Iron Age settlements have so far been recorded, some of which have been investigated.

A few settlements (Babino,[50] Nezvysko,[51] etc.) yielded pottery of 'Komarów' type with marked 'Trzciniec' features; these were evidently the earliest Komarów-Biały Potok settlements which probably dated from period A of that culture. More numerous were settlements typical of which was a well-made and baked ware with a black, sometimes dark brown, highly polished surface, very similar to the Central European Hallstatt ware. Accordingly, the name 'Thracian-

TABLE 25. Tentative Chronological Scheme of the Biały-Potok – Holihrady Remains

Komarów and Biały-Potok periods		Biały-Potok – Holihrady Remains			Equations
		Slab-cists and flat graves	barrow-graves	settlements	
I		See Table 15, p. 54	—	Tripolye D-pottery	Alpine Bronze Age B-2, C Montelius Bronze Age II Salka cemeteries Füzeszabony culture Trzciniec culture Early Srubna connections
II	A	Beremiany 3 Biały-Potok gr. 1/2 Trembowla Żeżawa	—	Babino Nezvysko Nowosiółka-Kostiukowa	Alpine Bronze Age D Montelius Bronze Age III Bohemian Tumulus culture Čaka culture
III	B	Biały-Potok gr. 3 Czernelica Horodnica Aa & Ad Nagórzanka Podgórzany	Barh Nenia Semenów	Holihrady culture	Hallstatt A, B Montelius Bronze Age IV Lusatian influence Noua elements
IV	C	Ivanye-Zołote Uwisła 2 Rakówąt	Luka-Vrublivetska Mervintsy Uście Biskupie	Holihrady culture	Hallstatt B, C Montelius Bronze Age V Wysocko culture

do okresu wędrówek', *Prehistoria Ziem Polskich*, Kraków 1939–48, pp. 214 ff.

[46] M. Petrescu-Dimboviţa, Конец бронзового и начало раннежелезного века в Молдове в свете последних археологических раскопок, *Dacia*, vol. NS IV, 1960, p. 151.

[47] See note 28.

[48] Sulimirski (op. cit., note 18), pp. 103 f.

[49] T. Sulimirski, *Scytowie na zachodniem Podolu*, Lwów 1936.

[50] T. C. Пассек, Стоянка комаровской культуры на среднем Днестре, Ксиимк, по. 75, 1959, pp. 1954 ff.

[51] Г. И. Смирнова, Ксиимк, no. 67, 1957. Id., Підсумки досліджень верхніх шарів незвиського поселення, Мдапв, vol. 2, 1959, pp. 87 ff.

Hallstatt' culture is usually given to these remains in Soviet archaeological literature;[52] recently the name of the 'Holihrady' culture has been applied to it by Svešnikov[53] who devoted to it a special study. The culture equated partly with the third, but mainly with the fourth period of the Komarów culture, or with stages B and C of the Biały Potok group (Table 25). According to Svešnikov, the culture developed during the period from the tenth to the seventh century B.C.

West Podolian black-polished 'Holihrady' ware has been regarded as exclusively characteristic of both 'pre-Scythian' and 'Scythian' periods, which correspond with Hallstatt periods C and D in Central Europe. An earlier appearance of this pottery in our area has not been taken into account,[54] and the gap between the 'Komarów period' and the 'Holihrady-pre-Scythian period' has been regarded as filled in by the Noua culture.[55] In fact, however, settlements of the Noua type were not found north of Mahala near Černivtsi,[56] the cemetery of Ostrivets near Horodenka mentioned above being the northernmost site of that culture.

On the other hand, black pottery, although not yet highly polished, was found in the settlement of Komarów and in the few barrow-graves there (e.g. Fig. 29:7), dating already from the first period of the Komarów culture. The highly polished black ware formed the bulk of pottery of the hut investigated at Nowosiółka Kostiukowa, where it was dated by two bronze fibulae of Peschiera type;[57] the date of these fibulae is debatable[58] but they possibly date from a period before 1200 B.C. and definitely before 1100 B.C. A fluted black polished ware very similar to the Holihrady pottery was typical of the Füzesabony culture in the eastern part of the Hungarian Plain dated from the Hungarian Bronze Age period III, equated with Reinecke's period B.[59] The early date of this pottery in our region has also been evidenced by the vessel from Gruszka in which was hidden a bronze hoard of the fifth period of the Bronze Age (Montelius),[60] a period prior to the 'pre-Scythian' period.

The 'Holihrady' culture was clearly complementary to the Biały Potok graves in some of which (Uwisła, no. 220; Uście Biskupie, no. 219) 'Hallstatt' pottery was found (Fig. 32:6; Plate 22:6); both were vestiges of the same people who inhabited West Podolia during the Middle and Late Bronze Age and Early Iron Age. They were descendants of the Tripolye culture (Globular Amphora people respectively) as has been confirmed by the position of Tripolyan pottery (D-ware) in the settlement of Komarów and, above all, at Nowosiółka Kostiukowa. The latter also indicates the final date of the Tripolye sequence.

During its long existence, the Biały Potok-Holihrady culture was subjected to various cultural trends. At first, in periods I and II (A), this was the trans-Carpathian influence, the same which contributed with the Trzciniec culture to the formation of the Komarów culture proper to the adjoining Sub-Carpathian region; only slight Trzciniec influence reached West Podolia. In the subsequent development, in period III (B), strong ties connected West Podolia with Moldavia and the area further south, including Transilvania; they were evidently based on ancient tradition going back to early Tripolyan times. Elements borrowed from the Monteoru and in particular the Noua cultures can be clearly distinguished, and the latter reached even further north, to Volhynia (Dubno, Voytsekhivka); nevertheless, as emphasized by Melyukova,[61] Holihrady ware differed from Romanian pottery which shows many features in common with the 'Early Hallstatt' pottery of the Theiss region on the other side of the Carpathians.

The settlements with the 'Scythian' pottery are distinguishable by their kitchen-ware which, unlike that of the earlier periods, was of 'Bilohrudivka' type; its appearance was clearly due to eastern influence and possibly to an influx of eastern ethnical elements caused by political events of about 800 B.C., which initiated period IV (C).

BRONZE HOARDS AND FINDS

All the above changes, the crossing of different currents and their superseding one another, are well reflected in the stray bronze objects and hoards found in our area. The Trzciniec and Lusatian bronzes were proper to the northern part of our territory; they expanded eastwards and later southwards along the Dnieper (Fig. 35). Only a few Lusatian bronzes, or hybrid forms, were found in the Sub-Carpathian region and West Podolia, both being proper to the 'Hungarian' bronze industry. The latter bronzes give the territory of the Komarów and Biały-Potok-Holihrady cultures the character of a 'Hungarian' province.

The earliest 'Hungarian' bronzes of Koszider type (Montelius period II) reached far to the east, some being found beyond the Dnieper.[62] Those of period III had a smaller extent and in periods IV and V they were confined to West Podolia and the adjoining area.[63] At that time Lusatian bronzes proceeded southwards along the Dnieper to be checked by eastern, Uralian types, the appearance of which followed the expansion of the Srubna culture,[64] which crossed the Dnieper and established itself in the eastern part of the grassland within the Territory. The hoard from Borodino[65] in South Bessarabia, dating probably from *c.* 1300

[52] E.g. Тереножкин (op. cit., note 20: 1961), pp. 208 ff.

[53] І. К. Свешніков, Пам'ятки голіградського типу на західному Поділлі, Мдапв, vol. 5, 1964, pp. 40–66.

[54] А. И. Мелюкова, Памятники скифского времени лесостепного среднего Поднестровья, МИА, no. 64, 1958, pp. 25 ff. Id., Исследование памятников предскифской и скифской эпох в лесостепной Молдавии, Миаюз, 1960, p. 140.

[55] Тереножкин (op. cit., note 20: 1961), pp. 196, 208.

[56] Г. И. Смирнова, Поселение позднебронзового века и раннего железа возле с. Магала, Ксиимк, no. 70, 1957, pp. 105 ff.

[57] T. Sulimirski, 'Tripolyan Notes', *PPS*, vol. XXX, 1964, pp. 56 ff. Id. (op. cit., note 1), pp. 49 f., Fig. 2. Мелюкова (op. cit., note 54), pp. 22 ff., Figs. 3–5.

[58] V. G. Childe, 'Notes on the Chronology of the Hungarian Bronze Age', *Acta AASH*, vol. VII, 1956, pp. 298 f.

[59] A. Mozsolics, 'Der Tumulus von Nyirkarász-Gyulaháza', *Acta AASH*, vol. XII, 1960, pp. 116 ff.

[60] K. Żurowski, 'Skarb brązowy z Gruszki, pow.tłumacki', *Prz.A.*, vol. VI, 1937–9, pp. 204 ff. Id. (op. cit., 41), pp. 159 ff., 199 f.

[61] See note 54.

[62] Tallgren (op. cit., note 9), pp. 137 f. 190, 146, Figs. 80; 101:12; 107; 81. Тереножкин (op. cit., note 20: 1957), p. 58. Sulimirski (op. cit., note 2), pp. 183 ff.

[63] See note 60.

[64] See note 37.

[65] See notes 2 and 36.

B.C., marks the end of the ancient order in the Pontic region. A local bronze industry had developed by then in the area on the Lower Dnieper, in which various traditions blended together: Lusatian, 'Hungarian', Srubna, and later a strong Caucasian (Koban) and Transcaucasian current also left its imprint.[66]

The eighth century B.C. was a turning-point in the development of our area. At this time many settlements in the valleys of the rivers in the steppe were abandoned and destroyed and new ones founded. This was the period of the 'Thraco-Cimmerian' bronzes in West Podolia.[67] A series of French and Italian imported objects from this area and the country further east[68] reflect the extent of commercial connections in this period via the Hungarian Plain.

The sixth century B.C. witnessed a new change, caused by the Scythian conquest. To the early part of that century the earliest 'Scythian' barrow-graves belonged in the steppe west of the Dnieper. West Podolia was conquered at a slightly later date. The gold hoard from Michałków on the Dniester,[69] evidently the property of a local 'Thraco-Cimmerian' ruler deprived of his princedom by the invaders, gives the date of this occurrence. The background of all these changes and transformations, their reason and their consequences, have been discussed by me in another volume.[70]

[66] Кривцова-Гракова (op. cit., note 37), pp. 132 ff. А. А. Йессен, Некоторые памятники VIII–VII вв. до н.э. на северном Кавказе. Вопросы скифо-сарматской археологии, Moscow 1955, pp. 112 ff.

[67] Sulimirski, 'Die thrako-kimmerische Periode in Südostpolen', *Wiener Prähistorische Zff.*, vol. XXV, 1938, pp. 129 ff.

[68] A. Szlankówna, 'Kilka importów staroitalskich i zachodnio-europejskich z południowo—wschodniej Polski i Ukrainy', *Światowit*, vol. XVII, 1938, pp. 302 ff. Terenozhkin (loc. cit., notes 9 and 20:1961), unjustly denies the western origin of socketed bronze axes found in the Ukraine; they represent the genuine Armorican (French) type of socketed axes. See Рыбалова (op. cit., note 9), p. 91.

[69] K. Hadaczek, *Złote skarby michałkowskie*, Kraków 1904. *Reallexikon-Ebert*, vol. VIII, pp. 180 ff., Pls. 52–6.

[70] T. Sulimirski, *Prehistoric Russia*, London (John Baker Publishers Ltd.) (in press).

PART II

Description of Graves and Reports on Excavations

SECTION I

Barrow-grave Cemetery and Settlement of Komarów

1. THE CEMETERY
(Plan 1)

A FAIRLY high ridge of hills runs west of the village in a SW–NE direction, forming the water-shed between the rivers Łukwa and Łomnica, tributaries of the Dniester which terminates a few kilometres further to the NE, in the Dniester valley. For the most part, these hills are covered with woods in which clearings occur in some areas: hamlets have been established in these clearings. Numerous barrow-graves are situated along a fairly narrow belt on the summit of these hills and these are part of several villages. A total of sixty-eight barrow-graves occur in the main line of graves in an area belonging to Komarów village. This line is about 2·5km long. Two of the barrow-graves (nos. 63 and 'e') are in fact a little over the border and in the territory of two neighbouring villages. Four more barrow-graves occurred somewhat lower down, in the hills nearer Komarów village.

As a rule, the barrow-graves on the hill-top were in groups of two or four, though some groups of six to ten mounds also occur. The belt along which they were distributed was about 50m wide, extending to 250m at the widest part of the hill-top. The distance between individual groups did not exceed 150m.

Four barrow-graves in this cemetery, near the Kryłos border at the eastern end of the hill, were investigated in 1886 by T. Ziemięcki.[1] I carried out a control investigation of three of these (nos. 2, 3, 4) in 1936, identifying them by the description. Sixty-two barrow-graves in this cemetery were investigated in 1934–6 by the present writer and Dr J. Grabowski, the then Director of the 'Pokuckie Muzeum', Stanisławów, with the assistance of Miss I. Siwek and Mr K. Żurowski, then students of the Prehistoric Institute, Lwów University, the latter at present Professor of Prehistoric Archaeology at the University of Poznań. Six barrow-graves in this cemetery, marked 'a'–'f' on the plan, were not investigated. At the same time, Dr J. Pasternak was excavating a barrow-grave known as the 'Nastasyna Mohyła' which formed part of this cemetery but was situated in the area of the neighbouring village of Kryłos (no. 48), 50m east of barrow-grave 4. In addition, two barrow-graves in fields situated lower down (nos. 41 and 64) were investigated by us, while Dr J. Pasternak investigated another (no. 43). One ('g') was not investigated. Only brief notes[2] were published: full details were prepared for the printer but did not survive the war.

Numeration of the barrow-graves investigated starts at no. 5, since this was included in the numeration of the barrow-graves excavated by T. Ziemięcki. The material Ziemięcki excavated was deposited in the Archaeological Museum, Cracow, while that deriving from our excavations went partly to the Pokuckie Muzeum, Stanisławów and partly to the Prehistoric Institute of Lwów University.

The large extent of the Komarów cemetery and the formation of the terrain indicate that it does not constitute a single entity. The dead buried in the Komarów cemetery barrow-graves must have belonged to several family groups, perhaps clans, and they probably dwelled in separate hamlets not far from their burial place. One of these settlements uncovered in the 'Dworzyska' field lay nearer the western end of the Komarów cemetery, and was within easy reach and access. Despite a search, however, it proved impossible to discover the sites of other settlements particularly of the settlement which had been inhabited by those buried in the central part of the cemetery, in graves of the Bronze Age. The distance as the crow flies from these barrow-graves to the settlement in the 'Dworzyska' field was over 3km, and deep ravines between the barrow-graves and the settlement increased this distance considerably. It follows from this that those buried in these barrow-graves were not inhabitants of the settlement we discovered.

Most of the skeletons had undergone entire disintegration, and only the positions and arrangements of the objects found indicated the site where the grave must have been. Traces of the skeleton were preserved only in exceptional cases. The arrangement and number of objects found made it likely that each mound had usually contained one burial, though several mounds contained two, undoubtedly those of a man and woman, coeval. Secondary burials were very rare, and occurred only in two groups (nos. 28, 33, 34, 37, 38); these derived from the Late Bronze or Early Iron Age, and had been dug in Neolithic or Middle Bronze Age barrow-graves.

The orientation of the graves was usually W–E or NW–SE, occasionally NE–SW and one only (no. 47) was N–S. The heads were placed to the west as a rule. The dimensions of graves and arrangement of objects show that the dead were buried in a somewhat contracted position. A certain number of the graves, several of these neolithic, were cremation burials. Cremation took place on the spot, as a rule the calcined bones were not moved and the mound was erected upon them and the fragments of pyre. The orientation of the

[1] T. Ziemięcki, *ZWAK*, vol. XIV, 1887, p. 56.

[2] T. Sulimirski, 'Das Hügelgräberfeld in Komarów und die Kultur von Komarów', *Bulletin Internationale de l'Académie Polonaise,* Cracovie 1936, pp. 172 ff. Id., 'Cmentarzysko kurhanowe w Komarowie koło Halicza i kultura komarowska', *Spr.PAU*, vol. XLI, 1936, pp. 273 ff. Id., 'Kurhany komarowskie', *Złoty Szlak*, no. 4, Stanisławów 1939, pp. 1 ff. J. Pasternak, 'Moje badania terenowe w 1935 r.', *ZOW*, vol. XI, 1936, p. 132.

cremation burials did not differ from that of the inhumation burials.

The graves were almost invariably in the centre or near the centre of the mounds. In some Neolithic graves, the dead were lying in shallow shafts, but they were usually placed on the ancient level, particularly in later periods. They were generally placed on oak logs, though traces in some barrow-graves appear to indicate that the dead had been lying in a kind of wooden box.

All the Komarów graves contained a large quantity of charcoal, scattered in lumps throughout the area of the mound and often in the mound itself. Traces of burned hearths round the graves were often found, this indicating the importance of fire in the burial rite.

Single river pebbles (or sometimes several), deliberately arranged, were found in the barrow-graves of the Komarów period. In barrow-grave 11, five pebbles marked the boundary of the grave. Larger accumulations of stones occurred less frequently. Two larger accumulations in barrow-grave 20 formed something not unlike a stone surround: the grave area in barrow-grave 45 was marked by large pebbles, while the dead body in barrow-grave 48 had been lying on a layer of carefully arranged stones. The stone construction in barrow-grave 14 was unique, though its date could not be established owing to the absence of grave goods.

Flint flakes, sometimes in large quantities, were found in all barrow-graves no matter what their date. Odd potsherds were also found in many graves, though not deriving from vessels in the grave. The potsherds were usually very small. Lumps of ochre were found in some Neolithic graves, while lumps of calcined earth dust were used in others instead of ochre.

One or two vessels were found in the Neolithic graves, though pottery was often absent. Provisions for the journey after death were undoubtedly given to the dead on platters of wood or other organic material. The quantity of clay vessels increased in later graves. The finding of broken incomplete vessels in some Bronze Age barrow-graves, particularly cremation burials (e.g. nos. 34, 47) and found next to complete vessels, is curious.

The Komarów barrow-graves were not coeval. In addition to the barrow-graves containing typically Neolithic grave goods, barrow-graves of the Middle and Late Bronze Ages also occurred here, containing highly characteristic pottery and other grave goods. The latter belonged to the culture named 'Komarów culture', by the present writer, after this cemetery.

The Neolithic barrow-graves were scattered, sometimes in groups varying from two or three in number, or sometimes singly, across the entire area occupied by the cemetery. However, the Komarów period barrow-graves were only found in the centre of the cemetery, where they formed two larger groups in the 'Lis' field, each containing about ten graves. A few Komarów graves dating from the Late Bronze Age, were at the west of those referred to above. These were mainly secondary burials in the Neolithic and Middle Bronze Age barrow-graves. The distribution of the barrow-graves investigated in individual groups is shown in Table 26.

A closer study of the relative position of barrow-graves of different periods revealed that those of the Komarów type were always grouped around a Neolithic, or early Bronze Age barrow; the latter usually lay on the eastern periphery of the group concerned, and the 'Komarów' graves were placed west of it.

TABLE 26. Groups of barrow-graves at the cemetery of Komarów and their date

Group	Neolithic and Early Bronze Age	Komarów culture	Not specified
A	39, 40, 42		57
B	59		30, 58
C-a	31	55	56
a	16, 17, 18		
c	37, 38, 52, 63	37/s, 38/s	
d	49, 50		
D-a	53		54
b			60
c			61, 62
E-a	32	33, 33/s, 34, 34/s, 36, 47, 48	
b	25, 26	35	
F-a	24	19, 20, 21, 22, 23, 37, 51	
b	29	45, 46	
c	44	6, 7, 8, 9, 10, 11, 14, 15, 28	
d	5	12, 13	
G-a	2		1, 3
b	65		4
H	64		
J		43	41
Total	25	28+4 secondary	12

This chronological arrangement is clearly visible in the easternmost group of barrow-graves of the Komarów period (group F-c), which adjoined the Late Neolithic, or Early Bronze Age barrow 44. Close to its eastern side lies barrow 28 of period II, but all other mounds were south or south-west of it. The nearest were barrow-graves 8 and 6, situated close to each other, both richly furnished, and dating from the very end of period I. A little further south, in the same row, lay barrow 9 likewise of period I. Close to these, to the south-west, were barrow-graves 10 and 7, forming the second row, both of period II. West of these, on the perimeter of the group, were barrow-graves 11, 14, 15, all of period III.

The arrangement was similar in the neighbouring group F-b, which was initiated by the Neolithic, or Early Bronze Age barrow-grave 29, situated on the eastern periphery of the group. West of it lay barrow-grave 46 of Komarów period II, and close to it, a little further north, was barrow-grave 45 of period III; another pair of barrow-graves was south of the above: barrow 12 of period II was nearer to the Neolithic mound, the other, no. 13 of period III, was behind it to the south. The Neolithic or Early Bronze Age barrow 24 of the next group F-a lay likewise on the eastern periphery of the group. Close to it was barrow 21 of Komarów period I, and mound 27, a little later in date, of the transitional stage from periods I to II, lay a little apart to the north-west. Near by, north of barrow-grave 24, was barrow 23 of period II, and barrow 19 of period III lay on the western periphery of the group; on the other hand, another barrow of period III (no. 20) was placed in the centre of the group.

The position in the next group E-a differs in that the Neolithic or Early Bronze Age barrow-grave lies on the northern periphery of the group instead of on the eastern, but otherwise the distribution of barrow-graves exhibits the same patterns. Barrow-grave 34 (original grave) of the transitional stage between periods I and II, lies south-east of the Neolithic mound. East of it was barrow-grave 36 of period II. Barrow-grave 48, of period III, was raised on the western periphery of the group. Barrow-grave 33 of period IV was placed in the centre, close to the Neolithic mound, and so also was the secondary burial of the same period in barrow 34. Finally, barrow 47 of period IV lay a little outside the group, on its western side.

Below is given the description of all barrow-graves excavated at Komarów. The following Section II contains a list of all vessels found in these barrows; their measurements and other particulars are also indicated. The report on the investigation of the settlement situated in the field 'Dworzyska' has been included in Section III.

The excavation of the entire barrow-grave cemetery at Komarów gave results such as had been expected before investigations began. It emerges from these results that the custom of erecting mounds over graves prevailed in this area from the Neolithic to the start of the Early Iron Age. Continuity in the use of the cemetery was also established, showing continuity of settlement in this region.

Description of Barrow-graves

Barrow-grave 1 formed part of a group of three mounds (nos. 1–3) all excavated by T. Ziemięcki, in 1886. It was 24m in diameter, 1·5–2m high. It was cut across with a trench 8m long, 1·6m wide and 2·6m deep. Only one flint was found at a depth of 1·05m.

Barrow-grave 2 (Plan 16:1). 14m in diameter, 40cm high, originally higher. T. Ziemięcki found there only a flint knife. I excavated it again in 1936. In the centre the grave-shaft was uncovered (f), dug about 20cm into the ancient surface, orientated NW–SE, about 1·8m long. More than half of it had been destroyed by the trench dug by T. Ziemięcki. It was filled in with loose red fired clay, charcoal and calcined human bones. In a few places on the ancient surface around the grave were found a few flint flakes (b), lumps of charcoal and a single potsherd (c). This last was of Tripolyan 'D-ware' type, thick-walled, and bore traces of red paint. South of the grave a few calcined bones lay on the ancient surface (a).

Barrow-grave 3.14m in diameter, 40cm high. Nothing was found in it by T. Ziemięcki. It was excavated by me again in 1936. On the ancient surface, NE of the centre, a few flint flakes and one potsherd were found. The sherd was of Tripolyan 'D-ware' type and did not differ from pottery excavated in the settlement on the 'Dworzysko' field.

Barrow-grave 4. Situated close to the border with Kryłos, about 50m west of the barrow-grave there excavated by J. Pasternak, dating from the Early Bronze Age. It was 16m in diameter, 50 cm high. According to T. Ziemięcki, in the southern part of the area excavated a vessel 'filled in with ashes' which disintegrated was found. Inside was a flint and near it lay a 'pointed' flint. I excavated this mound in 1936. Only two small potsherds were found, which originated from the vessel mentioned by T. Ziemięcki. This was a small beaker, its body hemispheric, undecorated.

Barrow-grave 5. Excavated by me in 1934, and one of the larger mounds, situated on a clearing. It was 18m in diameter, 1m high. In its mound a few very small potsherds, flint flakes and three trimmed implements were excavated. On the ancient surface, about 1·5–2m E of the centre, two vessels stood, both very brittle, crushed; (a) a larger amphora with two lugs and (b) a beaker or bowl. The latter had a high neck, and an everted rim. Its decoration consisted of incised fishbone patterns on the body and a few horizontal rows of short oblique, alternating incisions on the neck. Drawings of both went astray during World War II and I was unable to recover them. Recently, the drawing of the bowl has been published by J. Machnik.[3] Close to these vessels lay an axe (Fig. 16:11) made of black flint of 'Bug' variety, its cross-section being an irregular quadrangle.

The cross-section of this mound was as follows: 30cm grey arable soil, then about 50cm of mound earth, grey in colour, darker in its lower part nearer to the centre. It lay on the ancient fossil humus nearly black in colour, which at a depth of 30cm (1·1m from the top of the mound) became increasingly brownish, and at a depth of about 1·7m from the top of the mound the pure yellow subsoil appeared. The same sequence of layers has been attested in all mounds excavated at Komarów.

Barrow-grave 6 formed part of a larger group of mounds situated on a clearing. It was 19m in diameter, 70cm high (Plan 12:1). In the centre of the surface covered by the mound, contours of the ancient grave pit (j) were uncovered, about 2 by 1m in area, orientated nearly E–W. It was only 25cm deep. On its bottom lay the skeleton, head to E, of which only slight traces, mainly of the skull (d) were discernible. In the SE corner near the head stood a cup and a bowl (i-1, 2) (Plate 16:6); the latter had a slanting fluted decoration on the body, but it disintegrated: it was similar to that from barrow-grave 11/a-2. On the chest of the skeleton lay a bronze pin (h) (Fig. 26:7), and along the eastern side of the grave outside it, stood three vessels: a tulip-shaped pot (a); a smaller beaker (e) (Plate 16:2) with a raised band on the neck covered with a row of punctures below its incised ornament; a small tulip-shaped pot (f) which disintegrated. Along the western side of the grave lay almost completely decayed timber logs (c), covering an area about 2m long, 50cm wide, possibly the platform of another (male?) grave. On the southern end of the logs a small bronze dagger in a wooden sheath (b) (Fig. 26:9) was found, and about 2m E of it lay a small gold earring (g) (Fig. 26:8).

Barrow-grave 7 was 16m in diameter, 40 cm high, ploughed up. About 1m S of the centre, on the ancient surface, a vessel was found (a), and nearly 2m NW of it lay a flint scraper (b). Both objects marked the site of the grave, the skeleton of which had completely decayed.

[3] J. Machnik, *Studia nad kulturą ceramiki sznurowej w Małopolsce*. Wrocław-Warszawa-Kraków 1966, Pl. XLV:c3.

Barrow-grave 8 (Plan 12:2) belonged to a group of three mounds including nos. 6 and 7 described above. It was 16m in diameter, 40 cm high, almost completely ploughed up, the grave being partly ruined. The grave was in the centre, orientated nearly SW–NE. It was well marked by loose earth which filled in a shallow hole dug in the ancient surface. On its three corners stood six vessels. One of these was an undecorated tulip-shaped beaker (b) (Plate 16:1); two others were two handled cups, one of which (d) almost completely destroyed by the plough, was similar to that from barrow-grave 12/b, and the other (e) (Plate 16:10) was decorated with four protuberances on the body encircled by semicircular grooves. Three other vessels stood in the eastern corner: a small decorated goblet (c-1) (Plate 16:8), a small cup (c-2) and small bowl (c-3) (Plate 16:7) both undecorated. In the eastern part of the grave, on its bottom lay an oak box (f)[4] which contained several bronze and gold personal ornaments. One gold pendant (a) was found about 2m E of the grave, in the arable soil, evidently displaced by the plough. Bronze ornaments in the box were (Fig. 26:1–6): a pin, 37cm long, with a round perforated massive head, 4·5cm in diameter; the pin was round in its upper part, square and torqued in the lower half; a massive bracelet 7·7cm in diameter, made of a bar round in section, 1·5cm thick, its wide open terminals thinner, the surface covered with several groups of deep-cast grooves; a torque made of a round bar, 6mm thick, 14·2cm in diameter, the terminals wound in spirals; and finally, two identical sets of head, or ear, ornaments consisting of several tubular beads made of bronze wire, of two rings each, 2cm in diameter, with their terminals wound in spirals, each consisting of two bell-shaped pendants, with a long tubular shaft to which a small gold pendant was attached, 1·6cm in diameter. The fourth gold pendant was of the same type but larger, 5cm high. All these objects were well arranged in the box, the pin lying diagonally.

Barrow-grave 9 (Plan 12:3). 17m in diameter, 60cm high, ploughed up. Five vessels found on the ancient surface east of the centre probably marked the site of the burial, orientated S–N, the skeleton of which had completely decayed. Three of the vessels were in the northern end of the grave, i.e. an undecorated bowl (a-1) (Plate 16:13), a decorated cup (a-3) (Plate 16:9), and a tulip-shaped cup (a-2) (Plate 16:5). On the eastern side was a bowl similar to that above (b), and at the southern end was a beaker (c) (Fig. 28:7) decorated with horizontal grooves and herring-bone patterns.

Barrow-grave 10 (Plan 12:4). 16m in diameter, 40 cm high, ploughed up. Eleven vessels (NW of the centre) placed in a line from SW to NE, evidently marked the site of the burial, about 3m long, 2m wide. Two vessels were at the SW end, i.e. a tulip-shaped pot (a-1) (Plate 18:5) with a raised band, and a small cup (a-2) (Plate 18:16). East of the latter were two vessels, a small beaker (c-1) (Plate 18:7) and a bowl (c-2) (Plate 16:20), and at the NE end a tulip-shaped pot with decorative grooves on its neck (d-1) inside which was found another, smaller pot of the same type (Plate 18:3), and two bowls (d-2, 3) (Plate 16:18). Along the northern end a crushed beaker (e) (Fig. 28:5) and a tulip-shaped pot (f) (Plate 18:8) stood, and about 2m SE of the vessels above was another tulip-shaped pot (b).

Barrow-grave 11 (Plan 13:2). 16m in diameter, 40cm high, much ploughed up which resulted in the upper part of many vessels and part of the grave itself being destroyed or badly damaged. The burial was near the centre on the ancient surface; it covered an area about 3m long orientated almost NW–SE. The corpse most probably was buried in an extended position and the pyre laid over it. Bones were only partly calcined, those which had survived indicated the position of the burial. Over the whole area lay charcoal, which also formed small concentrations outside the area of the grave proper. The corpse was laid head to NW, as indicated by the remains of the skull (c). In the NW corner of the grave stood two bowls (a-1, 2) (Plate 17:1, 10), a larger and a smaller, both with fluted decoration on the body, and further south stood a tulip-shaped pot (b) upside down, the description of which is missing. Near the feet lay two small cups (p-1, 2) (Plate 18:18), and a larger, handled and decorated cup (p-3) (Plate 17:4). Around the eastern end of the grave lay five pebbles (j) and within an area 20cm in diameter lay over one hundred small flint flakes (m) heaped up to 10cm high, mixed with charcoal; a few potsherds were also found in this heap, which belonged to vessels scattered along the northern side of the grave (d, k, m) i.e. a bowl with a fluted decoration (Fig. 27:5) and a tulip-shaped pot (Fig. 28:2). Along the other, south, side of the grave sherds of a bowl with a fluted decoration were found (e, f), also scattered (Fig. 27:10).

Barrow-grave 12·20m in diameter, 80cm high. A flint flake was found in the mound, and on the ancient surface, about 1m S of the centre, lay a crushed tulip-shaped pot with a raised band on the neck. No traces of any skeleton were discerned.

Barrow-grave 13 (Plan 13:4). 15m in diameter, 30–40cm high, ploughed up, vessels and the grave partly ruined. South of the centre, on the ancient surface, a layer of almost completely decayed timber logs, or planks in line from W to E, lay over an area 1·7m long and 1m wide (h). One perpendicular log lay at the eastern end of the grave. Under the timber cover a layer of dark, loose earth extended about 5cm deep. In its western part slight traces of the skeleton were perceptible, in particular of the skull (g), near which lay a lump of fired clay, apparently as substitute for red ochre. Around the grave, mainly in its corners, stood four vessels: a small undecorated cup (a) (Plate 21:9) on the eastern side; in the NE corner was a decorated, handled cup (b) (Plate 21:8) with a high, funnel-shaped collar; in the NW corner another, destroyed, handled cup (c); finally, in the SW corner was a beaker (e) (Plate 21:10) upside down, with a flat rim and fluted horizontal decoration covering its entire body. Close to it lay its lid (d), its surface dark-brown, well polished (Plate 21:11).

Barrow-grave 14 (Plan 13:3). 17m in diameter, 60–70cm high. At a depth of 30cm, in the mound itself, three groups of large pebbles (a, b, c) were found at a distance of about 2m from each other. Deeper, in the area enclosed by these pebbles, upper stones of a peculiar stone construction ap-

[4] O. Seidl, 'Les différentes espèces de charbon et de bois trouvées dans quelques stations préhistoriques', *Académie Polonaise, C.R.M. des séances de la Classe des Sc. Math. et Nat.*, no. 10, Cracovie 1935.

peared. This was a kind of square cist built of small boulders (e) laid in 3–4 layers in two rows, about 40cm high above the ancient surface, orientated NW–SE, SW–NE, approximately 1·2 by 1·1m in area. Its cobbled bottom (f) was funnel shaped and sunk about 50cm in the ground. From the southern corner of the stone construction was a kind of wall built of smaller pebbles laid in two rows, about 25cm wide, 20cm high, 80cm long (d). Nothing was found either in the construction, or around it and beneath it.

Barrow-grave 15. 16m in diameter, 30cm high, completely ruined by ploughing. Only a few flints and potsherds were found in the arable soil. The latter belonged to a large red vessel made of clay paste tempered with crushed stones and fired clay, which was probably of a type and size similar to the large vessel from barrow-grave 20.

Barrow-grave 16 (Plan 13:1) belonged to a group of three Neolithic barrow-graves (nos. 17 and 18), near the western end of the cemetery, in the 'Wąski tryb' forest, close to the border of Medynia. It was 12m in diameter, 60cm high, NW of the centre; on the ancient surface a layer of timber logs or planks (probably beech) (c) almost completely decayed, was uncovered. They were about 1·8m long and covered an area 70cm wide, orientated NW–SE. Nothing was found either around or beneath this layer. Further north, about 2m from the centre, also on the ancient surface, calcined human bones were found on two heaps, 10–15cm thick, mixed with cinders, charcoal and fired earth, covering an area 130 by 30cm, orientated NW–SE (a). No traces of the pyre in which the corpse was cremated were found. In the eastern heap of bones a flint knife, 10cm long (b) was found and another 8cm long, lay about 1m SW of the grave on the ancient surface (e). At the SE end of the area with calcined bones, was a lump of red fired clay, 20cm in diameter (d).

Barrow-grave 17. 16m in diameter, 80cm high. In the central part a few lumps of charcoal were found on the ancient surface within an area 2 by 1m. North of this a flint flake (a), and west of it a large flint blade, probably a knife or dagger (b), 12cm long, were found on the ancient surface.

Barrow-grave 18 (Plan 15:1). 27m in diameter, about 2·5m high. Traces of a pit dug by treasure hunters were well marked in the centre (g). Fortunately they had not reached the grave. About 3m NE of the centre, at a depth of 60–80cm (in the mound earth) four flint blades, some of them trimmed, a lump of charcoal and a small lump of red ochre were found (a). The grave was uncovered on the ancient surface at a distance of about 1m NE of the centre (f). This was a shallow shaft, 1·6m by 80cm in area, rectangular in plan, orientated NW–SE, not more than about 25cm deep. In its western corner were found a few calcined bones and a few more lay scattered along the middle of the shaft, along with a few pieces of charcoal. In the eastern corner of the grave a flint point was found sticking in the side of the shaft (e); this was probably the head of a digging stick. A flint blade, partly trimmed, was found in the western corner of the shaft (b). West of the grave, on the ancient surface, charcoal was strewn over an area about 2 by 1m wide (d). Two metres NE of the grave, a few lumps of ochre were found (c) in the mound earth, at a depth of 1·2m. No pottery was excavated.

Barrow-grave 19 formed part of a larger group of mounds situated in the central part of the cemetery. It was 19m in diameter, about 50cm high. A flint knife (a) 8·2cm long, was found 2m NE of the centre at a depth of 30cm. Some odd potsherds lay in a few places in the mound at depths of 20–30cm. About 2·5m NE of the centre, at a depth of 25cm, was an area about 1m in diameter covered with small lumps of fired clay, over which lay a large potsherd of a large vessel (b). It was of the same type as that found in barrow-grave 20, its slipped walls, 16mm thick, were reddish in colour.

Barrow-grave 20 (Plan 14:3) was 18m in diameter, 50cm high, and had a somewhat complicated structure. In the mound, at a depth of about 15–20cm, a few flint flakes (a) and small odd potsherds (b) were found. The ancient surface occurred at a depth of 30cm from the top of the mound. At about 3·3m NW of the centre (f), charcoal was found strewn on this level, beneath which the grave-shaft was uncovered, dug 40cm in the ancient ground (70cm below the top of the mound). At this depth a layer of almost completely decayed timber logs appeared (f). These were 1·5m long, 60cm wide, forming a rectangle orientated NW–SE. This was probably the floor of the grave. The following objects were found on this timber platform: near its eastern end was a handled cylindrical cup (f-2) (Fig. 29:8) or tankard, near which lay a small stone battle-axe (f-3) (Fig. 35:15), 9.2cm long. Near the vessel, and towards the western end, calcined human bones, concentrated chiefly within an area 70cm long, lay on the platform. In the SE corner, but outside the grave, a flint arrow-head (f-1) was found (Plate 9:15).

On the ancient surface, about 1·5m W of the above grave, an area 1m in diameter was uncovered, within which the ground surface was hard, red-fired; this was a hearth from which cinders and charcoal had been removed. In the centre lay a very large vase (j) (Fig. 29:7) with a flat rim, with four warts on the body, walls partly matt, reddish, partly black, slightly polished, made of tempered clay paste, brittle. Near the vessel lay two pebbles, and a third under it. The vessel had been broken into small pieces.

At a distance of 2·5m SSW of the centre, a concentration of boulders tightly laid in two layers appeared (d), about 1·6 by 1m in area. The lower layer was dug into the ancient ground, the upper layer reached about 30cm above the ancient surface. Beneath the boulders were found a few lumps of charcoal. About 1m S of this one, another concentration of stones was uncovered (g). Large, but thin, pebbles laid close to each other with their narrow sides upwards, forming a crescent about 4m long, 90cm wide on its western side, thinning out towards its eastern end. Nothing was found here apart from stones, but an area about 50cm in diameter (h) of fired ground, on which charcoal lay was joined to its western end. A similar area (i) was found halfway between this and that on which lay the large vessel (j).

Barrow-grave 21 (Plan 14:1). 16m in diameter, 50cm high. In various points in the mound a few odd potsherds and flint flakes were excavated. About 3m N of the centre a group of five large pebbles was uncovered (d) which lay within an area 1m in diameter. The grave (A) (no traces of the skeleton were left) was north of the centre, and marked by grave goods lying on the ancient surface, 40cm under the top of the mound. They consisted of: two decorated handled cups, one larger (a-1) (Plate 16:4) than the other (a-2) (Plate 16:14), both with four protuberances on the body encircled by semi-circular grooves, the larger on a hollow stand, or ring; an undecorated cup with an everted rim (a-4) (Plate 16:11); a tulip-shaped pot (a-3); a flint arrow-head (b) (Plate 9:18) 2·5cm long with a convex base, made of light brown flint, found about 50cm NE of the group of the above vessels; and finally a handful of charcoal scattered 50cm NE of this group.

Barrow-grave 22. 17m in diameter, 40cm high. A few odd potsherds were found in the mound, while an almost completely crushed vessel (b) which disintegrated was lying on the ancient surface, at a depth of 30cm, about 50cm NW of the centre.

Barrow-grave 23 (Plan 14:2). 18m in diameter, 50cm high. In several points in the mound a few odd potsherds and flint flakes were excavated, and about 1m SE of the centre, at a depth of 20cm, just under the arable soil, lay a bone point 14·6cm long (d). Two metres SW of the centre a small concentration (a) of potsherds and a lump of ochre lay on the ancient surface, at a depth of 24cm. Close to it, a little to the NW, another concentration of potsherds (b) was found on the same level. They belonged to a very large broken vessel of a type similar to that from barrow-grave 20 (j). Its walls were about 1cm thick, reddish on the outside, black inside, and large decorative warts were present on a few sherds. Sherds in concentration 'a' belonged to the same vessel. At a distance of 3·5m N of the centre, two tulip-shaped pots (c-1, 2) (Plate 18:10) were found at a depth of 40cm, apparently placed in a hole; they probably marked the site of the burial. Both were badly crushed, and only one could be reconstructed.

Barrow-grave 24. The mound had been destroyed several years previous to the excavation and its earth used to fill some cavities in the ground near by. What remained of the mound was investigated, but only a few flint flakes and a flint axe (Fig. 15:7), evidently displaced, were found. The axe was well-made of black flint, rectangular in section, 7·8cm long.

Barrow-grave 25 belonged to a group of two mounds west of those described above. It was 20m in diameter, 50cm high. At a depth of 40cm, on the ancient surface, several irregular flint blades, some of them worked, flint flakes and a few small odd potsherds, were found all over the area covered by the mound. No traces of the skeleton were found, or of the grave-shaft but the site of the burial was marked by a completely crushed vessel, a cup (a) or beaker, which disintegrated, lying on the ancient surface 1m NE of the centre, and a stone battle-axe found at the same level close to the centre at a distance of about 1m from the vessel. The battle-axe, 10cm long, was made of the lower part of a typical Fatyanovo axe, with a new shaft-hole bored after the original axe had been broken.

Barrow-grave 26 was 19m in diameter, 60cm high, and belonged to the same group as the above. About 1m NW of the centre, at a depth of 50cm, on the ancient surface, lay a charred piece of log, some 50–60cm long, orientated SW–NE. Near it, but at a level about 15cm higher, a single potsherd was found (a-2), and another on the ancient level, lay 3·5m west of the centre (a-1). Both potsherds were of Neolithic character, made of tempered clay paste, reddish on the outside, the paste being dark, or black.

Barrow-grave 27 belonged to the larger group of mounds described before the two above. It was 16m in diameter, about 40cm high. In a few places in the mound itself, and under it on the ancient surface, a few odd potsherds and small flint flakes were found. At a distance of about 3m N of the centre, at a depth of 45–50cm, an area was uncovered, about 5 by 1m orientated roughly W–E, on which lay reddish fired clay with charcoal. Both ends of this area (a, b) about 1m in diameter, had a much larger admixture of charcoal, and in the eastern end a potsherd was found (a). It originated from a large vessel, reddish, surface smoothed.

At a distance of nearly 1m SE of the centre, a tulip-shaped pot was found in a shallow hole (c) (Plate 18:14) decorated with nine parallel grooves around the neck. Inside this vessel lay a flat pebble, 16·5cm long, 9·5cm wide, 2·5cm thick, with one end flattened. It was reminiscent of a flint axe and seems to have been chosen because of its shape. Some 25cm south of the vessel a large boulder lay on the ancient surface, 25cm long, 12cm wide, nearly square in section, with its sides deliberately cut to form a cube.

Barrow-grave 28 (Plan 15:2) formed part of another group of mounds. It was 14m in diameter, 30cm high, much ploughed up. It lay on the northern slope of the hill. A few odd potsherds and a flint flake were found in the mound or on the ancient surface, mainly in the NE part of the mound. At one point (a) a few potsherds of a large vessel lay. At a depth of 15–20cm, a little above the ancient surface, near the northern and north-eastern periphery of the area investigated, patches about 1m in diameter were uncovered over which charcoal dust and lumps were strewn. Under the northern of these (d) (Fig. 28:11), a straight-sided cup was found in a hole dug about 35cm in the ancient ground (about 70cm, from the top of the mound). About 2m NE of the centre, at a depth of 70cm, two vessels were found near each other: one was a very large vase (b) partly crushed, its rim flat, with a raised band under it (Fig. 28:8), sherds found in place marked 'a' belonged to the same vessel; the other (c) was an undecorated cup.

In the centre two burial sites were uncovered on the ancient surface, both marked by vessels laid in their corners. Grave I, at a distance of about 1m SE of the centre, was rectangular in plan, about 2 by 1m, orientated NE–SW. On its northern side stood an undecorated beaker (f); in its eastern corner lay two small decorated bowls (e) (Fig. 28:9), one of which (e-2) was crushed and disintegrated. In the SW corner lay a gold ear-pendant (Fig. 26:11) bearing traces of having been repaired in antiquity 3·5cm long (g) and a crushed vessel. The other grave II was perpendicular to this, also about 2 by 1m in area, orientated NW–SE, situated at a distance of about 60cm NW of the former. In the southern corner was an undecorated bowl (h). The western corner was marked by a cup (i) (Fig. 28:10) oval in section, with sides decorated by horizontal and vertical grooves. The vessel from the northern corner (j) was a vase with two handles (Plate 17:13) having horizontal grooves on the neck and shaded triangles on the upper part of the body.

Barrow-grave 29 (Plan 15:3). 16m in diameter, 45cm high, ploughed up. In a few places on the ancient surface odd potsherds and flint flakes were found, and about 2m N of the centre lay a small crushed vessel (a) which disintegrated.

Barrow-grave 30 (Plan 16:3) lay on a field situated on a lower hill nearer the village, outside the main cemetery. It was 14m in diameter, 80cm high. In the central part of the mound lumps of charcoal appeared just under the arable soil. South of the centre, at a depth of 50–70cm, charred timber logs or sticks were found heaped, crossing each other, covering an area about 4 by 2m, orientated SW–NE (a). In a few places, at various depths, odd potsherds were found. They were of a Neolithic character.

Barrow-grave 31 (Plan 17:2) was situated in the western part of the cemetery, in a part of the forest known as 'Maliniska', and it formed a group with mound 55. It was 16m in diameter, 1m high. Three potsherds were found on the ancient surface in the central part under the mound. About 1·5m SE of the centre, within an area 1·5 by 1m on the ancient surface charcoal was strewn in a very thin and uneven layer. On the eastern end of this area stood two vessels, and near the SW corner lay a flint implement 5·5cm long, damaged by fire. One of the vessels (a-1) was a Thuringian amphora broken into small pieces, many of them being completely crushed. It was made of tempered clay paste and was very slightly baked, very brittle, it could not be reconstructed. The other vessel (a-2) was a beaker (Fig. 9:2) made of tempered clay paste, very brittle. Both vessels stood on a level slightly lower than that of the charcoal. This was the site of the burial, but no traces of skeleton were noticed.

Barrow-grave 32 (Plan 18). A third of this mound was destroyed by a forest road cut across it. It was 20m in diameter, 1·8m high. It formed part of a group of three barrow-graves (nos. 33 and 34), situated in a part of the forest known as 'Mała Sośnina'.

At a depth of 70–90cm, odd potsherds, a flint flake and lumps of charcoal were found, scattered mainly around the central part of the mound. The upper part of a broken hammer made of siliceous slate, 7cm long, nearly rectangular in section, also lay about 2m W of the centre (b) (Fig. 16:24).

More remains were found deeper, at a depth of 1·4 to 1·6m. Odd potsherds lay scattered all over the ancient surface, and in many places small flint flakes and parts of broken implements were lying; among the latter was the edge of an axe. North-west of the centre, an area 2 by 1m was found covered with densely strewn charcoal (I), and another similar area (II), a little larger, 2·5 by 1m, lay 2·5m NE of the centre; both were orientated NW–SE. On the first of these lay two potsherds. These large patches of charcoal marked probably the sites of the burials, but no skeletons were discernible here. At a distance of about 2m from the second of these patches, on the edge of the destroyed part of the mound, two small, crushed vessels (a) were excavated at a depth of 1·4cm. Both were undecorated cups, made of tempered clay paste, insufficiently baked, brittle, and both disintegrated.

Barrow-grave 33 (Plan 17:1). 18m in diameter, about 1·5m high, situated close to the above. At a depth of 25cm, under the forest soil, several small potsherds and a few flint flakes were found scattered over the whole mound. In the central part of the mound, in its eastern part, a layer of reddish, fired earth occurred at this depth. It extended over an area oval in plan, 5 by 4m, orientated N–S, 25cm thick at its circumference, about 50cm nearer to its centre. The reddish earth was mixed up with cinders, charcoal, while calcined human bones were also found in it, mainly in its central part. Under this layer lay a group of eight vessels within an area 2·5 by 1·5m, orientated NNW–SSE (vessels I–IX, XI). Among these were a tulip-shaped pot (Plate 21:12), bowls (Plate 21:15) and two cups, with high pointed handles (Plate 21:14, 16), typical of the Early Iron Age. On the sherds of a crushed vessel (an urn) (IV/IX) lay many calcined bones, which were also scattered about; among these were found two light-green glass beads, 9·5mm in diameter, and three amber beads of the same size, two being unperforated (Plate 21:13). The tulip-shaped vessel and some others, also the glass beads, were deformed by fire. Within this area two small concentrations of small, brittle potsherds also lay (F, G). About 1·5m west of this group, another crushed vessel (x) was found on the same level, which disintegrated. Under it lay a broken flint blade.

Deeper, at a level 80cm to 1·1m, apparently on the original surface many potsherds, flint flakes and a few worked flint implements, lay scattered all over the entire area under the mound, whilst charcoal was also strewn in the northern part of this area in particular. Some of the flints and potsherds lay slightly deeper, up to the depth of 1·2m from the top of the mound. A flint knife was found at that depth (c) about 3m NE of the centre.

Vessels of the central group were typical, in both shape and make, of the Early Iron Age; vessel 'x', found outside this group, was probably a tulip-shaped pot made with a different technique, typical of the Komarów culture; it had a slip cover. It seems that the Iron Age grave was a secondary burial which had ruined the original Bronze Age (Komarów), or Late Neolithic burial.

Barrow-grave 34 (Plan 19:2). 14m in diameter, 60cm high. Under the forest humus at a depth of 20cm, many odd potsherds and flint flakes and a few damaged trimmed blades were found. At the same level, in the centre of the mound, a concentration of calcined bones was uncovered, about 1·5m in diameter (d). Many potsherds were found in it originating from at least four or five vessels: a bowl or deep dish with an inverted rim, a large spherical vessel, one or two bowls with an everted rim, and a large dark vessel with fluted decoration. All sherds were damaged by fire, many warped. This was probably a secondary cremation burial.

Deeper, at a depth of 70cm, beneath the above burial, six halved boulders, 20 to 60cm long, enclosed an area about 1·5m square. Along its eastern side lay three vessels in one row (II–III, IV, VII), a bowl (Fig. 31:8), a beaker and a cup, all crushed. About 1m E of these an undamaged large deep dish (I) with an inverted rim lay in a vertical position. Also in this area, three shallow holes were found, filled with charcoal, and in the NE corner of the area enclosed by the boulders lay a flint arrow-head (s) with its tip broken off (Plate 9:16). This was undoubtedly the site of the main grave (A) orientated NW–SE, but no traces of skeleton were found.

About 2m NW of this grave, another grave (B) was found. It was marked by similar boulders laid in three rows, enclosing an area about 2m square. On its western side a shallow hole filled with charcoal was uncovered, with three vessels standing in its southern part; a beaker (Plate 16:3), a cylindrical cup (Plate 16:12), both decorated, and a decorated bowl with an everted rim which disintegrated (v, vi, viii). These vessels were typical of the transitional period from the Early to the Middle Bronze Age period. No traces of skeleton were found.

On the ancient surface, at a depth of 60–70cm, many scattered potsherds and flints were found all over the area covered by the mound. A fragment of the damaged edge of a stone battle-axe was also found and a few scattered pebbles, mainly east of grave A.

Barrow-grave 35 (Plan 22:3). 16m in diameter, 60cm high. At a distance of about 4·5m SE from the centre an undecorated wide beaker or bowl was found under the forest humus, at a depth of 20cm (a). Close to it, but at a depth of 90cm, lay a halved boulder (f) in a small hole dug in the ancient ground.

About 2m E of the centre, and again 3m S of the centre, lumps of charcoal, about 1cm thick, and lumps of fired clay were found (d), 4·5m N of the centre was a hole (b), about 50cm in diameter, dug some 10–20cm in the ancient ground filled with fired clay, ashes and charcoal, and in another small hole (c), 2m W of the centre, a lump of ochre was found. About 3·5m NE of the centre placed NW–SE on the ancient surface lay a charred timber log, 2·5m long, 40–60cm wide (e).

Barrow-grave 36 (Plan 22·2) 16m in diameter, 50–60cm high. About 1·5m SE of the centre a boulder was found (c) at a depth of 20cm, just under the forest humus. It marked the site of the burial on the ancient surface, at a depth of about 50–60cm. At its western end, 1m NE of the centre of the barrow, lay a decorated bowl (b) (Plate 17:5), and close to it, somewhat higher (40cm from the top of the mound) lay an upside-down clepsydra-shaped cup (a) (Plate 18:19). The vessels probably stood near the head, and the other side of the grave was marked by a large patch of charcoal and red ochre (d) about 10cm thick, extending 1·5–2m from the two vessels; however, no traces of skeleton were found.

Over the whole ancient surface, covered by the mound, but in particular in its SE part (d), very small pieces of fired clay were strewn. About 4m W of the centre lay a few small worked flints at the same level.

Barrow-grave 37 (Plan 20). 16m in diameter, 2·5m high. At a depth of 40–60cm from the top of the mound, in the central part of the barrow, charcoal, lumps of fired clay and ashes were strewn more or less densely over an area about 5 by 3m, orientated S–N. They were concentrated in particular on peripheries of this area. Single calcined human bones were also found within this area, but they formed three larger concentrations (i, ii, iii) along its eastern side, 2m long, each about 50cm in diameter. Two of these lay at a little deeper level, which seems to indicate that the bones were shovelled into small holes about 30–40cm deep. In the northern part of this area, about 1m N of the centre of the barrow, the largest concentration of calcined bones (v) was uncovered; it was 1m long, about 50cm wide, and consisted solely of animal bones.

At a distance of 4m E of the centre, another concentration of calcined bones (iv) was uncovered at a depth of 1m; it was about 50cm in diameter. Near it lay a small flint point (g) (Plate 9:27).

At a distance of 7m N of the centre, on the level 1·40m below the top of the mound, but actually at a depth of 40cm, a flint axe (a) irregular (Fig. 16:27), but somewhat oval in section, 10·5cm long, was found, and at a distance of 6m SW of the centre, at about the same level, lay a flint knife and close to it a hole filled in with charcoal, reaching a depth of 1·6m from the top of the mound, were found (f). Flint flakes and a few worked blades lay at a depth of 1·5–1·9m around the circumference of the mound in several places. Differing depths in which the various objects mentioned above were found, and also cross-sections of the mound drawn by Dr J. Grabowski who excavated it, suggest that the mound was raised on a small natural elevation. At the first stage a low flat mound was formed, not more than 8m in diameter, the earth being taken from the area around it. On it the pyre was laid and the corpses probably of three persons at least were cremated along with some animals placed on the northern part of the pyre. After cremation, the calcined bones were shovelled to the various points marked by their concentrations, and a larger mound was raised covering the whole area. This accounts for the flints and the axe at the periphery occurring on a lower level: the earth from this area was used for raising the first elevation.

The burial seems to date from the Early Iron Age, although no grave goods were found to confirm this dating. The axe and other flint implements may have belonged, however, to an earlier grave which had been destroyed during the construction of the cremation burial. Perhaps the first, the lower mound, on which the pyre was laid, belonged to the original, Neolithic grave. This seems to be confirmed by the circumstances revealed by the excavation of the next barrow-grave, 38, situated 30m to the NE.

Barrow-grave 38 (Plan 21). 18m in diameter, 2m high. In the centre, at a depth of 80cm to 1m, an area 4m in diameter was uncovered (A) within which charcoal, fired clay and ashes were more or less densely strewn. A flint flake, a number of odd potsherds of a large, reddish vessel with an incised decoration, were found at the same level. About 3m S of the centre, or 1m S of the area described above, lay a small concentration of calcined human bones, 50cm in diameter, at a depth of 70cm (g).

Deeper, at 2m, 4m E of the centre, the following objects lay close to each other, possibly in a shallow shaft orientated NW–SE(?): two flint axes (c, d) (Figs. 15:12; 16:10), 8·5 and 8cm long, one rectangular, the other nearly oval in section (hybrid type); a flint point 2cm long (e), perhaps an arrowhead; and a decorated bowl, or wide beaker (a). One metre NW of these lay a well-polished battle-axe (b) of a greenish variety of stone, 12cm long, of type *y*-1 (East European) (Fig. 13:8). These objects apparently marked the site of the grave, the skeleton of which had completely decayed (Plate 2:4). Several flints and lumps of charcoal were found scattered at the level 160–80cm, which was probably the original surface of the ground.

The Neolithic grave was evidently the original grave; its mound has been re-used and raised higher by a cremation burial of a later period, probably of the Early Iron Age.

Barrow-grave 39 (Plan 19:1) formed part of a group of four mounds with nos. 40, 42 and 57. It was 14–15m in diameter, 1·4m high; in its SE part were traces of a trench of World War I.

In the northern part, in the mound, a few flint flakes were excavated. In the centre, on the ancient surface, at a depth of 1·2m, the site of the burial was uncovered. It was apparently orientated N–S. Its southern end was marked by an almost completely decayed timber log, traces of which were clearly visible, about 75cm long, lying W to E. On its northern side, near the eastern end, stood a decorated bowl (or wide beaker) (a) (Plate 6:4), and on its western side were four flint arrow-heads (f) (Plate 9:17, 23, 24, 26) one with the tip broken off, and a flint knife, 11cm long, trimmed along its edges (g). Close to the arrow-heads lay two clay tubes (*e*-1, *e*-2) (Fig. 12:8), one 6·8cm long, the other a little larger. North of these, along the western side of the supposed grave, lay the upper part of a battle-axe of type *y*-2, 7cm long, made of a greenish variety of stone, well polished, its edge missing (d), and somewhat further was a large flint flake reminiscent in shape and size of an axe, 9·5cm long (c), its edge blunt.

At the same level, 3·5m W of the centre, and 4m SW of it, patches of scattered charcoal, 50cms and 1m in diameter respectively, were uncovered, and in some other places a few flint flakes were found.

Barrow-grave 40 (Plan 22:1) formed part of the above group, the westernmost of this cemetery to be excavated. It was 12m in diameter, 50cm high. At 1m S of the centre, on the ancient level, at about 60cm from the top of the mound, the grave-shaft was uncovered, marked by charcoal strewn over an area over 1m square (A). The grave-shaft under the charcoal reached to a depth of 1m, being dug some 40cm in the ancient ground. Its size was not established. In the shaft a flint axe of Lindø type (s) (Fig. 15:16), 10·2cm long, and a stone battle-axe which perished (t) were excavated. On the ancient surface a few flints (b) were found scattered, and two small potsherds (a) were found at a depth of 20cm at about 4·5m S of the centre.

Barrow-grave 41 lay on the field called 'Łuniów', at a distance of about 1·5km S of the cemetery, on the lower part of the mountains, nearer the village. It was 12m in diameter, 30cm high, ploughed up. Nothing was found in it.

Barrow-grave 42 (Plan 23:3). One of the group described above, almost completely ploughed up; only its central part, 6m in diameter, was excavated.

The grave was uncovered in the centre (A). This was a shallow shaft undamaged by the plough. Along its eastern side, from SW to NE at a depth of 80cm, lay an almost completely decayed timber log about 2m long (b). On its southern end traces of a very short section of a perpendicular log were visible. West of the long beam, at the same depth in the grave itself, lay a flint axe (Fig. 16:19), 9·5cm long, nearly rectangular in section, well polished (d), a large trimmed flint flake, probably a knife (e), 9cm long, and a flint flake (c). South-west of the grave, at a level about 20cm higher, a concentration of charcoal was uncovered (a) about 50cm in diameter.

Barrow-grave 43 lay on the 'Kreczkówka' field, at a distance of about 100m W of mound 41. It was much ploughed up. All the still visible mound, 6m in diameter, was investigated by Dr J. Pasternak in 1935.[5] His description of this grave was to have been published in my book on the Komarów culture; it perished during the War along with my typescript.

According to a draft note which survived, made after the description by Dr J. Pasternak, twelve vessels were excavated in this grave. Under the arable soil, at a depth of 25–30cm, and all over the whole area investigated traces of a large pyre were well visible: the ground was red-fired to a depth of a few centimetres, and over it lay charcoal, lumps of red clay and ashes. The vessels mentioned above stood in groups around its centre, about 1·5m in diameter.

Only part of a large urn of Villanova type (1) was deposited in the grave; its surface was smoothed, black, but not polished, and it was somewhat lighter inside. In it were calcined bones, among which half a small, very rusty, oval iron ring was found. Next to it was a large dish (2), badly damaged, with a low inverted rim, light grey in colour. Near it lay a smaller bowl (3) of which only the lower part survived. Further down, in a corner, was a medium-sized dish, or bowl (4) with an inverted rim, surrounded by many calcined bones; a crescent-shaped flint saw, or knife, was also found here, badly damaged by fire. At some 50cm from this vessel, stood two handled cups (5, 6) both reddish in colour, one oval in section, with a high pointed handle. At a distance of 50cm, in another corner, lay a large dish (7), similar in size and shape to dish '4' near which two handled cups were found (8, 9); one had a high pointed handle. Close to these vessels, on the outside, was a hole 50–60cm in diameter, 25cm deep, filled in with earth, charcoal and a few lumps of hard baked clay. Between this group of vessels and the urn '1', stood another urn (10), ovoid in shape, reddish in colour, with a low, slightly everted neck, having four decorative warts on the body. In it calcined bones were found. The position of the two remaining vessels, a medium-sized bowl (11) with a slightly inverted rim, and a similar, but larger vessel (12), has not been established. Both had been broken by the plough and the sherds displaced over a wider area.

A 'dark', evidently bronze, bit was found in this mound in 1913 when ploughing. Unfortunately it perished. This barrow-grave dated from the Early Iron Age.

Barrow-grave 44 (Plan 23:2). 19m in diameter, 40cm high, ploughed up, so that furrows have spoiled the grave. On the ancient surface at a depth of 35–40cm a few flint flakes and lumps of charcoal were found at various points in the area covered by the mound. The grave was in the centre. Within a rectangular area, about 1·5 by 1m, orientated N–S, loose earth was uncovered which reached some 20cm below the ancient surface (A) marking a shallow grave-shaft; in the middle of its northern side a large boulder lay on the ancient surface (i); no traces of skeleton were found. Grave goods lay east of the grave on the ancient surface, and the order in which they lay and the distances between them suggest they must have belonged to a burial situated on the ancient ground close to the shaft (B). These grave goods were: a battle-axe of type *y*-3 (g) made of a greenish variety of stone, 11·5cm long, which lay close to the NE corner of the shaft; a beaker almost completely destroyed by the plough (f), which lay 1m east of the battle-axe; and a flint axe (d) (Fig.

[5] Pasternak, loc. cit., note 2.

16:13) 9cm long, which lay about 50cm N of the battle-axe.

Barrow-grave 45 (Plan 23:1) formed part of a group of three mounds (nos. 29 and 46), 20m in diameter, 50cm high, ploughed up, many vessels ruined by the plough. On the ancient surface, at a depth of about 30–40cm a large cube boulder (k) was found about 3m NE of the centre. In the mound, and over the whole area under it, were scattered many flint flakes, fragments of broken flint implements, odd potsherds and small pieces of charcoal. They were concentrated especially in an area 3 by 6m, east and south-east of the centre (m). Potsherds found here belonged to a few vessels, including a large vase with thick walls (f), reddish in colour, the interior dark, and a decorated bowl, while one sherd was a typical Tripolyan D-ware.

The grave was placed on the ancient surface, at a distance of 1·5m NW of the centre. It was marked by eleven boulders laid in three rows, forming a rectangle 5·5 by 3m in area, orientated SW–NE. The original number of stones must have been greater but they were probably removed when ploughing. In the SW part of this area lay slightly calcined bones (j) and charcoal. Around the grave, in the row of stones on the SE side, and along the NE and NW sides, but outside the area enclosed by these, nine vessels were found (b, g-1-8); a tenth vessel, a decorated beaker (d) (Fig. 30:5) badly damaged by the plough, lay at the same level about 2m NE of the grave. Among these vessels was one tulip-shaped pot (g-8) (Plate 21:5) with a raised band on the neck; a richly decorated, almost cylindrical single-lugged mug (*Zapfenbecher*) its base decorated (g-6) (Plate 21:4); a richly decorated bowl (g-3) (Plate 21:1), a similar one undecorated (g-7) (Plate 21:2) and a third one which disintegrated; a small decorated bowl (g-5) (Fig. 30:3); a decorated handled bowl (g-1) (Plate 21:6), and a simple undecorated bowl or deep dish with sides widened upwards (g-2) (Plate 21:7); finally a decorated handled cup (g-4) (Plate 21:3).

Barrow-grave 46 (Plan 24:1). 18m in diameter, 55cm high. A series of vessels mostly decorated, were uncovered on the ancient surface, at a depth of 35cm, but some were a little deeper, 55cm from the top of the mound, at a distance of 2m NW of the centre. They were arranged in two parallel rows, about 1·5m wide, over 2m long, orientated NW–SW, marking the site of the burial (G). On the western side were three bowls (A, B, C) (Fig. 27:4, 2), on the eastern side a bowl and two cups (g, h, j) (Plate 18:9) and further down a tulip-shaped pot and a bowl (k, l) (Fig. 27:1, 3). A double-handled bowl (F) (Plate 17:8) which lay between the two rows marked the southern end of the grave (G). North of the grave, a little outside the eastern row, lay another bowl (i) (Fig. 27:9). Two other vessels, a flowerpot-shaped cup with its base decorated (E) (Plate 18:13) and a tulip-shaped pot (D), lay over 2m S of the centre, at a depth of 30cm; they were badly damaged by the plough. This was probably the site of another burial (H) but no traces of skeleton were found.

Barrow-grave 47 (Plan 24:2). 16m in diameter, 40cm high, ploughed up. In the arable soil, over the whole central part of the mound (a) loose red fired earth, hard-baked lumps of clay, fragments of broken stones and a few flint flakes were excavated. They were concentrated in particular within an area 3 by 2m S of the centre (b), where they formed a layer up to 20cm thick. This lay on the ancient surface over the site of the burial, orientated N–S. The site of the burial was well marked by four holes, 40–50cm in diameter (d-1-4), dug into the ancient surface about 50cm deep. The holes were filled in with fired clay, ashes, charcoal, and a few calcined bones were also found in them, but calcined bones lay mainly over the surface enclosed by the holes, those of the skull being found on its southern end (e). Between two southern holes, on the ancient surface, lay upside down a large deep dish (c) (Fig. 31:7) broken into pieces; the upper part only of a large vessel, its neck covered with parallel fluting (f) (Fig. 31:9) was found in the middle between the two western holes and close to the SW hole lay a larger accumulation of charcoal (g).

Barrow-grave 48 (Plan 24:3). 16m in diameter, 50cm high. The site of the burial was uncovered at a depth of 70cm, about 1m W of the centre. It covered an area 2·3 (W–E) by 1·9m (N–S), sunk about 10cm in the ancient ground. Its northern half (b) was thoroughly cobbled with boulders 20–25cm in diameter and in the western part with two layers of smaller stones. The southern part (c) encircled by similar boulders, was covered by a large sandstone slab or by a layer of hard cemented sand with the surface well smoothed. Two vessels, a handled cup and a bowl (b-1, 2) (Fig. 30:9) stood at the eastern end of the northern side of the grave, and near by lay a narrow stone battle-axe (Fig. 35:13), 12cm long, well executed, of a late type (b-6). In the SW corner were found vessels, three tulip-shaped pots (4a, 4, 5) (Fig. 30:2, 7; Plate 19:4), and one two-handled vase (b-3) (Fig. 30:1). In the middle of both northern and southern sides of the grave lay larger accumulations of charcoal (d). This must have been a double burial but no traces of skeletons were found.

Barrow-grave 49. 15m in diameter, 60cm high. Only a few flint flakes, single lumps of fired clay, very small pieces of charcoal and a few very small odd potsherds were found on the ancient surface, at a depth of 40cm, scattered over an area 4m in diameter in the centre of the mound.

Barrow-grave 50 (Plan 25:2) lay close to the above, forming a distinct group with it. It was 19m in diameter, 1m high. Just under the humus cover, in the centre of the mound, at a depth of 35cm, lay a flint axe (d) (Fig. 16:17), 9cm long, rectangular in section, and a stone battle-axe (e) of type *y*-2 (Fig. 13:9), 10cm long, which seemed to have been in fire. Deeper, at a depth of 70cm, in the central area (c), about 6·5–7m in diameter, potsherds (b), lumps of fired clay and small pieces of charcoal were found scattered on the ancient surface. On the southern edge of this area, 4m S of the centre, small accumulations of calcined human bones (g), a few potsherds of a large vessel (f) and a crushed, large, deep bowl with an inverted rim (i) (Fig. 31:2) were found. Potsherds found over the whole area (b) and those from its southern edge (f) belonged to the same vessel of unknown shape.

About 2m SE of the centre, eight small boulders were found on the ancient surface forming a circle nearly 1m in diameter (h) filled in with charcoal; a potsherd of the large vessel mentioned above (bf) was also found here.

Barrow-grave 51. 16m in diameter, 55cm high, partly destroyed by a field road across it. Only charcoal was found here at a depth of 30–40cm, 2·5m south of the centre, thinly scattered over an area 2·5m long and 50cm wide. In the mound only three potsherds were excavated, those of a large thick-walled vessel with a black, polished surface, similar to the large jar from barrow-grave 20.

Barrow-grave 52 (Plan 25:1). 16m in diameter, 85cm high. Close to the centre, on the top of the mound, just under the humus cover, a large boulder was excavated (a). In the central area under the mound, at a depth of about 70cm, on the ancient surface, a layer was uncovered, 3·5 by 2m, orientated NW–SE, of powdered charcoal and larger lumps of charred wood, in which calcined human bones and several broken flint implements were found (b).

Barrow-grave 53 (Plan 26:1) formed a group with no. 54. It was 20m in diameter, 1m high. About 2·5m N of the centre a large boulder was found (d) just under the humus cover. About 3m E of the centre, at a depth of 40–50cm, in the mound, charcoal (b) was found scattered over an area about 50cm in diameter, and a few metres further SW, also in the mound, lay a few pieces of charcoal.

On the ancient surface at a depth of 70cm, about 2·5m N of the centre, under the boulder, lay a flint scraper, or knife (g) and a handful of charcoal. A similar handful of charcoal lay 2·5m SE of the centre, on the ancient surface (e), and near by a lump of red ochre (d) and another flint scraper, or knife (f) were excavated at the same level. No traces of skeleton were discerned.

Barrow-grave 54. 15m in diameter, 50cm high. A large boulder was found just under the upper humus, at a distance of 2m SE of the centre, and W of the centre a handful of charcoal at the same level. Nothing else was found, either in the mound or under it.

Barrow-grave 55 formed part of a group of two, with no. 31. It was 16m in diameter, 60–5cm high. On the ancient surface, at a depth of 65cm an almost completely crushed cup (a) lay at a distance of 2m N of the centre. Sherds of an incomplete, larger vessel lay at the same level 2m E of the centre (b), and a deep decorated dish (c) (Fig. 27:7) lay 2m S of the centre. No traces of skeleton were found.

Barrow-grave 56 was an isolated mound on the border of the forest of Medynia, 16m in diameter, 45cm high. Nothing was found in it.

Barrow-grave 57 formed part of the westernmost group of mounds investigated in this cemetery, along with nos. 39, 40, 42. It was 15m in diameter, 50cm high, ploughed up. Only a flint flake and a flint scraper were found, the latter 3m E of the centre, in the arable soil.

Barrow-grave 58 belonged to a group of two, with no. 30, situated outside the cemetery, on a lower part of the hills. It was 15m in diameter, 35cm high, much ploughed up. Four metres S of the centre, in the arable soil, a flint flake was found, and at a distance of 1·5m E of the centre a hole, triangular in plan, was uncovered, dug in the ancient surface. It was about 60–65cm in diameter, 50cm deep (80 from the top of the mound), and was filled in with charcoal and red fired clay.

Barrow-grave 59 (Plan 27:2) lay some 150m S of the above group, also outside the cemetery. It was 24m in diameter, 1m high, but a large portion of its SW part was eroded by a stream. In the centre, on the top of the mound just under the arable soil, traces of a hearth (a), 1m in diameter, were uncovered. A layer about 10cm thick, of fired clay, cinders and charcoal lay here. On the top of the mound, under the arable soil, about 3·5m SE of the centre a large flint core in the shape of a blunt axe, or hammer (b), was excavated, 9cm long. On the ancient surface, at a depth of 60cm, an area 3·5 by 2m, orientated W–E was uncovered, within which small pieces of charcoal were scattered (f), in its western part particularly. About 2m N of this, at a level some 10cm higher (50cm from the top of the mound) lay a very roughly executed axe made of yellow siliceous slate (c), 10cm long. Further north, at a distance of 5m from the centre, on the ancient surface, an area littered with charcoal, about 2 by 1m in area, was uncovered (d). Finally, 5m E of the centre, at the same level, a flint flake lay (e). No traces of skeleton were found.

Barrow-grave 60. A single mound in the central part of the cemetery. It was 15m in diameter, 40cm high. A few small pieces of charcoal were found in the mound, and on the ancient level at a depth of 40cm, in the centre of the mound, a handful of charcoal lay. Nothing else was found.

Barrow-grave 61 (Plan 26:2) formed a group of two mounds with no. 62. It was 15m in diameter, 40cm high. South-east of the centre seven boulders (a), about 10cm in diameter, were found at a depth of 20cm, under the forest humus. Five of these formed an irregular circle 2m in diameter with a sixth boulder in its centre. Under these stones, at a depth of 40cm, on the ancient surface an area was uncovered nearly rectangular in plan with its corners rounded (c), about 1·6m by 80cm, the surface of which was red fired to a depth of 20cm, 60cm from the top of the mound. However, no cinders, charcoal etc. were found over it: it had been cleared of any remains of pyre. No grave goods or traces of the skeleton were found. Only about 2m SW of the above area, at the same level, on the ancient surface, lay a handful of charcoal (b).

Barrow-grave 62. Near the above. It was 15m in diameter, 40cm high. Nothing was found in it except charcoal which lay on the ancient surface at a depth of 50cm, 1·5m SE of the centre, in a layer 1cm thick, about 1m long, a few centimetres wide.

Barrow-grave 63 (Plan 26:3) formed part of a group of four mounds (nos. 37, 38, 52) but lay just over the border in the forest of the neighbouring village of Medynia. It was 15m in diameter, 55cm high. On the ancient surface, at the depth of 55cm, close to the centre, an almost completely decayed skeleton in a crouched position, head to W, was uncovered (a). Near its head lay a stone battle-axe (b) (of type *y*-3), made of a greenish stone, 11cm long, well polished, with a flint scraper or burin (c) near by.

Barrow-grave 64 (Plan 16:2) lay outside the cemetery, on a slope, at a distance of some 450m E of the large group of Bronze Age mounds. It was 18m in diameter, 40cm high, ploughed up. In various points a few odd potsherds of Neolithic character were found under the arable soil (a); they originated from a medium-sized beaker with thick walls. At a distance of 2m SE of the centre, the site of the grave (b) was uncovered, 2m long, orientated SW–NE, which was only 60cm wide, its SE side being destroyed by a drain-pipe trench. On the NE edge of the grave lay a large lump of charcoal (c). The site of the grave was marked by a much darker earth extending over the area, only a few centimetres thick. No traces of skeleton were found.

Barrow-grave 65. This was a single mound about 75m SW of mound 4, near the border of Kryłos, 15m in diameter, 40cm high, ploughed up. Traces of previous excavation in the form of a trench cut across the mound from W to E 2m wide were uncovered; across the eastern part of the mound ran a drain-pipe trench. The SW corner of the grave was found (b), at the junction of the two, about 1 by 1m in area. The grave was orientated N–S, and was sunk a few centimetres in the ancient ground surface. In the loose, dark earth which filled the grave, calcined bones lay scattered but no grave-goods. A large flint flake (a) lay on the ancient surface about 1·5m west of the grave, on the edge of the ancient trench.

2. LIST OF VESSELS

No.		Vessel	Height	Diameter			Illustration	Remarks
				upper	body	base		
	Barrow-grave 4							
1		beaker						disintegrated
	Barrow-grave 5							
2	a	amphora, 2 lugs						drawing perished
3	b	beaker or bowl[6]						
	Barrow-grave 6						Plan 12:1	
4	a	tulip-shaped pot	29·5	20	20	7·5		brittle
5	e	tulip-shaped beaker	12·5	11·2	12·5	7	Plate 16:2	decorated
6	f	small tulip-shaped pot				6		disintegrated
7	i-1	cup	4·7	6·5	7·8	3·8	,, 16:6	
8	i-2	bowl						disintegrated
	Barrow-grave 7							
9	a	vessel ?						description missing
	Barrow-grave 8						Plan 12:2	
10	b	tulip-shaped beaker	13·7	13·2	13·5	8	Plate 16:1	raised band
11	c-1	goblet	3·3	4·2	2·7	3·1	,, 16:8	decorated
12	c-2	small cup	4·5	6		3·5		
13	c-3	small bowl	4	6·8		3	,, 16:7	
14	d	handled cup				4·5		disintegrated
15	e	handled cup	9·5	9·5	12	5	,, 16:10	decorated
	Barrow-grave 9						Plan 12:3	
16	a-1	bowl	11·5	16·7	17·5	8·5	Plate 16:13	
17	a-2	tulip-shaped beaker	12	11·2	12	6	,, 16:5	
18	a-3	cup	8·8	8·5	8·5	4·4	,, 16:9	decorated
19	b	bowl similar to a-1				9		disintegrated
20	c	beaker	12·5	10·4	10·4	5·8	Fig. 28:7	decorated
	Barrow-grave 10						Plan 12:4	
21	a-1	tulip-shaped pot	20				Plate 18:5	raised band
22	a-2	cup	3·2	6		4·3	,, 18:16	
23	b	beaker	13	12·5	12·2	6·5		decorated
24	c-1	small beaker	8	11·8	13	6·5	,, 18:7	decorated
25	c-2	bowl	9	14	15	10	,, 16:20	decorated
26	d-1α	tulip-shaped pot	19·5	14	16	7		decorated
27	d-1β	tulip-shaped pot	12	10·5	10·5	4·6	,, 18:3	decorated
28	d-2	bowl	9·8	20		7·8	,, 16:18	
29	d-3	bowl as above		20		8·9		disintegrated
30	e	beaker	13	10			Fig. 28:5	decorated
31	f	tulip-shaped pot	16·5	11·5	11	6	Plate 18:8	
	Barrow-grave 11						Plan 13:2	
32	a-1	bowl	12·2	19·8	20	10·5	Plate 17:1	decorated
33	a-2	bowl	12·5	13·8	16	7·5	,, 17:10	decorated
34	b	vessel ?						description missing

[6] See note 3.

No.	Vessel		Height	Diameter upper	Diameter body	Diameter base	Illustration	Remarks
35	p-1	small cup	4	4·5	6·5	3·7	Plate 18:18	
36	p-2	small cup	4·5	5·2		3·5		
37	p-3	handled cup	7·8	8·7	10·9	4·7	,, 17:4	decorated
38	ef	bowl with 2 lugs	14·2	15·2	16·6	7·8	Fig. 27:10	decorated
39	dmk	bowl	12	15	16·2	6·2	,, 27:5	decorated
40	dmk	tulip-shaped pot	16·6	12·4	13·5	7	,, 28:2	
	Barrow-grave 12							
41	a	tulip-shaped pot	23		18	7		raised band
	Barrow-grave 13						Plan 13:4	
42	a	cup	5·2	6·8	9·8	5·3	Plate 21:9	
43	b	handled cup	12·8	14	14	5·6	,, 21:8	decorated
44	d	lid	2		9	5·3	,, 21:11	
45	e	beaker	7·6	8·3		4·7	,, 21:10	decorated
	Barrow-grave 19							
46	b	very large vessel						a few potsherds
	Barrow-grave 20						Plan 14:3	
47	f-2	handled cup	12	10			Fig. 29:8	
48	j	very large vase	65	40	60	17	,, 29:7	four warts
	Barrow-grave 21						Plan 14:1	
49	a-1	handled cup	12·2	13	13·5	5·5	Plate 16:4	decorated
50	a-2	handled cup	8·5	8·5	9	4·1	,, 16:14	decorated
51	a-3	tulip-shaped pot	14	9	14	6		
52	a-4	cup	7·5	7·2	8	3·5	,, 16:11	
	Barrow-grave 22							
53	b	vessel ?	6		9·5	3·5		crushed
	Barrow-grave 23						Plan 14:2	
54	b	a very large vessel						sherds only
55	c-1	tulip-shaped pot	18	16	15	8	Plate 18:10	
56	c-2	tulip-shaped pot						crushed
	Barrow-grave 25							
57	a	cup				8·5		crushed
	Barrow-grave 27							
58	c	tulip-shaped pot	20·5	18	17	9	Plate 18:14	decorated
	Barrow-grave 28						Plan 15:2	
59	b	very large vase			45		Fig. 28:8	crushed
60	c	cup	8	8		5·5		
61	d	cup	8	8		5	,, 28:11	decorated
62	e-1	small bowl	9	12	13	6	,, 28:9	decorated
63	e-2	small bowl						crushed
64	h	bowl	9·5	13·8		6·5		
65	f	beaker or cup	7·5	8		3·5		
66	i	cup	9	7·7×9		6	,, 28:10	decorated
67	j	vase with 2 handles	11·7	12·7 ×14·5	17	7	Plate 17:13	decorated
	Barrow-grave 29						Plan 15:3	
68	a	vessel ?				7		
	Barrow-grave 31						Plan 17:2	
69	a-1	Thuringian amphora		25		9		disintegrated
70	a-2	beaker	11	12	12·5	4	Fig. 9:2	decorated

No.	Vessel		Height	Diameter upper	Diameter body	Diameter base	Illustration	Remarks
	Barrow-grave 32						Plan 18	
71	a-1	small cup	10			3·9		crushed
72	a-2	small cup	10			3		crushed
	Barrow-grave 33						Plan 17:1	
73	I	tulip-shaped pot	24	23×14	23×18	9	Plate 21:12	damaged by fire
74	II	handled cup	6·5	11·5		8	,, 21:16	handle 11 cm
75	III	handled cup	11×9	10·5	13	8	,, 21:14	handle 12·5 cm
76	IV	ovoid vessel		16	23			identical with IX
	IX	urn						description missing
77	V	bowl	10			8		description missing
78	VI–VII	bowl		17				crushed, disintegrated
79	VIII	vessel ?						
80	X	tulip-shaped pot?						only a number of potsherds found
81	XI	bowl	7·4	15×13	17×15	9	,, 21:15	
	Barrow-grave 34						Plan 19:2	
82	I	deep dish	*c.* 10		*c.* 30	*c.* 10		description missing
83	II–III	bowl	13	16·5	18·5	8·5	Fig. 31:8	decorated
84	IV	small beaker		8				disintegrated
85	V	beaker	9·4	9	9·2	5·5	Plate 16:3	decorated
86	VI	cylindrical cup	6	7·8		7·3	,, 16:12	decorated
87	VII	cup	7		8	5·5		disintegrated
88	VIII	bowl				8		disintegrated
89	d	large deep dish						
90	d	spheric vessel						a few potsherds
91	d	bowl (or two)						of each –
92	d	a large vessel						damaged by fire
	Barrow-grave 35						Plan 22:3	
93	a	bowl	13	22	22	10		
	Barrow-grave 36						Plan 22:2	
94	a	clepsydra-shaped cup	7	7·5	5	6·5	Plate 18:19	
95	b	bowl	13	16	19	7	,, 17:5	decorated
	Barrow-grave 38						Plan 21	
96	a	bowl	8	15				crushed
97	f	a large vessel?						only scattered potsherds found
	Barrow-grave 39						Plan 19:1	
98	a	bowl	9·5	13	12·2	5	Plate 6:4	decorated
	Barrow-grave 43							
99	1	Villanova urn	31?					decorated
100	2	dish	11	27				
101	3	bowl				8·5		
102	4	bowl	9×11	26·5		10·3		
103	5	handled cup						disintegrated
104	6	handled cup	8·1	9×11	10	6·5		handle 11 cm
105	7	deep dish	11×12	33×34		12·5		
106	8	handled cup	9	8·6	10	6·5		handle 12 cm
107	9	handled cup	7	8·2	9·3	6		handle 8·2cm
108	10	ovoid urn	24·8	11	19·8	10·8		decorated
109	11	bowl or dish	9·5	?28		10		
110	12	vessel similar to no. 10	20?					only a number of sherds left

No.	Vessel		Height	Diameter upper	body	base	Illustration	Remarks
	Barrow-grave 44						Plan 23:2	
111	f	beaker or cup				10		disintegrated
	Barrow-grave 45						Plan 23:1	
112	b	bowl				7		decorated, crushed
113	d	beaker	11·2	10	10·2	5·8	Fig. 30:5	decorated
114	f-m	thick-walled						} in scattered sherds
115	f-m	bowl decorated						
116	g-l	handled bowl	9	10·8	12·5	4·5	Plate 21:6	decorated
117	g-2	deep dish or bowl	16·5	14·5		7	„ 21:7	decorated
118	g-3	bowl	10	14	16	5·5	„ 21:1	decorated
119	g-4	handled cup	10·5	12·5	14	6·5	„ 21:3	decorated
120	g-5	bowl	7·2	12·8	13·1	5	Fig. 30:3	decorated
121	g-6	single-lugged mug	15	14 × 15		11	Plate 21:4	decorated
122	g-7	bowl	9·4	13	16	6·5	„ 21:2	decorated
123	g-8	tulip-shaped pot	20	13	13	7	„ 21:5	raised band
	Barrow-grave 46						Plan 24:1	
124	a	bowl	9·4	15	14·8	6	Fig. 27:4	decorated
125	b	bowl				7·5		disintegrated
126	c	bowl	10·5	16	15	8	„ 27:2	decorated
127	d	tulip-shaped pot				9		raised band, disintegrated
128	E	cup flower-pot-shaped	8·5	10		8·7	Plate 18:13	decorated
129	F	two-handled bowl	13	15·5	19·5	8	„ 17:8	decorated
130	g	cup	9	8·7	9·2	5·6	„ 18:9	decorated
131	h	bowl	5	7·5	8	5		
132	i	bowl	8·6	14	14·2	6·5	Fig. 27:9	
133	j	cup	6·5	6·6	4·8			
134	k	tulip-shaped pot	24	14	18·5	8	„ 27:1	raised band
135	l	bowl	11·5	16	16	8	„ 27:3	decorated
	Barrow-grave 47						Plan 24:2	
136	c	dish	9·7	29·5	30·5	12	Fig. 31:7	
137	f	large vessel	30?	19	25?		„ 31:9	only a few sherds, decorated
	Barrow-grave 48						Plan 24:3	
138	b-1	handlcd cup						crushed
139	b-2	bowl	11·4	13	13·2	5·5	„ 30:9	decorated
140	b-3	two-handled bowl	12	13	14·8	7?	„ 30:1	
141	b-4a	tulip-shaped pot	19·5	14·8	15·5	9·7	„ 30:2	raised band
142	b-4b	tulip-shaped pot		14·7	16·5		„ 30:7	decorated, lower part missing
143	b-5	tulip-shaped pot	14	11·5	12	7	Plate 19:4	
	Barrow-grave 50						Plan 25:2	
144	b-f	very large vessel				16?		scattered sherds
145	i	bowl	12	21·5	24	7	Fig. 31:2	
	Barrow-grave 51							
146		large vessel similar to that from mound 20(j)						scattered sherds
	Barrow-grave 55							
147	a	cup	10			7		crushed
148	b	larger vessel						only a few sherds
149	c	deep dish	5·8	20		9	Fig. 27:7	decorated
	Barrow-grave 64						Plan 16:2	
150	a	beaker ?						scattered sherds

3. THE SETTLEMENT
(Plans I and 7)

It has been already mentioned that on the surface of the 'Dworzyska' and 'Łuniów' fields were lying potsherds, stones, lumps of fired clay, etc., which were obviously traces of a settlement. A copper shaft-hole axe, a copper or bronze knife (Fig. 35:8, 9) and a fragment of a 'wire' were found there before 1885.[7] I investigated this settlement during my excavation of the cemetery in 1935; lack of funds prevented me from undertaking this work on a larger scale.

The area chosen for the investigation was situated in the lowest part of the 'Dworzyska' field, where most of the portions of fired clay and fragments of pottery occurred over an area 100 by 30m. There was a slight oblong-shaped elevation 50 by 20m in the middle of this area, in the centre of which the broken blade of a stone battle-axe had been ploughed up some days before the excavation started. Two squares were dug in the centre of this elevation, each 10 by 10m, one of which was later widened out on the southern side, and a longer trench dug in the same direction.

Most objects were found beneath the level of ploughed soil, at a depth from 20 to 40cm. The soil in which they occurred did not differ from the ploughed soil either in colour (greyish-yellow) or structure, though it was harder. Under the level containing objects was a layer of completely dark earth, 10–15cm in depth, clearly differentiated from the first level. Still deeper, at 50cm and over, was virgin soil, light ash in colour, marbled, and gradually merging into increasingly yellow clay.

After the ploughed soil had been removed, red friable soil appeared, containing harder 'brick' in some places. This occurred in a narrow layer, hardly visible in some places, but occurring in thicker and relatively hard accumulations towards the southern boundary of the excavation: it did not occur in the northern section of the excavation.

In the southern part of the area under excavation, a fairly large number of stones of various dimensions occurred, mostly river pebbles of up to 25cm in diameter, among the accumulations of lumps of fired clay. In many places these stones had formed distinct lines, sometimes coinciding with the lines of the accumulations of fired clay. Closer inspection of these lines showed that they formed the boundaries of the walls of the dwellings. Unfortunately they provided an incomplete picture, since the larger stones, of which the upper portions had extended into the layer of ploughed soil, had long since been removed by the owners of the fields.

The clearest outlines were those of the dwelling situated more or less in the centre of the site (dwelling I). This was oblong in shape, some 5 by 4m facing N–S. The stones revealing the lines of the former walls had acted as supports for the foundation beams which, laid horizontally had formed supports for the framework of the dwelling. This type of erection, i.e. having its foundations placed on stones without fixing piles into the ground, is still widely used today throughout the Sub-Carpathians.

The construction of the walls could not be established. Probably the framework of the house had been of oak, as they still are in this neighbourhood, particularly in farm buildings, but having walls of wattle and daub, plastered with clay. An argument in favour of this hypothesis is the relatively thick layer of lumps of fired clay found more particularly alongside the line of stones and in the corner area. The charred remains of oak piles were found in some places in the corners, though there were no holes into which these piles might have been driven. Some cavities which were discovered in the settlement were rubbish dumps or used for ashes by the hearth. The oak piles, therefore, must have been placed vertically to the foundation beams.

Near the N–E corner of the dwelling a remarkably thick accumulation of lumps of fired clay (p) was found, covering a wider area than usual. These were fragments of a clay hearth, of the baker's oven type, built in the same way as similar ovens in other settlements of the Tripolye culture. Pieces of a broken pot (n) were found among the remains of the oven on the broken hearth, and beneath the clay, closer to the northern wall was a hole 50cm deep, full of fired clay potsherds and ash (d). A large storage vessel was found under the eastern wall (z): it was broken. Its sides were 2cm thick, and the clay contained a large admixture of broken rubble, but the vessel itself was very well fired. Its outer side was brick-red, while its interior was covered with a thin layer of slip 2–3mm thick, dark and smooth. This vessel, like fragments of similar vessels found under the southern wall, particularly in the S–W corner, was decorated with vertical ribs running from the shoulder curve to the widest part of its convexity (Fig. 20:2). Some of the fragments derived from vessels made of more silted clay, and had inner walls spread with a fine layer of smoother, brown slip, sometimes bearing a slight polish. In addition to the large storage vessel referred to above, a broken bowl was found, made in a similar manner; this bowl (Fig. 20:1) coincided exactly both in make and shape with the bowls from the barrow-graves of the Komarów type of the Middle Bronze Age. This pottery clearly indicates that dwelling I was contemporary with the Komarów barrow-graves, and dates from the Middle Bronze Age.

Dwelling I stood on the site of an earlier hut destroyed by fire (dwelling II), as was clearly shown by the well-defined line of the earlier wall at some distance from the western wall of dwelling I. This line was marked by stones, fired clay and the remains of charred piles (w). It was also fairly easy to distinguish the southern wall of this dwelling, whereas the eastern and northern walls were more difficult to discern, since they were inside the area of the later dwellings I. Dwelling II was almost square, 4 by 4·5m. Some flint implements were found near its northern corner, while a large, broken storage vessel, was found within its circumference, and halfway along the western wall, its lower portion buried in the ground (r). It was of the type common to the Tripolye culture, with an everted rim, made in accordance with the technique char-

[7] M. Much, *Die Kupferzeit in Europa*, 2nd ed., Jena 1893, p. 45, Fig. 40. J. Kostrzewski, 'Z badań nad osadnictwem wczesnej i środkowej epoki brązowej na ziemiach polskich', *Prz.A.*, vol. II, 1922–4, p. 197. The shaft-hole axe of another type (Fig. 35:10), published by W. Antoniewicz, *Archeologia Polski*, Warszawa 1928, Pl. XIV, was not found at Komarów but in the neighbouring village of Sapohów. Two socketed bronze lance-heads of 'Hungarian' type (both 20cm long) were found at Komarów in unknown circumstances. They are at present at the Natur-Historisches Museum in Vienna (No. 33102). They date from about 1000 B.C., the turn of the Komarów periods II and III.

acteristic of the D-ware,[8] its exterior was not painted. A large number of potsherds of Tripolye D-ware were found near the S–E corner (c), as well as a large, damaged (Fig. 12:12) clay masculine figurine (h). Various dishes and other vessels with everted rims were distinguished among these fragments.

One wall of a third dwelling (III) could be perceived to the west of the above dwellings: it faced NE–SE. Beside it were found the remains of charred oak piles (b), a quantity of lumps of fired clay and small flint implements, including a scraper and saw (e). A small female figurine was also found here (i) (Fig. 12:13). However, it was difficult to determine the position of the other walls of this dwelling. They probably ran S–E underneath dwellings I and II.

Traces of more dwellings were found beyond the western wall of dwelling III, but their outline could not be discerned. Lumps of clay, stones, numerous fragments of D-ware type pottery and flint implements (k) were found here. It is likely that another dwelling (IV) lay to the east of dwelling I, beneath both it and dwelling II. This is indicated by the larger accumulations of fired clay slabs (p) and flint implements here. The absence of stones may be due to their having been removed during ploughing. Traces of yet another dwelling were apparent along the eastern boundary of the excavation.

Reconstruction of the outlines of the dwellings show that dwelling I stood on the site of several earlier dwellings. As a result of building several successive dwellings on the same site, lumps of fired clay plaster accumulated and the elevation, visible on this site before excavation began, was formed. A large quantity of charcoal occurring in many places beside the clay lumps show that the settlement was frequently subject to fires.

The finding here of a fairly large number of small calcined bones (a) is of interest. These were subjected to analysis before World War II by Professor A. A. Bandt of the Lwów Veterinary Academy (College), who showed that all were of animal origin: no human bones were found. These animal bones lay scattered about, both within the area of the dwellings and outside it, beneath the clay lumps and outside their extent. In some places they were found in the rubbish pits (d). It is possible that part of them originate from animals burned during the fires.

No accurate stratigraphic observations could be made to determine the order in which the dwellings were erected, and whether the remains found within their areas appertained to them. This was because the upper layer, 20cm thick, containing objects had been damaged by ploughing. However, it is certain that, apart from the type of the finds, dwelling I was the most recent of the dwellings, the remains of which occurred on this one site.

Although limited in range, the investigation of the above settlements provided valuable results. They confirmed that the settlement was contemporaneous with the barrow-grave cemetery, or at least with part of its barrow-graves. The dwellings containing pottery of the Tripolye type D-ware provided many small flint implements, arrow-heads (Plate 9:28, 29), and even a fragment of a stone battle-axe, none of which differed typologically, materially or in technique of manufacture, from similar implements found in the barrow-graves. The fragments of D-ware found in some of the barrow-graves (nos. 2, 3, 45) also show that the settlement was contemporaneous with the Neolithic barrow-graves or those of the Early Bronze Age.

The fact that the settlement continued to be inhabited in the Middle Bronze Age was also confirmed. Pottery from dwelling I (Fig. 20:1–3) corresponds entirely, both in technique of manufacture and form, with sepulchral pottery of the Komarów type: there can be no doubt they are contemporaneous. The type and the mode of construction of the 'Komarów' hut I did not differ in any respect from those of its preceding huts on the debris of which it was built.

[8] The term 'D-ware' I have given to a particular type of pottery characteristic of the Tripolyan settlements of the final stage of the development of that culture. It was a sand-gritted or grog-gritted ware; the surface had a thin, smooth slip and was undecorated. It was very 'soft', easily 'washed off', the edges of sherds being therefore rounded, deformed, which renders the reconstruction of the vessels difficult. All types of vessels usually found in Tripolyan settlements were represented among this pottery.

SECTION II

Barrow-graves of Sub-Carpathian Culture[1]

I. THE PRZEMYŚL GROUP

1. *Balice* district of Mościska

Nineteen barrow-graves were excavated about 1902 by A. Chizzola,[2] two of which (unspecified) lay in the territory of the adjoining villages of Moczerady and Nowosiółki. Thirteen of these barrow-graves formed a single group. I visited this site in 1935; it was situated on common pasture land close to a forest. Seven large mounds, *c.* 30m in diameter, 4–5m high, and two smaller mounds lay in a slightly curved line, and another lay close to these in the forest of Nowosiółki. All bore traces of excavation. Only a few mounds were described in the report by A. Chizzola; all the grave goods were at the Prehistoric Institute of the University of Lwów before the war. Barrow-graves II, III, IX, X, XII and XIII were not mentioned in the report nor were any of their grave goods represented in the collection. The report also mentions that fragments of animal bones were excavated in a few mounds.

Barrow-grave I. (a) A small axe, 7cm long, made of dark-grey slate; (b) a flint blade scraper, 7cm long; (c) a diorite battle-axe, badly damaged by fire, 7·5cm long; (d) a small flint knife.

Barrow-grave IV. A handled, cord-decorated cup (Plate 6:24) 9·5cm high; a drawing by Chizzola and copied by Kozłowski, is wrong.

Barrow-grave V. At a depth of 3m, an extended skeleton on its back, head to NW. It lay on a layer of brown earth and was surrounded by timber logs, traces of which were well visible. No grave goods were reported.

Barrow-grave VI. At a depth of 3m, an extended skeleton on its back, head to N. Grave goods: (a) a flint knife 13cm long; (b) a dagger made of 'Bug' variety of flint (Plate 11:3), 12cm long, base matt, 4·5cm wide, otherwise two-thirds of its surface shining; (c) a small polished battle-axe made of light-grey slate (type *x*-3; Fig. 13:5), 8·5cm long.

Barrow-grave VII. One of the smaller mounds in the group. At a depth of 1·7m an extended skeleton on its back, head to NE. This was the most richly furnished grave: (a) an undecorated Miechów amphora with four lugs, 27cm high, its body 31cm in diameter (Plate 3:6); (b) a small pedestalled bowl, found between the legs of the skeleton, 6cm high, its rim bore a row of slanting incisions, the stand plain with a flat base, 6·5cm in diameter, a raised finger-tip decorated band around the stand (Plate 3:2); (c) the blade of a granite battle-axe damaged by fire, 5cm long; (d) a flint axe, 9·5cm long, rectangular in section; (e) two flint arrow-heads, only one of which was in the collection; (f) three flint implements (knives); (g) a lead ring found on a finger of the left hand, made of a band 12mm wide, 7cm long (Fig. 19:22); (h) an open bronze bracelet undecorated, 7·5cm in diameter, made of a round bar, found near the knuckle of the left foot (Fig. 19:17); (i) a damaged bronze dagger with traces of three rivet holes, 4·3cm long, originally about 8cm, found near the right elbow (Fig. 19:18); (j) a damaged bronze pin found near the dagger, 7·8cm long, head missing (Fig. 19:14). Chemical analysis made before the last war in the Chemical Institute of the University of Lwów[3] gave the following results: Cu 92·85 per cent, Sn 5·46 per cent, traces of lead; (k) a few flint flakes.

Barrow-grave VIII. At a depth of 3·4m an extended skeleton on its back, head to N. No grave goods reported.

Barrow-grave XIV. A small straight-sided, cord-decorated cylindrical cup, with a flat base, its upper part missing, 6·5cm high.

Barrow-grave XV. (a) A Thuringian amphora, 28cm high, body 29cm in diameter, two lugs on the body, the cylindrical neck has three wide, flat, horizontal parallel grooves (Plate 4:2); (b) a battle-axe made of sandstone, 10·6cm long, of type *y*-1 (Fig. 13:2).

Barrow-grave XVI. At a depth of 3·5m an extended skeleton on its back, head to W (Plate 1:3). Grave goods: (a) flint dagger in the right hand (Plate 11:2), 16cm long, its surface shining; (b) a very well polished battle-axe made of a greenish variety of stone, 11cm long, in the left hand (Plate 10:10); (c) a mace-head made of granite, very well polished, 10cm long, found near the right arm (Plate 10:9); (d) a small axe made of yellow slate, 8·2cm long, found near the right elbow; (e) a large, undecorated amphora of which only a few sherds survived had three or four lugs under the neck on the upper part of the body; (f) a wide open basin (Plate 6:11) 6·5cm high, 14·5cm wide; (g) two flint implements, probably knives.

Barrow-grave XVII. A small undecorated handled cup, published by A. Chizzola, but missing in the collection.

Barrow-grave XVIII. At a depth of 4m a considerably decayed skeleton over which many heaped human bones were found. Grave goods: (a) an axe oval in cross-section, 7·5cm long, made of a dark variety of flint; (b) a narrow flint point or burin, 3·6cm long.

Barrow-grave XIX. According to A. Chizzola, a medium-size pot (a) was found with a low, well-modelled body, a relatively small mouth, an everted rim, decorated with primitive

[1] The districts are indicated according to the pre-war administrative division of the country, except sites excavated and published after 1945.

[2] A. v. Chizzola, 'Prähistorische Funde aus Westgalizien', *Jahrbuch d.k.k. Zentral Kommission,* vol. I, Wien 1903, pp. 142 ff., Figs. 180–4. L. Kozłowski, *Młodsza epoka kamienna w Polsce (neolit)*, Lwów 1924, p. 188, Pl. XXVII:14, 15. Id., *Wczesna, starsza i środkowa epoka bronzu w Polsce,* Lwów 1928, p. 35, Pl. XIII:11, 13, 14.

[3] I am indebted for this analysis to Professor W. Kemula, at present of the University of Warsaw.

zigzag patterns. In the vessel remains of corn of various kinds were found. The vessel was missing, but other grave goods not mentioned by A. Chizzola were: (b) a flint dagger (Plate 11:10) 11cm long, the base matt, 4·5cm wide, the surface shining; (c) a flint knife made of a blade 13·3cm long; (d) a small flint blade.

In 1933 a barrow-grave was excavated by Skibniewski at a site called 'Załucze'. At a depth of 2m a layer of black, dusty 'cinders' was found, which contained no charcoal. Nothing else was excavated. It is important to note that A. Chizzola remarks that the kernel of the large mounds consisted of black, rich earth, of a kind nowadays unknown in this part of the country. The 'cinders' from Załucze barrow-grave were undoubtedly of the same category.

2. *Brusno* district of Lubaczów

Before the war the following objects were in the Dzieduszycki Museum in Lwów; they were probably found in a barrow-grave near a quarry, not in a cist-grave as mentioned by L. Kozłowski[4] (Plate 3:3–5): a large 'Miechów' amphora with three lugs under the neck, the neck cord decorated, a very large body and very small base; another small amphora with two lugs on the junction of its cylindrical neck with the body, and the neck cord decorated; and a cord-decorated bowl with a flat base and slightly everted rim; a flint axe, quadrangular in cross-section, of Bundsø type (Fig. 15:4).

3. *Brzezinki* district of Lubaczów

A cemetery of six barrow-graves situated in a meadow was excavated by A. Dzieduszycka-Machnikowa and J. Machnik in 1957 and 1958.[5] All the mounds were built of sand.

Barrow-grave 1. About 11m in diameter, 40cm high. Traces of a few hearths on various levels. In the centre the grave-shaft was uncovered, 1m deep, over 1·5m wide, lined and covered with oak logs. Logs of the cover were charred, probably by the pyre built over it, traces of which, or of a large hearth, were clearly visible on the ancient surface. On the bottom of the shaft lay a wide beaker and an amphora, the latter base upwards. The beaker had a flat base, the neck slightly widening upwards, decorated with four horizontal rows of short oblique incisions. The amphora, of the Miechów type, was undecorated, and provided with four small lugs on the shoulder. Many decorated potsherds were excavated in the mound, among which were those of a beaker similar to that above.

Barrow-grave 2. 11m in diameter, 30cm high, flattened. In the centre the grave-shaft 1·6 by 2m rectangular in plan, reaching to a depth of 1·1m from the top of the mound. Around it several post-holes were uncovered, probably of wooden construction which had not survived. Only a few potsherds and one worked flint were found in the filling of the shaft.

Barrow-grave 3. Originally the largest of all mounds but the sand of its mound has been used for industrial purposes. Presumably 15m in diameter. Four rectangular shafts were uncovered, one in the centre, all within an area about 10m and encircled by a band of dark sand, 50cm deep, 20cm wide. Similar enclosures, about 4m in diameter, encircled two shafts. The central shaft was 2·4 by 1·5m. In one corner stood a vessel, near which lay charcoal and calcined bones. In another corner lay sherds of a few vessels, flint blade, charcoal and calcined bones, and near by was a stone battle-axe. In the somewhat deeper north-eastern shaft, 2·5 by 1·6m, a vessel, stone battle-axe, flint axe, two flint arrow-heads and a few other flints were excavated. In the north-western shaft, similar to the above, lay three vessels, a flint axe and a few flint blades. In the eastern shaft (grave 3) three more vessels were found and a large flint flake. One of these was a high vase with a spherical body, a short cord-decorated neck and an everted rim. The other vessel was a 'flowerpot' beaker with three rows of oblique incisions and the third one, likewise a beaker, had a short cord-decorated neck and a spherical body. All vessels were flat-based.

Barrow-grave 4 (Plan 9:2). Originally a large mound probably about 12m in diameter, destroyed like the preceding. In the centre was a shaft surrounded by a band of dark sand, similar to that in barrow-grave 3, rectangular; it contained two worked flint blades, a large undecorated 'Thuringian' amphora with four lugs on the body, and a beaker with a spherical body, the neck covered with three rows of incised chevron patterns. Inside the amphora were two more vessels, a miniature cup and a small beaker with nearly vertical sides covered entirely with rows of alternately oblique incisions. The central area, 8m in diameter, was encircled by three concentric bands of dark sand of the same type and depth as those in barrow-grave 3. In the eastern part of the area covered by the mound, partly outside the area encircled, partly on the encirclement itself, a second grave-shaft was uncovered quadrangular in plan, 35cm deep on the bottom of which lay a few flint blades and two larger vessels with a smaller one inside of each of these.

At a distance of about 7–8m respectively from the centre of the mound, two holes, round in shape were uncovered, outside the extent of the mound. In one of these, south of the mound, 80cm in diameter, 1·20m deep, two small cord-decorated vessels lay on the bottom and a few flints, the hole being filled in with dark sand with a large admixture of powdered charcoal. The other hole in which two vessels were also found as well as pieces of charred logs[6] was similar.

Barrow-grave 5. Almost completely destroyed by industrial excavation. Two vessels and two flint blades were found on the bottom of the central shaft.

Barrow-grave 6. 6m in diameter, 10cm high. The single central shaft was nearly oval in plan and encircled by a narrow belt of dark sand, running at a distance of about 50cm to 1m from the edge of the shaft. A vessel was found near the centre of the shaft at the depth of 60cm, and on its bottom, at a depth of 1·1m, lay a flint scraper.

[4] Kozłowski (op. cit., note 2: 1924), p. 190, Pl. XXVII:9, 17, 18.

[5] J. Gromnicki, 'Neolityczne cmentarzyska kurhanowe w miejscowościach Łukawica i Brzezinki, pow.Lubaczów', *W.A.*, vol. XXV, 1958, pp. 386 f. A. Dzieduszycka & J. Machnik, 'Badania archeologiczne na cmentarzyskach kurhanowych w Łukawicy i Brzezinkach, pow.Lubaczów, *Spr.Arch.*, vol. VIII, 1959, pp. 12 ff. A. Dzieduszycka-Machnikowa, 'II Sprawozdanie z badań wykopaliskowych na cmentarzysku kurhanowym kultury ceramiki sznurowej w Brzezinkach, pow.Lubaczów', *Spr.Arch.*, vol. X, 1960, pp. 9 ff. J. Machnik, 'Untersuchungen über die schnurkermische Kultur in Südostpolen', *Archaeologia Polona*, vol. IV, 1962, p. 139, Pls. I:1, 3; II:1–3. Id., *Studia nad kulturą ceramiki sznurowej w Małopolsce*, Wrocław-Warszawa-Kraków 1966, pp. 240 ff.

[6] J. Machnik, 'Badania archeologiczne w Rostoczu Lubelskim w 1959 r', *Spr.Arch.*, vol. XII, 1961, pp. 90 f.

Pottery from these mounds consisted of amphorae, beakers and other vessels, cord decorated or with incisions. Chevron patterns were very common. No detailed description of these grave goods was published in the preliminary reports.

4. *Chłopice* district of Jarosław

Sherds of a few cord-decorated vessels, probably from a grave, are at the Archaeological Museum in Cracow. Among these are fragments of a deep bowl and a handled cup of 'Złota' type.[7]

5. *Czarna* district of Łańcut

A 'neolithic site' was uncovered. At the part of the village known as Podbórz. At a depth of 1·2m, in a sandy layer, a flint axe, a stone battle-axe, a flint blade and two large sherds of a small bowl (Fig. 12:7) were accidentally excavated. No other remains were found there during subsequent investigations by K. Moskwa, M.A.[8]

The spherical bowl (Fig 12:7), 11cm in diameter, 5cm high, was brownish in colour, undecorated. The flint axe, 9·3cm long had a wide butt, and the battle-axe, of the 'simple' *x*-2 type, 10·8cm long. This find seems to have been a grave, probably a barrow-grave in origin, as is indicated by the character of its assemblage.

6. *Czyszki* district of Mościska

A barrow-grave was excavated in the nineteenth century similar to that at Komarowice near Dobromil (no. 15) but no particulars are available.[9]

7. *Dobrostany* district of Gródek Jagielloński

In 1908 K. Hadaczek investigated two barrow-graves,[10] and found flint chips, flint knife and a terracotta weight in one. Before the war the following objects from these excavations were preserved at the Dzieduszycki Museum in Lwów: a fragment of the body of a large vessel and another fragment of the rim with a row of perforations; a fragment of a small battle-axe made of slate; a flint knife or scraper, 7cm long, and a flint flake.

8. *Gdeszyce* district of Przemyśl

Ten barrow-graves of a group of twenty-five situated in a forest on the border with Czyszki were excavated in 1887 by Bishop J. Stupnicki.[11] They were 16–20m in diameter, 30cm to 1·5m high, crossed by two trenches dug 1m wide. In five of these entirely in the centre (nos. IV, V, VI, VII, XV), 'remains of sepulchral vessels and ashes' were found; in barrow-grave XXI three broken vessels and a flint flake were excavated, and in barrow-grave XXII, two broken vessels, a flint dagger and a flint hammer while nothing was found in the three remaining mounds (VIII, XVIII and XX). Vessels are said to have been wide in the middle, with a narrow mouth and base, dark-grey or light-brown in colour; rims were either flat or slightly everted, only one vessel is reported to have been decorated (by horizontal grooves around the rim).

9. *Handzlówka* district of Łańcut.

Two 'neolithic sites' were uncovered here.[12]

Site 1 was on a small hill. Four flint axes and a stone battle-axe were found. Axes were 10cm, 11·2cm, 7cm and 6cm long, all with a polished surface. The battle-axe, 7·6cm long, was of the simple *y*-type.

Site 2 lay about 150m north of the above. Three flint axes and a flint blade knife were found. Two axes (10 and 10·6cm long) were lenticular in section, and the third (8·8cm long) was of banded flint, rectangular in section. The knife, 10·6cm long, had its edges well trimmed.

The position of these sites on the hills seems to suggest that they were graves, probably barrow-graves, which were completely ploughed up.

10. *Hartfeld* district of Gródek Jagielloński

A barrow-grave in the field known as 'Au' was excavated by me in 1935 (Plan 8:3). It was about 29m in diameter, 1·2m high, its north-western part ruined by trenches of the First World War. The cross-section of the mound was as follows: 20cm arable soil; 1·1m dark, loose mound earth which lay on the ancient surface, formed by dark humus in which many hamster holes were clearly visible; in its lower part this layer gradually changed to yellow virgin soil, which formed a continuous stratum at a depth of 1·6–1·7m.

The grave-shaft (A) was in the centre; it was dug to a depth of 90cm in the ancient level, reaching to the yellow virgin soil, to the depth of 2·2 from the top of the mound. It was 3 by 2m in area, orientated W–E, quadrangular in plan with rounded corners; it was smaller on the bottom, which was only 2 by 1·1m in area (B). No traces of the skeleton were visible, it had decayed entirely. In the NE corner of the shaft, a little below the ancient level, a flint scraper was found (e) and close to the corner, on the ancient surface, lay a few potsherds (d), among these the fragment of a lug of a Thuringian amphora (b). A few more fragments of the neck and rim of the same vessel and of other parts of its body including another lug, were found scattered on the ancient surface north of the grave (a, c). The neck had wide, shallow grooves. No decorated sherds were found.

11. *Hruszatyce* district of Przemyśl

In 1896–7, two burial mounds in a group of three were excavated by W. Demetrykiewicz,[13] who dug 1m wide trenches across each. Layers 'of cinders' (evidently loose mound earth) some charcoal, small fragments of bones and small sherds of badly fired vessels were found.

[7] *ZOW*, vol. VIII, 1933, p. 24. J. Machnik, 'Ze studiów nad kulturą ceramiki sznurowej w Karpatach polskich', *Acta AC*, vol. II/1–2, 1960, p. 64, Fig. 7:a, b.

[8] K. Moskwa, *ZOW*, vol. XXIV, 1958, pp. 406 f. Mr K. Moskwa, M.A., has very kindly sent me the drawings and photographs of the objects excavated. J. Machnik (op. cit., note 5, 1966), p. 250, Pl. XXIII:2.

[9] J. Stupnicki and A. Lubomirski, *Protocolle über die IV. Conserv. Conferenz in Krakau*, Wien 1889, pp. 63 ff. B. Janusz, *Zabytki przedhistoryczne Galicyi Wschodniej*, Lwów 1918, p. 174.

[10] Janusz (op. cit., note 9), p. 108.

[11] Stupnicki and Lubomirski, loc. cit., note 9. Janusz (op. cit., note 9), p. 181. See also note 23.

[12] K. Moskwa, *ZOW*, vol. XXIV, 1958, pp. 330 f., Fig. 8.

[13] W. Demetrykiewicz, 'Kurhany w Przemyskiem i Drohobyckiem', *Materiały antropologiczno-archaeologiczne i etnograficzne*, vol. II, Kraków 1898, pp. 123 f. Janusz (op. cit., note 9), p. 182.

12. *Kańczuga* district of Przeworsk

About 1888, a burial mound was excavated by local peasants. A small copper bowl, a copper helmet and a stone battle-axe are said to have been excavated.[14]

13. *Kniażyce* district of Przemyśl

A grave situated on the top of a hill was uncovered in a quarry in 1939 and partly destroyed. It was subsequently investigated by me.[15] At a depth of 1·2m lay a double burial in a shaft dug into the lime rubble of the subsoil. It was 2m long. Bones which remained *in situ* indicated that both skeletons (man and woman) lay in a contracted position, heads to S. Near the man's head stood three vessels: a crushed cord-decorated beaker, 14cm high, base 14cm in diameter, a small cup, and another large crushed vessel, probably an amphora, 20cm in diameter. Near the female skeleton lay two vessels, an amphora half of which was destroyed at the discovery of the grave, about 19cm high, body 18cm in diameter, the cord-decorated neck 10cm in diameter; and a small undecorated semi-spheric cup, 3cm high, 6cm in diameter, which lay with the base upwards. Two more vessels were found in this grave at the time of its discovery.

14. *Komarno* district of Rudki

In 1936, a barrow-grave was excavated by Dr J. Pasternak.[16] This was a double cremation burial in which an amphora, a battle-axe made of diabase, a flint axe rectangular in section, a bone awl and a flint scraper were found. The amphora was of 'Lubaczów' type, 22cm high, 28cm in diameter, base slightly concave, 7·5cm in diameter; it had four lugs on the upper part of the body, and its ornament consisted of large fish-bone patterns incised on both sides of the body.

15. *Komarowice* district of Dobromil

In 1895, a large mound known as 'Ostra Górka' was excavated by W. Demetrykiewicz,[17] and another smaller close to it, which had already been excavated in 1863. The larger one was in fact a small medieval earthwork. In the smaller one clay vessels, partly calcined human teeth and a lead band were said to be found. Demetrykiewicz found in one of these mounds a flint implement and Neolithic potsherds. Both were probably Neolithic burial mounds on the site of which later a small mediaeval fort was built.

16. *Korczyna* district of Krosno

In 1949, during the construction of a road on top of the hill, a contracted skeleton was found at a depth of 2m, head to E; near it lay a flint knife.[18]

17. *Koropuż* district of Rudki

In 1935, I excavated a mound 26m in diameter, over 1m high, and situated on the summit of a hill in a field known as 'Pod Mogiłą' (Plan 8:1).[19] Three deep shafts dug for survey posts and block were uncovered in different parts of the mound. A trench running north–south crossed the eastern side, near the centre: this was 60cm wide and 60cm deep (A).

A rectangular grave-shaft (B) 1·9m by 1m occurred in approximately the centre of the mound; it was some 80cm deep, dug about 40cm into the ancient soil and orientated, roughly, west–east. It was paved with oak logs. A crouching skeleton, almost entirely decayed and barely visible, was lying at the bottom on its right side, its head westwards. The head had been resting on material of some kind, traces of which were visible round the skull. A crushed Thuringian amphora (e) (Plate 3:1) was lying in the north-west corner of the shaft, near the head, with a flint blade (f) (Plate 3:1) beside the skeleton's trunk. The skeleton was thickly strewn with red and yellow ochre, and had a large lump of charcoal by its knees. The shaft had been covered over with oak logs, traces of which were clearly visible.

A number of lumps of charcoal, forming larger heaps particularly towards the east, surrounded the grave-shaft on the ancient level in a semicircle on the south, east and north-east over an area of about three to four metres in width (c). An odd potsherd (a) was found near the southern edge of this area, while a large charcoal lump with dust of calcined earth near it, 30cm in diameter, was found in another spot.

The remains of a burned hut (D) were found 4·5m east of the grave-shaft, along its axis. It was square, sides 4m in length, orientated south–north and was some 40cm deep in the earth. The walls were of wood. Their foundations consisted of single, thick logs of about 20cm diameter, placed horizontally. Thick planks placed vertically upon them had formed the walls of the hut. Heavily calcined remains of the lower portion of the western and northern walls had been preserved to a great extent. It was impossible to determine the construction of the upper portions, or to distinguish accurately where the entry into the hut had been situated.

A hearth (g) 1m in diameter was inside the hut: somewhat calcined animal bones, including a stag's antler as well as several dozen fragments of pottery (Plate 3:1), were lying round the hearth and were also scattered throughout the hut. An ornamented perforated bone disc (h) (Fig. 19:19), several fragments of broken saddle-quern and over a dozen calcined fragments of stone of various sizes (sandstone) were also found.

A pile of calcined earth covering an area of 1 by 1·1m was situated in the south-western corner, by the wall (i). Its origin could not be determined: it may have been the remains of a second hearth or stove, or some form of construction smeared with clay, which had been burned during the conflagration of the hut. The north-east corner of the hut had been destroyed by a shaft dug later, possibly for a survey tower. A large quantity of charcoal was found throughout the hut and its filling, as well as in the elevation above it.

The orientation of the hut and the grave, both of which

[14] *Mitteilungen d. Central-Kommission*, vol. XIV, Wien 1888, p. 122.

[15] Machnik (op. cit., note 7), p. 60, and (op. cit., note 5, 1966), p. 250.

[16] J. Pasternak, 'Moje badania terenowe w 1936 r', *ZOW*, vol. XII, 1937, p. 109. Id., Нові археологічні набутки Музею Наук. Тов. ім. Шевченка у Львові, 1933–6, off-print, p. 15. J. Machnik, (op. cit., note 5, 1966), Pl. XLV:c7.

[17] Demetrykiewicz (op. cit., note 13), pp. 116 ff. Janusz (op. cit., note 9), pp. 102 ff.

[18] *ZOW*, vol. XVIII, 1949, p. 54.

[19] T. Sulimirski, *Polska przedhistoryczna*, part II, London 1957–9, p. 229, Fig. 56. Id., ' "Thuringian" Amphorae', *PPS*, vol. XXI, 1955, Pl. VI:D.

lay along the same axis and were orientated similarly, the uniformity of the elevation upon both, as well as the charcoal deriving from the calcined walls of the hut, which was scattered on the ancient level almost up to the grave itself, all clearly indicate that the grave and hut were connected and contemporary. The hut was obviously burned down at the time of the burial and the mound raised upon both.

The pottery found in the hut (Plate 3:1) was different from that found in the grave. It was typical Funnel Beaker ware, while in addition some cord-decorated potsherds of vessels characteristic of Corded Ware were found in it. The hut must have been deliberately left before the funeral, and everything of value removed from it. No implements of any kind were found in it, while the several dozen potsherds found were not connected and formed part of a larger number of broken vessels.

Searches outside the hut and round the mound in order to find a settlement of the Funnel Beaker culture proved fruitless.

Objects found in this mound are shown in Plate 3:1. The amphora was 19·5cm high, its body 20·5cm in diameter, brownish-yellow in colour, well baked. Its cylindrical neck had four parallel grooves made by cord impressions. On the shoulder under the neck was a row of triangular stamped impressions around the vessel, from which bands consisting of four cord-impressed grooves descended obliquely to the body, thus forming, when seen from above, a five-pointed star pattern. The blade-knife, 9·2cm long, was made of 'Bug' variety of flint. The bone disc (Fig. 19:19) was 36mm in diameter, 8mm thick. Potsherds of the Funnel Beaker ware were reddish-grey, or light brownish in colour with the surface well smoothed and slightly polished. A few potsherds were of funnel beakers, a few of bowls and of other vessels typical of the Funnel Beaker pottery; several had a stamped ornament on the rim, or under it, characteristic of that culture.

18. *Krosno*

Two flint axes and a flint dagger were found near crouched skeletons.[20]

19. *Lipie* district of Lubaczów

Two barrow-graves were investigated by J. Machnik in 1958.[21] They lay in the valley of a small stream.

Barrow-grave 1. 8m in diameter. Nothing was found in it.

Barrow-grave 2. 15m in diameter, 50cm high, raised of sand. In the mound itself, in the central part, two vessels and a fragment of a worked flint were found; one of these vessels was a cord-decorated beaker typical of the early stage of the Corded Ware culture. Under the mound, in the centre, the grave-shaft was uncovered, nearly quadrangular in plan, 3·25 by 2·20m, 1·20m deep. On its bottom lay two small amphorae and a beaker with a chevron ornament, and a flint blade knife. In the filling, though mostly on the bottom of the shaft, small pieces of charcoal and calcined bones were excavated. In two corners of the shaft traces were visible of posts supporting some structure over the grave. Around the shaft, at a distance of 3m, ran a small ditch, 20–40cm wide, 30cm deep.

20. *Łukawica* district of Lubaczów

In 1957 and 1958 a group of three barrow-graves were excavated by J. Machnik.[22] They lay on a sandy elevation over the meadows extending along a small tributary of the Tanew.

Barrow-grave I. 12m in diameter, 70cm high. In its centre was a shaft, 80cm deep (180cm from the top of the mound), its bottom 1m in diameter; its sides partly collapsed. Over it, on the ancient ground level, a cord-decorated beaker was found, and another vessel lay near the bottom of the shaft. The shaft was surrounded by a ditch 25cm wide, 40cm deep, which encircled an area 9m in diameter. The sand of the ancient surface and the bottom of the shaft were reddish in colour, the result of intensive fires. Many calcined human bones, charcoal and lumps of fired clay were found in the mound and in the filling of the ditch. Outside the ditch four pits were uncovered, about 50–70cm in diameter, 60cm deep, filled in with sand and numerous pieces of charcoal. Many small potsherds typical of Corded Ware and two clay whorls proper to the Funnel Beakers were also excavated in the mound.

Barrow-grave J. This lay close to the above and was 19–20m in diameter, 1·5m high. Its mound had been partially ruined by industrial excavation of sand. Under the mound a pit was uncovered in the centre, 2m long, 1m wide, 80–90cm deep from the ancient surface. It was surrounded by an irregular ditch. Over the pit traces of another, dug subsequently, were uncovered; on its bottom were two vessels typical of Corded Ware, two flint axes, a stone battle-axe and a few small flint implements. In the mound many scattered potsherds were found. Most were characteristic of the Funnel Beaker culture but a large proportion were proper to the Corded Ware. The largest concentration of these potsherds and also of various stone and flint implements and waste, and also of pieces of animal bones were found in the central part of the area under the mound. In this layer calcined human bones were also found; this layer evidently consisted of the remains of a funeral pyre. The central pit had been dug after the cremation took place, through the layer of the remains of the pyre. The secondary pit was dug after the mound had been raised and the grave goods deposited then.

Barrow-grave K. This was about 100m from the above. It had been largely destroyed by the industrial excavation of sand. It was 14m in diameter, 80cm high. In the centre, under the mound, a shaft was uncovered, the sides of which had collapsed. It was 60cm deep (130cm from the top of the mound) and its bottom was 120 cm in diameter. It was encircled (10m in diameter) by a ditch 25cm wide. The sand of the area encircled on the ancient surface and also the filling of the shaft had a strong admixture of small pieces of charcoal,

[20] Machnik (op. cit., note 7), p. 81.

[21] Machnik (op. cit., note 5, 1962), pp. 145 f., Pls. 1:2; II:5, and (1966), p. 246, Pl. XXIII:3,4. Id. (op. cit., note 6), pp. 91 ff., Figs. 1–3.

[22] Dzieduszycka and Machnik (op. cit., note 5), pp. 9 ff., Figs. 1–4. Gromnicki, loc. cit., note 5. J. Machnik, 'II Sprawozdanie z badań na cmentarzysku kurhanowym kultury ceramiki sznurowej w Łukawicy, pow.Lubaczów', *Spr. Arch.*, vol. X, 1960, pp. 17 ff. Id. (op. cit., note 5, 1962), p. 145, Pl. II:4, and (1966), pp. 247 ff., Pl. XXIV. Id. (op. cit., note 6), pp. 89 f.

and in the ditch still more charcoal was found. In the central shaft, traces of a post were visible. At a depth of 90cm, probably on the ancient cover of the shaft, lay a crushed beaker with a wide body and narrow neck, and a large part of another beaker with a nearly flat base, decorated with cord impressions on its upper part and with rows of alternately slanting incisions on its lower part of the body. On the bottom of the shaft were found a flint axe, flint knife blade and a stone battle-axe. Outside the ditch a hole was uncovered, filled with sand mixed with charcoal. In the mound traces of small hearths on various levels, many small potsherds typical of the Corded Ware and Funnel Beakers were found in a few places, and in the northern part, in a small hole, a number of similar potsherds and two clay whorls. The excavator considered both barrow-graves were cremation burials. The Funnel Beaker potsherds originated from a settlement of that culture on the site of which the barrow-grave was raised.

21. *Małoszynka-Surmaczówka* district of Lubaczów

Two small undecorated amphorae (Plate 5:10, 11) were found on a small elevation like a barrow-grave, both at present at the Archaeological Museum in Cracow. One (no. 3175/2) 15cm high, 16cm in diameter, the other a little smaller (no. 3175/1) 11cm high, 11cm in diameter, both provided with small perforated lugs on the body.

22. *Miżyniec* district of Przemyśl

A barrow-grave was excavated by K. Hadaczek in 1912.[23] At the depth of 2·4m, near the edge of the mound, a pit was uncovered filled in with earth mixed with charcoal. It was 3m long, 50cm deep. A small pot was found in it. Near by, in the centre of the mound, a badly cracked urn stood containing calcined bones and a small bowl. A small collared flask (Plate 7:10), 13·5cm high, body 10cm in diameter, preserved at the Dzieduszycki Museum before the war (no. 1762), originated from this mound. It is a vessel typical of the Funnel Beaker culture.

23. *Moczerady* district of Mościska. See *Balice*.

24. *Morawsko* district of Jarosław

In 1856, a burial mound was excavated and grave goods found there given to the Archaeological Museum in Cracow (nos. 3178, 3211). These are: (a) a large beaker with missing upper part (Plate 6:21) 11·5cm high, body 12·5cm in diameter, its upper part having a chevron incised decoration; (b) a diorite battle-axe, 13·5cm long of type *A* (Plate 10:2); (c) two flint blade knives, and (d) a wide flint scraper.

25. *Nowosiółki* district of Przemyśl

In 1916, a barrow-grave was excavated, on a hill (point 311), east of the village. At a depth of 3m a badly decayed skeleton was uncovered, near which a small cord-decorated beaker (Plate 6:2) lay, later given to the Museum in Przemyśl. It was 10cm high, body 10cm in diameter, its upper part covered with an ornament made by impressing a simple cord round the vessel in a spiral direction, forming ten lines.

[23] Janusz (op. cit., note 9), p. 181, wrongly reported as excavated at Gdeszyce.

26. *Orzechowce* district of Przemyśl

In 1886 a Neolithic grave was uncovered on a hill. The skeleton was found in yellow clay, lying on its back, head to NW, at a depth of 2m, with legs 50cm lower. There was a stone battle-axe by its chest, a 'bone polisher' by its left leg, and two flint scrapers and flint axe at its hip. The objects were lost, but have been described by G. Ossowski:[24] (a) battle-axe made of diorite, 10·5cm long; (b) flint axe 9cm long, quadrangular in cross-section; (c) flint scrapers (in fact knives) 8·5 and 11·5cm long, about 2cm wide; (d) the 'bone polisher' was evidently a dagger; it was 16cm long, made of a long animal bone, the end flat, the surface well polished.

27. *Ostrowiec* district of Lubaczów

In about 1890, two barrow-graves situated in the 'Na Ostrowie' forest, were excavated. In one of these a clay vessel was found.

28. *Rakowa* district of Sambor

Twenty-eight burial mounds were found in the forest of Rakowa forming six groups, extending from SW to NE, over a distance of about 1,700m (Plan 2). The groups consisted of from two to four mounds except one, the largest, which included eleven barrows. The distance between the separate groups varied from 150 to 500m. At least nine mounds bore traces of previous excavation. It was said that in one of these, in the south-westernmost group, a stone battle-axe and a flint axe were found.

In 1937, seven mounds were excavated by a team of students of Prehistory of the University of Cracow under my direction with the assistance of Dr R. Jamka. Five of these formed part of the largest group in the area called Pod Horisznem; two others (nos. VI and VII) belonged to two different smaller groups. The material excavated was given to the Archaeological Museum in Cracow.

Barrow-grave I (Plan 10:4). About 20m in diameter, 2m high. A few large trees growing on it prevented us from excavating the whole mound. The ancient ground surface was at a depth of 1·3m from the top of the mound. Three metres SE of the centre a layer of charcoal lay on the surface covering an area 2 by 1m. A rectangular shaft-grave (A) was uncovered 10cm under it, 2 by 1m in area, orientated nearly SW–NE, 25cm deep. Nothing was found in it. One metre N of its NW corner, directly in the centre of the area covered by the mounds, the lower part of an undecorated tulip-shaped pot (vessel I-1-2) (Plate 23:6) lay on the ancient surface while other sherds of this pot were scattered further north over an area of 2 square metres. The pot was 26cm high, body 16–17cm in diameter. At a distance of 1m NE of the grave lay (also broken in sherds) an undecorated bowl (vessel 1-4), probably 17cm high, its aperture 17cm in diameter, base *c.* 7·5cm in diameter. Both vessels were made of a tempered clay paste, with a small admixture of crushed shells, both were poorly baked and very brittle. They were brown in colour, their surface covered with a thin layer of slip, smoothed.

Several loose sherds of the two above vessels and probably

[24] G. Ossowski, *ZWAK*, vol. XIV, 1890, pp. 24 f. Kozłowski (op. cit., note 2: 1924), p. 191.

of a third similar one also, were scattered over the ancient surface, mainly NE and W of the centre of the area covered by the mound. The area was also strewn with charcoal. In its western part was found the only flint object, a knife or scraper, made of a small flake.

Barrow-grave II (Plan 10:3). 14m in diameter, 50cm high. Several small potsherds were found scattered over an area 3m in diameter in the centre of the mound of the ancient surface, at a depth of about 70cm. Many lumps of charcoal and of fired clay, a fragment of whetstone made of limestone, and a flint blade (knife) 9·2cm long, the sole flint object, were also found here. The latter was made of banded flint. Traces of a very shallow shaft (grave) were visible in the centre of the area, but neither its size nor shape could be established. A few odd potsherds lay around the area. They belonged to at least two vessels. One of these, brown in colour, had walls about 12mm thick, its rim 14mm wide, flat; the body had a raised 'thickening' round the vessel. The other vessel must have been much smaller, its base 5cm in diameter, and an incised chevron decoration was visible on a fragment of the wall. The larger vessel was made of tolerably well silted clay paste, the surface covered with a thin layer of slip; the smaller was brittle, made of tempered clay paste in the manner proper to the Corded Ware.

Barrow-grave III (Plan 10:1, 2). 12m in diameter, 60cm high, close to the barrow-grave II. Very small odd potsherds, lumps of fired clay and charcoal only were scattered mainly on two levels, at 30–40cm deep, and again at a depth of about 50–60cm, evidently on the ancient ground surface. They formed two loose agglomerations, one in the northern part of the area covered by the mound, mainly at a depth of 30–40cm, the other on the lower level, mainly SW of the centre. In each a single small flint was found. No traces of any grave were noticed, but the two concentrations described above suggest they were sites of two burials, the skeletons of which had decayed completely and disappeared.

Barrow-grave IV (Plan 11:1). Situated near barrow-grave I, NE of it; this was one of the largest mounds, 33–20m in diameter. A trench 29m long, 1·4m wide, widened to 4·5m in two places in the centre, was dug across the barrow from W–E. The funds available did not allow us to engage on excavation of the whole mound. Only a few concentrations of charcoal, a few animal bones and a polished stone were found.

Barrow-grave V (Plan 11:2). Situated east of the above, 13m in diameter, 60cm high. Only small lumps of charcoal were found, scattered over the ancient surface at a depth of 60cm, mainly in the eastern part of the area under the mound; in addition a few odd potsherds—one consisting of a rim with a row of short nail incisions—a badly damaged axe made of yellow slate, 7cm long, and a sole flint blade (knife) were found there. The last-named lay in the southern part of the area, at a depth of 90cm somewhat deeper than other objects mentioned above. It probably marks the site of the grave, but no traces of any burial were actually found.

Barrow-grave VI. This formed part of a group of four mounds at a distance of about 230m SW of the barrow-grave I. It was 12m in diameter, about 50cm high. Here only lumps of charcoal scattered over the northern part of the area under the mound, on the ancient surface at a depth of 40cm, were found.

Barrow-grave VII (Plan 11:3). This lay in a section of the forest known as 'Na jedlinie', about 600m SW of barrow-grave VI, and formed part of a group of four mounds. It was 14m in diameter, about 70cm high.

In the mound itself, lumps of charcoal appeared in several places. On the ancient ground surface, at a depth of 40–50cm, the whole central area, irregular in plan and about 7m in diameter, was copiously strewn with small lumps of charcoal, or charcoal crushed almost to powder. In a few places charcoal, as dust or in lumps, appeared in a continuous layer and in two places, A and B, formed well-marked concentrations. One of these in the western part of the area uncovered (B), was nearly 2 by 1m in size, orientated W–E. The other was in the central part, a little north of the centre (A). Beneath it was a shaft, about 70–80cm deep, reaching to a depth of 1·25m from the top of the mound; it was nearly oval in plan, 3 by 2m in area, orientated SW–NE. It was filled with earth strongly mixed with crushed charcoal or charcoal lumps. No traces of any skeleton were noticed. In a few places, mainly near the two concentrations of charcoal, lay small potsherds. The two concentrations undoubtedly mark the sites of burials.

29. *Rzeplin* district of Jarosław

Two barrow-graves, about 16m in diameter, 30–40cm high, situated close to the border of Siennów, were investigated by me in 1935.[25] Nothing was found in either of them.

30. *Siedliska* district of Przemyśl

In 1886, during the construction of a fort by the Austrian Army, graves were uncovered on the top of a hill, point 302. They were probably low barrow-graves. Skeletons found at a depth of 3m were in a crouched position and some grave goods were found near them. Most of the latter were given, in two parts, A and B[26] to the archaeological collection of the Jagiellonian University in Cracow.

Objects in group A, which probably originated from a single barrow-grave, consisted of: (a) one damaged, thin axe made of dark flint, 8·5cm long (Fig. 16:25); (b) another axe with a thick butt, rectangular in section, made of a brownish spotted variety of flint, 10cm long; (c) a small battle-axe of dark diorite, 9·5cm long, very well made and polished with a low placed shaft-hole.

Group B consisted of the following eight objects: (a) a cord-decorated beaker with the base wider than the aperture, 10cm high (Plate 6:18); (b) two miniature cups (Plate 6:13, 14), undecorated, 3·4 and 3·5cm high; (c) small battle-axe of type *z-1* (Fig. 14:5) made of yellow slate, 8cm long; (d) axe made of yellow slate, rectangular in section, 7·4cm long (Fig. 15:8); (e) axe made of 'Bug' variety of flint, nearly rectangular in section (Fig. 16:21), 8cm long; (f) axe made of a similar variety of flint, nearly triangular (oval) in section (Fig. 16:8), 8 cm long; (g) a boar tusk, unperforated.

[25] T. Sulimirski, 'Ziemianka starszej kultury ceramiki wstęgowej i kurhany w Rzeplinie, pow. Jarosław', *Acta AC*, vol. II, 1960, pp. 126 ff.

[26] W. Demetrykiewicz, 'Neolityczne groby szkieletów t. zw. siedzących w Przemyskiem i Krakowskiem', *Materiały antropologiczno-archeologiczne i etnograficzne*, vol. III, Kraków 1898, pp. 78 ff. Kozłowski (op. cit., note 2: 1924), p. 193.

In 1902, A. Chizzola[27] excavated three barrow-graves. Nos. II and III contained skeletons but no grave goods. The skeleton in grave I was almost entirely decayed: by it were six vessels, two stone battle-axes, flint axe, a copper or bronze ring and another of lead. The fate of these objects is unknown, but their description was given by A. Chizzola: (a) two beakers, 13 and 14cm high with flat bases, undecorated; (b) a handled cup 8·5cm high with a few horizontal ribs; (c) a vessel 9cm high with an everted rim; (d) a handled vessel (jug?) with a large body, 10cm high, its upper part below the neck decorated with horizontal incisions (grooves); (e) an undecorated vessel, 8cm high, with a large body, provided with two opposite lugs, base narrow, neck cylindrical; (f) stone hammer-shaped mace-head 11cm long, both ends blunt; (g) stone battle-axe 11cm long; (h) flint axe 7·3cm long; (i) oval copper or bronze ring, 4·5cm wide, round in section, 8mm thick, ends thinner; (j) lead ring 4·5cm in diameter.

31. *Siennów* district of Przeworsk.

A barrow-grave in the 'Mogiły' field, some 400m N of two mounds excavated by me at Rzeplin, was investigated by me in 1935.[28] This was 26m in diameter, 50cm high. A few potsherds were found on the ancient surface, under the mound, at a distance of 4m E of the centre. The grave-shaft (Plan 9:1) was uncovered about 3·5m N of the centre. It was rectangular in plan with rounded corners, 1·9 by 1·5m in area, orientated N–S about 55–60cm deep. In its filling, mainly in the northern part, two animal teeth and a few Neolithic potsherds were excavated. On the bottom of the shaft a layer of planks appeared; they were almost completely decayed but well visible. They were placed obliquely across the grave, sinking westwards. A deepening of the shaft by a further 40cm was found under them (i.e. to about 1·2m from the top of the mound) and excavated in the sand constituting a substratum under the yellow loess. This lower portion was recessed under the western wall of the grave-shaft and was 1m wide. No traces of the skeleton were found; it had decayed completely.

32. *Sierakośce* district of Przemyśl

A cord-decorated amphora with two lugs on the upper part of the body (in the Museum at Przemyśl) seems to have originated from a destroyed grave.[29]

33. *Sobiecin* district of Jarosław

Three vessels were in the Dzieduszycki Museum in Lwów before the war (Plate 7:11–13) presumably found in a barrow-grave, all typical of the Funnel Beaker culture. These were an amphora with two lugs, a two-lugged beaker and a large handled jug, all undecorated.[30]

34. *Stare Sioło* district of Lubaczów

In a barrow-grave two destroyed vessels and a flint axe of Valby-type (Fig. 15:18), 15cm long, and a battle-axe very thoroughly made of a green variety of stone, 12·5cm long, were excavated.[31] The two latter were in the Dzieduszycki Museum (nos. 62, 61) before the war.

35. *Stojańce* district of Mościska

A barrow-grave, 20m in diameter, 1·2m high, situated in the small 'Gaik' forest, was excavated by me in 1935 (Plan 8:2). Its mound consisted of nearly black, very hard and compressed earth with an admixture in some places of yellow earth. The ancient surface occurred at a depth of 1·15m from the summit of the mound. It was comprised of a 20cm layer of brown humus, which gradually became of an increasingly yellow colour further down, and pure yellow loess started at a depth of 1·8m. Some fragments of pottery (b), lumps of fired clay and a flint knife (a) (Fig. 12:6) were found at the top, under the forest loess and in the mound, on the northern side; S of the centre, at a depth of 50–70cm, a few potsherds (b) and small scattered accumulations of lumps of fired clay, or irregular bricks, lay in the mound in several places especially SW of the centre (c); deeper under these 'bricks' at a depth of about 1·2m the contour of the grave-shaft appeared on the ancient surface (g). It was about 2·3 by 1·4m in size, rectangular in plan, orientated W–E. It was about 60cm deep, its sides narrowing, and the floor was only 1·95 by 1·1m in area, lined with planks, which were still recognizable although almost completely decayed. Three small potsherds were found here, but no traces of skeleton.

About 2m north of the grave, an accumulation of loose, red fired clay was uncovered on the ancient surface (d); it formed a layer about 60cm in diameter, 5–10cm thick, and evidently marked the site of a hearth plastered with clay. Near it lay a few decorated and undecorated potsherds typical of the Funnel Beaker culture (e) (Fig. 12:1, 2), and further east a small flint knife or scraper, 4cm long (f). This was very probably the site of a funeral hut or other sepulchral structure destroyed during the funeral. No details of its construction were apparent.

All the material excavated was given to the Prehistoric Institute of the University of Lwów. Larger lumps of fired clay, irregular bricks, bore imprints of palling, rods, etc. The potsherds belonged to a few vessels, each of which was represented by a single or sometimes two or more fragments. The following were distinguished: a large vessel made of a tempered clay paste, dark inside, covered with a thin reddish slip on the outside; a similarly made smaller vessel; a few fragments belonged to a large vessel, most probably a Thuringian amphora; a few small potsherds were made in a manner typical of Corded Ware. Of particular interest, however, were a number of potsherds characteristic of the Funnel Beaker pottery (Fig. 12:1, 2). There was a large fragment of a nearly cylindrical, undecorated beaker, a rim with a row of vertical incisions (a decoration proper to the Funnel Beaker pottery), and a few more sherds of this type. All these potsherds were found in the area north of the grave, near the ruined hearth. Besides pottery, and the two knives mentioned previously, only a few flint chips and a flint hammer were excavated.

[27] Chizzola (op. cit., note 2), pp. 139 f.
[28] Sulimirski, loc. cit., note 25.
[29] Machnik (op. cit., note 7), p. 65, Fig. 1:3.
[30] Kozłowski (op. cit., note 2: 1924), p. 194, Pl. XXVII:4, 8, 13.
[31] Ibid., p. 194.

36. *Tarnawka* district of Łańcut

In a barrow-grave 12m in diameter, 1m high, excavated by local peasants, a flint axe and potsherds were found.[32] According to information kindly given by Dr G. Leńczyk, the potsherds, three in all, were undecorated and much resembled pottery excavated in the barrow-graves at Rakowa, described previously (no. 28), in type and character of the clay paste used.

37. *Zagórzyce* district of Ropczyce

A light-grey flint axe (Fig. 16:1) lenticular in section, was given to the Archaeological Museum in Cracow. It was found in a barrow-grave.

2. THE SUB-CARPATHIAN GROUP

A. Graves

38. *Błudniki* district of Stanisławów

A burial-mound was excavated by Dr Szaraniewicz in 1884. It was 1·5m high, and only one flint knife was found in it.[33] This was in the collection of the Ukrainian Narodnyi Dom in Lwów before the war. A flint axe, presumably found in a barrow-grave, is at the State Archaeological Museum in Warsaw.

39. *Bolechowce* district of Drohobycz

There were two groups of burial mounds here, one in the forest, the other on the summit of a hill which extended between Bolechowce and Stebnik. In the latter group about thirty mounds were counted, one of which, on point 331, was excavated by Dr M. Roska[34] in 1916–17. It was nearly 2m high, 35 by 51m in diameter, but the study of its cross-sections published by Dr M. Roska reveals that in fact it was less than 24m in diameter. The archaeological remains excavated were deposited in the Museum at Cluj, Transilvania.

Dr M. Roska regarded this burial mound as the vestiges of a settlement on two levels, the uppermost having pottery mostly of coarse make, and the lower with Corded Ware. He published a number of cross-sections which are completely in agreement with the cross-sections of burial-mounds at Kołpiec which I investigated and which are situated at a distance of some three to four kilometres. These cross-sections show that the accumulation of the mound, under cultivation level, was fairly fine and grey in colour, whereas a core of black, beaten earth lying on virgin soil was in the centre of the barrow. In Roska's view, this earth was deliberately brought from a distance for building the settlement and was later beaten hard. In fact, however, this earth was brought from the immediate vicinity of the barrow. This black earth of *chernozem* type known in Podolia covered the entire Sub-Carpathians at this period, as is evident from the results of investigating barrows at various sites in the area. Climatic changes resulted in the humus it contained undergoing decomposition and the earth lost its dark colour. It survived only under the protective cover of the large mounds.

Roska's description shows that some dark-brown potsherds of handmade ware, made of clay paste tempered with sand, were found at the summit of the mound, under the cultivated earth at a depth of 50cm. These included a large fragment of a rim ornamented with a raised band with finger-tip impressions. Similar pottery was also found in the summit of Barrow-grave II at Kołpiec. Several traces of hearths were also found here. In the centre of the area covered with the mound, an area elipsoid in shape showing traces of having been fired was uncovered in the lower layer, i.e. (as appears from the description) on the ancient surface. It was approximately 20m long, 12m wide. A few holes were noticed in it, the largest being about 2m in diameter and situated in the centre of the mound. This was evidently the grave-shaft, but the skeleton was not found, as it had completely decayed and disappeared. Two cord-decorated vessels found on the periphery of the area under the mound probably mark the site of another grave. A flint axe, 6cm long, oval in section, a few flint flakes, a flint scraper or knife 8cm long, and a flint arrow-head 1·4cm long, triangular in shape, were also found here. One of the vessels of which only the base, 6cm in diameter, has survived, was probably a beaker. Another is presumed to be an amphora with a cylindrical neck, with horizontal cord-impressed lines, made of well-silted clay paste, dark grey inside, reddish-brown outside. A few cord-decorated potsherds from other vessels were also published by M. Roska.

40. *Bratkowce* district of Stanisławów

In 1935, a barrow-grave with a cremation burial was investigated by Dr J. Pasternak.[35] Vessels typical of the Komarów culture and a flint flake were found in it.

41. *Chromohorb* district of Stryj

A skeleton was uncovered presumably in a barrow-grave near which lay a flint axe.[36]

42. *Daszawa* district of Stryj

Over forty barrow-graves are situated on a high elevation to the south of the village: they are in groups varying from a few to over a dozen. They are connected with the burial mounds situated in the woods of the neighbouring villages of Jeseptycze and Oleksice. They are from 20 to 30m in diameter, and from 50cm to 3m in height. The mounds situated on cultivated land or clearings have been much ploughed. In 1930, a flint battle-axe of the Fatyanovo type, 20cm long and made of a greenish stone, was ploughed up in one of the mounds situated on the clearing. This was deposited in the Prehistoric Institute of the University of Lwów.

In 1932, I excavated[37] two barrow-graves situated on the

[32] G. Leńczyk, 'Nowe stanowiska przedhistoryczne w pow.rzeszowskim', *Spr. PAU*, vol. XLIX, 1948, pp. 167 f.

[33] Janusz (op. cit., note 9), p. 213.

[34] M. Roska, 'Glanement des antiquités de l'époque préhistorique en Galicie', *Dolgozatok-Traveaux*, vol. IX, Kolozsvar 1918, pp. 25 ff., Figs. 1–9.

[35] J. Pasternak, 'Moje badania terenowe w 1935 r', *ZOW*, vol. XI, 1936, p. 132. Id. (op. cit., note 16: 1933–6), p. 13.

[36] Kozłowski (op. cit., note 2: 1924), p. 190.

[37] T. Sulimirski, 'Sprawozdanie z działalności lwowskiego ośrodka prehistorycznego', *ZOW*, vol. X, 1935, p. 22. The 'Fatyanovo' stone battle-axe was published by me in *Polska przedhistoryczna* (op. cit., note 19), p. 229, Fig. 56.

border of Jeseptycze village, in a cultivated field of the Basiowka hamlet. These barrow-graves were part of a group of twelve, one of which was in the Jeseptycze area. Two other barrow-graves of this group had been destroyed, one during the erection of a house, the other having been cut across during the installation of a water-pipe.

Barrow-grave I. 22m in diameter, 70cm high. Crossed by a field road, the mound occurred 20cm below the forest humus: it was grey at first, while it became increasingly dark at a greater depth and particularly in the centre. Fossil humus at ancient ground level was found under the mound, 70cm in depth. It was blackish in colour in the lower layers, gradually becoming virgin soil. Several scattered, non-typical potsherds brick-red in colour, some lumps of ochre and one flint flake were found some 5m from the centre, on the ancient level and some 90cm in depth from the summit of the barrow-grave.

Barrow-grave II. This was situated 35m south-east of the other, much ploughed over, 18m in diameter, 50cm in height. Its cross-section was similar to the other. After removal of the mound and at a depth of about 65cm, three objects were found lying together in the centre of the grave and on the ancient surface: these were a totally crushed tulip-shaped vessel on its side, a bowl with two small lugs (Plate 17:7) and a cup, also totally crushed. A handful of charcoal was found about 2m from these, on the same level, while traces of a hearth about 60cm in diameter were found about 2m to the north of the objects. The earth here was calcined, with ash and charcoal dust in it, with a small flint flake near by. The grave must have been situated somewhere in the area between the objects and the charcoal lump: the burial had been placed in the ancient earth without a shaft being dug. However no traces of skeleton were found.

The tulip-shaped vessel was 26cm high, its lower diameter 19cm. It had an everted rim, a flat bottom, without ornament, made of clay with a large admixture of sand. The bowl (Plate 17:7) was 14cm high, with body diameter 19·5cm, having two perforated lugs on the body, placed opposite each other, and an incised chevron ornament under the rim. It was not possible to reconstruct it. All were made in the same way, were insufficiently baked and brittle.

43. *Horodyszcze* district of Sambor

Three barrow-graves forming a triangular group were excavated by Dr W. Kobilnyk[38] in 1932. They lay on common pasture grounds known as 'Mohyłki'. The remains were given to the Museum 'Boykivščyna' in Sambor.

Barrow-grave I. This was the largest of the group, 25m in diameter, 1m high. The upper 50cm layer was composed of fine clear humus, the other 50cm was fine, ash-coloured or blackish towards the centre of the mound. The ancient surface occurred at 80cm down and was formed of degradate chernozem, darker above but more ash-coloured below, gradually becoming virgin soil, 40cm thick altogether. Clear virgin soil occurred at a depth of 1·2m from the summit of the mound.

A fairly thick layer of charcoal was uncovered under the mound and in the centre of the grave at a depth of 75cm covering an area 5m in diameter a heap, about 30cm in diameter, of calcined human bones, appertaining to a young person was found under the charcoal layer. Below this, a regular circle 1m in diameter, formed by nine large stones (sandstone) varying from 10–25 and 25–40cm in size, dug in the ancient surface, was found at a depth of 1·25m. The shaft within this area contained a large amount of charcoal, while inside and on the bottom was found a spherical flint hammer: on the western side and on the stones were two bronze bracelets (Fig. 31:3, 4) an iron pin (Fig. 31:6) and two kaolin beads. Two clay vessels were about 20cm from these objects, on the ancient surface under the stones (Fig. 31:1, 5).

Soon after these investigations were terminated, I dug a pit in an unexplored part of the mound to check its cross-section. At 3m east of the centre of the mound, an urn filled with calcined human bones was uncovered. This lay at a depth of 35cm and its upper part had been broken by ploughing. Another vessel, totally destroyed by ploughing, was beside it. Both clearly derived from a secondary burial.

One of the vessels found near the circle of stones was a tulip-shaped cup (Fig. 31:5), 14·5cm high, diameter of body 11·1cm. Its edge was obliquely marked on the outside with four parallel lines encircling the vessel on the neck. Made of tempered clay paste, its surface was covered with thin slip, brownish in colour and in the characteristic manner of the Komarów culture. It was highly brittle. The other vessel (Fig. 31:1) near it was of similar type but larger in size, made in the same manner. It was about 26cm high, diameter of the body about 19cm, and had two slightly marked raised bands round the neck. Both bronze bracelets (Fig. 31:3, 4) were of the same type with overlying thinner terminals 58 and 64mm in diameter and made of ingots almost circular in cross-section from 8 to 9mm thick. The iron pin (Fig. 31:6) about 8cm long, was very much rusted and broken into three. Both kaolin beads were disc-shaped, 4mm in diameter, 2·5mm thick, while the scraper was made of a blade of the 'Bug' variety of flint.

The urn had a flat bottom, 16·5cm in diameter, the sides thick (1·2cm) and not ornamented: it was made of a strongly-tempered clay paste, highly brittle. Its rim was flat. The other vessel found near it appeared to be a large bowl, with a flat bottom 13cm in diameter, the rim entirely smooth, made of strongly-tempered clay paste, and very brittle.

Barrow-grave II. This was 25m in diameter, 75cm high. A road cut it in two and one half was excavated. Only a few potsherds characteristic of the Late Bronze Age and a few calcined human bones were found.

Barrow-grave III. This was 25m in diameter, 80cm high, much damaged by ploughing. A quantity of charcoal and calcined human bones extending over an area of one square metre was found under the cultivated level, at a depth of 35cm. Two entirely broken vessels were found near the bones, with a third about 1·1m away, also entirely broken. These vessels were of the same manufacture and type as the vessel in Barrow-grave I. One appeared to be a tulip-shaped vessel, with a flat rim about 1cm wide, of the same type as the vessels in the Rakowa barrow-grave. The second was smaller, with a rim obliquely cut. Only some disconnected fragments remained of the third vessel. All three were similar in

[38] В. Кобільник, Могила ч. I, II, III в Городищі, Літопис Бойківщини, vol. 2, Sambir 1933, pp. 31 ff., Pl. III.

manufacture to the vessel in which a bronze hoard of the Late Bronze Age was found at Sambor.[39]

44. *Kałusz*

A flint axe, 9cm long (Fig. 15:5), presumably found in 1875 in a barrow-grave is in the Archaeological Museum in Cracow (no. 3208). A large barrow-grave cemetery has been recorded in the neighbourhood of the town.[40]

45. *Kavsko* district of Medenice

In 1956–7, six mounds situated in swampy meadows, scattered over an area of 1 square kilometre, in the wide valley of the Stupnica, were excavated by K. V. Bernyakovyč.[41] Shallow holes, irregularly oval or round in plan, from 50cm to 2·9m in diameter, 10 to 23cm deep, were uncovered on the ancient surface under the mounds; they were filled in with ashes, charcoal mixed with earth, and potsherds, sometimes various implements were found in them. Several dark patches of various size, round or oval in plan, from 45 × 148cm to 60 × 195 cm in diameter, were distinguished on the ancient surface. No traces of any skeleton were found in the mounds but in one (no. 5) a cremation burial was uncovered in a hole. Remains found in the mounds were of two types. In each mound flint axes, lenticular in cross-section, stone 'hammer-axes' or battle-axes, and vessels, entire or in sherds, etc., were excavated which did not differ in any respect from the usual grave-goods of the Sub-Carpathian barrow-graves. In addition to these, potsherds, flint implements, quern stones, etc., which do not form part of the usual endowment of burial mounds, were excavated here.

The above mounds are considered by Bernyakovyč and Sviešnikov[42] to be the remains of a settlement, or rather traces of seasonal encampments on pasture grounds. However, I do not share these views, and am inclined to regard them as burial mounds perhaps of a similar nature to those excavated by me at Koropuż or Stojańce. The absence of skeletons is no evidence against these views: this is a phenomenon attested in most Sub-Carpathian barrow-graves; the acidity of the soil resulted in the complete decomposition of all bones except those which were, at least partly, calcined. Pottery excavated in these mounds has never been found in the remains of undisputed settlements and flint axes and stone battle-axes represent typical grave-goods of the Sub-Carpathian barrow-graves. The fact that in one mound (no. 5) a burial was actually uncovered also points to the character of these relics. Patches of charcoal and small holes were found by me in the ancient surface in several barrow-graves I excavated, e.g. at Rakowa, where the size of the mounds leaves no room for doubts as to their sepulchral purpose.

In the description below, particulars concerning the mounds investigated and objects excavated are taken from the brief reports published so far; Mr I. K. Sviešnikov has very kindly supplemented them in some details in his correspondence with me.

Mound 1. 18–20m in diameter, 86cm high. Three 'hearth-holes' and a few patches strewn with charcoal were uncovered on the ancient surface. A stone battle-axe of type *x*-1, a stone mace-head, three flint axes, eight flint implements (knives and scrapers), twenty-two flint flakes, flint core, two 'querns' and fifty-seven potsherds were excavated. Of the latter, a cord-decorated bowl with a flat base has been reconstructed. According to a sketch plan of this mound, kindly shown me by Mr Sviešnikov, all these remains were found on two levels: those in the north-western part of the area lay at a depth of 40–60cm, probably on the ancient surface, whereas those further east lay at a depth of 80–100cm. Their distribution is somewhat confusing, but the distance between the axes, battle-axe and concentrations of potsherds seems to suggest that there were at least two graves about four metres apart, both orientated SW–NE, one on the ancient surface, the other some 40cm deeper.

Mound 2. 13–14m in diameter, 64cm high. Nine 'hearth-holes' and traces of a large hearth were uncovered. Holes reached to a depth of about 90cm whereas the hearth extended to a depth of 40cm, evidently over the ancient surface. On the same level lay two vessels, but the third and a few concentrations of potsherds lay a little deeper. The objects excavated were: one stone battle-axe, two flint axes, six flint knives, scrapers, etc., two flint cores, nineteen flint flakes, one fragment of saddle-quern, seventy-one potsherds and three vessels. Besides, seven trapezoid points were found which differed in no respect from Tardenoisian arrow-points; they are, however, considered to be inlays of composite sickles, as they all have the edge shinning, evidence that they were used for a purpose other than an arrow-head. The vessels were: (a) a wide, low cord-decorated bowl with a rounded base similar to that from barrow-grave VIII at Kołpiec (Fig. 12:14); (b) a flask-shaped vessel with a flat base and a cylindrical cord-decorated neck (Fig. 12:15); (c) a flat based, undecorated vessel, apparently a deep bowl, the upper part of which is missing.

Mound 3. 22·5 by 24m in diameter, 60cm high. One 'hearth-pit' and traces of two hearths on the ancient surface were uncovered. The following objects were excavated: flint dagger (Plate 11:4), flint axe, two flint knives and seven other flint implements, three flint cores, thirty flint flakes, three trapezoid 'arrow-points' (or parts of a composite sickle), fragment of a saddle-quern, one vessel and forty-nine potsherds. The vessel was a small undecorated cup.

Mound 4. 14m in diameter, 48cm high. One 'hearth-pit' and traces of four hearths were uncovered. The objects excavated were: a broken flint knife and ten other flint implements, one flint core, thirty flint flakes, five trapezoid 'arrow-points' (inlays), two vessels and 172 potsherds. One of the vessels was a wide deep bowl (Fig. 29:1) with a rounded body, everted rim, and a flat base; its only decoration was a raised band round the upper part of the body. The other vessel was an undecorated small handled wide-mouthed

[39] В. Кобільник, З археології Бойківщини, Літопис Бойківщини, vol. I, Sambir 1931, pp. 39 ff., Pls. I, II. K. Żurowski, 'Zabytki brązowe z młodszej epoki brązu i wczesnego okresu żelaza z dorzecza górnego Dniestru', *Prz.A.*, vol. VIII, 1949, pp. 197 f.

[40] Janusz (op. cit., note 9), p. 153.

[41] К. В. Берняковин, Роботи прикарпатської археологічної експедиції в 1956–1957 рр. Археологічні роботи музею, Lviv 1959, pp. 29 ff., Pls. I–III. Id., 'Sidliště lidu se šňůrovou keramikou na hornim Dněstru a Sanu', *Arch.R.*, vol. XI, 1959, pp. 692 ff., Figs. 262–4.

[42] И. К. Свешников, Памятники племен бронзового века Прикарпатья и западной Подолии, Moscow 1958, p. 9.

cup with a narrow base, calling to mind Unetice types (Fig. 29:4).

Mound 5. 12m in diameter, 45cm high. Four patches were uncovered consisting of cinders, and also a shaft, 4·45 by 3·7m wide, filled in with ashes, charcoal and calcined human bones. The latter is said to have been a secondary cremation burial, which does not seem convincing. Cremation took place on the spot and the bones were not completely calcined. Fragments of the skull (of a person 30–35 years of age) lay in the southern part of the shaft. Some 90cm north of the shaft, at a depth of 25cm on the ancient surface, was found a decorated handled cup typical of the Komarów culture (Fig. 29:5). Other objects excavated were: nine flint implements, one saddle-quern, one flint flake, two vessels and eighty-six potsherds. One of the vessels was a deep undecorated beaker or bowl (Fig. 29:2) similar to that from mound 4, but somewhat smaller, a beaker with a flat rim, decorated with a raised band around the neck (Fig. 29:6).

Mound 6. 14m in diameter, 25cm high. No hearths were found under the mound: the following objects were excavated: two flint knives, five flint flakes, a cylindrical single-handled, cord-decorated mug (Fig. 12:11), typical of the late stage of the Corded Ware culture, and eighteen potsherds of some other vessels.

46. *Kołpiec* district of Drohobycz

On high ground over the valley of the Tyśmienica, in the 'Dąbrowa Kołpiecka' forest was a large barrow-grave cemetery (Plan 3:2). Several mounds were destroyed in 1907 during the construction here of reservoirs and only eight mounds at the eastern end of the area, and one at its western end, at a distance of about 600m from the above group, survived. Seven of these (nos. 2–8) at the eastern end were investigated in 1932 by me jointly with Dr M. Śmiszko, assisted by students of prehistory of Lwów University.[43] About 1·5km east of this group and in the same woodland, two very low barrow-graves were situated: both of these were investigated by us (nos. 9, 10). The third group, consisting of two barrow-graves, was about 3km from the woodland, south of Kołpiec village and on common pasture-land forming a wedge in fields of the neighbouring Stebnik and Solec villages. One of these barrow-graves was excavated in 1916 by M. Roska and published as the Stebnik barrow-grave (no. 55): the other, excavated by us in 1932, will be described as Stebnik Barrow-grave II, to avoid confusion. The archaeological materials from the barrow-grave we excavated are now in the Lviv Historical Museum.

Barrow-grave 1. This, 21m in diameter, 2m high, was not investigated.

Barrow-grave 2 (Plan 28:1). This was 28m in diameter and 3m high. It was overgrown with large oak trees, so that investigation was restricted to making a trench 4m wide, widened in the centre to 5m. The cross-section was as follows: under the forest humus layer (40cm deep) was a mound 2·7m deep (reckoning from the top of the barrow-grave). Its upper section was fairly fine, ash-coloured and, in places, yellowish, turning darker and becoming almost black as the depth increased: in the deeper portions it was also harder and closer-packed, particularly in the centre for the last 70cm. A layer of fossil humus extended under the mound. It was comprised of black, very hard rich earth, about 40cm thick, gradually becoming virgin soil underneath.

In the centre of the barrow near the edge of the mound and the ancient surface, was a layer of yellow clay, arched in shape and extending for 3m. The clay was about 20cm thick, and had been excavated from the bottom of the grave-shaft, which reached into virgin soil. The grave-shaft (a) in the centre of the area covered by the barrow was rectangular 1·8 by 1·3m, orientated north-east by south-west, and dug 1m into the ancient surface, about 60cm being in virgin soil. Its bottom was 3·7m in depth, reckoning from the summit of the mound.

Traces of hearths comprising charcoal and ashes and potsherds were uncovered at several points on the summit of the mound where it bordered with forest humus, and also in the lower section of the forest humus itself. The pottery was hand made, brittle, made of clay paste with a large admixture of crushed stone, the sides thick. Lumps of charcoal varying in size and some flint flakes were also found and a few potsherds (e, f) at various points in the mound itself, especially west of the centre, at a depth of 1·10m (g). Under the mound and on the ancient surface, at 6m west of the grave shaft was found a small broken vessel (b) which could not be reconstructed nor its shape determined: some charcoal and traces of ash were with it. Around the grave were traces of a layer of logs(?) about 7–8m in diameter (h).

The grave shaft contained no traces of skeleton, as it had decomposed entirely. An axe (c) (Fig. 16:4) 9·5cm long, lenticular in cross-section, carefully polished and made of dark flint with lighter patches, was found in the north-west corner of the shaft. Lumps of red ochre occurred at several points on the bottom of the shaft. The shaft had been covered with oak logs, the imprints of which were well preserved on the edges of the shaft (d).

Barrow-grave 3 (Plan 29:3). This was 18m in diameter, 1m high, cut across by a pathway. Its cross-section resembled that of the large Barrow-grave 2, except that the degradation of chernozem was more advanced due to the protective layer being thinner. The mound of the barrow, 50cm deep, lay under a 40cm layer of forest humus. The fossil humus under the mound, at a depth of 90cm from the top of the mound, was grey instead of black and gradually became virgin soil as the depth increased.

Three small vessels next to each other were found in the centre of the mound on the ancient surface: these were a handled cup (a-1), a bowl (a-3) and beaker (a-2) with a flint scraper (a-4) near by and a battle-axe (a-5) of type *y*-3 about 60cm away. A lump of ochre occurred about 1m SE of the vessels (c) but no traces of skeleton were found, nor was there a grave-shaft. The burial must have been on the ancient surface. Finally, *c.* 3m NE of the vessels some charcoal was strewn (b).

The handled cup, being excessively fragile, disintegrated. Its diameter was about 4cm on top. The bowl was fairly wide, cord decorated and with a circular bottom. The beaker, also cord decorated, was about 10cm in diameter. All three vessels were a sand-gritted ware, insufficiently baked, highly fragile. Their reconstruction was not practicable. The battle-

[43] Sulimirski, loc. cit., note 37.

axe was of yellow slate, 10·5cm long, very flat, carelessly made.

Barrow-grave 4 (Plan 29:4). This was 18m in diameter, 40cm high. Several fragments of hand-made vessels, a sand-gritted ware were found 3m NW of the centre, immediately below the forest humus (a). Deeper, at 45cm a flat flint axe (Fig. 16:2), very carefully made of light-coloured, white-spotted flint, 12·7cm long, lenticular in cross-section (b), and a larger flint blade (c) (a dagger) (Plate 11:5) were found next to each other. The blade was made of a broad flake, 11cm long, 3·8cm wide at one end, and 1cm at the other. Both lay over the grave-shaft (A) which was 1·60 by 1m, orientated SW–NE, dug about 50cm in the ancient ground. Nothing was found in it.

Barrow-grave 5 (Plan 28:4). This was 30m in diameter, 50cm high, cut across by a trench 5m wide, widened to 7m in the central part. Several fragments of rough pottery and traces of hearths about 50cm in diameter were found in the centre, at a depth of 80–90cm, on the ancient surface (c, d, e). The grave-shaft (k) occurred in the centre: it was rectangular, 2m by 1·7m orientated W–E, dug 75cm into the ancient surface and extending to virgin soil. A flint knife (h) was uncovered on the edge of the shaft, at the ancient level on the north-west side: a flint axe (a) was found on the opposite edge (Plate 8:2d). No trace of skeleton was found, though there were clear traces of red ochre on the bottom of the shaft. The shaft had been covered in with a layer of oak logs 2·6 by 2·2m in area, traces of which were visible on the edges of the shaft.

Traces of a hearth in the form of small pieces of charcoal, a lump of calcined clay and potsherds were found on the ancient surface 3m west of the shaft (i). About 3m further in the same direction, and on the same level, were heaped calcined animal bones covering an area of 30 by 40cm mixed with earth (b). The remains of another hearth about 20 by 30cm were found on the opposite side of the grave-shaft, about 7m to the east (g). A small vessel with two lugs (Plate 8:2c) was found at a depth of 1·2m in a shallow hole on a somewhat thin layer of calcined clay, with a necklace of greenish faience beads near it (Plate 8:2a, b). Three metres further off, almost on the periphery of the mound and on the same level, was a small entirely crushed vessel reddish in colour (f) unusually poorly baked and brittle. Its reconstruction was not practicable.

The two-lugged vessel (g), being unusually brittle, disintegrated. However, it was possible to reconstruct its shape from the earth which had filled it and was fairly hard (Plate 8:2c). It was 8·5cm high, body diameter 10·2cm with lugs under the rim placed on opposite sides, a circular bottom, dark in colour and not ornamented. There were very few brittle fragments of pottery in the neighbourhood of the hearth on the western side of the shaft: they were reddish in colour and made of sand-gritted clay. The potsherds on top of the mound were of another type: they were also reddish in colour and thick, but had a strong admixture of grains of crushed quartz and were stronger than those previously described. The axe (Plate 8:2d) was small, made of a dark 'Bug' variety of flint, 5·5cm long, oval in cross-section, the surface almost entirely polished. The flint knife was of the same material, trimmed on one side, 9cm long. The beads, of which there were over fifty, were of two kinds: most (about forty) were irregular discs, 3 to 4mm long and 6mm thick, while the others were segmented beads from 1 to 3cm long. A chemical analysis carried out by the Chemical Institute of Lwów University showed: SiO_2 91·49 per cent, PbO 2·32 per cent; Al_2O_3 1·61 per cent; Fo_2O_3 1·01 per cent; CaO 1·43 per cent; MgO 0·83 per cent; CuO traces.

Barrow-grave 6 (Plan 28:2). This, with the two following (nos. 7 and 8) formed a group, triangular in shape, at some 20m from one another. It was 20m in diameter, 1·5m high. A trench was cut across it 3m wide, extending to 8m in the centre. Its cross-section was like that of the others.

A larger vessel (a) and, near it, a flint flake (b), were found 3m E of the centre of the barrow on the ancient level. Traces of a hearth about 60cm in diameter, on which a layer of calcined clay (c) several centimetres in thickness and some charcoal (d, e) was found, occurred some 4·5m SW from the centre, also on the ancient level. No traces of skeleton or grave-shaft were found. The vessel referred to above was entirely destroyed. It was the lower portion of a large, tulip-shaped vessel, body diameter about 20·5cm, but preserved only to a height of 14cm. It was made of clay mixed with sand, very brittle and reddish in colour.

Barrow-grave 7 (Plan 29:2). 20m in diameter, 80cm high, cut across like the above. An entirely destroyed vessel (c), unusually brittle, was found in the centre of the mound, under the forest humus at a depth of 50cm. It was not possible to extricate it or determine its shape. It was reddish, badly baked, made of clay with a very large admixture of sand.

A grave-shaft (d) was found in the centre, under the mound: it was 1·8m by 1·2m orientated SW–NE, dug about 70cm in the ancient level and extending down to virgin soil. Traces of red ochre and several lumps of ochre were scattered on its bottom, but the skeleton had disintegrated entirely. A layer of entirely decayed oak logs was traced about 30cm from the bottom: of these, as in other cases in other graves, only very slight, brownish traces and an imprint in the clay revealed the wooden structure. Lumps of charcoal were scattered about 50cm west of the shaft at the ancient level (b), over an area of about 1m. There was also a flint flake (a) and an entirely destroyed vessel (e). This was made of clay similar to that used for the vessel from the upper part of the mound: it was unusually brittle and disintegrated.

Barrow-grave 8 (Plan 29:1). Diameter 20m, height 80cm, cut across like the other two in this group. Traces of a large hearth were found in the top of the mound, under the forest humus (a). A cord-ornamented beaker (d) (Fig. 11:3) 14cm high, body 10cm diameter, lay under the mound at the ancient level: this beaker was cord-ornamented and had a low raised lug on the neck, the upper portion cylindrical, the lower flask-shaped, the bottom rounded. A handful of charcoal fragments lay near it. A group of four vessels (bowl, beaker, small cup and a larger vessel of some kind), and flint scraper 6·5cm long were found about 2m west of the centre of the mound and on the same level as the objects referred to above (c). There was no trace of skeleton, nor was a grave-shaft found. The bowl (Plate 7:8) was 11cm high, lower diameter 16cm, sides vertical, a wide base, its rim curved, with five parallel lines impressed by cord under the rim. This vessel, like the beaker and the three other vessels, was a strongly sand-gritted ware, very insufficiently baked and unusually brittle. These vessels were entirely destroyed and it was not possible to reconstruct them.

Barrow-grave 9 (Plan 28:3). This mound and mound 10 constituted a separate group, situated 1·5km from the mounds described above. It was 12m in diameter and 30cm high. Fragments of coarse vessels were found at a depth of 20cm, immediately under the forest humus (d). The outline of a grave-shaft (e) occurred under the mound, orientated NE–SW: it was not possible either to measure or to excavate this on account of the roots of a large oak tree and part of its trunk, which we were not allowed to remove. A bowl (a) with flat bottom (basin) (Plate 7:4), 6·5cm high, its sides widening upwards, diameter of opening 10·6cm, was found close to the most southerly corner of the shaft on the ancient level. Under its rim was an ornament of four parallel lines impressed by cord. It was standing on a thin layer of ashes and small lumps of charcoal, with a flint burin or knife (c) 9·8cm long next to it: this was made of a dark 'Bug' variety of flint. Some centimetres away, several entirely crushed vessels (f) were found in a shallow hole: it was not possible to reconstruct them. Like the bowl described above, they were made of sand-gritted clay, poorly baked, very brittle, reddish in colour: some bore cord decoration.

Barrow-grave 10. This was 12m in diameter, 30cm high, poorly visible, with the centre destroyed some time ago by extraction of a tree trunk growing on it. A bowl was found lying on its side in the centre of the mound, on the ancient level, with a flint axe next to it. The bowl disintegrated but was reconstructed on the basis of the hard earth inside it (Plate 7:9). It was 1·1cm high, sides parallel, diameter 1·2cm, the lower portion semi-spherical. It was made of clay strongly admixed with sand, poorly baked, extremely brittle. The axe was of dark flint, 10cm long, lenticular in cross-section.

47. *Komarów* district of Stanisławów

The description of sixty-four barrow-graves and the settlement investigated here is given in the preceding Section.

48. *Kryłos* district of Stanisławów

A large number of barrow-graves occur in various parts of the fields. There were over twelve in the 'Nad Bidunem' forest, some of which were excavated in 1883–6 by Dr I. Szaraniewicz.[44] The following description is derived from published material, in the order of their excavation.

Barrow-grave 1. Excavated in 1883 and designated as '10a'. Under the mound an area 14 by 15m in extent was cobbled. The pebbles were missing at two points, where it had perhaps been at some time excavated. In this mound were found a portion of a flint knife, fragments of broken red and black vessels and an object 'shaped like a button', black in colour, like 'petrified lava'. Szaraniewicz provided a plan of the pebble arrangement which he considered to be the foundation of a construction of some kind.

Barrow-grave 2. This was excavated in 1883 as no. 11, and was the largest (4m high). It was composed of black earth with white streaks. The black earth ceased at 3m deep and gave way to yellow, hard, beaten clay. Nothing was found except for small pieces of red brick and a flint arrow-head.

Barrow-grave 3. This was excavated in 1883 as no. 10c. It was also cobbled. It was cut across by a diagonal trench. It consisted of clay mixed with black earth to a depth of 1·4m then yellow clay appeared. Nothing was found except some small fragments of pottery.

Barrow-grave 4. Situated in the 'Na Czahniowie' wood, this was excavated in 1884 by a diagonal trench. A large number of river pebbles were found here, lying at random through the entire mound. The earth uncovered in the walls of the mound excavation was black, as though 'brought from else-where' and had streaks which appeared to be a mixture of earth and ash (in fact degradate chernozem). It contained many holes (almost certainly those of hamsters). Virgin soil occurred at a depth of 2m. The description does not refer to any findings.

The objects deriving from Szaraniewicz' excavation were deposited in the Lviv Narodnyi Dom and Instytyt Stauropigianski. It has only been possible to identify the flint knife 8·5cm long, almost certainly deriving from barrow-grave 1.

Barrow-grave A. In 1883, T. Ziemięcki[45] excavated a mound situated in the earthwork and called it the 'Hałyczyna Mohyła'. It was 36m in diameter, 2·5m high. A few scattered fragments of pottery, charcoal and one small bone were found in the upper portions of the mound at a depth of 1·9m. The description states that a 'lenticular layer of sand' 30cm deep was found just over the virgin soil: this was presumably traces of the grave-shaft, which Ziemięcki failed to observe, dug in the ancient level and extending to the virgin soil.

In 1935 and 1936 Dr J. Pasternak[46] excavated six mounds here, providing only a brief note on them.

Barrow-grave I. In the 'Dubrowa' forest. A skeleton strewn with red ochre.

Barrow-grave II. Situated as above. A cremation burial of the Bronze Age.

Barrow-grave III. In the 'Glinna' forest. Cremation burial. Corded Ware and a bronze pin with a spiral head (three windings).

Barrow-grave IV. 'Stawiska' field. Inhumation burial of the Early Bronze Age.

Barrow-grave V. Inhumation burial of the Early Iron Age. A large yellow bead of glassy paste with blue eyes in a white ring.

Barrow-grave VI called 'Nastasyna Mohyła', situated in the 'Dubrova' forest close to the border of Komarów, investigated in 1936.[47] This was 30m in diameter, 3·5m high. In the mound were found charcoal, lumps of fired clay and small odd potsherds, some of which had an incised ornament. In the eastern part of the mound, at a depth of 1·12m, two horse leg-bones and five horse teeth were excavated, but no skull was found.

At a depth of 2m, 3·7m S of the centre, a human skeleton lay on a layer of oak planks, of which only slight traces were left. It was also covered with a black layer, the nature of which could not be established. The skeleton lay on its back, legs con-

[44] I. Szaraniewicz, *Przegląd Archeologiczny*, vol. III, Lwów 1883, p. 3, and plan; vol. IV, Lwów 1888, p. 88.

[45] T. Ziemięcki, *ZWAK*, vol. VIII, 1884, p. 93; vol. XI, 1887, p. 52. Janusz (op. cit., note 9), pp. 216 f.

[46] Pasternak, loc. cit., note 35 (1936), and note 16 (1937).

[47] Я. Пастернак, 'Настасина могила' у Крилосі. Літопис Національного Музею за 1936 р. Lviv, pp. 14 ff.

tracted towards the left side. Near the feet three fairly small hearths were uncovered; they formed a regular triangle. Near the skeleton several grave goods were excavated (Fig. 11:1): (1) part of a thin bronze torque, 14·5cm long the wire 4mm thick on the neck; (2) fragments of two lead spiral bands, 1·5cm in diameter; (3) a beaker near the feet, 14·5cm high, 13–14 cm in diameter with an incised chevron decoration on its high neck; (4) a diorite battle-axe, 12·5cm long, of *y*-2 type, which lay near the left elbow; (5) a flint axe, rectangular in section, 10cm long, found near the beaker; (6) three flint arrow-heads, one of these thick and of an unusual form; one arrow-head was found near the ribs, the other in the hip bones; (7) five flint flakes were found near the flint axe.

49. *Kulczyce Szlacheckie* district of Sambor

Two groups of barrow-graves occur here, the smaller consisting of six large mounds in the forest: the other, which is larger, contains fifteen mounds situated on common pasture land (Plan 3:1). Both groups are situated on the summit of hills and extend approximately in a line running west–east, at distances varying from some dozen to a few metres from one another. Their diameters vary from 20 to 30m, heights being from 50cm to 2m. In 1932 and 1933 I excavated[48] three mounds here in the pasture land (nos. I–III). In 1933 Dr J. Pasternak[49] excavated the fourth mound on the same pasture land (no. IV) as well as two others in the forest (nos. V and VI) belonging to the other group. The material excavated from all mounds was deposited in the 'Bojkiwszczyna' Museum in Sambor, except for Barrow-grave II, the material of which I deposited in the Prehistoric Institute of Lwów University. A few more barrow-graves were excavated in 1949, but no reports have yet been published.[50]

Barrow-grave I. This was 27m in diameter, 1·5m high, its cross-section as follows: under 30cm of humus, the mound (extending to a depth of 80cm) consisted of fine, light ash-coloured earth, looking like ash particularly where it had an admixture of sand: it was darker and less fine in proportion to depth. It was situated on the fossil humus, which was entirely black, very hard in the upper 25cm, and gradually gave way to virgin soil. At a depth of 1·5m pure yellow virgin soil occurred.

The grave-shaft was found almost in the centre of the mound: it was 1·7m by 80cm, orientated SW–NE dug approximately 55cm into the ancient ground and penetrating about 15cm into virgin soil. A slightly contracted skeleton was found on the bottom, on its right side, head SW: only whitish and poorly visible traces were to be seen. It was scattered over with a fine layer of ochre, the head being most thickly scattered, with several lumps of ochre round it. Traces of a layer of logs, probably oak, were found about 15–20cm above the skeleton. A flake of 'Bug' variety flint was found some 4m from the centre of the mound, on the ancient level, and a small flint axe of rectangular cross-section (Fig. 15:14) 6·2cm long, was found near the grave.

Barrow-grave II (Plan 30:2). This was 28m in diameter, 60cm high. Its cross-section was similar to the above. A crushed Thuringian amphora (F) (Plate 5:4) was found under the mound on the ancient level: a blunt axe, made of sandstone (C) (Fig. 15:17) was lying 4m SE of the centre on the same level, while a large quantity of charcoal occurred at about 2·5m S of the centre (D). Clear traces of two oak planks (E), placed one by the other on an eminence a few centimetres high, placed in a NE–SW direction, together 50cm in width and about 2m long, were found some 2m NE of the centre. One log was supported on a large lump of sandstone. This was probably the site of the second burial, but the skeleton had disintegrated and no trace was found.

The grave-shaft (A), 2 by 1·2m was in the centre of the mound: it was orientated NE–SW, dug about 65m into the ancient ground and penetrating about 30cm into virgin soil. No traces remained of the skeleton, except that some ochre was found on the SW side (M), where the head had probably been. Traces of a layer of oak logs, which had at one time covered the entire shaft, occurred 10cm above the bottom.

The Thuringian amphora (Plate 5:4) was not ornamented, 16cm high, body diameter 17 cm. The axe (Fig. 15:17) was fairly carefully made of flat sandstone, 11cm long and bore clear traces of use on the blade. Its central thickness was 1·6cm.

Barrow-grave III (Plan 30:1). This was situated near the above, 24m in diameter, 50cm high, ploughed over. The cross-section was similar to the preceding graves. The original diameter of the mound was 15m, and must therefore have been much higher.

A large number of undecorated fragments of a large vessel, probably a red amphora, were found at various depths in the mound, beginning at the top and mainly on the west side (A). This vessel had been broken deliberately and its sherds scattered. A number of lumps of charcoal were found (E) with these, which had also been scattered over a wider expanse and at varying depths in the mound.

The remains of a crushed and incomplete Thuringian amphora were found in the western portion of the mound on the ancient level (D). The neck of the amphora was lying about 3m away (F): the fragments found in the mound and referred to above (A) belonged to this vessel. About 3m from the amphora was a large handful of charcoal, while a larger lump of ochre was lying nearer the centre.

The grave-shaft (G) was about 3m SE of the centre of the mound: it was orientated NE–SW, 2·4 by 1·2m, about 65cm deep, penetrating to virgin soil into which it was dug about 35cm. A cord-decorated beaker with semi-spherical bottom, the upper part narrowing to the outlet, was standing in the shaft's NE sector (H). A broken stone battle-axe (T) of type *x*-1, much damaged, was lying near the southern corner at the bottom of the shaft: two flint arrow-heads were found nearer the centre of the shaft, with a flint scraper near them (K) and a flint axe (S) (Fig. 16:14) near the vessel. No traces of skeleton were found. Judging by the arrangement of the grave goods, the skeleton was in a slightly crouched position, on its right side, head to SW. The battle-axe was near its hand, the arrow-heads in the stomach cavity, the scraper near the thighs, while the axe and vessels were standing near its feet. There was no ochre. The battle-axe was 11cm long,

[48] Sulimirski, loc. cit., note 37.

[49] Я. Пастернак, Доісторичні Кульчиці, Діло, no. 221, Lviv, 24, VIII, 1933. Id., Шнурова могила в Кульчицях, Літопис Бойківщини, no. 7, Sambir 1936.

[50] І. К. Свешніков, Підсумки дослідження культур бронзової доби Прикарпаття і західного Поділля, Lviv 1958, p. 15.

its blade very blunt, the surface very rough. The axe, 9·4cm long, had a lenticular cross-section and was made of dark flint with a somewhat brownish tinge slightly speckled. Both flint arrow-heads had a convex base and were about 1·7cm long, one with a broken tip.

Barrow-grave IV. This was about 20m in diameter, low, excavated by Pasternak. Some fragments of pottery and lumps of charcoal were found in the mound. The grave-shaft was in the centre, but contained no trace of skeleton, its base being covered by a very thin layer of ochre. Two flint scrapers appear to have been found on the ancient level.

Barrow-grave V. This was situated in the forest, in the other group from those described above. It was 25m in diameter, 3m high. In the mound a few potsherds were found and lumps of charcoal. Under the mound, at a depth of 1m, the contour of the grave-shaft appeared but its outline was poorly visible. It was only about 50cm deep and its bottom had not reached the yellow subsoil of the fossil humus. A cord-decorated beaker (Fig. 11:2), typical of the Corded Ware culture, was found over the shaft. It was 10·4cm high. Under it lay a flint knife, near by lay a part of the base of a Thuringian amphora, and at a small distance lay a few sherds of the body, including a perforated lug of the same amphora. No traces of skeleton were noticed. Potsherds found in the mound belonged to several vessels, some of which were cord-decorated.

Barrow-grave VI. This lay at a distance of about 50m from the above, and was smaller in size. In its mound a few potsherds, some cord-decorated, and a few lumps of charcoal were excavated. Traces of the grave-shaft were found but no exact measurement could be taken. Nothing was found in it.

In barrow-grave 2–1949, a small debased Thuringian type amphora *c.* 8cm high and a bowl *c.* 15cm in diameter were excavated, both with incised patterns. Those of the amphora had horizontal grooves and zigzag lines reminiscent of the ornament typical of Thuringian amphorae; the neck of the bowl had three horizontal bands of chevron patterns separated by horizontal grooves.

Settlement. An area of several dozen square metres was investigated in 1933 by Pasternak at the entrance gate of a very large earthwork, some 120 by 900m in area. At a depth of 20–40cm a layer dating from the eleventh to twelfth century A.D., of the Mediaeval East Slavonic type was uncovered. The same site was then further investigated by Kobilnyk.[51] At a depth of 140–75cm, under a sterile stratum, another layer of occupation was found, dating from the Late Bronze Age and attributable to the Komarów culture.

Two pit-dwellings were uncovered in this layer. One of these had a round hearth 1–1·20m in diameter, paved with flat river pebbles, and was plastered with clay. Over the whole area of the hut, about 6m in diameter, lay many potsherds, animal bones, clay whorls, a few flint implements, etc., also lumps of clay plaster; the latter bore impressions of timber logs of the overstructure of the hut. Chaff was added to the clay plaster, which implies some acquaintance with agriculture by the inhabitants of the settlement. Flint not available in the region must have been brought here from the western border of Podolia, a distance of about 100km. Animal bones were identified as those of cattle, horse, pigs, roedeer and a large bird. Pottery was of two kinds. One was coarse kitchen ware (mainly high tulip-shaped pots) made of strongly-tempered clay paste, badly fired, the inner surface of the vessels dark, well smoothed; decoration consisted of raised bands around the neck or under the rim, often finger-tipped, or with a row of perforations. The other pottery was well made, brownish in colour, the surface smoothed; it comprised mainly deep bowls or dishes, and handled cups (Plate 22:3, 4). This pottery shows many features characteristic of the Lusatian pottery.

50. *Łotatniki* district of Stryj

In 1931 two barrow-graves on the 'Mogiła' field were excavated, probably by members of the staff of the Agricultural School at Bereźnica. The description of these and grave goods ultimately reached the Prehistoric Institute of the University of Lwów.

Barrow-grave 1. Small in size. At a depth of 60cm a layer of red, fired clay, about 1m in diameter was uncovered, evidently the site of a hearth.

Objects from this barrow-grave deposited at the Prehistoric Institute were: (a) an axe (Fig. 16:7) 10·2cm long, thin, with narrow sides, flat, and the wide ones convex, made of grey white-spotted flint; (b) a small flint knife 7·5cm long; (c) the blade of a narrow chisel made of yellow slate, 6cm long, nearly square in section, 1·4 by 1·7cm; (d) three irregular flint flakes.

Barrow-grave 2. This was situated west of the above. It was larger in size. It was cut by a trench 4m wide, running E–W. At about 1·3m from the centre, at a depth of 1·2m, lay two decorated vessels and near by a flint axe, flint knife and stone battle-axe.

The grave goods deposited at the Prehistoric Institute were: (Plate 6:3, 15, 16) (a) a dark, handled bowl with three rows of cord impressions under the rim, lower part semi-spheric, the handle wide; (b) a beaker 9·5cm high with, an everted rim, wide base, body 11·5cm in diameter, greyish-brown in colour, incised chevron pattern under the rim; (c) a dark, wide bowl, or deep dish, with a flat base, 6·5cm high, the aperture 16·5cm in diameter, the rim flat; (d) a battle-axe of yellow slate (Plate 10:8), 11cm long, with a small shaft-hole placed close to the wide end of the axe; (e) a thin flint axe (Fig. 16:3), lenticular in section, 10·5cm long, well made of a dark variety of flint; (f) a large flint blade, probably a knife, 9·5cm long.

51. *Medynia* district of Stanisławów. See Komarów barrow-grave 63 (p. 115).

52. *Niegowce* district of Kałusz

A battle-axe of type *y*-5 (Fig. 14:3) 10·5cm long, made of greenish stone, was found in 1885 in a barrow-grave.[52]

53. *Ozimina* district of Sambor

Two barrow-graves were excavated by me in 1932.[53] They were situated in a meadow in the wide valley of the Bystrzyca,

[51] В. Кобільник, Відкриття доісторичних землянок в Кульчицях, Літопис Бойківщини, no. 3, Sambir 1934, pp. 12 ff., Pls. I–VI.

[52] Kozłowski, op. cit., note 2: 1924), p. 191.

[53] Sulimirski, loc. cit., note 37.

a tributary of the Dniester, close to the border of the village of Horodyszcze, at a distance of about 500m SSW of the three barrow-graves at that village excavated by Dr V. Kobilnyk. The archaeological material was deposited in the 'Bojkiwszczyna' Museum, Sambor.

Barrow-grave I. This was 21m in diameter, 60cm high, much ploughed over. A mound 50cm deep occurred under 30cm of humus: this mound was not uniform in structure being looser and ash-coloured at the top, darker further down. The mound was on fossil humus, 25cm thick, and was black, very hard, gradually becoming virgin soil underneath.

The grave-shaft, some 2m SE of centre, was fairly shallow and did not penetrate to virgin soil. Its limits were erased and its dimensions could not be measured with accuracy. No traces of skeleton were found. The only object found in the grave was a flint splint, found in the centre of the upper layer of the mound.

Barrow-grave II (Plan 30:3). This was 20m north of the previous grave, and of the same dimensions. Its cross-section was like that of the previous grave. A small splint of hornstone was found in the summit of the mound of the grave, with a small flint knife near it, 8cm long, very well made (a). A small potsherd of a vessel bright red in colour outside, black in cross-section, very brittle and poorly baked, was found a few centimetres away. An irregular rectangular grave-shaft, 1·9 by 1·1–0·85m, 60cm deep, and dug in the virgin soil was found under the mound and also in the centre, on the NW side. Clear traces of an almost entirely disintegrated skeleton occurred on the bottom, of which the skull was relatively better preserved (Plate 1:1). The skeleton was slightly contracted, on its right side, head to SW. The head was on the wider side of the shaft. Some lumps of ochre were found near the skull and chest, while the entire bottom and the skeleton was scattered with ochre. A layer of logs, precisely similar to those in the Kulczyce barrow-graves was found over the skeleton.

54. *Podgrodzie* district of Stanisławów

In 1936 Dr J. Pasternak excavated a barrow-grave here in which a cremation burial of the Komarów culture was found. No details have been published.[54]

55. *Stebnik* district of Drohobycz

Two barrow-graves were found in pasture land belonging to the village of Kołpiec, which formed a wedge between fields of the neighbouring villages Stebnik and Solec, somewhat below the top of the hill. One was excavated in 1916–17 by Dr M. Roska[55] who published the results of his investigation and called it the Stebnik barrow-grave. I have adopted this name here for the second barrow-grave which I investigated in 1932 while investigating the barrow-graves at Kołpiec described above (no. 46).

Barrow-grave I. This was oval, 15·5 by 13m in diameter, 78cm high, raised of sandy clay. Lumps of charcoal were found at three points, while potsherds and flint splints were scattered throughout the entire mound. The potsherds were very small, generally very brittle, red or darker in colour. Many had a strong admixture of quartz grains in the clay. M. Roska distinguished a nucleus and a well-made scraper among the flints. In addition, the butt of an axe, rectangular in cross-section and a stone for polishing were also found. Roska considered this barrow-grave to be the remains of a settlement.

Barrow-grave II. This was 12m in diameter, 35cm high. It was built of very loose, dark-yellow earth, like forest humus in appearance. Some scattered potsherds and several lumps of charcoal were found 70cm deep in the centre of the mound. They were clearly arranged in a semicircle and most probably lay round the grave-shaft or the spot where the skeleton had been placed: traces of skeleton and outline of grave-shaft could not be identified. The potsherds were deposited in the Prehistoric Institute of the University of Lwów: they were a sand-gritted ware, dark in colour and very brittle.

56. *Wacowice* district of Drohobycz

In 1898, W. Demetrykiewicz excavated three barrow-graves in the 'Kogucik' wood.[56] The material found is in the Archaeological Museum, Cracow.

Barrow-grave I. This was 24m in diameter, 3m high. The upper layer consisted of humus 30–40cm deep, then the mound described as 'ashes' by W. Demetrykiewicz, mixed with lumps of charcoal while hardened earth occurred underneath: this, as appeared from the similarity with barrow-graves excavated by me in the same region was fossil humus. Small, brittle fragments of poorly baked vessels were found here and there in the mound. A group of vessels, 'a concentration of potsherds', found in the southern part of the mound were destroyed. A flint axe 7cm long (Fig. 16:6), lenticular in cross-section was found near them, and a flint blade knife, 12cm long, was found nearer the periphery of the mound. All the potsherds now in the Museum derive from vessels red in colour and made of clay with a strong admixture of sand, poorly baked, very brittle, cord decorated. Fragments of a beaker with wide bottom, similar to one found in the Siedliska barrow-grave could be distinguished among them.

Barrow-grave II. This lay in the centre of the group, and was 8m in diameter, 1m high, cross-section similar to the above. Similar very brittle potsherds and lumps of charcoal were found in it.

Barrow-grave III. This was the largest, being 30m in diameter, 4m high, raised as the above of loose ash-coloured earth which W. Demetrykiewicz described as 'ashes'. 'A large concentration of reddish potsherds', i.e. crushed vessels, was discovered near the centre of the barrow-grave 'on the lowest layer of clay'. None was preserved. One flint flake was also found.

57. *Wiktorów* district of Stanisławów

A large number of barrow-graves occur here, scattered in various parts of the fields. In 1878, one was excavated by Dr Lenz of Vienna, who found 'several urns and a flint knife' in it. Some years later, several of the graves were excavated by a Mr Pniewski, a local agronomist.[57]

Barrow-grave A. This was excavated jointly by Pniewski and

[54] Pasternak, loc. cit., note 16 (1937).

[55] Roska (op. cit., note 34), pp. 28 f., Figs. 10, 11.

[56] Demetrykiewicz (op. cit., note 13), pp. 124 ff. Janusz (op. cit., note 9), pp. 107 f.

[57] Janusz (op. cit., note 9), p. 200.

Dr Lenz: it is situated on the 'Huszcza' field. It was excavated to a depth of 1·59cm and potsherds, calcined human bones, charcoal and a flint knife *c.* 14cm long, with another, smaller, were found in it. Dr Lenz removed both knives to Vienna.

Barrow-grave B. This was excavated in 1883 and is situated in the 'Huszcza' field. A broken flint knife and two smaller flints found in it were presented to the Archaeological Museum, Cracow (I was unable to identify them).

In 1886, T. Ziemięcki[58] excavated nine barrow-graves situated on the border with Kryłos, in the forest and in the fields. The material was deposited in the Archaeological Museum, Cracow (no. 2694).

Barrow-grave I. This was the largest, being 26m in diameter, 5m high. It was excavated by a diagonal trench 7m long, 2m wide, 4·5m deep. A layer of pulverized charcoal mixed with calcined human bones was found about 3m deep near the eastern periphery of the mound, with some calcined clay and a few potsherds. A flint axe 11·2cm long (Fig. 16:15) of a hybrid form, was lying in the centre of this layer, with a flint knife 11cm long outside the layer of charcoal and bones.

Barrow-grave II (Plan 27:3). This was situated near the above, 20m in diameter, 115m high. A trench 1·1m wide was cut across it. In the middle, at a depth of 1·5m, heaped calcined human bones were found, among which lay a diorite battle-axe of type '*y*-4' (Fig. 14:2), 9·5cm long and cracked due to being in a fire, a small bronze ring, and a fragment of a bronze object, probably a bracelet. A little to the west lay a flint axe 8cm long (Fig. 16:16) of the hybrid type.

In 1934 I investigated this barrow-grave again, by excavating its central part which was 6m in diameter. Traces of the trench dug by Ziemięcki were clearly visible (a) and the site in which calcined human bones lay was identified (f). My excavation showed that the grave was 2m long, over 1m wide, orientated W–E, situated near the centre of the mound. The northern side of the grave, about 50cm wide, was left untouched by the trench (e). In this part, calcined human bones and small lumps of charcoal lay scattered on the bottom of the shallow grave-hole. On the other side of the trench dug by Ziemięcki, at a depth of 35cm, in the centre of the mound a fine battle-axe of type *x*-1 (Fig. 13:1) was found, made of a greenish variety of stone, 10cm long, and near it was a flint knife, 6·5cm long (b) (Fig. 12:4). In the mound earth a few small potsherds undecorated, mainly reddish in colour, were excavated. North of the grave lay a flint burin (d) (Fig. 12:5). These objects were given to the Archaeological Museum in Cracow.[59] On the southern periphery of the mound heaped pebbles were found within an area 2 by 1m (c).

Barrow-grave III. Nothing was found in this.

Barrow-grave IV. This was 18m in diameter, 1m high, situated on the border of Kryłos, intersected by a trench 4m long, 1·5m wide. A flint knife 11cm long was found at a depth of 1·66m in a layer of charcoal, ash and calcined bones.

Barrow-graves V–VI. These lay a little further away, while *barrow-grave* VII, somewhat lower on a slope, was entirely destroyed during the First World War. These barrow-graves were about 20m in diameter, 1–1·5m high. A layer of large pebbles was found in both, at a depth of from 1·2 to 2m, arranged as though in two or three layers. No material or charcoal was found here, as a result of which excavation was stopped without disturbing the pebbles. The construction of these barrow-graves, as is evident from the description was entirely similar to those I found in some Bronze Age Komarów barrow-graves situated some kilometres from the above.

Barrow-grave VIII. This was situated beside a road into the forest, much ploughed over, excavated by a trench 4m long, 1·25m wide. A broken 'urn' full of 'ashes and human bones' was found at a depth of 1·74m, in a layer of fat chernozem (probably on the ancient level): a flint knife 6·5cm long was next to it, and a flint axe (Fig. 16:18) 8·5cm long, trapezoid in cross-section, was found near by. The 'urn' was in fact a debased Thuringian amphora (Plate 5:6) about 30cm high. It had a very wide opening, with an ornament of parallel lines impressed by cord and ending in two rows of small stamped impressions on the shoulder. No traces of calcined bones or charcoal were found by me at the Museum in the earth deriving from this vessel, which was ash-coloured and resembled dust. It was certainly not a cremation burial.

Barrow-grave IX. This was situated in the field 'Na Obszarkach' and was 20m in diameter. Nothing was found in it.

In 1934 I excavated two further barrow-graves.[60] The material was deposited in the Institute of Prehistory in Lwów.

Barrow-grave X. Situated in the 'Bandurówka' site, 20m in diameter, 80cm high, it had already been excavated, probably by Pniewski as was evident from a trench 4 by 2·5m in area, orientated S–N. About 1m NE of the NE corner of this trench, at a depth of 20cm, a broken flint scraper was found and in the other corner of the trench a few potsherds and a handful of charcoal were excavated on the ancient surface. The potsherds belonged to a larger vessel, reddish in colour, made of a strongly tempered clay paste. A decoration of irregular shallow grooves was visible on these sherds.

Barrow-grave XI (Plan 27:1). Situated in the 'Na Kuciłiwce' forest. This was 18m in diameter, 1m high. In the centre, at a depth of 80–90cm and on the ancient surface, charcoal and loose fired clay and lumps of baked clay appeared scattered over an area about 1·5m in diameter (a); they were concentrated in particular on the eastern side of this area. On its southern side a fragment of a broken flint axe (b) was found, and near by was a small flint flake (c). In the SE corner of the central area contours of a square pit, 1·2 by 1·1m were uncovered, probably dug by treasure seekers (d).

58. *Załukiew* district of Stanisławów.

A bronze bracelet (Fig. 19:9) 75mm in diameter, was in the collection of the Ukrainian Narodnyi Dom in Lwów before the War. It seems to have originated from a destroyed barrow-grave.

3. THE LWÓW–OPOLE GROUP

59. *Bybło* district of Rohatyn

In 1886 a barrow-grave was excavated in which a Neolithic burial had been destroyed by an early medieval secondary

[58] Ziemięcki (op. cit., note 45: 1887), pp. 53 ff. Janusz (op. cit., note 9), pp. 220 f.

[59] Sulimirski, loc. cit., note 37. See also J. Machnik, 'Zabytki z kurhanów kultury ceramiki sznurowej w Wiktorowie', *Mat.Arch.*, vol. II, 1960, pp. 69 ff., Pls. I–III.

[60] Sulimirski, loc. cit., note 37.

burial. Of the Neolithic grave only calcined bones and two flints were found.[61]

60. *Czyżyków* district of Lwów

Two barrow-graves were excavated by Dr M. Śmiszko, the first one with the assistance of Miss I. Siwek, M.A.

Barrow-grave I (Plan 31:1). Situated in a field belonging to W. Bogdanowicz, investigated in 1935–6; the archaeological material was deposited in the Prehistoric Institute of the University of Lwów.[62] The mound was 20m in diameter, 2m high. Near the southern periphery of the area under the mound, and on the ancient surface, two vessels typical of the Komarów culture stood close to each other (N); these were a deep bowl (Plate 16:19) 9·8cm high, 15·2cm in diameter (the aperture), and a tulip-shaped decorated beaker (Plate 18:2) 11cm high, 10cm in diameter. About 50cm N of these was an undecorated bowl (Plate 17:12) 6·4cm high, 10·1cm in diameter (aperture) near which lay a bronze awl, 13·7cm long, made of bronze wire 3·5mm in diameter, one half round in section, the other square, both ends pointed. In the NE part of the area under the mound a bone button with a thin bronze sheet covering was excavated (Fig. 26:10). It was 2·6cm in diameter, round, 8mm thick, provided with a round massive tang 9mm in diameter, 4mm long with traces of a broken-off loop. In the central part of the mound, at a depth of about 1·5m, ochre was found, strewn on the same level over small areas (a). About 1·50m S of one of these was a patch of fired clay, about 50cm in diameter; this was probably the site of the burial. In the mound itself a few odd potsherds and one flint flake were found (c).

Barrow-grave II. This was investigated in 1955.[63] It had been largely destroyed by industrial excavation during which a richly furnished secondary grave of the Lipica culture (first century B.C. to first century A.D.) was uncovered. The original Early Bronze Age grave lay in the western part, probably on the ancient surface, or in a very shallow hole. Only the legs of the crouched skeleton survived, near which a flint knife, 10·8cm long, was found. About 1·4m NW of the legs lay a small cord-decorated, handled cup (Fig. 12:10) about 6cm high, 8cm in diameter, under which two small bronze earrings with one end flattened were found, one about 2·5cm in diameter, the other somewhat smaller (Fig. 19:12, 13).

61. *Dusanów* district of Przemyślany

A Neolithic barrow-grave, 15m in diameter, was investigated by Dr J. Pasternak in 1934,[64] in which only a fragment of an amber disc was found. The barrow had been damaged by previous excavation.

62. *Dziedziłów* district of Kamionka Strumiłowa

In the nineteenth century, during the construction of a road, a barrow-grave was destroyed in which a flint axe was found. In 1897, a skeleton grave was excavated by Professor Siemiradzki in which a cord-decorated, handled cup (Plate 6:23) was found, given to the Dzieduszycki Museum in Lwów.[65] It was 6·7cm high, 8·7cm in diameter.

63. *Jaktorów* district of Przemyślany

Five barrow-graves were excavated in 1933–5 by Dr J. Pasternak,[66] the fifth dating from the late Hallstatt period.

Barrow-grave I. 15m in diameter, 1·4m high, in the Yavornya forest. In the mound a flint burin 6·2cm long and a flint knife 4·3cm long were found. In the south-eastern part of the mound, at a depth of 1·63m, a poorly preserved contracted skeleton was uncovered, which lay on its right side, head to E, in a shallow hole 35cm deep. Under its feet remains of a hearth with charcoal were visible and a fragment of an animal bone lay here. On a finger of the right hand was a bronze 'nap-ring' 2·1cm in diameter, made of thin wire (Fig. 19:11).

Barrow-grave II. Near the above, 10m in diameter, 1·35m high. In the centre at a depth of 1·55m, a handled cord-decorated cup (Plate 7:2) was found, 7·9cm high, 8·8cm in diameter. The body was covered with radial vertical cord impressions nearly reaching the base. No traces of the skeleton were found.

Barrow-grave III. Situated near by, yielded no remains whatever.

Barrow-grave IV. In the 'Moczary' forest 500m NE of the above group. This was 18m in diameter, 80cm high. Under the upper forest humus, 20–5cm deep, the mound earth was uncovered; it was hard, nearly black in some parts, with an admixture of yellow clay. At a depth of 80cm lay the ancient surface, on which a layer of charcoal and cinders spread over almost the entire area covered by the mound. On this layer in the southern part of the mound, a cord-decorated handled cup (Plate 7:3) was found, 8·6cm high, near which lay a flint scraper, 8·4cm long. No traces of skeleton were found.

64. *Janczyn* district of Przemyślany

A barrow-grave on the 'Mohyłki' field was excavated in 1933 by Dr J. Pasternak.[67] It was 26m in diameter, much ploughed over. At a depth of 16cm in the centre of the mound, two skeletons in an extended position, both badly damaged by ploughing were uncovered. They lay parallel to each other at a distance of 2m. Near the feet of the left skeleton (male) stood a handled cup 7·6cm high, 10cm in diameter, with slanting fluting on the body, and near the head of the other (female) was an undecorated cup, 12·5cm high, 12·5cm in diameter, with a narrow neck. Both were of the Komarów culture.

65. *Karaczynów* district of Gródek Jagielloński.

In the nineteenth century a barrow-grave was excavated in which a skeleton and a flint axe were found.

[61] I. Szaraniewicz, *Mitteilungen d. Central-Commission*, Wien 1887.

[62] Sulimirski, loc. cit., note 37.

[63] М. Ю. Смишко, Богатое погребение начала нашей эры в львовской области, Сов. Арх., vol. I, 1957, pp. 243 ff., Pl.I:7–12.

[64] Sulimirski, loc. cit., note 37. Я. Пастернак, Перші археологічні розкопкі. Богословіа, vol. XIV, Lviv 1936, p. 176.

[65] Kozłowski (op. cit., note 2: 1924), p. 190, Pl. XXVII:12.

[66] Sulimirski, loc. cit., note 37. Я. Пастернак, Перша бронзова доба в Галичині, Lviv 1933, pp. 67 ff. Id., loc. cit., note 16 (1937).

[67] Sulimirski (op. cit., note 37), p. 23. Я. Пастернак (op. cit., note 64), pp. 172 ff.

66. *Kołokolin* district of Rohatyn.

On a low hill close to the road to Bukaczowce, seven barrow-graves lay forming two groups, one of three mounds the other, situated north of it, of four (Plan 4:1).

In 1934, one mound of the latter group (B), later named barrow-grave IV (or B/1) by us, was largely destroyed by local inhabitants and a richly furnished, secondary grave was uncovered at that time. In 1935, one barrow-grave of the first group (A) was partly excavated by me, and later by Dr M. Śmiszko, who also investigated five more mounds.

Barrow-grave I (A–I) (Plan 31:3). About 21m in diameter, 80cm high. A small flint knife (b) was found in the mound in the southern part of the barrow. At a depth of 60cm, on the ancient level two entirely crushed vessels (a, c) stood about 3m SE of the centre, 2m from each other, in a line SW–NE. They probably marked the site of a burial (grave 1). The site of another burial (grave 2) was uncovered south of the centre. This was a shaft dug about 50cm deep in the ancient ground, the contours of which could not be well established. It was about 2 by 1m in area, orientated W–E. At its western end stood two vessels (M, N) (Plate 6:1, 9) a cord-decorated beaker 10·3cm high, 9·8cm in diameter, and a smaller one, undecorated, 10cm high, 8·3cm in diameter, and near them two flint flakes. At the eastern end stood a Thuringian amphora (K) (Fig. 10:1), 26cm high, 29cm in diameter, with a zigzag ornament under the neck and vertical chevron patterns over the lugs, reaching the neck, and near it was a bowl (L) (Plate 6:20) 6·5cm high, 12cm in diameter, with the upper part missing, and two cord-impressed grooves around the neck. The rim was slightly everted. In the centre of the grave near the amphora, were calcined human bones (f), and among and partly a little over these, in the black earth of the filling of the shaft, were found a flint arrow-head (g) (Plate 9:25) 2·5cm long, a small, very thin flint axe, probably about 6cm long, of which only a part, badly damaged by fire, remained, and a decorated potsherd typical of the Globular Amphora culture (Fig. 12:9). Three metres to the NE of the centre, a flint scraper was found on the ancient surface (e) and 4·50m N of the grave 1, at the same level, lay a small fragment of a polished flint axe (d).

Barrow-grave II (A–II) (Plan 32:1). Close to the above, 12m in diameter; 20cm below the turf, in the centre, an alabaster slab (b) of local origin 40 × 35 × 15cm in size, was uncovered. It lay over the grave which was in a shaft dug into the ancient ground and reaching to the yellow subsoil. Its size, depth and orientation were not indicated in the original report; apparently it was orientated NE–SW (f). In the eastern end of the grave was a deep bowl (c) (Plate 7:6) 13cm high, 18cm in diameter, with a slightly inverted rim, bearing on the upper part of the body, a decoration of two parallel grooves, the space between them being covered with short, slanting incisions. On the northern edge of the grave lay two flint knives (e) (Fig. 17:8) 12·4 and 9·8cm long, while on the southern edge a flint axe (d) (Fig. 15:9) 10cm long, nearly rectangular in section, was excavated. Near the NW circumference of the mound, on the ancient level, a beaker (a) (Plate 7:7) was found. It was 8·5cm high, 9cm in diameter. No traces of skeleton were found. In the mound a larger flint flake burin (Fig. 17:7) and blade were excavated.

Barrow-grave III (A–III) (Plan 31:2). This belonged to the same group, although situated at some distance from the two above. It was 12m in diameter. About 3m W of the centre and at a depth of 40cm, two wheel-made vessels of the Lipica culture (first century A.D.) were found (a-1) which probably belonged to a secondary grave. At a depth of 1m (from the top of the mound), on the ancient surface, sites of three graves were uncovered. Burial 1, the main grave, lay in the centre. This was a shaft dug some 40cm into the ancient ground, about 2m by 80cm in area, orientated W–E. On the bottom of the shaft a little charcoal was strewn (1), and a sandstone laid (e-1). On the eastern side, close to the shaft, were the following grave goods: a small cord-decorated cup (k-1) (Plate 6:19), 5·4cm high, 7·8cm in diameter, base rounded, the handle covered with two double cord-impressed lines along its entire length; a large wide flint flake trimmed on the edges (k-2) (Fig. 17:6) 8·5cm long; the upper part (butt) of a flint axe rectangular in section (a-2) 6·5cm long; a stone battle-axe (i) (Plate 10:3) originally about 14cm long, with its edge broken off and missing. Close to the northern edge stood a small vessel (e-2) completely crushed, of which only the base, 4·8cm in diameter, survived.

The probable grave II, in which no skeleton was found, as in the shaft of grave 1, lay 2m NNW of the former. It was marked by a large deep bowl (b) (Plate 7:5) which was badly crushed, its upper part missing. Its actual height was 12·5cm, 20·5cm in diameter, with an incised decoration on the shoulder consisting of a double row of vertical incisions. At a distance of nearly 2m NNW of it, an axe, 8·3cm long, rectangular in section, made of siliceous slate, lay on the same level, on the ancient surface (f).

Grave III lay at a distance of about 2m W of grave 1, on the ancient surface. This was a cremation burial, apparently orientated NW–SE. In its eastern part lay a small heap of calcined bones (g). At a distance of 1m W of it, a battle-axe made of a greenish stone of type *y*-4 (Fig. 14:1) was found (d) 10·5cm long and over 1m to the N lay part of a handled cord-decorated cup (Fig. 10:2) near which calcined bones were scattered (c); it was about 7cm high, about 8cm in diameter.

Barrow-grave IV (B–I). This belonged to the second group of mounds. It was originally 19m in diameter but had been excavated for industrial purposes. On that occasion a richly furnished grave of the first to second centuries A.D. was destroyed and only part of its grave goods recovered.

In the central part of the mound, probably on the ancient surface, or in a shallow shaft, lay a large decorated Thuringian amphora (a) (Plate 4:1) and a large stone battle-axe near it (b) (Plate 10:1). No traces of skeleton were noticed. The amphora was 28·5 cm high, 31·5cm in diameter, very brittle. It was decorated with incised grooves in patterns characteristic of these vessels: a large band around the body between the two lugs (reconstruction was not properly executed), and four sets of vertical grooves between this band and the neck. The axe was 15·5cm long, very heavy of a 'Baltic' type.

A number of grave goods, many damaged, were excavated in the damaged part of the mound. They undoubtedly either belonged to one or two graves coeval with the above, or belonged to the latter or formed part of secondary burials. These objects were: a well-polished flint axe 11·2cm long, rectangular in section (c) (Fig. 15:1) of Bundsø type; a small fragment of a well-polished axe, rectangular in section and mad eof banded flint, originating from the Krzemionki, or similar mines in Central Poland (d) (Fig. 17:4); a stone battle-axe type *x*-3 (Fig. 13:6) 10cm long, with part of its butt missing (e); two (f) small and thin sherds of a vessel with a deep incised decoration, apparently of the Globular Amphora culture; a large spherical flint hammer (g), 7cm in diameter, battered over its whole surface; a fragment of a flint axe (h) used as a hammer (Fig. 17:3) 5cm long; a small thin flint axe, rectangular in section, polished all over the surface (i) with its edge missing (Fig. 17:2), 4·5cm long, and a similar one, a little larger, with its butt missing (g) (Fig. 17:1) 4·5cm long; burin (k) (Fig. 17:5) made of 'chocolade' variety of flint; two blades (m) and a flake (l); a sherd of a vessel, the base of it 4cm in diameter (o).

Barrow-grave v (B–II). At a distance of 11m from the above, 16m in diameter, 80cm to 1m high. A trench 17·5m long, 2m wide was dug across it; the plan is missing. In the centre of the barrow at a depth of 40cm a broken flint knife was found (e), 3cm long, and 2m N of it was a flint axe (a) (Fig. 16:12) 9cm long, irregular in section, an undecorated potsherd of a cup, grey in colour, and a stone battle-axe (d) of 'Baltic' type (Plate 10:5) well made of a greenish variety of stone, 15cm long. In another unspecified place near by, a decorated potsherd was found, characteristic of the Globular Amphora culture (Fig. 12:3).

Barrow-grave vi (B–III) was not investigated. This was 19m in diameter.

Barrow-grave vii (B–IV) (Plan 32:2). This was 23m N of the previous grave, 18m in diameter. A large portion of the mound had been destroyed and its earth removed for industrial purposes; thus the eastern perimeter was completely cleared, and much of the mound in the western part already taken.

The description of investigation and the position of the grave goods excavated suggest that two graves were uncovered, although in neither were any traces of skeletons found; they had evidently decayed entirely.

Grave i was situated about 1·5m SW of the centre, probably in a very shallow hole. Its site was marked by the following objects: a flint arrow-head 2·2cm long, with its tip broken off (B), another flint arrow-head 3·4cm long, found at a distance a little over 1m SE of the above (C) (Plate 9:19, 22), and a vessel (A) red-yellowish in colour, of Neolithic character, insufficiently baked, of which only a few very brittle sherds were recovered. Near it, or in it, lay a part of a perforated pendant-disc, about 4cm in diameter (A-2) made of clay (Fig. 19:20).

Grave ii was situated about 2m NW of the above, at about 3m W of the centre. It was marked by a cord-decorated mug (F) (Fig. 10:3) of which only a number of sherds of the lower part had survived (6cm high, base 5·5cm in diameter), and a mutilated axe (S) 8·4cm long, made of siliceous slate, which lay at 1·5m N of the mug, both on the ancient surface.

At about 4m SW of the centre of the mound, under the humus, was an accumulation of charcoal and red fired clay, about 15cm in diameter, 20cm thick (P).

67. *Krasów* district of Lwów

A group of six barrow-graves occur here in the forest near the Miedziaki hamlet (Plan 5:2). They are situated on the summit of a hill all in one line, running W–E for some 360m. All were excavated by me in 1935–6. Two mounds at the eastern end were Neolithic, all others belonged to the Komarów culture of the Bronze Age. The material was deposited in the Prehistoric Institute of the University of Lwów.

Barrow-grave i (Plan 33:2). This was situated on the western periphery of the group and was 18m in diameter and 1·2m high. An area approximately square in shape, with sides 3m long, dug 30cm into the ancient ground and orientated SW–NE was uncovered in the centre (A) at a depth of 80–90cm. Its western corner was covered by a thick layer of charcoal (h), about 1·1m by 50cm wide, orientated S–N. Small pieces and lumps of charcoal were likewise scattered over the whole of the central area but particularly along its borders (e, j, f, l). Close, and perpendicular, to the layer of charcoal, south of it and already outside the central shaft, lay a large sandstone slab 1m long, 40 by 40cm diameter, its surface fired (a). A few calcined bones were found near the northern corner of the shaft (b). Sherds of a broken Thuringian amphora (Fig. 9:1) were scattered over the whole area of the central shaft (c, d, g, k, n). There were also two small vessels found: a ribbed beaker (p) (Fig. 9:3) in the centre, and a small entirely crushed cup (i) near the southern corner. An axe made of siliceous slate also lay in the centre (m) (Fig. 9:4).

The axe above was 11cm long, almost round in cross-section. The beaker (p) (Fig. 9:3) its surface covered entirely by horizontal ribs, was 9·5cm high, 13cm in diameter, and was very brittle, being made of clay with a large admixture of sand, dark in cross-section and its outer wall covered with a thin layer of brownish slip. The amphora (Fig. 9:1) was about 31cm high, 32cm in diameter, with a row of triangular incisions under the shoulder and on the body, with several repeated vertical stripes linking both rows of incisions and consisting of four parallel grooves. Only a dozen or so fragments of this amphora survived, scattered at various points round the grave, on its bottom, as in other places. The small cup (i) had a rounded bottom, was not baked and could not be extricated.

Barrow-grave ii (Plan 33:3). This was about 40m west of the above, 16m in diameter, 60cm high. Its cross-section was similar to the above: a loose dark ash-coloured mound was found under the forest humus 25cm thick. The ancient level occurred at a depth of about 55cm. It was formed of hard, beaten earth, black above, with the lower layers gradually giving way to darker brown, then to virgin soil. It was excavated to a depth of 1·2m where the earth still had a somewhat blackish tinge.

A trimmed flint flake (a) and an odd potsherd (b) were found in the mound at a depth of about 40cm south of the centre. A broken Thuringian amphora (e) (Plate 4:5) with some fragments lying about 1m away to the east (c) was found at a depth of 70cm, most probably in a small, shallow shaft dug about 15–20cm into the ground, at 2m west of the centre. A small, well-polished flint axe (f) (Fig. 16:22) 7·1cm long was lying near the amphora, with a flint knife 10cm long, very well made, its edges trimmed (Fig. 17:9) at 50cm from it, to the east (g). The Thuringian amphora was 22·5cm high, 24cm in diameter, and was decorated with an incised ornament typical of these amphorae. It was not possible to determine the edges of the shaft with any accuracy. The amphora had evidently been standing at its western end, while the flint knife was undoubtedly lying by the hip of the skeleton, which had completely decayed. East of the centre of the mound a lump of charcoal lay on the ancient surface (d).

Barrow-grave III (Plan 33:1). This was situated at the western end of the entire group, was 16m in diameter and 40cm high. The grave-shaft (C), traces of which were only slight, was in the centre of the mound. It was about 2·8 by 1·8m, dug 30cm into the ground, orientated W–E. A handled cup (b) (Plate 19:11) 9·5cm high, 9·8cm in diameter, not decorated, was found in the centre, near the eastern end at a depth of 60cm from the top of the mound. Two bowls and a small cup (A) (Plate 19:9) were standing in the SE corner of the shaft, on the ancient level. One bowl (A–1) (Plate 20:10) was 12cm high, 17·5cm in diameter, with narrowing outlet, four small parallel grooves encircling it on the shoulder, the bottom very clearly marked. The second (A-2) (Plate 20:8) was 10·3cm high, 17cm in diameter, and had a short shoulder, with narrow outlet and six symmetrically placed protuberances on the body, made from within. The cup (A-3) (Plate 19:9) was 3·7cm high, 6·3cm in diameter with smooth sides widening towards the top. No traces of skeleton were found.

Barrow-grave IV (Plan 34:2). This was situated 92m east of the above. It was 16m in diameter, 50cm high. The handle of a Roman amphora (a) was found immediately under the forest humus on the north side, with a large quantity of fragments of the amphora near it (b). An oval area (e) about 5 by 3·5m orientated approximately N–S, occurred in the centre of the grave under the mound, at a depth of 40–50cm. Small lumps of charcoal were found scattered on this area, though they did not form a continuous layer. The shaft (f) about 1m in diameter, dug 40cm into the ancient ground i.e. 85–90cm from the top of the mound, occurred on the north side of this area, about 2m from centre of the mound. Poorly calcined human bones mixed with charcoal were found at the bottom. They were covered with almost entirely decayed logs. Two smaller shafts of 20cm diameter were east of this shaft, with entirely calcined posts (d) placed vertically in them. An oval shaft (g) 1m long, dug 20cm into the ancient ground was about 1m SW of the centre, in the SW corner of the above-mentioned area. A large bowl, upside down (g-2) (Plate 19:13), was standing in the centre of this oval shaft with a bronze pin (g-4) on its bottom. A small red, entirely crushed and extremely brittle, vessel stood near the bowl: it could not be extricated (g-1). A sandstone whetstone or more probably an unperforated hammer (g-3) (Fig. 35:16) 10cm long was on the other side: one side of it was entirely flat, with traces of polishing. The bronze pin (g-4) was 9cm long, made of circular wire 2·5cm in diameter, its head enclosed in a spiral shield 16mm in diameter; it was entirely eaten away by patina and disintegrated. The large bowl (g-2) (Plate 19:13) was 15cm high, 26cm in diameter, with eight parallel grooves round it and fluted ornamentation placed diagonally and wide apart led from them to the upper portion of the body, with groups of incised grooves between and parallel to them.

Barrow-grave V (Plan 34:1). This was 62m ENE of the above, 14m in diameter, 30cm high. A large number of scattered small lumps of charcoal were found on the ancient level at a depth of 30–35cm, after removal of the mound: they were scattered round the centre and to the south of it, about 4–5m in diameter (d), while some potsherds were found on its southern periphery, about 3m from the centre and covering an area about 1·5m long. The fragments were those of a larger vessel, probably a bowl (b). Two fragments (e), probably of this vessel, were found on the eastern periphery of this area. They were a sand-gritted ware covered with a slip. A handled cup 7cm high, 9·3cm in diameter, handle slightly raised above the rim and with four parallel grooves encircling it was found on the NE periphery of this area and 2m from centre (c). A large handled jug (a-1) (Fig. 30:8) and small cup (a-2) were standing approximately in the centre of the central area. The jug was 20cm high, 23cm in diameter, the upper part cylindrical, the bottom concave. The body bore a broad fluting, the handle being rectangular with raised edges. The surface of the vessel was carefully slipped. The cup disintegrated into powder. Both vessels had been grown across by roots of a tree which stood on the mound above them. No traces of skeleton were found.

Barrow-grave VI. This was 55m ENE of the above and 155m W of Barrow-grave II, and was 24m in diameter, 1m high. It bore traces of excavation by a trench 6m long, 1·2m wide, running W–E. A layer of calcined oak logs 50cm long, 60cm wide, placed W–E, was found immediately under this trench, 2m W of the centre at a depth of 60–70cm.

68. *Krymidów* district of Stanisławów

One of the several barrow-graves there was excavated in 1856. Near the skeleton polished implements were found.[68]

69. *Lwów*

A cord-decorated 'Złota' handled cup was found, presumably in a destroyed grave, 7·5cm high.[69]

70. *Mitulin* district of Złoczów

In barrow-graves situated on the 'Mogiłki' field, vessels and flint implements were found.[70]

71. *Mogilany* district of Żółkiew

Flint implements are said to have been found in a barrow-grave.[71]

72. *Niesłuchów* district of Kamionka Strumiłowa

In a barrow-grave situated on the border with Żelechów, a few stone objects and a fine flint celt were found. The latter is reported to have been given to the Dzieduszycki Museum in Lwów, but I have been unable to identify it.[72]

[68] Kozłowski (op. cit., note 2: 1924), p. 190.

[69] J. Głosik, 'Wołyńsko-podolskie materiały z epoki kamiennej i wczesnej epoki brązu w Państwowym Muzeum Archeologicznym w Warszawie', *Mat.St.*, vol. VIII, 1962, p. 151, Pl. IX:7.

[70] Janusz (op. cit., note 9), p. 281.

[71] Ibid., p. 292.

[72] A. Schneider, *Notatki archeologiczne* (a nineteenth-century manuscript in the possession of Dr A. Czołowski, which I was kindly allowed to read and make appropriate notes).

73. *Nowosiołki Liskie* district of Kamionka Strumiłowa

Three vessels, found in a barrow-grave destroyed by industrial excavation, were given to the Ševčenko Museum in Lwów before the war. They were found in an inhumation grave along with a flint dagger (a 'saw').[73] The vessels were: an amphora reminiscent of a Thuringian amphora (Plate 5:2) but with the lugs near the neck on the upper part of the body. Its decoration followed patterns typical of the Thuringian amphorae, and consisted of a raised band around the body, cord decoration around the neck and a series of groups of three vertical cord-impressed grooves between them; the two outer grooves in each group terminated in spirals. The second vessel was an undecorated beaker with a high body, and the third was a wide cup, with a raised finger-tip decorated band around the rim (Plate 6:7, 8).

74. *Olszanica* district of Złoczów

A flint axe of Valby type(?) (Fig. 15:13) 8cm long, found in an excavated barrow-grave was at the Dzieduszycki Museum in Lwów (no. 499) before the war. It was made of banded grey and brownish flint very thoroughly polished (including the narrow sides), the butt nearly square in section.

75. *Płaucza Wielka* district of Brzeżany

Here a group of seventeen barrow-graves occurred on the ridge of an extensive hill over a distance of about 120m (Plan 6). Two mounds situated at either end of this group were excavated in 1937 by Dr R. Jamka assisted by students of Prehistory of the University of Cracow.[74]

Barrow-grave I. This dated from the early mediaeval period.

Barrow-grave II. At the eastern end of the group. Two burials were uncovered, both with skeletons in a contracted position, heads to W. The skeleton in grave 1 (Plate 1:2) was well preserved; near its feet lay a handled cord-decorated jug of Unetice type (Plate 6:22) 10·5cm high, 10·5cm in diameter, brown in colour, well baked; on the bones (or close to them) of the skeleton lay two flint arrow-heads, a boar-tusk (halved, unperforated), and half a stone battle-axe, damaged by fire. In grave 2, the skeleton of which was in a poorer state, a flint scraper and a stone battle-axe of type *z*-1 (Fig. 14:4) near the knees were excavated. All the grave goods were deposited in the Archaeological Museum in Cracow.

76. *Podciemne* district of Lwów

In 1935, three barrow-graves were excavated by Mr Ryński, a forest attendant. In the largest several flints and clay vessels were found. In the second, smaller in size, a flint knife and vessels were excavated, and the third also small in size, yielded only vessels.

77. *Podwysokie* district of Brzeżany

A barrow-grave of a group of several mounds situated on the 'Mogiłki' field was excavated in 1874.[75] Human bones, a few flints and potsherds were found, which are said to have been deposited at the Archaeological Museum in Cracow. I was unable to find or identify them there.

78. *Polana* district of Lwów

During road construction between Polana and Huta Szczerzecka, a barrow-grave was cut through. Two polished flint axes, ashes and charcoal were found here.[76]

79. *Putiatyńce* district of Rohatyn

Three bronze pins and a vessel were found in 1896 during the construction of the railway line.[77] They evidently originated from destroyed barrow-graves, a number of which were recorded in that locality. One of the pins was of the 'Cypriot' type of the Early Bronze Age (Fig. 19:15). Two others (Fig. 26:14, 15) and the vessel (Plate 16:17) were of the Middle Bronze Age Komarów culture. Both were of the same type made of bronze wire, one having the upper part square in section, the heads being formed of a thin, round convex sheet decorated with protuberances and perforated. The vessel in which calcined bones were found had its neck covered with three parallel grooves and the upper part of the body bore hanging shaded triangles. The body had protuberances, one of these with a vertical perforation.

80. *Remenów* district of Lwów

In 1918, a large thin flint flake, 9 by 6cm in size, was found by Professor Siemiradzki near a contracted skeleton, probably in a barrow-grave.[78]

81. *Rohatyn*

Before the war the Lubomirski Museum in Lwów possessed an undecorated handled cup of Mad'arovce type (Plate 7:1) 6·5cm high, 6·5cm in diameter. It probably originated from a barrow-grave.

82. *Rokitno* district of Lwów

Sixteen mounds were found on the ridge of 'Hryniówka-Zielony Garb' hill, in the forest. Similar mounds also lay on the territory of the adjoining village of Polany in the district of Żołkiew. In 1933 I excavated six of these mounds[79] with the assistance of Mr K. Wardzała, a student of Prehistory of the University of Lwów. All the material excavated was deposited at the Prehistoric Institute of the University of Lwów.

Barrow-grave 1. 16m in diameter, 1m high. This had been excavated previously by Dr S. Iszkowski who found two flint axes and a flint chisel. The larger axe of Bundsø type (Fig. 15:3) 12·1cm long, was nearly rectangular in section, polished over its entire surface, made of light grey flint, slightly banded. The second axe was small, 8·1cm long, flat, very well polished, rectangular in section, made of the same variety of flint (Fig. 16:26). The chisel, 12·5cm long, made of the

[73] Pasternak (op. cit., note 35), p. 131, and note 49.

[74] T. Sulimirski, 'Sprawozdanie z badań wykopaliskowych w Małopolsce Wschodniej i na Wołyniu'. *Spr.PAU*, vol. XLII, 1937, pp. 226 f.

[75] Kozłowski (op. cit., note 2: 1924), p. 191.

[76] *ZOW*, vol. XI, 1936, p. 17.

[77] J. Kostrzewski, 'Z badań nad osadnictwem wczesnej i środkowej epoki brązowej na ziemiach polskich', *Prz.A.*, vol. II, 1922–4, p. 191. Kozłowski (op. cit., note 2: 1928), p. 99, Pl. XIII:2, 3, 12.

[78] Id. (op. cit., note 2: 1924), p. 192.

[79] Sulimirski, loc. cit., note 37. M. Śmiszko, 'Osady ludzkie z przed trzech tysięcy sześciuset lat w okolicy Lwowa', *Z Bliska i z Daleka*, no. 1, Lwów 1934, pp. 3 ff., Figs. 1, 2. *IKC*, no. 104 of 16.IV. 1934 (Dodatek Literacki).

same variety of flint, was nearly square in section, 1·7cm thick (Fig. 16:28).

I excavated this mound again. Its cross-section was as follows: under the forest humus, 40cm thick, was the mound earth, quite loose and dark in colour, 1m deep. It lay on the ancient humus, dark with a brownish shade, 60cm thick, which gradually changed to the yellow sub-soil. The grave lay on the ancient surface as indicated by the ruined skeleton; axes were found close to it.

Barrow-grave 2 (Plan 35:1). This was situated about 30m NW of the above and was 12m in diameter, 50cm high. Its cross-section was similar to the above. A flint burin (a) 5cm long was found in the centre of the mound, immediately underneath the forest humus, while a flint arrow-head (b) was found deeper, at 50cm and immediately on the grave-shaft. A shallow grave-shaft about 30cm deep, the limits of which could not be determined, orientated SW–NE, was found under the mound, in the centre of the area covered by the mound. Two irregular lumps of soft sandstone (c) 20–30cm in diameter, 1m apart in a NW–SE line, were found halfway down the shaft, on either side and on the ancient level. Half a crushed Thuringian amphora (d) (Plate 5:8) was lying on the bottom of the grave-shaft, at the NE end, about 1m N of the eastern stone, at a depth of 1·1m from the top of the mound. A flint axe (e) (Fig. 15:2) was by it. An amber pendant (f) (Fig. 19:21) was found above the amphora, on the edge of the shaft and lodged vertically in the earth. A stone battle-axe (g) was found in the shaft, between the two stones. A stag tooth (h) was lying 20cm E of it, and an unworked flint blade-knife (i) 12·4cm long was found immediately beside the stone. Another wide flint flake (j) 10cm long, was lying approximately halfway across the area between the amphora and the western stone. A small pebble was lying by it, nearer the centre of the grave (k). No traces of skeleton were observed.

The amphora (Plate 5:8) was 20·5cm high, 24·5cm in diameter, and was red, with a large admixture of sand, poorly fired, very brittle. The rim was raised and finger-tip decorated, with a seven-cord impressed horizontal line on the shoulder encircling the vessel. It had two lugs on the body. The flint axe (Fig. 15:2) 11cm long of Bundsø type(?) was made of a black variety of flint, rectangular in section, slightly polished. The battle-axe was made of granite, but had been badly damaged by fire and disintegrated. It was of type *x*-1, very similar to that from Barrow-grave III at Kulczyce Szlacheckie. The amber pendant was rectangular, with a perforation in the middle, undecorated, and 3·5 to 2·5cm in size.

Barrow-grave 3 (Plan 35:5). This formed a separate group with Barrow-grave 4 some 500m N from the above. It was 15·5m in diameter, 1m high. Traces of shaft 1·5m square, 1·2m deep, occurred on the NE side (a). Its cross-section was as follows: the barrow-grave mound 90cm thick was found under forest humus 30cm deep. Fossil humus 60cm deep and very degradate blackish-yellow in colour as in the mound itself, occurred under this, gradually giving way to virgin soil. Numerous traces of hamster holes were found in the lower humus.

A fairly well-preserved strongly contracted skeleton of a woman (b), on its left side, head to W was under the mound on the ancient level and near the centre (Plate 1:5). It was covered with a fairly thick layer of charcoal (c), and a large fragment of the left jawbone and some teeth from the upper jawbone of a young male lamb (*Ovis L*) (d) were found[80] by the head: a large fragment of a beaker of the same type as the Morawsko beaker (Plate 6:21), dark-red in colour, well-fired, and covered with cord decoration lay near the feet (e). The skeleton was lying on the periphery of the grave-shaft, at the south side. The shaft (f), which was 1·8 by 80cm and orientated W–E, was under the centre of the mound and dug 80cm into the ancient ground. A very decayed strongly contracted male skeleton, head to E, on its right, with no grave goods present, was lying on the bottom of the shaft. Both burials were coeval, placed parallel, with heads in opposite directions and lying on different sides.

Barrow-grave 4. This was 12m W of the above, 9m in diameter, 50cm high. The grave-shaft 1·3 by 1·2m, dug about 60cm into the ancient ground and penetrating to virgin soil, was situated under the centre of the mound. An almost entirely decayed male skeleton, much contracted, on its right side, head to W was lying on the shaft bottom. No grave goods were present.

Barrow-grave 5. This was a single mound some 500m NW of the above, 10·5m in diameter and 60cm high. One flint flake, 4cm long and a few lumps of charcoal were found on the ancient level, near the centre, around a shallow grave-shaft 20cm deep. Nothing was found in it. Its limits could not be determined.

Barrow-grave 6 (Plan 35:4) was situated 1km N of the above, and belonged to a larger group of mounds in the forest, near the forester's house. It was 11·5m in diameter, 1m high. Its cross-section was as follows: a mound 1m deep, relatively dark, occurred under 40cm of forest humus. This was lying on highly degradate fossil humus, which merged without clear limit into virgin soil.

A highly contracted male skeleton, head to E was lying 165cm from the top of the mound and in the centre of the mound, in a very shallow shaft of some 20–30cm depth, the limits of which could not be determined with any accuracy (a). Two flint axes (Fig. 15:10, 11) and the butt of a third were lying by one another near the skeleton's hands (b) with three points made of horn by them (Plate 11:13, 14). A flint knife (c) 10·7cm long was lying by its elbow, with another knife 11·3cm long 30cm SW of its knees (d). A broken Thuringian amphora (e) (Plate 5:9) was standing immediately behind the skeleton, by its hip bones. A loose human left leg (f), bent at the knee, was lying on the hip and thighs of the skeleton so that its thigh was lying on the hip of the skeleton, its shin across the shins and thighs of the skeleton, and its foot immediately behind the feet of the skeleton. The bones of this leg were very decayed, as was the skeleton under it. A larger stone (g) was found some 2m E of the centre of the mound, on the ancient level, close to the SE corner of the shaft and close to the NW corner charcoal was strewn (h).

The Thuringian amphora (Plate 5:9) was 20cm high, 12cm in diameter and had two lugs on opposite sides of the body.

[80] I am much indebted to Dr K. Myczkowski, before the war of the Institute of Topographic Anatomy of the Veterinary Medicine College (Akademia Medycyny Weterynaryjnej) in Lwów, for identifying these bones.

The shoulder bore one row of vertical incisions. It was brownish-red in colour, not very carefully fired or made. The larger flint axe (Fig. 15:11) was 11·3cm long, flat, made of dark flint as was the other, smaller axe (Fig. 15:10) 10cm long. This axe was flatter, while both were nearly rectangular in cross-section, though provided with small elevations of the long edges. Only the butt was found of the third axe: it was 5·6cm long, made of the same flint, but thicker than the others. Only two points of horn, both with broken ends, both about 12cm in original length could be preserved (Plate 11:13, 14).

83. *Romanówka* district of Brody

A decorated bowl, at present in the Historical Museum at Lviv, was found in a barrow-grave on the Styr. It was 10·5cm high, 16cm in diameter, its decoration consisting of thirteen horizontal grooves around the neck, and a row of groups of three concentric semicircles below them, on the upper part of the body. The vessel was typical of the Trzciniec culture.

84. *Rusiłów* district of Kamionka Strumiłowa

A barrow-grave, 30m in diameter, 80cm high, was excavated by Dr J. Bryk[81] in 1930. At a depth of 90cm, in the centre of the mound, a secondary burial was uncovered with a contracted skeleton near which a fibula typical of the fourth century A.D. was found. The original burial was found 75cm deeper, under the above, in a depression or hole, 12m in diameter (?), 30cm deep, which extended over the entire centre of the barrow-grave. The skeleton lay crouched on its right side, head to W (Plate 1:4). The following grave goods (Plate 8:1) were deposited at the Prehistoric Institute of the University of Lwów: a flint dagger with the tip broken off and missing (it was wedged in the abdomen of the skeleton), a large stone battle-axe, 14·5cm long, three flint arrow-heads, one with the tip broken off, and a few flint blade knives. Near the left ear lay a gold ear-pendant of Irish type, with traces of having been repaired in prehistoric times, and provided with a small bronze wire which evidently replaced the original damaged or broken-off gold catch.

85. *Rypniów* district of Milatyn Nowy

A cord-decorated handled jug and a bronze ear-pendant of Stubło type were found in a burial, probably in a barrow-grave.[82]

86. *Sarniki* district of Bóbrka

A group of six barrow-graves in a line running SE–NW for 700m was situated on the summit of a hill in the 'Kamionki' forest (Plan 5:1). More barrow-graves on the same hill lay in the territory of the neighbouring villages Łanki Małe (to SE) and Żabokruki (to NW). I excavated three of these barrow-graves in 1931 and 1935,[83] as well as a fourth in the 'Grabowiec' forest. All grave goods were deposited in the Institute of Prehistory of Lwów University.

Barrow-grave I (Plan 36:1) was the largest, situated in the centre of the group and 27m in diameter, 2·5m high. It was overgrown with large beech trees so that investigation was restricted to digging across (SE–NW) a trench 3m wide, widened in the centre to 5m. A battle-axe of granite, 9·3cm long, a flat almost triangular bronze dagger (Fig. 19:23) 9cm long with no middle rib, bearing three rivet holes, a flint scraper 4·4cm long were found near the centre of the barrow (a), at a depth of 60cm in the mound: they were side by side. The grave-shaft, 2 by 1·5m, rectangular, with rounded corners and orientated W–E was found under the mound, in the centre of the barrow. It was dug some 50cm into the yellow subsoil and reached to a depth of 3m from the top of the mound. Nothing was found, nor was it possible to discern any traces of the skeleton.

Barrow-grave II. This was the most easterly of the group, and was 20m in diameter, 50cm high. Its cross-section was as follows: 20cm of ashy forest humus, then a dark ash-coloured mound 35cm deep. Fossil humus occurred under this at a depth of 55cm and reached to 90cm depth, being dark, entirely black in places, with a very large number of hamster holes. Below, it gradually gave way to an increasingly yellow colour, with hamster holes. Pure virgin soil occurred at 1·2m from top of the mound. Nothing was found in this barrow-grave.

Barrow-grave III (Plan 36:2) was situated 80m NW of barrow-grave I, and was 18m in diameter, 60cm high. Its cross-section was similar to that of barrow-grave II. Some scattered lumps of charcoal (e) and several calcined sandstones (h, j) lay near the centre on the ancient surface, irregularly covering an area of about 2 by 1·5m, orientated approximately W–E. This was undoubtedly the position of the burial though no traces of skeleton could be discerned. A flint knife (c) (Fig. 17:10) 9cm long was lying 3·5–4m N of this spot, with a flint scraper (f) (Fig. 17:15) 6cm long at a distance of 1m from it, to the SW. Several potsherds (a, d) were found about 2m W of the grave, also on the ancient surface. They derived from one large vessel, made of grog-gritted clay, black inside and the exterior being streaked with red slip.

Barrow-grave IV (Plan 36:3, 3a). This isolated barrow-grave was in the 'Grabowiec' forest, on a hill west of the village. It was 18m in diameter, 1m high. Small lumps of charcoal, small single potsherds and flint flakes were found both in the top of the mound and deeper in it. They occurred mainly in a circle about 6m in diameter around the centre of the mound. The rectangular grave-shaft (A) 1·6 by 1·1m, orientated NE–SW and dug about 25cm into the ancient ground was found at 1m depth, on the ancient level. Four vessels were standing on its bottom, along the SE wall: these were a tulip-shaped beaker (h) (Plate 18:1) in the north corner, which was 14·6cm high, 13cm in diameter, with five grooves round the shoulder and a raised band; one larger bowl (j) (Plate 17:3) 12·5cm high and 19cm in diameter, with six parallel grooves round the neck and a zigzag line, shaded triangles, oblique impressions and dots immediately on the upper part of the body. A smaller bowl (i) (Plate 17:6) was standing in

[81] J. Bryk, 'Kurhany w Rusiłowie i Krasnem.' *Materiały Prehistoryczne*, vol. I, Kraków 1934, pp. 85 ff., Figs. 1–4, Pl. XV. See also J. J. Butler, 'The Late Neolithic Gold Ornament from Bennekom', *Palaeohistoria*, vol. V, Groningen 1956, Pl. X.

[82] J. Machnik, 'Uwagi o wczesnej fazie epoki brązu w dorzeczu górnej Wisły i Dniestru', *Sprawozdania z posiedzeń Komisji PAN*, Kraków, VII–XII, 1960, Fig. f.

[83] Sulimirski, loc. cit., note 37. See also loc. cit., note 19 (1957–9).

the southern corner of the grave: it was 11cm high, 17·5cm in diameter, with six parallel grooves on the shoulder and the body covered by deep oblique fluting. The surface was carefully polished, shining in some places. An ornamented beaker (n) (Plate 18:11) 9·5cm high, 9·6cm in diameter was standing near the previous bowl; it was entirely covered with an incised ornament consisting of groups of vertical grooves divided by strips filled with oblique lines. It was carefully made. No skeleton was found, though slight traces warranted the hypothesis that it had been lying head SW.

87. *Stratyn* district of Rohatyn

Several groups of barrow-graves were situated here. One, consisting of several mounds, was in the 'Pohrebiska' forest, and another, of eight graves, was in the 'Piaseczna' forest. They were distributed on the summit of a hill in a NE–SW direction, reaching into the area of other villages (Wulka, district of Brzeżany, and Dubryniów district of Rohatyn). These barrow-graves averaged about 20m in diameter, and were from 80cm to 2m high. In 1933 I excavated two barrow-graves here in the 'Piaseczna' forest.[84] The material was deposited in the Institute of Prehistory in Lwów University.

Barrow-grave 1. This was the smallest, being 14m in diameter, 1m high. Its cross-section was as follows: the mound, about 95cm deep, lay under forest humus 35cm thick. It was lying on fossil humus which was very hard and brownish in colour, about 50cm thick. This humus gave way with no clear dividing line to increasingly yellow sub-soil.

A flint scraper 4·8cm long, a flint flake and a handful of charcoal were found approximately in the centre of the mound, under the forest humus at a depth of 40cm. A two-lugged Thuringian amphora (Plate 5:1) 14·5cm high, 16cm in diameter, not decorated, very fragile and red in colour, with shoulder and rim broken was found at a depth of 1·4m on the ancient level and about 1m E of centre. The base of this amphora was dug about 10cm into the ancient ground. A flint blade knife 9cm long was lying near it, with some lumps of calcined clay, red in colour, scattered by it. There was no grave-shaft, nor could traces of skeleton be discerned.

Barrow-grave 2 (Plan 34:3) was situated about 30m from the above, 20m in diameter and 1·2m high. Its cross-section was similar to the above, except that the mound had a somewhat larger admixture of sand which does not occur in the proximity of the mound. A rectangular grave-shaft 2m by 90cm, orientated NE–SW, dug about 50cm into the ancient ground was found under the mound at a depth of 1·5m in the centre of the barrow-grave (a). An entirely smashed Thuringian amphora (b) (Plate 5:5) in a somewhat leaning position, was standing in the south corner of the shaft: it was not decorated, had two lugs on the body and was 26·5cm high, with body diameter 26cm. Nothing else was found, nor were traces of skeleton discerned.

88. *Tenetniki* district of Rohatyn

A group of barrow-graves up to 1·5m high occurred on a high elevation between Tenetniki and Bukaczowce. One was excavated *c.* 1880 during the building of a road, while four others were excavated in 1889 by G. Ossowski.[85] The material was deposited in the Archaeological Museum, Cracow.

Barrow-grave I was the largest of the group, 12m in diameter, 1·5m high and dug across for an extent of 6m wide. Clay vessels containing calcined human bones (?) were found at a depth of 50cm, at three points near the circumference. One was entirely destroyed, the other two could be reconstructed. One was a tulip-shaped undecorated pot 21·5cm high, 16·4cm in diameter, reddish-grey in colour, made of clay with a strong admixture of sand and very brittle. This vessel has not been preserved in any museum collection. The second vessel was an unornamented jug, 17cm high, 17·7cm in diameter, dark brown in colour, with the inside black and the surface polished. It had a smooth lug on the body extending to the rim. The third vessel was a similar jug.

Barrow-graves II–IV were somewhat smaller in size. Several vessels were found in each, but they were so damaged that they could not be preserved. They were similar in type to the vessel in Barrow-grave I. One vessel only had an ornament consisting of a few short incisions encircling it. Some flint flakes were also found.

89. *Trościaniec Mały* district of Złoczów

A group of eighteen mounds, situated on high ground SE of the village and about 1–2m high, of which six were excavated in 1875 by F. Marynowski. Only 'ashes and clay' were found in three of these, while potsherds were excavated from the other three.[86]

90. *Ubynie* district of Kamionka Strumiłowa

An undecorated Thuringian amphora (Plate 5:3) found in a barrow-grave here was deposited in the Shevchenko Museum, Lwów (no. 23079) before World War II.[87]

91. *Wolica* district of Podhajce

A group of eleven barrow-graves extending in a SW–NE direction for about 150m was situated on a hill in the 'Okrągły Garb' forest (Plan 4:2). Four of these mounds were excavated in 1935 by Miss I. Siwek and K. Żurowski,[88] then students of the Institute of Prehistory, Lwów University. The archaeological material was deposited in the Institute of Prehistory, Lwów University.

Barrow-grave I (Plan 35:3) was situated on the SE periphery of the group, 12m in diameter, and about 1m high. The forest humus was 25cm deep. Flint flakes, some calcined, and single pottery fragments were found under the humus and in the grave mound, with lumps of charcoal and single calcined human bones in addition. A group of four vessels placed approximately in a square 1m in size was found at a depth of about 1·5m, on the ancient level and on the east side of the central portion of the mound. A large, broken bowl (i) (Plate 20:13) about 16·5cm high and 21cm in diameter was standing on the west side, almost in the centre of the mound. Four symmetrically placed lugs, horizontally perforated were between shoulder and body, with a raised band triangular in

[84] Sulimirski, loc. cit., note 37.

[85] G. Ossowski, *ZWAK*, vol. XIV, 1890, pp. 38 ff. Janusz (op. cit., note 9), p. 196. R. Rogozińska, 'Cmentarzysko kultury komarowskiej w Bukównie', *Mat.Arch.*, vol. I, 1959, p. 112, Pl. VIII:5.

[86] Janusz (op. cit., note 9), p. 289.

[87] Pasternak (op. cit., note 16: 1933–6), p. 16.

[88] Rogozińska (op. cit., note 85), p. 112.

section on their base, from which groups of oblique flutings extended upwards. A handled cup (l) (Plate 19:5) 6·5cm high and 8·8cm in diameter was standing about 1m N of this, bearing an ornament on the upper part of the body consisting of groups of three wide oblique grooves varying in direction. A tulip-shaped beaker (j) (Plate 20:3) 11cm high and 9·8cm in diameter, with a low raised band on the neck was standing about 50cm E of it. A small undecorated bowl or large cup (z) (Fig. 28:6) 10·5cm high and 13cm in diameter, was standing 1·2m SE of the bowl: it had a flat bottom, was brownish in colour and partly red. A small heap of human calcined bones (k) was lying between this bowl or cup and the tulip-shaped beaker.

Barrow-grave 2 was situated 30m SW of the above. It had been destroyed at some time in the past. Only a few small flint flakes and some small odd potsherds were found in it.

Barrow-grave 3 was situated at the NW periphery of the group on the far side of the forest road: it was 18m in diameter and about 1·5m high. Several odd potsherds and flint flakes, some trimmed at the edges, and one flint scraper 3·5cm long were found in the mound. A large, handled jug (D) (Plate 19:10) 11cm high, 13cm in diameter, was found at a depth of 1·2m on the ancient level and in the centre of the mound. It had a wide handle raised over the rim. The only decoration consisted of warts on the body. These were not counted as the vessel had been severely crushed. Nothing else was found.

Barrow-grave 4 (Plan 35:2) lay at the far end of the other group, at a distance of 26m NW of no. 1 and 25m N of no. II. It was 15m in diameter and 60cm high. Some flint flakes were found in the mound. A layer of charcoal 3cm deep, 1·5m in length, being the remains of a charred log lying W–E was found in the centre of the mound, at 45cm deep (k). Somewhat lower, at 60cm deep and on the ancient level and 3m S of centre, were found seven vessels placed in two groups along a line running SW–NE: one group consisted of four vessels viz. a large handled bowl (g) (Plate 19:7); two decorated bowls (a, b) and a beaker (c) (Plate 19:8). The second row consisted of three vessels viz. a tulip-shaped pot (d) (Plate 20:4); a small cup, entirely crushed (e) and a larger cup (f) (Plate 19:12). Two other vessels, two handled cups (h, i) (Fig. 30:4, Plate 19:6) were at a distance of *c.* 1·5m SE of the centre, *c.* 1m N of the cup 'f'. No traces of any skeleton were noticed.

The bowl 'a' was 14cm high, 17cm in diameter. Two grooves encircled the neck, and the body was adorned with five bosses pressed from inside, each encircled by concentric fluting; the intervals between the bosses had vertical fluting. A large, wide protuberance occurred on the upper part of the body. The second bowl 'b' was similar in size; it was very brittle, disintegrated and its reconstruction was not practicable. The beaker 'c' (Plate 19:8) was 11cm high, 11·5cm in diameter, S-shaped profile; the decoration consisted of three horizontal grooves on the border of the neck and the body below, which consisted of groups of alternating slanting incisions, three in each group. The tulip-shaped pot 'd' (Plate 20:4) 13·5cm high, 12cm in diameter, had a raised band around the neck provided with four double warts. The cup 'f' (Plate 19:12) 9cm high, 10cm in diameter, has four horizontal grooves round the neck and seven bosses on the body, each encircled by a double fluting, the rim flat. The handled bowl 'g' (Plate 19:7) 13cm high, 13·5cm in diameter, had a wide trough-shaped handle, and was decorated with four wide bosses with three or four semicircular flutings around each. The handled cup 'h' (Fig. 30:4) 9cm high, 11cm in diameter, was decorated with five horizontal grooves around the neck, three bosses on the body, the intervals between them covered with a slanting fluting. The other handled cup 'i' (Plate 19:6) 10cm high 12cm in diameter, had the body covered with vertical fluting.

92. *Wyrów* district of Kamionka Strumiłowa.

An inhumation burial was uncovered in 1924 on an elevation west of the village during the erection of survey posts (point 217): this was undoubtedly in the low mound. The grave was investigated in 1927 by B. Janusz.[89] It had been much damaged by the post-holes. He found from the position of the undisturbed bones that the skeleton was contracted. A lump of earth with traces of a small brass or bronze object was found near it, as well as a flint dagger, carefully made, 15·2cm long. No pottery was found.

93. *Żelechów Wielki* district of Kamionka Strumiłowa

K. Hadaczek excavated a large barrow-grave here on an elevation[90] in 1897. It appears from the description that the grave was rectangular, 1·16m by 80cm, dug in the ancient level of the mound in the centre. No skeleton was found, as it had evidently decayed entirely. A secondary burial was also found, in an extended position, on its back, head to W, which had been destroyed by later digging, presumably by a treasure-seeker. The bones in this grave were displaced, with only the head and extremities of legs retaining their original position. Apart from some flint flakes and odd potsherds nothing else was found in this barrow-grave. The following objects from this site were deposited in the Dzieduszycki Museum, Lwów, before the Second World War: some flint flakes, the bottom of a small vessel (perhaps a cup), the fragment of a dish with inverted rim and several fragments of a larger vessel (probably a tulip-shaped pot), which derived from its bottom and rim, under which was a raised, finger-tip decorated band and row of nail-tip impressions. All the vessels were hand-made ware, well-made and well-baked, red in colour. The places where these objects were found is not recorded: they undoubtedly derive from the secondary burial.

94. *Zvenyhorod* (*Dzwinogród*) district of Bóbrka (see no. 420)

The early Bronze Age cemetery on the 'Hoyeva Hora' site, ascribed to the Lublin Painted pottery culture, has been investigated in 1953–54. In 1955,[91] a cremation burial of the Corded Ware and an inhumation burial of the Komarów culture were excavated there, but no description has yet been published. In 1955, three graves of the Komarów culture and

[89] B. Janusz, *W.A.*, vol. x, 1929, p. 266. Głosik (op. cit., note 69), p. 171, Pl. XXVII:10.

[90] Janusz (op. cit., note 9), p. 159.

[91] І. К. Свешников, Археологічні роботи музею в 1952–7 pp. Lviv 1959, pp. 15 ff.

one dating from the Early Iron Age were uncovered on the 'Zahuminky' site. The latter, a double inhumation burial, lay at a depth of 40cm, and was damaged. Near the heads a large tulip-shaped pot with raised band and a row of small impressed holes were found.

4. THE HORODENKA GROUP

95. *Baliñce* district of Kołomyja

In barrow-graves on the 'Mogiłki' and 'Żałoby' fields, skeletons were excavated near which bronze rings and flint implements were found.[92]

96. *Beremiany* district of Tłumacz (see no. 484)

In 1827 a large barrow-grave built of earth and stones with a slab-cist built of six slabs was excavated. In it lay five human skulls and almost completely decayed bones, but according to another report, three skeletons lay here with a flint axe near each.[93] One of the axes of Valby type (Fig. 15:19) 16cm long, made very thoroughly, all four sides thoroughly polished, was at the Lubomirski Museum in Lwów (no. 5/12) before the war.

A number of slab-cist graves of the Globular Amphora culture were found at various points within the confines of this village (see no. 484). In 1932, I excavated four barrow-graves here which I considered to belong to the West Podolian group of Scythian remains.[94]

97. *Bukówna* district of Tłumacz

Forty-six barrow-graves were counted here by Dr J. Bryk, thirteen in the fields, thirty-three in the forest. They were situated on a long ridge where they were scattered in groups usually of three mounds each, forming a continuous line to which barrows in the territories of the neighbouring villages were adjoined, at either end. In 1931, six barrow-graves were investigated by Bryk, two in the field near the church (nos. 3, 4) and four in the forest (nos. 14, 15, 16, 17). Only a short report on these excavations has been published.[95] All the archaeological material has been deposited at the Archaeological Museum in Cracow. A detailed description of all mounds and their grave goods was included in my work on the Komarów culture, the typescripts of which with all plans, drawings, photographs etc., perished during the last war. Recently, thirty-eight vessels (almost all) and other grave goods at the Museum in Cracow were published by Mrs R. Rogozińska.[96]

Barrow-grave 3 (*later renamed* II) was 1m high. Six 'graves' were uncovered under the mound, each of which yielded one to two vessels, described and published by R. Rogozińska; I refer here (in square brackets) to her publication. Grave 1: a decorated vase and an undecorated bowl with inverted rim [pl. I, 5, 4]; grave 2: a vase [pl. I, 1]; grave 3: a black decorated cup [pl. I, 2] with a neck and wide everted rim; grave 4: no vessels in the collection; grave 5: a tulip-shaped, decorated beaker [pl. I, 3] with two lugs on the junction of the neck and body. According to a note in my possession, the undecorated beaker with a wavy rim [pl. II, 3] was found in grave 6 of this mound, whereas Rogozińska included it in grave 7 of barrow-grave IV.

Barrow-grave 4 (*renamed* I) situated near the preceding, was 1m high, and its central part encircled by a low wall of loose limestones, about 1·3m wide, 30cm high. In the centre, on the ancient surface, traces of a large hearth were uncovered under the ground, about 4m in diameter. Around this area stood ten urns with cremations, each with some additional vessels and other grave goods. At one point outside the stone circle, but close to it, lay a few fragments of an animal skull (cow or sheep).

Vessels and other grave goods found near most of these urns, and published by Rogozińska, were—grave 1: a large, decorated single-handled vase; a handled decorated cup, and a polished axe made of siliceous slate [pl. IV, 5, 2, IX, 2]. Grave 2: a decorated bowl [pl. III, 2]. Grave 3: a decorated bowl; a pot with horizontal fluting; a small decorated beaker with four lugs; a clay spoon; flint axe and two flint knives [pl. III, 4, IV, 4, V, 2, IX, 3, 1; fig. 3]. Grave 4: a decorated bowl (unpublished); a beaker with horizontal fluting; a bowl with a raised band under the rim [pl. V, 4, 3]. Grave 5: a decorated beaker; a decorated bowl [pl. VI, 5, II, 1]. Grave 6: a decorated bowl [pl. III, 1]. Grave 7: a decorated and an undecorated beaker; a decorated beaker with two vertically perforated lugs; two decorated bowls with rims everted; an undecorated bowl with a flat rim; a small undecorated bowl; a wide undecorated cup; a decorated handled cup [pl. VI, 1, 4, 2, IV, 1, III, 2, 5, II, 4, V, 5, 1, III, 6]; a single handled decorated bowl,[97] two small unpublished bowls or cups.

Barrow-grave 14. Situated in the forest, 1m high. A few vessels were found on the ancient surface. Rogozińska published the following grave goods: a decorated double-handled bowl, a decorated bowl [pl. VII, 2, 3], half a battle-axe made of siliceous slate, and a hoe of the same material.

Barrow-grave 15. Near the preceding, 1m high. At a depth of 1m, a single vessel, a decorated bowl [Rogozińska, pl. VII, 1], was excavated, and also a few flints.

Barrow-grave 16. 1·2m high. At a depth of 60cm a few vessels were excavated, and deeper, on the ancient surface, a double animal grave was uncovered: skeletons of two young horses lay side by side, legs towards one another. Three vessels from this grave were published by Rogozińska: an undecorated beaker, a decorated bowl with the rim everted, and another one with a short undecorated neck, rim wide, flat [pl. VI, 3, VII, 5, 4].

Barrow-grave 17. This was 1m high. Only a few potsherds and a few flint flakes were found in it.

In 1937, seven more barrow-graves were excavated by Dr M. Śmiszko and Miss I. Siwek, M.A., six being situated at the northern end of the barrow-grave cemetery, in the forest (nos. I–IV), and one in its southern group (no. VII). A short

[92] Schneider (op. cit., note 72).

[93] Janusz (op. cit., note 9), p. 256. Kozłowski (op. cit., note 2: 1924), p. 185.

[94] T. Sulimirski, *Scytowie na zachodniem Podolu*, Lwów 1936, pp. 62 ff.

[95] J. Bryk, 'Tymczasowe sprawozdanie z badań archeologicznych w Bukównie, pow.tłumacki', *Spr.PAU*, vol. XXXVII, 1932, pp. 21 f.

[96] Rogozińska (op. cit., note 85), pp. 97 ff., Pls. I–IX.

[97] L. Kozłowski, *Zarys pradziejów Polski południowo-wschodniej*, Lwów 1939, Pl. XIV:18.

report on these excavations was published,[98] and a detailed description included in my work, mentioned above. Only draft plans of three mounds survive in my notes,

The archaeological material from these graves is at present at the Historical Museum in Lviv, but some vessels were not properly identified after the disorganization of the collections during the war.

Barrow-graves I and II–1937. Both on communal ground. Only small hearths and charcoal, but no traces of burial were found.

Barrow-grave III–1937 (Plan 37:2). This lay in a small wood close to the road to Miłowanie. About 3·5m south of the centre, on the ancient surface, a hole (A) was uncovered, *c.* 30cm deep, nearly quadrangular in plan. It was *c.* 3 × 1·5m in area, orientated W–E, filled in with red fired clay, and in its central part, 1 square metre in area (B) 10cm deeper, lay charcoal and calcined human bones. The following grave goods were found in the hole: a bronze spiral-headed pin which disintegrated (c) found at the northern edge; south-west of it lay a bowl (d) (Plate 17:2) decorated with four horizontal grooves round the neck and a row of shaded triangles above, the whole body being covered with slanting fluting; near it lay sherds of another vessel (a). In the central square (B) among calcined bones lay: a bronze pin (g) (Fig. 26:12) 31cm long, with a disc-shaped perforated head, another spiral-headed pin (g) and a bronze spiral arm-band (i) (Fig. 26:13) 7·2cm in diameter, 13cm high with its terminals wound in spirals; a decorated cup (j) (Plate 18:12) its ornament consisting of groups of two horizontal grooves round the body, separated by bands of short slanting alternating incisions. In the SE corner of the grave stood a crushed vessel (h). In the mound several flint flakes were excavated.

Barrow-grave IV–1937 (Plan 37:1). North of the manor house, on the 'Skiba' field. On the ancient surface, 3m west of the centre, a layer 5cm thick was uncovered, about 1m in diameter which consisted of fired clay mixed with charcoal (A); lumps of charcoal were also found in other parts of the area (L). Some 3m north of the centre was a hole, 60 × 40cm in area, 20cm deep, filled with charcoal and fired clay, in which four vessels were found, three brownish in colour, undecorated (B, C, E): a tulip-shaped pot, 16cm in diameter, its upper part missing, a cup (Plate 20:7) 7cm high, 8·5cm in diameter, its sides straight and widening upwards, and a small bowl, or saucer (Fig. 30:6) 7·5cm high, 12·5cm in diameter; the fourth vessel was a bowl (D) (Plate 20:11) brownish in colour, 11cm high, 15·5cm in diameter, provided with two small unperforated lugs on the base of the neck, the neck decorated with two horizontal grooves, and the upper part of the body covered with vertical fluting. At a distance of *c.* 2·5cm south of the centre stood an undecorated bowl (G) (Plate 20:5) or saucer 8·2cm high, 17cm in diameter, and 1m further south another bowl (F) (Plate 19:14) with the neck covered with five horizontal grooves and the body with slanting fluting. Almost 2m E of these vessels lay, on the same ancient level, a lump of charcoal, and another lay 1·50m NE of the bowl 'G'. At a distance of 3m W of bowl 'G', 3·50m SW of the centre of the mound, a flint scraper was found (K).

[98] I. Siwek, 'Tymczasowe wyniki badań terenowych w Bukównej, pow.tłumacki', *ZOW*, vol. XIII, 1938, pp. 67 ff.

Barrow-graves V and VII–1937. The first of these was situated in the court of the manor, the other in a field near the church. Only potsherds and flint flakes were found in both.

Barrow-grave VI–1937 (Plan 38:3). 1·50m high, situated in the forest. Six vessels in three pairs were excavated, all at a depth of 90cm to 1m from the top of the mound; all were crushed. Two lay 2m N of the centre (c, d); another two (a, b) were at a distance of over 2m E of the centre, and the third pair (e), a little over 3m S of the centre. Vessel 'a' was an undecorated tulip-shaped beaker (Plate 20:2) 15·6cm high, 14cm in diameter. One of the southern vessels (e) (Fig. 28:4) of which only a few sherds remained, was a large pot brownish in colour, undecorated, with a slightly everted rim, provided with four vertically perforated lugs at the junction of the neck and the body. Another vessel from this mound, preserved in the collection, is a handled cup (Plate 19:1) 8·5cm high, 11cm in diameter, two parallel grooves around the neck, the rim flat, six flat bosses on the body, encircled by two concentric flutings each.

98. *Capowce* district of Zaleszczyki

In 1878, a barrow-grave was excavated by A. Schneider.[99] A slab-cist grave was found in which lay two skeletons of a 'mother and of a child'. A diorite battle-axe of type *z*-3 (Fig. 14:8) 'excavated at Capowce', was presented by Schneider in 1878 to the Lubomirski Museum, in Lwów; it may have originated from the above grave. It was 9cm long (no. 27–1661).

99. *Chocimierz* district of Tłumacz.

In the forest called 'Lipki', out of a group of three barrow-graves, two were excavated by A. Schneider and A. Kirkor in 1874.[100] One of these proved to have been previously excavated. In the second one, the largest in the group, a stone battle-axe of type *y*-4 and five other stone implements were found at a depth of 80cm. Over a dozen similar stone and several flint objects were found at a depth of 2m in the centre of the mound: these included a 'small, ground hammer with four sides' (?). No traces of skeleton were found.

Some of these objects were deposited in the Cracow Archaeological Museum. I was able, on the basis of the dimensions given by Kirkor, to identify only a battle-axe of sienite (no. 731), well ground, 9cm long. An axe (no. 112) (Fig. 16:9) is also to be found at the Museum, deposited at the same time as the battle-axe and made of dark yellow stone, apparently a mixture of sandstone and slate, 8·7cm long, oval in cross-section, carelessly made. Schneider is believed to have deposited seven stone objects and the urn excavated here in the Lubomirski Museum, Lwów.

100. *Dobrotów* district of Delatyn

Before the last war a local teacher, Mr Bagger, excavated a barrow-grave in which the following grave goods were found: a dark, or black, handled jug, a small black bowl, a black 'urn' 12–14cm high, and two other larger 'urns'.

[99] Janusz (op. cit., note 9), p. 258.
[100] Janusz (op. cit., note 9), p. 236.

101. *Gwoździec Stary* district of Kołomyja

Single barrow-graves occur here in various parts of the fields, sometimes in pairs. I excavated two mounds here in 1935. The material was deposited in the Prehistoric Institute, Lwów University.

Barrow-grave I (Plan 39) formed part of a group of two barrow-graves on the border with Podhajczyki and was the larger of the two. The border between both villages passed across its centre. It was much ploughed, about 30m in diameter and 1·5m high. I was unable to excavate it entirely because of sugar-beet planted over a part of its area. A trench 13m was dug running W–E, 28m long i.e. from end to end of the present mound, and crossing the centre and northern section of the mound. A section 13m long and 13m wide, in the SE section of the mound, was also excavated.

An area of yellow clay about 2m in diameter and clearly distinguishable from the black earth of the mound was found about 10m NW of the centre, at 70cm deep under the actual surface (K). It was undoubtedly the place of a secondary burial which had been destroyed by ploughing. A very rusty iron chisel (d) was found about 2·5m in the same direction from the clay area, at 1m deep, and an iron nail (e) 50cm deep was found 4m further in the same direction i.e. at 18m NW of centre.

The original grave (L) was in the centre of the mound on the ancient surface, at a depth of 1·3–1·4m. Close investigation of cross-sections and position of objects gave the following structure of the mound: a central area nearly circular about 4·5m in diameter seems to have been set with timber logs or planks of which only very faint traces had been left, although these enabled the extent of the area to be discerned. Lumps of charcoal were scattered throughout this area, and there lay a fragment of a broken, well-made flint implement (m) (Fig. 17:12). The actual grave was on the west side of this area, though no traces of skeleton could be found: it had disintegrated entirely. This grave was marked by a layer of timber logs, thicker in this spot and forming a kind of low platform (M) 2 by 1·2m, orientated NE–SW. This layer was more thickly scattered with charcoal than the surrounding area. A lump of red ochre was found in the south side of the grave. No objects or charcoal were found around the entire central area. The area set with timber logs lay in the middle of the central sector (p) *c.* 13m in diameter, the outer periphery of which was very clearly marked with an abrupt hollow of some 30–40cm in the ancient level. It was evident that the entire centre was the base on which the original mound had been erected. The lowering of the ground outside its extent had occurred as the result of digging the earth to form the mound.

The distribution of the various potsherds (c) and a relatively large number of flint flakes (b) and fragments of broken flint implements (f) and small differences visible in a few points of the almost uniform mound consisting of black earth made it possible to determine the height of the original mound. They were found in the central part of the mound, over the central area, at a depth of 70–80cm above the level of the grave: this was the altitude of the original mound. Pebbles and flints occurred outside the central area at a depth of 1·3m. They were scattered on the bottom of the area from which earth had been taken to form the mound.

The mound had been added to later, probably for the secondary burial, from which the iron objects referred to above on the NW side of the mound derived (d, e). The altitude of the secondary mound had been much decreased through ploughing and the objects which were not destroyed had been displaced by the plough.

The blade of a broken battle-axe (Plate 10:4) 7cm long was found on the west periphery of the present mound (a), in the layer of ploughed ground. This battle-axe blade was well made of green stone. It must have derived from the central portion of the mound and from the summit of the original mound, but had been displaced first by the secondary burial, then by ploughing. The potsherds found in the mound were fairly thick, brick-red in colour, dark inside and of Neolithic character. Traces of a herringbone ornament were visible on one somewhat larger fragment; it may have derived from an amphora.

Barrow-grave II (Plan 40:3) was 500m W of Barrow-grave I, in the 'Korczunek' field: it was 28m in diameter, 1m high, and much ploughed. Some objects were found close together about 4·5m S of the centre: these were a small trimmed flint blade (a) at 30cm deep, a larger dark potsherd (b) somewhat deeper (at 40cm), and a lump of hard fired clay (d) at 60cm deep. A larger flint flake (g) was lying 2m SW of the centre, with two larger fragments of a thick vessel (f) and another flint (n) 2m further away and about 5m from the centre a lump of charcoal (e) was found, all at 60cm deep.

The grave (G) was 2m NW of the centre, 80cm deep, on the ancient level. The slightly contracted skeleton was lying on its right side, head NW: a bronze ear-pendant (s) of the type of the ornaments from Perediwanie or Stubło was found on its skull (Plate 9:4), one end being sharp, the other broad. It was 6·5cm in diameter, strongly eaten away by patina so that only the wire survived, while the plate of the flattened end had disintegrated. Two vessels were standing by the head: a cord-decorated, handled jug (l) (Fig. 10:6) 13·5cm high, 12cm in diameter, and some kind of small, entirely crushed vessel (m) red in colour. About 50cm NE of the head was a tall, undecorated dark-coloured single-lugged mug (k) (*Zapfenbecher*) (Plate 9:5) 16cm high, 11·2cm in diameter with the lug placed under the rim. A flint burin (j) lay a little further away on the same level, with a flint blade in another spot (i). A larger lump of charcoal (w) was lying in the centre of the mound, also at 80cm deep, on the ancient level and a small potsherd (c) near by while 4m E of it was a dark-coloured vessel (h) with a carinated body (Plate 9:9), the neck and upper part of which disintegrated. The portion preserved is 6cm high, body 14cm in diameter, the base being slightly concave, 6cm in diameter.

102. *Horodenka*

Before the Second World War, a flint dagger (no. 383) length 13·5cm, lenticular in cross-section, very carefully made and found in a barrow-grave (an inhumation burial),[101] in 1913 was preserved in the Dzieduszycki Museum, Lwów. A bronze socketed axe 8·5cm long found in 1913 likewise in a barrow-grave (inhumation grave),[102] was also in this Museum. Both objects bore the same Indian-ink marking and had been

[101] Kozłowski (op. cit., note 2: 1924), p. 182.

[102] Żurowski (op. cit., note 39), p. 163, Pl. XI:9.

entered together in the Museum inventory. They undoubtedly derived from the same grave (Fig. 35:7, 12).

103. *Medwedowce* district of Buczacz

Flint implements were found in barrow-graves situated near the village.[103]

104. *Myszyn* district of Kołomyja

Two groups of barrow-graves occurred here on the summit of a hill, one of which dated from about the third or fourth century A.D.,[104] while the other, consisting of three graves, was on the summit of the hill but further south than the other, in the 'Pamirky-Polana' field. One was excavated in 1935 by Dr M. Śmiszko and the archaeological material was deposited in the Prehistoric Institute of the Lwów University.

The barrow-grave excavated (Plan 40:1) was 16m in diameter, 50cm high, and much ploughed. Its cross-section was as follows: 30cm of ploughed earth, 40cm mound consisting of humus mixed with black earth. The ancient level was 70cm under the mound, consisting of black earth 20cm deep, gradually giving way to virgin soil. Traces of vegetation and roots which had formed the ancient ground covering were observed in the centre of the mound, at the ancient level. A small rectangular pit about 1·8 by 1m (A) in which calcined human bones were found, occurred near the centre of the mound, to the NW. The bones were heaped in the western portion (b) while a damaged beaker (e) (Fig. 10:5) with a spherical base was standing on the calcined bones mixed with charcoal but outside the hollow. It was cord-decorated and there was a broken battle-axe under it (Plate 10:7). About 2m NE of these, and also in a small hollow was a similar heap of calcined human bones (f). Two butts of stone battle-axes (c) (Plate 10:6) were found side by side at about 3m W of the vessel and the battle-axe i.e. 4·5m W of the centre of the mound, on the ancient level. Some small undefined pottery fragments and lumps of charcoal were found in the mound and also the upper part of a cylindrical vessel (d) dating from the first centuries A.D. (it lay 5m SE of the centre), while three larger pebbles were lying side by side about 2m SE of centre (a).

Only the lower, semi-spherical part of the small vessel (Fig. 10:5) was preserved. It was almost black, made of clay with a very large admixture of sand, insufficiently baked and extremely brittle. It was covered with cord impressions extending obliquely from top to bottom, forming groups of two lines per group. The portion which was preserved was 7·2cm high and 8·7cm in diameter. The battle-axe (Plate 10:7) was 14cm long, while one of the battle-axe butts (Plate 10:6) found together was 8·5cm long, the other being 5cm. Two irregular flint flakes and a small scraper or flint knife were added to the material from this barrow-grave.

105. *Nagórzany* district of Zaleszczyki

In 1878 A. Schneider excavated four barrow-graves here, in which were found 'objects similar to those found in graves near Lwów'.[105] Before the Second World War, two flint axes (nos. 1663 and 1664) were preserved in the Lubomirski Museum, Lwów, which had come from Schneider and bore the indication 'excavated in 1878 at Zaleszczyki'. These objects most probably derive from the barrow-graves at Nagórzany, since Schneider did not excavate at Zaleszczyki itself.

106. *Okniany* district of Tłumacz

A score of barrow-graves were well visible situated in the forest and on its adjoining fields. One of these (I) was excavated by me in 1934, the other (II) by Miss I. Siwek at the same time.[106] The objects excavated were given to the Prehistoric Institute of the University of Lwów.

Barrow-grave I (Plan 38:2). This lay in the 'Rososz' forest, and was about 22m in diameter, about 2m high. Near the centre, on top of the mound, a battle-axe (d) of type *x*-4 (Fig. 13:7) was found, made of granite 10·5cm long. In the central part, under the mound on the ancient surface, the grave shaft (A) was uncovered. It lay NE of the centre, and was about 70cm deep in the ancient ground which consisted of chernozem. In a few places only did it reach the yellow subsoil beneath the chernozem and the contours of the shaft were therefore very difficult to establish. The shaft was some 3 by 2m wide, orientated SE–NW. No traces of skeleton were found in it; only a few large flint flakes (e), some trimmed, lay on the bottom. Over the shaft, probably on its timber cover, a number of grave goods were excavated; in the eastern part, at a distance of over 1m from each other stood two vessels, a cord-decorated single-lugged mug (a) (*Zapfenbecher*) (Plate 9:14) 16cm high, 13·5cm in diameter, reddish in colour, insufficiently baked, brittle, and an entirely crushed smaller vessel (b) probably a cup, dark in colour, which disintegrated. In the centre lay a small battle-axe well made of a greenish variety of stone (c) of type *y*-3 7cm long. Two other battle-axes were close to each other on the western side of this area; one of these (j-2) of type *x*-2 (Fig. 13:4) 10cm long, was well made and polished, of a greenish variety of stone, the other (j-1) of type *x*-4 9cm long, was of a dark variety of stone (granite ?) unfinished, unpolished.

Outside the grave, about 2m NW of it, three larger limestones (g) lay on the ancient surface, and about 1·5m W of these a flint point (k) was found. At a distance of about 2m SW of the grave, a few boulders lay on the ancient surface forming a single line (h) and 2m S of these, on the same level, a flint arrow-head (f) was found. A few large flint flakes were found in various parts of the mound.

Barrow-grave II (Plan 38:1). Situated in the 'Kamienne Laski' forest, 20m in diameter, 2m high. In the upper part of the mound many odd flints were found. The mound reached to a depth of some 1·30–1·40cm, and lay on the ancient brownish, degraded chernozem, 60–70cm thick, which gradually became yellow loess. Eleven vessels were excavated which formed two well-distinguished groups, both sunk a little in the ancient ground. One group, evidently grave goods of one burial, consisted of four vessels: a bowl with two small lugs (c) (Plate 16:16) which lay some 50cm west of the centre of the mound; at a distance of 1·2m north of it lay a bowl (d) (either Plate 16:15 or 18:15) and 60–70cm west of

[103] Kozłowski (op. cit., note 2: 1924), p. 191.

[104] М. Ю. Смішко, Карпатські кургани першої половини I тисячоліття нашої ери, Kiev 1960, pp. 27 ff.

[105] Janusz (op. cit., note 9), p. 269.

[106] Sulimirski, loc. cit., note 37.

the bowl 'c' stood two tulip-shaped pots (a, b) one on the top of another (Fig. 28:3; Plate 18:6). The other group of buried vessels apparently the site of the second burial, lay east of the centre; at about 2m east of vessel 'c' lay vessel 'g', probably a tulip-shaped pot, of which only the lower part survived, the upper part having disintegrated. South of it lay a bowl 'v' (either Plate 16:15 or 18:15) and a large tulip-shaped pot 'f' (Plate 18:4) 50cm west of it. At a distance of 1m south-west of vessel 'v' was a group of three vessels: a double-handled vase 'h' (Plate 17:11), a handled cup 'i' (Plate 17:9), and another double-handled vase 'l' (Fig. 28:1). A few potsherds were found outside these groups (e). Three arrow-heads were excavated as well as pottery but their site has not been marked on the plan in the report. Two of these were typically triangular with slightly concave bases, the third one was made of a thick triangular blade (Plate 9:20, 21, 30).

The tulip-shaped pot 'a' (Fig. 28:3) 19cm high, 16·5cm in diameter, was reddish in colour, very brittle, its decoration consisted of a low raised band around the upper part of the body, with four oblong slanting bosses placed on it at regular intervals. The other tulip-shaped pot 'b' was 12·5cm high, 11·5cm in diameter, provided with a similar low raised band. The third and largest tulip-shaped pot 'f' (Plate 18:4) was 25·4cm high, 20cm in diameter, the rim flat, brownish in colour, provided with a raised band on the lower part of the neck. The bowl 'c' (Plate 16:16) 12·5cm high, 20cm in diameter, had two horizontal grooves on the junction of the neck and the body, and two horizontally perforated lugs. The body covered with vertical fluting. Vessel 'g' was probably a small tulip-shaped pot, of which only the base, 5cm in diameter, survived. It was very brittle, like the other vessels, and like them was made of strongly tempered clay paste. The vase 'h' (Plate 17:11) was 13·7cm high, 19 by 20cm in diameter, provided with two large handles. The neck covered with two parallel grooves and a punctuated line between. A similar band ran round the base of the neck, while below it, on the upper part of the body, was a row of triangles cut out on the surface. The second double-handled vase 'l' of which only a number of sherds survived, was 13cm high, 16·5cm in diameter (Fig. 28:1). Two horizontal grooves marked the junction of the neck and the body, and a row of shaded triangles was placed below them on the upper part of the body. The handled cup 'i' (Plate 17:9) 6·7cm high (8·7 with the handle) 9·3cm in diameter, was undecorated, greyish-brown in colour. The cup 'x' (Plate 18:17) 4cm high, 55cm in diameter, was undecorated.

Markings of the two remaining vessels are missing, and none can therefore be identified either with vessel 'd' of the western group, or vessel 'v' of the eastern group. One of these (Plate 16:15) was a carinated bowl, 8cm high, 16cm in diameter, the rim flat; it had three horizontal grooves on the neck with a band of vertical incisions over them. The body was covered with slanting incisions. The other (Plate 18:15) was an undecorated pot with a wide flat base, straight walls slightly widening upwards, 9·5cm high, 12cm in diameter.

The arrow-heads were 3 and 3·5cm long, the third being a pointed flint flake, 3·5cm long.

107. *Olejowa-Korolówka* district of Horodenka

In 1880 a barrow-grave about 20m in diameter, 1m high, was excavated.[107] It was situated on the top of a hill, close to the main Horodenka–Tłumacz road. Calcined human bones mixed with charcoal, sherds of a clay vessel and an axe made probably of siliceous slate (or of flint) were found.

108. *Pauszówka* district of Czortków

Two of the several mounds in this locality were excavated by K. Hadaczek in 1912.[108] In one a mediaeval burial was found, in the other five skeletons were uncovered, two being in a contracted position, the other three on their backs in an extended position.

109. *Harediwanie* district of Horodenka

A number of bronze ornaments were found near the skeleton[109] in a grave uncovered by chance. These were: two large ear-pendants 4·5 by 5cm in diameter with one end wide, flattened, and four naprings about 3cm in diameter, two of which were in fragments. These were in the Dzieduszycki Museum before the war (Fig. 19:1–8).

110. *Porchowa* district of Buczacz

A number of mounds lay on the fields and in the forest. On the field called 'Owsiańskie', a skeleton and a serpentine battle-axe were found. The latter was given to the Archaeological Museum in Cracow (no. 3206).[110]

111. *Stopczatów* district of Kołomyja

A barrow-grave was excavated here in 1936 by Dr M. Śmiszko. It lay on a hill about 100m NW of the main Kołomyja-Jabłonów road (Plan 40:2).

The cross-section was as follows: 40cm upper humus, with the mound beneath and the ancient level at 80cm deep, fossil humus below this differing little in colour from the mound and deeper merging into virgin soil composed of diluvial gravel. Traces of an oval hearth 2·5 by 2m, orientated SW–NE were found 60cm deep, near the centre of the mound on the southern side (A). Two heaps of calcined human bones with some pottery fragments among them were found on its eastern side (b, c). About 1m SW of them were two small pits about 35 and 45cm in diameter, 12 and 14cm deep, filled with remains of pyre and charcoal, calcined bones and pottery fragments (l, m). A much damaged bronze clasp was lying on the NE periphery of the hearth (f). Groups of charcoal and burned clay about 30cm in diameter were found NW of the hearth (e) and about 1m from the centre of the mound, with a heap of charcoal and burned clay about 1m further away in the same direction, among which half a bronze horse-bit was found (d). A larger fragment of a vessel was found on the SW periphery of the mound (k) under the humus. This grave dated from the sixth century, i.e. the Migration Period.[111]

The grave (A) described above was a secondary burial, placed on a barrow-grave of the Middle Bronze Age. Three vessels (i) (a small bowl (Plate 20:12) a handled bowl and a handled cup (Plate 19:2, 3)) were found standing side by side

[107] T. Ziemięcki, *ZWAK*, vol. I, 1878, p. 478.
[108] Janusz (op. cit., note 9), p. 100.
[109] W. Antoniewicz, 'Der in Stubło in Volhynien augefundene Bronzeschatz', *ESA*, vol. IV, 1929, pp. 140 f., Figs. 22–5.
[110] Janusz (op. cit., note 9), p. 95.
[111] See note 104, pp. 44 f.

in a small hollow reaching to the gravel 3m E of the centre. A tulip-shaped vessel (a) (Plate 20:1) was about 1m from them to the SE, lying on its side on the ancient level. Two small vessels, a small bowl and a cup (g) (Plate 20:6, 9) were standing in a small hollow penetrating to the gravel. All these vessels were typical of the Komarów culture. This was the site of the original grave (B).

The tulip-shaped vessel (a) (Plate 20:1) was 17·7cm high, its body diameter 15cm, the surface very rough, sand and stone gritted ware, poorly baked and brittle. The small bowl (i) (Plate 20:12) was 5·5cm high and 13·5cm in diameter, made in the same way. The handled cup (i) (Plate 19:3) found by it, was 12cm high, 15cm in diameter, covered with a thin layer of slip: it was decorated with four flutings placed horizontally on the neck, with vertical grooves on the upper part of the body. Protuberances symmetrically placed on the curve of the body were each encircled by semicircular double-fluted grooves. Its wide handle 3·5cm wide was ornamented with three fluted grooves running along it from top to bottom. The handled bowl (i) (Plate 19:2) was 10·5cm high, 16·5cm in diameter, made like the cup, the handle projecting above the rim. The ornament consisted of four curves, concentrically placed and repeated seven times on the upper part of the vessel. The second small bowl (g) (Plate 20:6) was 5cm high, 9·7cm in diameter, not ornamented, with a flat rim. The cup (g) (Plate 20:9) found near it was 5·2cm high, 9cm in diameter, very carefully made, covered with brown slip. The neck was narrowed, with an ornamentation of concentric half-circles on the upper part of the body, as on the handled cup (i-3).

[112] Janusz (op. cit., note 9), p. 242.

112. *Tłumacz*

In 1878 a barrow-grave was excavated by Dr Lenz.[112] The following objects found in it were given to the Natur-Historisches Museum in Vienna (nos. 3147–51): calcined human bones, three small flint flakes, a flint knife and two undecorated vessels, both thick-walled, brittle. One was a cup (3147) dark-brown in colour, 7cm high, wide open, 11·5cm in diameter, the sides provided with many perforations regularly distributed over the vessels in three rows (3148). This was evidently a cremation burial.

113. *Tracz* district of Kołomyja

In 1935, a barrow-grave was destroyed during the erection of a house. A flint axe, rectangular in section, and a flint knife found here were sold to the Museum in Toronto, Canada.

114. *Worwolińce* district of Zaleszczyki

A stone battle-axe of type *y*-3 (Fig. 13:10) 9·5cm long, found in a barrow-grave, was at the Dzieduszycki Museum in Lwów[113] before the war.

[113] Kozłowski (op. cit., note 2: 1924), p. 194.

SECTION III

North-western Barrow-graves and Settlements

1. THE LUBLIN-BUG SITES

(a) *Barrow-graves*

115. *Bondyrz* district of Zamość

A few potsherds typical of the Trzciniec culture and a fragment of a flint axe were found in a brownish occupation layer of a destroyed sandy mound, probably a barrow-grave.[1] The site is situated at a distance of 1·5km east of a group of barrow-graves at Guciów in the same district.

116. *Chobułtowa* district of Włodzimierz Wołyński

A barrow-grave cemetery in the forest. Some mounds were excavated and bronze objects were found.[2]

117. *Chotywel* district of Kowel

A 'Thuringian' amphora 27·5cm high at the State Archaeological Museum.[3] Its neck cord-decorated. It seems to have originated from a destroyed grave.

118. *Dominikanówka* district of Zamość

In 1958 one barrow-grave (no. 6) of a group of seven mounds was investigated.[4] It was situated on the edge of a low elevation over the river Wieprz. The mounds were 8–13m in diameter, 50–90cm high. The mound investigated was already partly ruined by a trench and by treasure hunters. On the ancient surface small pieces of charcoal lay strewn around the central part. Here too patches of darker sand were visible forming a circle about 2m in diameter; they were either traces of small hearth or of post-holes. In the central part potsherds lay strewn over an area 2·5m in diameter; they belonged to a large tulip-shaped vessel typical of the Trzciniec culture. Its only decoration consisted of a double raised band around the neck. No traces of skeleton or of cremation were noticed.

119. *Grzybowica* district of Włodzimierz Wołyński

A large flint point (dagger ?) was found in a barrow-grave.[5]

120. *Guciów* district of Zamość

A cemetery consisting of thirty mounds extending over the ridges of two hills in the valley of the Wieprz was investigated in 1959.[6] The mounds were round, 5–10m in diameter, up to 1m high and lay at a distance of 2–200m from each other. Seven mounds were excavated, but only a short preliminary report has yet been published. Charred timber constructions, calcined human bones and potsherds were found on the ancient surface of the mounds investigated. Calcined human bones and potsherds also lay in two or three holes under each mound near their circumference. The burial ritual was not everywhere identical. Cremation took place either on the spot in the centre, or the pyre was on the perimeter of the area subsequently covered by the mound, the calcined bones being scattered over the whole area covered. In some cases cremation took place outside the grave and calcined bones and remains of the pyre were laid in the central part of the grave. The pottery exhibits a variety of forms and decoration; it was typical of the Trzciniec culture but many vessels show features characteristic of the Komarów culture.

Five further mounds were excavated in 1961.[7] Four of these (nos. x, xi, xii, xv) were 10–13m in diameter and their construction and contents (cremations) did not differ from those mentioned above. One barrow-grave was of a different type:

Barrow-grave xiii. 14 by 15m in diameter, 30cm high. On the ancient surface were traces of a large hearth; many potsherds were scattered around. In the central area the grave-shaft was uncovered 1·60 by 1·2m, and 1·60m deep. It was surrounded by a number of vertical posts, about 15–20cm in diameter, charred remains of which were visible. North of the shaft, on the ancient surface lay charred remains of a layer of timber logs. Over the bottom of the shaft extended a layer of dark earth mixed with powdered charcoal and ashes; under it lay human bones probably of five persons, as indicated by the number of skulls. One of these, dolichocephalic, deformed, of an adult man, lay apart; the remaining ones, all with their front part (face) missing, were laid one inside the other and deposited on a heap of bones, mainly legs and arms. One of these skulls was brachycephalic, probably of a woman; another one, of an adult, had a small oval hole in its sinciput, and a small flint arrow-point was inside the skull. The third skull was of a child 8–10 years of age, and the fourth, trepanned, had an oval hole in the occiput. North of this heap of bones was another one, consisting mainly of ribs, and the

[1] J. Machnik, 'Badania archeologiczne w Roztoczu Lubelskim w 1959 r.' *Spr.Arch.*, vol. xii, 1961, pp. 98 ff.

[2] A. Cynkałowski, *Materiały do pradziejów Wołynia i Polesia Wołyńskiego*, Warszawa 1961, p. 89.

[3] J. Głosik, 'Wołyńsko-podolskie materiały z epoki kamiennej i wczesnej epoki brązu w Państwowym Muzeum Archeologicznym w Warszawie', *Mat.St.*, vol. viii, 1962, p. 131, Pl. ii:1. Cynkałowski (op. cit., note 2), p. 41.

[4] J. Machnik, 'Kurhan kultury trzcinieckiej z Dominikanówki, pow. Zamość', *Mat.Arch.*, vol. ii, 1960, pp. 79 ff.

[5] Cynkałowski (op. cit., note 2), p. 53.

[6] R. Rogozińska, 'Sprawozdanie z badań kurhanów trzcinieckich w Guciowie, pow.Zamość', *Spr.Arch.*, vol. xiii, 1961, pp. 45 ff. Machnik (op. cit., note 4), p. 83, note 18.

[7] R. Rogozińska, 'Sprawozdanie z badań stanowisk kultury trzcinieckiej w Guciowie i Bondyrzu, pow.Zamość, w 1961 r', *Spr.Arch.*, vol. xv, 1963, pp. 84 ff.

third heap (mainly hips) was south of the first one. In the south-eastern corner of the shaft lay a large part of a small ovoid vessel; the missing part of it was found in the cinders on the ancient surface near the grave. Close to the vessel lay a flat flint axe and small quarried quartzite and sand-stones. According to the Report, pottery found in this grave was reminiscent of comb-ware and also of that from the settlement of the Trzciniec culture in the neighbouring village of Bondyż.

121. *Hrubieszów*

A slab-cist was found under a mound; it contained a contracted skeleton, a small stone battle-axe of type *z*-4 (Fig. 14:9) and potsherds of unknown type.[8]

122. *Kałusów* district of Włodzimierz Wołyński

A stone axe typical of the Corded Ware was found in a barrow-grave.[9]

123. *Kropiszczyna* district of Włodzimierz Wołyński

A contracted skeleton, cord-decorated pottery and a diorite battle-axe were found in a barrow-grave.[10]

124. *Krzeczów* district of Włodzimierz Wołyński (see no. 609)

A stone battle-axe nearly quadrangular in section and a fragment of a cord-decorated neck of a vessel typical of the Strzyżów culture were found in a barrow-grave.[11]

125. *Markostaw* district of Włodzimierz Wołyński

Two contracted skeletons were uncovered in a barrow-grave excavated by a local peasant. Grave goods consisted of a few cord-decorated vessels which were destroyed, and a stone battle-axe.[12]

126. *Mikhale* district of Włodzimierz Wołyński

A flint axe rectangular in section and cord-decorated pottery were found in a barrow-grave.[13]

127. *Ostrobizh* district of Rawa Ruska

An almond-shaped stone axe was found in a barrow-grave.[14]

128. *Ostrów* district of Sokal

At a depth of 1·5m, apparently in a barrow-grave, a skeleton was uncovered near which lay a flint dagger (Plate 11:17) 11·5cm long, and a diorite battle-axe of type *y*-3 (Fig. 13:11) 11cm long.[15] Both were in the Dieduszycki Museum in Lwów before the War (nos. 236, 237).

[8] T. Malinowski, 'Nabytki b. Działu przedhistorycznego Muzeum Wielkopolskiego w Poznaniu w latach 1929–1932', *FAP*, vol. VI, 1956, p. 130, Fig. 8.

[9] Cynkałowski (op. cit., note 2), p. 211.

[10] Ibid., p. 48.

[11] Głosik (op. cit., note 3), p. 144.

[12] Cynkałowski (op. cit., note 2), p. 43.

[13] Я. Пастернак, Нові археологічні набутки Музею наук. тов. ім. Шевченка у Львові, 1933–1936, Записки наукового тов. ім. Шевченка, vol. CLIV, 1937, p. 255.

[14] Пастернак, loc. cit.

[15] L. Kozłowski, *Młodsza epoka kamienna w Polsce (neolit)*, Lwów 1924, p. 191.

129. *Osmihowicze* district of Włodzimierz Wołyński

A flint axe and a small dagger, or dart-head, were found in a ploughed up barrow-grave.[16]

130. *Siemnice* district of Tomaszów Lubelski

A flint spear-head and a stone battle-axe were found, most probably in a barrow-grave.[17]

131. *Sławinek* district of Lublin

A grave was investigated in 1960 by Z. Ślusarski.[18] It lay on an elevated site on loose soil, presumably under a ploughed-up mound. The skeleton was crouched on its left side. Grave goods consisted of three vessels: a large Lubaczów amphora with three small lugs on the shoulder with twisted, cord-impressed decoration on the upper part of the body; a beaker typical of the Cracow-Miechów Corded Ware with an incised decoration; and a handled jar. A spiral bronze ring 1cm in diameter was also found in this grave.

132. *Sokal* (see nos. 406 and 619)

In 1874 a skeleton was uncovered near the railway station, in brickwork and presumably under a mound.[19] Near it were a stone battle-axe and a flint axe, both later deposited in the Dzieduszycki Museum in Lwów. Before the last war this Museum had three objects marked as originating from this find (nos. 2156–8): a sand-stone battle-axe of type *z*-4 (Fig. 14:10) 9·5cm long, a larger flint axe of Valby type (Fig. 15:20) 17cm long, and a smaller one of Bundsø type (Fig. 15:6) 13cm long, both quadrangular in section.

133. *Stężaryce* district of Włodzimierz Wołyński

A clay vessel and two flint knives were found in a barrow-grave excavated by local peasants.[20]

134. *Szystów* district of Włodzimierz Wołyński

In a ploughed up barrow-grave, a granite battle-axe was found.[21]

135. *Zabuże* district of Luboml

A large stone battle-axe was found in a barrow-grave excavated by a local peasant.[22]

136. *Zakłodzie-Sąsiadka* district of Zamość

A barrow-grave 30m in diameter, 2m high, was excavated by Professor W. Antoniewicz in 1946.[23] Several burials were uncovered, mainly secondary. The central, original grave (no. 8) was partly destroyed by treasure hunters; it contained

[16] Głosik (op. cit., note 3), p. 161.

[17] S. Nosek, 'Materiały do badań nad historią starożytną i wczesnośredniowieczną międzyrzecza Wisły i Bugu', *AUMCS*, vol. VI F, 1951 (1957), pp. 255, 378.

[18] According to the information kindly given me by Mr Z. Ślusarski, M.A., Keeper of the Archaeological Section of the Lublin Museum. The site is being published by him.

[19] Kozłowski (op. cit., note 15), p. 194.

[20] Kozłowski, loc. cit.

[21] Cynkałowski (op. cit., note 2), p. 51.

[22] Głosik (op. cit., note 3), p. 174, Pl. XXXII:1.

[23] W. Antoniewicz, 'Neolithisches Hügelgrab im Dorfe Zakłodzie, Kreis Zamość, Wojewodschaft Lublin, Polen', *Acta AASH*, vol. IX, 1958.

human bones and a cord-decorated mug with two lugs under the rim. Near by lay the contracted skeleton of a child (grave 2), head to S, with a cord-decorated lugged mug (*Zapfenbecher*).

Other skeletons, all in an extended position on back, heads to SW, were of a later date. In grave 1, situated about 3m E of grave 2, only a flint flake was found near the male skeleton, the skull of which was of 'mediterranean-palaeoasiatic' type. Grave 4, about 5–6m SE of the central grave, contained the skeleton of a man approximately seventy years of age, 165·5cm tall, of a 'Cromagnon' type; a flint flake and three molar teeth were found here. Female grave 3 lay 4m SE of the centre. Its skull was of 'mixed mediterranean-palaeoasiatic' type; near the skeleton a flint scraper, and a few animal leg bones were found. North of this grave was a hole in which lay a skeleton of a dog, head to N, and near it was the point of a cattle horn with which it had been killed. The skeleton in grave 5 lay in a shallow hole, with a bone point under its left arm, a flint flake over the knee; half the skull and a few vertebrae and the left arm and shoulder were missing. Close to the above was grave 6 of a child, orientated NE–SE. It was badly ruined by ploughing; a small undecorated cup was found in it. Grave 7 lay 5m SW of the centre, orientated NE–SW; this was a shaft, 1·83m by 70cm in area, in which no traces of skeleton were found. Traces of a hearth were uncovered in the northern part of the mound, on the ancient surface.

137. *Zimno* district of Włodzimierz Wołyński (see nos. 401 and 632)

Two large stones were found in an isolated barrow-grave. In another place two barrow-graves were excavated in 1845, in which a flint axe and a small piece of amber were found.[24]

(*b*) *Settlements and graves of the Strzyżów culture* (*western section*)

Addenda: Nos. 601–45

601. *Dyniska Nowe*, district of Tomaszów Lubelski

Inhumation cemetery was uncovered.[25]

602. *Gródek Nadbużny*, district of Hrubieszów (see no. 403)

During investigation of the settlement of the Funnel Beaker culture, five graves were uncovered, three of which were considered to belong to the Strzyżów group of Corded Ware culture.[26] These graves lay in the occupation layer of the settlement[27] and did not much differ from two graves attributed to the Funnel Beaker culture. In 1957, a fourth grave of Corded Ware culture was uncovered here.[28] No shafts have been distinguished in any of these graves. The skeleton of grave 1 lay in an extended position on back, head to E, at a depth of 50–55cm. Two small vessels stood near the knees, and near the hips an amphora. Among the chest bones lay a bone pin with a hole in the head. The following objects were also found here but it has not been established whether they belonged to grave goods: a clay whorl near the knees, a horn (an antler) near the hips, and a bronze (or copper) earring in the eye-socket. One of the smaller vessels was a beaker with a 'brushed' surface, the other was a cup with a small flat base and a wide mouth having two vertically perforated lugs on the rim, decorated with tight horizontal cord-impressions which covered almost its whole surface. The amphora had a flat base, wide mouth and was provided with perforated lugs on the upper part of the body, the number of which has not been ascertained, a large part of the vessel being missing. Its rim and neck were covered with close parallel cord-impressions and the upper part of the body had an ornament proper to the Trzciniec culture of the Middle Bronze Age, consisting of parallel horizontal grooves and shorter grooves arranged in vertical or slanting groups. The skeleton of grave 2 (at a depth of 30–35cm) was in a crouched position on its left side, head to N. The palm of its right hand was missing, the left palm being under the head. Near the skull lay fragments of another human skull with no other bones. No grave goods were found. Grave 3 lay close to the former, its skeleton (at a depth of 40–45cm) in an extended position on back, head to W. Chest bones and the spine were disordered, the left foot missing and a fragment of a rib was sticking in the mouth. Under the jaw lay a triangular flint arrow-head, and around the skeleton lumps of baked clay. A bone dagger lay near the left hand, on the chest a small perforated shell, and three vessels stood along the left leg, and on the other side a fourth one with a cover. Near the left leg was a bone implement. The three vessels were a two-lugged amphora with a wide flat base, and a cylindrical neck covered with tight cord-impressions; a bowl with an everted rim, provided with four small handles on the upper part of the body, its lower part, similarly as the lower part of the amphora, was rough, brushed; the lower part of the beaker was also brushed, its neck and rim covered with tight cord impressions, it had a wide base and a wide mouth. The fourth vessel was a large beaker with single cord-impressions on the rim and the upper part of the body; its cover consisted of what was probably the upper part of a two-lugged amphora, the neck of which had a cord decoration. The skeleton of grave 4 (1957) lay in an extended position (at a depth of 35–45cm), head to E. The skull was detached and turned upwards, the jaw missing, ribs disordered. Green spots on both sides of the skull marked some copper (or bronze) objects, probably earrings, which had disintegrated. Near the left arm was a bone point, near the head three vessels: a shattered amphora with many sherds missing, a large beaker and a cup. The amphora had at least one lug under the rim, its neck and upper part rough, brushed. Similarly decorated was the beaker, the upper part

[24] Kozłowski (op. cit., note 15), p. 195.

[25] J. Gurba, 'Grób kultury sznurowej w Krzewicy w pow.tomaszowskim', *Prz.A.*, vol. XII, 1958, p. 18.

[26] J. Głosik, 'Uwagi o ostatnich odkryciach w Gródku Nadbużnym w woj. lubelskim', *Arch.R.*, vol. IX, 1957, pp. 660 ff., Figs. 272:1–5, 276. Id., 'Groby kultury ceramiki sznurowej w miejsc. Gródek Nadbużny', *W.A.*, vol. XXV, 1958, pp. 160 ff., Figs. 1–4, Pls. XXI, XXII. Id., *Spr.Arch.*, vol. VI, 1959, pp. 23 ff., Figs. 1–2.

[27] J. Kowalczyk, 'Sprawozdanie z badań osady kultury pucharów lejkowatych w Gródku Nadbużnym w 1956 r.', *W.A.*, vol. XXIV, 1957, p. 303.

[28] J. Głosik, 'Nowy grób kultury ceramiki sznurowej w Gródku Nadbużnym', *W.A.*, vol. XXV, 1958, pp. 382 ff., Figs. 1–5. Id., 'Czwarty grób kultury ceramiki sznurowej na st. 1 C w Gródku Nadbużnym', *Spr.Arch.*, vol. IX, 1960, pp. 81 ff., Fig. 1.

of its body being covered with parallel grooves in the manner typical of the Trzciniec culture. The cup, with two small vertically perforated lugs on the rim, had a flat narrow base and wide mouth. Its upper part was covered with horizontal parallel grooves proper to the Trzciniec culture. In addition to these graves, a few potsherds of the Corded Ware culture were found in the occupation layer of the settlement.[29] According to Głosik,[30] Corded Ware typical of the Strzyżów group was found in a pit together with pottery typical of the Trzciniec culture.

603. *Helenów*, district of Łuck

A settlement of the Corded Ware culture was found on the left bank of the Styr. Potsherds, flint and stone implements were found here on the surface of the field and deposited in the Museum at Łuck.[31]

604. *Hostynne*, district of Hrubieszów

Cord-decorated potsherds and fragments of two stone battle-axes, or hammer-axes, were found on a sandy bank of the Huczwa.[32]

605. *Hrubieszów*

Traces of a 'Late Neolithic' settlement were found on an elevated field, on the loess plateau over the Huczwa; they belonged at least partly to the Strzyżów culture.[33]

606. *Iżów*, district of Włodzimierz Wołyński

Corded Ware of Strzyżów type was found in the remains of a settlement of the Funnel Beaker culture.[34]

607. *Jezierna*, district of Tomaszów Lubelski

Cord-decorated potsherds, but also those of the Trzciniec and Lusatian types, fragments of flint axes, flint arrow-heads, and small flint implements were found on a sandy hill elevated over marshy meadows.[35] Several dark spots, 1–2m in diameter, evidently traces of pits, were visible on the surface of the field (possibly sites of cremation graves).

608. *Krasnystaw* (see no. 386)

Remains of a settlement were uncovered in a local brickworks. Pottery found here was of the same type as that from Raciborowice;[36] other objects included stone battle-axes, quern grinders and animal bones. Pig, goat and horse bones were identified.

609. *Krzeczów*, district of Włodzimierz Wołyński (see no. 124)

Corded Ware of Strzyżów type was found in the settlement attributable to the Funnel Beaker culture.[37]

610. *Krzewica*, district of Tomaszów

A cemetery situated on a hill was uncovered in 1959 and a few graves destroyed by their casual discoverers. During subsequent investigations by Gurba[38] a human burial and traces of a ruined horse burial were found. The human skeleton lay in a shaft 2m by 60cm in size, orientated W–E. The skeleton lay on its right side, legs very slightly contracted. A green spot on the skull indicated the presence of copper or bronze ornament (earring) which had disappeared due to decomposition. The following objects were found: a bracelet made of two boar-tusks perforated at both ends, three flint arrow-heads with a concave base, a large flint implement (scraper ?), and a large fragment of a bone awl or pin.

611. *Leżnica*, district of Włodzimierz Wołyński

Corded Ware of Strzyżów type was found in the remains of a settlement of the Funnel Beaker culture.[39]

612. *Mokre*, district of Zamość.

A cord-decorated handled cup found on a sand-dune is now in the Archaeological Museum in Lublin.[40]

613. *Nowostaw*, district of Horochów

An inhumation cemetery was uncovered on a small hill during the construction of a house. Pottery and flint axes were found near the skeletons.[41]

614. *Oborowiec*, district of Hrubieszów

In 1949 three complete vessels and one in sherds, and also a flint axe were found, probably in a grave which has been attributed probably erroneously to the Globular Amphora culture.[42] Vessels found in the grave exhibit features which connect them with pottery of the Strzyżów culture. One of these vessels, an amphora, had four warts (unperforated) on the upper part of the body, and four more below the rim; another was a two-lugged amphora with a large body and cylindrical neck covered with parallel horizontal cord impressions, while vertical double impressions covered the upper part of the body. The third vessel was also an amphora with four lugs on the body, with a rich incised decoration covering the upper part of the body and partly reaching down to its lower part, its neck missing. The fourth vessel was also an amphora with a cord decoration.

615. *Raciborowice*, district of Hrubieszów[43] (see no. 392)

In 1952 a flat grave was uncovered, in which four vessels and several personal ornaments were found. Among the vessels was an amphora decorated with cord impressions and short

[29] J. Kowalczyk, 'Badania osady kultury pucharów lejkowatych w Gródku Nadbużnym przeprowadzone w 1955 r.', *W.A.*, vol. XXIV, 1957, p. 49.

[30] Głosik (op. cit., note 28: 1958), p. 384.

[31] J. Fitzke, *IKC*, no. 166, 18.VI.1939.

[32] Nosek (op. cit., note 17), p. 247.

[33] A. Gardawski and Z. Rajewski, 'Znaleziska archeologiczne w Hrubieszowie i okolicy', *W.A.*, vol. XXIII, 1956, pp. 104 f.

[34] Głosik (op. cit., note 28: 1959), p. 26, n. 6. Id. (op. cit., note 3), pp. 139 f.

[35] Nosek (op. cit., note 17), p. 254. J. Machnik, *ZOW*, vol. XXV, 1959, p. 203; and op. cit., note 1, pp. 94 f., Fig. 5.

[36] J. Gurba, 'Osada kultury ceramiki sznurowej w miejscowości Krasnystaw', *W.A.*, vol. XXIII, 1956, p. 112.

[37] Głosik, loc. cit., note 34 (1959); and note 3, pp. 144 f.

[38] Gurba (op. cit., note 25), pp. 16 ff.

[39] Głosik (op. cit., note 28: 1959), p. 25. Id. (op. cit. note 3), pp. 147 f. Id., *W.A.*, vol. XXV, 1958, p. 164. J. Jazdowska-Król, *Mat.St.*, vol. VII, 1961, pp. 201 ff.

[40] J. Machnik, *Studia nad kulturą ceramiki sznurowej w Małopolsce*, Wrocław-Warszawa-Kraków 1966, Pl. XLIV:4.

[41] *IKC*, no. 352, 20.XII.1933. *ZOW*, vol. VIII, 1933, p. 83.

[42] Nosek (op. cit., note 17), pp. 235 f., Pls. XI:3, XIII.

[43] Ibid., p. 256. Głosik (op. cit., note 26: 1958), pp. 163 f. Kowalczyk (op. cit., note 27), p. 303. Z. Ślusarski, *ZOW*, vol. XXV, 1959.

incisions, provided with two larger lugs on the shoulder and two smaller under the rim; an ovoid, cord-decorated bowl; a handled cord-decorated cup, and a fourth vessel of which only a few small sherds survived. The personal ornaments consisted of a copper, or bronze disc with two holes in the centre and small bosses around the border; several beads of shells, faience and bone; the latter were tubular, segmented. In 1956–8 a score of graves were excavated by Z. Ślusarski. Pottery found in these graves was similar to that from the first grave and also from other graves of the Strzyżów group. It included two-lugged amphorae, beakers with a wide flat base, handled cups, cups with a small base, wide mouth and two vertically perforated lugs on the rim etc. (Fig. 2). Some beakers and cups also had the base decorated. Several personal ornaments were found, viz. faience beads, some segmented, and those made of shells; small copper ornaments; pendants of bone and horn (antler); plaques made of boar tusks with four holes in the corners or a single hole in the centre; two copper earrings with one end wide, leaf-shaped; pins; bracelets made of thin wire, etc. Elongated triangular flint arrow-heads, flint axes (only oval in section), flint drills, one stone battle-axe, whorls made of potsherds, etc., were also excavated in these graves. All these graves were found within the confines of a settlement of the same culture. At an earlier date the site had been occupied by a settlement of the Painted Linear pottery culture, and one grave mentioned above was dug into a pit-dwelling of the latter culture. Further important stratigraphic evidence was provided by a grave of the Globular Amphora culture, the only one found on this site, which lay under the western walling of a hut of the Strzyżów culture. The hut was built on the surface on a frame of vertical posts.

616. *Radków*, district of Tomaszów Lubelski

A flint saw, two flint axes and human skull were found; they probably originated from a cemetery of Corded Ware culture.[44]

617. *Skomorochy Małe*, district of Hrubieszów

In 1912 a grave was uncovered on a field known as 'Mogiły' (grave-mounds) and subsequently in 1935–7 and 1945 a few more were excavated by amateurs and in 1953 by Z. Ślusarski.[45] The grave uncovered in 1931 was surrounded by large stones, and near the skeleton a flint knife and a bronze bracelet were found. No particulars exist concerning the graves excavated in 1935–7; their grave goods included objects made of bronze, antler, bone and flint. In the graves excavated in 1945 which were covered with stones, a copper axe with a shaft-hole, a copper ear-pendant made of a wire quadrangular in section and two fragments of copper wire were found. No pottery was reported from any of these graves nor was any pottery found in four graves excavated in 1953 by Z. Ślusarski. All the latter graves were covered by stones which formed a kind of a low cairn. In grave 1, which was already ruined, stones covered an area 290 by 110cm, orientated W–E. In grave 2 they lay on a rectangular area 310 by 108cm, over a shallow shaft, the sides and bottom of which were paved with similar stones. In the grave lay a male skeleton on its back, head to E, with a female skeleton in a sitting position, head to W, near its feet. Both wore necklaces made of beads and shells (311 in all) on their necks, and the female skeleton had a flint arrow-head in its chest bones, evidently that of an arrow which had been the cause of death. Grave 3 was covered with stones over an area 220 by 60cm, orientated W–E, and the eastern part of the floor was paved. The bones had been displaced by rodents, but the skeleton probably lay head to E. Only one bead of shell was found here. The stone cover of grave 4 extended over an area 250 by 110cm, orientated W–E. The central part of the grave was ruined, its sides lined and the floor paved with stones. The skeleton lay on its back, head to E. Near the head were two copper ear-pendants, or rings, with one end flattened. A necklace consisting of 116 beads made of shells and eighteen of faience was round the neck. A flint arrow-head was found near the neck, and another near the hips, both with the tip broken off, while two undamaged lay under the left arm. More shell-beads and three boar tusks were found near the knees. Another two boar tusks were found in the ruined part of the grave. Each had a hole in the broad end.

618. *Sławęcin* district of Hrubieszów

During the construction of a railway line in 1943, remains of a settlement of the Corded Ware culture were found, a few pits and traces of several hearths being uncovered.[46] Among objects excavated here were oval flint axes, a flint 'sickle' or bent knife, a hammer, flint arrow-heads, potsherds, a thin bronze or copper object in the shape of a narrow leaf, animal bones, etc.

619. *Sokal* (see nos. 132 and 406)

A large number of potsherds, many typical of the Strzyżów culture and of the Globular Amphora culture also, flint axes quadrangular in section, various flint implements, etc., were found within the boundaries of the town. They were in the collection of the local Grammar School (*gimnazjum*) before the War. Similar potsherds and other objects found in the town and in its environments and on the Bug were in the Majewski Museum in Warsaw before the War.

620. *Starogród*, district of Sokal

Cord-decorated pottery and a flint axe, oval in section, were found on a field on the Bug.[47]

621. *Strzyżów*, district of Hrubieszów (see no. 395)

Remains of Corded Ware were found in several places.[48] In 1935–9 a settlement situated on a loess terrace of the Bug was investigated by Z. Podkowińska. Twenty-eight pits, some

[44] Nosek (op. cit., note 17), p. 254.

[45] Ibid., pp. 256 f., Pl. xx:4. Id., 'Znaleziska z wczesnej epoki brązu na Lubelszczyźnie', *Spr.PMA*, vol. IV, 1952, p. 94, Figs. 7, 8. Z. Ślusarski, *W.A.*, vol. xx, 1954, p. 436. Id., 'Cmentarzysko kultury mierzanowickiej w miejsc. Skomorochy Małe', *W.A.*, vol. XXIII, 1956, pp. 95 ff., Figs. 1–8. L. Gajewski, *ZOW*, vol. xx, 1951, p. 67.

[46] Gardawski and Rajewski (op. cit., note 33), pp. 106 f., Pl. xv.

[47] Nosek (op. cit., note 17), p. 248. B. Janusz, *Zabytki przedhistoryczne Galicyi Wschodniej*, Lwów 1918, pp. 211 f.

[48] Z. Podkowińska, 'Wykopaliska w Strzyżowie, przeprowadzone w 1935 r.', *ZOW*, vol. XI, 1936, pp. 72 ff., Figs. 1–4. J. Gurba, 'Grób psa kultury ceramiki sznurowej ze wsi Strzyżów, *AUMCS*, vol. v F, 1950, pp. 159 ff., Figs. 1–5. Nosek (op. cit., note 17), pp. 248 f., Figs. 27, 28. J. Głosik 'Osada kultury ceramiki sznurowej w Strzyżowie, w świetle badań w latach 1935–37 i 39', *Mat.St.*, vol. VII, 1959, pp. 112 ff.

of these dwellings with hearths, were uncovered, and also at least three graves. Pottery was of a special type, which has been called the Strzyżów group or culture, but pottery typical of the Trzciniec and Lusatian cultures were excavated also. Many oval flint axes, fragments of hammer-axes (or battle-axes), saddle querns, various implements and many animal bones were excavated. The floor of a few pit-dwellings was cobbled. Of the three graves uncovered, grave 1 contained a slightly contracted skeleton and yielded a flint dagger, six flint arrow-heads and a flint scraper and drill. Two other graves were child burials; in one twenty-one faience beads were found, in the other was one flint arrow-head and a bone point. In a different part of the village another settlement of the same culture was found, but was not investigated. In 1940 three skeletons were uncovered in a different site and clay vessels and some flint objects lay near by. In 1952 J. Gurba investigated a double burial situated in yet another site. Both skeletons lay in an extended position, one on its back, the other face down; near them a fragment of a handled cup was found. At about 7m from them, the skeleton of a dog was uncovered; at its sides stood two vessels: a two-lugged cord-decorated amphora and a handled cord-decorated cup. Of particular interest are two polished bone pins with perforated heads, both richly decorated with incised geometric patterns.[49]

622. *Teniatyska*, district of Tomaszów Lubelski

Traces of a settlement of the Corded Ware culture were found on sand-dunes surrounded by meadows extending along the Sołokija; they consisted of potsherds, and flint implements found on the surface.[50]

623. *Torczyn*, district of Łuck

In 1938 a cemetery consisting of nineteen flat inhumation graves in two groups was excavated by J. Fitzke.[51] All skeletons lay in a crouched position, on their right or left sides, all in shallow pits with their legs strongly contracted. Two skeletons had their feet cut off, and six graves were considerably ruined. Grave goods consisted of cord-decorated vessels, ornaments made of bronze, bone or shells, faience (beads), and weapons, e.g. flint daggers, flint 'sickles' and small arrow-heads; these last were found in chest bones which suggest that the persons concerned had been killed. Details are available in respect of a few graves only: In grave 1 a few tubular bone beads and a bronze ear-pendant with one end considerably widened were found. In grave 4, two vessels of different size and a bronze ornament were excavated. Grave 6 had a skeleton strongly contracted, its knees touching the chest, hand also contracted, palms under the head. Grave 13 yielded a large cylindrical bone pendant and three flint arrow-heads on which the resin serving to fix them to the arrow had been preserved. In graves 14 and 15 bronze ear-pendants with one end widened, flat, were found, and grave 18 was a burial of a child in which a few pendants made of boar tusks were excavated.

624. *Turkułówka*, district of Hrubieszów

A fragment of a large amphora with lugs on the upper part of the shoulder, a flint 'sickle' (dagger) and a stone battle-axe were found.[52]

625. *Uchanie*, district of Hrubieszów

A large part of a cord-decorated two-lugged amphora, a flint axe and a series of flint implements originating from a settlement were in the Lubomirski Museum in Lwów before the War. Another amphora found here was deposited in the State Archaeological Museum in Warsaw.[53]

626. *Ulwówek*, district of Sokal (see no. 398)

Traces of a settlement of the Corded Ware culture were found in 1930; potsherds and flint implements lay here on the surface of the soil. A cord-decorated handled cup from this site was in the collection of the Prehistoric Institute of the University of Lwów[54] before the War.

627. *Walentynów*, district of Łuck

In 1937 a grave was uncovered, the skeleton of which lay in a crouched position; near it three vessels were found, viz. a wide, deep bowl with two lugs under the rim, a beaker with two lugs on the shoulder and a jar with two lugs under the rim, a vessel typical of the Painted Linear pottery culture; all three vessels were richly decorated with cord impressions.[55] Near by, a settlement of the Corded Ware was found by J. Fitzke, who excavated a few pit-dwellings which yielded pottery typical of both the Painted Linear pottery culture and Corded Ware. Many flint implements, among them 'sickles', were found here. Corded Ware was reddish in colour, made of clay paste tempered with crushed lumps of fired clay, insufficiently baked, brittle. Rims were mostly thick and the upper part of the vessels covered with tight cord impressions.

628. *Werbkowice-Kotorów*, district of Hrubieszów

Four graves were investigated in 1959,[56] in which single crouched skeletons lay on their right side. Grave 1 was of a man *c.* 50 years of age (head to SE) strewn with charcoal. Its grave goods consisted of a cord-decorated beaker, a perforated, polished flint battle-axe on which traces of copper or bronze patina were visible, a bone 'polisher' (probably a

[49] J. Głosik, *ZOW*, vol. xxv, 1959, p. 190, fig. 4.

[50] J. Machnik, 'Archeologiczne badania powierzchniowe w południowej Lubelszczyźnie w 1957 r.', *Spr.Arch.*, vol. vii, 1959, p. 67.

[51] J. Fitzke, *IKC*, no. 130, 12.v.1937, and no. 298, 28.x.1937. Id., 'Cmentarzysko kultury ceramiki sznurowej w Torczynie pow.Łuck', *Spr. PAU*, vol. xliii, 1938, pp. 26 f. Id., *ZOW*, vol. xii, 1937, p. 81. T. Sulimirski, *Polska przedhistoryczna*, part II, London 1957–9, p. 235, Fig. 59.

[52] Nosek (op. cit., note 17), p. 249.

[53] Sulimirski (op. cit., note 51), p. 234, Fig. 57. J. Gurba, 'Przegląd ważniejszych badań nad kulturą ceramiki sznurowej we Wschodniej Lubelszczyźnie', *Arch.R.*, vol. xii, 1960, p. 406.

[54] Nosek (op. cit., note 17), p. 249. J. Machnik (op. cit., note 40), Pl. xliv:5.

[55] J. Fitzke, *IKC*, no. 76, 17.iii.1937. Id., *Spr.PAU*, vol. xliii, 1938, p. 26. Id., *ZOW*, vol. xii, 1937, p. 65; vol. xiii, 1938, p. 128. J. Podkowińska, 'Pierwsza charakterystyka stanowiska eneolitycznego na polu Grodzisko I we wsi Złota,' *W.A.*, vol. xix, 1953, p. 28, Pl. xii:5. И. К. Свешников, Культура линейно-ленточной керамики на территории верхнего Поднистровья и западной Волини, Сов. Арх., vol. xx, 1954, p. 107. Id., Могильник в селе Звенигород, Ксиимк, no. 63, 1956, p. 66, Fig. 27:1–3. Sulimirski (op. cit., note 51), p. 235, Fig. 58.

[56] T. Liana, T. Piętka-Dąbrowska, 'Sprawozdanie z badań ratowniczych przeprowadzonych w 1959 r. na stanowisku I w Werbkowicach-Kotorowie, pow.Hrubieszów.' *W.A.*, vol. xxvii, 1962, pp. 152 ff., Figs. 10–12, Pl. xxxiii:8–11.

dagger) and of two animal vertebrae. A boy, *c.* 11 years of age, was buried in the second grave (head to S) with no grave goods. Grave 3 of a woman (head to NW) has been considered to have belonged to the Painted Linear pottery culture; only a small perforated stone (chalk) amulet was found there. The skeleton and a cord-decorated vessel of Grave 4 were ruined by mechanical excavation.

629. *Wołajewice*, district of Hrubieszów

Many potsherds, flint implements, among them 'sickles', knives, axes, stone battle-axes, etc., were found here; they evidently originated from a settlement of the Strzyżów culture.[57]

630. *Wyszków*, district of Łuck.

In 1930 two vessels were found together near the boundary of Żydyczyn,[58] both being in the State Archaeological Museum in Warsaw at present. One of these is a large amphora with two large lugs on the upper part of the body and two warts, the neck covered with slanting alternating cord impressions; it is 34cm high. The other, a smaller vessel, thick-walled, heavy, with two handles below the everted rim, the upper part of the body covered with three rows of vertical impressions made with twisted cord, base flat, large.

631. *Zawisznia*, district of Sokal

Two vessels found here were at the Lubomirski Museum in Lwów before the War; they probably originated from a settlement of the Strzyżów culture. One of these was a large spherical vase with an everted rim, the upper part of its body being covered with cord impressions; the other was a bowl with two lugs on its upper part. It had a black-painted decoration.[59]

632. *Zimno*, district of Włodzimierz Wołyński (see nos. 137 and 401)

Pottery typical of the Strzyżów culture was found in the remains of a settlement of the Funnel Beaker culture.[60]

(*c*) *Other Corded Ware sites*

633. *Biskupice*, district of Lublin

A cemetery was destroyed during erection of a house. Two flint axes were found in graves; one skull had a green spot indicating the presence of a copper or bronze object which had disintegrated.[61]

[57] Gardawski and Rajewski (op. cit., note 33), pp. 108 ff., Fig. 2, Pls. XII, XIV. Głosik (op. cit., note 26: 1957), p. 648, Fig. 273:1.

[58] Głosik (op. cit., note 3), pp. 171 f.

[59] Kozłowski (op. cit., note 15), pp. 195, 198, Pls. XXVI:16, XXXI:7. Nosek (op. cit., note 17), p. 250. Sulimirski (op. cit., note 51), p. 234, Fig. 57.

[60] Ю. Н. Захарук, Поселение энеолитического времени в с. Зимно, Ксиак, no. 4, 1955, pp. 144 ff. Id., До питання про співвідношення і зв'язки між культурою лійчастого посуду та трипільською культурою, Мдапв, vol. 2, 1959, p. 60. J. Głosik, *W.A.*, XXV, p. 164; and op. cit., note 26 (1957), p. 647, Fig. 272:6.

[61] J. Gurba, *ZOW*, vol. XXV, 1959, p. 202, fig. 1.

[62] Nosek (op. cit., note 17), p. 262. J. Machnik (op. cit., note 40), Pl. XVIII:2.

634. *Dratów*, district of Lubartów (see no. 408)

A cord-decorated beaker found with two other vessels has been considered as belonging to the Mierzanowice culture of the Early Bronze Age.[62]

635. *Gozd Lipiński*, district of Biłgoraj

Traces of a settlement were found on a sand-dune; several pits, 2·50m in diameter, 60cm deep were excavated.[63]

636. *Hrebenne*, district of Tomaszów Lubelski

Cord-decorated potsherds and also a light-brown decorated bowl, similar to the vessels from Komarów barrow-graves of the third stage of the culture were found on a sand-dune.[64]

637. *Klemensów*, district of Zamość

A cord-decorated beaker found in unknown circumstances, has been attributed to the Mierzanowice culture.[65]

638. *Łęczna*, district of Lubartów (see no. 405)

A fragment of a jug and sherds of other cord-decorated vessels, and flint implements were found.[66]

639. *Myzowo*, district of Kowel

A laurel-shaped flint spear-head and a flint axe were found, originating probably from a ruined grave.[67]

640. *Podsośnina Łukowska*, district of Biłgoraj

An extensively ruined cemetery of Corded Ware was found on the Tanev.[68]

641. *Szczutków*, district of Lubaczów

Traces of a settlement of the Corded Ware culture were investigated; it was situated on a sandy elevation surrounded by marshy meadows. A few hearths, potsherds and flints were found.[69]

642. *Trójnia*, district of Lubartów (see no. 593)

Traces of a settlement of Corded Ware culture were found. They consisted of many cord-decorated potsherds and of a stone battle-axe of the boat-axe type.[70]

643. *Trzciniec*, district of Puławy

Potsherds of Corded Ware and of the Trzciniec culture were found together on a sand-dune.[71]

[63] J. Machnik and J. Potocki, 'Badania archeologiczne w widłach Sanu i Tanwi', *Spr.Arch.*, vol. V, 1959, p. 252.

[64] J. Bryk, 'Osady epoki kamiennej na wydmach nadbużańskich', *W.A.*, vol. IX, 1924–5, p. 57, Pl. III:13.

[65] Nosek (op. cit., note 17), p. 258, Pl. XX:1.

[66] Loc. cit.

[67] J. Fitzke, *IKC*, no. 276, 6.x.1937.

[68] Machnik and Potocki, loc. cit., note 63.

[69] Loc. cit.

[70] Gajewski, loc. cit., note 45.

[71] A. Gardawski, 'Wyniki prac wykopaliskowych przeprowadzonych w 1952 r. w miejscowości Trzciniec', *W.A.*, vol. XX, 1954, p. 381.

644. *Włostowice*, district of Puławy

Many cord-decorated potsherds were found on sand-dunes extending along the eastern bank of the Vistula; they evidently marked traces of temporary visits and encampments by the bearers of that culture.[72]

645. *Wola Lisowska*, district of Lubartów

Traces of an encampment of the Masovian and Corded Ware cultures, covering an area about 300 sq. m, were uncovered on a sandy hill surrounded by marshy meadows.[73]

Note: Besides those above, over one hundred sites have been recorded within the same area; they consisted of a few cord-decorated potsherds found on sand-dunes or on the surface of the arable fields.[74] In addition, a settlement of the Strzyżów culture was investigated at *Tarnogóra*, district of Krasnystaw.[75] Handled cups of the Chłopice-Véselé type have been found there.

2. WEST-VOLHYNIAN GRAVES

(*a*) *Barrow-graves*

138. *Agatówka* district of Równe

A flint axe and a flint dagger were found near the skeleton in a barrow-grave.[1]

139. *Boratyn Wielki* district of Łuck

In 1896 a skeleton was found in a Neolithic grave, possibly a barrow-grave, with a clay whorl near it and a stone battle-axe near the skull.[2]

A barrow-grave, 13·5m in diameter, 1·3m high, was excavated in 1938 by J. Fitzke.[3] A little below the ancient surface four crouched skeletons were uncovered, laying in two pairs, all the legs close to those of other skeletons, heads to E. One skeleton had the legs removed and lain on the chest; on its chest lay a bronze ornament with one end wound in a spiral, the other forming a figure similar to '8'. Another skeleton had a thin bronze band on its skull, 20cm long, 3·8cm wide, with its end gradually narrowing. The third skeleton had a bronze tubular ornament on the chest. The first skeleton, and the fourth which had no bronze ornaments, were spoiled; according to J. Fitzke they were spoiled when at some later period the two others were laid in the grave.

140. *Bronniki* district of Klewań (see no. 190)

A skeleton with a diorite battle-axe and clay vessel were found in a barrow-grave in 1858. This was one of a group of five mounds.[4] These objects were given to the Archaeological Museum in Kiev.

141. *Czersk* district of Kowel

A barrow-grave of the Middle Bronze Age was investigated in 1936 by J. Fitzke. A tulip-shaped vessel found in it is in the Museum at Łuck.[5]

142. *Dytynytsy* district of Dubno

In 1940 M. I. Ostrovski excavated five barrow-graves, some with inhumations others with cremation burials. In the graves were found pottery, particularly vessels with one handle and protuberances on the body and various bronze ornaments. Among the latter were bronze pins and fibulae. A bronze fibula lay on the ashes in one of the cremation burials. This was an '8'-shaped double-spiral fibula. This fibula and the pins from this cemetery were of the same type as those from the cemetery at Voytsekhivka in East Volhynia[6] (no. 236).

143. *Gródek* district of Łuck

In 1936 a barrow-grave situated on the top of a hill was excavated by J. Fitzke.[7] It was 1·3m high, 10m in diameter. In the centre of the mound were found a few animal bones, an antler, a flint arrow-head, a cord-decorated potsherd and the potsherd of a vessel with an everted rim. The original grave was ruined by a mediaeval secondary burial.

144. *Izyaslavl*

In one of the eight barrow-graves investigated by Byelaševskii,[8] lumps of charcoal and a stone battle-axe were found near a decayed skeleton. Another barrow-grave contained a cremation burial. Six barrow-graves were of the early mediaeval period.

145. *Jurkowce* district of Ostróg.

Several of the approximately forty barrow-graves here have been excavated by G. Ossowski, Z. Luba-Radzimiński, A. Gloger and others. Long-headed skeletons, and flint implements, many of them polished, were found in these graves.[9] This locality borders on Korytne and it is likely that three flint axes, all rectangular in section, 11, 11·5 and 10·5cm long, and a damaged stone battle-axe with the edge missing, originally about 12cm long, which were in the Lubomirski Museum in Lwów before the War, originated from these excavations (nos. 952–10, 953–11, 954–12, 955–13); all were the gift of Z. Luba-Radzimiński, and are marked in the Catalogue as from Korytne.

[72] A. Ruszkowski, *ZOW*, vol. xxv, 1959, pp. 206 ff.

[73] L. Gajewski, 'Ślady osadnictwa neolitycznego w Woli Lisowskiej, pow.Lubartów, *W.A.*, vol. xxvii, 1961–2, p. 399.

[74] Nosek, loc. cit., note 17. Machnik and Potocki, loc. cit., note 63. Machnik, loc. cit., note 50. J. Gurba, 'Neolithic Settlements on the Lublin Loess Uppland', *AUMCS*, vol. xv B, 1961, pp. 222 ff., Figs. 8, 9 (maps).

[75] J. Machnik, 'Archeologiczne badania powierzchniowe na niektórych schyłkowo-neolitycznych i wczesnobrązowych stanowiskach w Małopolsce', *Sprawozdania Komisji PAN*, Kraków 1964, i–vi, pp. 14–17.

[1] A. Cynkałowski, *Materiały do pradziejów Wołynia i Polesia Wołyńskiego*, Warszawa 1961, p. 224.

[2] L. Kozłowski, *Młodsza epoka kamienna w Polsce (neolit)*, Lwów 1924, p. 189.

[3] J. Fitzke, 'Tegoroczne badania archeologiczne na Wołyniu', *ZOW*, vol. xiii, 1938, p. 128, Fig. 2.

[4] Kozłowski (op. cit., note 2), p. 190.

[5] R. Rogozińska, 'Cmentarzysko kultury komarowskiej w Bukównie', *Mat. Arch.*, vol. i, 1959, p. 113.

[6] О. Лагодовська, Войцехівський могильник бронзової доби на Волині, Археологія-Kiev, vol. ii, 1948, p. 76. Cynkałowski (op. cit., note 1), p. 69.

[7] J. Fitzke, 'Badania archeologiczne w Gródku, pow.Łuck', *Światowit* vol. xvii, 1938, pp. 333 ff.

[8] В. Б. Антонович, Археологiческая карта волынской губернiи, Труды XI Археол., Сьезда, Moscow 1900, p. 103.

[9] Kozłowski (op. cit., note 2), p. 190.

146. *Korytne* district of Ostróg

A few barrow-graves were excavated by H. Breza and B. Rupniewski at Korytne and the neighbouring village of Siekierzyńce in 1849–50. Skeletons were found in these, along with one or two clay vessels, a battle-axe and in one case also a flint axe. A stone battle-axe, 16·5cm long 'found in a barrow-grave near a contracted skeleton', a flint axe, 13cm long and a flint dagger or spear-head (Plate 11:8) 8 cm long, both from a barrow-grave, which were at the University Museum in Tartu, Estonia[10] before the War, gifts of Mr W. Rupniewski in 1877, probably originate from these excavations.

In 1878, two barrow-graves were excavated by Z. Radzimiński and W. Rupniewski.[11]

Barrow-grave I. At a site known as 'Nadyszen' *c.* 9m (?) in diameter, *c.* 1m high. The skeleton had almost completely decayed, only slight traces of it were discerned. Charcoal, a little fired clay, very characteristic clay rolls, *c.* 5cm in diameter, and an undecorated Thuringian amphora[12] were found.

Barrow-grave II was about half a mile east of the above. On the ancient ground surface lay a crouched long-headed skeleton, head to E. The skull lay on a cushion of yellow clay, and near the feet stood an undecorated, double-handled vase, about 13cm high (Plate 23:2).

147. *Krzemieniec* (see no. 431)

In a barrow-grave, about 3km north of the town, a skeleton was found near the head of which lay two polished flint axes.[13]

186. *Molodove* III district of Dubno

Two skeletons were uncovered under a mound. Vessels and flint tools were found near these.[14]

148. *Nowy Dwór* district of Równe (see nos. 555, 658)

In 1856 three barrow-graves were investigated by Byelaševskii. Heaped calcined human bones were found in them.[15]

149. *Oderady* district of Łuck

Two cord-decorated vessels were found near a crouched skeleton in a barrow-grave.[16]

150. *Ostrożec* district of Dubno

In 1867 one barrow-grave in a group of five was investigated. A very fine flint dagger, or spear-head (Plate 11:1) was found, deposited in the Archaeological Museum in Cracow.[17]

[10] Nos. 3266, 1329/1, 2. I am indebted to the pre-war authorities of the Museum in Tartu for the photographs of these objects, and also for those of the two vessels mentioned below.

[11] Kozłowski (op. cit., note 2), p. 190.

[12] At the University Museum, Tartu, no. 1322/1. It was published by A. M. Tallgren, *ESA*, vol. II, 1926, p. 40, Fig. 35. Vessel from barrow-grave II was at the same museum (no. 1323).

[13] A. H. Kirkor, *ZWAK*, vol. I, 1877, p. 21.

[14] I. К. Свешніков, Пам'ятки культур шнурової кераміки в басейні р. Устя, Мдапв, vol. 4, 1962, p. 44.

[15] Антонович (op. cit., note 8), p. 39.

[16] Cynkałowski (op. cit., note 1), p. 44.

[17] G. Ossowski, 'Przyczynek do wiadomości o grotach krzemiennych znajdowanych na ziemiach dawnej Polski', *ZWAK*, vol. x, 1886, p. 28, Fig. 1. Kozłowski (op. cit., note 2), p. 191.

[18] Kozłowski, loc. cit.

151. *Pererosłe* district of Ostróg

A damaged and ploughed up barrow-grave was excavated in 1877 by Z. Radzimiński. The skeleton of an old man with a dolichocephalic skull was ruined. It was covered with rolls of yellow clay. A few fragments of flint knives were found near it.[18]

152. *Peresopnytsia* district of Równe (see no. 181)

The Ševčenko Museum in Lwów[19] had an oblong clay bead found on the neck of a contracted skeleton in a barrow-grave, also a clay vessel found in another barrow-grave, near a contracted skeleton.

153. *Płużne* district of Ostróg

A barrow-grave was excavated by Z. Radzimiński and W. Rupniewski[20] in 1878, numbered as III (nos. I and II were at Korytne). It was 17·5m in diameter, *c.* 2m high. At a depth of *c.* 60cm, a layer of strongly tempered rich earth with fragments of charcoal and calcined bones was uncovered. Two vessels, one inside the other, were found NW of this layer. This seems in fact, to have been a single large vessel, i.e. an amphora with its neck cord-decorated, the upper part of which was pressed down and appeared to be a different vessel. The 'smaller' vessel contained calcined bones. A flint axe 11·5cm long lay a few centimetres from the vessel, and near by was a damaged edge of another flint axe 6cm long.[21] The usual clay rolls appeared about *c.* 60cm deeper. They covered the crouched skeleton, which lay on virgin soil (probably in a shaft dug in the ancient ground surface), head to E. The skull was dolichocephalic. No grave goods were in the grave.

154. *Ponebel* district of Równe

A Neolithic barrow-grave was excavated here in 1897–1900.[22] In 1922 a barrow-grave was investigated by I. Sawicka. Small fragments of animal bones, a handful of charcoal and a small sherd of a vessel of the 'Komarów' culture were found.[23]

155. *Radzimin* district of Ostróg

Four barrow-graves were excavated by Z. Gloger, B. Rupniewski, and Z. Radzimiński in 1876. Four other graves were excavated by Radzimiński[24] in 1878. All the archaeological material was given to the Archaeological Museum in Cracow.

Barrow-grave I–1876. The largest in the forest about 20m in diameter and 3m high. A trench 2m wide cut across it.

[19] Я. Пастернак, Нові набутки музею тов. ім. Шевченка у Львові, 1933–1936, Записки наук. тов. ім. Шевченка, vol. CLIV, 1937, p. 256.

[20] Kozłowski (op. cit., note 2), p. 191.

[21] All objects are at the University Museum, Tartu, Estonia, given by Rupniewski: flint axe and a fragment of another one (no. 1244:1, 2); potsherds of a single large vessel, reddish, thick-walled, with a cord-decorated neck, probably of Thuringian amphora (no. 1244:3–12). I am much indebted to the pre-war authorities of the Museum for sending me the photographs of these objects.

[22] I. Sawicka, *Prz.A.*, vol. III, 1925–7, p. 205.

[23] J. Głosik, 'Wołyńsko-podolskie materiały z epoki kamiennej i wczesnej epoki brązu w Państwowym Muzeum Archeologicznym w Warszawie', *Mat.St.*, vol. VIII, 1962, p. 163.

[24] Kozłowski (op. cit., note 2), p. 122, Pl. XXVII:3, 6, 7.

Three skeletons were found in it. On the ancient surface lay an almost completely decayed skeleton of a child; 1·5m over it at a depth of 1·5m from the top lay skeletons of two adults, their heads to W. One of these lay at a level a little higher than the other. The upper lay facing the earth, its legs contracted under the body. Near the skeletons only a small potsherd, a broken flint knife, a flint flake and charcoal were found. The skeletons were covered with rolls of yellow clay laid across the burials. The skull of the upper skeleton was of a man fifty years of age, dolichocephalic.[25]

Barrow-grave II–1876. This formed a group of three barrows with nos. III–1876 and I–1878 and was in the forest, 1·5m high. The skeleton lay on the ancient surface on its back, head to W, arms on chest, legs crossed. Near it a few flints were found and about 75cm from the head stood two handled cups; both undecorated, one crushed and disintegrated, the other (Plate 24:9) was 7·5cm high, 8cm in diameter (deposited in the Archaeological Museum in Cracow). The skeleton was that of a man, thirty to forty years of age, 183cm tall, the skull ultra-dolichocephalic.[26]

Barrow-grave III–1876. Situated close to the above, 1m high. Only a skeleton was found in an extended position, head to NW, the head 30cm higher than the legs. No grave goods.

Barrow-grave IV–1876. 2m high. Two crushed vessels, one larger than the other, both provided with handles were found and an almost completely decayed skeleton.

Barrow-grave I–1878. 18m in diameter and *c.* 1·7m high, and forming part of a group with mounds II and III–1876. At a depth of a little over 1·2m, a double layer of thin slabs of limestone was uncovered on the ancient surface, covered with a larger slab *c.* 2·4m long, *c.* 60cm wide, and *c.* 30cm thick. Smaller slabs, partly crushed, formed the sides of the grave, orientated E–W. The skeleton in the cist lay on its back, head to W, the skull rested on two triangular stones, and under the knees lay a similar square stone. Near the left foot stood a large reddish-grey handled jug (Plate 24:12) 16·5cm high, 17cm in diameter, with a very fine incised decoration consisting of bands of horizontal, vertical and zigzag lines. Near it stood a pot (Plate 24:11) 17cm high, 12cm in diameter with raised and finger-tip decorated bands under the rim and on the body, and a row of small perforations under the rim. Near the jug stood a cup (Plate 24:10) 8·5cm high, 8cm in diameter, with a raised band finger-tip decorated and a row of perforations under the rim.

Barrow-grave II–1878. Nothing was found in this.

Barrow-grave III–1878. At a depth of *c.* 1m a skeleton copiously strewn with lime was uncovered, with no grave goods. Its skull was less finely made than others from this cemetery and differed from them in some respects.[27]

Barrow-grave IV–1878. This mound lay with the above, III–1878, near the farm. It was *c.* 12m in diameter, *c.* 1m high. A contracted skeleton on its right side, head to W, was uncovered. Near its right arm lay a well-polished small diorite battle-axe (Fig. 35:14) 9cm long, and near by sherds of a decorated vessel were found. They belonged to a bowl (Fig. 27:6) approximately 10cm high, 17cm in diameter, its incised decorative patterns consisting of horizontal parallel grooves and shaded triangles on the body. It was made of tempered clay paste, reddish in colour, well-baked.

In 1879, another mound was excavated but proved to be 'empty'.

156. *Siekierzyńce* district of Ostróg

In 1841–50 several mounds were excavated at this village and the neighbouring village of Korytne, as mentioned above. Later, four mounds were excavated, the descriptions of which were published.[28]

Barrow-grave A. Excavated in 1876 by Z. Radzimiński, about 1m high, ploughed up. Bones of two ruined long-headed skeletons were uncovered, and on the ancient surface stood a middle-sized vessel with a small handle, narrow, everted rim, an almost round base (handled cup). Near by lay a very well-made flint dagger, or spear-head, 12·2cm long.

Barrow-grave B. A skull was found in the 'Krucza' site in 1878. Subsequent investigations by Z. Radzimiński and H. Breza revealed that this was a ploughed up barrow-grave, which they excavated. Another long-headed skeleton was uncovered, that of a young man,[29] head to E, covered with rolls of white clay. Near its feet lay the remains of another skeleton and a crushed vessel, and on the other side a skull of a child.

Barrow-grave C. Situated in the forest and investigated in 1886 by A. Breza. At a depth of 20–30cm a, deep dish (Plate 24:6) was found, 5·8cm high, 15·6cm in diameter, with a row of bosses pressed from inside on the inverted rim (deposited in the Archaeological Museum in Cracow). It stood over a layer of limestones which formed a kind of two vaulted chambers in each of which lay a skeleton, one male, the other female (of an old woman) both dolichocephalic.[30]

Barrow-grave D. Situated close to the above and investigated by A. Breza in 1886, 6m in diameter. At a depth of 60cm two vessels were found at some distance from each other. Deeper, at a depth of 1·2m, lay a contracted long-headed skeleton on its right side, head to N, a child's skull in its arms. The skeleton was covered with rolls of yellow clay, which lay across it. One of the smaller vessels was a bowl, with a semi-spherical body, the other a cup, both undecorated.

157. *Siwki* district of Ostróg

Four barrow-graves were excavated here in 1876 and 1878,[31] and the archaeological material deposited in the Archaeological Museum in Cracow.

Barrow-grave 1876. Excavated by Z. Gloger, Z. Radzimiński and B. Rupniewski, 3m high originally, but later considerably ploughed up. At a very small depth a decayed skeleton was uncovered, near which were found sherds of a vessel and a fragment of a flint knife.

Barrow-grave I–1878. A few hundred metres from the above, considerably ploughed up. The contracted skeleton of a mature man on its left side, dolichocephalic[32] head to W, arms crossed over the head, was covered with rolls of clay laid across it. In its left hand was a flint knife with the top missing,

[25] I. Kopernicki, *ZWAK*, vol. I, 1877, p. 51.
[26] Ibid., p. 54.
[27] Id., *ZWAK*, vol. III, 1879, p. 117, Fig. 3, Pl. X.
[28] Kozłowski (op. cit., note 2), p. 193.
[29] Kopernicki (op. cit., note 27), p. 116, Pl. X:2.
[30] Loc. cit.
[31] Kozłowski (op. cit., note 2), p. 193, Pl. XXVII:1, 2, 5.
[32] Kopernicki (op. cit., note 27), p. 116.

10cm long. On its left side stood a beaker (Plate 6:6) 14cm high, 13cm in diameter, with a raised band decorated with a row of small holes on its neck; near the heaps stood a Thuringian amphora (Plate 5:7) 22·5cm high, 23cm in diameter, provided with two lugs on the body, the neck decorated with three pairs of horizontal cord impressions and a row of small triangular impressions on the upper part of the body. A fragment of a polished flint axe was also found.

Barrow-grave II–1878. Situated on an elevation near by, and considerably ploughed up, it proved to be 'empty'.

Barrow-grave III–1878. Situated in the forest bordering on Radzimin, 20m in diameter, *c.* 1·5m high. Bones in no anatomic order, probably those of two skeletons, were uncovered. Near the bones was a bowl (Plate 23:1) 16·5cm high, 17·5cm in diameter, the surface reddish, polished, covered with irregular, wide and shallow, incisions forming some triangular patterns. Near the bowl lay a fragment of a flint knife and a few sherds of another thick-walled vessel, and three flint flakes.

158. *Skurcze* district of Łuck (see no. 445)

A skeleton in an extended position was found in a small barrow-grave in 1892. The grave had no stone construction. Near the skeleton several bronze ornaments and two flint arrow-heads, both tanged were found[33] (Fig. 34:1–7). The following were the bronze ornaments: an oval armlet with an incised decoration, made of a bar oval in section; another armlet, round, made of a round bar, with overlapping terminals; a spiral bracelet of wide band, and another a little larger but lower, and a small spiral ring (earring).

159. *Stadniki* district of Ostróg (see nos. 446 and 662)

A small barrow-grave situated near the Prusy farm was investigated by Z. Radzimiński (on the right bank of the Horyn) in 1878. The skeleton had been destroyed. A few potsherds and flint flakes, also a fragment of a 'gold-brocade' were found.[34]

160. *Staryki* (?) district of Dubno (Sternia)

A number of barrow-graves some with cremation burials, were excavated by Ia. V. Yarotskii[35] in 1906. A stone battle-axe (Plate 23:4) *c.* 10cm long, four vessels (one in sherds) and calcined human bones originating from these graves are in the Hermitage Museum, Leningrad.[36] One of the vessels was a cord-decorated single-lugged mug (*Zapfenbecher*), *c.* 12cm high; two others were a handled cup (Plate 23:5) *c.* 11·5cm high with wide horizontal and vertical grooves on the upper part of the body and the neck, and a beaker (Plate 23:3) with a carinated body, about 8cm high, with an incised decoration all over the surface consisting of bands of alternating slanting incisions separated by horizontal grooves.

161. *Szepel* district of Łuck

A barrow-grave was excavated by J. Fitzke[37] in 1938. It was 16m in diameter, 1·6m high. In the centre a shaft was uncovered, 2·2m deep (from the top of the mound) in which two ruined skeletons were found, both in a contracted position, legs touching, one skeleton without skull. Near the skeletons were found a bronze ring, square in section, the spiral head of a pin, and a crushed vessel. Charcoal was strewn on the ancient surface around the grave.

162. *Szpanów* district of Równe

A battle-axe made of basalt was found in a barrow-grave.[38]

163. *Tomachów-Zderynowa* district of Ostróg

Three barrow-graves were excavated in 1889. In one of these a skeleton was found, near which lay a flint axe and a flint dagger, or spear-head.[39]

164. *Wilhor* district of Równe

A large Neolithic barrow-grave was investigated by J. Fitzke[40] in 1938.

165. *Wilia* district of Krzemieniec

A barrow-grave was excavated by Dr R. Jamka, and a group of students of prehistory of the University of Cracow in 1937. It was 26m in diameter, but only its southern half was excavated. A few animal bones and teeth were found in two places in the centre and in two other places further south.

166. *Zaborol* district of Równe (see no. 188)

A few dozen barrow-grave were found within the limits of this village. They formed groups of three to twenty-five mounds scattered on the fields and woods. Those situated on arable fields and on fresh clearings were ploughed almost flat. A number of these mounds were excavated more or less methodically by various persons, and part of the archaeological material found its way to the State Archaeological Museum in Warsaw.[41]

Eleven barrow-graves (nos. 1–11) in four different groups were excavated by me and a group of students of prehistory of the University of Cracow[42] in 1938. All the material excavated was deposited in the Archaeological Museum in Cracow. I also collected all the available data and records relating to previous excavations (nos. A–H).

Barrow-grave I (Plan 41:4). Situated in the part of the village known as 'Izydorówka' at a distance of 500m W of the manor house, 10m in diameter, 40cm high. Just below the arable

[33] J. Kostrzewski, 'Przyczynki do epoki bronzowej na Wołyniu', *Prz.A.*, vol. III, 1925–7, pp. 111 ff., Fig. 1. L. Kozłowski, *Wczesna, starsza i środkowa epoka bronzu w Polsce*, Lwów 1928, pp. 102 ff., Pl. XIII:4–8.

[34] Kozłowski (op. cit., note 2), p. 193.

[35] *W.A.*, vol. IX, 1924–5, p. 118. A. A. Йессен, Древние памятники западной Белоруссии, западной Украины, Польшии и Литвы в собраниях Эрмитажа, Сообщения гос. Эрмитажа, vol II, Leningrad 1940, p. 15, Fig. 3. К. Берняковић, Находка эпохи ранней бронзы на Волыни, Сообщения гос. Эрмитажа, vol. XX, Leningrad 1961, pp. 46 ff., 4 Figs. 'Sternia', the village in which the excavation is said to have been made, does not exist; this was possibly the village of Staryki near Krzemieniec.

[36] I am much indebted to the authorities of the Hermitage Museum, Leningrad, for the photographs of the vessels and the battle-axe (nos. 168:16, 90–2).

[37] Fitzke (op. cit., note 3), p. 128. Id., 'Wczesno-brązowe kurhany w Boratynie i Szeplu pod Łuckiem', *Spr.PAU*, vol. XLIV, 1939, pp. 273 ff.

[38] Cynkałowski (op. cit., note 1), p. 45.

[39] Kozłowski (op. cit., note 2), p. 194.

[40] Fitzke (op. cit., note 3), p. 126.

[41] J. Głosik, 'Grób ceramiki sznurowej w miejscowości Zaborol, pow. Równe', *Arch.R.*, vol. IX, 1959. Loc. cit., note 23.

[42] T. Sulimirski, 'Notatki z badań archeologicznych na Wołyniu', *Ziemia Wołyńska*, vol. II, Łuck 1939, pp. 36 f., Figs. 2, 3.

soil, flints (Fig. 18:3, 8, 9) and small potsherds were found, and near the centre a flint blade (i) and a fragment of another large one (j). Over 2m SW of the centre, on the same level, lay the upper part of a large crushed vessel, the base of which reached to a depth of 40cm from the top of the mound (a). This was a tulip-shaped pot, base about 16–17cm in diameter, the aperture about 20cm in diameter made of a clay paste strongly tempered with sand, brittle, pale reddish in colour; the rim flat. About 2m N of the centre a stone, a flint blade, and potsherds lay, among these several of a large decorated vessel (1) probably a tulip-shaped pot, its aperture about 14cm in diameter. Its flat rim was serrated and on its upper part, probably on the neck, was a decoration consisting of horizontal grooves and shaded triangles under these. One sherd had a raised band with short slanting incisions on it. Stones and potsherds which belonged to the two vessels above were also found scattered over the western part of the mound.

No traces of skeleton were found but it seems to have lain somewhere SW of the centre, as indicated by the distances between the flints and the vessel, and their distribution.

Barrow-grave 2. At 'Izydorówka' at *c.* 200m SWW of the above; it formed part of a group of three mounds in one row, one of which had been excavated previously. It was 16m in diameter, 40cm high, ploughed up. Only a few very small potsherds, flint flakes and pieces of animal bones were excavated. They were scattered over the northern part of the mound in the arable soil, which implies that the grave had been destroyed by the plough.

Barrow-grave 3 (Plan 42:2) was close to the above, 14m in diameter, 40cm high, ploughed up. Flint flakes, blades and one flint core were found scattered over the surface and in the mound. Many small potsherds were also found on the same level, mainly in the NE part of the mound. In the centre, under the mound, the grave-shaft was uncovered (A), rectangular in plan, 1·8 by 1·1m, orientated SW–NE, extending to the depth of 1·3m from the top of the mound, or 90cm from the ancient surface. Many small pieces of charcoal were found in the filling, but no traces of skeleton or grave goods.

Among potsherds found on the ancient level or in the mound were everted rims of at least three large tulip-shaped pots or pouch-shaped vessels; the base of a larger vessel, about 7cm in diameter, walls 7mm thick; and a fragment of a deep dish, about 15cm in diameter, with an inverted rim, cut flat, with a row of bosses under it pressed from inside (Fig. 29:3).

Barrow-grave 4 (Plan 41:5). Situated on the 'Olszynka' (Izydorówka) field near the manor house. It was excavated in 1935 and seven vessels were found, five of which were offered to the State Archaeological Museum in Warsaw. All these vessels were typical of the Komarów-Trzciniec culture: they consisted of a bowl (A) (Plate 24:3) 9·5cm high, 16·3cm in diameter, the body covered with slanting fluted decoration; a beaker (B-1) (Plate 24:5) 9cm high, 9cm in diameter, with horizontal grooves on the neck and a row of vertical incisions on the upper part of the body; an undecorated cup (B-2) (Plate 24:4) 7·2cm high, 10cm in diameter; a tulip-shaped pot (D) (Plate 24:1) 21cm high, body 16cm in diameter, with horizontal grooves on the neck and groups of alternating slanting incisions on the upper part of the body; a deep vase (C or E) (Plate 24:2) 16·5cm high, 21cm in diameter, horizontal grooves and a raised band on the neck, a band of three wavy grooves on the upper part of the body.

I excavated this mound again in 1938. Traces of the positions in which the vessels stood on the ancient ground under the sandy mound and remarks by the workers who took part in the previous excavation, enabled me to establish their original position in the grave. All these vessels formed a group south of the centre extending over a distance of about 3m, orientated NW–SE, as shown in the plan. Besides these vessels, a few flint flakes and odd potsherds were found scattered over the ancient surface. No traces of skeleton were noticed.

At a distance of about 200m west of the above, in the small wood of Izydorówka, was a group of three mounds, all excavated by a Mr H. Lessig and Mr M. Baranowski (nos. F–H). The vessels were given to the State Archaeological Museum in Warsaw.[43]

Barrow-grave F. A flat barrow-grave in which a tulip-shaped pot but no skeleton was found. The pot was reddish in colour, 22cm high, 15cm in diameter, a raised band under the rim with small bosses pressed from inside, but unperforated (Plate 24:8).

Barrow-grave G. Very flat. No skeleton and only a single vessel was found. This was a handled cup, 12cm high, 11·5cm in diameter, with traces of horizontal grooves on the neck (Plate 24:7).

Barrow-grave H. Only a single vessel was found, an undecorated tulip-shaped pot.

About 40m west of barrow-grave 4 (Izydorówka-Olszynka) was a small mound cut across by a trench. A flint axe was found in it, and deposited in the State Archaeological Museum in Warsaw.

In a different part of Zaborol, known as 'Głęboka', are over twenty-five mounds forming a large group situated partly in the forest, partly on its adjoining clearing (Plan 42:1). At least five of these (nos. A–E) had been excavated previously (Plate 23:8); three others were excavated by me (nos. 5–7).

Barrow-grave A. Excavated probably in 1935 by Dr R. Jakimowicz, the then director of the State Archaeological Museum in Warsaw. Results unknown.

Barrow-grave B. Excavated in 1934 by a Mr Baranowski. Two vessels were found in it, one of which disintegrated, and the other was given to the State Archaeological Museum in Warsaw. According to the description of one of the participants in this excavation, this vessel was provided with four lugs on the upper part of the body. Some of the cord-decorated potsherds published by J. Głosik[44] might have originated from this grave.

Barrow-graves C and D. Excavated by H. Lessig and J. Hoffman. Crushed vessels and some very delicate tissue was said to have been found in these; the latter disintegrated.

Barrow-grave E. A vessel 50cm high was found, an iron spear-head and a bronze button (tutulus), all deposited in the collection of the Monastery at Bielany near Warsaw.[45]

Barrow-grave 5 (Plan 42:3). 12m in diameter, 60cm high. At a depth of 25cm, under the arable soil, an iron spear-head

[43] Głosik (op. cit., note 23), pp. 172 f.

[44] Ibid., pp. 172 f., Pl. XXIX:6, 8–11, 13, 14, 16.

[45] *ZOW*, vol. VI, 1932, p. 87.

(b) was found in the northern part and a crushed vessel (a) in the southern part. A fragment of an iron object (g) was excavated a little deeper, and close to the iron spear-head; on the same level, west of the centre, lay a stone wedge (i). Under the mound, in the centre, the grave-shaft (A) was uncovered, rectangular in plan, 1·8m by 90cm, orientated SW–NE. Close to its southern corner stood a crushed vessel (d), and another (e), also crushed, was close to the NW side of the shaft. In the western corner lay a handful of pine charcoal (f). The shaft reached to a depth of 1–1·2m from the top of the mound, being 40–50cm deep. A few small potsherds, a little charcoal and calcined bones were found on its bottom. Calcined bones, potsherds and flints were also scattered over the whole area covered by the mound.

All vessels were of the same type (Plate 23:7), large pots pouch-shaped with a rounded base, a short everted rim, undecorated, made of a strongly tempered, insufficiently baked clay paste, covered with thin slip brownish in colour. They were about 23cm high, the aperture up to 17cm in diameter. Odd potsherds found in the mound and on the ancient surface originated from similar pots.

Barrow-grave 6 (Plan 42:4). 11m in diameter, 50cm high. A number of small potsherds, many decorated, and many small flint implements (Fig. 17:14; Fig. 18:2, 4–6) were found in the mound and also scattered on the ancient surface. Here, at a depth of 50cm, about 1m S of the centre lay a large crushed pouch-shaped vessel (N), near it heaped charcoal on the site of a small hearth (W). The sherds of the large vessel also lay at a small distance SE of it (B). At a distance of about 1m NW of the charcoal heap lay a concentration of small potsherds (a). The large vessel (N–B) was about 22cm high, 27cm in diameter, the base nearly rounded, the rim everted. It was made of a strongly tempered clay paste, brittle, the surface red, undecorated. On the upper part of the body were two small perforations near each other, about 8mm wide on the outside, only 3mm on the inside. Potsherds scattered in the mound and on the surface, including the small concentration (a), belonged to at least three vessels of the same type as that above. One of these was a large pot with a thickened flat rim, about 12cm in diameter, with horizontal grooves under it. The rim of another, smaller vessel was also flat, thick, and had double horizontal grooves under it with punctures between them. A few sherds were of the body of a vessel 14cm in diameter with a single horizontal groove from which groups of three concentric grooves descended on the body. All these sherds were made of silted clay reddish in colour.

Barrow-grave 7 (Plan 42:5). 11m in diameter, 40cm high. In the centre, under the mound, the grave-shaft was uncovered, rectangular in plan, 2 by 1·3m, 50cm deep (from the ancient surface). Only a few pieces of charcoal, a few potsherds, and flint flakes were found. Among the potsherds was a base 8cm in diameter, and the rim of a bowl or dish, 14cm in diameter.

Some twenty barrow-graves occurred in another part of the village, known as 'Biczal', particularly in the field known as 'Siszczuk' (Plan 41:1).[46] A few of these were excavated previously by Lessig and Hoffman; only a few potsherds, flint flakes and charcoal were found. In the neighbourhood of these mounds traces of a settlement were visible: a relatively large number of potsherds and clay plaster lay on the surface of the field here. Four more barrow-graves were excavated there by me (nos. 8–11).

Barrow-grave 8 (Plan 41:2). 11m in diameter, 60cm high. On the ancient surface were found a few potsherds, flint flakes, small implements (Fig. 18:1) and stones in various places. The grave-shaft was uncovered in the centre (A); it was rectangular in plan, about 2 by 1m, orientated nearly N–S, about 60cm deep. A few small pieces of charcoal were found in it, but no traces of skeleton. Potsherds found in this barrow-grave appear to have belonged to a single, large vessel, with a large body, everted rim, made of clay paste strongly tempered with sand and crushed flint, red in colour.

Barrow-grave 9 (Plan 41:3). 10m in diameter, 40cm high. Under the arable soil, at a depth of 20cm, a large crushed vessel lay (A, B), undecorated, with an everted rim, brownish in colour, about 17cm high, 18cm in diameter, base rounded. Near it lay a handful of charcoal and a large flint flake (C), and near by another crushed vessel with a flat, slightly rounded base. This was evidently the site of the burial which lay either on the ancient surface, or in a very shallow hole in the sand. No traces of skeleton were found.

Barrow-grave 10 (Plan 41:6). 8m in diameter, 60cm high. About 1m NE of the centre, at a depth of 40cm lay a large crushed vessel (A) close to which an area 75cm in diameter was copiously strewn with charcoal (W). This was the site of the burial, but no traces of skeleton were found. Near by a few odd potsherds were excavated. The vessel (A) was pouch-shaped, about 25·5cm high, 22cm in diameter, base very narrow, rounded, brown in colour, made of silted clay, but brittle, undecorated.

Barrow-grave 11. 10m in diameter, 60cm high. At a distance of about 100m NW of the above, on the 'Siszczuk' field. Only a few flint flakes and odd potsherds were found in it. It had been spoiled either by clearing a large tree which grew on it, or had been excavated previously.

167. *Załuże* district of Izaslyavl (Zasław)

A barrow-grave situated on top of a plateau was excavated by G. Ossowski[47] in 1869. The grave goods were deposited in the Archaeological Museum in Cracow. The mound was conic in shape, 12m in diameter, 7m high (?), and was cut across by a trench 1·5–2m wide, from W–E. In the centre a contracted skeleton was uncovered. It lay on its right side on the ancient ground surface, orientated W–E. Near the head was a small black doubled-handled vessel 12cm high, 11cm in diameter, with two parallel grooves made by cord-impressions around the neck and a row of vertical incisions on the upper part of the body (Plate 4:3) and a flint dagger, or point, 13cm long (Plate 11:6) (nos. 3170–1, 2).

168. *Zdolbunov*

In 1913, a stone battle-axe (Plate 10:11) and a flint spear-head (Plate 11:9), or dagger, were found at a depth of 1·5m near a skeleton.[48]

[46] Głosik (op. cit., note 23), p. 128.

[47] G. Ossowski, 'O niektórych zabytkach kamiennego wieku na Wołyniu', *W.A.*, vol. III, pp. 101 ff. Kozłowski (op. cit., note 2), p. 195.

[48] Отчет Археологической Коммиссіи за 1913–1915, Petrograd 1918, p. 199, Figs. 253, 254.

(b) *Flat graves and cemeteries*

169. *Borki* district of Krzemieniec (see no. 683).

A grave was uncovered in which cord-decorated pottery was found.[49]

170. *Dubno*

A skeleton was uncovered in the suburb Surmicze in 1896. It lay at a depth of 2m, presumably under a ploughed up mound, and near it lay two undecorated vessels, a beaker and a double-handled vase of Noua type (Plate 22:1, 2). Both were made of strongly tempered clay paste, both had thick walls, and both were in the Lubomirski Museum in Lwów[50] before the War.

171. *Góra Połonka* district of Łuck

A cord-decorated jug, probably from a ruined grave, was in the Museum at Łuck before the war.

172. *Gródek* (Horodok) district of Równe (see nos. 429, 650)

In 1926 a settlement ruined by a cemetery subsequently established on the side was investigated by I. Sawicka (site 'Gródek VII').[51] Three inhumation burials were uncovered near by, and investigated by M. Drewko.[52] One of these was ruined. The skeletons lay in a crouched position in shallow shafts with no stone lining. Grave goods consisted of a flint spear-head, or dagger, and a bone pin, and in one grave (no. 2) two pendants made of boar-tusks were excavated.

173. *Iserna* district of Krzemieniec

Bone beads, part of a necklace and a flint arrow-head with a concave base were found in an inhumation grave.[53]

174. *Karajewicze* (Karayevyči) district of Równe (see no. 651)

In a Neolithic grave an amphora 'of northern type' was found.[54]

175. *Lipa* district of Dubno (see no. 434)

Three graves were uncovered in 1939, all in a row at a distance of *c.* 70–80cm from each other.[55]

Grave 1. Crouched male skeleton on its right side, head to W. No grave goods.

Grave 2. A skeleton of a child in a crouched position, on its right side, head to W, lay in a quadrangular cist built of irregular quarried limestones. Near the head stood a small handled cup. Stones bore traces of fire.

Grave 3. A skeleton (probably female) on its left side, head to E, lay in a cist built in a similar manner to that above. Near the head were three ear-pendants made of flattened copper or bronze wire, and near the knees lay a triangular flint arrow-head.

176. *Łudzin* district of Krzemieniec

A grave with a skeleton in a 'sitting' position was uncovered.[56]

177. *Mokre* district of Dubno (see no. 438)

A number of graves were uncovered; some were investigated by M. Ostrowski.[57]

Grave 2. Near a skeleton ruined by ploughing a bronze ear-pendant (small ring) was found.

Grave 3. A crouched skeleton, head to N. Near its legs were a flint spear-head (or dagger) a flint axe and a scraper. Three limestone slabs, facing each other's wide side, stood upright near the head.

178. *Nowosiółka* district of Równe

A flat cemetery was uncovered.[58] Grave 3 yielded a crouched skeleton near which nine small beads (*c.* 1·5cm long) made of perforated animal teeth and eight beads made of small tubular animal bones (*c.* 7cm long) were found.

179. *Osada Krechowiecka* district of Równe

Parts of a cord-decorated 'flower-pot' beaker and a stone battle-axe, at present in the State Archaeological Museum in Warsaw, were possibly the furniture of a grave.[59]

180. *Ostróg* (see no. 442)

Near the skeleton in a flat grave were found: two stone battle-axes and near the head two clay vessels.[60]

181. *Peresopnica* district of Równe (see no. 152)

A score of crouched skeletons were found at site 'Zamostie'; some of the graves yielded beads made of thin tubular animal bones. In a grave published by A. Cynkałowski,[60] two skeletons lay (on their left side) in one line in the opposite direction, touching each other's crouched legs.

182. *Stavok* district of Teremno (see no. 665)

A settlement situated on the high plateau over the Styr valley, at site 'Vygadanka', was investigated by Iu. N. Zakharuk in 1952 and 1955.[61] A grave was uncovered near one dwelling. The skeleton lay in a crouched position on its right side, head to NE, with a flint flake near its feet, also a fragment of a flint implement and a potsherd.

183. *Stydnie* district of Kostopol

At the State Archaeological Museum in Warsaw are twelve large decorated vessels characteristic of the Trzciniec ('Ko-

[49] Cynkałowski (op. cit., note 1), p. 41.

[50] W. Przybysławski, *Repertorium zabytków przedhistorycznych Galicyi Wschodniej*, Lwów 1906, pp. 73 ff. Kozłowski (op. cit., note 33), p. 56, Pl. V:3, 6.

[51] Sawicka (op. cit., note 22), p. 206. Głosik (op. cit., note 23), pp. 135 f.

[52] M. Drewko, 'Sprawozdanie z działalności Konserwatora zabytków przedhistorycznych okręgu lubelskiego za lata 1927 i 1928', *W.A.*, vol. XIII, pp. 295 f.

[53] Cynkałowski (op. cit., note 1), Pl. VIII:3.

[54] Ibid., p. 224.

[55] Głosik (op. cit., note 23), pp. 148 f.

[56] Cynkałowski (op. cit., note 1), p. 225.

[57] Głosik (op. cit., note 23), p. 157.

[58] Ibid., p. 159.

[59] Ibid., p. 160.

[60] Cynkałowski (op. cit., note 1), p. 86, Pl. IX:5.

[61] Ю. Н. Захарук, Новое поселение культуры шнуровой керамики на Волыни, Ксиак, no. 7, 1957, pp. 38 f. Id., Нове джерело до вивчення культур шнурової кераміки на Волині, Мдапв, no. 3, 1961, pp. 22 ff. J. Głosik, *ZOW*, vol. XXIV, 1958, p. 223.

marów') culture and two flint chips found on a sand-dune.[62] The vessels seem to originate from a destroyed cemetery.

184. *Szumsk* district of Krzemieniec

A cemetery was probably destroyed at site 'Cegielnia'. Parts of a child's skeleton from this site are at present at the State Archaeological Museum,[63] and a decorated handled cup was published by A. Cynkałowski.[64] The latter mentioned also a necklace made of bone beads and published a tulip-shaped pot possibly from the same site.

185. *Tetylkowce* district of Krzemieniec

A flint spear-head (dagger?) was found near a skeleton in a flat grave.[65]

186. See p. 163—after no. 147

187. *Unijew-Werników* district of Ostróg

In 1856 several skeletons close to each other (a cemetery?) were uncovered during the building of a house. Near the skeletons lay clay vessels and bronze bracelets and other bronze ornaments, all of which perished.[66] One bracelet with spiral terminals (Fig. 34:8) 10cm in diameter, was deposited in the Lubomirski Museum in Lwów (no. 977–121).

188. *Zaborol* district of Równe (see no. 166)

In 1933 about ten graves were uncovered during the construction of a road,[67] all of which were destroyed except one. They lay on an elevation and were scattered over a relatively small area. The burial which escaped destruction was in a rectangular shaft, 2 by 1m, at a depth of 1m. The skeleton lay in an extended position on its back, head to N; near it stood a vessel with four lugs on the junction of the neck and the body. Its neck and the upper part of the body had an ornament consisting of horizontal cord-impressed lines (Plate 4:7). On the chest lay a bone bead, and outside the shaft a number of animal bones and a few cord-decorated potsherds were found. At the 'Karier' site, a stone battle-axe was found near a skeleton.

A cemetery situated further south should be also mentioned here:

189. *Poczapy* district of Złoczów

Three graves situated in a sand-dune were excavated by Dr J. Pasternak.[68] Skeletons were in a crouched position, heads to NW or W. In grave 1 several bronze ornaments were found: three small ear-pendants with one end flattened, one pendant in the form of a double spiral, two bronze buttons perforated in the centre, and a necklace consisting of many tubular beads made of a thin spiral band, and a number of discoid beads. In addition a bone point (awl) was found here. Grave 2 contained a small fragment of bronze wire, a bone point, while a green spot on the skull indicated that another bronze earring must have disintegrated. In grave 3 a small bronze arrow-head lay near the left arm of the skeleton; it was made of a thin flat piece of bronze. A few bronze earrings, nap-rings were previously found on this sand-dune; they probably originated from destroyed graves.

(c) *Settlements (mainly of the Zdovbytsia and Strzyżów cultures)*

190. *Bronniki* district of Klevan (see no. 140)

A settlement of the Zdovbytsia culture has been found.[69]

191. *Chilczyce* district of Złoczów

Cord-decorated potsherds were found on a sand-dune, a fragment of a handled cup among them. A small bronze axe with low flanges found on a sand-dune was at the Dzieduszycki Museum in Lwów before the last war.[70]

Addenda: Nos. 646–69

646. *Chwojanka*, district of Kostopol

Traces of a settlement of Corded Ware.[71]

647. *Czudwy* district of Klevan

Several concentrations of Neolithic flints and of cord-decorated pottery were found on the surface of sand-dunes on the Horyn.[72] Traces of settlements of both the Zdovbytsia and Strzyżów cultures have been recorded.[73]

648. *Dzików* (*Dykiv*) district of Równe

Traces of a large Late Neolithic settlement, situated on the right bank of the river Stubło were found; many potsherds typical of the Funnel Beakers and of the Strzyżów culture lay on the surface of the soil here.[74]

649. *Gaje Lewiatyńskie* district of Krzemieniec

Cord-decorated potsherds and those of other cultures were found on sand-dunes along with many flint implements.[75]

650. *Gródek* (*Horodok*) district of Równe (see nos. 172, 429)

In 1926 a settlement of Corded Ware was investigated by I. Sawicka[76] (site 'Gródek VII'). Several pits uncovered here, in particular pits nos. 2 and 6, yielded many flint implements,

62 Głosik (op. cit., note 23), p. 167.
63 Ibid., pp. 167 f.
64 Cynkałowski (op. cit., note 1), p. 92, Pl. IX:1, 2.
65 Ibid., pp. 56, 225.
66 J. Kostrzewski, 'Z badań nad osadnictwem wczesnej i środkowej epoki bronzowej na ziemiach polskich', *Prz.A.*, vol. II, 1922–4, p. 182. Kozłowski (op. cit., note 33), p. 103, Pl. XIII:15.
67 Głosik (op. cit., note 41), pp. 711 f., Fig. 273, 5; op. cit., note 23, p. 172, Pl. XXIX.
68 Я. Пастернак, Перша бронзова доба в Галичині. Записки наук. тов. iм. Шевченка, vol. CLII, Lviv 1933, pp. 64 ff., Figs. 1–7.
69 Op. cit., note 14, p. 48.
70 J. Bryk, *Kultury epoki kamiennej na wydmach zachodniej części południowego Wołynia*, Lwów 1928, p. 52, Pl. III:14. Kozłowski (op. cit., note 33), p. 37. Пастернак (op. cit., note 68), p. 74.
71 T. Sulimirski, 'O poleskiej praojczyźnie Słowian', *ZOW*, vol. XIV, 1939, p. 37.
72 Sawicka (op. cit., note 22), p. 208. Głosik (op. cit., note 23), p. 132.
73 Свєшніков (op. cit., note 14), pp. 48, 50.
74 J. Fitzke, *IKC*, no. 276, 6.x.1937. Свєшніков (op. cit., note 14), p. 50.
75 Bryk (op. cit., note 70), p. 54.
76 Sawicka (op. cit., note 22), p. 206.

mostly broken or damaged, implements and ornaments made of bone, pendants of mollusc shells and many cord-decorated potsherds similar to those found near Cracow. Saddle querns and fragments of them, remains of corn, fish scales, and a fragment of a bronze or copper pin were also found. A settlement in another part of the village (field 'Kurhany') was investigated in 1957–8.[77] Ten huts built on the ancient surface and six pits connected with some husbandry purpose were uncovered. Pottery was of the pre-Strzyżów type, similar to that found in a number of similar early Corded Ware sites in the same region. It showed many agreements with the Masovian (Dnieper-Elbe) pottery and some vessels call to mind those of the Dnieper-Desna culture.

651. *Karayevyči* district of Równe (see no. 174)

A settlement similar to that of Horodok was investigated.[78] Two more settlements or encampments of the Corded Ware culture were found in other parts of the village. One of these was of the Strzyżów culture.

652. *Kołki* district of Sarny

A large fragment of a cord-decorated vessel typical of the Strzyżów culture was found on a sand-dune.[79]

653. *Kostyanets* district of Dubno

A settlement of the 'Komarów' culture (or Trzciniec culture) of the Middle Bronze Age was investigated by I. K. Sviešnikov;[80] it was situated on a low terrace extending along a swampy meadow. Three hearths and two pit-dwellings were excavated which yielded also late Tripolyan and cord-decorated pottery.

654. *Majdan Mokwiński* district of Kostopol

A hut of Corded Ware culture was investigated by T. Sulimirski in 1938.[81] The hut of shanty type lay on a sandy elevation surrounded by marshy meadows, close to a lake, non-existent at present. It was trapezoid in plan, 7m long, 6 and 3m wide. It was supported by seven posts. The entrance was on the SE side. In the centre was a hearth, about 2·5m in diameter. Over the area between the post-holes, over the floor of the hut, lay an occupation layer 40–60cm thick which implies a long period during which the hut was inhabited. In the layer many animal bones, potsherds and various flint and bone tools were found. Among the latter were two flint axes, knives, bone awls, and a whistle made of antler. Pottery was a grey sand-gritted ware, coarse, decorated with simple cord-impressions; semicircular impressions typical of the Gorodsk culture appeared on some vessels. There were several handled amphorae of Strzyżów type, Bones were identified mainly as those of cattle; less frequent were pigs, and a few bones were of goat or sheep, boar and roe-deer.[82]

655. *Młyniv* district of Dubno (see no. 437)

A settlement of the Strzyżów culture was uncovered.[83]

656. *Myrohošča* district of Dubno (see no. 436)

Traces of a Corded Ware settlement were uncovered.[84]

657. *Nowyj Dwir-Kwasilow* district of Równe

A number of potsherds and flint and stone implements were found on an elevated site on the swampy bank of the river Uście (*Sumpfinsel*) between these two villages. They were deposited in the Prehistoric Institute of the University of Vienna.[85] Among them are potsherds typical of the Strzyżów culture, of the Globular Amphora culture, and also of the Middle Bronze Age.

658. *Nowyj Dwir-Równe* (see nos. 148, 555)

Many potsherds typical of the Strzyżów culture were found along the eastern bank of the river Uście between the above village and the town of Równe; they were deposited in the Prehistoric Institute of the University of Vienna.[86]

659. *Piwcze* district of Dubno

Cord-decorated potsherds and flint implements found at site 'Wiatrak' are at present in the State Archaeological Museum, Warsaw.[87]

660. *Sapanów* district of Krzemieniec

Cord-decorated and other potsherds and many flint implements were found on sand-dunes.[88]

661. *Shepetyn* near Krzemieniec

Corded Ware was found, also flint implements.[89]

662. *Stadniki* district of Równe (see nos. 159 and 446)

Potsherds typical of Corded Ware of Strzyżów type and various flint implements originating from a settlement are now in the State Archaeological Museum in Warsaw.[90]

663. *Staryi Mylsk* district of Zdołbunów (see no. 558)

Many potsherds typical of the Strzyżów culture, those of the Funnel Beakers and sherds of painted Tripolyan type ware, also potsherds typical of the Globular Amphora culture, many stone and flint implements, etc. were found in two sites.

[77] Свєшніков (op. cit., note 14), pp. 46 ff. Id., Поселение культуры шнуровой керамики у с. Городок, Ксиаан, no. 97, 1964, pp. 127 ff.

[78] Свєшніков (op. cit., note 14), pp. 45 ff.

[79] Głosik (op. cit., note 23), p. 142.

[80] I. К. Свєшніков, Розкопки в с. Костянці на полі Лиственнщина, Арх. Пам., vol. IV, 1952, p. 131, Pl. I:9, 10.

[81] Sulimirski (op. cit., note 71), pp. 36–8, Figs. 3–6. Id., 'Notatki z badań archeologicznych na Wołyniu', *Ziemia Wołyńska*, vol. II, Łuck 1939, pp. 37 f., Figs. 4–5. B. Ginter, R. Rogozińska-Goszczyńska, 'Przyczynki do poznania wschodnich grup kultury ceramiki sznurowej (na podstawie stanowiska w Majdanie Mokwińskim pow. Kostopol)', *Mat.Arch.*, vol. VI, 1965, pp. 33–55, 12 Plates.

[82] Mrs R. Rogozińska, M.A., Cracow, kindly arranged for the identification of the osseous material, at present in the Archaeological Museum, Cracow.

[83] Свєшніков (op. cit., note 14), p. 50.

[84] Ibid., p. 48.

[85] Nos. 24070–110.

[86] Nos. 24111–15.

[87] Głosik (op cit., note 23), p. 163.

[88] Bryk (op. cit., note 70), p. 54, Pl. IX:15, 19.

[89] М. Я. Рудинський, Дубно-кременецька палеолітична експедиція, Арх. Пам., vol. IV, 1952, p. 144.

[90] Głosik (op. cit., note 23), p. 166, wrongly considered as originating from the slab-cist grave investigated here. Professor A. Gardawski very kindly sent me drawings of a number of these remains.

They were presented to the Prehistoric Institute of the University of Vienna[91] (Figs. 20:4, 5; 21:6).

664. *Stavok* district of Teremno (see no. 182)

A settlement situated on the high plateau over the Styr valley, called Vyhadanka, was investigated by Iu. N. Zakharuk[92] in 1952 and again in 1955. Two occupation layers were uncovered, one of the Strzyżów group of the Corded Ware culture, the other of the 'Komarów' culture, in fact of the Trzciniec culture. Several pit-dwellings of the Strzyżów culture, oval in plan, 3·2 by 2m in area, and other pits about 2m in diameter were excavated, in which many remains were found. Vessels were of the same type as those of the Strzyżów culture at Strzyżów itself and other sites. Many amphorae with two lugs on the shoulder, flint implements, flint arrow-heads, a battle-axe, flint spear-heads, also personal ornaments were excavated. The last-named included tubular beads made of bird bones, animal teeth, boar tusks and mollusc shells. Pottery was cord decorated in the usual manner, typical of the Strzyżów culture. A grave was uncovered near one dwelling.

665. *Velykyi Oleksyn* district of Równe

Traces of a settlement of the Corded Ware culture were found.[93]

666. *Wólka Radwaniecka* district of Kamionka Strumiłowa

Cord-decorated potsherds were found on a sand-dune.[94]

667. *Zastawie* district of Klewań

Cord-decorated potsherds found on a sand-dune.[95]

668. *Zdolbitsa* (*Zdovbytsia*) district of Zdołbunów (see no. 451)

A settlement of a local branch of Corded Ware, called the Zdovbytsia culture after this site was investigated in 1957–8.[96] Two pit-dwellings were uncovered. They were rectangular in plan, about 2·5 by 3·5m in area. Many flint implements, bone tools, animal bones and potsherds were excavated. The most typical vessels were large double-handled amphorae with the neck and shoulder covered by horizontal cord-impressed lines.

669. *Zoziv* district of Równe

Traces of Corded Ware settlements were found in three different sites of the village. One of these, at site 'Kut', was investigated in 1961[97]. A semi-pit-dwelling (no. I) of the Zdovbytsia culture was uncovered; it was oval in plan, about 2·5 by 3m in area, and a hearth was on the ancient ground surface near its northern edge. The dwelling was partly ruined by semi-pit-dwelling no. II, of the Strzyżów culture built on the same site. In both many flint and bone tools, animal bones and pottery typical of the two subsequent Corded Ware cultures were excavated.

3. PODOLIAN BARROW-GRAVES

192. *Barh* district of Mohylev

In 1882 a skeleton was found in an extended position, head to E in a barrow-grave situated on a hill near the junction of a stream called Zaboryce with the Lodava. On its head was a bronze diadem, 15cm in diameter, made of round wire 4mm thick, with its terminals wound in spirals, 3cm in diameter, and a bronze spiral bracelet was on its arm (Fig. 34:11, 12). The bracelet was 5·5–6cm in diameter, made of a band 8mm wide, flat inside, outside convex. Both ornaments were at the Lubomirski Museum in Lwów before the War (nos. 164–1884, 165–1881).[1]

193. *Biała* district of Kamenets Podolskii

In 1903 a barrow-grave was excavated by local peasants and subsequently investigated by E. Sicynskyi.[2] The central area, 7m in diameter, was encircled by stone slabs. One of these, 1·47–1·08 by 1·12m in size, 16–20cm thick, had some marks incised on its corners. In the grave three skeletons were found in a sitting or crouched position. Near one of the skeletons lay an undecorated cup, 9·3cm high, with a narrow neck 5·8cm in diameter, with two small perforations close to each other under the rim, large, low body 9·4cm in diameter, and a rounded base. In the mound was found a sherd of a rim with a row of perforations of a vessel destroyed during an earlier excavation.

194. *Buhłów* district of Krzemieniec

In 1937 two barrow-graves were excavated by me jointly with a group of students of prehistory of the University of Cracow.[3] The archaeological material was given to the Archaeological Museum in Cracow.

Barrow-grave I (Plan 43:1). About 30m in diameter, 1m high. It was partly ruined by the Army Survey when a triangulation tower was built on it.

About 25cm under the present surface, 2·5m SE of the centre, a burial (a) was uncovered (Plate 2:3). Its legs were cut off and lay along the body on both sides. At about the same depth 1m N of the centre, at a distance of nearly 3m from burial (a), another burial (b) was uncovered. It was almost completely ruined by the shaft of a triangulation post. Over the whole area both under the mound and in the mound

[91] Nos. 24031–47, described in the Catalogue as originating from a settlement near the limestone quarry; Nos. 24048–59, described as *geschlossener Siedlungsfund*.

[92] Захарук, loc. cit., note 61.

[93] Свєшніков (op. cit., note 14), pp. 45 ff.

[94] Bryk (op. cit., note 70), p. 55, Pl. III:12, 15.

[95] Głosik (op. cit., note 23), p. 175, mistaken for a village of the same name in Podolia.

[96] И. К. Свешников, Памятники культуры шнуровой керамики у с. Здолбица, Ксиаан, no. 85, 1961, pp. 55 ff. Id. (op. cit., note 14), pp. 44 ff.

[97] Ibid., pp. 45 ff., Fig. 3, Pls. I, II.

[1] J. Kostrzewski, 'Z badań nad osadnictwem wczesnej i środkowej epoki bronzowej na ziemiach polskich', *Prz.A.*, vol. II, 1922–4, p. 182, note 97.

[2] Є. Сіцінский, Нариси з історії Поділла, vol. I, Vinnitsa 1927, pp. 61 f., Figs. 44–6.

[3] T. Sulimirski, 'Sprawozdanic z badań wykopaliskowych w Małopolsce Wschodniej i na Wołyniu', *Spr.PAU*, vol. XLII, 1937, pp. 226 f. Id., 'Notatki z badań archeologicznych na Wołyniu', *Ziemia Wołyńska*, vol. II, 1939, pp. 36 f., Figs. 2, 3.

itself, a large number of small flint flakes and pieces of animal bones were excavated, but no grave goods were found.

Barrow-grave II (Plan 43:2, 2a). 16m in diameter, 70cm high, situated on the 'Za Lasem' site. At a depth of 25cm, traces of a hearth, 50cm in diameter, were uncovered at a distance of 2m W of the centre (b). About 2m E of the centre, at a depth of about 45–50cm, probably on the ancient surface, lay badly decayed human bones (a). They appeared to belong to a skeleton orientated NW–SE, the skull of which was missing (grave 1). Two metres further east, on the same level, a female burial (c) was uncovered (grave 2) (Plate 2:1, 2). The skeleton lay on its back, orientated NW, but the skull was missing; it lay near by in a hole dug in the ancient ground, at a depth of 65cm from the top of the mound, its base upwards (g). The legs had also been cut off the body and lay along the skeleton, the feet missing. Close to the abdomen stood a cord-decorated single-lugged mug (*Zapfenbecher*) (Plate 9:6) 10cm high, 9·5cm in diameter (d). Near both arms lay seven bone beads and two silver spiral rings (e, f) (Plate 9:10–11) both of the same size, about 2·5cm in diameter, made of wire 1mm thick.[4] A flint scraper was also found on the ancient ground surface near the centre of the mound (h).

195. *Chorostków* district of Kopyczyńce (see no. 487)

On the top of an elevation was a group of three barrow-graves, all considerably ploughed up. Two of these were investigated by G. Ossowski[5] in 1889. The archaeological material was given to the Archaeological Museum in Cracow.

Barrow-grave I. 18m in diameter, 1m high. At a depth of 50cm a number of small limestone slabs were uncovered beneath which lay the skeleton; its bones were in disorder so that the original position of the skeleton could not be established. Among the bones was a cord-decorated handled mug (Plate 9:1) 1·4cm high, 13·2cm in diameter, and an amber disc, 7·5cm in diameter, with a hole in the centre and a perforation near the circumference (Plate 9:2).

Barrow-grave II was 2m high, and only half was excavated. Only odd potsherds were found in the mound and a polished point made of roe antler.

196. *Grzymałów* district of Skałat

A handled jug (Fig. 32:8), flint arrow-heads, a flint chisel, axe and scrapers were found at the end of the nineteenth century in a barrow-grave situated in a forest.[6]

197. *Kačkovka* district of Yampol

Three skeletons, all in a contracted position, were found in a barrow-grave. They lay on each other, strewn with ochre; near one skeleton potsherds were found.[7]

198. *Kaczanówka* district of Skałat

In 1927 five barrow-graves were excavated by J. Bryk,[8] the fifth, a cremation burial, being of the Scythian period.[9] The archaeological material was given to the Prehistoric Institute of the University of Lwów.

Barrow-grave I had a stone circle under the mound around the grave. It had been excavated previously and it was said that only a skeleton was found in it but no grave goods.

Barrow-grave II lay on the 'pod Monasterychą' field and proved to have been excavated previously; a vessel was said to have been found in it. The mound was built of gravel mixed with earth.

Barrow-grave III. Situated near by, about 20m in diameter, 1·2m high. It was also partly excavated previously. At a depth of 1·3m a cord-decorated single-lugged mug (*Zapfenbecher*) (Plate 9:7) was found (a), 10cm high, 10cm in diameter. Ten centimetres deeper, under the mug, lay a skeleton in a contracted position, head to S, partly ruined by previous excavation. Behind the skull lay potsherds (b) with a stamped decoration (Plate 9:8) and a large flint knife 11cm long. In the mound a few flint flakes were excavated.

Barrow-grave IV. 20m in diameter, 1·1m high. At a depth of 80cm in the mound, an undecorated mug (a) was excavated (Plate 8:4b). Deeper, at 1·1m on the ancient ground surface, lay a granite battle-axe (b) of type *z*-5 (Fig. 14:11) 11cm long and near it was a cord-decorated mug with its upper part missing (c) (Plate 8:4a, c); its actual height was 8cm. The skeleton was uncovered, in a contracted position on its left side, head to N, on the same level, it was partly spoiled by previous excavation.

199. *Klimkowce* district of Zbaraż (Plan 44:1)

A barrow-grave, called 'Tarnowa Mogiła' (Plan 44:1) 21m in diameter, over 1m high, was investigated in 1937 by Dr R. Jamka and a group of students of prehistory of the University of Cracow.[10] The archaeological material was given to the Archaeological Museum in Cracow.

A field road 2m wide ran across the mound. A grave was uncovered at a depth of 40cm about 2m SW of the centre (grave 1) (a), and about 1m N of it was another one (grave 2) (b). In grave 1, only a few bones lay, not in anatomical order and mainly in the northern part of the grave which covered an area of about 2·5 by 1·5m, orientated NNW–SSE. At the southern end stood a cord-decorated single-lugged mug (*Zapfenbecher*) (a-6) (Fig. 10:4) 10·5cm high, 9·5cm in diameter; on both sides of the grave lay two stone battle-axes (a-1, a-2) types *x*-2 (Fig. 13:3) and *z*-1 (Fig. 14:6) 9·5 and 8cm long, and three flint arrow-heads were found (a-3-5) between the axes and the vessel. Grave 2 covered a somewhat smaller area 1·8 by 1·4m; only a few human bones in no anatomic order lay there with charcoal, and the following grave goods: a stone battle-axe (b-1) of

[4] B. Burchard, 'Zabytki z grobu kultury ceramiki sznurowej z Buhłowa na Wołyniu', *Archeologia*, vol. VIII, Warszawa 1956 (1958), pp. 177 ff., Fig. 2.

[5] L. Kozłowski, *Młodsza epoka kamienna w Polsce* (Neolit). Lwów 1924, p. 190, Pl. XXVII:10, 11.

[6] B. Janusz, *Zabytki przedhistoryczne Galicyi Wschodniej*, Lwów 1916, p. 199. The drawing of the jug was in the stencilled catalogue of a private collection (Skarbowski) at Touste.

[7] A. A. Спицын, Записки имп. русск. археол. общества, vol. XI, 1899, p. 114.

[8] J. Bryk, 'Neolityczne kurhany ze szkieletami skurczonemi w Kaczanówce w pow.skałackim', *Memorial Volume Prof. Demetrykiewicz*, Poznań 1930, pp. 135 ff.

[9] J. Bryk, 'Scytyjski kurhan w Kaczanówce', *Lud*, vol. x, Lwów 1932. T. Sulimirski, *Scytowie na zachodniem Podolu*, Lwów 1936, p. 84.

[10] Sulimirski (op. cit., note 3), pp. 226 f.

type *z*-1 in the northern edge, four flint arrow-heads (b-2-5) on the western side, and a boar tusk (b-6) in the centre. Close to the latter lay a flint scraper.

At about 3m NW of the centre, north, but close to grave 'b', a site of a large hearth was uncovered (d). Charcoal, large pieces of charred wood (e) and loose, red fired clay, lay over an area 3–3·5m in diameter forming a layer up to 1m thick, reaching to a depth of 1·5m from the top of the mound; this implies that the layer filled a hole dug about 40–50cm in the ancient ground. Its SW side adjoined an accumulation of calcined animal bones (c), about 60–70cm in diameter, which lay at a depth of 80cm from the top of the mound, apparently in a shallow hole. The identity of these bones has not been established, but a fragment of stag antlers was found here.

South-west of the centre, about 2m W of grave 1, a number of human bones were found at a depth of 80cm, within an area 1·5 by 1m (f) apparently those of an almost completely decayed skeleton in a contracted position (grave 3). On the NE and SW side of this area lay small accumulations of charcoal. A few more human bones and charcoal (grave 4) were found within an area a little over 1m in diameter (g) about 1·5m SE of grave 3 at a depth of 40cm. Several small flint implements were found in the mound (Fig. 17:11, 13; Fig. 18:7, 10, 11).

200. *Kosikovtsi* district of Ushitsa

A cemetery in which fifteen skeletons in a sitting position were found, was uncovered. Near the left arm of the skeletons lay a stone axe.[11]

201. *Kuźminczyk* district of Proskurov

Two graves situated on a field known as 'Mohyły' were excavated by A. Breza.[12] The archaeological material was given to the Archaeological Museum in Cracow.

Barrow-grave I. Only large boulders were found at a depth of 20–30cm, in the trench 1m wide dug across the mound.

Barrow-grave II, situated on the top of the hill, had been partly excavated in 1886. A large stone, 80 by 90cm in size, 50–60cm thick, lay in its centre at a depth of 30–40cm. It was on a layer of flat boulders which formed a kind of arch, or cover beneath which were clay rolls. About 10cm under the stones, in the western side of the grave, a crushed bowl, or dish, was found, decorated with a row of small lugs, and at a distance of 60–70cm from it lay a flint axe (Fig. 16:20) 7·5cm long, rectangular in section, very flat, of a type proper to the Globular Amphora culture. A large potsherd of the vessel survived, 30cm long, 20cm wide. A little deeper a layer of horse bones was uncovered, including four horse skulls. No traces of human skull were found but a few thin bones, finger and ribs, may have been human.

202. *Liczkowce* district of Kopyczyńce

Four barrow-graves situated on the field called 'Diwicz' were excavated by A. H. Kirkor[13] in 1877. A large Tripolyan settlement also extended over this field.

Barrow-grave I. 21m in diameter, 1·7m high, the largest in the group. At a depth of 1m a female skeleton (skull brachycephalic) was uncovered in a secondary burial. It lay in an unusual position, head to W, legs to N. An accumulation of lumps of baked clay, *c.* 1m in diameter, 60cm thick, mixed with charcoal and animal bones lay east of it. Deeper, at 2·16m the original grave was uncovered. A badly preserved skeleton lay on its back, head to N. Near it were seven flints, some trimmed on the edges, a stone 'hammer or rather a wedge' (probably an axe), and a flint 'sling'. Near the skeleton lay sherds of a large painted vessel and a small bowl made of tempered clay, insufficiently baked. Deeper still, at 2·7m, two more accumulations of fired clay, charcoal, animal bones and many sherds of painted vessels were uncovered. In the mound itself many painted potsherds were also excavated which evidently originated from a Tripolyan hut on the site of which this mound was erected.

Barrow-graves II–IV were smaller in size. Almost completely decayed skeletons were found in all (one with a dolichocephalic skull) and barrow-grave IV also contained a child's skull from a secondary burial. Unpainted potsherds but nothing else were found in all.

203. *Lisieczyńce* district of Zbaraż

In 1937 a barrow-grave (Plan 43:3) situated on the 'Mohyła' field was excavated by me and a group of students of prehistory of the University of Cracow.[14] The archaeological material was given to the Archaeological Museum in Cracow.

The mound was 20m in diameter, much ploughed up. We were able to excavate its western half only. The grave was uncovered at a distance of about 1m W of the centre at about 45cm. It was marked by a patch of very dark earth, about 2·5m in diameter, which differed from the surrounding chernozem (A). Over this irregular area were scattered lumps of charcoal; a crouched skeleton on its right side lay head to W in its eastern part (C). On its abdomen was a large stone (g) and about 50cm SW of the skull was a Thuringian amphora sunk in the ground (a) (Plate 4:4). The amphora was 22cm high, 24·5cm in diameter; its decoration consisted of incisions and cord impressions and was typical of these vessels. Close to the amphora lay a lump of lime (i) 20cm in diameter. Both the amphora and the skeleton were in a shallow shaft dug in the ancient surface.

About 1m NW of the skeleton a large piece of charcoal, or of charred wood (b) 20cm long, 8cm thick, lay on the ancient surface, and near by was a flint knife (j). At 1m W of the skeleton, at a depth of 55cm, on the ancient surface, a few bones (L) were excavated, the identity of which was not established. They were badly decayed. Some 3m S of the skeleton a skeleton of a sheep or lamb (K) lay on the ancient surface. The hind part with legs lay apart, having evidently been cut off the body.

204. *Łuczka* district of Tarnopol

A few barrow-graves situated in the forest were excavated in 1926 by B. Janusz. They were very similar to those at

[11] Е. Сецинский, Археологическая карта подольской губернии. Труды XI археол. сьезда 1899, vol. I, Moscow 1901, p. 298.

[12] A. Breza, *ZWAK*, vol. XII, 1888, pp. 56 f.

[13] A. Kirkor, 'Sprawozdanie i wykaz zabytków z wycieczki archeologiczno-antropologicznej w 1877 r.', *ZWAK*, vol. II, 1878, pp. 12 f. J. Kopernicki, 'Uwagi tymczasowe o starożytnych kościach i czaszkach z Podola galicyjskiego', *ZWAK*, vol. III, 1879, p. 125.

[14] Sulimirski (op. cit., note 3), pp. 226 f.

Chorostków, and Uwisła.[15] In one of these, 12m in diameter, 60cm high, a grave of the Roman period was uncovered. In 1935 I excavated two isolated mounds situated in a different part of the forest.

Barrow-grave I. 12m in diameter, 1m high. Only a handful of charcoal was found on the ancient surface under the mound.

Barrow-grave II (Plan 44:2). 12m in diameter, 50cm high, situated at a distance of 150–200m south of the above. The ancient surface lay at a depth of 40cm. Its central part, about 3m in diameter (A), was lightly strewn with charcoal; more charcoal was found in the northern section of that area (c), where also small lumps of fired clay appeared. Right in the centre of the area (b) lay a large sherd of a large bowl (Fig. 32:2). It was brownish in colour, about 13cm high, 30cm in diameter, the rim inverted and decorated with small bosses pressed from inside. A little over 1m east of these, on the perimeter of the area strewn with charcoal, lay a few sherds, including the base (7cm in diameter) of the same bowl and a number of sherds of at least two other vessels (d): a deep dish (Fig. 32:1) reddish in colour, 33cm in diameter, the rim slightly inverted, undecorated, and an undecorated pot (Fig. 32:7) with a slightly everted rim, about 17cm in diameter, reddish in colour. Calcined human bones were found scattered between the two accumulations of potsherds and north of these (a); they formed a small heap near the eastern accumulation.

205. *Luka Vrublivetska* district of Kamenets Podolskii

On the 'Plyty' site on a lower terrace of the Dniester was a cemetery consisting of eight mounds; they lay close to a Tripolyan settlement. All these mounds were excavated in 1947–1951 by S. N. Bibikov, I. G. Shovkoplyas and others.[16] A. I. Melyukova[17] dated these graves as of the eighth to seventh century B.C.

Barrow-grave 1 was 10m in diameter, 50–60cm high. Its mound consisted of shapeless quarried limestones. Under it a shaft was uncovered in the centre, dug in the ancient ground, nearly rectangular in plan, 3 by 1·4m, about 60cm deep, orientated SSE–NNW, filled with limestones. The floor was stamped except for its central part, on which lay the burial. A chamber probably built of timber stood over this shaft but had collapsed under the pressure of the cairn.

Four skeletons lay in the grave-chamber. Two were in a crouched position, on their right side, heads to NNW. The third skeleton had its legs contracted and the fourth lay on its back, head to SSE, close to the feet of the other three. All skeletons bore traces of red paint. A small undecorated handled cup lay in the middle of the grave, upside down, a similar cup was found in the mound over the grave, probably in a secondary burial, traces of which were apparent. Many potsherds were excavated in the mound: these were of vessels with a raised and finger-tip decoration, many with perforations under the rim, typical of the Pre-Scythian period.

Barrow-grave 2. About 7m in diameter, 50cm high. Under a 20cm layer of earth was a 1m high cairn of limestones. Under it, at a depth of 52cm, was a surface 2 by 1m covered with slabs, orientated SSE–NWW, on which at least five very poorly preserved skeletons lay in a crouched position. No grave goods but a few sherds were found.

Barrow-grave 3 lay at the northern end of the cemetery, 7m in diameter, 50cm high. This was a cairn 60cm high under which, at a depth of 65cm, east of the centre, heaped bones of four skeletons lay on a platform built of slabs similar to that in barrow-grave 2, 2 by 1m in area. The slabs lay on a small mound about 3·5m in area, 15cm high over the ancient surface. In various parts of the mound scattered potsherds of a bowl and a large spheric vessel, also a whetstone, were found. A copper ring made of a flat band lay in the centre of the grave.

Barrow-grave 4. The largest in the centre of the entire group, 15–17m in diameter, 60cm high. Its stone cairn was 1m high and was encircled by stones. Six graves were uncovered. Grave 1: a stone pavement, 1 by 2m in area, at a depth of 65cm, on the ancient surface. Two crouched, very poorly preserved skeletons lay in it in opposite directions, perpendicular to the pavement, which was orientated NNW–SSE. About 2m west of the grave, on the ancient surface, lay a potsherd. Grave 2: two crouched skeletons on a similar stone pavement of slabs, 2 by 1m in area, at a depth of 75cm, orientated NNW–SSE. No grave goods. Grave 3: on the eastern border of the cairn, at a depth of 46cm. No regular pavement, but a number of flat stones marked the platform on which lay six skeletons, very poorly preserved. They were in a crouched position orientated three in one, the other three in the opposite direction. The grave was orientated NNW–SSE, and was 2m by 80cm in area. About 1·5m west of it a small area cobbled with small stones was uncovered on the ancient surface, on which lay a well-made black deep dish broken in sherds. Sherds, stones and earth around bore traces of an intensive fire. Grave 4: a shaft 60cm deep in the western part of the central area, 1·3 by 2·75m, orientated NNW–SSE. Its three edges were covered with clay rolls 10–20cm thick. The bottom of the shaft, paved with small slabs, was only 1·55m by 88cm in area and five skeletons lay on it in two layers, all in a crouched position. Two skeletons lying on their right side covered the central part of the grave, their heads to NNW. The third skeleton lay beneath these in a sitting position near the northern side of the shaft. The fourth lay on its right side on the bones of the two central skeletons in the southern part of the grave, and close to its skull lay the fifth skeleton facing downwards. Two potsherds were found near the eastern wall of the shaft. Grave 5: a pavement of small slabs, 1 by 2m in area, in the SE part under the cairn. Three very badly preserved skeletons in a contracted position lay on it. The grave was orientated NNW–SSE. No grave goods were found. Close to the grave, two broken vessels were excavated both made of silted clay but insufficiently baked; they had a row of perforations under the rim. Grave 6 was at 1·5m E of grave 4. This was a rectangular shaft, 1·3m by 85cm, 65cm

[15] B. Janusz and A. Czołowski, *Przeszłość i zabytki województwa tarnopolskiego*, Tarnopol 1926, p. 6.

[16] І. Г. Шовкопляс, Курганний могильник передскіфського часу на середньому Дністрі, Арх. Пам., vol. IV, 1952, pp. 5 ff. Id., Середньодністровська експедиція 1949–1955 рр., Арх. Пам., vol. VI, 1956, pp. 34 ff. І. Г. Шовкопляс and Е. В. Максимов, Дослідження курганного могильника передскіфського часу на середньому Дністрі, Археологія-Kiev, vol. VII, 1952, pp. 89 ff.

[17] А. И. Мелюкова, Памятники скифского времени лесостепного среднего Поднестровья, МИА, no. 64, 1959, pp. 12 ff.

deep from the ancient surface. On the bottom lay a contracted skeleton on its right side, near it a potsherd. Over the shaft lay a few small slabs, and a fragment of a polished stone battle-axe lay about 1m from the shaft.

Pottery from this mound was very similar to that of the Scythian period, but it also showed features of pottery of the Late Bronze Age. On the ancient surface, under the cairn, and in the mound, lay scattered potsherds (171 were collected), lumps of charcoal and fragments of animal bones.

Barrow-grave 5. Situated at the southern end of the cemetery, 8·5m in diameter, 25cm high, its cairn 6·8m in diameter and 65cm high. In the eastern part of the area under the mound, a small stone pavement was uncovered, orientated NNW–SSE. On it lay two vessels broken in sherds, i.e. a black dish with an inverted rim, and a spheric vessel. In the mound many potsherds of a large spherical vessel were excavated. In the central part of the cairn badly preserved bones of a secondary burial were uncovered; half a copper bracelet, a small vessel and a clay whorl were found near by. In the NE periphery of the mound many potsherds were found on the ancient surface, and in the southern periphery lay several stones which did not form any kind of 'platform'. A few potsherds and a clay whorl were found here. In the centre, about 20cm under the ancient surface, human bones were found within an area 1 by 2m, also potsherds of Komarów type and a horse tooth. The authors are of the opinion that the latter remains were of an earlier date and belonged to a grave spoiled by the cairn raised later on the same site.

Barrow-grave 6. Close to the above, 8m in diameter, 30cm high. A few concentrations of potsherds were found over the grave. This was a communal grave (grave 1) NW of the centre. Very poorly preserved bones probably of seven contracted skeletons lay on a stone pavement 2·1 by 1·3m, 20cm high, orientated NNW–SSE. On the northern edge of the pavement a bronze (copper) needle was found and many potsherds lay among bones and round the grave. At a depth of 32cm from the top of the mound, and close to the grave, stood a few crushed vessels, among these a small handled cup 3·5cm high, 6·5cm in diameter, and a spheric vessel, 7·5cm high, aperture 8cm in diameter. Grave 3: at a distance of 1m W of grave 1, was a slab 25 by 25cm, 3cm thick, on which a large hand-made urn stood upside down; it had bosses on its body, 32cm high, 19cm in diameter, and was filled in with calcined human bones. Grave 2: a few large slabs lay on the ancient surface east of grave 1; under it was a shaft 1·9 by 1m, 30cm deep, orientated NNW–SSE. On the bottom lay two very poorly preserved crouched skeletons. Near one of these was a whetstone, 10·5cm long. Clay rolls 10cm high lay along three edges of the shaft.

Barrow-grave 7. Irregular in shape, 5 by 11m in diameter. Very large stones up to 100–120kg of weight, formed a circle around the central cairn. Four graves were uncovered. Grave 1 was in the NE part. Only traces of a crouched skeleton, orientated NNW–SSE were found on the ancient surface; it was surrounded by small stones. Grave 2 was on the northern circumference a shaft 1·2m by 80cm, 60–70cm deep, lined and paved with small slabs. No traces of skeleton were found here. Grave 3 was situated in a western extension of the mound with a small mound over it. About ten contracted skeletons lay heaped on a small area paved with slabs, the skulls of which were in various points of the grave. They were covered by heaped stones. The authors expressed the opinion that this was a tribal burial place with successive interments, the bones of the earlier burials being displaced by later ones. However, the description of the grave does not support this assumption. Near this grave many potsherds were excavated, among which were those of a small bowl with inverted rim. A cup was found with a few calcined bones inside the grave. Grave 4 was in the centre. A crouched skeleton lay on the ancient surface, on its right side, head to NW; no grave goods. Close to grave 2 a round hole, 1m deep, was found; it was filled in with large stones. A few broken vessels were excavated in the central part of the mound, among which was a small handled cup and a high pot with a row of perforations under the rim.

Barrow-grave 8. South of the above, 9m in diameter. A hole was uncovered NW of the centre, 40cm in diameter, 30cm deep, in which stood an urn filled with human calcined bones (grave 1). South of it a contracted skeleton (grave 2) with no grave goods, lay on the ancient surface. A communal grave (grave 3) was uncovered under a heap of stones NW of the centre of the mound. The skeletons, the number of which could not be ascertained owing to their bad state of preservation, lay on a platform of slabs. Sherds of a broken black polished bowl and of a number of decorated vessels were found among the bones and above the grave. This pottery was similar to that from the settlement at Dunayok in the neighbourhood of the cemetery, which dated from the Pre-Scythian period.

206. *Mervintsy* near Mogilev-Podolskii

Two barrow-graves were investigated here by M. I. Artamonov[18] in 1953.

Barrow-grave 1 was raised of earth and stones under which a small grave-shaft, 30cm deep, was uncovered. Pottery found in the grave exhibits features characteristic of the Pre-Scythian period. It included a cup with vertical fluting; another with horizontal fluting, both with the surface well-polished; handled cups of a type proper to the Moldavian barrow-graves of the eighth to seventh century B.C. and also a fragment of iron horse-bits typical of Hallstatt C period of Central Europe, dating from the second half of the seventh century B.C.

Barrow-grave 2. A stone circle 12m in diameter, 1m wide, was uncovered under the mound raised of earth; in its centre was a stone slab-cist. Pottery found here was characteristic of the Pre-Scythian period, but of an earlier type than that from barrow-grave 1. A tulip-shaped pot was found, decorated with a raised horizontal band on the neck, the ends of which did not meet but were bent downwards. An iron knife was also found here.

207. *Mielnica* district of Borszczów

In 1901 a barrow-grave in the forest 'Stara Dąbrowa' on a slightly sloped ridge, was excavated by K. Hadaczek.[19] It was 15m in diameter, 90cm high. It was built of very hard, dark-

[18] М. И. Артамонов, Археологические исследования в южноий Подолии в 1952–1953 гг., Ксиимк, no. 59, 1955, pp. 100 ff. Мелюкова (op. cit., note 17), pp. 13 ff.

[19] Janusz (op. cit., note 6), p. 70.

yellow clay, in which single small lumps of charcoal, small lumps of hard fired clay and flint flakes were found in various points, as well as sherds of hand-made vessels of Neolithic character, made of clay paste strongly tempered with sand, badly baked, brittle.

208. *Mogilnica* district of Trembowla

Barrow-graves in the forest were excavated *c.* 1890; stone and bronze objects were found.[20]

209. *Muszkatowce* district of Borszczów.

A bronze socketed axe[21] is believed to have been excavated from a barrow-grave in the forest here in 1893.

210. *Myszków* district of Borszczów

Two barrow-graves were excavated here by G. Ossowski[22] in 1891. They were situated on a high plateau south of the village.

Barrow-grave 1 was 7–8m in diameter, 1m high. The area under the mound was divided by stone slabs, placed vertically and forming four-sided figures; the largest 3m by 1·5, smaller ones 1m in length or less. All the divisions were filled in with clay earth dust, burned red. Nothing was found either in the mound or in the divisions and under them.

Barrow-grave 2. Dimensions as above. A skeleton, on its back, head S, bones entirely decayed, was lying in the centre on the ancient level. A small fragment of a bronze plate was found near the fingers of one hand, the bones of which were covered with green verdigris. A handled cup, 8cm high, 10cm in diameter, dark in colour with thick walls, made of tempered clay paste, surface somewhat coarse and undecorated, was standing at the feet of the skeleton.

211. *Nemia* near Mogilev-Podolskii

Two double burials in a barrow-grave were excavated[23] in 1891. One of these was in a shaft, 1m deep, covered with stones. Two bronze bracelets with overlapping ends, an animal tooth and a double-handled vessel were found in it. A bronze neck-band and a small battle-axe made of diabase were excavated in the second grave.

Addendum: 592. *Nowa Sieniawa* district of Lityn (see no. 462)

A cord-decorated single-lugged mug, 8cm high, was ploughed out on a field probably from a destroyed barrow-grave (Plate 9:3); it was given to the Archaeological Museum, Cracow.[24]

212. *Nowosiółka Jaruzelskich* district of Skałat

Three barrow-graves were excavated in 1927 by J. Bryk;[25] they were published in the report as 'Kaczanówka', nos. v, vi, and vii. They all lay in the 'Malnik' forest. The archaeological material was given to the Prehistoric Institute of the University of Lwów.

Barrow-grave i(v). 20m in diameter, 90cm high. An almost completely decayed skeleton lay in a contracted position on its left side, head to NW; it had no grave goods. At a depth of 1·5m in the centre lay another skeleton in a contracted position on its left side, dolichocephalic head to W, a flint knife 9cm long near its feet and three flint flakes near by. This skeleton lay on the yellow clay of the sub-soil which indicated that the grave had been dug in the ancient surface.

Barrow-grave ii(vi) (Plan 45). 24m in diameter, 1·1m high. A cairn was uncovered 5·5m in diameter, 30–40cm high, under the 20cm cover. It was surrounded by a stone circle 2·5m from it, built of irregular quarried limestones. A mound of black earth was raised over the whole area encircled and the cairn. Large stones lain around the perimeter had to protect the mound from collapse.

Under the cairn a skeleton lay at a depth of 80cm in a contracted position on its left side, head to N. Near the legs was a stone battle-axe of type *z*-2 (Fig. 14:7) 9cm long, near the feet stood a crushed, small, very late Thuringian amphora (Plate 4:9), undecorated, 17·8cm high, and a flint scraper. Two flint knives were found in the mound.

Barrow-grave iii(vii). 18m in diameter, 1·1m high. In its centre, a cairn was uncovered, 1·2m high surrounded by large limestones forming a kind of circular wall, 10m in diameter. Under the centre of the cairn lay a skeleton on a pavement (platform) built of limestones 1·9 by 1·2m in area; along its longer sides vertical stones, raised above the level of the pavement, marked the border. The skeleton was crouched on its left side, head to E, while near it stood a small undecorated vessel with two lugs on the body, reminiscent of a Thuringian amphora, 9·5cm high (Plate 4:8). A few flints were excavated in the mound.

213. *Ostapie* district of Skałat

In 1929 six barrow-graves situated on the 'Polana' field were excavated by Dr J. Bryk.[26] The archaeological material was given to the Prehistoric Institute of the University of Lwów.

Barrow-grave 1. Oval in plan, 27 by 13m in diameter, 80cm high. A large low wall construction built of limestones was uncovered under the mound. It encircled the central part and had a pear-shaped enlargement on the northern side, and a smaller, nearly quadrangular, on the other. The length of the whole construction was 18·5m, orientated SW–NE; the two larger ones, connected, were 15m long, the smaller, which was not connected but had one common wall, was 3m in diameter and had a break 1·4m wide on its southern side. A large stone, 75 by 45cm, 40cm thick, lay in the middle of it. Within the large enclosure were three graves (nos. 1–3), dug in the ancient ground, one in the centre of the northern part, the second in the junction of the two parts, and the third in the middle of the central part. All were covered with a cairn, approximately 2·7 by 2m in area, about 1m high and a single crouched skeleton on a stone pavement, on its right side, head to SW, lay in each. Near the northern one a wide flint and a flint arrow-head (in the bones of the left foot) were found, in the second lay a flint burin and a boar tusk, and in

[20] Ibid., p. 245.

[21] K. Żurowski, 'Zabytki brązowe z młodszej epoki brązu i wczesnego okresu żelaza z dorzecza górnego Dniestru', *Prz.A.*, vol. viii, 1949, p. 167.

[22] G. Ossowski, *ZWAK*, vol. xvi, 1892, pp. 92 f., Fig. 16.

[23] A. M. Tallgren, 'La Pontide préscythique', *ESA*, vol. ii, 1926, p. 40.

[24] G. Ossowski, *ZWAK*, vol. xiii, 1890, p. 44, Fig. 3.

[25] Bryk (op. cit., note 8), pp. 140 ff.

[26] J. Bryk, 'Badania archeologiczne w Ostapiu na Podolu', *Światowit*, vol. xvi, 1934–5, pp. 117 ff., six plates.

the third grave a flint knife and a flint arrow-head were excavated (Plate 8:3a–c).

At a depth of 65cm in the centre of the mound, an undecorated single-lugged mug (*Zapfenbecher*) and a small undecorated cup were found (Plate 8:3e, f). Deeper, near the junction of the two larger enclosures, partly over grave 1, a double burial was uncovered (grave 4), evidently a secondary burial. Two crouched skeletons on their right side lay in opposite directions, one head to N, the other to S, their legs close to each other. On the arm of the southern skeleton lay the base of a large vessel; this grave also contained a simple beaker with two raised bands, one under the rim, the other on the body, both with finger-tip impressions, a bone awl, or point, and another made of roe antler (Plate 8:3d, g, h, i).

Barrow-grave 2. 16m in diameter, 1·1m high. At a depth of 1·1m, about 1m north of the centre, a crouched skeleton on its left side, head to E, was uncovered. Near its left arm a bone point and a flint dagger (Plate 11:7) 10cm long were found, on the chest lay a pendant made of a perforated *Pectunculus* shell. On the other side of the mound on the same level a bronze disc, or a fragment of a round sheet, 6·5cm in diameter, was excavated. Analysis carried out by the Chemical Institute of the University of Lwów[27] gave the following results: Cu 76·79 per cent; Pb 2·78 per cent; Sn 18·39 per cent; traces of Ag and Al established spectrographically. At a depth of 1m, a few potsherds were found in another place in the mound. One was of a large reddish vessel with a raised band on the body with finger-tip impressions.

Barrow-grave 3. 23m in diameter, 1·2m high. In the centre, at a depth of 2m, a contracted skeleton on its right side, head to W, was uncovered. It probably lay in a shallow shaft. Near its feet stood an undecorated cup (Plate 6:10) 6·5cm high, 7·5cm in diameter. At about 5·6m south of the centre, at a depth of 1·5m, probably on the ancient surface, was a double-handled vase, cord-decorated, 11cm high, 13cm in diameter (Plate 4:6).

Barrow-grave 4. 18m in diameter, 70cm high. At a depth of 60cm, near the centre, a single-lugged undecorated mug (Plate 9:13) was found, 8cm high, 11cm in diameter, and about 2m away lay two fragments of a bronze ornament with cast bronze decoration (Plate 9:12). Both objects lay on the ancient surface. Beneath the vessel, at a depth of 1m from the top of the mound, a shallow shaft was uncovered in which a contracted skeleton lay on its left side, head to E. Nothing was found near it. The chemical analysis carried out by the Chemical Institute of the University of Lwów[28] gave the following results: Cu 74·09 per cent; Pb 9·40 per cent; Sn 4·24 per cent; traces of Al, Ag and Au attested spectrographically.

Barrow-grave 5. 17m in diameter, 1m high, situated close to barrow-grave 4. At the depth of 1·35m, in the centre, probably on the ancient surface or in a shallow shaft, lay a contracted skeleton on its right side, head to W. Near its right shoulder was a bone point, or rather dagger (Plate 11:11) 13·5cm long, near the hips a cord-decorated beaker (Plate 6:5) 13·5cm high, the very wide aperture 15cm in diameter; near it lay a flint axe 11·5cm long, rectangular in section, another bone point or dagger (Plate 11:12) 13·5cm long, and a flint knife, 14cm long.

Barrow-grave 6. 11m in diameter, 60cm high. A circular construction of quarried limestones, about 6m in diameter, was uncovered under the mound. The stone circle, 1 to 1·2m wide, 40cm high, was 1m wide open in its NE side. Inside the enclosure two burials were excavated. In the centre lay the main grave under a cairn 1·7 by 1·2m: a contracted skeleton on its left side, head to SW, near it a point made of antler (Plate 11:16) 8cm long, a flint scraper and potsherds probably of a single large vessel of amphora type among fragments, those of the base 7·8cm in diameter, and a perforated lug. In the south-western part of the enclosure, close to the stone circle, was the site of the second grave. A contracted skeleton lay on a well-made stone pavement, 2 by 1·1m, on its right side, head to NE. The skull was halved, evidently slashed with a sword, one half of it laying on the shoulder. Between the two halves of the skull lay a bone point (Plate 11:15) and behind the skeleton lay sherds of an undecorated large vessel with its upper part missing (Plate 6:17). The actual size of the vessel was 12·5cm, its diameter 14cm. It was well made, the the wall, thick, well baked, reddish in colour. Both graves were evidently contemporaneous.

214. *Postołówka* district of Kopyczyńce

A flint axe and a clay vessel were found in a barrow-grave in the forest. The axe was 14cm long, rectangular in section.[29]

215. *Rąkówkąt* district of Kopyczyńce

A skeleton was uncovered at a depth of 80cm in 1886. It lay in the earth and near it a stone battle-axe 8·5cm long, and a flint axe 16·2cm long, rectangular in section were found,[30] both given to the Archaeological Museum in Cracow.

216. *Semenów* district of Trembowla (see no. 512)

One of the two large mounds was investigated by W. Demetrykiewicz in about 1900,[31] about 5·5m high, 20m in diameter. A trench was dug across it and at a depth of 4m a human jaw was found and at a depth of 2m in the centre a grave was uncovered. The skeleton lay in a rectangular chamber built of timber logs, head to W, and near its head was a deep bowl 9·5cm high, 14·5cm in diameter, yellowish in colour (Plate 22:5). At a distance of 1m to the W, a similar chamber of timber logs was uncovered. The bowl was reddish-yellow in colour, decorated with two shallow incised horizontal lines around the rim, and the body covered with similar slanting parallel lines reaching nearly the base.

217. *Stawki* district of Skałat

In an inhumation grave a large granite battle-axe of type *x*-3, 11·5cm long, was found. This was probably a barrow-grave.[32] The axe was at the Museum in Tarnopol before the war.

218. *Tokarivka* district of Lityn

In 1889 a barrow-grave was excavated in which was uncovered a grave built of two vertical slabs and covered with a

[27] I am indebted to Professor W. Kemula, at present of the University of Warsaw, for this analysis.

[28] See note 27.

[29] Kozłowski (op. cit., note 5), p. 192.

[30] Loc. cit.

[31] W. Demetrykiewicz, 'Poszukiwania archeologiczne w pow.trembowelskim w Galicyi Wschodniej', *Materiały antropologiczno-archeologiczne i etnograficzne*, vol. IV, Kraków 1900, p. 120, Fig. 23.

[32] Kozłowski (op. cit., note 5), p. 194.

third one. Inside lay a polished stone battle-axe. Another barrow-grave was excavated in 1886 in which two polished flint axes, potsherds and traces of some wooden objects were found.[33]

219. *Uście Biskupie* district of Borszczów

Two barrow-graves about 100m apart were situated on a plateau above the Dniester valley, in a field known as the 'Nowa Tłoka' or 'Werhorodia'. I excavated the larger in 1935: it was 20m in diameter, 70cm high, much ploughed (Plan 44:3).

A layer of gravel forming a kind of small cairn occurred 70cm deep and in the centre. The grave-shaft (a) was found underneath this: it was 1·8 by 1·2m, dug about 70–80cm into the ancient ground for about 1·6m from the present summit of the mound, and orientated N–S. The bottom of the shaft was fairly thickly scattered with lumps of charcoal: an iron knife (c) (Fig. 32:5), 5cm long, lay on this in the north part of the grave. No traces of skeleton were found, as it had entirely disintegrated. The shaft had been covered by logs, now entirely decayed, which were halfway down the shaft. A fine layer of charcoal was lying on these logs, with a large piece of the body of a vessel in it (b) (Fig. 32:6). This was about 23·5cm in diameter, with protuberances on the body, the surface black and smoothed, well made and baked.

220. *Uwisła* district of Kopyczyńce (see no. 518)

A skeleton was found here in 1889, crouched, lying in the earth, on its right side, head E. This was in the northern part of the village. An axe of red-deer antler lay near its ribs.[34]

221. *Zaścianka* district of Tarnopol

A. Kirkor[35] excavated three barrow-graves in the 'Mohyłka' field here in 1877. All three contained large stone slabs. In one, removal of one slab revealed another somewhat smaller and narrower, under which were smaller slabs carefully arranged side by side. A stone, 90cm high, stood on the northern side. A layer of earth 9cm thick occurred underneath, beneath which were entirely crushed bones. The skeletons in all the graves were in a crouched position and lay on the north side: one was sprinkled with lime. No objects were found.

222. *Zawadyńce* district of Kamenets Podolskii (see no. 523)

In 1888–9 a barrow-grave, 16m in diameter, 1·25m high, situated on the top of a hill, was excavated by F. Pułaski.[36] At a depth of 50–60cm in various points, but mainly in the southern part of the mound, thirty-four potsherds, black, grey or red, were excavated. Only one sherd had a decoration consisting of parallel grooves.

Close to the northern circumference of the mound sixteen slabs were uncovered, the largest being 1m–65cm wide, 25cm thick. Several slabs were in a vertical position, and they had evidently formed a grave chamber originally. However, no traces of skeleton were noticed. Two contracted skeletons were found in the centre of the barrow at a depth of 90cm. One of these, a dolichocephalic male, lay on its right side, head to W, with knees nearly reaching the chin. It lay on a layer of hard stamped earth and was surrounded by very hard plaster. Near it lay two lumps of red ochre, a small worked animal bone (apparently an amulet), a handled cup, undecorated and brittle, 6cm high, 7·5cm in diameter, a flint knife 11·5cm long, a flint axe 11cm long, oval in section, found 60cm south of the skeleton, a bone point, 15cm long, found close to the axe.

The second skeleton lay at a distance of 4·5m SW of the first one. It was considerably decayed and badly damaged by roots of a large tree; its position could not be well established. Only charcoal and a few animal bones were found near it.

In the centre of the mound were found: a fragment of a flint knife, 4·5cm long, 4·8cm wide, another flint knife, 35cm long, excavated at a level 50cm deeper than the skeleton, also several small flint flakes. On the southern periphery of the mound two flint arrow-heads were found, one with a small concave base, the other, 2·2cm long, provided with a small tang.

[33] Є. Сіцінський, Матеріяли до археології західнього Поділля. Записки всеукраїнского археол. комітету, vol. I, Kiev 1930.

[34] Kozłowski (op. cit., note 5), p. 195.

[35] A. Kirkor, *ZWAK*, vol. II, 1878, pp. 9 f. Janusz (op. cit., note 6), p. 233.

[36] F. Pułaski, *ZWAK*, vol. XIV, 1890, pp. 4 ff.

SECTION IV

Eastern Barrow-graves

1. EAST VOLHYNIAN BARROW-GRAVES

223. *Hlumča Mala* district of Novograd Volynskii

About one hundred barrow-graves occurred. Two were excavated in 1887.[1] In one a flint spear-head (or dagger), a diorite battle-axe and clay whorl and carnelian beads were found.

224. *Hlumča Velyka* district of Novograd Volynskii

Sixty-nine barrow-graves occurred. In one excavated in 1887, a polished stone battle-axe was found.[2]

225. *Kupyšče* district of Korosten

A few barrow-graves were excavated in 1928 but no reports published. The Museum in Zhitomir had a number of vessels of various size from these barrow-graves before the War. They were ovoid in shape, had a pointed or rounded base, carinated and everted rim and were undecorated. During my visit to Zhitomir in 1934 I photographed three of these: a beaker (no. II–354–1928) with a small base, 14cm high, 14cm in diameter; a smaller beaker (Plate 24:13) with a large funnel-shaped neck, pointed base, 12cm high, mouth 8·2cm in diameter (no. II–355–1928); a cup with a pointed base, 6·3cm high, 5cm in diameter, yellow in colour.

226. *Kurbativka* near Zhitomir

A cemetery consisting of fifty-five mounds extended over the southern slope of the low terrace of the Teterev, on the 'Hremyače' site. Twelve of these barrow-graves were excavated by S. Hamčenko in 1924. No report on these investigations has been published. According to a brief note by E. Makhno,[3] the mounds contained mainly cremation burials. Grave goods consisted of pottery. Characteristic were pouch-shaped vessels made of a tempered clay paste, undecorated, with a carinated everted rim, and a rounded base, their surface coarse, dark-yellow or brown in colour. In 1934 I photographed and described two of these vessels, then at the Museum in Zhitomir. One of these (no. 2080–1924) was 15·5cm high (Plate 24:17), the other (no. 2101–1924) a beaker (Plate 24:16) 13·5cm high, both yellow-reddish in colour.

In 1945 five more mounds of the above cemetery were excavated.[4] They were 6–8m in diameter, 15–25cm high; the distance between the mounds was 15–25m. Under the mounds, at a depth from 3 to 75cm, calcined bones, potsherds of broken vessels and flint flakes were usually found on the ancient surface. Only one barrow-grave was described and its plan published.

Barrow-grave 1. In the central area under the mound was a small heap of calcined human bones, among which a bronze pin was found, 13cm long, with a few sherds of a small hemispheric bowl close to it. Cremation most probably took place outside the grave and calcined bones were then deposited on the ancient surface and a mound raised over them. The bowl was 5·5cm high, 13·5cm in diameter, walls 8mm thick; its decoration consisted only of a row of punctures under the rim.

227. *Kurilivka* district of Khmilnyk

A cemetery of over twenty mounds extended close to the border of Sandraki. The mounds had been ploughed up and on the site of one of these were found potsherds of which a vessel was reconstructed. It was ovoid in shape, the base rounded, the neck narrow, widening upwards and on its carinated junction with the body was a row of small warts pressed from inside. In 1950, nine barrow-graves were excavated[5] and dated by the investigators as the Scythian period, the fourth to third century B.C.

228. *Kustowce* district of Starokonstantinov

In 1852 a small barrow-grave was excavated in which bones of at least two skeletons were uncovered. Two vessels and several bronze personal ornaments were found[6] (Fig. 33:A). One was a double-handled vase, undecorated, the other a single-handled vase with four warts arranged in two pairs on the body and groups of four slanting incisions on the lower part of the body. Both were reddish in colour. The personal ornaments excavated were a diadem with terminals wound in spirals, a similar armband, another spiral armband and a double spiral, probably a fibula. Both J. Kostrzewski and L. Kozłowski dated this grave as the third period of the Bronze Age (Montelius).

229. *Narodyči*

In 1927 two small barrow-grave cemeteries were investigated by I. Levyckyj,[7] extending over sand-dunes at the site called

[1] В. Б. Антонович, Археологiческая карта волынской губернiи, Труды XI Археол. Сьезда, Moscow 1900, p. 25.

[2] Loc. cit.

[3] Е. Махно, Двi пам'ятки бронзової доби в басейнi р. Тетерева, Арх. Пам., vol. II, 1949, p. 205.

[4] Ibid., p. 204 ff., Pls. 1–4; Fig. 1.

[5] О. Ф. Лагодовська, Р. І. Внєзжев, Ф. Б. Копилов, Кургани скiфського часу в с. Курилiвцi, Арх. Пам., vol. VI, 1956, pp. 17 ff., Fig. 1.

[6] J. Kostrzewski, 'Przyczynki do epoki bronzowej na Wołyniu', *Prz.A.*, vol. III, 1925–7, pp. III ff., Fig. 1. L. Kozłowski, *Wczesna, starsza i środkowa epoka bronzu w Polsce*, Lwów 1928, pp. 103 ff.

[7] I. Левицький, Стацiя в ур. Пiщаному бiля Народич, Антропологiя, Kiev, vol. IV, 1930, pp. 227 ff., Figs. 35–8.

'Piščane'. Seven graves situated close to each other, covered with small mounds 35cm high, were uncovered in *Cemetery* I:

Grave 1. Shaft 3 by 5m, orientated N–S, 25–30cm deep. It contained calcined bones, sherds of six or seven vessels and of a hemispheric bowl, also two clay whorls and a lump of fired clay modelled as a 'human head'.

Grave 2. Oval shaft 4·5 by 2·5m in area, its bottom 98 by 30cm, orientated W–E. Near the N and SE edges traces of hearths were visible, and the following objects lay: sherds of eight vessels, two clay whorls, several flint chips and broken stones.

Grave 3. Shaft oval in plan, 4 by 2m, bore slight traces of firing. Over the SE end sherds of a vessel and a bowl lay heaped, and at the other end were two whorls.

Grave 4. Oval shaft, orientated N–S, 4·5 by 2·5m in area. Over the SE and NW edges were traces of hearths; near the latter were found sherds of tulip-shaped pots and near the southern end of the grave lay a fragment of a large clay net-weight.

Grave 5. Only its western part had survived, orientated W–E. Around the shaft were traces of hearths. On the western side lay sherds of four tulip-shaped pots and of two bowls. A fragment of a net-weight and chipped sandstone were also found here.

Grave 6. A few calcined bones, sherds of two decorated vessels and three small, heart-shaped tanged flint arrow-heads were found.

Grave 7. Ruined. Potsherds of three to four vessels and bowls.

No reference is given to vessels published from this cemetery (Fig. 33:B); the most common type were high tulip-shaped pots very similar to those of the Trzciniec culture with an incised decoration consisting of a horizontal or zigzag band of two or three incisions around the neck, groups of various length with slanting incisions below the horizontal lines, often forming triangular patterns. Sometimes triangles were shaded. Of particular interest were groups of three concentric triangles, or semicircles round the neck, a motif characteristic of the Globular Amphora culture. The second type of vessel were bowls often decorated in a similar manner to the pots, but many had a row of small bosses pressed from inside around the rim, which was always inverted. Unique was an undecorated large vessel of which the neck and the rim are missing.

Cemetery II was situated on the northern slope of the dune. Four of these mounds were excavated, but no detailed description of these has been published. Burials were cremations in oval shafts 3·5 by 2m or less in size, orientated W–E or SW–NE. Five to seven vessels usually lay over the SE corner of the shaft, close to a hearth, and in the NE corner lay sheep and horse teeth. In the shaft lay personal ornaments, either broken or at least damaged. They consisted of two spiral-headed pins (only the heads survived), a fragment of a flanged bronze axe (grave 3) and a bronze pin of a late type (grave 4). A few rims published from these graves were comb-stamp decorated and had a row of pits under the rim; other vessels mentioned by the author were ovoid in shape with rounded base. E. Makhno[8] mentions that vessels found in this cemetery were similar to those excavated at Kurbativka (Hremyače; no. 226). In 1934 I photographed one of these vessels at the Museum at Zhitomir (no. 7597–1925) (Plate 24:14) which was apparently identical with the fragment published by Levyckyj (his Fig. 39:7). It was 16cm high, ovoid in shape, the base rounded, rim carinated and everted, decorated with a row of small warts pressed from inside round the junction of the body and the neck. This vessel was found with a lump of ochre and a broken stone; it was typical of the Milograd culture.

230. *Polonne* near Shepetovka

In 1927 two barrow-graves were excavated by S. Hamčenko.[9] Both were 15–20m in diameter, 50cm to 1·5m high.

Barrow-grave 1. Contracted skeletons were uncovered in four shafts. Flint knives, scrapers, spear- and arrow-heads also artifact of a microlithic character were found near them.

Barrow-grave 2. A granite hammer, a fragment of a fired stone and small potsherds were excavated in this grave. The potsherds were made of a tempered clay paste with quartzite, insufficiently baked, reddish-yellow in colour. The reconstruction of the vessels was not practicable. They were 'typical of the Volhynian barrow-graves with contracted skeletons'.

231. *Psyšče* near Zhitomir (see no. 474)

A few barrow-graves in a cemetery consisting of twenty-two mounds were investigated by S. Hamčenko (1895–1920). Their pottery was of the same type as that excavated in the graves of Kurbativka (Hremyače; no. 226).[10]

232. *Raiki* near Berdichev

According to P. Kourinny,[11] barrow-graves with contracted skeletons were found here. In 1926 an isolated mound, 2m high, was excavated by him. Under the mound in the centre a layer of chernozem 17m in diameter was uncovered; at present chernozem is to be found at a distance of more than 1km from the mound. The grave was in the centre but had been ruined by a shaft of treasure hunters. This was a cist built of six large slabs sunk in the ancient ground. It contained a skeleton probably in a contracted position. Only a small bronze plaque was found outside the grave, within the shaft dug by the treasure hunters.

The mound was raised over the remains of a Tripolyan settlement of 'Raiki' (Gorodsk) type, dating from a late Tripolyan period. The date of the mound has not been established, but Kourinny considered it to be 'of Scythian type'. Its slab-cist is reminiscent of the East Volhynian group of Globular Amphora culture.

233. *Selets* district of Korosten

In 1926 a few barrow-graves were excavated by I. Levyckyj, but no reports on these were published.[12] In 1934 I photographed one vessel originating from these graves, then at the Museum in Zhitomir (no. 684–1926) (Plate 24:15). It was

[8] Махно (op. cit., note 3), p. 209.

[9] С. Гамченко, Могильний некропіль біля ст. Полонного на Волині, Хроніка археол. та мистецтва, vol. I, Kiev 1930, pp. 27 ff.

[10] Махно (op. cit., note 3), p. 209.

[11] П. Курінний, Раєцька могила на Бардичівщині, Коротке звідомлення за 1926 рік, Kiev 1927, pp. 72 f.

[12] Махно (op. cit., note 3), p. 209.

pouch-shaped, the base rounded, grey in colour, 16·5cm high, its neck cylindrical. The only decoration consisted of a row of warts pressed from inside round the junction of the neck and the body.

234. *Sokolova Hora* near Zhitomir

A few barrow-graves of a large cemetery of thirty mounds were excavated by S. Hamčenko (1895–1920), but no reports were published. According to E. Makhno[13] pottery found in these was of the same type as that from Kurbativka (Hremyače; no. 226).

235. *Troianiv* (*Trojanów*) near Zhitomir

Two bronze armbands with terminals wound in spirals were found in an inhumation barrow-grave.[14] Before the War they were in the Polish Army Museum, Warsaw.

236. *Voytsekhivka* near Miropil (see no. 460)

Four groups of barrow-graves were recorded at this village, all situated on an elevated plateau along the left (western) bank of the Sluch, at a distance of 2km from that river. Group I consisted of sixteen mounds, group II of two, group III of five and group IV of seven. In 1924 six barrows in group I were excavated by S. Hamčenko, as well as one in group II, situated some 500m NEE from group I. No indication was given in the report as to which of the seven barrow-graves described belonged to group II. Grave goods were deposited in the Museum in Zhitomir and the Historical Museum in Kiev. Part of this material perished during the War. Unfortunately the vessels were not marked and thus none could be attributed to a particular grave. The report on these excavations was published by O. Lahodovska;[15] she was only able to indicate the type of the vessels found in the graves. While in Zhitomir in 1934 I photographed a few vessels from this cemetery, some of which were not subsequently published by Lahodovska. The unpublished arrow-heads were, according to the latter author, either oblong and leaf-shaped, or smaller and tanged. Barrow-graves 4 and 7 were raised on the site of a settlement of the Gorodsk ('late Tripolyan') culture. Male burials were in the central part under the mound; female burials often accompanied by a child, were under the periphery.

In 1949 six more barrow-graves, all in group I, were investigated by O. F. Lahodovska and Iu. M. Zakharuk.[16]

Barrow-grave 1. 7m in diameter, 30cm high. The grave-shaft 1·8 by 1·5m, orientated E–W, 26cm deep. Only traces of the skeleton were visible. Close to the shaft, on the ancient surface, were two groups of vessels: NE of the grave were a tulip-shaped pot, or beaker, a large-handled cup, or jar, and a double-handled vase; SW of the grave a similar tulip-shaped pot was found, also a similarly shaped beaker or cup, a single-handled jug, and a large pot which disintegrated.

Barrow-grave 2. 18m in diameter, 1·24m high. Many potsherds were found in the mound. Three shaft-graves were uncovered on the ancient surface, one in the centre, the others north and south of it respectively. Near each stood a few vessels. The central *shaft* 1, 1·8m by 50cm, 40cm deep, contained an almost completely decayed skeleton, head to W. Near the feet were four vessels viz. a bowl, another smaller, wide bowl and a tulip-shaped cup. In the northern *shaft* 2, 1·5m by 40cm, 40cm deep, lay a female skeleton in crouched position, head to N. Two bronze ornaments made of thin bronze wire were found near it: a spiral pendant and a spiral armlet or bracelet. Near the grave were four vessels: a double-handled vase, a beaker, a single-handled cup or jar, and a tulip-shaped cup. A whorl was also found here. In the southern *shaft* 3, 1·66m by 50cm, 45cm deep, lay a female skeleton in a crouched position near which two bronze ornaments were found: a pin and a bracelet with spiral terminals. Outside the shaft lay a clay whorl where three vessels also stood: a larger bowl, a tulip-shaped beaker and a small hemispheric bowl.

Barrow-grave 3. 10m in diameter, 40cm high. In the grave-shaft in the centre, orientated E–W, traces of a skeleton were visible. On both sides of it sherds of a few vessels were lying.

Barrow-grave 4. This was a double barrow, one 2m high, the other 1·7m high. In the mound were found remains of the Gorodsk culture originating from a settlement on the same site. On the ancient surface under the larger of the two mounds lay a crouched skeleton, head to W. Near the feet were traces of a hearth, and similar hearths were also near the head and on one side of the skeleton. Near its feet lay bones of sheep and pigs, and two horse teeth. Under the lower mound three female graves were uncovered: in the centre lay a crouched skeleton on its right side, head to W, near which stood three vessels: a pot (beaker), a bowl, and a large vessel. In the northern part was a female skeleton in a crouched position, head to W, while near its feet lay the skeleton of a child on its right side, head to S, also in a crouched position. Near the head of the woman stood a large vessel, with a small vessel and a bowl near her feet and a beaker close to the skeleton. The third skeleton, that of a young person in a crouched position, head to S, lay in the western part of the mound. A bowl and a large vessel were found near it. Both skeletons of adults were green stained, which implies the presence of some bronze objects, ornaments, which had disintegrated.

Barrow-grave 5. 18m in diameter, 1·5m high. On the ancient surface under the centre of the mound were traces of hearth, 1m in diameter, beneath which was the grave-shaft, 2·6 by 1·6m, nearly 60cm deep; on the bottom lay a crouched skeleton on its right side, head to W. A flint arrow-head was found among the pelvis bones. In the NW part of the mound was another shaft, 2·24m by 82cm, 25cm deep in which lay three skeletons; two girls lay in a crouched position on their left sides close to each other, heads to E. Near by lay a pot with a large body and a cylindrical neck, two bracelets made of thin bronze wire, a spiral-headed bronze pin 30·5cm long and bones of pigs and cows. The third skeleton lay near the feet of the girls in a crouched position on its right side, head to W. Near it lay a bowl made of the calotte of a human skull, and pig and cow bones.

[13] Loc. cit.

[14] Kozłowski (op. cit., note 6), p. 10. Mentioned by O. Lahodovska in Археологія-Kiev, vol. II, 1948, pp. 76 ff.

[15] О. Лагодовська, Войцехівський могильник бронзової доби на Волині, Археологія-Kiev. vol. II, 1948, pp. 62 ff.

[16] О. Ф. Лагодовська and Ю. М. Захарук, Нові дослідження войцехівського могильника, Арх. Пам., vol. VI, 1956, pp. 69 ff.

Barrow-grave 6. 18m in diameter, 1·17m high. Potsherds were found in its mound. At a depth of 90cm a bronze fibula made of double spiral was found, probably displaced by roots of trees. Three graves were uncovered on the ancient surface: *Burial* 1 was in the NW part. This was a crouched skeleton on its right side, head to NWW, which lay in a shallow hole. Two flint arrow-points were found near its back-bone. *Burial* 2 was in the NE part. The skeleton lay in a crouched position, head to NEE, on its left side, in a very shallow hole. A bronze pin 16·5cm long and the spiral fibula mentioned above belonged to this burial. *Burial* 3 was in the northern part, also in a shallow hole. Nothing was found near the crouched skeleton which lay on its left side, head to E. Traces of a hearth (charcoal and ashes) extended between burials 2 and 3.

Barrow-grave 7. 14m in diameter, 90cm high. In the mound were many potsherds, flints and other remains of the 'late Tripolyan' (Gorodsk) settlement which previously occupied this site. Under the mound in the centre traces of a hearth were uncovered, about 60cm in diameter. Beneath it lay a crouched skeleton on the right side, head to W. Nothing was found near it.

Barrow-grave 8–1949. 22m in diameter, 1m high. The grave had been destroyed by treasure hunters. The skeleton probably lay in the centre of the barrow, head to W.

Barrow-grave 9–1949. 15m in diameter, 60cm high. A double burial was uncovered in the centre. Very badly preserved skeletons lay in a contracted position placed in opposite directions, with legs of skeleton 2 on those of the other. Skeleton 1 (male) lay on its right side, head to W, near the head lay a fragment of a bronze button with a loop, 2cm in diameter; the other skeleton (female) lay on its left side, head to E. North and south of the grave charcoal and ashes were strewn. Near skeleton 2 the following grave goods were found: a spiral bronze pendant 1·5cm in diameter, a very small piece of gold sheet (found near the teeth), bronze rings with terminals wound in spirals (on the feet), a small cup (near the head) 4·2m–4·5cm high, undecorated. Both skulls were dolichocephalic. In the western part of the mound another grave with three skeletons was uncovered. Two lay in a contracted position in opposite directions, the feet touching. The male skeleton (no. 4) lay on its right side, head to W, the female (no. 5) on its left side, head to E. The third skeleton (no. 3) lay on its back with legs slightly contracted, close to skeleton 4, head to W. Its left leg lay on the bones of skeleton no. 5; under its right foot was a large patch of ochre, 33cm in diameter, and near by stood two vessels, a double-handled vase 9cm high, and a small wide-mouthed bowl, its upper part decorated with short incisions arranged in groups in alternating directions. A tulip-shaped pot was found on the ancient surface in the northern part of the mound. In this part of the mound many late Tripolyan (Gorodsk) remains, potsherds etc., were found.

Barrow-grave 11–1949. 16m in diameter, 40cm high. Its centre had been destroyed by a pit dug by treasure hunters. In the NE part of the mound a shaft 2·3 by 1·4m, 1·1m deep, was uncovered, which contained a double burial. One skeleton (no. 2) lay in a contracted position on its left side, head to E; near the left arm a bronze spiral ornament was found made of thin wire, 1·2cm in diameter. Near its feet lay telescoped bones of the second skeleton (no. 3) which had originally been laid in the grave in a sitting position. This was a secondary burial, the shaft of which had almost completely destroyed an earlier grave; only a few bones of an almost completely decayed skeleton of this grave (no. 1) were visible, and no grave goods attributable to it were found. In the SE part of the mound at a distance of 3m from the centre a fourth skeleton was found at a depth of 1·30m; it lay in a contracted position on the left side, head to W, and had no grave goods.

Barrow-grave 12–1949. 14 min diameter, 50cm high. A double burial was uncovered in the centre at a depth of 1·20m from the top of the mound. Both skeletons lay in a contracted position in opposite directions, the feet touching. The male skeleton lay on its right side, head to W, while skeleton no. 2 lay on the legs of the male skeleton; it was considerably spoiled by skeleton no. 3. Near the first skeleton a small fragment of a ring made of bronze band was found, and near skeleton 2 lay a small bowl with a wide base. About 2·5m E of the centre on the ancient surface stood two small undecorated bowls of the same type as that from barrow-grave 9, and near these lay a bronze pin. The large part of a base of a large vessel was found close to them, another sherd of the same base was found on the ancient surface under mound 11, which was situated close to barrow-grave 12. This implies that barrow-grave 11 was of a little later date than barrow-grave 12. West of the centre a ruined burial no. 3 was uncovered. A few potsherds of a spheric vessel were found near the double burial at a depth of 75cm, and another potsherd lay on the ancient surface about 2·85m east of the centre.

Barrow-grave 15–1949. 40cm high, ploughed up so that its diameter could not be established. In its mound potsherds of Gorodsk type were found. Under the mound in the NE part, at a depth of 1·25m, a contracted skeleton was uncovered which lay on its left side, head to W. Nothing was found near it. Two vessels were uncovered SE of the grave at a depth of 90cm. These were a beaker, the neck of which was decorated with five parallel grooves and a low raised band, and a small bowl (or cup) 4·5cm in diameter.

Barrow-grave 16–1949. 10m in diameter, 50cm high. On its surface lay potsherds of Gorodsk type. At a depth of 40cm, probably on the ancient surface, west of the centre was an area 2·70 by 2·60m, the colour of which differed from the surrounding soil. This was the site of the grave. South of it at a depth of 1·08m, a fragment of a human bone was found, and at a depth of 1m a leaf-shaped flint arrow-head was excavated.

237. *Zubkoviči* district of Ovruch

In a barrow-grave excavated in 1898 a skeleton was found in a shaft, head to W, near which lay lumps of charcoal, and a polished diorite battle-axe (hammer-axe).[17]

[17] Антонович (op. cit., note 1), p. 22.

2. BARROW-GRAVES OF THE MIDDLE DNIEPER CULTURE[1]

(a) *West of the Dnieper*

Addendum: 670. *Berkozovka* district of Starčenko (Kanev)*

238. *Bielilovka* district of Berdychev (see no. 747)

Ochred skeleton and a polished battle-axe found in a barrow-grave.[2]

Addendum: 671. *Budkiva* district of Gorodišče*

Addendum: 672. *Burty* district of Kagarlyk*

Addendum: 673. *Drači* district of Rzhyščev*

239. *Dubrovka* district of Tetievka

240. *Gamarnya* (*Hamarnya*) district of Kanev

Thirteen barrow-graves were excavated by D. Samokvasov.[3] Some were of a later period, e.g. barrow-grave I of the Srubna type, most had secondary burials. The following were of the period dealt with in this book:

Barrow-grave 3. Three crouched skeletons in the mound. Two crouched skeletons of an adult and a child in the shaft.

Barrow-grave 4. A crouched skeleton in the shaft. Near it a fragment of a cow's skull.

Barrow-grave 7. In the mound: a crouched skeleton and another one in an extended position with a stone battle-axe and a cord-decorated vessel. In the shaft: a 'painted' crouched skeleton, head to SW.

241. *Gatnoe* (*Hatne*) district of Kiev

Addendum: 674. *Gorokhovatka* district of Kagarlyk*

242. *Griščintsy* district of Kanev

A Thuringian amphora found in a shaft-grave together with a flint axe (Fig. 1:1).

243. *Iwachny* district of Lipovets

In barrow-grave 72: a crouched skeleton on the ancient ground, head to W. Near the head a bone 'hammer-headed' pin and a disc made of a thin bronze sheet, with a perforation in the middle.[4]

244. *Jackowica* (*Yatskovitsa*; recently renamed Dolinka) district of Lipovets[5]

Besides barrow-graves nos. 29, 41, 44, 48, 55, 56 and 60, quoted and attributed by both T. S. Passek and A. Häusler to the Middle Dnieper culture, the following graves should also be attributed: nos. 36, 38, 43, 45, 46, 49, 50, 52, 57, 58, 59, 61, 62 and 65 (Fig. 4).

245. *Kagarlaki* district of Bila Tserkov

An ochred skeleton was uncovered in a barrow-grave.[6]

Addendum: 675. *Kazarovka* district of Kanev*

246. *Khalepye* district of Kiev

An ochred skeleton was found in a barrow-grave raised over the remains of a Tripolyan hut of period B-2.[7]

247. *Kononoč* district of Kanev

Six skeletons were uncovered either in shafts or on the ancient surface of the ground. Four were crouched, two in an extended position. Near one of these lay potsherds, and near two others lumps of ochre.[8]

248. *Krasna* district of Vasylkiv

A crouched, ochred skeleton was found in a barrow-grave. Grave goods consisted of a flint implement, a small silver earring and a vessel.[9]

249. *Lipovets*

Three barrow-graves were investigated.[10]

Barrow-grave 1. Near a crouched skeleton a bone disc of the usual type was found with a perforation in the centre.

Barrow-grave 2. A crouched skeleton on its left side in a shaft, head to W.

Barrow-grave 3. Human bones in no anatomic order were found in a shaft; head was to N. A stone battle-axe was found there.

Addendum: 676. *Lipovets* district of Starčenko (Kanev)*

250. *Łosiatyn* district of Bila Tserkov

A shaft-grave was uncovered in the centre of a large barrow-grave investigated by G. Ossowski.[11] A skeleton lay on its back, legs contracted, head to W. Near the head stood a large black decorated globular amphora, 22cm high (Plate 14:12). The shaft was covered with timber planks.

Addendum: 677. *Maslovka*, district of Starčenko (Kanev)*

251. *Medvin* district of Boguslav

252. *Netrebka* district of Kanev

[1] If not stated otherwise, graves were described by Т. С. Пассек, К вопросу о среднеднепровской культуре, Ксиимк, no. XVI, 1947, pp. 34 ff.; and/or by A. Häusler, 'Die kulturellen und wirtschaftlichen Beziehungen der Bevölkerungsgruppen Mittelrusslands am Ende der jüngeren Steinzeit', *Wissenschaftliche Zft der M. Luther Universität*, vol. V–I, Halle 1955, pp. 70 ff. Most of the sites have been recently mentioned by И. И. Артеменко, О памятниках раннего этапа среднеднепровской культуры, Ксиаан, no. 93, 1963, pp. 38 ff.; and by Id., Среднеднепровская культура, Сов. Арх., vol. 1963–2, pp. 12 ff. He also quotes ten other sites in which barrow-graves of the Middle Dnieper culture were excavated; they have been additionally included in the list below, and marked by an asterisk *. Their marking on Map VI was not practicable.

[2] А. А. Спицын, Курганы с окрашенными костякам, Записки имп. русс. археол. Общества, vol. XI, 1899, pp. 114, 125.

[3] Д. Я. Самоквасов, Описание археологических раскопок, Труды XIV археол. сьезда, Moscow 1908, pp. 8 ff. See also A. M. Tallgren, 'La Pontide préscythique', *ESA*, vol. II, 1924, p. 42.

[4] A. Bydłowski, *Światowit*, vol. VI, 1905, pp. 26 f., Figs. 37, 38, 50b.

[5] Ibid., pp. 10 ff.

[6] Op. cit., note 2, p. 125.

[7] П. Курінний, Хроніка археології та мистецтва, vol. 2, Kiev 1930, p. 29.

[8] Op. cit., note 3 (1908), pp. 9 f.

[9] Op. cit., note 2, pp. 115 f.

[10] Loc. cit.

[11] G. Ossowski, *ZWAK*, vol. XIII, 1889, p. 12, Pl. II:4–7.

253. *Nowosiółka* district of Lipovets

Of a series of barrow-graves excavated by A. Bydłowski,[12] the following ones may be attributed to the Middle Dnieper culture: nos. 10, 19, 21, 24, 25, 26 (Fig. 4).

254. *Piatyhorce* district of Taraščа

A porphyry battle-axe, a flint axe (Fig. 16:5) and a small diorite hammer (Fig. 16:23) were found near a burial in a barrow-grave.[13]

255. *Piliptsi* district of Bila Tserkov

An ochred skeleton was found in a barrow-grave.[14]

256. *Podwysokie* district of Lipovets

Barrow-graves nos, 74, 75 and 76, excavated by A. Bydłowski,[15] may be attributed to the Middle Dnieper culture.

257. *Popówka* district of Vinnitsa

In a barrow-grave with a late secondary burial on the perimeter of the mound, a shaft-grave was found at a depth of 1·8m in which human bones lay in disorder, and near these a few potsherds and a flint dagger (or spear-head).[16]

258. *Raygorod* district of Cherkasi

A decorated beaker with a large body, presumably found in a barrow-grave, was in the Khanenko Collection in Kiev.[17]

259. *Rossava* district of Kanev

A crouched skeleton lay in a shaft dug in the ground, and near it lay lumps of ochre. Another crouched skeleton lay on the ancient surface near the periphery of the mound. A clay vessel stood near it, and a clay hammer, a polished stone grinder and two handles made of antler.[18]

260. *Samhorodok* district of Skvira

Three barrow-graves were investigated in 1875.[19]

Barrow-grave 1. A handful of charcoal and a few potsherds were found.

Barrow-grave 2. Very small and low. Four skeletons lay on the ancient ground on their right side; two close to each other, heads to E, the other two were likewise close together, heads to W. The fifth skeleton lay between the two pairs, the head touching the legs of the second pair, the legs close to the heads of the other pair; near it stood a well-made vessel with finger-tip decoration.

Barrow-grave 3. 3m high. In the mound a number of potsherds were found. At a depth of 2·5m lay a skeleton, head to S, near which stood two black vessels, one with an incised decoration, the other with a finger-tip ornament. Near the latter lay a stone battle-axe, three flint arrow-heads, a fragment of bronze wire, and two boar tusks. Near by stood a third undecorated vessel in which calcined human bones were found.

261. *Sinyavka* district of Kanev

A larger barrow-grave cemetery was excavated. Mainly Scythian period graves were uncovered.[20]

Barrow-grave 29. On the ancient surface a crouched child skeleton, head to W, was found. Near by lay an adult in an extended position, head to W, and another one, a female, with slightly 'painted' bones. Nothing was found in the grave-shaft; near by lay a fourth skeleton, of a woman, on its back, legs contracted, near it nine beads of perforated animal teeth and three tubular beads made of bone. In the second shaft lay a female skeleton, slightly contracted, head to W, near it lumps of ochre.

Barrow-grave 30. A crouched skeleton in a shaft, strewn with ochre. Near it was a whorl and a flint scraper.

262. *Sokołówka* district of Bila Tserkov

A skeleton was uncovered in a shaft dug in the eastern part of a barrow-grave.[21] It lay on its back with legs contracted. Another burial was uncovered in the eastern part of the barrow; its head was to E, but some of its bones were displaced. A secondary burial in the mound itself was of a later date.

263. *Stanisławka* district of Bila Tserkov

A male skeleton in crouched position on its left side, head to NE, was uncovered in a shaft in the southern part of a barrow-grave investigated by G. Ossowski.[22] The head of the skeleton was cut off and lay a little apart from the body.

264. *Stretivka* district of Kiev

265. *Ščudovka* district of Kiev

A crouched skeleton in a shaft was uncovered in a barrow-grave.[23]

266. *Šandra* district of Rzhyščev

267. *Šulaki* on the Ross, district of Zaškov

268. *Tadievka* district of Skvira

Three skeletons in a crouched position were uncovered in a barrow-grave.[24]

269. *Tripolye* district of Kiev

An ochred skeleton was uncovered in a barrow-grave.[25]

270. *Yankoviči* (recently renamed Ivankoviči) district of Kiev

[12] A. Bydłowski, *Światowit*, vol. v, 1904, pp, 59 ff. J. Głosik, *Mat.St.*, vol. viii, 1962, p. 159, Pl. xxv:2.

[13] Before the war in the collection of the Prehistoric Institute of the Yagiellonian University, Cracow, nos. 8557–9.

[14] Op. cit., note 2, pp. 115, 125.

[15] Bydłowski (op. cit., note 4), p. 28, Figs. 39, 40. A large sherd of a richly decorated bowl, typical of the Middle Dnieper culture, was in the Majewski Museum in Warsaw before the war (no. 16239).

[16] F. Pułaski, *ZWAK*, vol. xvii, 1893, p. 44, Figs. 1, 2.

[17] Khanenko Collection, vol. ii, Kiev 1899, Pl. xxxiv:674.

[18] Op. cit., note 3 (1908), p. 10.

[19] B. Popowski, *ZWAK*, vol. vi, 1882, pp. 11 ff.

[20] А. Бобринской, Курганы и случайныя археологическия находки близ м. Смиелы, vol. iii, St Petersburg 1901, p. 105.

[21] Ossowski (op. cit., note 11), pp. 9 ff., Pl. ii:2.

[22] Ibid., pp. 6 ff., Pl. i:3, 5.

[23] Op. cit., note 2, p. 116.

[24] Ibid., pp. 115, 126.

[25] Ibid., p. 125.

Addendum: 678. *Yanovka* district of Starčenko (Kanev)*

Addendum: 679. *Zabara* district of Kagarlyk*

271. *Zelenki* district of Starčenko (Kanev)

(b) *Related graves east of the Dnieper*

272. *Brasovo* province of Orel

273. *Belynets* (*Vščizh*)

274. *Evminka* district of Oster

275. *Grečaniki* (*Hrečanyki*) district of Pereyaslav

In a barrow-grave excavated by V. Ščerbakivskii[26] a copper battle-axe was found with pit-comb decorated potsherds, and at another point lay a stone battle-axe with a cord-decorated pot. The latter had a light-grey slip and was made in a technique proper to the Tripolye pottery although it was not painted.

276. *Krupol* district of Pereyaslav

A barrow-grave with an inhumation burial was excavated by V. Ščerbakivskii. Three cord-decorated vessels were found in the grave: a bowl 10cm high, 17cm in diameter, a single-lugged mug 11·5cm high, and a pot with its rim missing, now 105cm high, the body 135cm in diameter.[27]

277. *Rečitsa* province of Briansk

A Thuringian amphora, two flint axes and a whetstone were found in a barrow-grave.

278. *Sednev* district of Chernigov

A copper spear-head (dagger), an amber bead and a flint arrow-head were found in a barrow-grave.[28]

3. CHERKASI-KIROVOGRAD-UMAN GROUP OF BARROW-GRAVES

279. *Alexandrovka* district of Kirovograd

Five skeletons lay on the ancient surface; grave goods consisted of handled and cord-decorated vessels.[1]

280. *Arsenyevka* district of Kirovograd

In the mound skeletons were uncovered on their backs with legs contracted, heads to N; near the head of each stood a vessel. Two shaft-graves were under the mound; each contained a crouched skeleton, head to W, strewn with ochre but no grave goods.[2]

281. *Dubova* district of Uman

A Yamna type burial in a barrow-grave.[3]

282. *Grečkovka* near Smyela

The original burial in Barrow 249[4] was a shaft under the southern part of the mound with a 'painted skeleton' and no furniture. The secondary burial, likewise in a shaft, consisted of two skeletons covered with timber planks, both partly calcined, heads to NE; lumps of ochre lay around, and a few granite stones over the grave. Grave goods were: a bronze object which disintegrated, a few clay beads, and an amber bead. Another secondary burial in the mound was of a later date.

283. *Gulay-Gorod* (*Hulay Horod*) near Smyela

Two extended skeletons lay close to each other on the ancient surface near the periphery of the mound no. 41.[5] Near each was a large bronze pin with a rhomboid head and three small beads, or pendants, made of a thin bronze sheet. In a shaft near by only animal bones were found. A secondary burial of Scythian period was uncovered in the mound.

284. *Kamenno-Pototske* district of Alexandriya

A stone battle-axe and a copper vessel were found in a barrow-grave.[6]

285. *Kobrynova* district of Zvenigorodka

Twelve graves in shafts were uncovered in a barrow-grave investigated in 1887.[7] The central grave 2, probably the main one, contained a crouched skeleton on its right side, head to W, but no grave goods. On its axis, at a distance of 4m, was another shaft with two skeletons in an extended position, side by side, face downwards, with no grave goods. In other shafts lay crouched skeletons; near some of them ornaments, made of bone, and vessels were found. Two graves (nos. 3 and 4) yielded necklaces consisting of tubular bone beads, many covered with an incised spiral groove aiming at imitating bronze spiral wire beads; a bone hammer-headed pin formed part of each of the necklaces.

286. *Kočerzhintsy* district of Uman

Yamma type graves were uncovered in which bronze buttons and a vessel were found.[8]

287. *Kolodistoe* district of Uman

Twelve barrow-graves were excavated.[9] In barrows nos. 1, 2, 10 and 12 crouched skeletons were found in shafts, strewn

[26] V. Schtscherbakiwskyj, Кам'яна доба в Україні, München 1947, p. 47. The vessel published by A. Äyräpää, *ESA*, vol. VIII, 1933, p. 125, Fig. 127, and after him wrongly reproduced by both T. S. Passek and A. Häusler (note 1), was found in fact at Krupol.

[27] Schtscherbakiwskyj (op. cit., note 26), p. 46. The vessels were in the Museum at Poltava before the war (nos. 1931, 1932, 1936).

[28] Op. cit., note 2, p. 125.

[1] В. И. Гошкевич, Клады и древности херсонской губернии, vol. I, Kherson 1903, p. 94.

[2] Loc. cit.

[3] *Bulletin du Laboratoire d'Anthropologie et d'Ethnographe*, Kiev 1925, p. 22.

[4] А. А. Бобринскии, Курганы и случайные археологические находки близ м. Сьмелы, vol. III, St Petersburg 1901, pp. 52 ff.

[5] Ibid., vol. I, 1887, p. 102, Pl. IX:7, 8, 14–16.

[6] Op. cit., note I, p. 13.

[7] G. Ossowski, *ZWAK*, vol. XII, 1888, pp. 58 ff., Pls. IX, X. A. M. Tallgren, 'La Pontide préscythique', *ESA*, vol. II, 1924, pp. 42, 99.

[8] Op. cit., note I, p. 22.

[9] А. А. Спицын, Раскопка курганов близ с. Колодистаго, Известия имп. Археол. Комм., vol. 12, 1904, pp. 119 ff. Tallgren (op. cit., note 7), p. 44, Fig. 36.

with ochre, heads mostly to W. Near some of these lay flint arrow-heads and a small polished stone. In each mound secondary burials of later periods were uncovered. Barrow-grave 8 had several cremations in urns on the surface and a crouched skeleton strewn with ochre. Vessels were of Tripolyan character but some authors consider them Hallstatt.[10] Burials were within a stone ring. A similar stone ring was uncovered in barrow-grave 9 in which on the ancient surface of the ground lay two skeletons side by side and cremations. In Barrow-grave 11 a vessel with a pointed base lay on the ancient surface under the mound; no shaft was found there.

288. *Kompanievka* district of Kirovograd

A crouched skeleton lay in a shaft, near its head lumps of ochre. Secondary burials were in the mound itself.[11]

289. *Konstyntinovka* near Smyela.[12]

Barrow-grave 361. A Scythian secondary burial in the mound. Four shafts were dug in the ground, in three of which crouched skeletons of adults and in one that of a child were found, all strewn with ochre ('painted'), with no grave goods.

Barrow-grave 362. Shafts were uncovered in which crouched skeletons lay strewn with ochre. In one shaft a vessel with a pointed base was found (Fig. 7:1).

290. *Korzhova* district of Uman

In barrow-grave 1 a Yamna type burial in a shaft was found. A lump of ochre and a small vessel lay near the skeleton.[13]

291. *Marianki* district of Uman

A 'coloured' skeleton was found in a barrow-grave.[14]

292. *Martonoša* district of Kirovograd.[15]

Barrow-grave 1. Three graves in shafts under the mound; skeletons on their backs with legs contracted, skulls strewn with ochre. In the mound itself four crouched skeletons, heads to W, each of them with lumps of ochre; one had a small bronze spiral ring. Another skeleton in the mound was of a later date.

Barrow-grave 2. A crouched skeleton in the mound, near it a child's skeleton and a dark vessel. In the shaft under the mound a skeleton on its back, strewn with ochre, legs contracted, head to NW.

Barrow-grave 3. In the mound a crouched skeleton; the jaw and the upper row of teeth missing, a small hole in the skull. Near it a dark vessel. In the shaft under the mound a crouched skeleton with lumps of ochre near the skull.

293. *Novo-Nikolayevka* district of Kirovograd

A large, thick-walled, dark ovoid vessel with a pointed base, two handles and a cylindrical neck with the rim incised was found in a barrow-grave. It was in the Museum at Kherson before the War (no. 4225). It was *c.* 26cm high.[16]

294. *Olšanka* (*Bilšanka*) district of Novoarchangelsk

Six barrow-graves excavated.[17]

Barrow-grave 3. A crouched skeleton in the shaft, head to E, near the feet lumps of ochre. Grave goods consisted of a necklace of thirty-one perforated animal teeth and four vessels. Two of these were thin-walled, black, polished and cord decorated. Their upper part was red painted in a manner met with on some Tripolyan vessels of period B-2. Accordingly T. S. Passek attributed the grave to the Usatovo culture, as also the following grave.

Barrow-grave 9 had two shafts, situated at a small distance from each other. In one lay a crouched skeleton on its left side, head to SE, with no grave goods. In the other shaft lay two crouched skeletons on their left and right sides respectively, heads to N and E, both strewn with ochre. Grave goods were a flat copper axe and an axe (or hoe) made of perforated antler. The shaft was covered with stones and the mound was within a stone ring ('cromlech').

295. *Rogova* district of Uman

A Yamna burial was uncovered in a barrow-grave. Near the skeleton lay a stone battle-axe.[18]

296. *Rotmistrovka* near Smyela

A Tripolyan vessel was found in a barrow-grave excavated by A. Bobrinskii.[19]

297. *Rubanyi Most* district of Uman

In a barrow-grave investigated in 1883 two vessels, one of these provided with handles, and a polished stone battle-axe were found near human bones.[20]

298. *Ryzhanivka* (*Ryżanówka*) district of Zvenigorodka

Several barrow-graves, mainly of Scythian period, were excavated by G. Ossowski[21] and D. I. Samokvasov.[22] Mention should be made of at least two barrows of the earlier periods.

Barrow-grave 5. Excavated by G. Ossowski. It contained a number of secondary graves of later periods. In the main shaft-grave in the centre a crouched skeleton lay on its left side, head to W, with no grave goods. In another grave (no. 11) on the ancient surface, the skeleton, in an extended position on its back, head to NE, had a bronze ring on its finger; the ends of the ring were flattened. Near the feet stood two vessels, a small undecorated bowl or cup, and a spherical vase with an incised decoration of shaded triangles over its whole surface. A skeleton of a young woman lay near the smaller vessel. It was richly strewn with ochre.

[10] Tallgren, loc. cit., note 9.
[11] Op. cit., note 1, p. 95.
[12] Op. cit., note 4, pp. 26 f.
[13] Op cit., note 3, p. 22.
[14] А. А. Спицын, Курганы с окрашенными костяками, Записки имп. русск. археол. общества, vol. XI, 1899, p. 124.
[15] Op. cit., note 1, p. 96.
[16] The vessel was published in *Prähistorische Zft*, vol. IV, Leipzig 1912, p. 441, Fig. 1.
[17] Т. С. Пассек, Периодизация трипольских поселений, МИА, no. 10, 1949, pp. 202 ff.
[18] Op. cit., note 3, p. 22.
[19] Op. cit., note 4, vol. II, 1894, Pl. VI:7. Пассек (op. cit., note 17), p. 201.
[20] Op. cit., note 14, p. 124.
[21] G. Ossowski, *ZWAK*, vol. XII, pp. 30 ff., Pls. VII, VIII.
[22] Д. Я. Самоквасов, Описание археол. раскопок, Труды XIV археол. съезда, Moscow 1908, pp. 12 ff. Tallgren (op. cit., note 7), p. 44.

Barrow-grave II. Excavated by D. Samokvasov. A Scythian secondary burial was uncovered. Under the mound, in the centre, a skeleton lay in an extended position, and near it was a diorite battle-axe and a small bowl.

Barrow-grave IV. Two skeletons in 'a sitting position' were uncovered in the mound, and a crouched skeleton lay in another part of the mound. A small cup, lumps of ochre and flint chips lay in the centre of the mound.

299. *Serezlievka* district of Novoarchangelsk

Twelve barrow-graves were investigated; all had stone circles ('cromlechs') around the mound and skeletons were mostly in a crouched position. Two graves have been attributed to the Usatovo culture by T. S. Passek:[23]

Barrow-grave 4. A skeleton on its back, legs contracted, head to E, was found in a shaft. Over it lay a small Tripolyan vessel with a black-painted ornament typical of period C-1.

Barrow-grave 7. In the shaft in the centre lay a skeleton in an extended position on its back, head to E. Near its hand were found a large lump of ochre and a schematic clay human figurine of the Usatovo type.

300. *Smyela*

A considerable number of barrow-graves, mainly of the Scythian period, were investigated by A. Bobrinskii in the vicinity of the town.[24] Of the earlier ones the following deserve mention, all dated by T. B. Popova to the Catacomb period.[25]

Barrow-grave 1. It yielded twelve burials. In two of these, nos. 4 and 9, bone hammer-headed pins were excavated.

Barrow-grave 56. In the central shaft under the mound lay a crouched skeleton of a child strewn with ochre, near it an undecorated ovoid vessel with a pointed base (Fig. 7:3). Another child's skeleton, crouched and strewn with ochre, was found in the mound.

Barrow-grave 59. Three 'coloured' crouched skeletons lay in three shafts under the mound. Near one of these an undecorated ovoid vessel with a pointed base was found.

Barrow-grave 70. Four shafts were uncovered under the mound. In one of these lay a crouched male skeleton, in three others skeletons of three children in a similar position. All were strewn with ochre. In the three latter shafts undecorated vessels, ovoid with a pointed base, were found. A Scythian secondary burial was in the mound.

Barrow-grave 71. A female and a child's skeletons were uncovered in two shafts under the mound. Over them in the mound an undecorated ovoid vessel with a pointed base was found.

301. *Suškivka* district of Uman

A barrow-grave was raised over the remains of a Tripolyan hut. The shaft was at the SE end of the hut. In the shaft lay a skeleton on its back, legs contracted, its knees upwards, strewn with ochre. No grave goods were present.[26]

302. *Teklino* near Smyela

In barrow-grave 347[27] a female skeleton lay on the ancient surface. Near it were found: a small decorated vessel, a bronze arm-ring with spiral terminals, a bronze spectacle-shaped spiral brooch, a large clay whorl and a small polished granite. No grave-shaft was found.

303. *Verbovka* district of Chigirin

Three barrow-graves excavated by A. Bobrinskii were recently attributed to the Middle Dnieper Culture by A. Häusler.[28] Two of these had stone circles ('cromlechs'). That in barrow-grave 1 was built of twenty-nine slabs, seventeen of which had an incised geometric ornament and schematic human figures; the incisions call to mind those on the North-west Caucasian slab-cists.[29]

304. *Volodymirivka* district of Uman.

In the centre of the large Tripolyan settlement a few barrow-graves were situated. One of these was excavated. In its shaft lay a skeleton in the 'Yamna' position, on its back, legs contracted, with no grave goods. In its secondary burial a 'Srubna' type vessel was found near the skeleton.[30]

305. *Voynovka* district of Alexandriya

A skeleton, head to S, lay on the ancient level under a low mound. Under it, in a shaft, lay another 'red coloured' skeleton in a crouched position.[31]

4. LIST OF THE STEPPE BARROW-GRAVES

(a) *The Eastern Division (east of the Ingul)*

306. *Arkhangelskoe* district of Kherson.[1] Three barrow-graves.

307. *Belozerka* district of Kherson. Twenty barrow-graves were investigated.[2] In one of these (no. 8) was found a vessel considered by T. S. Passek to be typical of the Usatovo culture.[3]

308. *Folievka* district of Kherson.[4] Two barrow-graves.

309. *Hruškivka* district of Apostolovo.[5] Fourteen barrow-graves.

[23] Op. cit., note 17, pp. 201 f.

[24] Op. cit., note 4, vol. II, 1894, pp. 24 ff., Pl. VI:15, 21–4.

[25] Т. Б. Попова, Племена катакомбной культуры, Moscow 1955, p. 17.

[26] В. Козловська, Точки трипільської культури біля с. Сушківки, Трипільська культура на Україні, vol. 1, Kiev 1926, pp. 45 f.

[27] Op. cit., note 4, vol. III, 1901, p. 18, Pl. II:4, 9, 6; Fig. 4a.

[28] A. Häusler, 'Die kulturellen und wirtschaftlichen Beziehungen der Bevölkerungsgruppen Mittelrusslands am Ende der jüngeren Steinzeit', *Wisschenschaftliche Zft d. M. Luther Universität*, vol. v–1, Halle 1955, pp. 78 f.

[29] А. А. Формозов, Изображения на плитах из кургана у с. Вербовки, Ксиак, no. 5, 1955, pp. 71 ff.

[30] Т. С. Пассек, Ксиимк, no. 26, 1949, pp. 49 f., Figs. 17, 18.

[31] Op. cit., note 1, p. 9.

[1] В. И. Гошкевич, Клады и древности херсонской губернии, vol. 1, Kherson 1903, p. 109.

[2] Ibid., pp. 97 ff.

[3] Т. С. Пассек, Периодизация трипольских поселений, МИА, no. 10, 1949, p. 201.

[4] Op. cit., note 1, pp. 106 f.

[5] Д. Т. Березовець, Курганний могильник в с. Грушівка, Арх. Пам., vol. x, 1961, pp. 56 ff. Д. І. Бліфельд, Курган епохи бронзи в с. Грушівка, Арх. Пам., vol. x, 1961, pp. 46 ff.

310. *Ivanovka* district of Dneprovskii (south of the lower Dnieper).[6] Two barrow-graves.

311. *Kamenka Blazhkova* district of Kherson.[7] Two barrow-graves.

312. *Kherson*. One barrow-grave.[8]

313. *Khutor Khmelnitskii* district of Nikopol. A niche-grave in a barrow.[9]

314. *Kičkas* near Zaporozhe. A few barrow-graves with stone circles.[10]

315. *Kozatskoe* district of Kherson. Three barrow-graves.[11]

316. *Krivoy Rog* (*Kryvyi Rih*). A few barrow-graves,[12] in one of which a vessel made in the Tripolyan technique was found.[13]

317. *Kut* district of Apostolovo. Thirty-three barrow-graves investigated.[14]

318. *Marianske* district of Apostolovo. Six barrow-graves.[15]

319. *Mikhailovka* district of Kherson. One barrow-grave.[16]

320. *Mogilna* district of Dneprovskii, south of the Lower Dnieper. One barrow-grave.[16]

321. *Nikopol*. About thirty barrow-graves investigated.[17]

322. *Perevizky Khutory* district of Nikopol. One barrow-grave.[18]

323. *Pervomaivka* on the left (southern) side of the Dnieper, near the junction of the Konka. Seven barrow-graves investigated.[19]

324. *Shandrovka* (*Chandrovka*) near Zaporozhe. A barrow-grave.[20]

325. *Sirko* district of Nikopol. Forty graves investigated.[21]

326. *Snihurivka* (*Snigirevka*) district of Kherson. Several barrow-graves.[22]

327. *Sofievka* district of Dneprovskii, south of the Lower Dnieper. One barrow-grave near the sea-shore.[23]

328. *Staryi Kodak* near Dnepropetrovsk. Barrow-grave 'Storozhevaya Mogila'; remains of a two-wheeled cart found in the secondary grave.[24]

329. *Ust-Kamianka* district of Apostolovo. One barrow-grave investigated.[25]

(b) '*Flat*' *cemeteries*

330. *Červona Hryhorivka* district of Novo-Vorontsovka.[26]

331. *Havrylivka* district of Novo-Vorontsovka.[27]

332. *Leontynivka* district of Novo-Vorontsovka.[28]

333. *Mykhailivka* district of Novo-Vorontsovka.[29]

334. *Mykilske* (*Nikolskoe in Russian*) near Dnepropetrovsk.[30]

335. *Oleksivka* district of Novo-Vorontsovka.[31]

336. *Osokorivka* district of Novo-Vorontsovka.[32]

337. *Zolota Balka* district of Novo-Vorontsovka.[33]

(c) *The Western Division* (*Boh-Ingul*) *barrow-graves*

338. *Čornyi Tašlyk* near Pervomaisk. Seven barrow-graves.[34]

339. *Domanevka*. A number of barrow-graves excavated by local peasants.[35]

340. *Dymovka* district of Kherson. Seven barrow-graves.[36]

[6] Op. cit., note 1, pp. 129 f.

[7] Ibid., pp. 108 f.

[8] Ibid., pp. 110 ff.

[9] І. П. Костюшенко, Могильник епохи бронзи поблизу хут. Хмельницького, Арх. Пам., vol. IX, 1960, pp. 88 ff.

[10] В. Козловська, Археологічні досліди на території Дніпрельстану, Хроніка археології та мистецтва, no. 1, Kiev 1930, pp. 14 ff.

[11] Op. cit., note 1, pp. 112 f.

[12] I. Fabritius, ' "Tsaréva mohila" près de Kryvoi Rog', *ESA*, vol. IV, 1929, pp. 126 ff.

[13] О. Ф. Лагодовська, Пам'ятки усатівського типу, Археологія-Kiev, vol. VIII, 1953, p. 106, Fig. 3. Пассек, loc. cit., note 2.

[14] Д. Т. Березовець, Розкопки курганного могильника епохи бронзи та скіфського часу в с. Кут, Арх. Пам., vol. IX, 1960, pp. 39 ff.

[15] Д. Т. Березовець, Е. Ф. Покровська, А. І. Фурманська, Кургани епохи бронзи у с. Мар'янського, Арх. Пам., vol. IX, 1960, pp. 102 ff.

[16] Op. cit., note 1, pp. 113 f., 130.

[17] Л. Д. Дмитров, Археологічне вивчення Нікопольщини в 1935–1936 pp. Наукові записки, vol. II, Kiev 1946, pp. 55 ff. Id., Археологія-Kiev, vol. III, 1950, pp. 160 ff., Pls. I–III. О. А. Кривцова-Гракова, Погребения бронзового века и предскифского времени на никопольском курганном поле, миа, no. 115, 1962, pp. 5–55.

[18] Op. cit., note 9, pp. 100 f.

[19] В. А. Іллінська, Г. Т. Ковпаненко, Е. О. Петровська, Роскопки курганів епохи бронзи поблизу с. Первомаївки, Арх. Пам., vol. IX, 1960, pp. 127 ff. В. И. Капивец, Курган раннего бронзового века у с. Первомаевки на Херсонщине, Ксиак, no. 5, 1955, pp. 75 ff. Г. Т. Титенко, Каменная стела из с. Первомаевки, Ксиак, no. 5, 1955, pp. 78 f.

[20] A. M. Tallgren, 'La Pontide préscythique', *ESA*, vol. II, 1924, pp. 88, 101.

[21] Б. Граков, Підсумки і перспективи робот нікопольської експедиції, Археологія-Kiev, vol. II, 1948, pp. 208 f. Id., Інформачійний звіт нікопольської археологічної експедиції за 1946 р., Археологія-Kiev, vol. II 1949, pp. 112 ff.

[22] Т. Б. Попова, Племена катакомбной культуры, Труды ГИМ, no. 24, Moscow 1955, pp. 17 f. І. Г. Шовкопляс, Археологічні дослідження на Україні (1917–1957), Kiev 1957, p. 132.

[23] A. Bertrand, 'Tumulus de la Tauride', *Revue Archéologique*, vol. NS 25, Paris 1873, pp. 203 ff., Figures. Objects excavated at present at the Musée St. Germain-en-Laye, nos. 18680–6.

[24] А. И. Тереножкин, Скифская днепровская правобережная экспедиция, Ксиимк, no. XXXVII, 1951, pp. 117 ff. Id., Курган Сторожова могила, Археологія-Kiev, vol. V, 1951, pp. 183 ff., Figs. 1–9.

[25] Е. В. Махно, Розкопки пам'яток епохи бронзи та сарматського часу в с. Усть-Кам'янці, Археологія-Kiev, vol. IX, 1960, pp. 14 ff.

[26] О. Г. Шапошникова, Могильники епохи ранньої бронзи на нижньому Дніпрі, Арх. Пам., vol. X, 1961, p. 10.

[27] Ibid., pp. 6 ff.

[28] Ibid., pp. 4 ff.

[29] О. Ф. Лагодовська, О. Г. Шапошникова, М. Л. Макаревич, Михайлівське поселення, Kiev, 1962, pp. 127 ff.

[30] Д. Я. Телегин, Никольский могильник эпохи неолитамеди в Надпорожье, Ксиак, no. 11, 1961, pp. 20 ff. A. Häusler, 'Die Grabsitten der mesolithischen und neolithischen Jäger- und Fischergruppen auf dem Gebiet der UdSSR', *Wissenschaftliche Zft d. M. Luther Universität*, Halle, vol. XI/10, 1962, pp. 1164 ff.

[31] Op. cit., note 26, p. 10.

[32] Ibid., pp. 3 f. В. Д. Рибалова, Могильник епохи бронзи в с. Осокорівці, Арх. Пам., vol. IX. 1960, pp. 5 ff.

[33] А. В. Добровольський, Розкопки ділянок "А" і "Г" та могильника и золотобалківського поселення рубежу нашої ери в 1951 і 1952 pp., Арх. Пам., vol. IX, 1960, pp. 141 ff. М. І. Вязьмітіна, Могильник епохи бронзи біля с. Золота Балка, Арх. Пам., vol. X, 1961, pp. 64 ff.

[34] Ф. А. Козубовський, Археологічні дослідження на території Богесу, 1930–1932, pp. Kiev 1933, p. 21.

[35] И. В. Фабрициус, Археологическая карта Приченоморья Украинской ССР, Kiev 1951, p. 99, Pl. V:3.

[36] Op. cit., note 1, pp. 107 f.

341. *Horozheno* (*on the Ingul*) district of Kherson. At least one barrow-grave.[37]
342. *Kamenyi Most* near Pervomaisk. A few barrow-graves.[38]
343. *Katerinovka* near Pervomaisk. A few barrow-graves.[39]
344. *Konstantinovka* district of Pervomaisk. One barrow-grave.[40]
345. *Kovalivka* on the Boh. Barrow-grave 'Popova Mohyla'.[41]
346. *Mayaki-Didova Khata* near Nikolaev. A barrow-grave.[42]
347. *Mostovoe-Lyakhovo*. A number of barrow-graves excavated.[43]
348. *Ostrovka-Maritsino* on the Boh Liman. A few barrow-graves.[44]
349. *Pervomaisk*. Six barrow-graves.[45]
350. *Ternovatoe* near Nikolaev. Three barrow-graves.[46]

(d) *The Usatovo barrow-graves*[47]

351. *Ananiev*. One barrow-grave.
352. *Čobruči* district of Tiraspol. One barrow-grave.
353. *Glinne* district of Tiraspol. One barrow-grave.
354. *Karagaš* district of Tiraspol. Two barrow-graves.
355. *Krasnohorka* district of Tiraspol. Two barrow-graves.[48]
356. *Olaneşti* near Akkerman, Bessarabia. Barrow-grave.[49]
357. *Parkany* district of Tiraspol. Eighteen barrow-graves.[50]
358. *Ploske* district of Parkany. Five barrow-graves.[51]
359. *Serbka* (*Sadove*) district of Tiraspol. One barrow-grave.
360. *Severynovka* near Odessa. One barrow-grave.
361. *Slobidka-Romanovka-Odessa*. One barrow-grave.[52]
362. *Sukleia* district of Tiraspol. Three barrow-graves.[53]
363. *Šabalat* near Akkerman, Bessarabia. Two barrow-graves.[54]
364. *Ternovka* district of Tiraspol. Thirteen barrow-graves.[55]
365. *Tiraspol*. Sixteen barrow-graves.[56]

Addendum: 596. *Tudorovo* district of Olaneşti. One barrow-grave.[57]

366. *Usatovo* near Odessa. Two barrow-grave cemeteries.[58]
367. *Zagorie*. A large barrow-grave.
368. *Zatišče* district of Tiraspol. One barrow-grave.

(e) *Cemeteries*

369. *Skinyany* near Soroca, Bessarabia. A Tripolyan type beaker decorated in a manner characteristic of the Usatovo culture was in the Museum in Odessa before the War. It was presumably found in a grave.
370 (and 366). *Usatovo*. A 'flat' cemetery.[59]
371. *Vykhvatyntsi* near Rybnitsa. A cemetery[60] (Fig. 1:4, 5, 8).

[37] A. Äyräpää, 'Über die Streitaxtkulturen in Russland', *ESA* vol. VIII, 1933, pp. 81 f., Fig. 86.
[38] Op. cit., note 35, p. 101.
[39] Loc. cit.
[40] Ibid., p. 82; op. cit., note 34, p. 42, Pls. 16; 18:2.
[41] Op cit., note 35, pp. 82 f. Tallgren (op. cit., note 20), p. 48.
[42] Op. cit., note 35, p. 79.
[43] Ibid., p. 99.
[44] Ibid., p. 71. M. Ebert, *Prähistorische Zft*, vol. III, 1911.
[45] Op. cit., note 35, pp. 94 ff.
[46] Ibid., p. 82.
[47] Almost all sites were quoted and described by I. V. Fabritius (op. cit., note 35), and by V. I. Goškevič (op. cit., note 1).
[48] Op. cit., note 3, p. 208.
[49] Лагодовська, loc. cit., note 13.
[50] Op. cit., note 3, p. 205; op. cit., note 37, p. 71, Fig. 73; op. cit., note 35, pp. 48 ff.
[51] Op. cit., note 3, p. 206.
[52] Ibid., pp. 194 ff. M. Gimbutas, *The Prehistory of Eastern Europe*, part I, Cambridge (Mass.) 1956, pp. 85 ff., Figs. 47–9.
[53] Op. cit., note 3, pp. 195, 206.
[54] Д. Я. Самоквасов, Описание археологических раскопок, Труды XIV археол. сьезда, Moscow 1908, pp. 21 ff. Пассек (op. cit., note 3,) p. 205.
[55] Op. cit., note 3, pp. 196, 206.
[56] Ibid., p. 206.
[57] Лагодовська (op. cit., note 13), p. 105.
[58] Op. cit., note 3, pp. 194 ff. Gimbutas (op. cit., note 52), pp. 108 ff. О. Лагодовська, Усатівська експедиція 1946 р., Арх. Пам., vol. III, 1949, pp. 201 ff.
[59] See note 58.
[60] А. Е. Алихова, Выхватинский могильник, Ксиимк, no. XXVI, 1949, pp. 69 ff. Т. С. Пассек, Ксиимк, no. 56, 1954, pp. 76 ff. Id., Ксиимк, no. 70, 1957. Id., Раннеземледельческие (трипольские) племена Поднестровья, МИА, no. 84, 1961, pp. 146 ff. Gimbutas (op. cit., note 52), pp. 105 ff., Fig. 58.

SECTION V

The Globular Amphora Culture

I. THE PUŁAWY GROUP

(a) *List of Graves*

Grave[1] (all in the district of Puławy)	No. of skeletons	Grave fired	No. of vessels	Kuyav. amphora	Ovoid amphora	Various amphorae	Small amphorae	Bowls	Cups	Large pots	Other vessels	Lids	Flint axes	Flint blades	Bone implements	Boar tusks	Amber beads	Other grave goods and remarks
372. Drzewce		+	5	1									1					
373. Klementowice A-I	1	+	4	1				1		2			2	2				partly ruined; 2 bovidae
,, B-I	4		15	3	3		4	1	3	1			4	6	2	4	1	partly ruined; pig jaw
,, B-II													2					ruined
,, B-III																		unpublished[2]
,, B-IV																		unpublished[2]
374. Las Stocki C-I				1									3	3				
,, C-II	1	+	9	3			3				2	1	2	1				additional skull
,, C-III	2	+	5		1	2			1	1			2	2				
,, C-IV	2	+					1		1	1			1	1			2	ruined
,, C-V	2				1				1	1		1				1		ruined
,, G-I	3		7	2	1		3						2	3	2	1	7	schist plaque
375. Nałęczów				1														several graves
376. Parchatka	2		1							1					1			2 bovidae
377. Stok A-I	2		6	1	1		1		1		1		3	4		2		3 arr. heads clay disc

Graves were shallow pits surrounded and covered by medium-sized slabs of quarried limestone, some with a cobbled floor. Skeletons were in a contracted position.

[1] All sites, except a few, were described by Nosek in his publications, and the literature concerned quoted there: S. Nosek, 'Kultura amfor kulistych na Lubelszczyźnie', *AUMCS*, vol. v F, 1950, pp. 55 ff. Id., 'Materiały do badań nad historią starożytną i wczesnośredniowieczną międzyrzecza Wisły i Bugu', *AUMCS*, vol. vi F, 1951 (1957), pp. 233 ff.

[2] J. Kowalczyk, 'Osada i cmentarzysko kultury pucharów lejkowatych w miejscowości Klementowice, pow.Puławy', *Mat.St.*, vol. ii, 1957, p. 175.

(b) *Other sites*[3]

378. *Bochotnica* district of Puławy.

379. *Buchałowice* district of Puławy.

380. *Kosiorów* district of Opole.

381. *Włostowice* district of Puławy

Traces of temporary encampments marked by potsherds of the Globular Amphora culture were found on sand-dunes.[4]

2. THE HRUBIESZÓW GROUP[5]

(a) *Graves*

382. *Bezek* district of Chełm

Vessels were found in a slab-cist grave.

383. *Branica Suchowolska* district of Radzyń

Two slab-cist graves were found in 1875, both rectangular in plan. In one potsherds and a flint knife were found, in the other four vessels which were destroyed. One was a Kuyavian amphora, another was an undecorated spheric bowl, and the two remaining were small amphorae, one decorated, the other undecorated. The decoration consisted of stamped patterns.

384. *Chotiaszów* district of Włodzimierz Wołyński

A slab-cist grave was uncovered in which lay a human skeleton and a spherical black vessel.[6]

385. *Huta* district of Chełm

Two small potsherds and a flint axe were found in a cist grave built of twelve granite slabs, uncovered in 1916.

386. *Krasnystaw* (see no. 608)

A burial attributable to the Globular Amphora culture was uncovered at the local brickworks.[7]

387. *Kryłów* district of Hrubieszów

Two slab-cist graves were uncovered before 1913 and destroyed. The site was investigated by A. Cynkałowski in 1934, according to whom[8] the grave lay at a depth of 27–29cm. It was 1m wide, 2·5m long, built of slabs but the NW wall was of smaller stones. A contracted skeleton lay on the cobbled floor, head to NW. Near the head stood a Kuyavian amphora (Fig. 21:1) 26·5cm high, *c.* 29cm in diameter; its deep-stamped and white-encrusted decoration followed patterns typical of the Globular Amphora culture. Other objects found were a well-polished flint axe (missing), two boar tusks, a small flint point 2·8cm long, and a fragment of a pig jaw.

388. *Litowierz* district of Włodzimierz Wołyński

A slab-cist grave was uncovered before the War. Two crouched skeletons lay in it and the following grave goods: black vessels with an incised scale ornament, one of these spherical, with the incisions filled in with white paste; and a well-polished flint axe, 15cm long.[9]

389. *Miedniki* district of Hrubieszów

A nearly square slab-cist grave, 1·5m wide, was uncovered in 1930. It contained two contracted skeletons and a few vessels of which only one was saved, a Kuyavian type amphora the decorative patterns of which were cord impressed (Fig. 23:7).

390. *Okalew* district of Radzyń

Two completely ruined cist-graves built of granite boulders were found in 1873, both situated on the top of a hill. Three flint axes were found in it only one of which, made of banded flint, was saved.

391. *Poniatówka* district of Chełm

A slab-cist grave situated near the top of an elevation was uncovered in 1934. It contained one contracted skeleton, head to N, a richly decorated bowl with an unperforated lug and a flint axe near its head, and two crushed vessels near the feet.

392. *Raciborowice* district of Hrubieszów (see no. 615)

A burial attributable to the Globular Amphora culture was uncovered within the settlement of the Strzyżów culture.[10] It lay partly under the remains of a hut of that culture. Its grave goods consisted of three vessels: a Kuyavian amphora provided with four lugs, decorated by deep-stamped patterns typical of the Globular Amphora culture; an undecorated amphora provided with two lugs on its body, reminiscent of late debased Thuringian amphorae of type IIc; a deep bowl with a row of small bosses under the rim. Cow and sheep bones were also found in this grave.

393. *Stadarnia* district of Chełm

In 1957 a grave attributable to the Globular Amphora culture was found on a sandy elevation, the skeleton of which had completely decomposed.[11] Its grave goods consisted of an ovoid amphora *c.* 17cm high, 17cm in diameter, adorned with a stamp decoration; a vase, or a deep bowl, the neck and shoulders of which were covered with a stamped decoration typical of the Globular Amphorae; a thick-butted axe, quadrangular in section, very well polished all over its surface, made of light-grey flint; fragments of a few cow teeth.

[3] Sites quoted by J. Gurba, 'Neolithic Settlements on the Lublin Loess Upland', *AUMCS*, vol. xv B, 1960, p. 220.

[4] A. Ruszkowski, *ZOW*, vol. xxv, 1959, p. 207.

[5] All sites, if not stated otherwise, were quoted and described in the works by Nosek cited in note 1.

[6] A. Cynkałowski, *Materiały do pradziejów Wołynia i Polesia wołyńskiego*, Warszawa 1961, p. 38.

[7] According to information kindly given me by Mr Z. Ślusarski, M.A., Lublin.

[8] Cynkałowski (op. cit., note 6), p. 38. Professor A. Gardawski, Lublin, has kindly sent me the drawings of the remains preserved at the State Archaeological Museum in Warsaw and a copy of the accompanying note by A. Cynkałowski.

[9] Cynkałowski (op. cit., note 6), p. 39.

[10] Z. Ślusarski, *ZOW*, vol. xxv, 1959, p. 208, Fig. 13 (Kuyavian amphora).

[11] S. Skibiński, 'Znalezisko zabytków kultury amfor kulistych w Stadarni, pow. Chełm', *W.A.*, vol. xxv, 1958, p. 384 f., Figs. 1, 2. See also *ZOW*, vol. xxvi, 1960, p. 370, Figs. 10, 11.

394. *Stołpie* district of Chełm

A slab-cist grave contained five vessels typical of the Globular Amphora culture, and an axe made of banded flint. Only the axe was preserved.

395. *Strzyżów* district of Hrubieszów (see no. 621)

In 1958 a grave attributable to the Globular Amphora culture was uncovered and subsequently investigated by L. Gajewski and J. Gurba.[12] The skeleton lay in an extended position, at a depth of 1·65–1·9m in a shallow pit, some 25m below the ancient surface, head to SE, facing north. Near the head stood two vessels, both representing Kuyavian amphorae which departed from their prototype, both with four lugs on the shoulder. The larger one, 21cm high, 29cm in diameter, was richly decorated with deep stamped patterns proper to the Globular Amphorae culture; the other vessel, 19cm high, 21cm in diameter, was undecorated. Near the shoulder lay a flint axe made of the Volhynian flint. Near the hips lay a boar tusk.

396. *Terespol* district of Zamość

A slab-cist grave was uncovered, of which only a flint axe was preserved.

397. *Tworyczów* district of Zamość

In 1937 a slab-cist grave was uncovered, three vessels of which were saved: a Kuyavian amphora with a typical stamped and cord-impressed decoration; an undecorated ovoid amphora and a deep bowl decorated in the same manner as the amphora, provided with a few bosses on the body (Plate 13:8–10).

398. *Ulwówek* district of Sokal (see no. 626)

Three slab-cist graves are said to have been uncovered here. One of these, grave II (Plan 46:1) investigated by B. Janusz in 1923, contained two skeletons, two stamp-decorated black Kuyavian amphorae, another amphora and a bowl, a flint axe and a pig jaw (Plate 12:1, 2).

399. *Wola Gródecka* district of Tomaszów

A slab-cist was uncovered in 1930. Near the head of the single skeleton stood three vessels of which only a deep bowl was saved, provided with a double lug on the body, horizontally perforated, its upper part richly decorated by cord impressions in a style closely connected with that of the Złota culture (Plate 13:5).

400. *Wytyczno* district of Włodawa

A grave attributable to the Globular Amphora culture was uncovered in 1952, and subsequently investigated by J. Gurba.[13] It was situated on sandy soil. The position of the skeleton was not established as it was destroyed during the accidental discovery. Its grave goods included at least four vessels and a miniature clay model of an adze. One of the vessels was a Kuyavian amphora with a richly stamped decoration following the usual patterns of the Globular Amphora culture; it was 23cm in diameter, its neck missing. Other vessels were in sherds and reconstruction was not practicable. Among these was a deep bowl and at least one more amphora. Vessels were stamp decorated in the usual manner, but some had also cord-impressed decoration, and one had a raised band with finger-tip impression around the neck.

401. *Zimno* district of Włodzimierz Wołyński (see nos. 137 and 632).

A slab-cist grave was uncovered in which a Kuyavian amphora was found with a stamped decoration typical of the Kuyavian vessels of this type.[14]

(b) *Settlements*

402. *Biłgoraj*

Potsherds typical of the Globular Amphora culture were found on the surface of sandy soil in the environment of the town.[15]

403. *Gródek Nadbużny* district of Hrubieszów (see no. 602)

Potsherds typical of the Globular Amphora culture were found.[16]

404. *Harasiuki* district of Biłgoraj

Potsherds of the Globular Amphora culture were found on the surface of sand-dunes.[17]

405. *Łęczna* district of Lubartów (see no. 638)

Potsherds found on a sand-dune.

406. *Sokal* (see nos. 132 and 619)

Before the Second World War the Grammar School (*gimnazjum*) at Sokal had a large collection of potsherds and flint implements, mainly axes, found in a few sites in the town itself. Among these were cord-decorated potsherds typical of the Strzyżów culture, and others characteristic of the Late Bronze Age, but a number were of the Globular Amphora culture. Some of the latter were lugs and larger fragments of Kuyavian amphorae with deep-stamped and fish-scale decoration.

Addendum: 593. *Trójnia* district of Lubartów (see no. 642)

Potsherds found on a sand-dune jointly with those of the Corded Ware and 'Masovian' cultures.[18]

[12] L. Gajewski and J. Gurba, 'Sprawozdanie z prac ratowniczych prowadzonych w 1958 r. w Strzyżowie, pow.Hrubieszów', *Spr.Arch.*, vol. x, 1960, pp. 98 ff., Figs. 2, 4.

[13] J. Gurba, 'Materiały do badań nad neolitem Małopolski', *AUMCS*, vol. IX F, 1954 (1957), pp. 195 ff., Figs. 34–7.

[14] J. Kostrzewski, 'Od mezolitu do okresu wędrówek', *Prehistoria Ziem Polskich*, Kraków 1939–48, p. 151. I. K. Свєшников, Мегалітичні поховання на західному Поділлі, Lviv 1957, p. 21.

[15] M. Pękalski, 'Znaleziska neolityczne z okolic miasta Biłgoraja', *Mat St.*, vol. II, 1957, pp. 207 f.

[16] Nosek (op. cit., note 1: vol. VI), p. 235. Z. Rajewski, 'Sprawozdanie z badań na Grodach Czerwieńskich w 1954 r.', *Spr.Arch.*, vol. II, 1956, p. 49. Z. Podkowińska, 'Badania w Strzyżowie, pow.Hrubieszów, *Arch.P.*, vol. v, 1960, p. 71. J. Głosik, *Mat.St.*, vol. VII, 1961, pp. 118, 121, 124, etc.

[17] Pękalski (op. cit., note 15), p. 209.

[18] L. Gajewski, *Prz.A.*, vol. IX, 1953, p. 334, note 18.

(c) *Other sites*[19]

407. *Dobryniów-Kolonia* district of Krasnystaw
408. *Dratów* district of Lubartów (see no. 634)
409. *Głuszczyzna* district of Lublin
410. *Kębłów* district of Lublin
411. *Lublin*
412. *Łopiennik Dolny Kolonia* district of Krasnystaw
413. *Majdanek* district of Tomaszów Lubelski
414. *Mełgiew* district of Lublin
415. *Piaski* district of Lublin
416. *Skomorochy* district of Hrubieszów
417. *Świdniki* district of Hrubieszów.
418. *Turowiec* district of Chełm

3. THE LWÓW GROUP

419. *Dublany* district of Lwów

A slab-cist grave was uncovered in 1866 in which the following objects were found: two vessels, two gold(?) finger-rings, and a few flint artifacts. All these grave goods perished except a flint dagger (Plate 15:11) 13cm long, the top of which is missing. It was in the Lubomirski Museum in Lwów (no. 17) before the War.[20]

420. *Dzwinogród* district of Bóbrka (see no. 94)

A slab-cist grave was uncovered, vessels of which agreed both in form and decoration with those of the West Polish Globular Amphora culture.[21]

421. *Hołosko* district of Lwów

A slab-cist grave was ruined by its casual discoverers before the last War.

422. *Lany* district of Bibrka

A tightly contracted skeleton of a young person was found in a slab-cist; near it lay a stone battle-axe and two flint flakes.[22]

423. *Mikołajów* district of Radziechów

A few vessels characteristic of the Globular Amphora culture were presented in 1917 to the Natur-Historisches Museum in Vienna.[23] They evidently originated from one or more burials (slab-cist?). These vessels are: (1) a typical Kuyavian amphora with four lugs on the shoulder, stamped and cord decorated in a manner proper to those vessels, 20cm high, 21cm in diameter (Fig. 21:2). (2) base (9cm in diameter), a large part of the neck (11cm in diameter) and a few sherds of the decorated body (*c.* 20cm in diameter) of an amphora (*c.* 25cm high) provided with two lugs on the shoulder (Plate 14:2); the deep-stamped decoration consisted of patterns typical of Kuyavian amphorae rows of zigzag lines, short incisions and groups of parallel slanting lines. (3) a large undecorated ovoid amphora provided with four lugs on the base of the neck, 31cm high, *c.* 22cm in diameter (Plate 13:1). (4) a similar ovoid undecorated amphora, 26·5cm high, 20·5cm in diameter (Plate 13:3). (5) a deep bowl (Plate 13:4) 12·5cm high, 18cm in diameter, the neck adorned by cord-impressed patterns typical of the Globular Amphora culture. (6) a small globular amphora with the neck decorated, provided with two lugs on the junction of the neck and the body (Plate 13:6). All the vessels had a black, or nearly black surface (except the small amphora which had dark-brown patches) and were slightly polished.

424. *Podlipce* district of Złoczów

In 1871 a large slab-cist grave was uncovered when extracting earth from a hill (barrow-grave?). Two skeletons were found in it, of an adult in a 'sitting position' and a smaller one near by (of a child?).[24] A point made of roe antler, 14cm long, and a narrow flint-axe (Fig. 15:15), quadrangular in section, 9·8cm long, found in this grave, were given to the Archaeological Museum in Cracow (nos. 3156, 3157).

425. *Sukhodoly* district of Zabolotse

In 1937 a slab-cist grave was uncovered. A clay vessel found in it was destroyed by the casual discoverers of the grave.[25]

520. *Żaderewacz* district of Dolina

A slab-cist grave which contained flint implements is said to have been uncovered there.[26]

426. *Żulice* district of Złoczów

In 1934 I uncovered a slab-cist grave[27] (Plan 46:3) which lay 2·55m north of a similar grave completely destroyed by its discoverers. The grave investigated lay at a depth of 70cm under irregularly heaped small limestone slabs. It was a regularly built cist, orientated NNW–SSE, only slightly ruined, about 2·4m long (outside measurements), 90cm wide at the southern end and 80cm at the other, about 40cm high. Its sides were of small size limestone slabs irregular in shape, and the floor was similarly paved. The grave was already ruined and its covering stones heaped mainly over the southern part of the cist. Only the skull (jaw missing) (d) and the lower part of the legs were *in situ* (b). Their position indicated that the skeleton had lain in an extended position on its back, head to S. Near the left shoulder a vessel probably stood, two sherds of which were found near the skull (c) and a few more among the heaped stones over the grave (c); they were proper to the Wysocko culture. A small flint also lay near the skull (a), and a handful of charcoal was found near

[19] These sites were quoted by Gurba, loc. cit., note 3, but no particulars were given regarding these.

[20] L. Kozłowski, *Młodsza epoka kamienna w Polsce (neolit)*, Lwów 1924, p. 186.

[21] Kostrzewski, loc. cit., note 14.

[22] Я. Пастернак, Нові археологічні набутки музею наук. тов. ім. Шевченка, Записки наук. тов. ім. Шевченка, vol. CLIV, 1937, p. 11 (off-print).

[23] Nos. 49143–51, 49057. T. Sulimirski, *Polska przedhistoryczna*, part II, London 1957–9, Fig. 69:11–19.

[24] Kozłowski (op. cit., note 20), p. 187.

[25] Свєшников (op. cit., note 14), p. 22.

[26] B. Janusz, *Zabytki przedhistoryczne Galicyi Wschodniej*, Lwów 1928, p. 106. Kozłowski (op. cit., note 20), p. 188.

[27] T. Sulimirski, *ZOW*, vol. x, 1935, p. 23.

the feet and a small polished stone near the eastern wall (e). The grave probably dated from the Late Bronze Age or Early Iron Age (Wysocko culture).

4. THE DUBNO-OSTRÓG GROUP

427. *Białokrynica* district of Krzemieniec

A dark globular amphora with two small lugs, cord decorated, now at the State Archaeological Museum (Plate 13:7). No particulars are available concerning this vessel. It may originate from a grave.

428. *Dermań* district of Krzemieniec

The blade of an extremely well-polished flint axe, at present at the Archaeological Museum in Cracow, was possibly found in a slab-cist grave.[28]

429. *Gródek* (*Horodok*) district of Równe (see no. 172)

Four slab-cist graves are said to have been uncovered here,[29] in which potsherds, flints and bronze ear-pendants of Stubło type were found.

430. *Koźlin* district of Równe

A small globular amphora with two lugs on the upper part of the body and incised ornament of short vertical and zigzag lines on the neck and the upper part of the vessel, a flint axe, a flint chip and a large clay whorl, were probably found in a slab-cist grave.[30]

431. *Krzemieniec* (see no. 147)

A slab-cist grave is said to have been found here.[31] Two polished stone axes were found near the head of its skeleton.

432. *Lachów* district of Zdołbunów

In 1939 a slab-cist grave was uncovered, 1·5 by 0·8m wide, 70cm high. On its floor covered with slabs lay two contracted skeletons. Grave goods consisted of six vessels (two of which were near the feet, four near the heads), a granite grinder and a fragment of a pig jaw, and also a fragment of a copper or bronze wire.[32] The above vessels[33] were (Fig. 23:3–5, 10, 11): (1) a small black globular amphora with two lugs on the base of the neck, the neck decorated with four horizontal rows of short incisions; (2) a deep dark bowl, undecorated and provided with two small lugs; (3) a dark-brown undecorated vase; (4) a bowl with a series of raised horizontal unperforated lugs around the neck, the neck decorated with four horizontal rows of short incisions; (5) an undecorated vase with smooth sides; (6) an undecorated amphora with two lugs on the shoulder.

433. *Lepesivka* district of Krzemieniec

Three vessels from a slab-cist grave (grave 1) were published by I. Lewyckyj,[34] all representing the Podolian variety of the Kuyavian amphorae (Fig. 22:3, 7) decorated in fish-scale patterns incised and white encrusted. In another slab-cist (grave 2) investigated by A. Cynkałowski[35] lay two crouched skeletons of adults and one of a child. Grave goods consisted of black vessels, one of these with a fish-scale ornament, and of two well-polished flint axes.

434. *Lipa* district of Dubno (see no. 175)

A slab-cist grave was investigated in 1938. Its grave goods were similar to those from cist-graves at Zdolbitsa.[36]

435. *Międzyrzec* district of Ostróg

In 1900 a slab-cist grave was uncovered[37] which contained a single skeleton in a contracted position. Three amphorae and three flint axes stood near its feet. Two amphorae had globular body and cylindrical neck and were provided with two lugs each on the base of the neck. One (Plate 12:3), 14cm high, 8cm in diameter, was decorated with stamped zigzag patterns typical of the Globular Amphora culture on its neck but with cord-impressed patterns on the shoulder; the other amphora, 10cm high, had a similar decoration executed solely by cord impressions. The third amphora, 9cm high, of a similar type and similarly decorated, had a very wide flat base, 8cm in diameter. Flint axes were all of the same type (Fig. 25:13, 14, 19) thick-butted, quadrangular in section, very well polished, 19, 13 and 15cm long. The last had its sides less thoroughly polished than the others.

436. *Mirohoszcza* district of Dubno (see no. 656)

In 1935 a grave built of large sandstones was uncovered, in which a skeleton was found with a small 'pretty' vessel. Another slab-cist grave was uncovered in 1937.[38] Two skeletons, one destroyed, the other in an extended position on its back, head to NW, lay on the floor paved with slabs. Stones were ostensibly red-fired and charcoal was found over the skeleton. No grave goods were present.

437. *Młynów* district of Dubno (see no. 655)

In 1938 a slab-cist grave was uncovered in which a spear-head, stone battle-axe, flint axe and 'needles' were found.[39]

438. *Mokre* district of Dubno (see no. 177)

In 1937 a burial of a child covered with a stone slab was investigated; near the skeleton were found a small amphora and a bronze or copper oval earring (or pendant) made of wire with one end flat widened.[40]

[28] Cynkałowski (op. cit., note 6), p. 65.

[29] I. Левицький, Пам'ятки мегалітичної культури на Волині, Антропологія, vol. II, Kiev 1929, p. 194.

[30] J. Głosik, 'Wołyńsko-podolskie materiały z epoki kamiennej i wczesnej epoki brązu w Państwowym Muzeum Archeologicznym w Warszawie', *Mat.St.*, vol. VIII, 1962, p. 143, Pl. VIII:4–7.

[31] Свєшников (op. cit., note 14), p. 22.

[32] J. Fitzke, *ZOW*, vol. XIV, 1939, p. 104. Id., *IKC*, no. 166, 18.VI.1939.

[33] Свєшников (op. cit., note 14), pp. 30 f., Pl. III:4–9.

[34] Левицький loc. cit., note 29, and Pl. III:10, 13, 16.

[35] Cynkałowski (op. cit., note 6), p. 39.

[36] И. К. Свешников, Памятники культуры шнуровой керамики у села Здолбица, Ксиимк, no. 85, 1961, p. 64.

[37] Kozłowski (op. cit., note 20), p. 187. Свєшников (op. cit., note 14), p. 30, Pl. III:10, 11. Głosik (op. cit., note 30), p. 154, Pl. XXIV:1–3. One amphora was wrongly attributed to the Corded Ware by Głosik in *Arch.R.*, vol. IX, 1957, p. 662, Fig. 273:4.

[38] A newspaper note in the *IKC*, Kracow, no. 360, of 30.XII.1935. Свєшников (op. cit., note 14), p. 30. Głosik (op. cit., note 30), p. 154.

[39] A newspaper note in the *IKC*, no. 344, of 31.XII.1938. All objects were given to the State Archaeological Museum, Warsaw.

[40] Свєшников (op. cit., note 14), p. 30.

439. *Nowomalin* district of Ostróg

A quadrangular slab-cist grave was uncovered in 1887. It contained two clay vessels.[41]

440. *Obycz* district of Krzemieniec

Two well-polished flint axes were found in a slab-cist grave destroyed by its casual discoverers.[42]

441. *Okniny* district of Ostróg

A slab-cist grave with a single skeleton was found in the nineteenth century.[43]

442. *Ostróg* (see no. 180)

A slab-cist grave was uncovered in 1939.[44]

443. *Rakowiec Mały* district of Krzemieniec

A human skeleton was found in a destroyed slab-cist grave.[45]

444. *Rydoml* district of Krzemieniec

A human skeleton and a well-polished flint axe were found in a slab-cist grave uncovered in 1933.[46]

445. *Skurcze* district of Łuck (see no. 158)

A slab-cist grave was uncovered with a single skeleton which had two bronze bracelets.[47]

446. *Stadniki* district of Ostróg (see nos. 159 and 662)

A skeleton was found in a slab-cist grave uncovered before the last war.[48] Grave goods consisted of several personal ornaments but no pottery: bronze, or copper, ear-pendants of Stubło type, small spiral earrings of thin wire, spiral beads made of bronze or copper wire, biconic bone beads and faience beads. Before the war all these objects were at the State Archaeological Museum in Warsaw.[49]

447. *Świniuchy* district of Krzemieniec

A human skeleton was found under stone slabs.[50]

448. *Varkovytsia* district of Dubno

A Kuyavian amphora decorated in a manner typical of the Globular Amphora culture (Fig. 22:1) was found in a slab-cist grave.[51]

449. *Volytsia Staklivska* district of Dubno

A few years before the last war, a slab-cist grave was uncovered in which human bones and clay vessels were found.[52]

450. *Wierchów* district of Ostróg

Two slab-cist graves were uncovered in 1892.[53]

451. *Zdolbitsa* district of Zdolbuniv (see no. 668)

In 1957 a combined burial was uncovered. The main, male, skeleton lay in a crouched position, head to W, in a grave built of larger stones; near it a stone battle-axe of type *z*-1 and a flint dagger were found. Near the feet of this skeleton was a slab-cist which contained a female skeleton, head to W, with a copper earring of Stubło type and a cord-decorated amphora of Strzyżów type with two lugs on the junction of the neck and the body. A third skeleton of a young woman, lay in a crouched position, head to W over the slab-cist; no grave goods were found near it. At a distance of 1 and 2m respectively two further burials with crouched skeletons were uncovered in graves with no stone construction. Near one of these a few cord-decorated potsherds were excavated. Sviešnikov[54] attributed this grave to the Corded Ware.

5. THE SLUCH GROUP

452. *Aneta* district of Novograd Volynskii

The cist built of gneiss slabs investigated by I. Lewyckyj[55] in 1927 was 2m long, nearly 1m wide at both ends but 1·15m in the middle, being slightly oval in plan; it was 75–60cm high, the eastern side being a little lower. It contained two skeletons, that of a man 18–20 years of age, and of a woman 16–18 years of age, which lay in a contracted position, heads, resting on small slabs, to E; both skulls were dolichocephalic. The floor under the male skeleton, especially the part under the head, was profusely strewn with charcoal. Near the skeletons lay two flint axes (II.12) 14 and 7·8cm long, of 'Bug' type, and fragments of amber beads. Close to the feet of the female skeleton was a small heap of white clay, and near by lay a skeleton of a pig and three vessels. The latter were: a decorated Kuyavian amphora (Plate 14:3) 21cm high, 27cm in diameter, provided with two vertically perforated lugs on the shoulder; and two undecorated amphorae of the hybrid type provided with four lugs each. One of these, published by Lewyckyj (IV.4), was 21cm high, the aperture 8·5cm in diameter.

453. *Kolodiazhne* district of Polonnoe (see no. 750)

A slab-cist was uncovered[56] but no particulars are available.

454. *Kośków* district of Izyaslavl

A layer of round flat stone slabs, 3m long, 1·5m wide was uncovered; its surface was dark red painted. No bones or grave goods were found there.[57]

[41] Kozłowski (op. cit., note 20), p. 188.
[42] Cynkałowski (op. cit., note 6), p. 39.
[43] Kozłowski (op. cit., note 20), p. 188.
[44] J. Fitzke, *ZOW*, vol. XIV, 1939, p. 104.
[45] Cynkałowski (op. cit., note 6), p. 40.
[46] Loc. cit.
[47] В. Б. Антонович, Археологическая карта волынской губернии, Труды XI археол. сьезда, Moscow 1900, p. 52.
[48] Kostrzewski (op. cit., note 14), p. 206.
[49] Objects described and published by Głosik (op. cit., note 30), p. 166, Pl. XXVI:6–8), allegedly found in a slab-cist grave investigated by J. Hoffman in 1930, originated probably from a settlement of the Strzyżów culture.
[50] Cynkałowski (op. cit., note 6), p. 40.
[51] Левицький (op. cit., note 29), p. 194, Pl. III:12.
[52] Свєшников (op. cit., note 14), p. 30.
[53] Kozłowski (op. cit., note 20), p. 188.
[54] Op. cit., note 36, pp. 55 ff.
[55] Op. cit., note 29, pp. 200 f.
[56] Ibid., p. 194.
[57] *Wiadomości Numizmatyczno-Archeologiczne*, 1890, p. 97.

455. *Kykova* district of Novograd Volynskii

A slab-cist grave was investigated by I. Lewyckyj[58] in 1928. It was quadrangular in plan, orientated W–E, 1·8m long, 85cm wide, 60–75cm high, the eastern side being a little lower. It contained a cremation burial (perhaps more than one?). Ashes, charcoal, lumps of ochre and of white clay were found in its centre. The grave goods were: three polished flint axes, one 13·2cm long; another polished flint axe chipped into small pieces was strewn over the floor; a flint scraper and a large number of small flint chips; nine vessels. Among the latter were five ovoid amphorae, two of which were cord decorated in zigzag patterns; one of these (Fig. 22:4) was provided with two lugs, 20cm high, 18cm in diameter. Another vessel was a Kuyavian amphora (Fig. 22:8) with a stamped decoration. Two small decorated spheric amphorae were provided with two lugs each; one of these (Plate 15:5) was 9·5cm high, 10·2cm in diameter, the other one a little larger, 14·5cm high. A hemispheric bowl with an inverted rim, 13cm high, 18cm in diameter, was also among the vessels (Plate 13:11).

456. *Ostrozhok* district of Novograd Volynskii

Two slab-cists were found which contained vessels filled in with ashes.[59]

457. *Serbinovka* on the upper Teterev

A slab-cist was uncovered in which clay vessels were found.[60]

458. *Staryi Myropil* district of Polonnoe

A cord-decorated beaker (Fig. 21:5) from a slab-cist, found in 1924, was published by I. Lewyckyj.[61] It was at the Museum in Zhitomir before the last war (no. 2773). It was 9·8cm high, 10·8cm in diameter, the neck decorated with two horizontal bands consisting of two or three rows of punctated lines each, with a triple zigzag cord-impressed band between them.

459. *Suyemtsi* district of Baranivka

Two slab-cist graves were found here, both subsequently investigated by I. Lewyckyj[62] in 1926.

Slab-cist 1. 2m long, 92cm wide in the NE side, 1·2m in the SW side, orientated NE–SW; 75–98cm high, the SE end being a little lower. It was built of two large slabs and smaller stones connected with clay mortar, and covered with a large slab. It contained five skeletons: a man, three women and a child five to seven years of age. The adults were all forty to sixty years of age, except one woman between twenty to thirty years of age; the index of the male skull was 76.66. The following grave goods were found: two polished flint axes 16 and 13cm long (II. 10, 13), a battle-axe made of basalt with the shaft-hole unfinished (Fig. 24:10); one flint scraper, two flint flakes, bones of two pigs, and seven vessels. Among the latter were: two stamp-decorated amphorae of a somewhat debased Kuyavian type (Plate 14:1; Fig 22:11), the larger of these 20cm high, the aperture 13·5cm in diameter, reddish in colour; a debased, lugged, undecorated amphora of a similar type (Plate 14:7); two globular amphorae with an incised decoration (Plate 14:5, 6), one of these 12cm high, 11·8cm in diameter; finally, three small spheric vessels (bowls?) the largest 7·8cm high, 7·7cm in diameter.

Slab-cist 2. Quadrangular in plan, orientated NE–SW, 2·26m long, the NE width 1·09m, that of the other end 86cm, 89–98cm high. The two narrow sides were of a single slab each. Inside five skeletons were found: two men (forty to sixty years of age) close to the eastern side, both in a sitting position, and the contracted skeletons of two women in the centre, the lower (forty to sixty years of age) on its right side, the upper (thirty to thirty-five years of age) on its left side, the latter with a child three to four years of age. Skulls were sub-dolichocephalic, indexes: 75.00 (man), 75.67 and 77.05 (women). One of the male skeletons and the upper female skeleton with the child were a secondary burial. Around the central skeletons were strewn ochre and lumps of white clay.

The following grave goods were excavated: two polished flint axes, 11·6 and 11·8cm long (Fig. 25:17); six spheric flint and granite hammers; chips of several polished flint axes (destroyed); a fragment of a decorated bone ornament, a pendant of bear tooth; and seven clay vessels. The latter were: a large black debased Kuyavian amphora with a narrow base and the neck stamp decorated (Plate 14:2) 24·8cm high, 34·5cm in diameter; three black or dark-yellow amphorae with large bodies; a small richly decorated globular amphora provided with four lugs made of reddish clay dark-grey painted; two decorated lids, one (Fig. 21:4) with an incised ornament consisting of a five-point star. Small pieces of bones of two pigs lay along the walls of the grave, and also in the large amphora which stood near the heads of the two central skeletons.

Only the latter vessel has been described as belonging to the secondary burial: its base lay some 15–20cm over the lower skeletons of the primary burial. No such distinction has been made in respect of any other grave goods.

460. *Voytsekhivka* district of Polonnoe (see nos. 236 and 756)

Two slab-cist graves were uncovered here.

Slab-cist 1. Investigated in 1924 by I. Lewyckyj.[63] This was a quadrangular cist built of large slabs, orientated W–E, its chamber 2·26m long, 1·28m wide at the eastern side, 1·18m at the other end, and about 97cm to 1·1m high. The floor was paved with large slabs 6cm thick, and plastered with a layer of clay 4cm thick. The cist contained ten skeletons, all buried at one time: a man (forty-five to fifty years of age) sitting close to the western wall (skull index 77.54); two women on the floor on both sides of the male skeleton, facing each other, one forty-five to fifty years of age (index 72.52), the other forty to forty-five years of age, each with two children, two to nine years of age; near their feet lay two skeletons, of a girl sixteen to eighteen years of age (index 79.77) and of a boy fourteen to sixteen years of age (index 77.77). All skeletons were in a contracted position, heads to W. The tenth

[58] Левицький (op. cit., note 29), pp. 201 f.
[59] Ibid., p. 194. Антонович (op. cit., note 47), p. 29.
[60] Антонович (op. cit., note 47), p. 6.
[61] Левицький (op. cit., note 29), p. 194.
[62] Ibid., pp. 196 ff.
[63] Ibid., pp. 126 ff. Id., Домовина кінця неолітичноï доби на побережжі середньоï течіï р. Случі, Записки всеукраïнського археологічного комітету, vol. 1, Kiev 1930, pp. 162 ff. Т. С. Пассек, Периодизация трипольских поселении, МИА, no. 10, 1949, p. 219.

skeleton, similarly in a contracted position, lay head to S in a special annexe at the entrance to the main chamber, on its eastern side; this was evidently a male serf, or slave, about thirty years of age, its brachicephalic skull (index 82.38) differed from those of all skeletons in the main chamber. All skeletons, except that of the main male, were richly sprinkled with ochre, especially their heads and chests.

The following were the grave goods: six flint axes one of which perished, 13·8, 12·3 and 10·3 cm long, made of black variety of flint, one 9·9cm long made of grey flint and one 11·1cm long made of white flint with a wide, thick butt; one of these axes was found under the amphora in the annexe; a flint chisel 10·4cm long, similarly found in the annexe in its northern corner; five small, polished flint points and blades; a decorated bone blade or point 8cm long, 1·6cm wide, 5mm thick; three pairs of boar tusks; finally, seven vessels; those found in the main chamber were all decorated and stood along its western wall, except the largest amphora which was near the feet of the main male skeleton, being filled in with some kind of corn. Flint implements lay on these vessels. One large undecorated amphora was found in the central part of the annexe. Many sherds of kitchen ware and also chips of destroyed flint implements were found scattered over the whole chamber.

Only three vessels escaped destruction by the accidental discoverers of the cist, all the others being reduced to small sherds and their reconstruction not practicable. The following types of vessels have been distinguished: a large globular amphora (found near the feet of the main skeleton) 22·4cm high, 17cm in diameter, black in colour, with two vertically perforated wide lugs (Plate 15:6); its neck and shoulder covered with a complicated stamped decoration consisting of rows of short vertical lines, fish-bone patterns and zigzag lines. The other large undecorated ovoid amphora (found in the annexe) was 21·1cm high, 17·5cm in diameter, provided with two lugs on the shoulder. The third entire vessel was a small globular amphora provided with two vertically perforated lugs, its neck and shoulder decorated with horizontal cord-impressed lines. Two of the remaining vessels seem to have been medium size amphorae, probably of Kuyavian type; one of these was probably 17·5cm high, 12cm in diameter and had a flat base; it was stamped and cord decorated; the other one was about 11·7cm in diameter, its surface reddish, polished, and the neck decorated with stamp impressions. Only a few sherds were left of the remaining vessels. One of these was black and had a cord ornament; the other, reddish with a polished surface, had the neck adorned with rows of short vertical stamped lines separated by a row of shallow pits.

Slab-cist 2. Situated at a distance of some 230–50m from the above; this was found before 1917, and investigated by S. Hamčenko in 1924.[64] No reports or descriptions published.

6. THE BOH GROUP

461. *Holodky* district of Khmelnik

In the museum at Vinnitsa there is a well-polished flint chisel, nearly square in section, 12·5cm long, made of a whitish flint, typical of the Globular Amphora culture; it was possibly found in a destroyed slab-cist grave (no. 5995–2093).

462. *Nowa Sieniawa* district of Lityn (see no. 592)

Within a small area on the top of a hill a few entire 'urns', invariably surrounded by stones, also potsherds, were excavated at a depth of 60–90cm. Animal bones, mouldered wood and charcoal were found near the urns, but no metal objects.[65] One of the smallest 'urns' published by G. Ossowski was a debased globular amphora (Fig. 22:2) 12·5cm high, about 15cm in diameter, dark brown in colour, provided with two vertically perforated lugs on the base of the neck. The neck and the shoulder adorned with horizontal rows of short stamped lines with a punctated zigzag line in between. A large fragment of another vessel, large in size, was similarly decorated.

463. *Šabelnya* district of Illintsi

Two well-polished axes probably found in a destroyed slab-cist grave are in the Museum at Vinnitsa (nos. 7687–57, 7689–57). Both made of a whitish flint typical of the Globular Amphora culture; the smaller one 8cm long, nearly flat, the larger one *c.* 5·5cm wide at the blade, the upper part missing.

464. *Tartaki* near Mezhirov (Vinnitsa)

Two skeletons, heads to E and W were uncovered in a quadrangular slab-cist, the floor of which was paved with smaller stones. Near one of the skeletons were found two vessels, and a third near the other one.[66] One of the pots was a debased Kuyavian amphora (Plate 14:11) 24·5cm high, 11·5cm in diameter, provided with four lugs on the shoulder; its cord-impressed decoration differed from that of the genuine Kuyavian amphorae, though reminiscent of it.

465. *Vinnitsa*

A small debased 'globular' amphora, with a flat base (Plate 14:8), 11cm high, found in the environments of the town, is at the museum at Vinnitsa. It is provided with two small lugs on the upper part of the shoulder, its neck and the upper part of the body covered with deep-stamped decoration in patterns typical of the Globular Amphora culture. Under the rim a row of small perforations. The vessel is very reminiscent of similar amphorae of the Masovian group.

466. *Žahnitkova* district of Olgopol

Human skeletons surrounded by stone slabs were found.[67]

7. THE ZHITOMIR GROUP

467. *Davydivka* on the Irsha

In 1890 a slab-cist was uncovered in which an axe and a hammer-axe (battle-axe) of labrador were found.[68]

[64] Левицький (op. cit., note 29), pp. 194 ff. Id., note 63, pp. 162 ff.

[65] B. Ossowski, *ŻWAK*, vol. XIII, 1890, p. 43, Figs. 1, 2.

[66] Є. Сіцінський, Матеріяли до археології західнього Поділля. Записки всеукраїнського археологічного комітету, vol. 1, Kiev 1930, pp. 28 f., Fig. 7.

[67] Ibid., p. 28.

[68] Антонович (op. cit., note 47), p. 9.

468. *Dovhynyči* near Ovruch

A cist was uncovered built of granite slabs in which cremations, flint knives and a scraper were found.[69]

469. *Fasova* district of Černyakhiv

A slab-cist was uncovered in which vessels were found similar to those from Voytsekhivka.[70]

470. *Hlynytsia* (*Glinnica*) on the Teterev

About 1810 a few slab-cist graves were uncovered in which stood vessels with calcined bones and lay polished axes and hammers.[71]

471. *Kamyanyi Brid* district of Černykhiv

A slab-cist grave was uncovered.[72]

472. *Karabačyn* near Korostyšev

A slab-cist grave was uncovered.

473. *Mininy* district of Radomysl

A decorated amphora of a debased Kuyavian type with a lid (Fig. 22:10); it was wrongly published by A. Äyräpää as originating from a catacomb grave near Kharkov.[73]

474. *Psyšče* near Zhitomir (see no. 231)

A slab-cist grave was uncovered.[74]

475. *Skolobiv* on the Irsha

A cist grave built of gneiss slabs was uncovered in 1914 and investigated in 1927 by I. Lewyckyj.[75] It was oval in plan, the chamber 2·15 by 1·18m, 33–45cm high, orientated NEE–SWW; at the entrance, on the NE side, was a kind of porch, 45cm long, built of two vertical slabs covered with a third. The chamber contained cremation burials, supposedly in two urns which stood near the western wall; this part of the floor was sprinkled with ochre.

Eleven vessels were found in this cist. One of these was a stamp-decorated Kuyavian type (Fig. 22:5) and the other was an ovoid amphora of the hybrid form (Plate 14:4) with a stamped decoration in chevron patterns on the high neck, provided with four lugs on the shoulder, 20·5cm high; both vessels reddish in colour. The other two vessels were small globular amphorae both with the neck covered with a simple stamped decoration consisting of rows of short vertical lines and zigzag lines, one of these (Fig. 22:6) with a cylindrical neck had two perforated lugs on the base of the neck, the other, 96cm high, had the neck narrowed and was provided with two unperforated lugs on the shoulder (Plate 15:12). A further vessel was a two-lugged bowl (Fig. 21:7) 10·5cm high, 16·3cm in diameter, the upper part of which had a stamped decoration consisting of rows of short vertical strokes and a double zigzag line in between, reddish in colour. The remaining six vessels were reduced to small sherds by the casual discoverer and their reconstruction was not practicable; they were mainly small in size.

Other grave goods consisted of twelve flint axes and chisels; twelve flint chips and small flakes, some trimmed on the edges, and also chips of polished axes purposely destroyed and strewn over the floor of the chamber; one tanged flint arrow-head, 2·8cm long, found among the calcined bones; and finally three amber beads.

476. *Velednyki Nove* near Ovruch

In 1892 a slab-cist grave was excavated. It contained four skeletons, flint knives and scrapers and a slate cube.[76]

477. *Volodarske-Horoški* on the Irsha

Polished axes made of labrador were found in a slab-cist grave.[77]

478. *Vysoke* district of Zhitomir

In 1926 a slab-cist grave was uncovered and subsequently investigated by I. Lewyckyj.[78] It was orientated W–E, the chamber 1·5m by 70cm wide, 80–90cm high. The eastern side had a kind of porch, *c.* 50cm long. Near the western wall stood a Kuyavian amphora of a somewhat debased form, cord decorated with wavy lines on the neck, dark reddish in colour, 16·5cm high (Fig. 22:9); it served as a cinerary urn. It was covered by a clay lid with a decoration consisting of a five-pointed star. Decoration of both the above vessels was white encrusted. Along other walls of the chamber stood four smaller vessels, namely ovoid and globular amphorae and a shallow dish. There were also three flint axes, 14·3, 12·6 and 13·7cm long, and two chisels, one broken, the other 10cm long.

479. *Vyševyči* on the Teterev

In 1885, a quadrangular cist built of granite slabs was found. It contained vessels with cremations, three thick-butted flint axes and hammers.

In 1889 a second cist grave was uncovered at a distance of three miles from the above. It was built of twenty-nine slabs covered with three slabs, and was 1·89m long, 81cm wide, 92cm deep. In it stood five vessels filled in with calcined bones and ashes, near which lay a polished flint axe and a piece of amber.[79]

480. *Zbranky* near Ovruch

A cist was uncovered built of granite slabs in which urns with ashes (cremation burials) and a flint axe were found.[80]

[69] Ibid., p. 19.

[70] Левицький (op. cit., note 63), p. 176.

[71] *ZWAK*, vol. I, 1877, p. 21. В. Б. Антонович, Археологическая карта киевской губернии. Древности, vol. XV, Moscow 1895, p. 10. Пассек (op. cit., note 63), p. 219.

[72] Op. cit., note 29, p. 194.

[73] A. Äyräpää, 'Über die Streitaxtkulturen in Russland', *ESA*, vol. VIII, 1933, p. 120, Fig. 118. Пассек (op. cit., note 63), pp. 220 f.

[74] Op. cit., note 29, p. 194.

[75] Ibid., pp. 199 f.

[76] Op. cit., note 47, p. 17.

[77] Ibid., p. 9.

[78] Op. cit., note 29, p. 199.

[79] Антонович (op. cit., note 71), p. 9. Пассек (op. cit., note 63), p. 219.

[80] Op. cit., note 47, p. 19.

481. (*Zhitomir*)

According to S. Hamtchenko[81] slab-cist graves, some with inhumation burials and others with cremations, were found in a few places in the central part of the town, on a hill near the junction of the Rudava with the Kamyanka; they were all orientated W–E and yielded dark-grey pottery and polished flint implements. A more detailed, but general description of such graves has been given by Hamtchenko, but it probably relates to all cist graves investigated by him within the whole East Volhynian region. According to this report cremations were in urns which stood in the central part of the cist surrounded by two to three smaller vessels often turned upside-down. On the top of the urns and of other vessels were usually deposited flint axes, chisels and other implements, among these bent flint knives and 'sickles', obviously daggers. The inhumation graves contained amphorae of a slightly debased Kuyavian type about 15cm high, the skeleton of the main male, usually in a sitting position close to the western wall, and of his two wives at his feet, both lying in a contracted position facing each other. Near the eastern wall lay the fourth skeleton, of a serf or slave, similarly in a contracted position but differently orientated, head to N. In both western corners, and also in the central part of the cist, stood several vessels and lay various flint implements of the same types as those from cremation cists.

8. THE SOUTH-EASTERNMOST GRAVES

482. *Berybisy* (*Gulyaipole*) near Zvenigorodka

In 1882 a slab-cist was uncovered in which lay a skeleton and a clay vessel.[82]

483. *Reymentarovka* near Smyela

A slab-cist grave was uncovered in which stood vessels with calcined bones.[83]

9. THE PODOLIAN GROUP AND BIAŁY POTOK GRAVES

484. *Beremiany* district of Buczacz (see no. 96)

At least five slab-cist graves have been uncovered here. One of these, found under a large mound in 1827, has been described in the Section devoted to the Barrow-grave culture (no. 96).

Slab-cist grave 2. Uncovered in 1877 on the field called 'Czerwona' and subsequently investigated by A. Kirkor.[84] It was destroyed even then, the slabs having mostly been taken away. The slab forming the floor of the cist was 1·53m long. Ruined human bones, potsherds, a few flints (Fig. 24:6) and an animal fang were found within the area of the ruined cist. All objects were given to the Archaeological Museum in Cracow (no. 3182). A handled jug (Plate 14:10), 13·2cm high, 11·5cm in diameter, was reconstructed from the sherds collected; its upper part was decorated by three triple cord-impressed lines around the vessel, and on its flat base a badly executed cross ornament. A large sherd of another vessel, the reconstruction of which was not practicable, is stamp decorated in fish-scale patterns.

Slab-cist grave 3. A slab-cist grave was uncovered and investigated in 1878 by A. Kirkor[85] on the same field 'Czerwona'; it was situated not far from cist 2. It was round in plan, built of large stones laid in a few layers and covered with a single slab 70cm long; the grave chamber was 55cm deep. It contained two skeletons, of a man and his wife, both in sitting positions on slabs which formed the floor. Near one of the skeletons was a small trimmed flint, and the other had a large bronze pin and earrings, or pendants, which had completely disintegrated and left only green spots on the skull. The pin similar to those from Putiatyńce (Fig. 26:14, 15) was 31cm long, its head round, made of a thin sheet, perforated. A few sherds of a broken vessel were also found. This was a double-handled vase (Fig. 32:3) typical of the Komarów culture, probably about 13cm high, the mouth about 9cm in diameter, reddish-yellow in colour. All objects are at the Archaeological Museum in Cracow (no. 4367).

Cist-grave 4. This was uncovered in 1932 on the field called 'u Wyłach'. It was 1·7m long. My attempt to refind and investigate it was unsuccessful.

A flint axe concavo-quadrangular in section, 11cm long, found in a destroyed slab-cist grave, was given in 1877 to the Archaeological Museum in Cracow[86] (no. 3812–1).

485. *Biały Potok* district of Czortków

Three graves were uncovered by J. Kostrzewski[87] in 1925, during investigation of a Tripolyan settlement. The whole archaeological material has been given to the Archaeological Museum in Poznań.

Double grave 1–2. A double burial was found at a depth of 25cm within a hut (no. 1) of the Tripolyan settlement dating from T. S. Passek's period C-1. Skeleton 1 lay on its back with legs strongly contracted, the other lay on its right side slightly contracted, both heads were to W. North of the skeletons lay a large oval stone. Near the skeletons were two vessels, a double-handled vase, 11·2cm high, 13cm in diameter, decorated in a manner typical of the Komarów-Biały Potok style, and a small undecorated bowl 6·5cm high. Over the skeletons and under them, up to the depth of 1m, many Tripolyan potsherds, lumps of fired clay and animal bones were excavated, which implies that the grave was dug into debris of a destroyed hut.

Grave 3. This lay at a distance of 2m from the above. The poorly preserved skeleton lay in a contracted position, on its left side, head to W; near the head was a deep bowl, 10·5cm high, 15·6cm in diameter, decorated with a row of bosses below the rim, and a similarly decorated cup, 11cm high, 11·2 cm in diameter; a third completely crushed vessel stood near the chest. At a distance of about 50cm from the head a flint axe was excavated, 10·5cm long.

[81] С. Гамченко, Житомир за перводжерелами передісторичної археології, Записки всеукраїнського археологічного комітету, vol. I, Kiev 1930, pp. 5, 15.

[82] Антонович (op. cit., note 71), p. 124.

[83] Ibid., p. 117.

[84] Kozłowski (op. cit., note 20), pp. 185 f.

[85] L. Kozłowski, *Wczesna, starsza i środkowa epoka bronzu w Polsce*, Lwów 1928, p. 101. Pl. XIII:1.

[86] A. Kirkor, *ZWAK*, vol. II, 1878, p. 6.

[87] J. Kostrzewski, 'Groby eneolityczne z skurczonymi szkieletami w Białym Potoku', *Prz.A.*, vol. III, 1925–7, pp. 9 ff., Pl. IV. Kozłowski (op. cit., note 85), pp. 55 f., Pl. V:2, 5, 14.

Grave 4. This lay in another part of the village. It was a slab-cist originally about 1·5m long, 1m wide, which had collapsed under the pressure of the earth. No grave goods were found but green spots on the teeth of the skeleton indicated the presence of some copper or bronze ornament which had disintegrated. The skeleton lay in a contracted position, head to S. Remains of a Tripolyan hut were found around the grave which was probably dug into its debris. The anthropological study of the osseous material[88] revealed that the main male skeleton in grave 1–2 was of 'Nordic' type, whereas the other, in a crouched position, was a woman of 'Laponoid' type. The person buried in grave 3 was of low stature, the skull badly crushed and reconstruction not practicable.

486. *Bratyszów* district of Tłumacz

In 1881, a slab-cist (no. 1) was uncovered which contained a skeleton.[89] In about 1894–6 another grave (no. 2) was uncovered built of regular slabs, situated on the field known as 'Hory', on the western slope of an elevation. Inside an axe was found which was taken by the local police.[90] A trapezoid axe made of 'milky' flint, typical of the Globular Amphora culture, which was given at about that time to the Archaeological Museum in Cracow (no. 111) probably originated from this grave (Fig. 25:2). It was 16·7cm long, very thoroughly flat-polished all over, quadrangular in section.

487. *Chorostków* district of Kopyczyńce (see no. 195)

A slab-cist grave, *c.* 2m long, *c.* 1m wide, was uncovered in 1864; in it lay two contracted skeletons.[91] The following were the grave goods: two clay vessels 'conical in shape', one larger than the other, which perished, two flint axes and one flint chisel (Fig. 25:6, 12, 15). Axes were flat, quadrangular in section, well polished all over; the smaller one (before the last war at the Dzieduszycki Museum in Lwów, no. 157) was nearly 12cm long, thick butted, made of a yellowish-grey flint. The other, 15cm long, thick butted, made of dark-grey flint, and the chisel, 10·7cm long, nearly square in section, dark-grey flint, were both before the last war at the Lubomirski Museum, Lwów (nos. 1239, 1240).

488. *Czarne Wody* district of Kamenets Podolskii

A slab-cist grave was uncovered in 1903.[92] A small globular amphora, 10cm high, 10cm in diameter, its decoration consisting of rows of triangles in fish-scale patterns, and two flint axes were found near the skeleton. Axes were typical of the Globular Amphora culture, extremely well polished all over their surface, flat, quadrangular in section, made of a 'milky' variety of flint.

489. *Czarnokońce* district of Kopyczyńce

In about 1860 a slab-cist grave was uncovered[93] in which a man's head (index 71.7) was buried; potsherds, a flint axe, small flint flakes and a decorated bone belt-buckle were found. The axe was of dark-grey flint (Fig. 25:7), 7·5cm long, thick butted, flat polished, quadrangular in section. Potsherds were decorated in fish-scale patterns. All objects were given to the Archaeological Museum in Cracow (no. 3189), except the axe which was at the Dzieduszycki Museum in Lwów (no. 156).

490. *Czernelica* district of Horodenka.

A slab-cist grave was investigated in 1878. It was 1·19m long, 61 and 55cm wide, and contained a contracted skeleton near which a vase was found.[94] It was typical of the Komarów-Biały Potok culture, decorated by several parallel horizontal lines around the neck and the upper part of the body, and a row of shaded triangles.

491. *Duliby* district of Buczacz

In 1907 a slab-cist grave was uncovered,[95] 2·2 by 1·2m in plan. In it were found human bones, four vessels which stood in the corners and two flint axes. Only one of the latter was saved (Dzieduszycki Museum in Lwów, no. 1765); it was slightly concavo-quadrangular in section, thick butted, well polished, 13·3cm long, made of dark-grey flint with darker spots (Fig. 25:11).

492. *Hlubičok* district of Borszczów

A slab-cist grave was uncovered in 1955.[96] It was 2·5m long, 1m wide, 1m deep, and contained three skeletons: of a man, woman and a child eight to ten years of age. The cist was orientated S–N, heads were all to N. Grave goods, given to the Historical Museum in Lviv, were as follows: five well-polished, thick-butted flint axes; two flint chisels; a bone point about 8·5cm long of unknown purpose; a small globular amphora, about 10cm high, with a spheric body provided with two lugs, the neck decorated by rows of vertical incisions separated by horizontal cord-impressed lines, and a row of concentric semicircles on the upper part of the body (Plate 12:7); fifteen sherds of a few greyish and black vessels with a well-smoothed surface, decorated by groups of small incisions, rhomboid, zigzag and other patterns; finally fragments of bones of two pigs.

493. *Horodnica* district of Horodenka

In 1877 five slab-cist graves were investigated by I. Kopernicki.[97] One of these dated from the first centuries A.D., four were of the Middle Bronze Age (Komarów-Biały Potok culture).

Cist Aa. Orientated NNW–SSE, 1·55m by 75–60cm. On the bottom was a decayed skeleton in an extended position, head to SSE. Near its skull a decorated handled saucer with a double-handled decorated vase near the feet, and a large

[88] K. Stojanowski, 'Resztki kostne z grobów eneolitycznych ze skurczonymi szkieletami w Białym Potoku', *Prz.A.*, vol. III, 1925–7, pp. 52 ff.

[89] Kozłowski (op. cit., note 20), p. 188.

[90] According to information given me, during my investigations there in 1934, of Scythian barrow-graves.

[91] Kozłowski (op. cit., note 20), p. 186.

[92] Ibid., p. 186, Pl. XXV:7, 8.

[93] Ibid., p. 186, Pl. XXV:4, 6.

[94] Kozłowski, as above, p. 186, dated it wrongly to the Neolithic. R. Rogozińska, 'Cmentarzysko kultury komarowskiej w Bukównie', *Mat. Arch.*, vol. I, 1959, p. 113, Pl. VIII:1.

[95] W. Antoniewicz, 'Z dziedziny archeologii ziem Polski', *Światowit*, vol. XVII, 1938, p. 394.

[96] Свбшников (op. cit., note 14), p. 27, Pl. II.

[97] I. Kopernicki, 'Poszukiwania archeologiczne w Horodnicy nad Dniestrem', *ZWAK*, vol. II, 1878, pp. 47 ff., Pl. III. Kozłowski (op. cit., note 85), p. 56, Pl. V:7–12, 15. Rogozińska (op. cit., note 94), pp. 112 f., Pls. VIII:3; IX:4, 5.

tulip-shaped pot with a raised band around the neck stood in the corner of the cist. Outside the grave, and close to its western slab, lay a flint arrow-head. Outside the eastern slab was a child's grave (B); near its skeleton lay a small undecorated bowl, base upwards, 5·2cm high, and a large pot almost completely crushed, made of tempered clay paste, insufficiently fired and brittle. The child's grave was covered with a slab, but had no slabs on the sides. North of the main grave was a third (C) which had only one slab on its eastern side and was covered with a large slab. Only a large tulip-shaped undecorated vessel provided with two lugs was found here.

Cist Ab. At a distance of 8m from cist Aa, 1·25 by 45–65cm in plan, 75cm high, orientated NNW–SSE. Pieces of charcoal and a pig tooth were found in its filling. On the bottom lay an almost completely decayed skeleton, head to N, near its feet a crushed vessel which disintegrated, and its reconstruction was not practicable.

Cist Ac. At a distance of 7m NNE from the above. Charcoal and potsherds were found in it, among the latter a base of a small vessel, 8cm in diameter, 12cm high. Two completely decayed skeletons lay on the floor, of an adult and of a child.

Cist Ad. At a distance of 3m SE of the above. In the upper part of the filling a few potsherds and charcoal were found. On the floor lay two skeletons aligned in opposite directions, heads to S and N respectively. Two vessels stood near each. One was a vase typical of the Komarów-Biały Potok culture (Fig. 32:9) about 12·5cm high, with a row of shaded triangles on the upper part of the body, apparently with lugs (two?) on the body.

494. *Horodnica* district of Kopyczyńce

A slab-cist grave was uncovered 1·4m by 80cm in plan.[98] It contained a skeleton in a sitting position near which stood a large black Kuyavian amphora (Plate 12:4, 5) 28cm high, decorated in stamped pattern typical of this type of vessel, and a bone object of unknown purpose.

495. *Horyhlady* district of Tłumacz

In 1898 a slab-cist grave was uncovered in which decayed human bones were found.

496. *Hubin* district of Buczacz

A slab-cist grave was uncovered in 1890 in which a stone axe was found.[99]

497. *Ivanye Zolote* district of Zališčyky

A slab-cist grave was uncovered in which a miniature vessel proper to the Early Iron Age was found, given (with the human skull found there) to the Ševčenko Museum in Lviv.[100]

498. *Keptyntsi* district of Kamenets Podolskii

In 1900 a slab-cist was uncovered and subsequently investigated by E. Sitzinsky.[101] Its chamber was 1·78m by 89cm in size; on its floor lay two skeletons, and near by two flint axes and a few vessels destroyed by the casual discoverer. One axe was also destroyed, the other one, 8cm long, was given to the museum at Kamenets Podolskii.

499. *Kociubińce* district of Kopyczyńce

A slab-cist grave, uncovered in 1876,[102] 1·90m by 99–85cm in plan, orientated S–N, contained three skeletons (two male, one female), all in a contracted position, heads to S. Skull indexes were: 73.4, 74.4 and 77.8 (female). Grave goods found there were: two amphorae (Fig. 23:8, 9), Kuyavian and ovoid, both provided with four lugs on the shoulder and decorated with rows of triangles in fish-scale patterns; three flint axes quadrangular in section; two pendants of boar tusks and a perforated amber disc (Fig. 24:5).

500. *Kolubaivtsi* district of Kamenets Podolskii

In 1934, in a field known as 'Kozavščyna', a slab-cist grave was uncovered and its contents given to the museum at Kamenets Podolskii. These were: a thick-butted flint axe quadrangular in section (Fig. 25:10), 12cm long, made of white flint with dark spots; a small undecorated amphora (or cup) with two lugs (Fig. 23:6), 8cm high; three potsherds of probably two vessels of a larger size, dark in colour, all decorated with rows of triangles in fish-scale patterns.

501. *Koszyłowce* district of Zaleszczyki

A quadrangular slab-cist grave 1·90m by 90–65cm in plan was uncovered in 1878, ruined by the casual discoverers and subsequently investigated by A. Kirkor.[103] Objects found in it (at the Archaeological Museum Cracow) include potsherds of at least three vessels; a small stone battle-axe, or mace-head (Fig. 24:9) 6cm long, made of a greenish stone variety; two small flint knives and one worked flake (probably an arrow-point). One of the vessels of which a base survived and a few sherds was probably an amphora decorated in fish-scale patterns and cord impressions. A fragment of a rim represented another pot which had a fish-scale ornament and cord-impressed shaded triangles. A large fragment of a neck with horizontal rows of cord impressions belonged to the third vessel.

In 1930 another slab-cist grave (grave 2) was uncovered in which a high cylindrical single-handled mug (Plate 14:9) typical of the late phase of the Corded Ware culture was found near the skeleton. It was 19·7cm high, 12cm in diameter, the rim flat, slightly inclined in a manner proper to the pottery of the Trzciniec culture. The upper part decorated by eleven parallel horizontal incisions and a row

[98] Antoniewicz (op. cit., note 95), p. 395. L. Kozłowski, *Zarys pradziejów Polski południowo-wschodniej*, Lwów 1939, Pl. VIII. Głosik (op. cit., note 30), p. 137.

[99] Kozłowski (op. cit., note 20), p. 188.

[100] Я. Пастернак, Нові археологічні набутки. Записки наук. тов. ім. Шевченка, Lviv 1937, p. 17 (off-print).

[101] Op. cit., note 66, p. 28.

[102] Kozłowski (op. cit., note 20), p. 186, Pl. XXV:5, 9, 10. Antoniewicz (op. cit., note 95), p. 392, Fig. 57.

[103] Kozłowski (op. cit., note 20), pp. 186 f. Kostrzewski (op. cit., note 14), p. 158. Свешников (op. cit., note 14), pp. 26 f.

of similar vertical, shorter incisions at the lower end of the decorative band.

In 1931 I excavated a third slab-cist grave in which nothing was found.

502. *Krowinka* district of Trembowla

In 1926 a slab-cist grave was uncovered at a depth of 65cm close to the road to Łoszniów. It was 2·2m long, 1·2m wide, 58cm high, and built of large slabs. Two skeletons were found inside.

503. *Latacz* district of Zaleszczyki

A slab-cist grave was uncovered in 1929, 2·1m long, 73cm high. Inside were found human bones and the following objects, given to the museum at Zaleszczyki (Fig. 24:1–4): a stone battle-axe, 10cm long, made of dark diorite, trimmed flint blade (knife) and two flint burins.

Another slab-cist grave was found a few years earlier on a different field. It also contained stone (flint?) implements but no pottery.

504. *Ładyczyn* district of Tarnopol

In 1914 a slab-cist built of six slabs was uncovered.[104] In 1931 another one built of large stones covered with large slabs was found. In it a bronze earring and a clay vessel typical of the Corded Ware were found. It had perforations around its upper part and its surface was black polished.

505. *Nagórzanka* district of Buczacz

In 1923 three slab-cist graves were investigated by L. Kozłowski.[105]

Cist I. Build of six slabs, its chamber 1m long, 40cm wide, 30cm high. No traces of skeleton were found, only an undecorated double-handled vase typical of the Komarów-Biały Potok culture, brownish in colour, lay on the floor; it was badly crushed.

Cist II. Ruined. It contained a skeleton only slight traces of which survived but no grave goods were present.

Cist III. This was built of three slabs only, one forming its cover. Nothing was found in it.

According to records in my possession, two more slab-cist graves were found on the same site. One was uncovered before 1923; its walls were built of five slabs, two slabs formed the floor and one large slab covered the grave. Inside were found one vessel and a stone battle-axe. Another grave (the fifth) was uncovered here in 1932. Potsherds were found in it.

506. *Niżniów* district of Buczacz

A slab-cist grave was uncovered in which lay a contracted skeleton, a stone battle-axe and red-painted vessels.[106]

507. *Ostrivets* district of Horodenka

In 1958 a flat cemetery was investigated; sixty-six graves with skeletons in a contracted position were uncovered. Its sepulchral pottery was very similar to that from the settlement at Mahala, district of Kelmentsi, of the Noua culture of Romania.[107]

Addendum: 594. *Podgórzany* district of Trembowla

A few cremation burials in urns were uncovered during the construction of the railway line. Two vessels, an undecorated tulip-shaped pot, 40cm high, and a double-handled vase of Noua type were among vessels taken by a private collector (Plate 22:7, 8). The site was subsequently investigated in 1899 by W. Demetrykiewicz,[108] who found many potsherds, three urns which disintegrated, and calcined human bones.

508. *Podhajczyki Justynowe* district of Trembowla

In 1895 a slab-cist grave was uncovered which contained skeletons of an adult and a child; a bone adze is said to have been found stuck in the skull of the latter.[109]

509. *Popovtsy* district of Tovste

Three slab-cist graves were uncovered, two of which were investigated by Iu. N. Zakharuk in 1953.[110]

Cist I. Built of slabs, orientated W–E, its chamber 1·2m by 64cm in plan, 60cm high. On its floor lay a badly preserved skeleton in a contracted position on its right side, head to E. Near its face was a flint knife, 7·8cm long, behind the skeleton stood a small cord-decorated double-handled cup, 5·5cm high, 7·5cm in diameter (Fig. 23:2).

Cist II. At a distance of 15m NW of the above, orientated W–E, built of slabs including the floor. Its chamber was 1·5m by 70–77cm in plan, the western side being shorter and 60cm high. Inside lay a contracted skeleton on its right side, head to E. Near its face was an undecorated cylindrical mug, 12·5cm high, 11·5×8cm in diameter (slightly oval), brownish in colour, made of a strongly tempered clay paste, insufficiently baked, which disintegrated. Near it lay eight triangular flint arrow-heads (Fig. 24:7) and near the arm of the skeleton lay a battle-axe of type *x*-2 made of a dark green stone (Fig. 24:8), 9·5cm long, and a broken flint knife, 7·5cm long.

510. *Rożniów* district of Śniatyn

A slab-cist grave was uncovered in about 1880, in which a stone battle-axe was found.[111]

511. *Ruzdwiany* district of Trembowla

In 1932 a slab-cist grave was uncovered and three vessels, all in sherds, found in it were given to the Grammar School (*gimnazjum*) at Trembowla. They were typical of the

[104] Antoniewicz (op. cit., note 95), p. 396.

[105] Kozłowski (op. cit., note 85), pp. 56 f., Pl. v:13, 16.

[106] Id. (op. cit., note 20), p. 197. A newspaper note: *Czas*, Kraków, 11.VII.1908.

[107] Е. А. Балагурі, Дослідження могильника пізньобронзового часу біля с. Остівець, станіславської області, Мдапв, vol. 3, 1961, p. 42, Figs. 1–4.

[108] W. Demetrykiewicz, 'Poszukiwania archeologiczne w powiecie trembowelskim w Galicyi Wschodniej', *Materiały antropologiczno-archeologiczne*, vol. IV, Kraków 1900, p. 100, Fig. 3c, e (the name of the site given wrongly as 'Podgórze').

[109] Ibid., p. 117. Kozłowski (op. cit., note 20), p. 187.

[110] Ю. Захарук, Погребения в каменных гробницах около с. Поповцев, тернопольской области, Ксиак, no. 8, 1959, pp. 129 ff., Fig. 1, Pl. I.

[111] Kozłowski (op. cit., note 20), p. 188.

Komarów-Biały Potok culture. Photographs and drawings of these perished during the last war and only a description has survived. These were: (a) a large vessel, about 40cm in diameter, walls 1·8cm thick, made of clay paste strongly tempered, dark grey, matt in colour, inside reddish-yellow; (b) a small vessel made in the same manner, walls covered with reddish slip slightly polished, the flat base 6·7cm in diameter; (c) a vessel of which only the base survived, and a small part of the lower part of the body, was very similar to a vessel from a slab-cist grave at Trembowla-Rakowica (no. 515).

512. *Semenów* district of Trembowla (see no. 216)

In 1866 a slab-cist grave was uncovered.[112]

513. *Słobódka Koszyłowiecka* district of Zaleszczyki

A slab-cist grave was uncovered in 1930 in which the following seven vessels were found;[113] a Kuyavian type amphora (Plate 15:8), brown in colour, the neck and shoulder decorated with rows of triangles in fish-scale patterns, 17cm high, 17cm in diameter; a small globular amphora with two lugs (Plate 15:7), decorated in a similar manner but white encrusted, with a spheric body and several double perforations around the rim, 12cm high, 12·5cm in diameter; a small globular amphora of the same type, 7cm high, 7cm in diameter, the fish-scale decoration white encrusted; another small amphora, ovoid in shape, provided with two lugs, 7·5cm high, 6·3cm in diameter, the base wide, the fish-scale decoration not encrusted; flat lids of the two larger amphorae decorated in the same manner as these (Plate 15:7, 8), the smaller one provided with perforations corresponding with those on the rim of the smaller amphora, 11·5cm in diameter, 4·5cm high and 9·5cm in diameter, 3·7cm high; a few sherds of some other vessel, decorated with fish-scale ornament.

514. *Strilče* district of Horodenka

A slab-cist grave was investigated in 1960 by I. K. Sviešnikov,[114] in which, near the contracted skeleton (head to S), a cord-decorated two-lugged amphora was found, a few beads and a flint arrow-head. Two other slab-cist graves uncovered there were already destroyed by their casual discoverers.

515. *Trembowla*

An ancient cemetery was destroyed during the construction of the railway line. The site was investigated by W. Demetrykiewicz[115] in 1899, who found a large part of a decorated bowl (Fig. 32:4) typical of the Komarów-Biały Potok culture, and a small brittle cup. The bowl was 12cm high, 16cm in diameter, the neck covered with horizontal lines around the vessel, and slanting fluting on the body reached the lower part of the vessel. The cup was reddish in colour and its body decorated by a row of shaded triangles. The Middle Bronze Age inhumation cemetery was partly destroyed by a cremation cemetery of the early centuries A.D. set up on the same site.

In 1932 in the Rakowica suburb two graves were uncovered.[116]

Grave 1. This was a cist built very thoroughly of thin sandstone slabs, trapezoid in plan, the chamber 2·3cm long, the western side 70cm wide, the eastern side 43cm wide, 65cm high. The floor was of stamped yellow clay. It contained a skeleton in an extended position, head to W; its knees rested on small stones, and small stones lay also close to the feet. The following grave goods, which before the war were in the Grammar School (*gimnazjum*) at Trembowla, were found: a larger vessel, of which only the base, 8cm in diameter, and a small part of walls escaped destruction by the casual discoverers, made of a strongly tempered clay, brittle, the outside covered with reddish slip; a cup, its base 5cm in diameter, flat, the body about 6·5cm in diameter, made in the same manner as the former one, and also only partly preserved; a whetstone of sandstone, 7·4cm long, 2·4cm wide, provided with a perforation at one end; a large flint flake. The vessels were typical of the Komarów-Biały Potok culture. Drawings of all these objects perished during the last war.

Grave 2 lay at a distance of 3m SE of the former. The skeleton in an extended position lay on a cobbled area oval in plan, and was covered by a cairn made of larger boulders (12cm in diameter), about 30cm high. Near the skeleton was an undecorated bronze armband 7cm in diameter, 5 by 2mm thick, its ends pointed and overlapping. Another object found was a lump of slag.

516. *Ułaszkowce* district of Czortków

In 1912 a very regularly built slab-cist grave was uncovered which contained human skeletons and the following grave goods (given to the Archaeological Museum in Cracow: no. 3172)[117] (Plate 15:1–4): an amphora with two lugs on the shoulder with a rich decoration in fish-scale patterns, dark in colour, 15cm high, 15·5cm in diameter; a small globular amphora similarly decorated but white encrusted, provided with two lugs on the base of the neck, base flat, 11cm high, 9·5cm in diameter; a bowl similarly decorated but not encrusted, provided with two lugs under the rim, 8·5cm high, 11·5cm in diameter; another bowl similarly decorated, white encrusted, with no lugs, 8cm high, 12cm in diameter; a thick-butted axe made of black flint, quadrangular in section, 12cm long (Fig. 25:18).

517. *Uścieczko* district of Zaleszczyki

A thin, dark-grey flint axe (Fig. 25:4), very well polished all over the whole surface, 12·3cm long, quadrangular in section, was preserved before the war in the collection of the Prehistoric Institute of the Yagellonian University in Cracow (no. 6799). It was found in a slab-cist grave.

518. *Uwisła* district of Kopyczyńce (see no. 220)

In 1890 a slab-cist grave (no. 1) was uncovered, and subsequently investigated by G. Ossowski.[118] Its chamber was

[112] Demetrykiewicz (op. cit., note 108), p. 31.

[113] Antoniewicz (op. cit., note 95), Figs. 61–6. Kozłowski (op. cit., note 85), Pl. VIII:9–12, 15.

[114] Information kindly given me by Mr I. K. Sviešnikov, Lviv.

[115] Demetrykiewicz (op. cit., note 108), pp. 93 ff., Figs. 1; 3d.

[116] *ZOW*, vol. VII, 1932, p. 76.

[117] Kozłowski (op. cit., note 20), p. 187, Pl. XXV:11, 12. Id. (op. cit., note 85), Pl. VIII:4–6, 8. Antoniewicz (op. cit., note 95), pp. 394 f.

[118] Kozłowski (op. cit., note 20), p. 187, Pl. XXV:1–3.

1·6m by 90cm in plan, orientated NW–SE. In the central part lay a skeleton on its back, of a woman, about fifty years of age, index 83.3, legs contracted, head to SE. Close to its left arm stood a small vessel, near by a flint knife and on the hips lay decorated bone belts (Fig. 24:11, 12). In the NW part of the grave lay two more skeletons, one of these of a man, head index 77.7, the other of a woman about forty years of age, index 80.9, heads to SW, and over their bones lay two amphorae. All vessels were broken by the discoverers, but a black amphora of Kuyavian type (Plate 12:6) was reconstructed, 27cm high, 22cm in diameter, two lugs, brownish in colour; it had a decoration consisting of rows of triangles in fish-scale patterns. The other amphora had a decoration of short stamped vertical incisions arranged in groups, and the third vessel, probably a small bowl, had also a fish-scale ornament. All objects were given to the Archaeological Museum in Cracow (no. 3218).

In 1933, I investigated a slab-cist grave (no. 2) (Plan 46:2) soon after its discovery. Its contents were already ruined by the casual discoverer. The grave was situated on the top of a hill, on a field known as 'pod Mazurówką'. The chamber was 1·8m long, 1m wide, orientated N–S, its western wall was a single large slab 1·9m by 60cm, 25–30cm thick; the eastern wall was formed by a few small stones and a large slab 1·5m by 60cm thick. The northern wall was built of a few layers of smaller stones, and the eastern half of the southern wall was similarly built. The floor was covered with two large but thinner slabs. South of the slab a kind of porch extended about 1·2m long, 60cm wide, its eastern wall only 60cm long, and the southern wall semicircular. A gap about 30cm wide was on its western side, and about 60cm wide on its eastern side, and there was no partition between the porch and the main chamber. The main chamber was covered with a single, very large slab which was broken and taken away by the discoverer of the grave. There was seemingly no stone cover over the porch. Only a few fragments of leg and feet bones were found in the northern part of the chamber (b), and a human tooth near its south-eastern corner (c) which suggest that the skeleton (or skeletons?) lay head to S (in a crouched position?). Outside the cist, close to its north-western corner a large vessel stood on a small cobbled area in a shallow pit (a). The vessel (Plate 22:6) was crushed and partly destroyed during the extraction of the covering slab. It was 24cm high, oval, 34·5 by 20cm in diameter, with a flat base. The surface bore traces of smoothing. Under the rim was a raised band running around the vessel, and on the body were a number of bosses. The vessel was made of a strongly tempered clay paste, but was well baked. It belonged to a late period of the Komarów-Biały Potok culture.

According to Sviešnikov,[119] a third slab-cist grave was uncovered in 1940. It contained human bones and clay vessels which perished.

519. *Velyka Mukša* district of Kemenets Podolskii

In 1926 a slab-cist was uncovered and subsequently investigated by E. Sitzinsky.[120] It was built of six large slabs, covered with a single large slab, and the floor covered with a few smaller slabs. The chamber was 1·58m by 73cm, 78cm high, orientated S–N. It contained two skeletons spoiled by the casual discoverers and their original position has not been established. They were accompanied by four vessels and five flint axes of which only four were given to the museum in Kamenets Podolskii. Close to the southern wall, outside the cist, lay a skeleton in a contracted position with no grave goods. The axes were very thoroughly polished all over, trapezoid in shape, 20, 15, 13·3 and 10·3cm long, quadrangular in section and made of white-grey flint (Fig. 25:1, 3, 16). The four vessels were: (a) a Kuyavian type amphora, 15.5cm high, 16·5cm in diameter, provided with four lugs on the junction of the neck, decorated with rows of triangles in fish-scale patterns (Plate 15:9); (b) a smaller amphora with two lugs, a flat base, similarly decorated, the neck missing, the surviving part 8cm high, 10·5cm in diameter; (c) a pedestalled bowl the upper part of which is missing (Plate 15:10), the surviving part, 5·5cm high, 9 cm in diameter, the stand hollow, black in colour, fish-scale decoration visible; (d) a larger sherd of a large vessel with the fish-scale ornament.

520. *Żaderewacz* district of Dolina. See p. 193.

521. *Żarwanica* district of Podhajce

A slab-cist was uncovered in about 1896–8.[121] It was regularly built, its floor covered with slabs, but no covering slab was found. No human bones were found inside but two flint axes lay on the floor (at the Dzieduszycki Museum in Lwów (nos. 284, 285) (Fig. 25:5, 9)). Both thick-butted, quadrangular in section, well polished all over the surface, made of whitish-grey flint, typical of the Globular Amphora culture, the larger being 13·5cm long, the other 9·3cm long, its butt missing.

522. *Żastawie* district of Tarnopol

Two slab-cist graves were uncovered.[122]

Cist 1. 1·3m long, 70cm wide, 90cm high, orientated W–E contained three skeletons in a contracted position: a man (dolichocephalic skull), a woman (skull brachicephalic) and the third undetermined. They were accompanied by two vessels and two flint axes. One of these was a Kuyavian type amphora with an ornament consisting of incised rows of concentric triangles, the other one, a globular amphora, had a fish-scale ornament. Both axes were quadrangular in section, one very well polished, the other, the smaller one, less thoroughly polished. Potsherds given to the museum belonged to at least one more amphora decorated in incised patterns similar to those of the Kuyavian amphora above.

Cist 2. Very large, its covering slab 1·72cm long, 1m wide, and the side slabs 97cm high. The cist contained skeletons of six to seven persons; several potsherds and unpolished flint implements were found there. They are said to have been black in colour and decorated in a manner similar to that of the vessels from Cist 1.

[119] Свешников (op. cit., note 14), p. 24.

[120] Op. cit., note 66, pp. 25 ff., Figs. 1–6.

[121] Kozłowski (op. cit., note 20), p. 188. Particulars concerning this grave were given me by Mr R. Ochocki who was present at its discovery.

[122] Kozłowski (op. cit., note 20), p. 187. Antoniewicz (op. cit., note 95), p. 397, Fig. 60.

523. *Zawadyńce* district of Kamenets Podolskii (see no. 222)

In 1888 a grave built of stones was uncovered on the top of a hill; no traces of any mound raised over it were visible.[123] The skeleton, in a contracted position (skull markedly dolichocephalic), orientated W–E, lay under a limestone cairn 60cm high, about 2·2 by 1·7m in area. The skeleton was covered with four rolls of clay 15cm wide, 10cm thick, which lay across it. A similar clay roll lay under the skull. Near the skeleton three flint flakes were found. The grave was cobbled with small slabs and under the skull lay two stones of a species not found in that region.

A fragment of a globular amphora decorated with fish-scale patterns originating from 'the neighbourhood of Zawadyńce', was published by Antoniewicz;[124] it may have originated from the above slab-cist grave.

524. *Zieleńcze* district of Trembowla

An inhumation slab-cist grave was uncovered, and a diorite battle-axe and beads (of caoline, chalcedon, and glass?) were found in this.[125] A deep bowl, typical of the Komarów-Biały Potok culture, was found in the village in unknown circumstances.[126]

525. *Żeżawa* district of Zaleszczyki

A double-handled vase, probably found in a grave, now at the Archaeological Museum in Cracow.[127] It was decorated with a row of shaded triangles on the upper part of the body; it was typical of the Komarów-Biały Potok culture.

10. THE MOLDAVIAN GROUP

526. *Cut* district of Piatra Neamț

A slab-cist was uncovered here[128] several years ago, its whole contents having been destroyed by the casual discoverers. The slab—reconstructed—is at the museum at Piatra Neamț.

527. *Dolheşti Mari* district of Fălticeni

In 1955 a slab-cist grave was uncovered, situated on a low river terrace.[129] It contained four skeletons, three flint axes, decorated bone objects and several vessels, the whole contents being destroyed by the casual discoverers. In 1957 a second slab-cist grave, situated in the vicinity of the first, was uncovered and investigated. This was a trapezoid slab-cist, orientated SEE–NWW, which contained two skeletons lying in opposite directions on their backs, legs contracted, head of the larger one to NW. The following grave goods were found in it: two small polished flint chisels, quadrangular in section, made of a grey variety of flint; five incised decorated bone belt-buckles; six brittle vessels, grey and black polished, reddish in colour. Among these were amphorae (Kuyavian type) (Fig. 23:12) provided with four lugs on the shoulder or body, and smaller globular amphorae (Fig. 23:13) and cups. Their decoration consisted of short incisions or stamp impressions, zigzag and other patterns, filled in with white paste, but some vessels had cord impressed horizontal lines and rows of concentric semicircles. This grave lay under a layer attributable to a settlement of the Gorodsk culture. Near the two slab-cist graves an animal burial was uncovered. Near the head of the animal (cervidae or bovidae) stood a vessel decorated with horizontal incisions and cord impressions, characteristic of the Globular Amphora culture.

528. *Gîrceni* district of Negreşti

In 1957 a slab-cist grave was investigated,[130] quadrangular in plan, its chamber 1·60m long, 65cm wide, orientated N–W. Its contents had already been completely destroyed. At a distance of 70cm from this cist, two small concentrations of stones were uncovered. Inside the larger of these stood a red vessel decorated with a slightly incised horizontal line and a row of crosses. At a distance of 16m SSE from the slab-cist, a large agglomeration of stones, quadrangular in plan, was found, near which three graves were uncovered. All skeletons were in a contracted position. In grave 1 a perforated bone disc was found, in grave 2 (orientated to S) a stone battle-axe, and near the third skeleton (head to NEE) five flint arrow-heads were excavated. Graves were dug into a layer with the remains typical of the Cucuteni B culture.

529. *Graniceşti* district of Rădăuți

In 1872 a slab-cist grave, 7 feet long, 4 feet wide, 3 feet deep, was uncovered on the top of a hill.[131] It contained two skeletons, one larger and the other smaller, which lay close to each other. Between the legs of the larger one stood two insufficiently fired clay vessels, spheric in shape, black in colour, walls thick. On the right side of the larger skeleton lay an axe very thoroughly made and evidently of whitish flint ('achate'). Remains of a 'wooden mace-head' and a few more potsherds were also found in the cist.

Another slab-cist grave was previously found near by and destroyed by the casual discoverer.

530. *Piatra Neamț*

A slab-cist grave was uncovered in 1955.[132] 2·2m long, 68–72cm wide, orientated E–W. It contained three skeletons accompanied by eight to nine vessels, three flint axes, one flint chisel, flint knife and flake, a small stone plaque and an undefined stone implement. Among the vessels was one Kuyavian type amphora decorated by cord-impressed horizontal lines around the neck and a row of concentric semicircles on the shoulders (Fig. 22:12). Another amphora provided with a few pairs of bosses on the shoulder, had its

[123] F. Pułaski, *ZWAK*, vol. XIV, 1890, pp. 1 ff. Свешников (op. cit., note 14), p. 28.

[124] Antoniewicz (op. cit., note 95), Fig. 69.

[125] Demetrykiewicz (op. cit., note 108), pp. 116 ff., Fig. 20b, e.

[126] Rogozińska (op. cit., note 94), p. 113.

[127] Kozłowski (op. cit., note 85), p. 56, Pl. V:1. Rogozińska (op. cit., note 94), p. 113, Pl. IX:6.

[128] C. Mătăsa, 'Decoperiri arheologic in raionul Piatra Neamț', *MCA*, vol. V, 1959, pp. 723 ff.

[129] M. Dinu, 'Sondajul arheologic de la Dolheşti Mari (r. Fălticeni, reg. Suceava)', *MCA*, vol. VI, 1959, pp. 213 ff. Id., 'Contribuții la problema culturii amforelor sferice pe teritoriul Moldovei', *Arheologia Moldovei*, vol. I, Iaşi 1961, pp. 46 ff., Figs. 1–7.

[130] A. Florescu and M. Florescu, 'Sondajul de la Gîrceni (r. Negreşti, reg. Iaşi)', *MCA*, vol. VI, 1959, pp. 221 ff.

[131] *Mitteilungen d. kk. Zentral-Kommission*, Wien 1880, p. LXXXV, no. 45.

[132] Mătăsa, loc. cit., note 128. Dinu (op. cit., note 129: 1961), p. 723 ff.

whole surface covered with rows of short incisions or stamps. There were at least two undecorated bowls, one provided with small lugs under the rim. A number of potsherds of some other vessels bore the typical fish-scale ornament. The flint axes were thoroughly polished, thick butted, trapezoid in shape, typical of the Globular Amphora culture, as was the chisel, the blade of which is missing.

531. *Scheia* district of Negreşti

A slab-cist grave was uncovered.[133]

532. *Stănceşti* district of Botosani

A slab-cist grave was uncovered.[134]

533. *Tăcuta* district of Vasului

A slab-cist grave was uncovered.[135]

534. *Tirpesti* district of Bacău

A whitish flat well-polished flint axe typical of the Globular Amphora culture, was found;[136] it probably came originally from a slab-cist grave.

11. TRANSILVANIAN SLAB-CIST GRAVES[137]

535. *Cacova* (*Aiud*)—tumulus[138]
536. *Cămpulung* (*Dămbovița*)[139]
537. *Carpinis* (*Sebes*)—tumulus[140]
538. *Helsdorf*—two graves
539. *Honigberg* (*Tartlaŭ*)
540. *Kronstadt*—two graves
541. *Moreşti*[141]
542. *Rosenau*
543. *Weidenbach*
544. *Weidenbacher Hattert*
545. *Zeiden*—two graves (Fig. 22:13)

12. BULGARIA

546. *Pekliuk* district of Sofia

A small pot and an amphora (Fig. 23:1) were found in an area 50cm in diameter, surrounded by a loose ring of stones; near the vessels lay five flint knives, two small polished stones and two perforated pendants made of bone. The amphora had an incised decoration and two small lugs on the base of the neck and was provided with a similarly decorated lid (Fig. 23:1); it represented a debased globular amphora. The grave has been regarded as a child's cenotaph.[142]

13. ELEMENTS OF THE GLOBULAR AMPHORA CULTURE IN THE REMAINS OF OTHER CULTURES (Map V)

(a) *Potsherds found in Settlements, Encampments and Graves*

547. *Černin* on the Dnieper north of Kiev

Potsherds from a site of Corded Ware.[143]

548. *Gorodsk* (*Horodsk*) on the Teterev (see no. 749)

Potsherds from the settlement of the Gorodsk culture.[144]

549. *Homel*

Potsherds from a Bronze Age site.[145]

550. *Kamenka* near Dnepropetrovsk

A well-polished chisel square in section, 9cm long, made of grey flint, typical of the Globular Amphora culture, found in the 'Late Neolithic' settlement with a stone battle-axe.[146]

Addendum: 595. *Kanev* (Velyke Horodyšče)

A few potsherds typical of the Globular Amphora culture found on a Bronze Age settlement.[147]

551. *Klementowice* district of Puławy (see no. 373)

Potsherds typical of the Globular Amphora culture found in a number of pits of the settlement of the Funnel Beaker culture.[148]

Addendum: 598. *Kołokolin* district of Rohatyn (see no. 66)

A number of potsherds typical of the Globular Amphora culture were found in barrow-graves I and V (Fig. 12:3, 9).

552. *Koszyłowce* district of Zaleszczyki (see no. 501).

A few sherds of Kuyavian amphorae, decorated with triangles executed in fish-scale patterns, found in the Tripolyan settlement. A similarly decorated sherd came from the rim of a large bowl, *c.* 24cm in diameter, provided with a wide lug horizontally perforated[149] (Fig. 21:3).

553 *Lučin* district of Rogačev (Homel)

Potsherds from site 'Zavalye' of Corded Ware.[150]

554. *Nevir* district of Kamień Koszyrski

Potsherds from a site of Corded Ware.[151]

[133] Mătăsa, loc. cit., note 128.

[134] Ibid.

[135] Ibid.

[136] S. Marinescu-Bîlcu, *SCIV*, vol. XIII–1, 1962, pp. 91 ff., Fig. 1.

[137] If not stated otherwise, the sites quoted here were described by A. Prox, *Die Schneckenbergkultur*, Kronstadt 1941, pp. 70 ff.

[138] *Istoria Romîniei*, vol. I, Bucureşti 1960, p. 78.

[139] J. Nestor, 'Der Stand der Vorgeschichtsforschung in Rumänien', *22 Bericht d. röm.-germ. Kommission*, Frankfurt a/M. 1933, p. 70.

[140] Loc. cit., note 138.

[141] K. Horedt, 'Șantierul arheologic Moreşti', *SCIV*, vol. VI, 1955, p. 658, Figs. 10, 16.

[142] Неделчо Петков, Едно символично погребение при с. Пеклюк, Археология-Sofia, vol. III–4, 1961, pp. 67 ff., Figs. 1–3.

[143] С. С. Березанська, Археологія-Kiev, vol. XII, 1961, p. 105, Fig. 2:3.

[144] Е. Ю. Кричевський, Трипільська культура, vol. I, Kiev 1940, pp. 401 ff., Figs. 86, 98.

[145] И. И. Артеменко, Ксиимк, no. 78, 1960, p. 38, Fig. 10:12, 17.

[146] At the Museum of Dniepropetrovsk before the war.

[147] Г. Г. Мезенцева, Археологiчнi розвiдки на територiї канiвського заповiдника в 1957 р. Матерiали до вивчення iсторiї та природи району канiвського заповедника, Kiev 1962, pp. 17 ff., Fig. 1:e, є.

[148] Kowalczyk (op. cit., note 2), pp. 182, 191 ff.

[149] K. Hadaczek, 'La colonie industriel de Koszyłowce', *Album des fouilles*, Kraków 1914, Pl. VII:46. Kostrzewski (op. cit., note 14), p. 158.

[150] И. И. Артеменко, Ксиаан, no. 88, 1962, p. 72, Fig. 19:9.

[151] Ю. В. Кухаренко, Первобытные памятники Полесья, Археология СССР, Б. 1–18, Moscow 1962, Pl. VI:6.

555. *Nowyj Dwir* district of Równe (see no. 658)

A large number of flint implements and potsherds, mainly typical of Corded Ware, were presented to the Prehistoric Institute of the University of Vienna in 1942.[152] Several potsherds of this collection were typical of the Globular Amphora culture and some had the characteristic fish-scale ornament. All these objects were found on the surface of a dry elevation in a swampy area (*Sumpfinsel*) between Nowyj Dwir and Kwasiłów.

556. *Seredni Stog*, Dnieper Rapids region

Potsherds typical of the Globular Amphora found in the upper layer (Seredni Stog II) of the standard site.[153]

557. *Solonoe* district of Zhlobin (Homel)

Potsherds typical of the Globular Amphora culture found in the Corded Ware site.[154]

558. *Staryj Mylsk* district of Zdołbunów (see no. 663)

In 1942 a collection of potsherds was given to the Prehistoric Institute of the University of Vienna[155] with a remark that they originated from a settlement (*ein geschlossener Siedlungsfund*). Potsherds typical of the Funnel Beaker culture (Fig. 20:4, 5), Corded Ware and of the Globular Amphora culture (Fig. 21:6) are included in this series.

559. *Strzyżów* district of Hrubieszów (see no. 395)

Potsherds typical of the Globular Amphora culture found in several pits of the settlement of the Strzyżów culture.[156]

560. *Terebin* district of Pińsk

Potsherds found on site of the Corded Ware.[157]

Addendum: 599. *Tuta Dmitrovskaya* district of Kanev

A small chisel square in section, made of 'milky' variety of flint, typical of the Globular Amphora culture. Historical Museum, Kiev, no. 2-119 (Fig. 25:8).

561. *Veleniči* district of Dawidgródek

Potsherds found on site of the Corded Ware.[158]

562. *Voytsekhivka* near Miropil (see nos. 236 and 460)

Potsherds typical of the Globular Amphora culture were found on the ancient surface under the Bronze Age barrow-graves nos. 8 and 15.[159]

563. *Zaborol* district of Równe (see nos. 166, 732)

Pottery typical of the Globular Amphora culture was found.[160]

In addition:

564. *Łosiatyn* near Bila Tserkov (see no. 250)

A globular amphora found in the barrow-grave of the Middle Dnieper culture (Plate 14:12).

(b) *Decorative Patterns on Pottery of other Cultures*

Addendum: 597. *Kalenske* on the Mostva

Incised zigzag decorative patterns of at least one vessel found in the middle layer were characteristic of the Globular Amphora culture.[161]

565. *Khalepye* near Kiev

Large vessels of the Tripolye culture.[162]

566. *Kolomiščyna* near Kiev

Vessels of the Tripolye culture.[163]

567. *Narodyči* (*Piščane*) (see no. 229)

Pottery of the Bronze Age barrow-graves of Cemetery I[164] (Fig. 33:B).

(c) *Slab-cists in Neolithic and Bronze Age Barrow-graves*[165]

568. *Beremiany* district of Buczacz (see no. 96)
569. *Belozerka* district of Kherson (see no. 307). Barrow-grave 9, secondary burial
570. *Capowce* district of Zaleszczyki (see no. 98)
571. *Domnitsa* district of Balta[166]
572. *Falievka* district of Kherson. Barrow 'Bliznitsa' (see no. 308)
573. *Hrubieszów* (see no. 121)
574. *Kherson* (see no. 312)
575. *Kovalivka* district of Kherson (see no. 345). 'Popova Mohyla', in a stone ring, 'cromlech'
576. *Krivoy Rog* (see no. 316). Barrow-grave 'Tzareva Mohila' in a stone ring, 'cromlech'
577. *Kuźmińczyk*, district of Proskurov (see no. 201). Barrow-grave II
578. *Marianske* district of Apostolovo (see no. 318). Grave 8 in Barrow 5
579. *Radzimin* district of Ostróg (see no. 155). Barrow-grave I-1878
580. *Raiki* near Berdychev (Late Bronze Age) (see no. 232)
581. *Slobodka-Romanovka-Odessa* in a double stone circle (see no. 361)

[152] Nos. 24070–102.
[153] Т. Г. Мовша, Сов. Арх., vol. 2, 1961, p. 194, Figs. 7:3, 4.
[154] И. И. Артеменко, Ксиаан, no. 84, 1961, p. 68, Figs. 20:22, 24.
[155] Nos. 24048–59.
[156] J. Głosik, 'Ślady osadnictwa kultury amfor kulistych w Strzyżowie nad Bugiem', *W.A.*, vol. XXVIII, 1962, pp. 133 ff.
[157] Op. cit., note 151, Pl. IV:2, V:6.
[158] Ibid., Pl. V:7.
[159] The relative material is in the collection of the Archaeological Institute of the Ukrainian Academy in Kiev.
[160] J. Głosik, 'Osada kultury ceramiki sznurowej w Strzyżowie, pow. Hrubieszów, *Mat. St.*, vol. VII, 1961, p. 157, note 48.
[161] І. Ф. Левицький, Дослідження стоянки на торфовищі Мостква в 1948 р., Арх. Пам., vol. IV, 1952, Fig. 2:2.
[162] At the Historical Museum, Kiev.
[163] Пассек (op. cit., note 63), p. 143, Fig. 76:3, 6.
[164] І. Левицький, Стація в ур. Піщаному біля Народич, Антропологія, vol. IV, Kiev 1931, pp. 214 (note 3), 230, Fig. 38:6, 7.
[165] Barrow-graves quoted here were described, or cited, in the relevant Chapters, and the numbers refer to their respective numbers there.
[166] Е. Сицинский, Археологическая карта подольской губ., p. 262.

582. *Šabalat* near Akkerman. Barrow-grave II (see no. 363)

583. *Tokarivka* district of Lityn (see no. 218)

584. *Unter-Horodnik* (*Horodnicul-de-Jos*) district of Rădăuti, Bucovina[167]

585. *Usatovo* near Odessa, Several barrow-graves (see no. 366)

586. *Zaścianka* district of Tarnopol (see no. 221)

587. *Zawadyńce* district of Kamenets Podolskii (see no. 222)

(d) *Slab-cist Graves of the Dnieper Rapids Region*

588. *Fedorivka*

In site 'Kruhlyk' a slab-cist was uncovered in 1946 under a 'stone cover'. It contained a contracted skeleton near which was a vessel typical of the Late Bronze Age.[168]

589. *Haduyča Balka*

Stone slab-cists were uncovered under a 'stone cover'.[169]

590. *Kičkas*

Two slab-cists contained contracted skeletons; near one of these was a spherical vessel and animal bones.[170]

591. *Osokorivska Balka* near Fedorivka

Slab-cist graves were found surrounded by a stone circle; in each a clay vessel was found. A leaf-shaped bronze arrow-head, a bracelet made of bronze wire and stone battle-axes ('perforated axes') were also found there.[171]

[167] *Jahrbuch d. Zentral-Kommission*, vol. I, Wien 1903, pp. 97 ff.

[168] А. В. Добровольський, Матеріали до археологичної карту дніпровського Надпоріжжя в межах запорізкої області, Археологія-Kiev vol. VII, 1952, p. 84.

[169] Ibid.

[170] Ibid., p. 85.

[171] Ibid., p. 84.

SECTION VI

Supplementary Lists of Sites

1. LIST OF ADDENDA

Sites with additional numbers will be found as follows:

592. p. 176, between nos. 211 and 212
593. p. 192, between nos. 406 and 407
594. p. 202, between nos. 507 and 508
595. p. 206, between nos. 550 and 551
596. p. 189, between nos. 365 and 366
597. p. 207, between nos. 564 and 565
598. p. 206, between nos. 551 and 552
599. p. 207, between nos. 560 and 561
601–45. pp. 157–62, Section III:1(b), (c), between nos. 137 and 138
646–69. pp. 169–71, Section III:2(c), between nos. 191 and 192
670. p. 183, Section IV:2(a), between nos. 237 and 238
671–3. p. 183, as above, between nos. 238 and 239.
674. p. 183, as above, between nos. 241 and 242
675. p. 183, as above, between nos. 245 and 246
676. p. 183, as above, between nos. 249 and 250
677. p. 183, as above, between nos. 250 and 251
678–9. p. 185, as above, between nos. 270 and 271

2. FLINT WORKSHOPS[1]

681. *Berek* district of Dubno
682. *Bodaki* district of Krzemieniec
683. *Borki* district of Krzemieniec (see no. 169)
684. *Borsuny* near Korosten[2]
685. *Buderaż* district of Zdołbunów
686. *Buszcza* district of Dubno
687. *Gaje Lewiatyńskie* district of Krzemieniec[3]
688. *Gurbiński Majdan* district of Dubno[4]
689. *Iserna* district of Krzemieniec
690. *Kuty Matwiejowce* district of Krzemieniec
691. *Listwin* district of Dubno
692. *Lisznia* district of Krzemieniec
693. *Ludwiszcze* district of Krzemieniec
694. *Lutka* district of Kowel
695. *Łozy* district of Krzemieniec
696. *Majdan* district of Dubno

697. *Mała Moszczanica* district of Dubno[5]

Traces of large workshops were found here. They specialized in various flint implements, the raw material being available from local natural outcrops of flint. Serpentine battle-axes were also manufactured there as is indicated by a large number of cones from perforated stone implements; serpentine rocks were found on the Goryn and the Sluch in the neighbourhood of the village.

698. *Mirohoszcza* district of Dubno
699. *Mukosiew* district of Dubno[6]
700. *Narajów* district of Dubno
701. *Niesłuchów* district of Kamionka Strumiłowa[7]

702. *Novostav* district of Velyke Dederkaly[8]

A workshop in which 'epipalaeolithic and neolithic' flints were found, but no pottery was recorded.

703. *Ostriv Varkovetski* district of Dubno[9]

A large flint workshop specializing in oval axes. Large flint blades, up to 10cm long, were also found. Pottery associated with this workshop was typical of the Bronze Age.

704. *Ostrów Kniahyń* district of Dubno
705. *Piwcze* district of Zdołbunów

706. *Połowla* district of Sarny[10]

A workshop specializing in knives and axes. Flint was mined in deep shafts which reached copious deposits of raw material.

707. *Przewodów* district of Sokal[11]

[1] Unless stated otherwise, the sites were recorded by A. Cynkałowski, *Materiały do pradziejów Wołynia i Polesia wołyńskiego*, Warszawa 1961.

[2] В. Данилевич, Археологічна минувшина Київщини, Kiev 1925, p. 28.

[3] J. Bryk, *Kultury epoki kamiennej na wydmach zachodniej części południowego Wołynia*, Lwów 1928.

[4] В. Б. Антонович, О каменном веке в западной Волыни, Труди XI археологическаго сьезда, 1899, Moscow 1901, vol. I, p. 142.

[5] A. Pawłowski, 'Wykopaliska moszczanickie', *Światowit*, vol. XVI, Warszawa 1934–5, pp. 175 ff.

[6] Антонович, loc. cit., note. 4.

[7] T. Sulimirski, 'Remarks Concerning the Distribution of Some Varieties of Flint in Poland', *Światowit*, vol. XXIII, Warszawa 1960, pp. 301 ff., n. 102.

[8] М. Я. Рудинський, Дубно-кременецька палеолітична експедиція, Арх. Пам., vol. IV, 1952, 144.

[9] Loc. cit.

[10] J. Fitzke, *ZOW*, vol. XII, 1937, pp. 81, 166.

[11] Sulimirski, loc. cit., note 7.

708. *Radzimin* district of Ostróg[12]

709. *Rudka* district of Dubno[13]

710. *Sapanów* district of Krzemieniec[14]

A huge mass of flint waste and unfinished or spoiled implements, sickles, knives, etc., lay on sand-dunes in the valley of the Ikwa. Implements were in various stages of completion and had apparently been rejected because of faulty execution. Smaller workshops in this area specialized in making of one type of implement or weapon only. M. Ia. Rudynskii[15] was able to distinguish at least two workshops specializing in 'crooked knives' (daggers). Many potsherds of various types of pottery were found, mainly typical of the Late Bronze Age and Wysocko culture, some proper to the Trzciniec culture.

711. *Stożek* district of Krzemieniec

712. *Stupno* district of Dubno

713. *Symonów* district of Ostróg[16]

714. *Tylawka* district of Krzemieniec

715. *Wielka Moszczanica* district of Dubno

716. *Wysock* district of Równe

717. *Zbranki* near Ovruch[17]

A workshop, the products of which were evidently for distribution over wider areas. The character of the implements found exhibits many archaic features. The pottery was very poor and found in very small quantity. Its decoration includes incised geometric patterns, pits, comb-stamp, straight and wavy lines, while raised bands were also a common feature.

718. *Żelechów* district of Kamionka Strumiłowa[18]

A very large number of sites on the sand-dunes were recorded in this part of the country where many implements, axes, daggers, sickles, arrow-heads, blades, knife-blades, scrapers, etc., were found and often also potsherds. The latter were mostly typical of the Middle Bronze Age (Trzciniec culture) or of the Late Bronze Age and early Iron Age (Wysocko culture), but Corded Ware potsherds were also found at least in some of these.

719. *Zielenica* district of Sarny

720. *Złoczów* environments of the town[19]

721. *Żołobki* district of Krzemieniec

3. FLINT HOARDS

722. *Beleluja* district of Śniatyn[20]

A hoard consisting of 23 blades 12–18cm long.

723. *Gamarna* near Kiev[21]

A hoard consisting of flint axes, arrow-heads and hammers was found in a large clay vessel in 1870.

724. *Ilkowce* district of Sokal[22]

A hoard consisting of about a dozen long blades, 13–19cm long, 2–3·5cm wide.

725. *Khomut* district of Dubno[23]

A hoard consisting of about forty 'sickles' found in a vessel of the 'Zaborol and Gródek' type.

726. *Kyslytske* district of Tomashpil (Vinnitsa)

A hoard of thirty-four axes and chisels made of greyish-white flint.[24] Axes and chisels were typical of the Globular Amphora culture.

727. *Ludyn* district of Włodzimierz Wołyński[25]

A hoard consisting of a large number of long blades of total weight of 32kg.

728. *Ostrów* district of Dubno[26]

A hoard consisting of a few larger and many smaller flint implements.

729. *Shistov* district of Włodzimierz Wołyński[27]

A hoard consisting of forty-six blades 20–21·5cm long.

730. *Świtarzów* district of Sokal[28]

A hoard consisting of a large number of long blades.

731. *Trembowla*

A hoard consisting of a few hundred long blades.[29]

732. *Zaborol* district of Równe[30] (see nos. 166, 563)

A hoard consisting of five 'sickle' knives.

4. STRAY LATE COPPER AND EARLY BRONZE OBJECTS AND HOARDS

733. *Adjask* near Odessa

A copper hoard consisting of nineteen flat axes, one shaft-

[12] Loc. cit., note 4.
[13] Loc. cit.
[14] Bryk, loc. cit., note 3. Id., *ZOW*, vol. XI, 1936, p. 93.
[15] Loc. cit., note 8.
[16] Loc. cit., note 4.
[17] Loc. cit., note 2.
[18] B. Janusz, *Zabytki przedhistoryczne Galicyi Wschodniej*, Lwów 1918, pp. 82 ff., 158 ff., 206 f., 278 f., 292 f. Bryk (op. cit., note 3), pp. 51 ff.
[19] Sulimirski, loc. cit., note 7. Janusz, loc. cit., note 18.
[20] J. Kostrzewski, 'Neolithische Depotfunde aus Polen und Litauen', *Prähistorische Zft*, vol. X, Berlin 1918, pp. 157 ff. T. Sulimirski, *Polska przedhistoryczna*, part II, London 1957–9, p. 313.
[21] A. M. Tallgren, 'La Pontide préscythique', *ESA*, vol. II, 1926, p. 42, n. 3. A. A. Формозов, Клады каменных орудий на территории СССР, *Arch.R.*, vol. X, 1958, p. 638, Fig. 245.
[22] Kostrzewski, loc. cit., note 20.
[23] Information very kindly given by Mr I. K. Svešnikov, Lviv, in his letter of 17 October 1961.
[24] M. Л. Макаревич, Клад крем'яних сокир. Археологія, vol. XVI, Kiev 1964, pp. 208 ff.
[25] О. Цинкаловський, Матеріяли до археології володимирського повіту, Записки наук. тов. ім. Шевченка, vol. CLIV, Lviv 1939, pp. 237 f.
[26] J. Głosik, 'Wołyńsko-podolskie materiały z epoki kamiennej i wczesnej epoki brązu w Państwowym Muzeum Archeologicznym w Warszawie', *Mat.St.*, vol. VIII, 1962, p. 160.
[27] Формозов (op. cit., note 21), pp. 643 f.
[28] Kostrzewski loc. cit., note 20.
[29] Loc. cit., Sulimirski (op. cit., note 20), p. 313.
[30] Głosik (op. cit., note 26), p. 172.

hole axe, and a massive chisel,[31] dating from the beginning of the second millennium B.C.

734. *Bussówno* district of Chełm

A flat copper axe, 12·8cm long, found in a peat-bog.[32]

735. *Bystryk* near Berdychev[33] (see no. 747)

A massive shaft-hole axe 13cm long and a flat axe 6cm long, both probably of copper, found in 1932; before the last war in the museum at Berdychev.

736. *Chilczyce* district of Złoczów

A small bronze axe with low flanges found on a sand-dune.[34] (Fig. 19:16).

737. *Chłopy* district of Rudki

In 1886 a pair of bronze ear-pendants or temple ornaments with one wide flattened end, of Stubło type, were found in a peat-bog. They were at the Lubomirski Museum in Lwów before the last war.[35] (Fig. 19:10).

738. *Hanna* district of Włodawa

A copper shaft-hole axe found on a field.[36]

739. *Kamenets Podolskii*

A stone mould for casting shaft-hole axes was found here.[37]

740. *Mamajestie* near Černivtsi, Bucovina

A bronze axe with low flanges 8cm long, at the Natur-Historisches Museum, Vienna, no. 36866.

741. *Mikhailovka* near Dnepropetrovsk

Four shaft-hole axes of the Caucasian 'Privolnoye' type were found here.[38]

742. *Munina* district of Jarosław

A small copper shaft-hole axe, 9·7cm long, was found here in 1951.[39]

743. *Pistyń* district of Kosów

A shaft-hole axe of copper, 14·5cm long, was found here.[40]

744. *Severynivtsi* near Kamenetz Podolskii

A small copper (or bronze) axe, 5·4cm long, with very low flanges, similar to that from Mamajestie, was in the museum at Kamenetz Podolskii before the last war (no. 231).

745. *Stubło* district of Dubno

A bronze hoard was found in 1927.[41] It consisted of two shaft-hole axes, two arm-bands made of thin bronze sheet, a thin pendant made of flat sheet, seven bracelets, ten ear-pendants with one end widened (of 'Stubło' type).

5. SETTLEMENTS OF THE GORODSK TYPE (Maps VI and VII)

(a) *Within the original territory in East Volhynia*

746. *Bystryk* near Berdychev (see no. 735)

Pottery and other remains in the museum at Berdychev before the last war.

747. *Bilylivka* (Belilovka) near Berdychev[42] (see no. 238)
748. *Gorodsk* (Horodsk) on the Teterev, district of Kostyshev[43] (see no. 548)
749. *Kolodiazhne* district of Polonnoe[44] (see no. 453)
750. *Nova Čortoriya* district of Lubar[45]
751. *Pavoloč* district of Popilnyany[46]
752. *Rayki* near Berdychev[47]
753. *Sandraki* district of Khmilnyk[48]
754. *Troyaniv* district of Zhitomir[49]
755. *Voytsekhivka* district of Polonnoe[50] (see no. 460)
756. *Yahnyatyn* near Berdychev[51]

(b) *In the central part of Podolia and further South*

757. *Horodiştea* on the Pruth, Moldavia[52]

[31] Tallgren (op. cit., note 21), p. 162. А. А. Иессен, Греческая колонизация северного Причерноморья, Leningrad 1947, p. 23.

[32] S. Nosek, 'Znaleziska z wczesnej epoki brązu na Lubelszczyźnie, *Spr. PMA*, vol. 4, 1952, pp. 93 f., Fig. 6. Id., 'Materiały do badań nad historią starożytną i wczesnośredniowieczną międzyrzecza Wisły i Bugu.' *AUMCS*, vol. VI F, 1951 (1957), p. 256, Pl. XX:7.

[33] T. Sulimirski, 'Copper Hoard from Horodnica on the Dniester'; *Mitteilungen d.Anthropologischen Ges.*, Wien, vol. XCI, 1961, p. 94.

[34] L. Kozłowski, *Wczesna, starsza i środkowa epoka bronzu w Polsce*, Lwów 1928, p. 37.

[35] W. Antoniewicz, 'Der in Stubło in Wolhynien aufgefundene Bronze-schatz', *ESA*, vol. IV, 1929, p. 140 L. Kozłowski, *Zarys pradziejów Polski południowo-wschodniej*, Lwów 1939, Pl XIII:5. Sulimirski (op. cit., note 20), p. 239, fig. 56.

[36] Nosek (op. cit., note 32, 1952), p. 93, and (1957), pp. 257 f., Pl. XX:2. J. Kostrzewski, 'Skarby i luźne znaleziska metalowe od eneolitu do wczesnego okresu żelaza', *Prz.A.*, vol. XV, 1964, p. 34, Pl. IX:8.

[37] Tallgren, loc. cit., note 21.

[38] Иессен (op. cit., note 31), p. 23.

[39] A. Żaki, 'Toporki miedziane na północnych stokach Karpat', *Acta AC*, vol. II:1–2, 1961, pp. 89 f., Fig. 1:b. Kostrzewski (op. cit., note 36), p. 51, Fig. 53.

[40] Żaki (op. cit., note 39), p. 90. Fig. 1:c.

[41] Antoniewicz, loc. cit., note 35.

[42] Т. С. Пассек, Периодизация трипольских поселений, МИА, no. 10, 1949, p. 171.

[43] Ibid., pp. 157 ff.

[44] Ibid., pp. 171 ff.

[45] Ю. М. Захарук, Пізньотрипільське поселення у верхів'ях р. Случі, Арх. Пам., vol. VI, 1956, pp. 130 ff.

[46] М. Л. Макаревич, Трипільське поселення біля с. Паволочі, Арх. Пам., vol. IV, 1952, pp. 96 ff.

[47] Пассек (op. cit., note 42), pp. 168 ff.

[48] О. Ф. Лагодовська, Пізньотрипілське поселення у с. Сандраках, Арх. Пам., vol. VI, 1956, pp. 118 ff. Id., Поселення часу пізньої бронзи в с. Сандраки, Арх. Пам., vol. IX, 1960, pp. 133 ff.

[49] М. М. Шмаглій, Кераміка поселень городського типу, Археологія, vol. XIII, Kiev 1961, pp. 22 ff.

[50] Е. Ф. Лагодовская, Войцеховское позднетрипольское поселение, Ксиак, no. 3, 1954, pp. 86 ff.

[51] Пасеек (op. cit., note 42), pp. 160 ff. М. М. Шмаглій (op. cit., note 49), pp. 25 ff.

[52] H. Dumitrescu, 'La station préhistorique de Horodiştea sur le Pruth', *Dacia*, vols. IX–X, 1944, pp. 127 ff.

758. *Kasperowce* district of Zaleszczyki

Many characteristic cord-decorated potsherds at the Natur-Historisches Museum, Vienna (nos. 49848–51).

759. *Koszyłowce-Tovdry* district of Zaleszczyki[53]

760. *Mitkov* district of Zastavna, Bucovina[54]

761. *Pečora* on the Boh near Vinnitsa[55]

762. *Tsviklovtsy* near Kamenets Podolskii[56]

763. *Zvenyačka* (Zvenyačin) on the Dniester, Bucovina[57]

6. LIST OF SITES PLOTTED ON MAP III

1. *Lublin Painted Pottery culture*

(a) *Westernmost sites*

Antopol (Puławy)
Czernięcin (Krasnystaw)
Jaszczów (Lublin)
Kamień (Puławy)
Łopatki (Puławy)
Siennica Różana (Krasnystaw)
Nałęczów (Puławy)
Trójnia (Lubartów)

(b) *Sites on the Middle Bug*

Ambuków (Uściuług)
Czerników (Włodzimierz Wołyński)
Czumów (Hrubieszów)
Gródek Nadbużny (Hrubieszów)
Kotorów (Hrubieszów)
Leżnica (Włodzimierz Wołyński)
Miedniki (Hrubieszów)
Ornatowice (Hrubieszów)
Piatydnia (Włodzimierz Wołyński)
Raciborowice (Hrubieszów)
Stepankowice (Hrubieszów)
Strzyżów (Hrubieszów)
Werbkowice (Hrubieszów)
Zimno (Włodzimierz Wołyński)
Żuków (Hrubieszów)

(c) *West Volhynian sites*

Antonówka (Łuck)
Buderaż (Zdołbunów)
Gródek (Horodok) (Łuck)
Gródek (Horodok) (Równe)
Hrydki (Kowel)
Jałowicze (Yaloviči) (Ostrożec)
Kostyanets (Dubno)
Lisznia (Krzemieniec)
Łuck
Nowomylsk (Zdołbunów)
Siedmiarki (Semaki) (Sienkiewicze)
Stary Mylsk (Zdołbunów)
Trostyanets (Dubno)
Ujście (Kostopol)
Walentynów (Łuck)

(d) *Southern sites*

Bolechowce (Drohobycz)
Kołokolin (Rohatyn)
Kukezov (Yaričiv)
Zvenyhorod (Bibrka)

2. *Masovian (Dnieper-Elbe) culture*

(a) *Lublin region*

Chlewiska (Lubartów)
Chodel (Lublin)
Łęczna (Lubartów)
Mierzwiączka (Puławy)
Piaski Luterskie (Lublin)
Włostowice (Puławy)

(b) *West Volhynia and Polesia*

Antonówka (Łuck)
Buyraz (Turov)
Chilczyce (Złoczów)
Dąbrowa (Sarny)
Dubrovka (Rokitno)
Gorodišče (Pinsk)
Ivančytsi (Zareče)
Khabarišče (Lubešov)
Khilčitsy (Turov)
Khotomel (David-Gorodok)
Klesów (Sarny)
Krymno (Kowel)
Kulczyn (Łuck)
Kuty (Krzemieniec)
Lelikowo (Kobryn)
Liblino (Stolin)
Lyakhoviči (Lubešov)
Mojnicze (Sarny)
Mulčitsy (Vladimerets)
Niewierz (Nevir) (Kamień Koszyrski)
Nobel (Zareče)
Ostrov (Pinsk)
Piatydni (Włodzimierz Wołyński)
Piszcza (Luboml)
Ryčevo (Pinsk)
Sleptsy (Turov)
Stanin (Kamionka Strumiłowa)
Starosiele (Łuck)
Terebin (Pinsk)
Tur (Kowel)
Turówka Stężarycka (Włodzimierz Wołyński)
Velemiči (Stolin)
Vetly (Lubešov)
Wólka Szczytyńska (Kamień Koszyrski)
Zakazanka (Brest)
Zawodnia (Równe)

(c) *East Volhynian sites*

Kalenske-Mostva (Korosten)
Khanev on the Teterev
Narodyči-Piščane
Rudnya Ozeryanska (Ovruch)
Yanivka on the Pripet junction

(d) *Region of Kiev*

Bortnyči
Čapayevka-Vita Litovska
Khotianivka
Levedievka
Mykilska Slobidka
Nizhnya Dubečna
Novosilki
Obolon
Pluti
Pohreby
Starosilya
Troyeščyna

3. *Tripolyan sites of periods* A *and* B-1

(a) *Western sites*

Babšin
Bernovo Luka
Braha
Černivtsi
Darabani
Fridrivtsi
Holihrady
Horodnica on the Dniester
Kadyivtsi

[53] В. П. Кравец, Изучение позднетрипольских памятников в верхнем Поднестровье, Ксиак, no. 4, 1955, pp. 133 ff.

[54] Т. С. Пассек, Раннеземледельческие (трипольские) племена Поднестровья, МИА, no. 84, 1961, p. 143.

[55] Е. К. Черныш, Многослойный памятник у с. Печоры на Южном Буге, Археологическй сборник Эрмитажа, no. 1, Leningrad, 1959, pp. 187 ff.

[56] Т. Г. Мовша, Новое позднетрипольское поселение Цвиковцы в среднем Поднестровье, Сов. Арх., vol. 1964–1, pp. 131 ff.

[57] Пассек (op. cit., note 54), p. 143.

Kelmentsy
Koroviya
Krutobrodintsy
Kudryntsi
Lenkivtsy
Luka Vrublivetska
Luka Ustyanska
Naslavča Luka
Nezvysko (Niezwiska)
Oknitsa
Ozaryntsi
Polivaniv Yar
Serafińce
Sokol
Stara Ušytsia
Stina
Vila Yaruzska
Voyevodčitsy

(b) *Sites of the Uman group*

Borysivka
Danylova Balka
Hunča
Kharpačka
Kolodiste
Krasnostavka
Mogilno
Plyskiv-Černyavka
Rakhny
Sabatynivka
Vyšnopil

(c) *Southern sites*

Alexandrivka
Cucuteni
Foltești
Holercani
Solonceni
Soroki
Zhury

4. *Sites of the Southern Bug (Boh) culture*

Bashkiv Ostriv
Gard
Hlynyšče
Kalamanzov
Ladyzhyn
Melnyča Kruča
Ostapkovtsy
Pečora
Raygorod
Samčyntsi
Savran
Ščurkovitsy
Skibentsy
Sokoltsy
Vorobievka
Zankivtsi

5. *Dnieper Rapids sites*

Durna Skela
Ihren (Igrin)
Mykilske (Nikolskoe)
Seredni Stog
Sobačky
Strelča Skela
Surskii Ostriv

6. *Eastern Flat cemeteries*

Mykhailivka
Osokorivka
Novoselitsa

Index of Sites and Geographic Names

Names in parenthesis mostly denote the district but often the region, or the river near which the site lay. Page numbers in italics denote listed sites.
Fig. – Figure; Pl. – Plate; Pn. – Plan; M. – Map

Index of Authors quoted

References to names cited in Russian characters will be found in the Russian Index following (see foot of page 223).

INDEX OF AUTHORS QUOTED

INDEX OF AUTHORS QUOTED

General Index

Page numbers in italics denote listed sites.

Maps, Plans and Figures

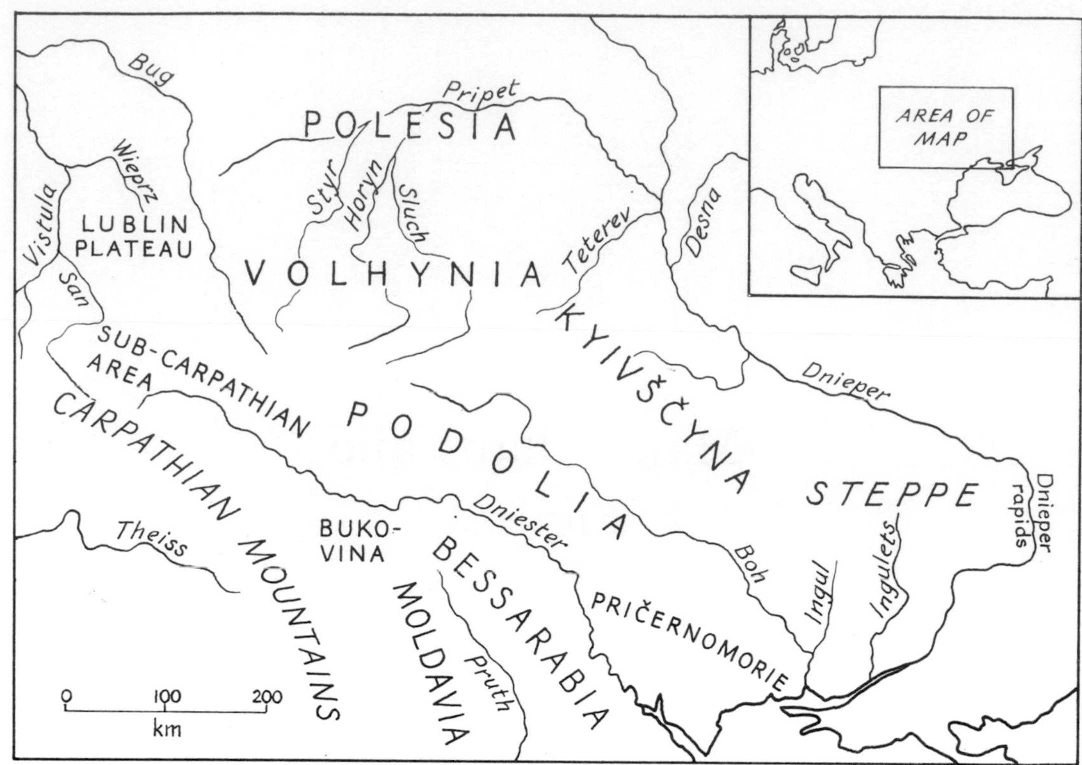

Map I. The extent of the territory dealt with in the work.
The position of the main geographical regions mentioned in the text is indicated.

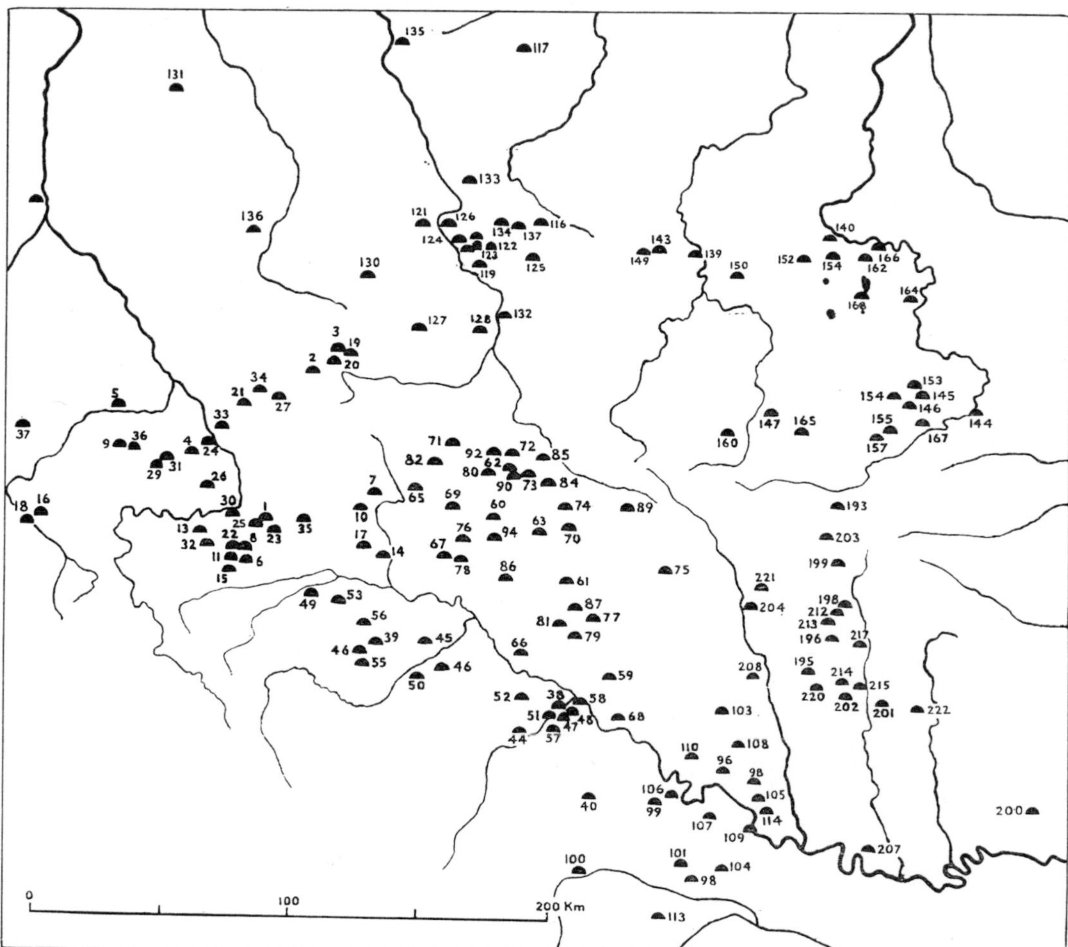

Map II. Diffusion of western barrow-graves of the Neolithic and Early Bronze Age (Sub-Carpathian culture and its related groups).
Numbers of sites correspond with those of the relative descriptions and reports in Part II of the volume.

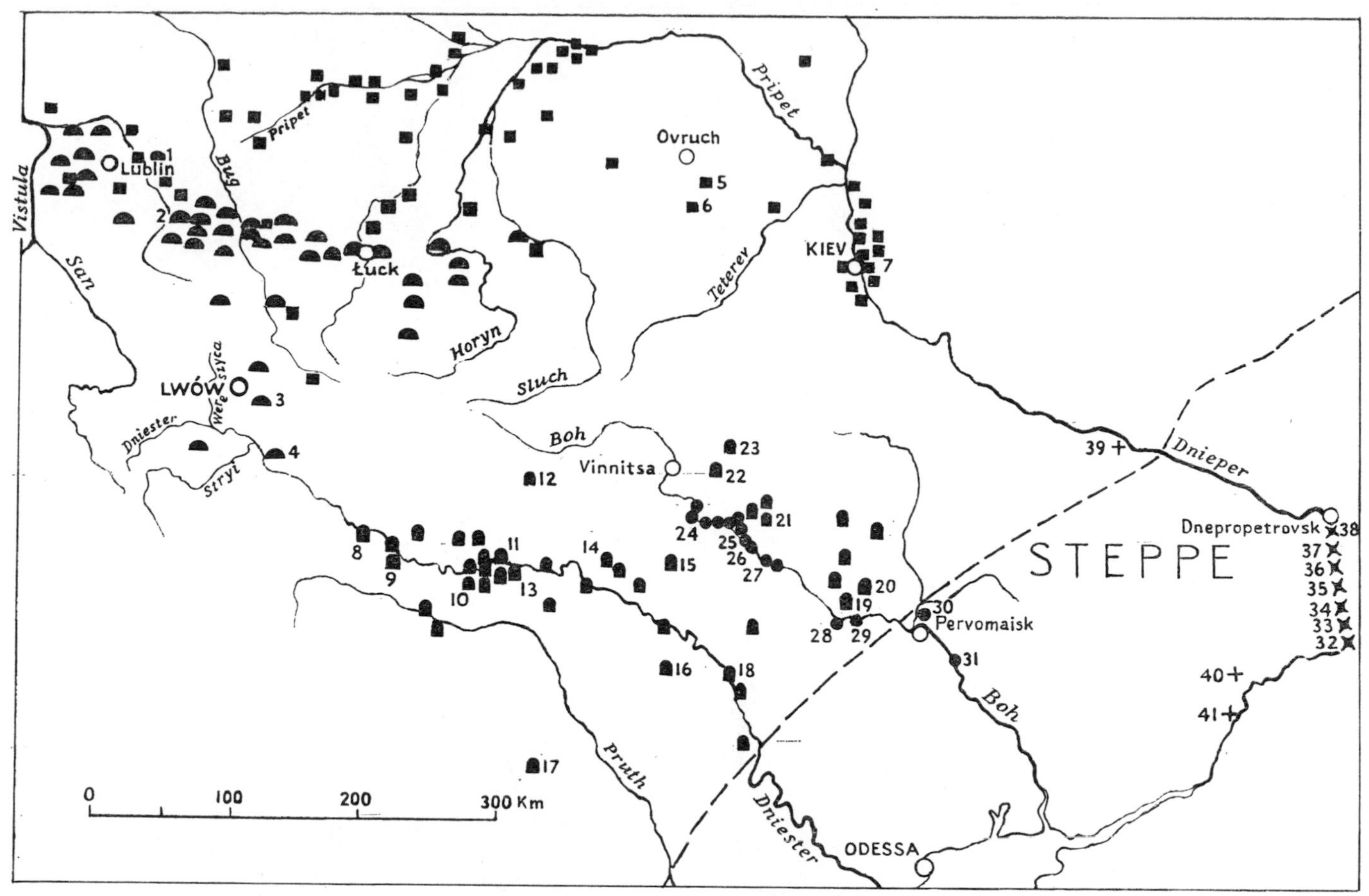

MAP III. Distribution of Neolithic cultures.

- Lublin Painted pottery culture.
- Masovian (Dnieper-Elbe) culture.
- Tripolyan sites of periods A & B-1.
- Southern Bug (Boh) culture.
- Sites of the Dnieper Rapids region.
- \+ Eastern flat cemeteries.

List of numbered sites is given below; for other sites see Part II, Section VI:6 (pp. 212 f.).

1. Jaszczów (Lublin)
2. Siennica Różana (Krasnystaw)
3. Zvenyhorod-Dźwinogród
4. Kołokolin (Rohatyn)
5. Narodyči-Piščane
6. Kalenske on the Mostva (Korosten)
7. Mykilska Slobidka (Kiev)
8. Nezvysko (Niezwiska) on the Dniester
9. Horodnica on the Dniester
10. Darabani, Bessarabia
11. Luka Vrublivetska (Kamenets Podolskii)
12. Krutobrodintsy
13. Polivaniv Yar
14. Ozaryntsi
15. Stina
16. Folteşti
17. Cucuteni (Moldavia)
18. Solonceni
19. Sabatynivka on the Boh
20. Danylova Balka
21. Rakhny
22. Borysivka
23. Plyskiv-Černyavka
24. Pečora
25. Sokoltsy
26. Samčyntsi
27. Skibentsy
28. Savran
29. Melnyča Kruča
30. Kalamanzov
31. Gard
32. Durna Skela
33. Seredni Stog
34. Sobačky
35. Mykilske (Nikolskoe)
36. Strelča Skela
37. Surskii Ostriv
38. Ihren (Igrin)
39. Novoselitsa
40. Osokorivka
41. Mykhailivka

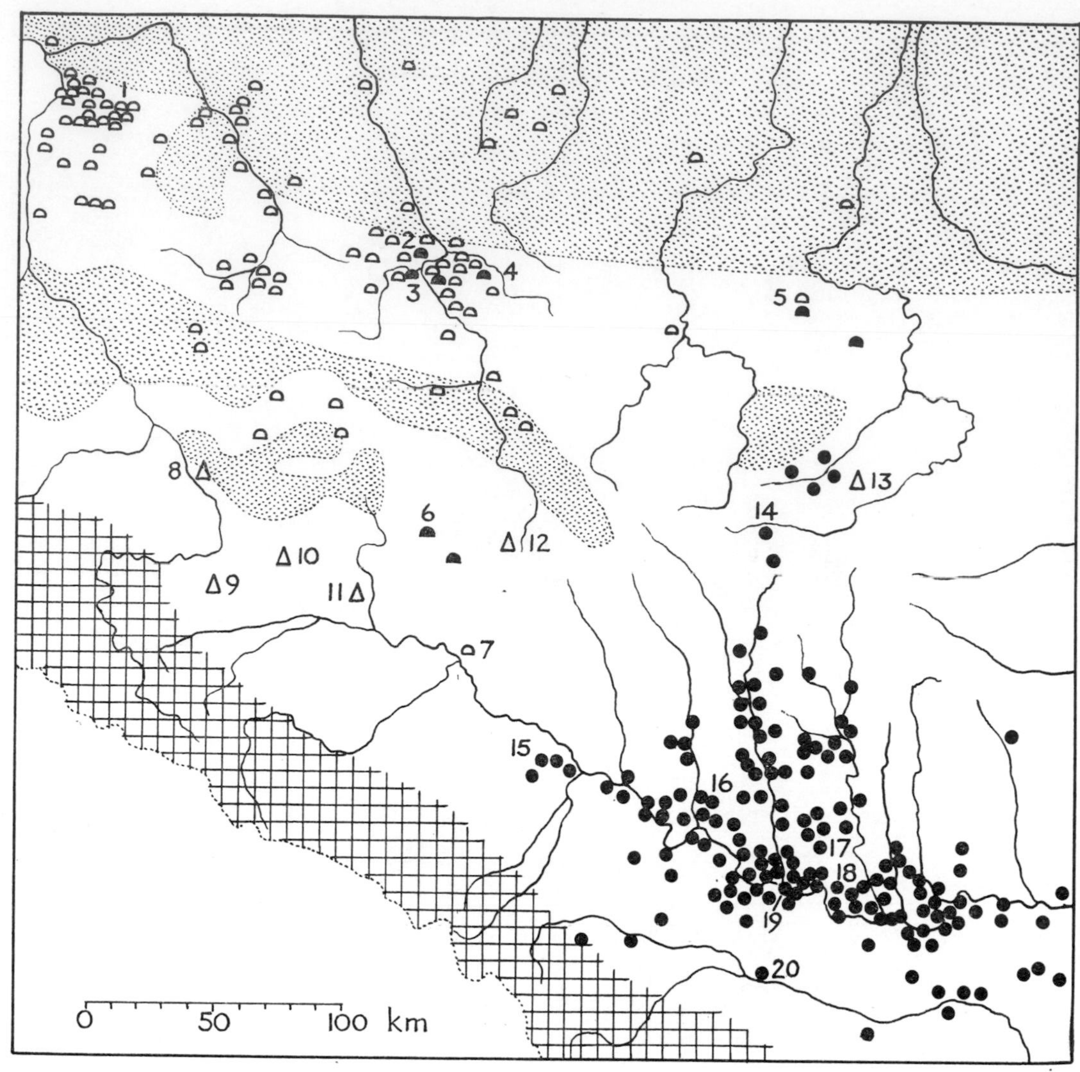

Map IV. Borderland of the Tripolye and Funnel Beaker cultures.

● Tripolyan settlements of periods B-2 and C (about 150 sites).

⌓ Sites of the Funnel Beaker culture (about 100 points).

⏺ Sites of the Funnel Beaker culture with Tripolyan pottery.

△ Sub-Carpathian barrow-graves, listed below, which yielded vessels or potsherds of the Funnel Beaker culture.

Dotted: sandy soils; *hatched:* Carpathian soils.

Selected sites of the Funnel Beaker culture:

1. Nałęczów (Puławy)
2. Strzyżów (Hrubieszów)
3. Gródek Nadbużny (Hrubieszów)
4. Zimno (Włodzimierz Wołynski)
5. Nowyj Dwir (Równe)
6. Grzybowice (Lwów)
7. Zalistsi (Bóbrka)

Barrow-graves with Funnel Beaker ware:

8. Sobiecin (no. 33)
9. Miżyniec (no. 22)
10. Stojańce (no. 35)
11. Koropuż (no. 17)
12. Nowosiółki Liskie (no. 73)
13. Siwki (no. 157)

Selected sites of the Tripolye culture:

14. Bodaki (Krzemieniec)
15. Komarów (Stanisławów)
16. Koszyłowce (Zaleszczyki)
17. Nowosiółka Kostiukowa (Zaleszczyki)
18. Bilcze Złote (Borszczów)
19. Zaleszczyki
20. Šypentsi

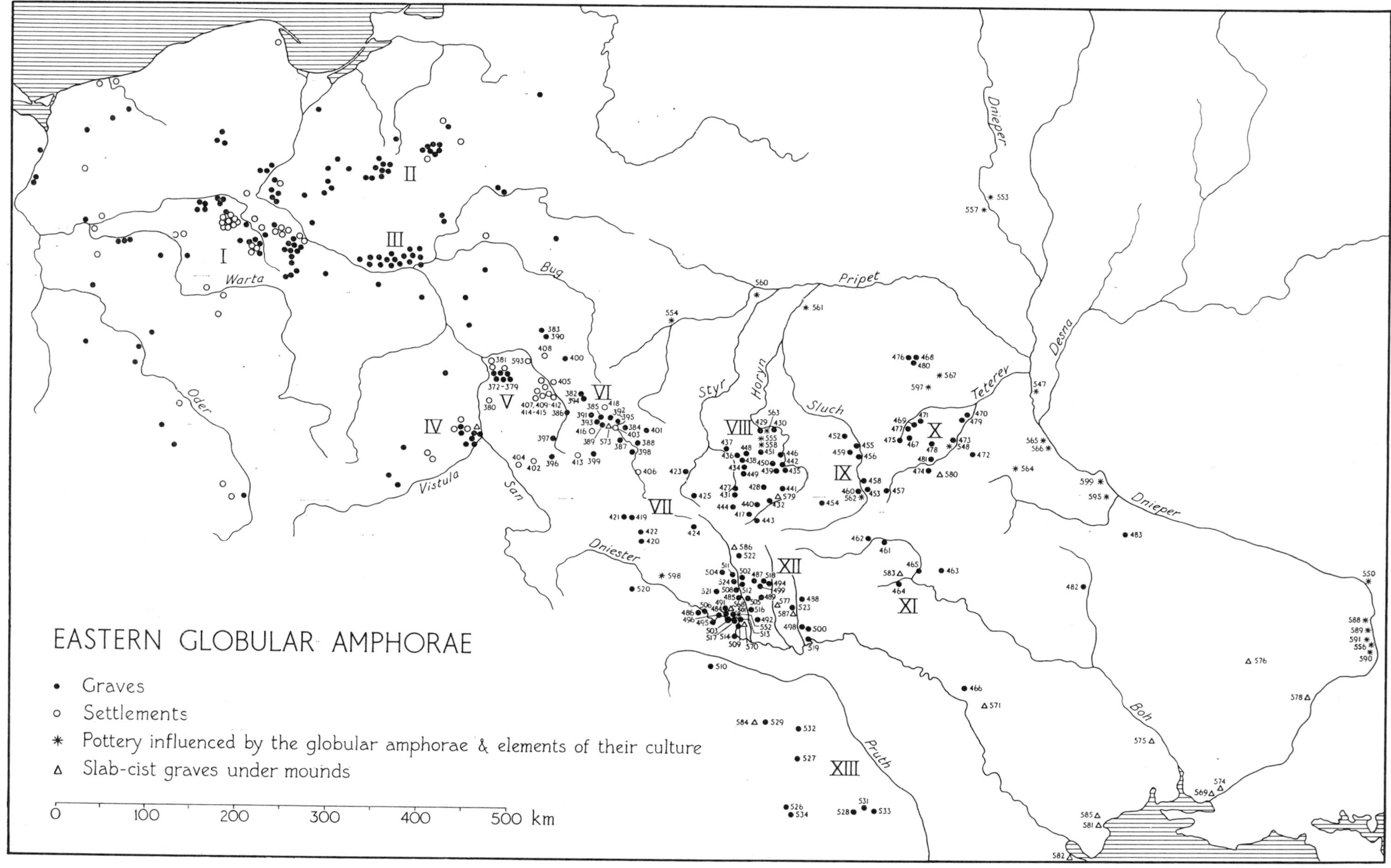

MAP V. Diffusion of graves and settlements of eastern Globular Amphora culture and of its elements in other cultures of the Territory, including slab-cists under mounds.

Numbers of sites correspond with those of the relative descriptions and reports in Part II of the volume.

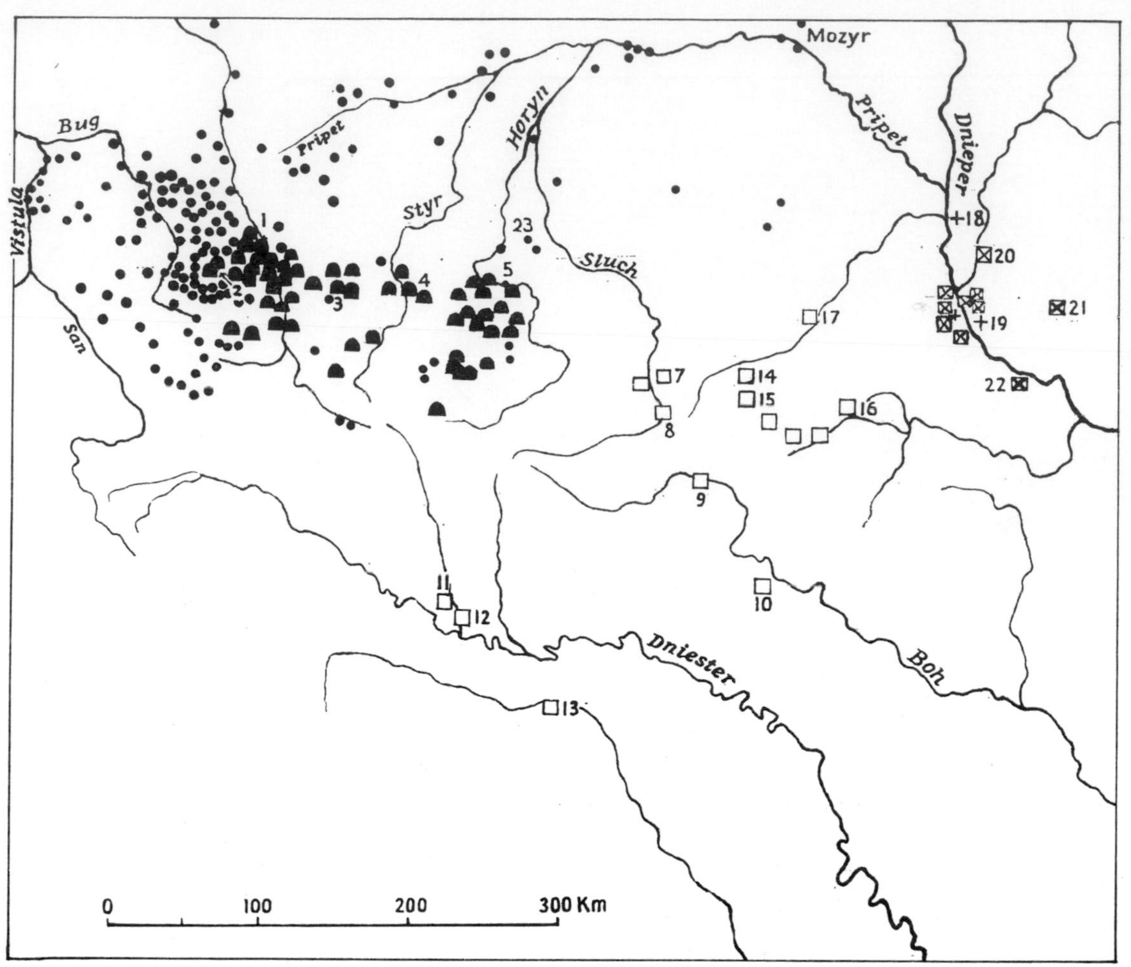

MAP VI. Distribution of various groups of Corded Ware.

- Strzyżów culture.
- □ Gorodsk culture.
- ⊠ + Settlements and graves of the Evminka-Sofiivka group.
- ● Sites of Corded Ware (about 150 points), chiefly on sandy soils or on sand-dunes.

Marked sites: 1, Raciborowice; 2, Skomorochy Małe; 3, Torczyn; 4, Stavok-Vyhadanka; 5, Gródek (Horodok) – Równe; 6, Zdolbitsa; 7, Kolodiazhne; 8, Nova Čortorya; 9, Sandraki; 10, Pečora; 11, Koszyłowce (Tovdry); 12, Kasperowce; 13, Horodiştea; 14, Troyaniv; 15, Rayki; 16, Pavoloč; 17, Gorodsk (Horodsk); 18, Černyn; 19, Sofiivka; 20, Evminka; 21, Lukaši; 22, Balyka; 23, Majdan Mokwiński.

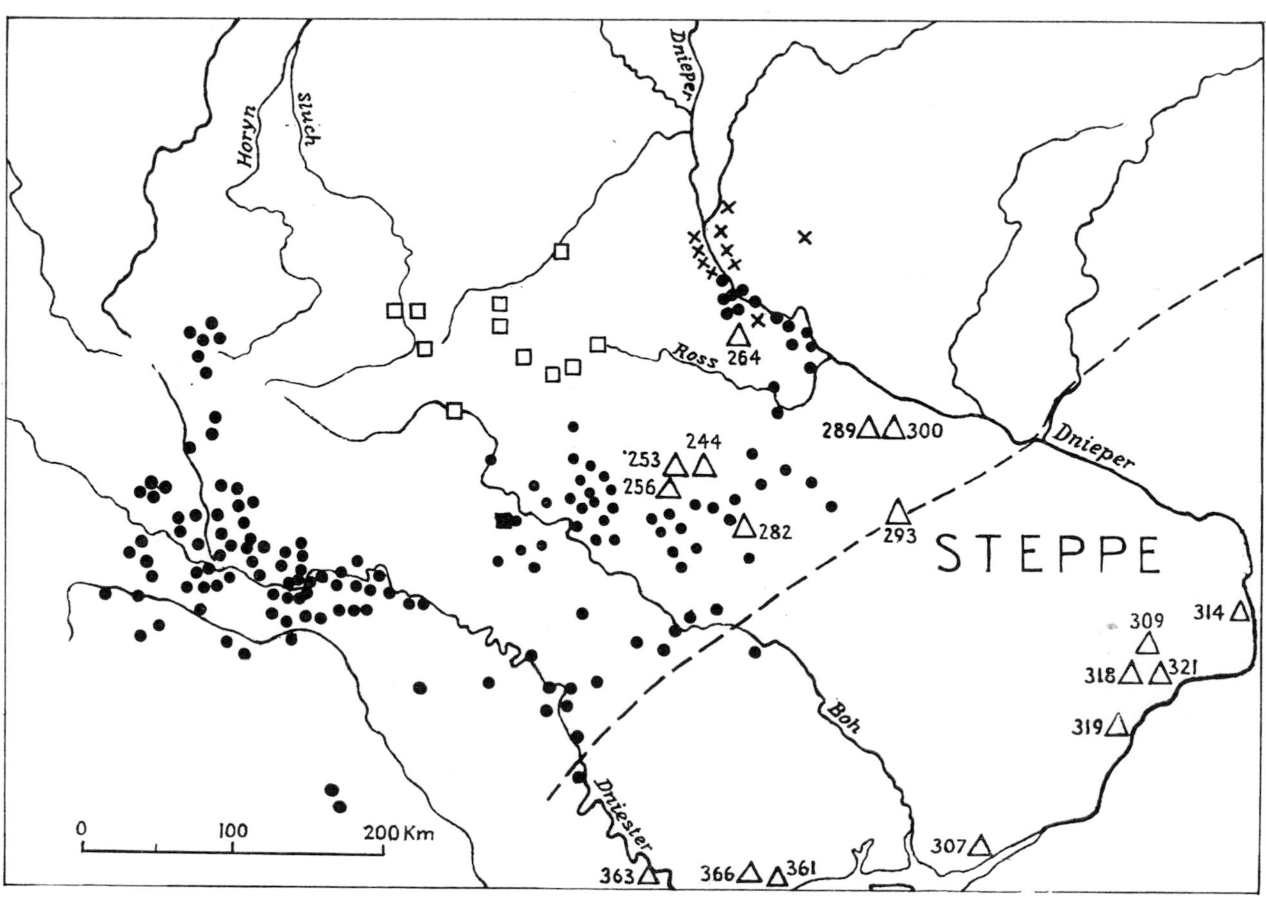

MAP VII. Geographical distribution of Tripolyan settlements of periods B-2 and C, and those of the Gorodsk and Evminka groups (see Map VI).

- ● Tripolyan sites.
- □ Settlements of Gorodsk type.
- × Settlements of Evminka type.
- △ Barrow-graves with 'Yamna' vessels with a pointed base (numbers of the latter correspond with those of the relative descriptions in Part II of the volume).

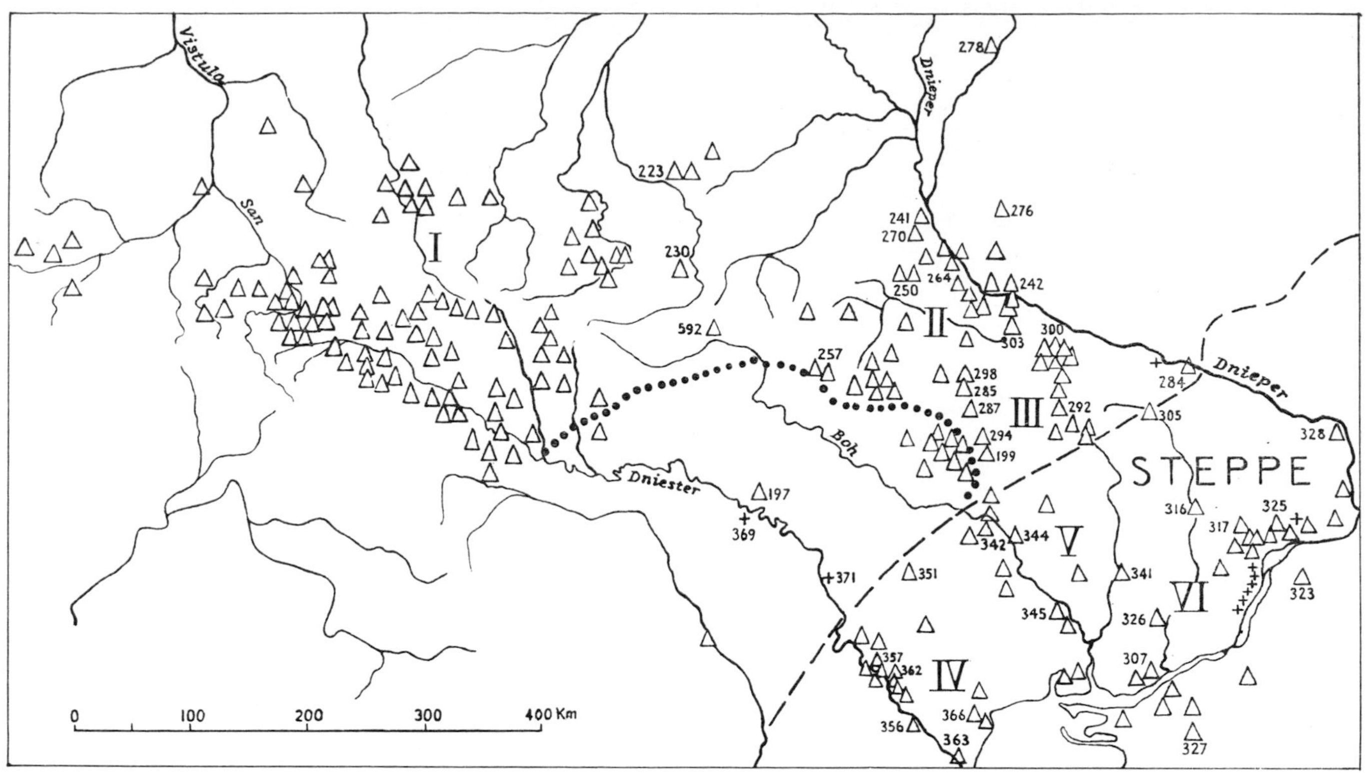

MAP VIII. Neolithic and Early Bronze Age barrow-graves within the Territory.

I–VI. Groups of barrow-graves (cultures) distinguished:
I. Western barrow-graves (see Map V).
II. The Middle Dnieper culture.
III. Cherkasi-Kirovograd-Uman group.
IV. Usatovo culture.
V. Western division of the steppe Ochre-Graves.
VI. Eastern Ochre-Graves (crosses denote 'flat' cemeteries).

Numbers of sites correspond with those of the relative descriptions in Part II of the volume; for western barrow-graves, see Map V.

Dotted line marks the northern reach of Tripolyan settlements of periods A and B-I (see Map III).

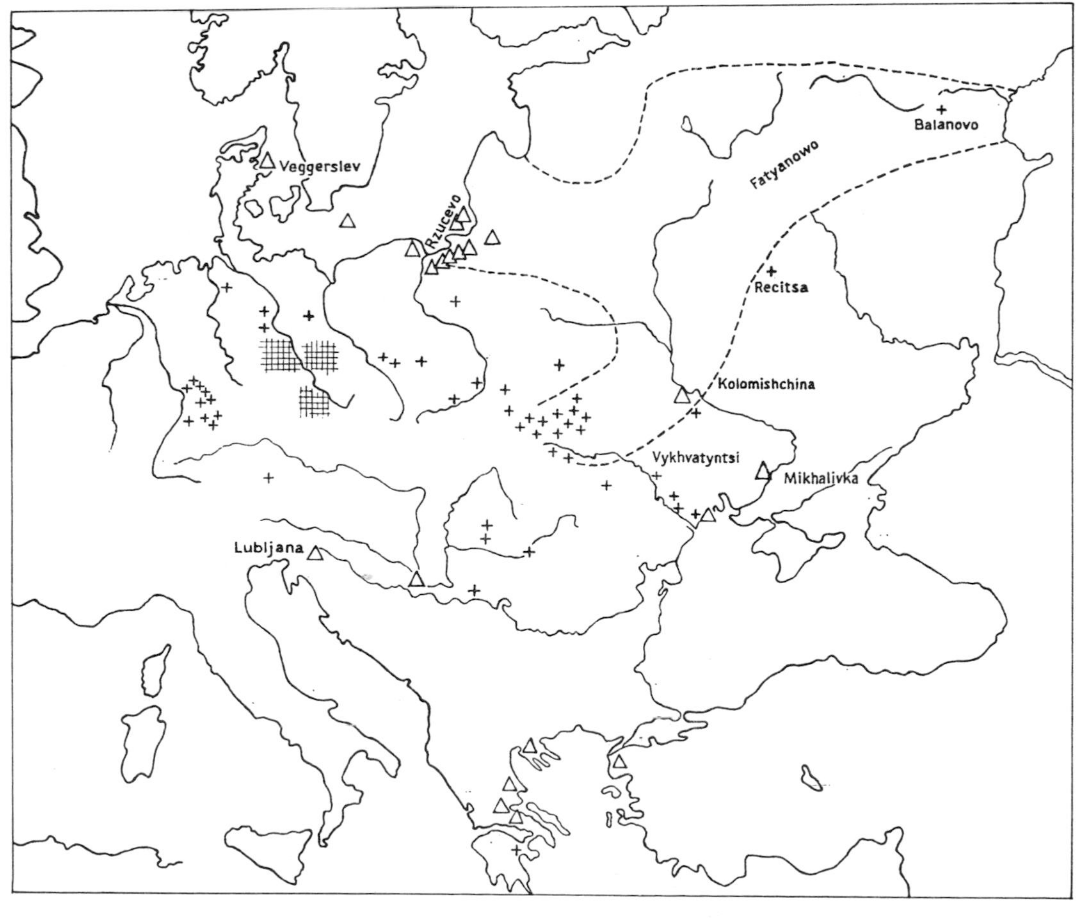

MAP IX. Geographical diffusion of the Thuringian amphorae.

+ Specimens found in graves.

Larger concentrations of graves with the amphorae.

△ Specimens found in settlements.

The area enclosed by the dotted line indicates the diffusion of the Fatyanovo battle-axes (after A. Äyräpää, *ESA* VIII).

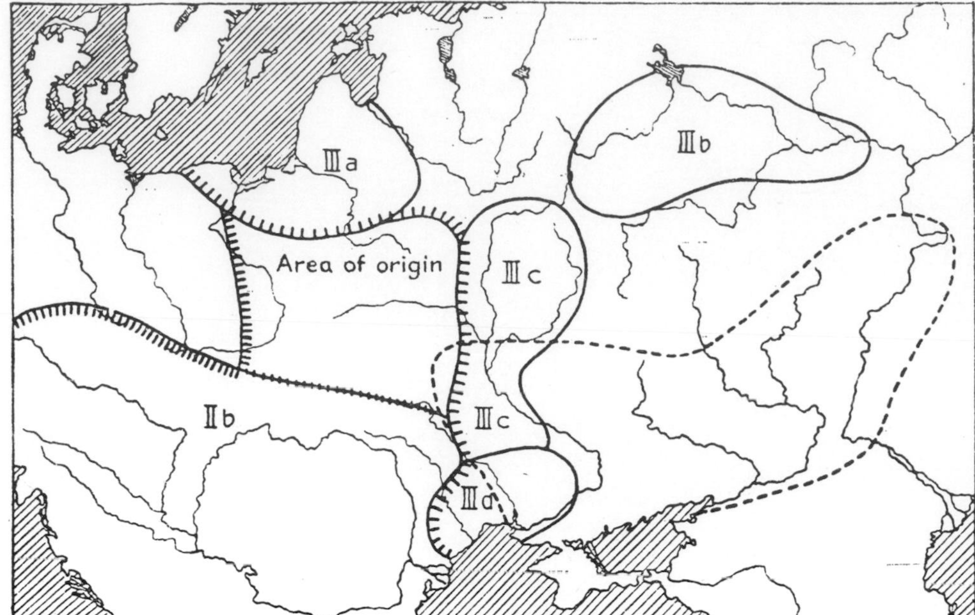

Map x. The spread of the Corded Ware from its assumed original area (according to L. Kilian, corrected).

Dotted line denotes the territory of the steppe Ochre-Graves. The section west of the 'Area of origin' should be marked IIa.

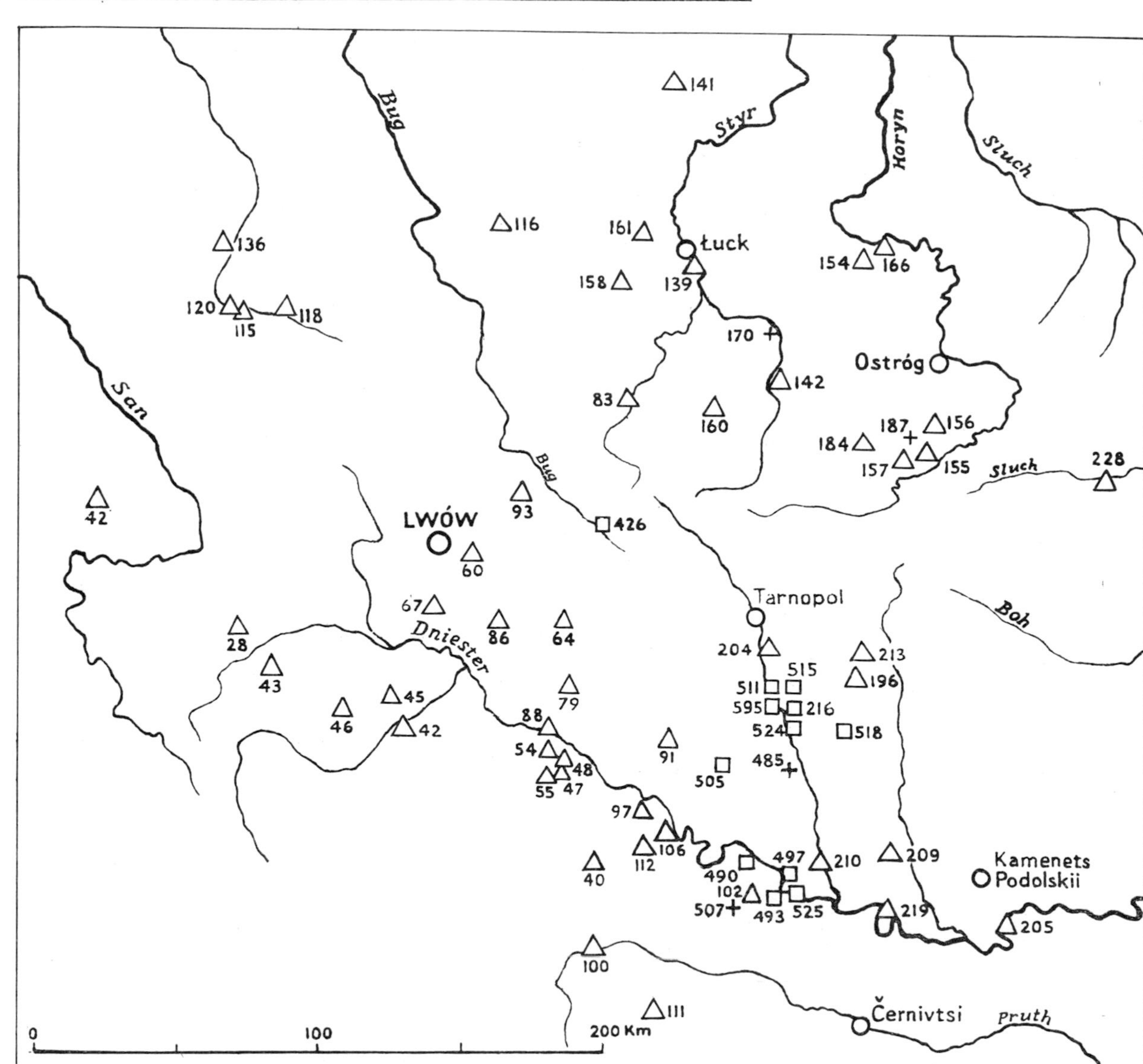

Map xi. Bronze Age and Early Iron Age barrow-graves in the western part of the Territory, and slab-cist and flat graves of the Biały-Potok group.

△ Barrow-graves □ Slab-cist graves + Flat graves or cemeteries

Numbers of sites correspond with those of the relative descriptions and reports in Part II of the volume.
Nos. 28–112, Komarów culture.
Nos. 115–36, Trzciniec culture.
Nos. 102, 196–219, 485–595, Biały-Potok group.
Nos. 83, 141–87, 228, Volhynian graves.

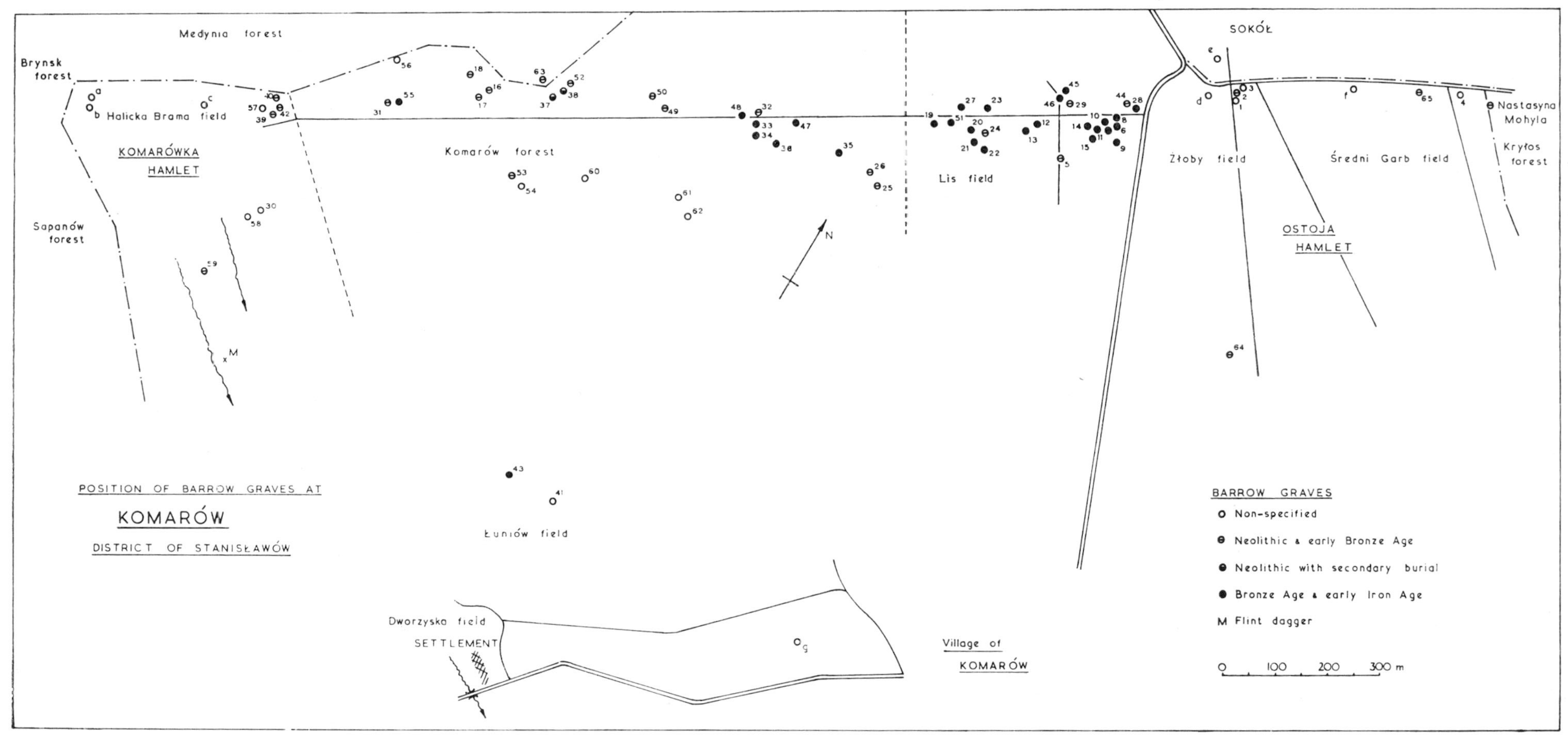

PLAN 1. The barrow-grave cemetery at Komarów.

The graves of different periods are differently marked, and the site of the settlement investigated indicated.

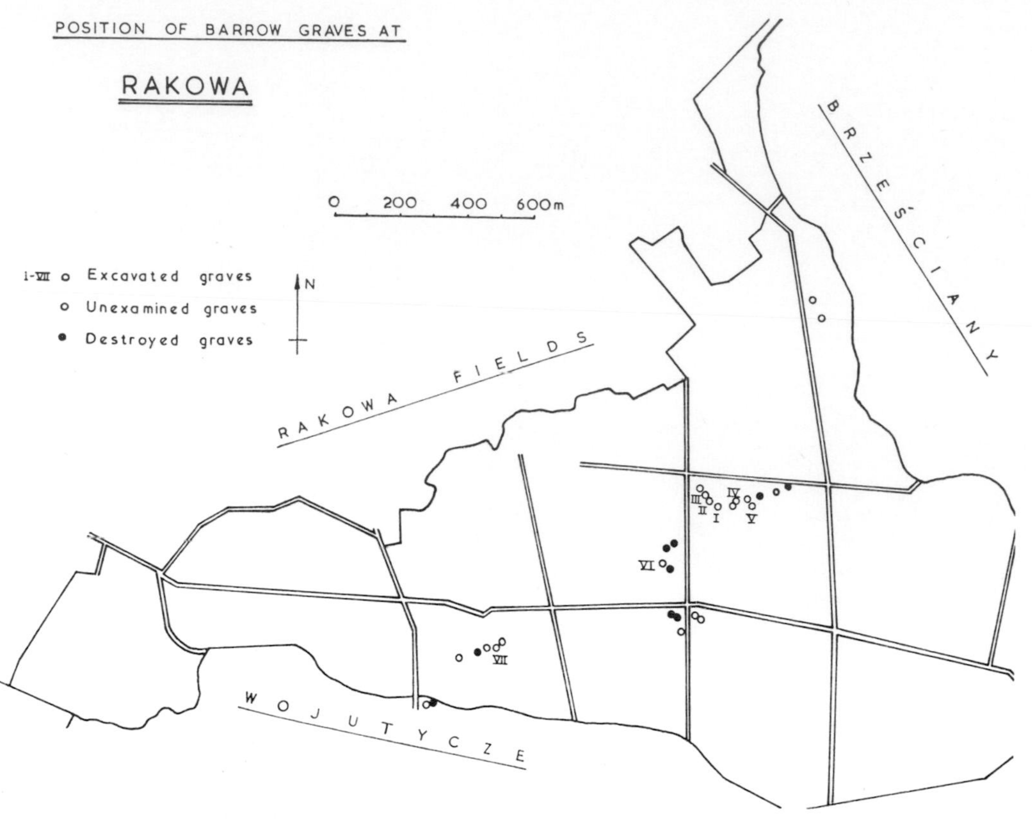

PLAN 2. The barrow-grave cemetery at Rakowa (no. 28). Mounds investigated are marked.

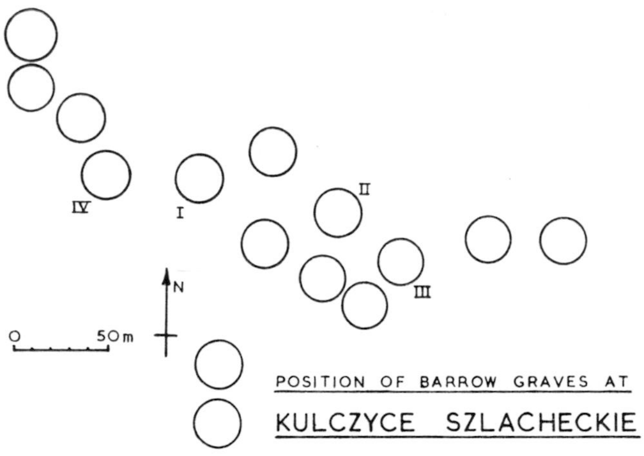

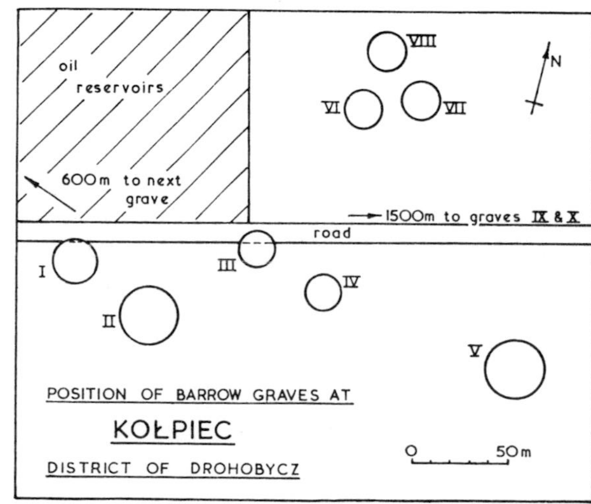

PLAN 3. Two barrow-grave cemeteries.
1. Kulczyce Szlacheckie (no. 49).
2. Kołpiec (no. 46).

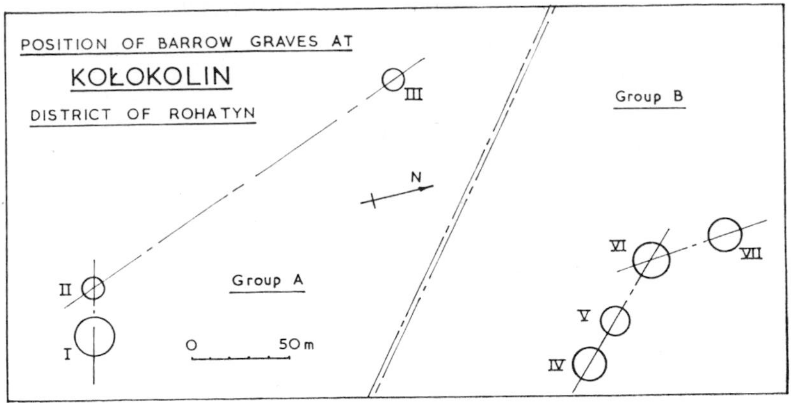

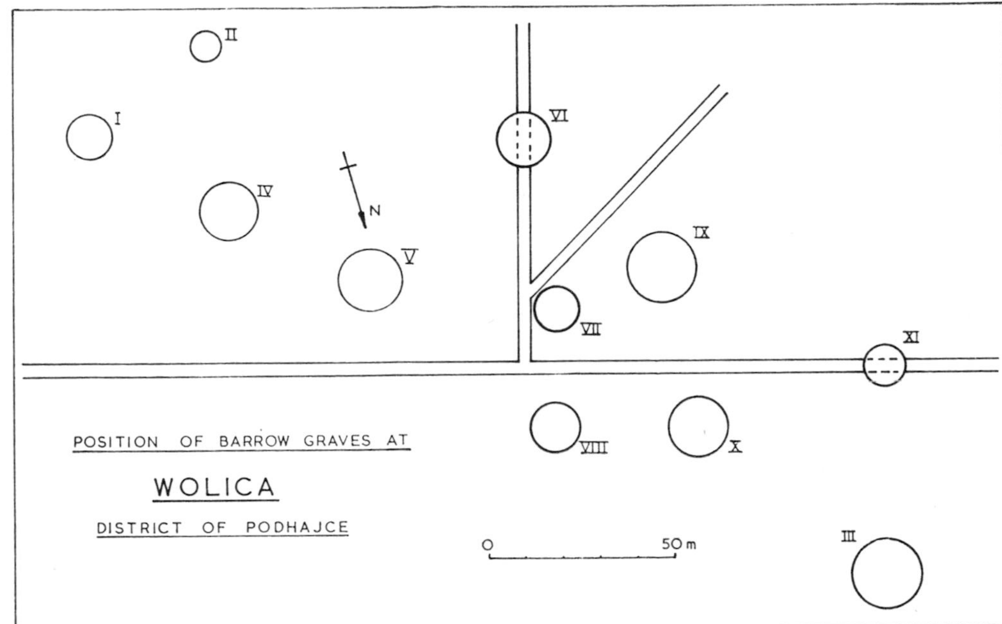

PLAN 4. Two barrow-grave cemeteries.

1. Kołokolin (no. 66).
2. Wolica (no. 91).

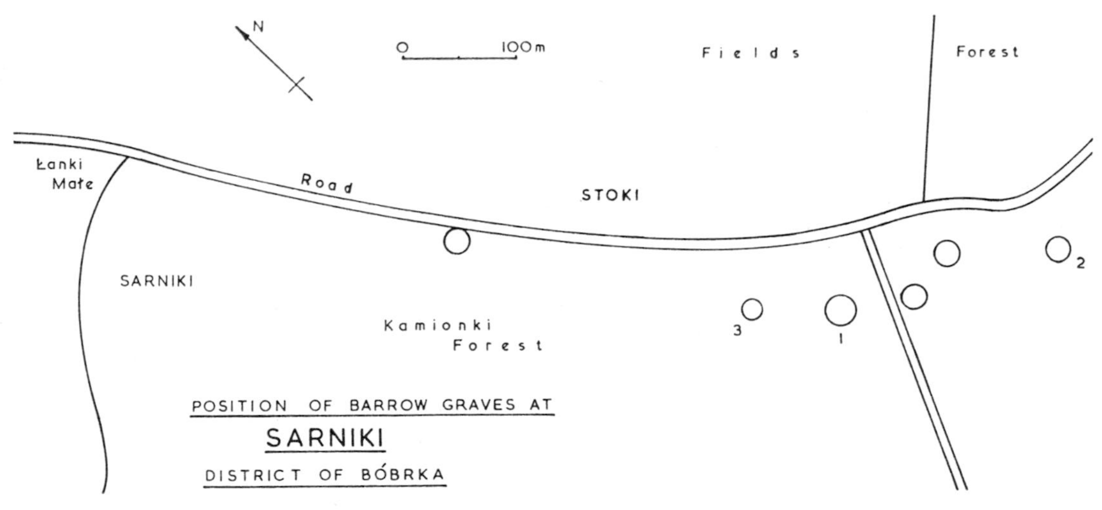

VI
24 m
II
16 m
I
18 m
V
14 m
III
16 m
IV
14 m
0 50 m
N

POSITION OF BARROW GRAVES AT
KRASÓW
DISTRICT OF LWÓW

PLAN 5. Two barrow-grave cemeteries.

1. Sarniki (no. 86).
2. Krasów (no. 67).

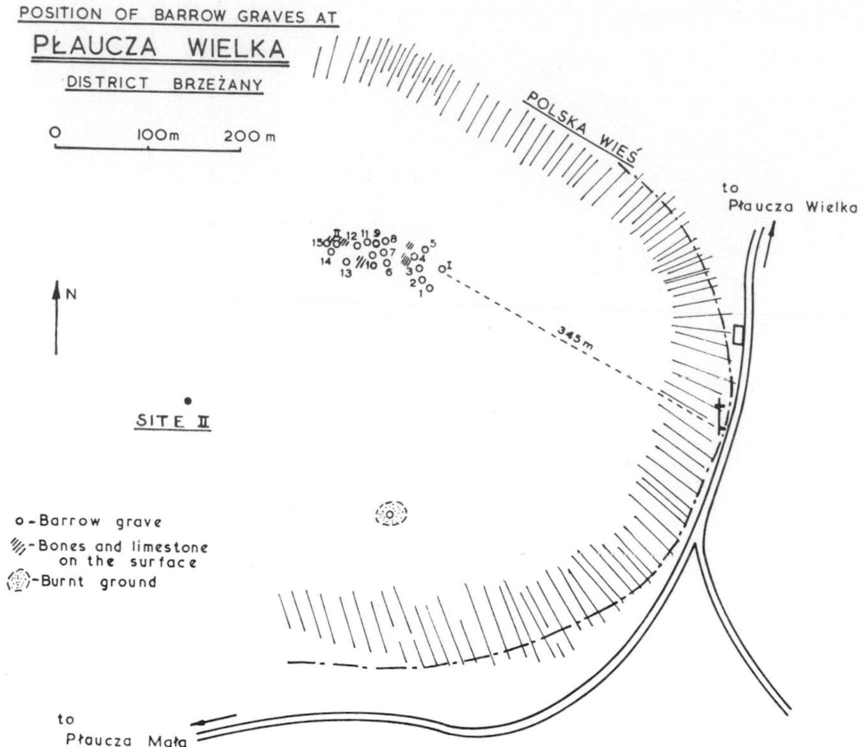

PLAN 6. The barrow-grave cemetery at Płaucza Wielka (no. 75).

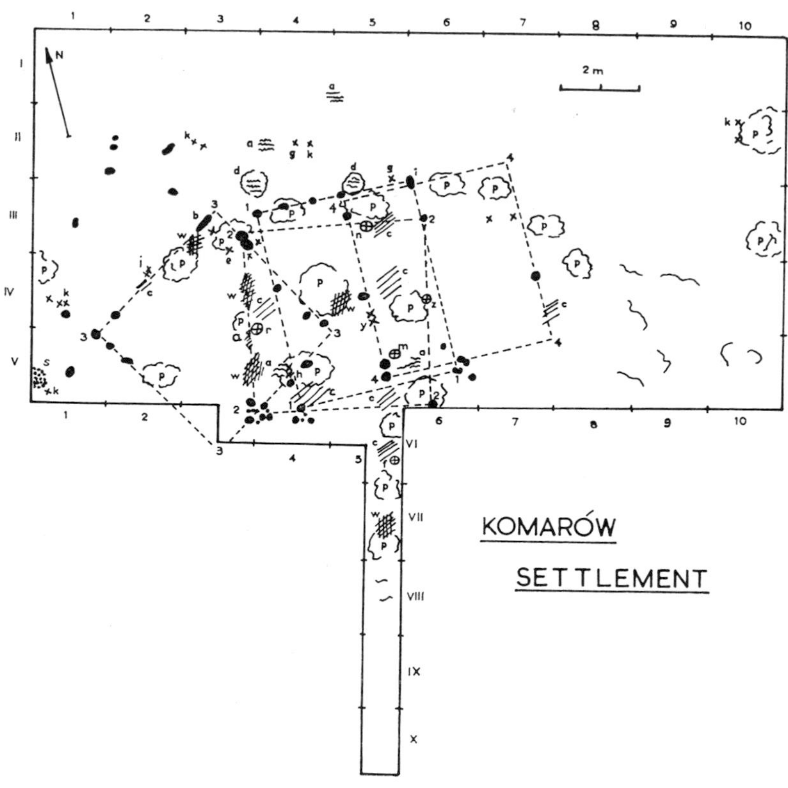

PLAN 7. The investigated part of the settlement at Komarów.

a, pieces of calcined bones; b, remains of a large charred beam; c, accumulated and single potsherds; d, hole, *c*. 50cm deep, filled in with lumps of fired clay, potsherds, and calcined bones; e, small flint saw; f, crushed larger vessel; g, two flint arrow-heads (Plate 9:28, 29); h, clay male figurine (Fig. 12:12); potsherds and calcined bones; i, small female clay figurine (Fig. 12:13), potsherds and calcined bones; k, (crosses) flint knives, scrapers and other small implements; m, n, crushed larger vessels; p, heaps of lumps of fired clay; r, large storage vessel; s, small heap of gravel; w, agglomerations of charcoal or remains of charred beams; y, two large flint blades damaged by fire; z, large storage vessel and bowl of a type proper to the Komarów culture (Fig. 20:1, 2).
1–4, corners of four huts (I–IV); black spots denote large stones which originally supported the foundation beams of the huts.

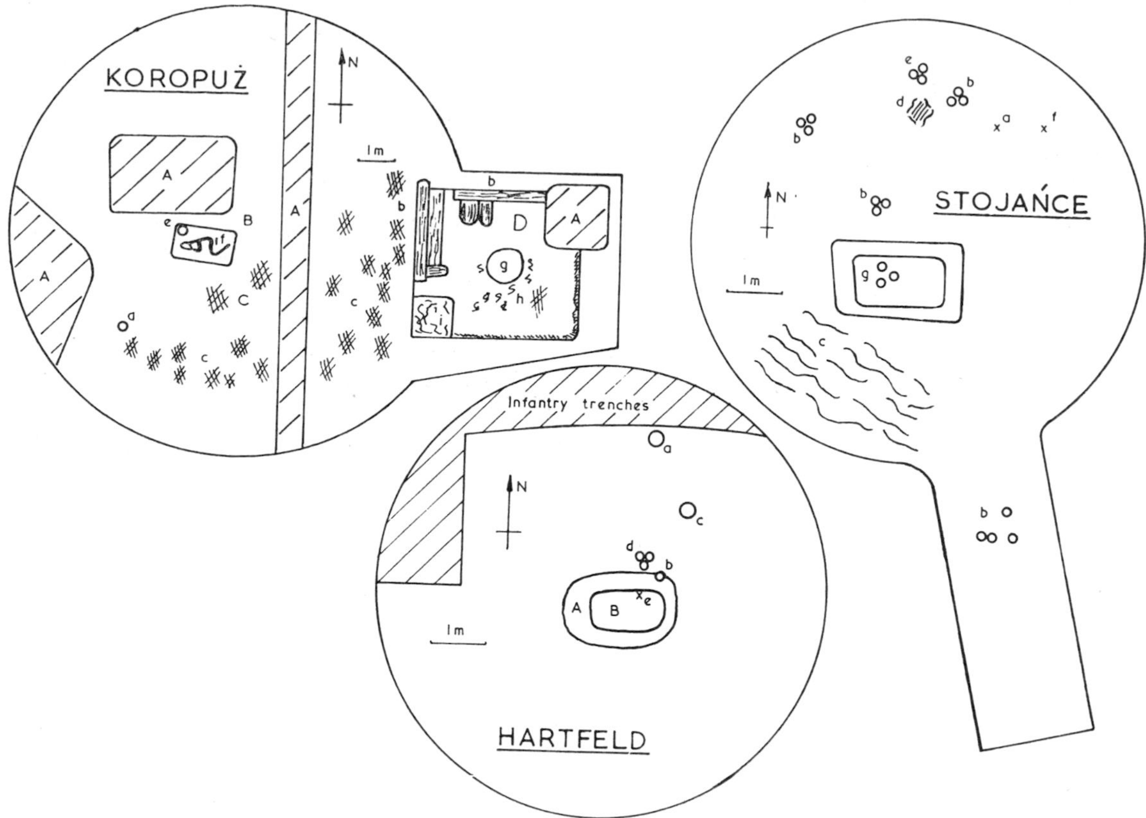

PLAN 8. Three barrow-graves.

1. Koropuż (no. 17) (Plate 3:1).
A, parts of the mound destroyed by survey posts and a trench; B, grave-shaft, 40cm deep; C, charcoal; D, remains of the hut; a, cord-decorated potsherd; b, charred oak logs; e, Thuringian amphora; f, flint knife; g, hearth; h, potsherds, bone disc (Fig. 19:19), fragments of saddle-quern, fragments of calcined stones, calcined animal bones and a stag's antler, scattered around the hearth; i, pile of calcined earth.

2. Stojańce (no. 35).
a, f, flint knife (Fig. 12:6) and scraper; b, c, potsherds (Fig. 12:1, 2); c, d, lumps of fired clay; g, grave-shaft with three small potsherds on the floor.

3. Hartfeld (no. 10).
A, B, upper and lower outlines of the grave-shaft; a, b, c, scattered fragments of a Thuringian amphora; e, flint scraper.

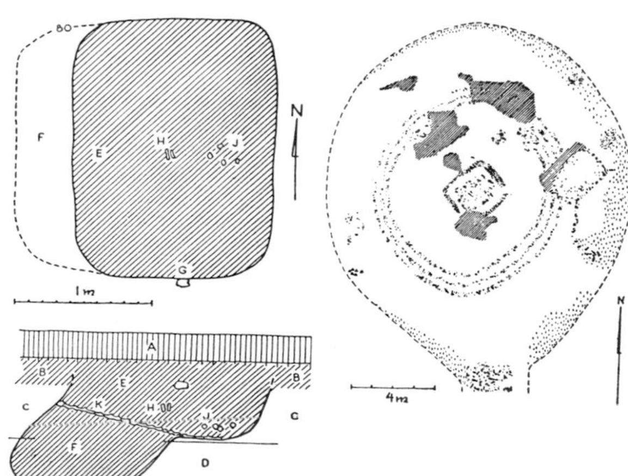

PLAN 9. Cross-section of two graves.

1. Siennów (no. 31), plan and cross-section of the niche-grave.
A, arable soil; B, dark-grey soil; C, yellow clay or loess; D, sand; E, grave-shaft; F, niche; G, dark potsherd; H, two animal teeth; J, small potsherd; K, layer of planks.

2. Brzezinki IV (no. 3) (after A. Dzieduszycka-Machnikowa).
- dark sand with remains of pyre;
- brown virgin sand;
- modern pits;
- potsherds of Corded Ware;
- limits of the area excavated.

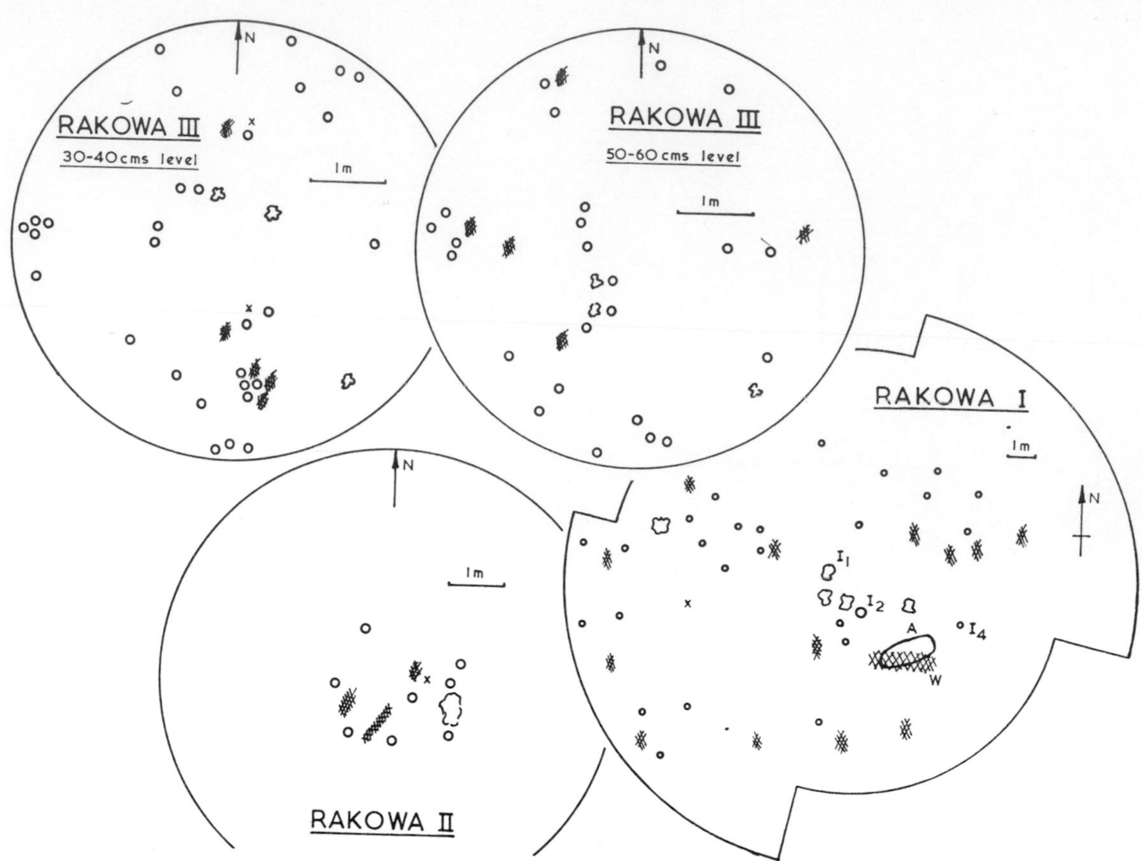

PLAN 10. Barrow-graves I, II and III at Rakowa (no. 28).

Circles: small potsherds; *crosses:* small flint implements or blades; *irregular marking:* agglomerations of fired clay; *hatched areas:* charcoal. A, shallow grave-shaft in Mound I; I-1, 2, tulip-shaped pot (Plate 23:6); I-4, bowl: both vessels in Mound I.

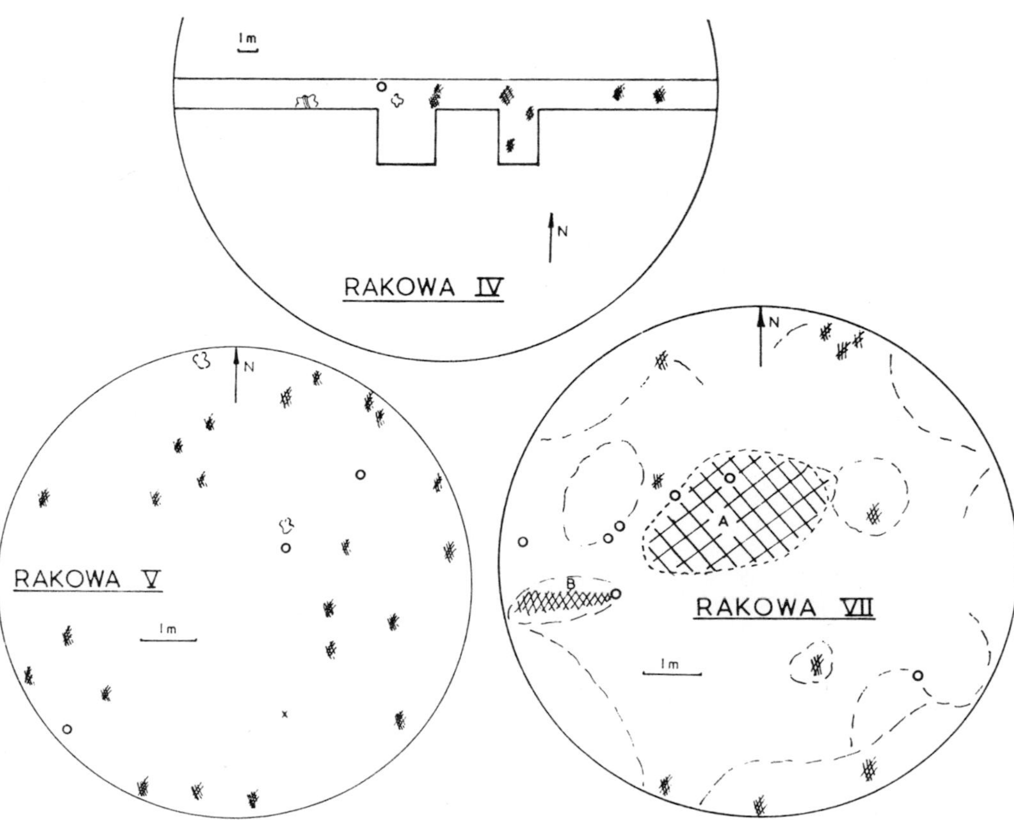

PLAN 11. Barrow-graves IV, V, VII at Rakowa (no. 28).

Markings as in Plan 10. A, B, charcoal, as dust or in lumps forming continuous layers.

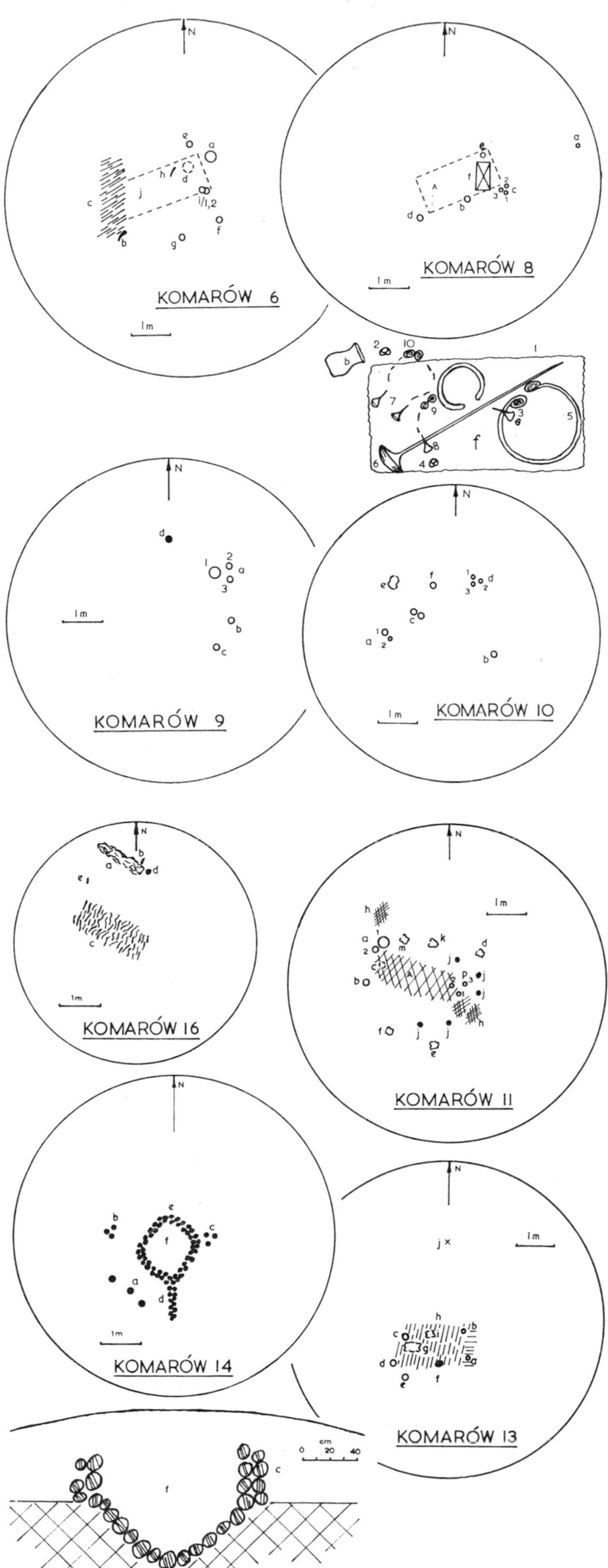

Plan 12. Four barrow-graves at Komarów.

1. Barrow-grave 6.

a, tulip-shaped pot; b, bronze dagger (Fig. 26:9); c, charred timber logs, possibly a platform of a male grave; d, faint traces of the skull; e, tulip-shaped beaker (Plate 16:2); f, crushed small tulip-shaped pot; g, gold ear-ring (Fig. 26:8); h, bronze pin (Fig. 26:7); i-1, 2, fragments of a bowl and a small cup (Plate 16:6); j, site of the grave.

2. Barrow-grave 8.

A, the grave; a, gold ear-pendant; b, tulip-shaped beaker (Plate 16:1); c-2, 3, two small cups (Plate 16:7); c-1, a small goblet (Plate 16:8); d, handled cup; e, handled cup (Plate 16:10); f, wooden box with jewellery (Fig. 26:1–6); 2, larger gold ear-pendant; 3, 4, small gold ear-pendants; 5, necklace; 6, pin; 7, 8, bell-shaped pendants; 9, 10, double spiral ornaments.

3. Barrow-grave 9.

a, group of three vessels (Plate 16:13, 9, 5): 1, bowl; 2, decorated cup; 3, tulip-shaped pot; b, bowl; c, decorated beaker (Fig. 28:7); d, larger boulder.

4. Barrow-grave 10.

a, tulip-shaped pot and small cup (Plate 18:5, 16); b, tulip-shaped pot; c, small beaker and bowl (Plate 18:7; Plate 16:20); d-1, 2, 3, group of three vessels: tulip-shaped pot with a smaller one inside (Plate 18:3), and two bowls (Plate 16:18); e, crushed beaker (Fig. 28:5); f, tulip-shaped pot (Plate 18:8).

Plan 13. Four barrow-graves at Komarów.

1. Barrow-grave 16.

a, calcined bones; b, flint knife; c, charred beech logs; d, large lump of fired clay; e, flint knife.

2. Barrow-grave 11.

A, earth mixed with charcoal, ash and calcined bones (the grave); a-1, 2, two bowls (Plate 17:1, 10); b, tulip-shaped pot; c, remains of the calcined skull; d, k, smashed bowl and tulip-shaped pot (Fig. 27:5; Fig. 28:2); e, f, sherds of another smashed bowl (Fig. 27:10); h, lumps of charcoal; j, five large pebbles laid around the eastern end of the grave; m, small flint flakes and a few sherds of vessels 'd' and 'k'; p-1, 2, 3, two small cups (Plate 18:18) and a larger one (Plate 17:4).

3. Barrow-grave 14.

a, b, c, three groups of three large pebbles each; d, e, stone construction with its centre sunk in the ground, as shown in the cross-section below.

4. Barrow-grave 13.

a, small cup (Plate 21:9); b, handled cup (Plate 21:8); c, handled cup; d, e, small beaker and its lid (Plate 21:10, 11); f, large pebble; g, faint traces of the skeleton; h, layer of timber logs covering the grave from W to E; i, lump of fired clay; j, flint chip.

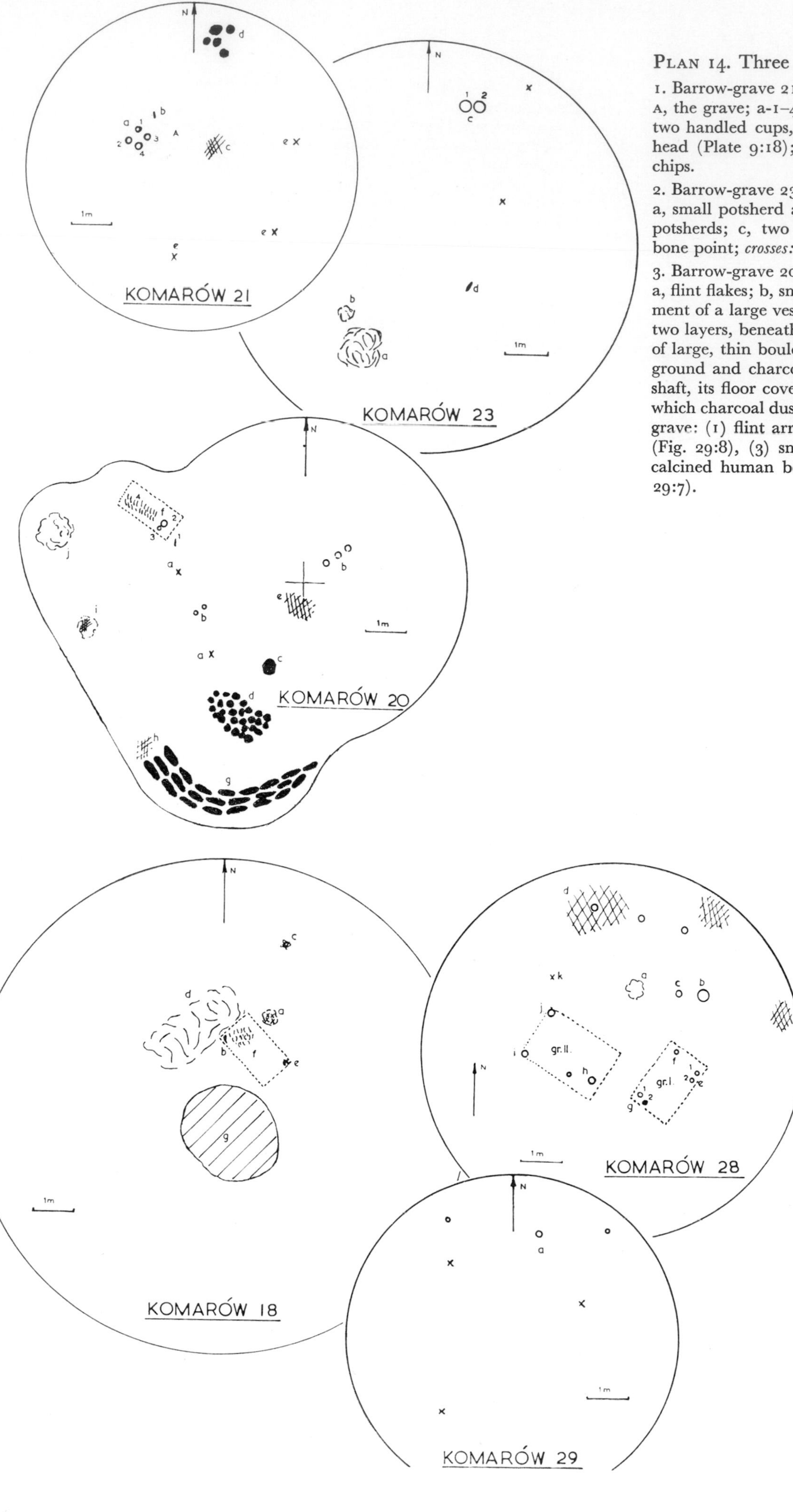

PLAN 14. Three barrow-graves at Komarów.

1. Barrow-grave 21.
A, the grave; a-1–4, group of four vessels (Plate 16:4, 14, 11); two handled cups, tulip-shaped pot and cup; b, flint arrow-head (Plate 9:18); c, charcoal; d, five large pebbles; e, flint chips.

2. Barrow-grave 23.
a, small potsherd and lump of red ochre; b, concentration of potsherds; c, two tulip-shaped pots (Plate 18:10); d, large bone point; *crosses:* flint chips.

3. Barrow-grave 20.
a, flint flakes; b, small odd potsherds; c, large pebble and fragment of a large vessel under it; d, concentration of boulders in two layers, beneath them lumps of charcoal; g, concentrations of large, thin boulders, their narrow sides upwards; h, i, fired ground and charcoal; e, lumps of charcoal; f, shallow grave-shaft, its floor covered by a layer of decayed timber logs over which charcoal dust was strewn; the following objects lay in the grave: (1) flint arrow-head (Plate 9:15), (2) handled tankard (Fig. 29:8), (3) small stone shaft-hole axe (Fig. 35:15); and calcined human bones (4); j, crushed large black vase (Fig. 29:7).

PLAN 15. Three barrow-graves at Komarów.

1. Barrow-grave 18.
a, four flint scrapers, lumps of charcoal and small lumps of ochre; b, flint blade; c, lumps of ochre; d, area strewn with charcoal; e, larger flint points; f, very shallow hole (the grave) with a few calcined human bones; g, area destroyed by a modern pit.

2. Barrow-grave 28.
a, few potsherds of a large crushed vase 'b' (Fig. 28:8); c, crushed cup; d, charcoal strewn on the ancient ground, in its centre a hole in which lay a cup (Fig. 28:11); goods found in grave I: e, two decorated bowls (Fig. 28:9); g, gold ear-pendant (Fig. 26:11) (1) and a crushed vessel (2); f, beaker; vessels found in grave II: h, bowl, and potsherds nearby over the grave; i, cup (Fig. 28:10); j, double-handled vase (Plate 17:13); k, flint chips.

3. Barrow-grave 29.
a, crushed vessel; *circles:* potsherds; *crosses:* flint chips.

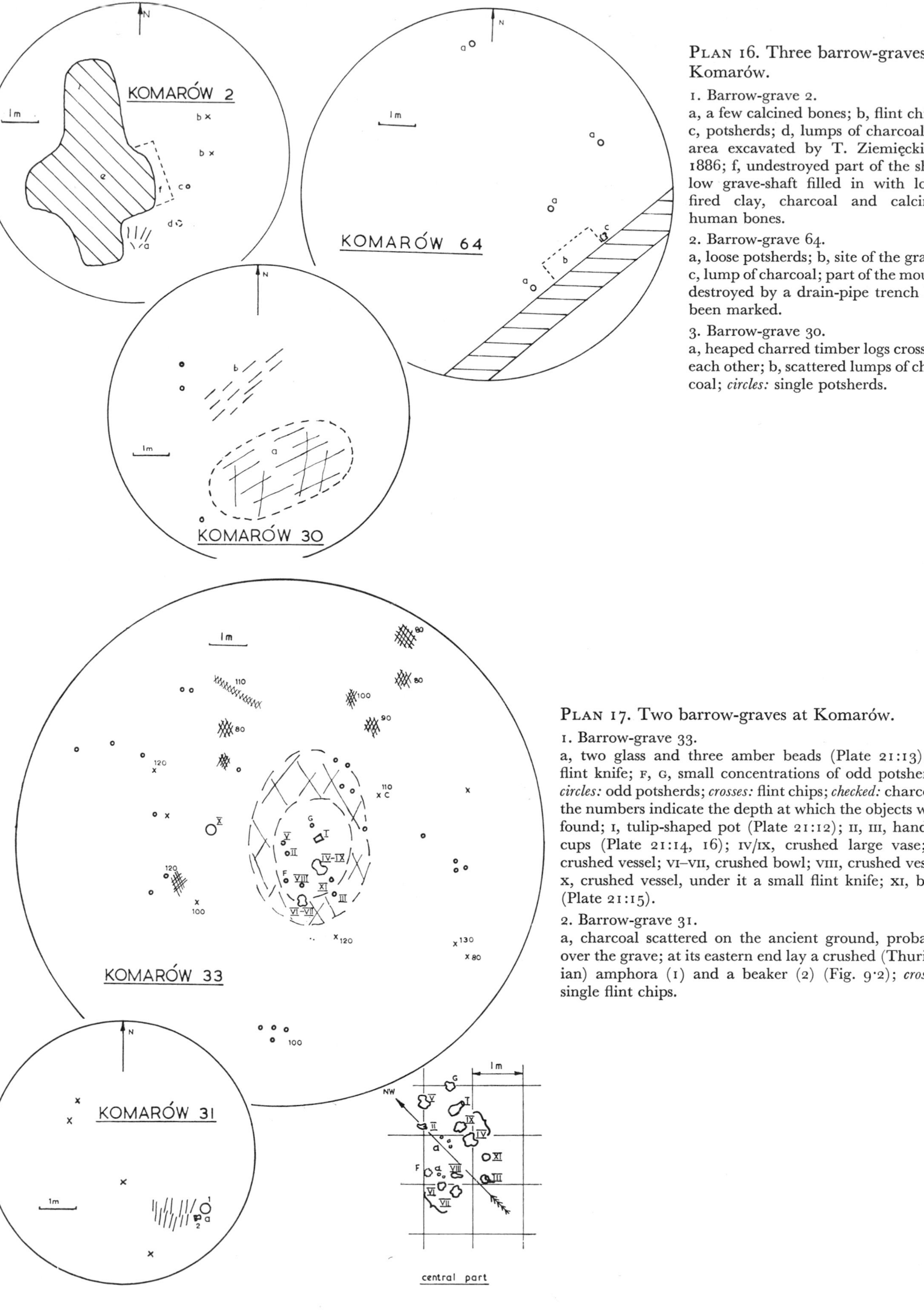

Plan 16. Three barrow-graves at Komarów.

1. Barrow-grave 2.
a, a few calcined bones; b, flint chips; c, potsherds; d, lumps of charcoal; e, area excavated by T. Ziemięcki in 1886; f, undestroyed part of the shallow grave-shaft filled in with loose fired clay, charcoal and calcined human bones.

2. Barrow-grave 64.
a, loose potsherds; b, site of the grave; c, lump of charcoal; part of the mound destroyed by a drain-pipe trench has been marked.

3. Barrow-grave 30.
a, heaped charred timber logs crossing each other; b, scattered lumps of charcoal; *circles:* single potsherds.

Plan 17. Two barrow-graves at Komarów.

1. Barrow-grave 33.
a, two glass and three amber beads (Plate 21:13); c, flint knife; F, G, small concentrations of odd potsherds; *circles:* odd potsherds; *crosses:* flint chips; *checked:* charcoal; the numbers indicate the depth at which the objects were found; I, tulip-shaped pot (Plate 21:12); II, III, handled cups (Plate 21:14, 16); IV/IX, crushed large vase; V, crushed vessel; VI–VII, crushed bowl; VIII, crushed vessel; X, crushed vessel, under it a small flint knife; XI, bowl (Plate 21:15).

2. Barrow-grave 31.
a, charcoal scattered on the ancient ground, probably over the grave; at its eastern end lay a crushed (Thuringian) amphora (1) and a beaker (2) (Fig. 9·2); *crosses:* single flint chips.

PLAN 18. Barrow-grave 32 at Komarów.

1. Deeper level, 140–160cm.
I, II, areas densely strewn with charcoal: sites of graves; a, two small cups; *circles:* odd potsherds; *crosses:* flint chips and broken implements.

2. Level of 70–90cm.
Potsherds, flints and concentrations of charcoal marked as above; b, broken hammer made of siliceous slate.

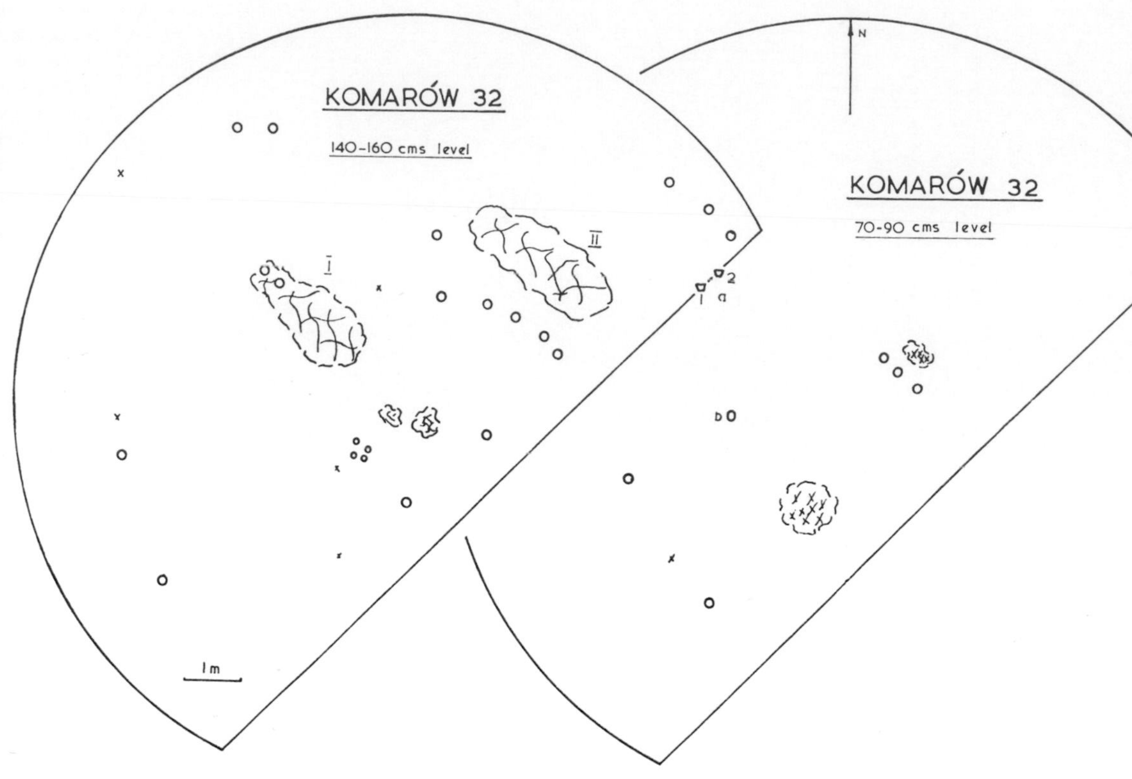

PLAN 19. Two barrow-graves at Komarów.

1. Barrow-grave 39.
a, beaker (Plate 6:4); b, decayed timber logs; c, flint axe; d, stone battle-axe; e-1, 2, two clay tubes (Fig. 5:8); f, four flint arrow-heads (Plate 9:17, 23, 24, 26); g, flint knife; h, patches of charcoal; *crosses:* flint flakes.

2. Barrow-grave 34.
A, site of the main grave; b, site of the second grave; a, roll of black, fat clay; d, concentration of calcined bones and of potsherds of *c.* five vessels; s, flint arrow-head (Plate 9:16); *black points:* larger pebbles; *circles:* odd potsherds; *crosses:* flint flakes; *checked:* patches of charcoal; I, deep dish; II–III, crushed bowl (Fig. 31:8); IV, crushed beaker; V, beaker (Plate 16:3); VI, cup (Plate 16:12); VI, crushed cup; VIII, crushed bowl.

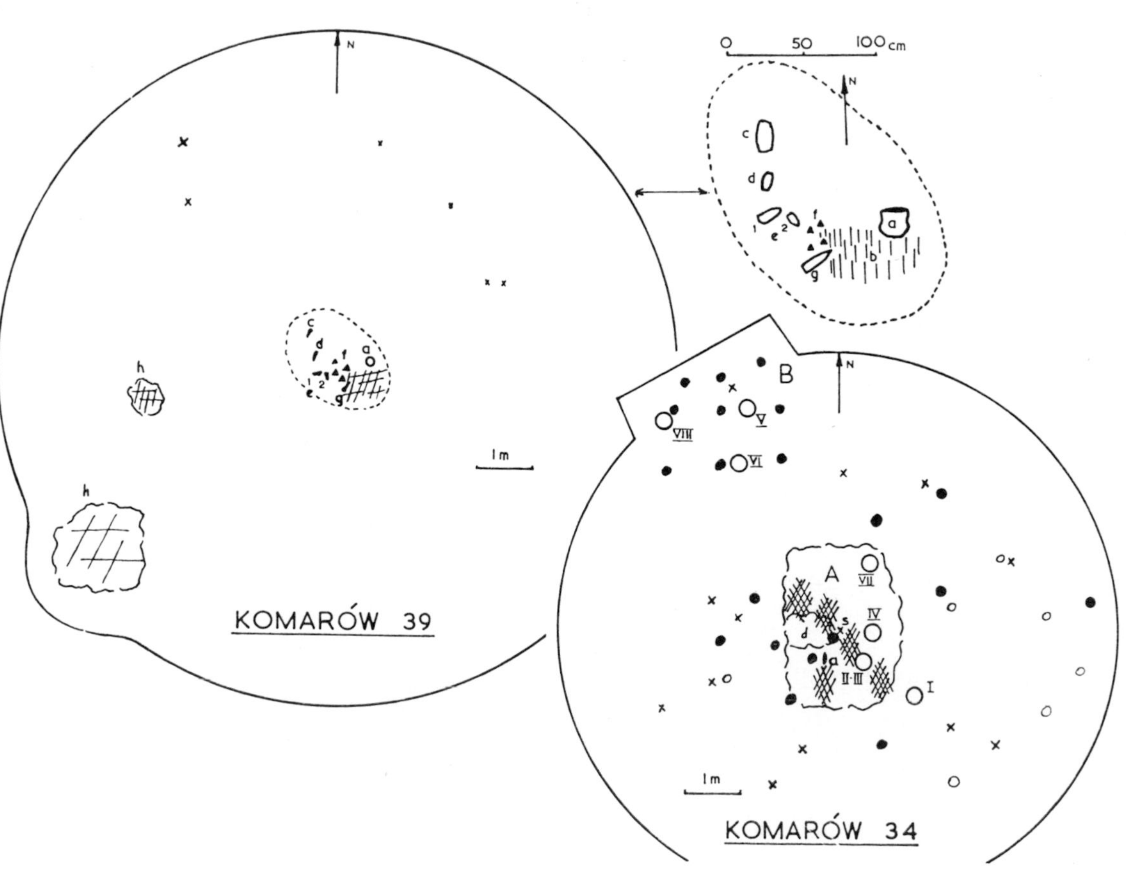

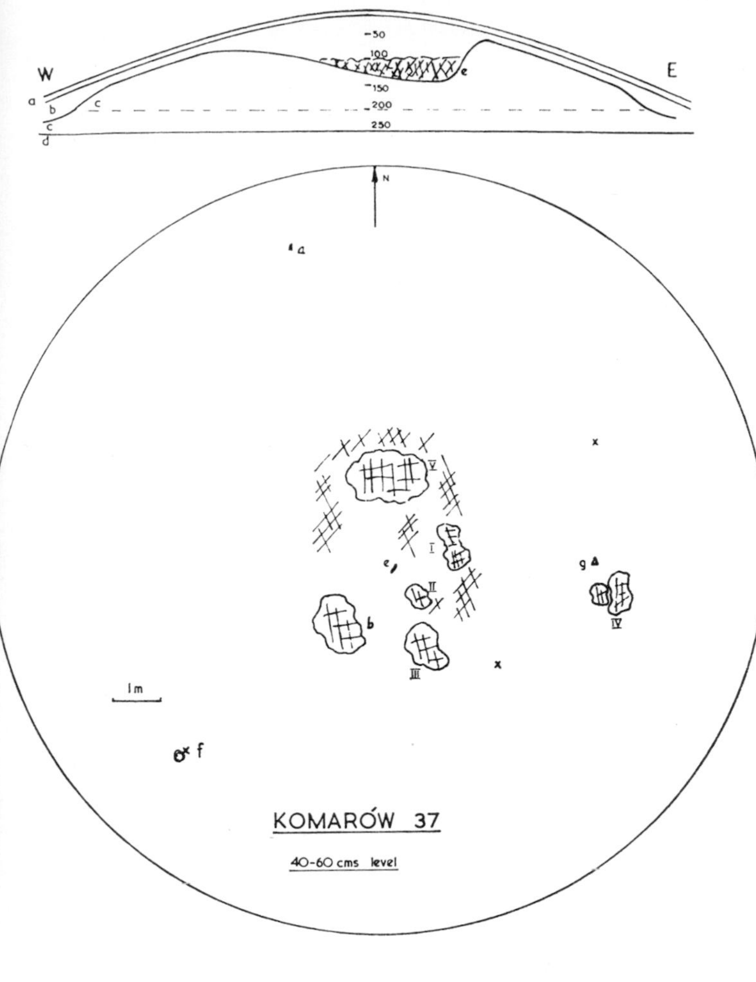

PLAN 20. Cross-section of barrow-grave 37 at Komarów.

1. W–E cross-section.

a, humus; b, yellow mound; c, black, fat clay; d, yellow virgin soil; e, fired clay, ash and charcoal.

2. Plan.

a, flint axe (Fig. 16:27); b, fired clay and charcoal; e, flint knife and a hole 1·6m deep filled in with charcoal; g, small flint point (Plate 9:27); I–V, concentrations of charcoal, ash, fired clay and calcined bones; *checked:* charcoal; *crosses:* flint chips.

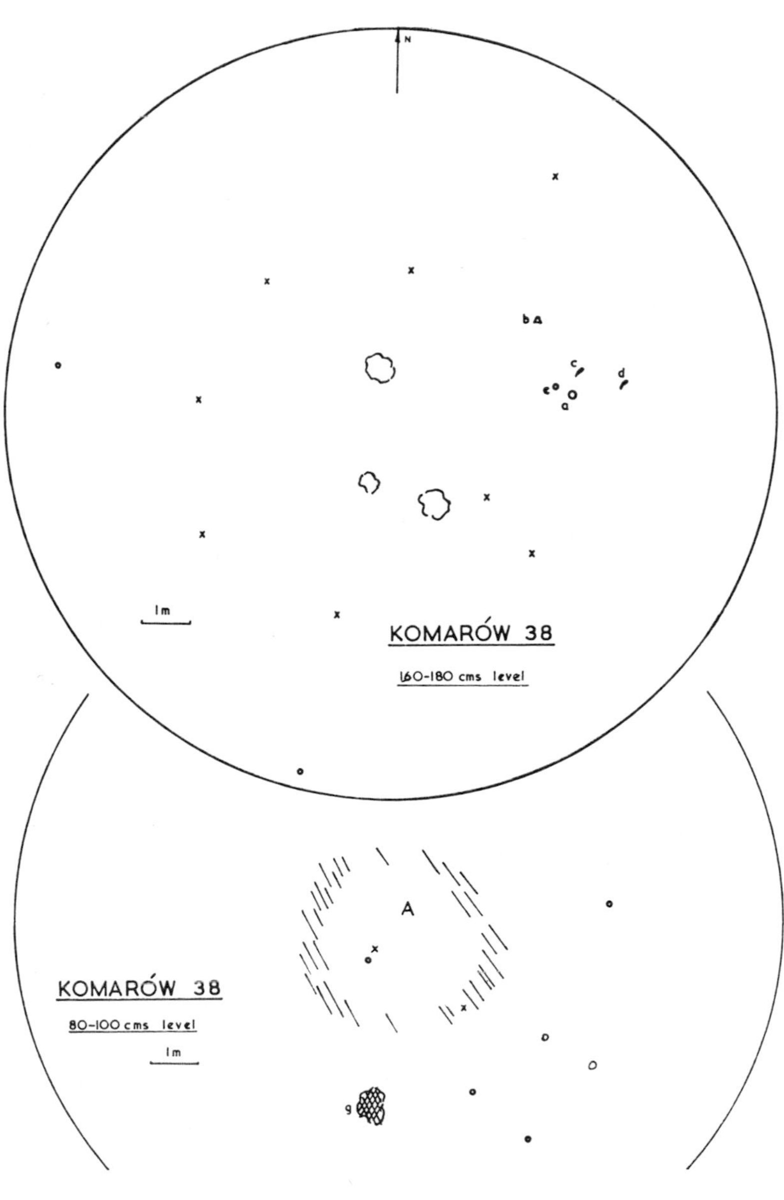

PLAN 21. Barrow-grave 38 at Komarów.

1. Level 160–180cm (Plate 2:4).

a, beaker; b, stone battle-axe (Fig. 13:8); c, d, flint axes (Fig. 15:12; 16:10); e, flint point; *crosses:* flint flakes; *circles:* odd potsherds; *irregular patches:* loose fire clay.

2. Level 80–100cm.

Crosses and circles: as above; A, area strewn with charcoal, fired clay and ash; g, concentration of calcined human bones.

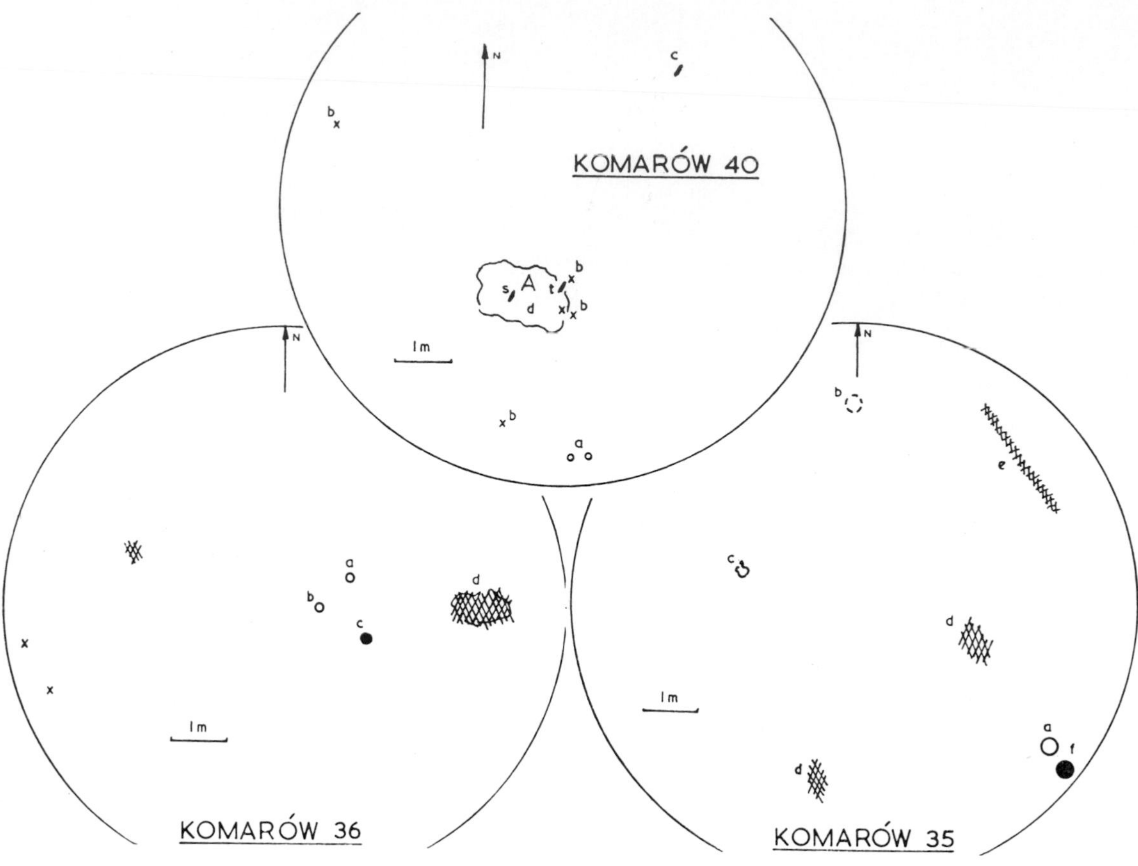

PLAN 22. Three barrow-graves at Komarów.

1. Barrow-grave 40.

A, grave-shaft; a, odd potsherds; b, flints; c, flint knife; d, small heap of charcoal; s, flint axe (Fig. 15:16); t, stone battle-axe.

2. Barrow-grave 36.

a, cup (Plate 18:19); b, bowl (Plate 17:5); c, large pebble; d, area strewn with charcoal, fired clay and ochre; *crosses:* flints; *hatched:* charcoal.

3. Barrow-grave 35.

a, beaker; b, hole filled in with charcoal, fired clay and ash; c, lump of ochre in a small hole; d, areas covered with charcoal, fired clay and ash; e, decayed timber log; f, halved boulder in a hole.

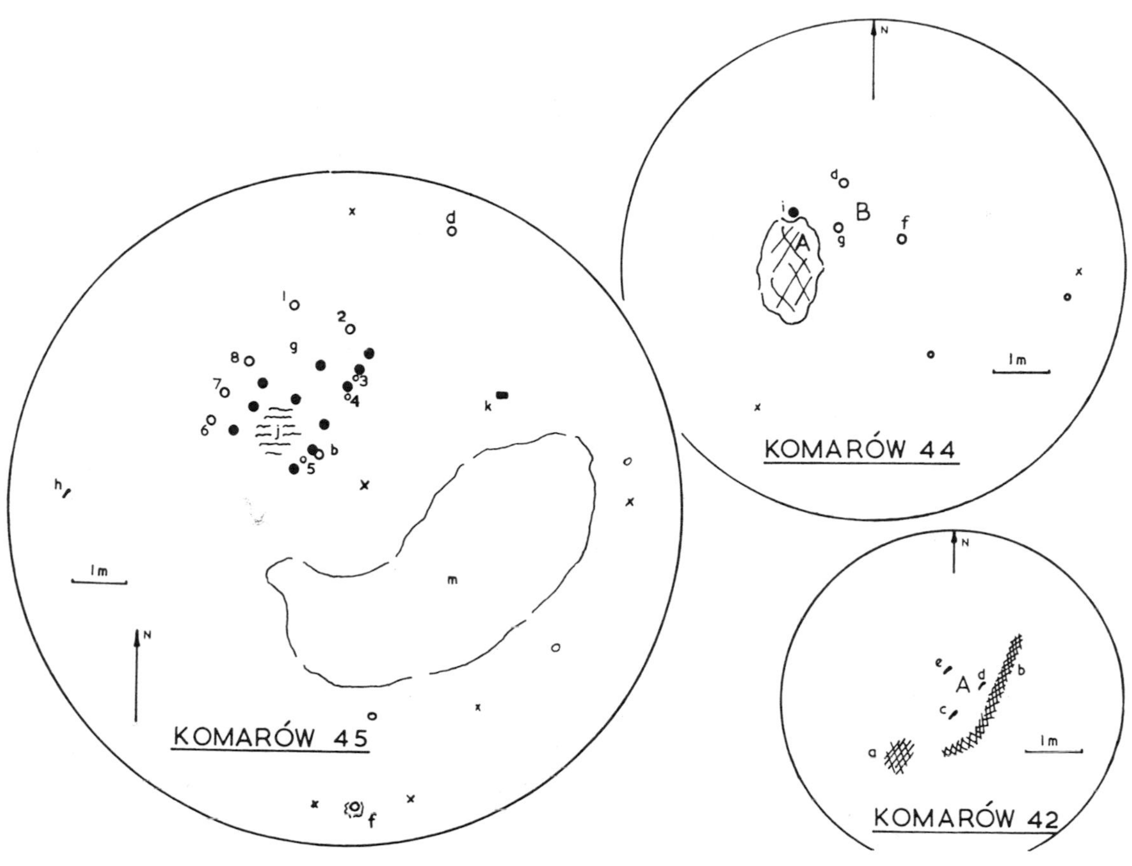

PLAN 23. Three barrow-graves at Komarów.

1. Barrow-grave 45.
b, crushed bowl; d, beaker (Fig. 30:5); f, few large sherds of a large thick-walled vase; g-1–8, eight vessels: (1) handled bowl (Plate 21:6), (2) deep bowl (Plate 21:7), (3, 5) decorated bowls (Plate 21:1; Fig. 30:3), (4) handled cup (Plate 21:3), (6) single-lugged mug (Plate 21:4), (7) undecorated bowl (Plate 21:2), (8) tulip-shaped pot (Plate 21:5); h, flint burin; j, calcined human bones; k, large cube boulder; m, area over which lay scattered lumps of charcoal, fragments of broken flint implements and odd potsherds, some of the same type as those further south (f), and one a late Tripolyan ware (D-ware); *crosses:* flints; *circles:* odd potsherds; *black points:* boulders.

2. Barrow-grave 44.
A, site of the burial in a very shallow shaft; B, site of the supposed second grave; d, flint axe (Fig. 16:13); f, crushed beaker; g, stone battle-axe; *crosses:* flints; *circles:* odd potsherds; i, large pebble.

3. Barrow-grave 42.
A, shallow grave-shaft; a, concentration of charcoal; b, decayed timber beam; c, flint flake; d, flint axe (Fig. 16:19); e, flint knife.

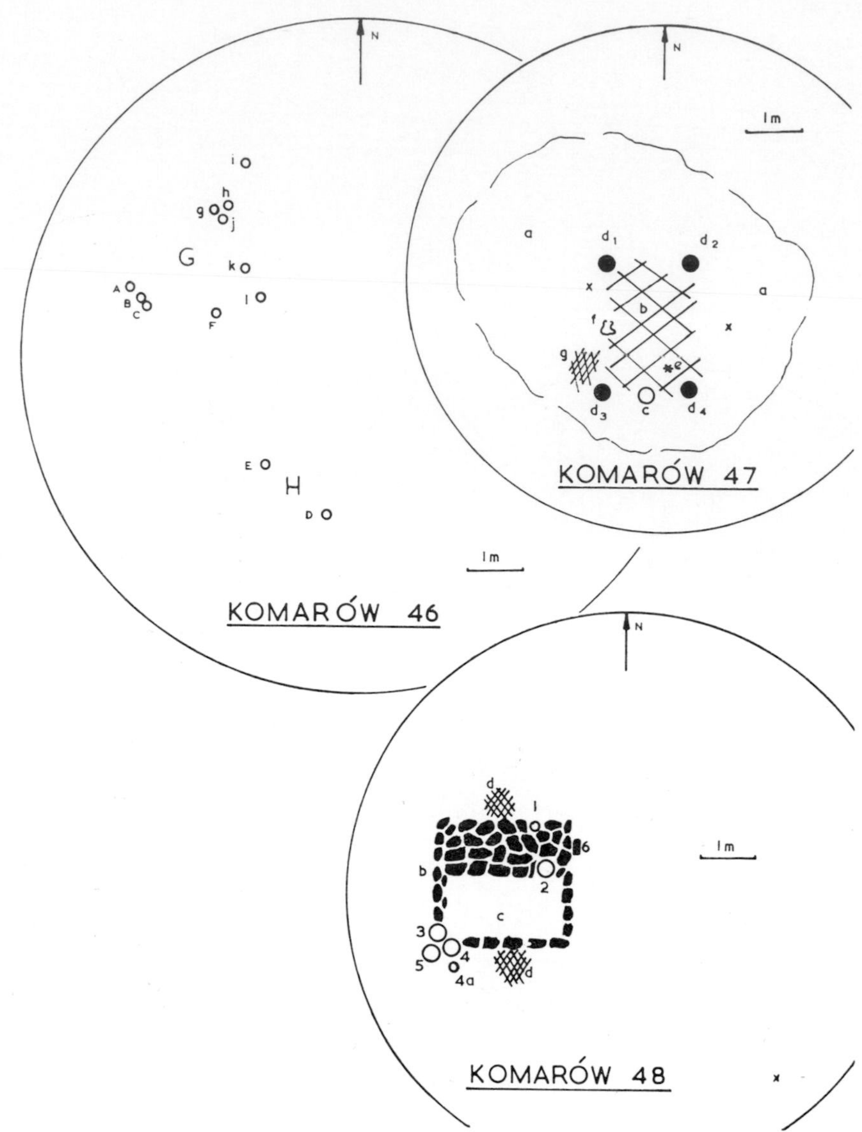

PLAN 24. Three barrow-graves at Komarów.

1. Barrow-grave 46.

A, B, C, three bowls (Fig. 27:2, 4); D, crushed tulip-shaped pot; E, flower-pot shaped cup with the base decorated (Plate 18:13); F, double-handled bowl (Plate 17:8); g, j, small cups (Plate 18:9); h, bowl; i, l, bowls (Fig. 27:9, 3); k, tulip-shaped pot (Fig. 27:1); G, H, sites of two burials.

2. Barrow-grave 47.

a, area over which (in the arable soil) lay scattered lumps of fired clay, fragments of broken stones and a few flint flakes; b, the area on the ancient ground within the above objects and deep loose red fired earth formed a layer up to 20cm thick; c, deep dish (Fig. 31:7); d-1–4, four holes, about 50cm deep, filled in with ash, charcoal, fired clay and a few calcined human bones; e, calcined bones of a human skull; f, upper part of a large, high vessel with a narrow mouth and everted rim (Fig. 31:9); g, accumulation of charcoal.

3. Barrow-grave 48.

b, square area encircled by stones, its northern part thoroughly cobbled, the southern part (c) covered by a layer of cemented sand; six vessels found there: (1) handled cup; (2) decorated bowl (Fig. 30:9); (3) double-handled vase (Fig. 30:1); (4) tulip-shaped pot (Fig. 30:7); (4a) smaller tulip-shaped pot (Fig. 30:2); (5) tulip-shaped beaker (Plate 19:4); c, stone battle-axe (Fig. 35:13); d, charcoal.

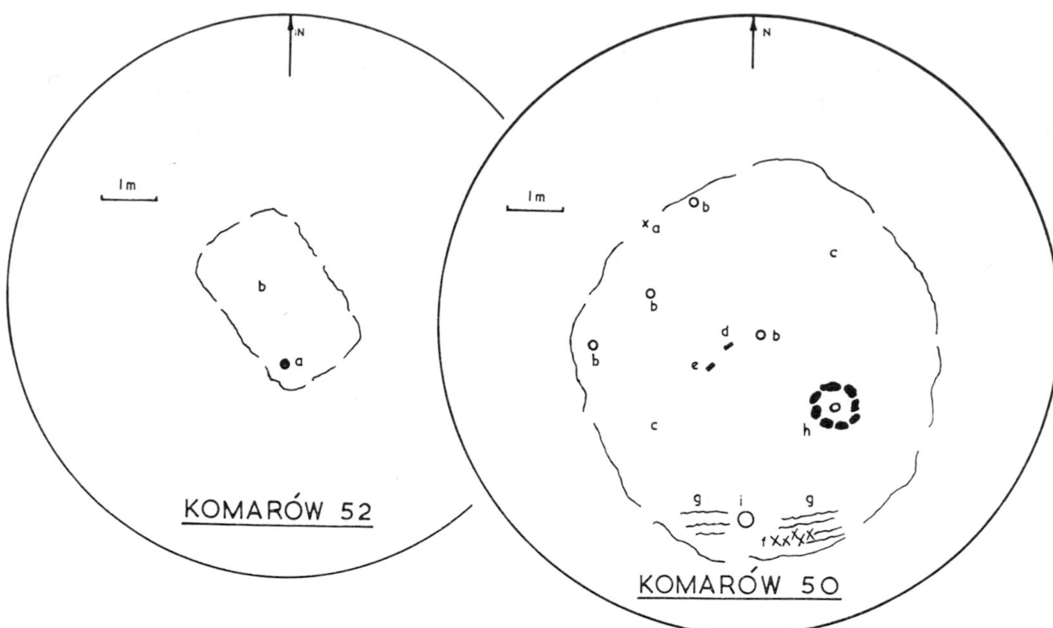

Plan 25. Two barrow-graves at Komarów.

1. Barrow-grave 52.
a, large boulder on the top of the mound; b, area on the ancient surface covered with a thin layer of powdered charcoal and lumps of charred wood, in which a few flints and calcined human bones were found.

2. Barrow-grave 50.
a, flint chip on the top of the mound; b, scattered potsherds; c, area littered with small lumps of fired clay, charcoal and loose fired clay; d, flint axe on the top of the mound (Fig. 16:17); e, stone battle-axe on the top of the mound (Fig. 13:9); f, a few potsherds of the large vessel 'b' mentioned above; g, small accumulations of calcined human bones; h, small ring of eight pebbles filled in with charcoal and a single sherd of the vessel 'b, f'; i, deep bowl (Fig. 31:2).

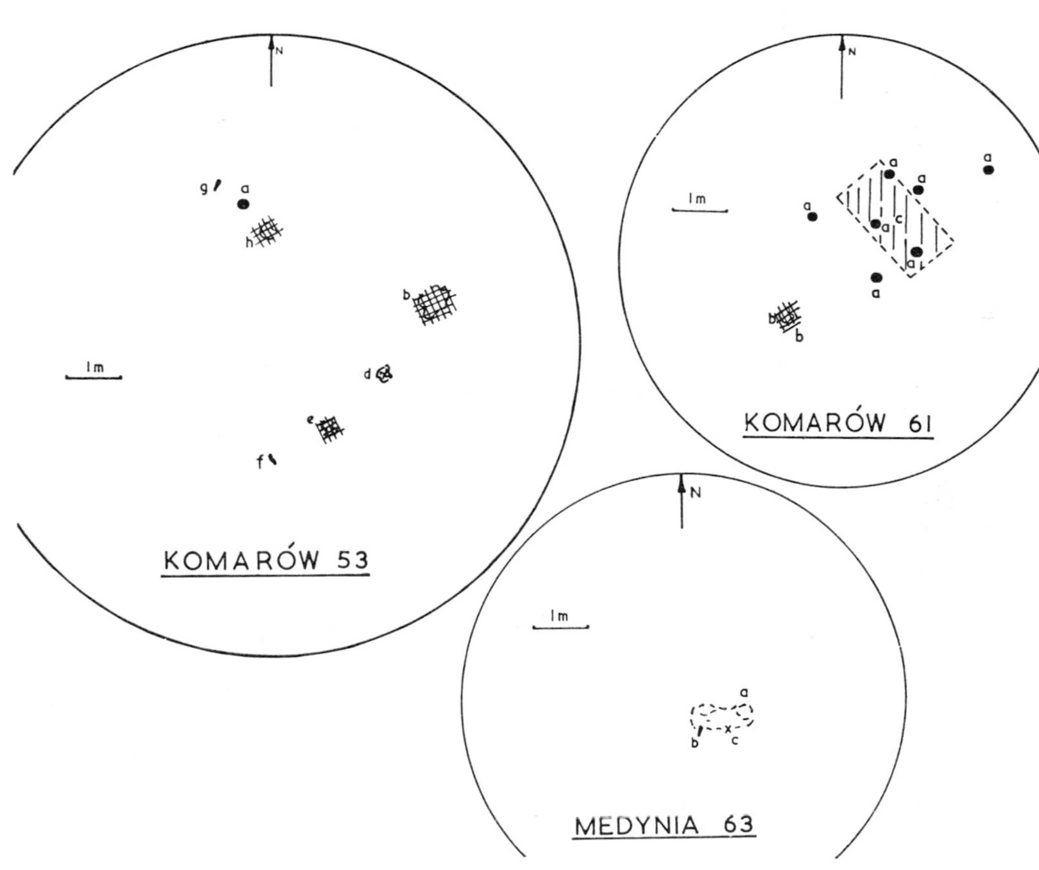

Plan 26. Two barrow-graves at Komarów and one at Medynia (no. 51).

1. Barrow-grave 53.
a, halved boulder on the top of the mound; b, e, h, large lumps of charcoal; d, lump of red ochre; f, g, flint scrapers.

2. Barrow-grave 61.
a, boulder on the top of the mound; b, accumulation of charcoal; c, red-fired area.

3. Barrow-grave 63 (Medynia).
a, area within which were found faint traces of a human skeleton (the grave); b, stone battle-axe; c, flint scraper.

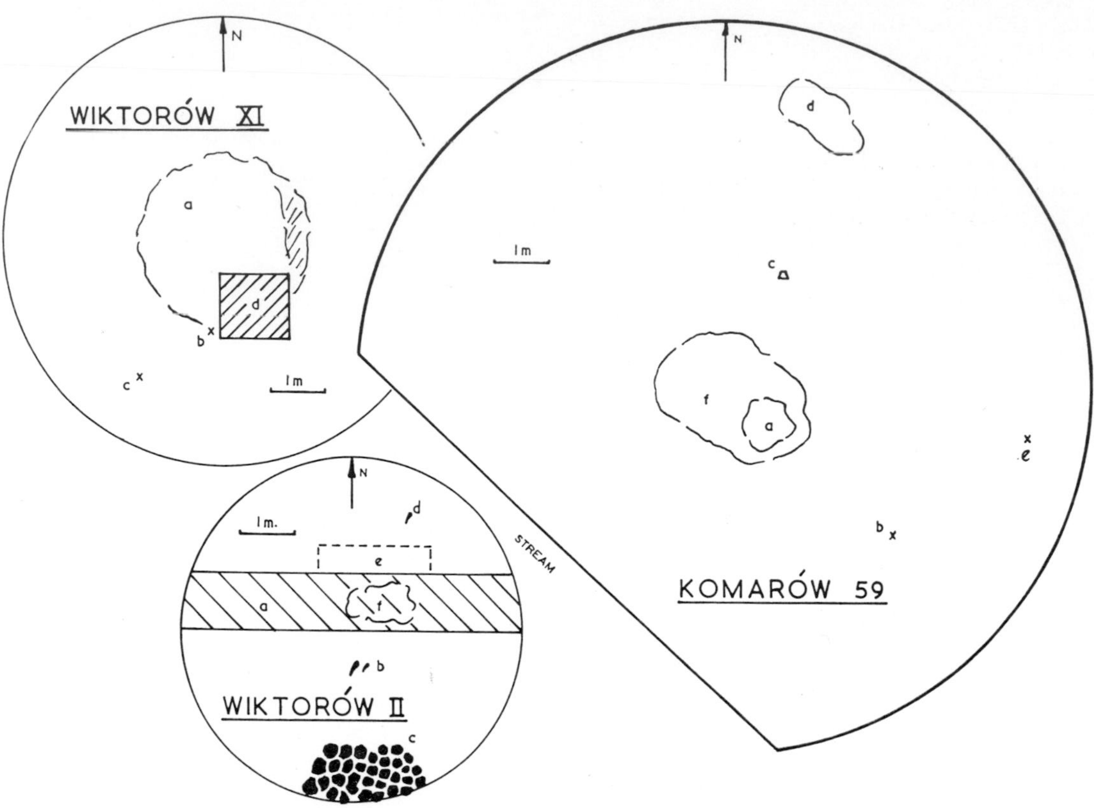

PLAN 27. Two barrow-graves at Wiktorów (no. 57) and one at Komarów.

1. Barrow-grave Wiktorów XI.

a, area littered with lumps of charcoal and backed clay; b, fragment of a flint axe; c, flint flake; d, modern pit.

2. Barrow-grave Komarów 59.

a, traces of a hearth on the top of the mound; b, flint hammer; c, axe made of siliceous slate; d, area littered with charcoal; e, flint flake; f, area littered with small pieces of charcoal strewn on the ancient surface of the ground.

3. Barrow-grave Wiktorów II.

a, trench dug by T. Ziemięcki in 1886; b, stone battle-axe (Fig. 13:1) and flint knife (Fig. 12:4); c, large heap of pebbles (modern?); d, flint burin (Fig. 12:5); e, part of the grave left undestroyed in 1886: shallow hole in which lay lumps of charcoal, loose fired clay and calcined human bones; f, calcined human bones left in the part excavated in 1886.

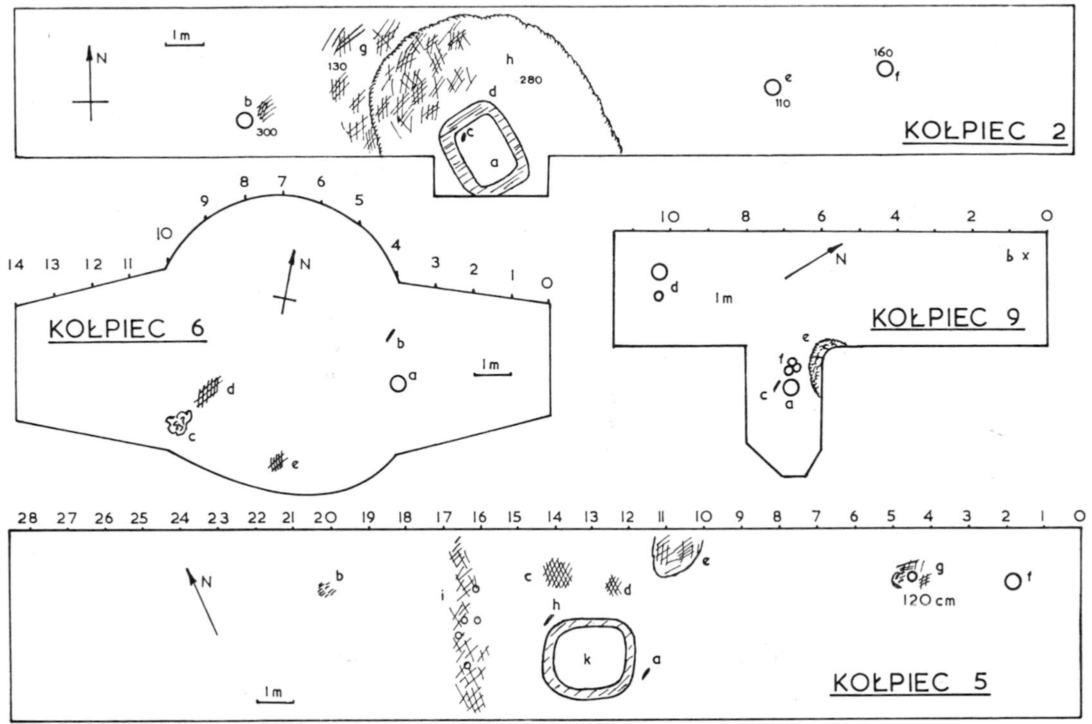

PLAN 28. Four barrow-graves at Kołpiec (no. 46).

1. Barrow-grave 2.
a, grave-shaft; b, broken vessel; c, flint axe (Fig. 16:4); d, imprints of oak logs covering the grave-shaft; e, f, odd potsherds; g (crossed), area within which lay scattered lumps of charcoal, small flint chips and a few odd potsherds; h, area seemingly covered by a layer of logs; numbers indicate the depth (in cm) at which the objects were found.

2. Barrow-grave 6.
a, tulip-shaped vessel; b, flint flake; c, fired clay; d, e, charcoal.

3. Barrow-grave 9.
a, bowl (Plate 7:4); b, flint flake; c, flint knife; d, fragments of coarse vessels on the top of the mound, e, grave-shaft; f, a few entirely crushed vessels in a small hole.

4. Barrow-grave 5 (Plate 8:2).
a, flint axe; b, heaped calcined animal bones; c, d, e, traces of hearths; f, entirely crushed vessel; g, small vessel with two lugs, and necklace of faience beads, found at a depth of 1·2m, in a hole filled in with calcined clay; h, flint knife; i, layer of charcoal dust, calcined clay and a few odd potsherds; k, grave-shaft with traces of oak logs covering it.

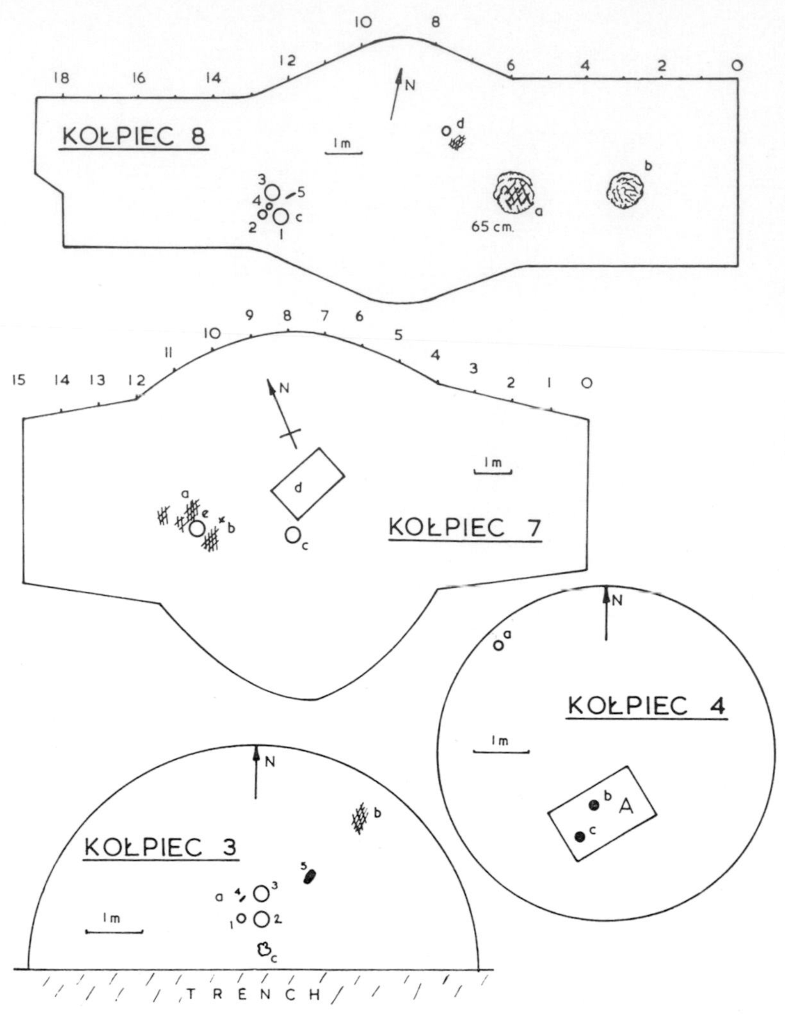

PLAN 29. Four barrow-graves at Kołpiec (no. 46).

1. Barrow-grave 8.
a, traces of a large hearth on the top of the mound; b, thick layer of black, fat clay; c, group of four vessels: bowl (Plate 7:8), beaker, small cup and a larger vessel, and a flint scraper (5); d, lugged beaker (Fig. 11:3) and lump of charcoal.

2. Barrow-grave 7.
a, charcoal; b, flint chip; c, destroyed vessel on the top of the mound; d, grave-shaft; e, destroyed vessel.

3. Barrow-grave 3.
a, group of three vessels: handled cup, bowl, flint scraper (4) and stone battle axe (5); b, charcoal; c, lump of ochre.

4. Barrow-grave 4.
a, few sherds of coarse vessels on the top of the mound; b, flint axe (Fig. 16:2); c, flint blade (dagger?) (Plate 11:5) (b and c were found in the mound); A, grave-shaft.

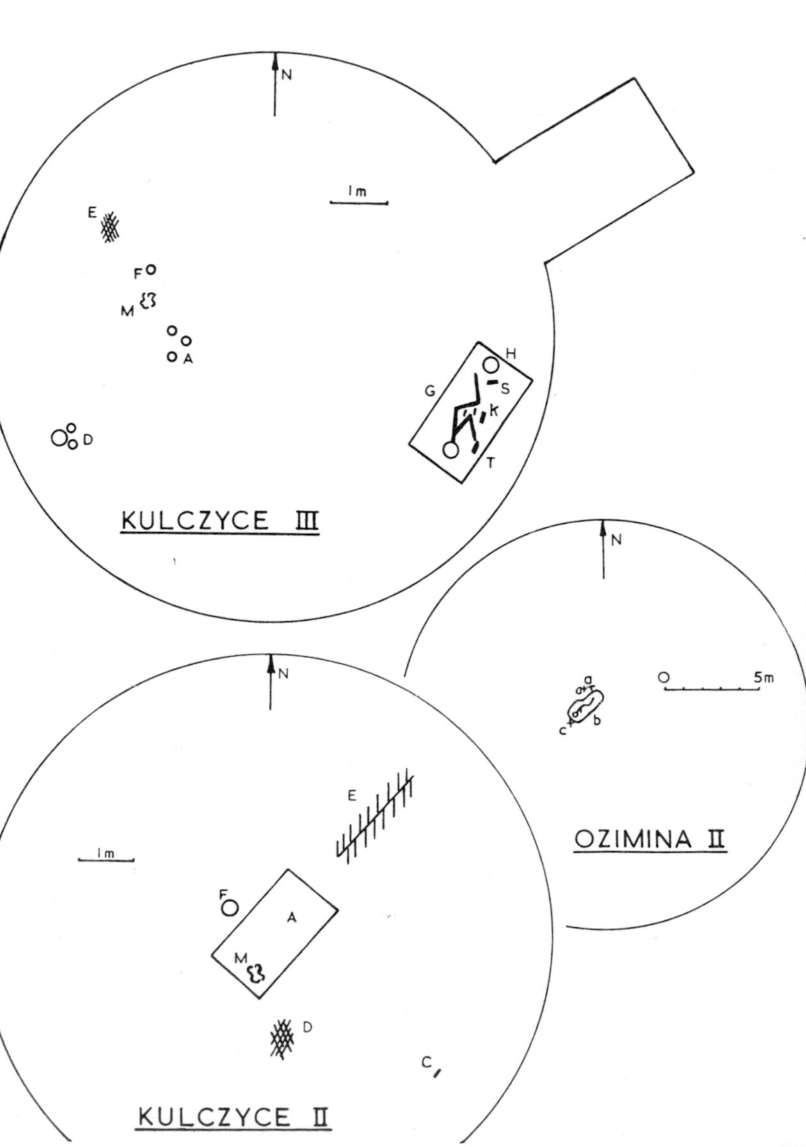

PLAN 30. Two barrow-graves at Kulczyce Slacheckie (no. 49) and one at Ozimina (no. 53).

1. Barrow-grave Kulczyce III.
A, D, F, sherds of a Thuringian amphora found at various depths in the mound and on the ancient ground; E, charcoal; G, grave-shaft; H, cord-decorated beaker; K, two flint arrow-heads and flint scraper; S, flint axe (Fig. 16:14); T, damaged halved stone battle-axe.

2. Kulczyce II.
a, grave-shaft; C, blunt axe made of sandstone (Fig. 15:17); D, charcoal; F, small Thuringian amphora (Plate 5:4); E, layer of oak planks, site of the second burial?; M, lumps of ochre.

3. Ozimina II.
a, splinter of hornstone, flint knife and small potsherd, both on the top of the mound; b, grave-shaft; c, flint chip.

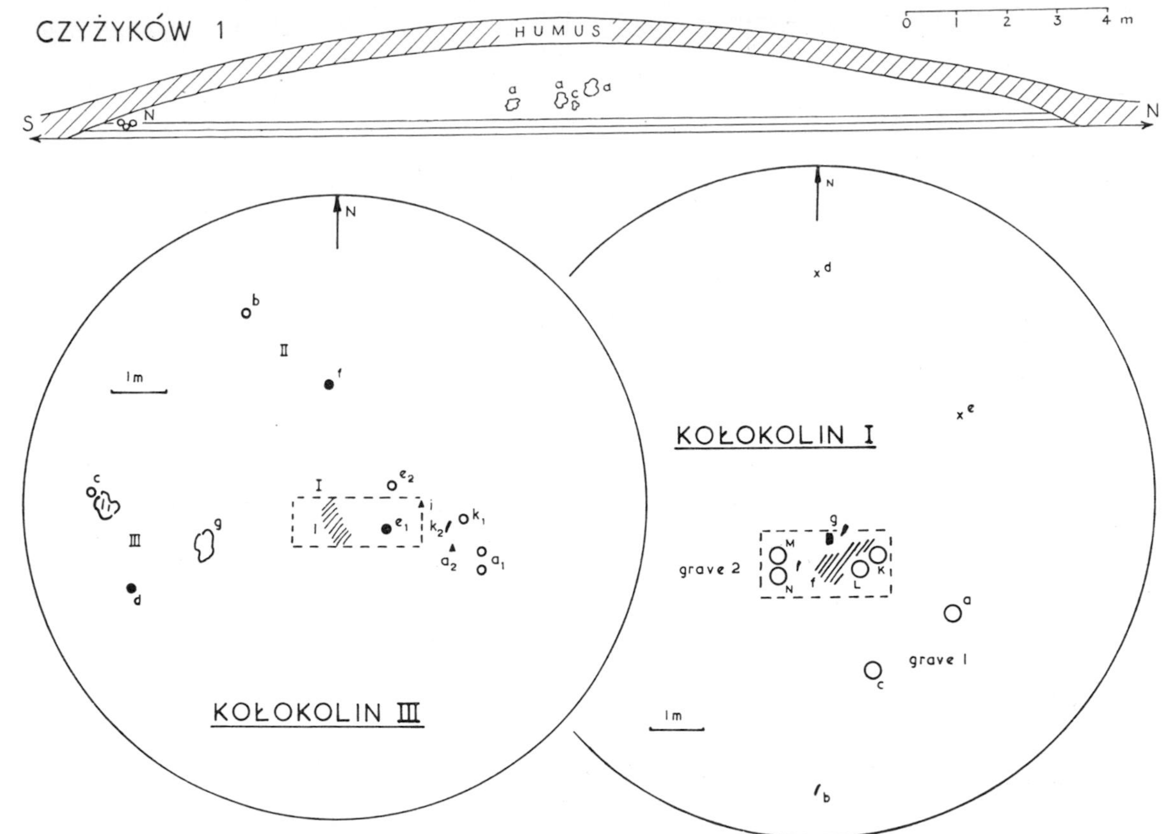

PLAN 31. Cross-section of barrow-grave I at Czyżyków (no. 60) and plans of two barrow-graves at Kołokolin (no. 66).

1. Czyżyków I.

a, lumps of ochre; c, potsherds; N, three vessels: deep bowl, tulip-shaped beaker and another bowl (Plate 16:19; Plate 18:2, 12), and a bronze awl.

2. Kołokolin III.

a-1, two vessels of the Lipica culture (Roman period) found in the mound; a-2, butt of a flint axe; b, deep bowl (Plate 7:5); c, handled cord-decorated cup (Fig. 10:2) and calcined bones; d, stone battle-axe (Fig. 14:1); e-1, sandstone; e-2, small vessel; f, axe made of siliceous slate; g, small heap of calcined bones; i, stone battle-axe (Plate 10:3); k-1, cord-decorated cup (Plate 6:19); k-2, large flint flake (Fig. 17:6); l, charcoal; I, II, III, sites of three burials.

3. Kołokolin I.

a, c, two entirely crushed vessels; b, small flint knife; d, fragment of a small polished flint axe; e, flint scraper; f, calcined human bones; g, flint arrow-head (Plate 9:25) and a thin small flint axe (Fig. 12:9); K, Thuringian amphora (Fig. 10:1); L, bowl (Plate 6:20); M, N, two beakers (Plate 6:1, 9).

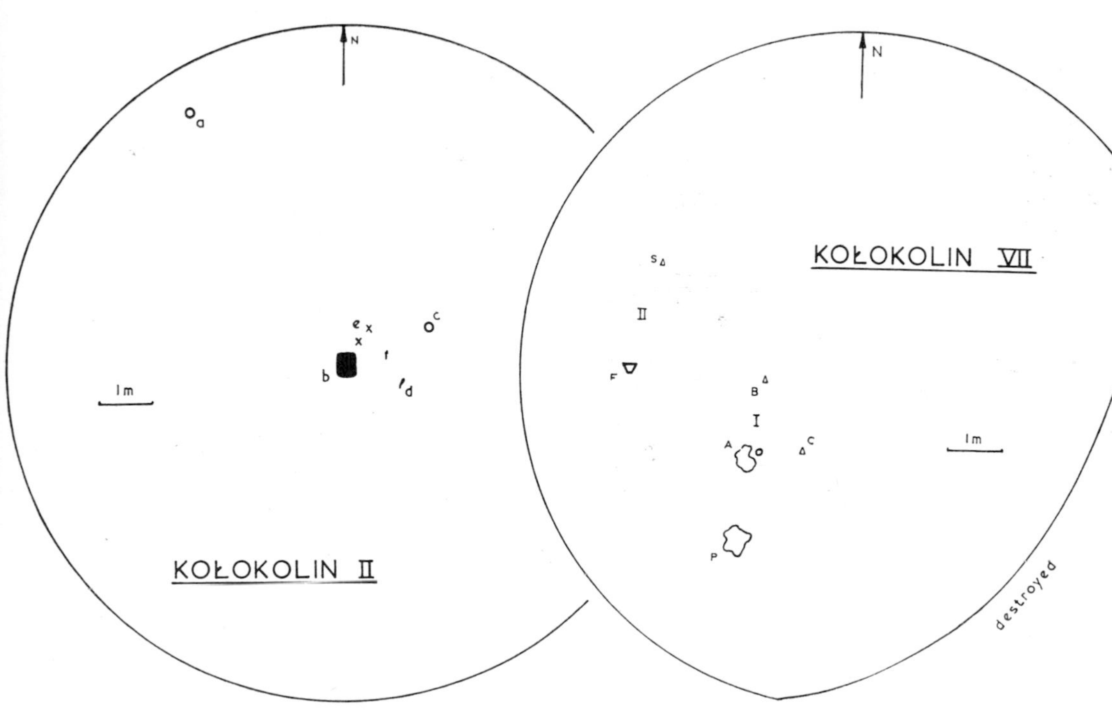

PLAN 32. Two barrow-graves at Kołokolin (no. 66).

1. Barrow-grave II.

a, beaker (Plate 7:7); b, alabaster slab on the top of the mound; c, deep bowl (Plate 7:6); d, flint axe (Fig. 15:9); e, two flint knives (Fig. 17:7, 8); f, site of the grave.

2. Barrow-grave VII.

A, crushed vessel, near it a perforated clay disc (Fig. 19:20); B, C, two flint arrow-heads (Plate 9:19, 22); P, accumulation of red fired clay and charcoal; F, cord-decorated mug (Fig. 10:3); S, mutilated axe made of siliceous slate.

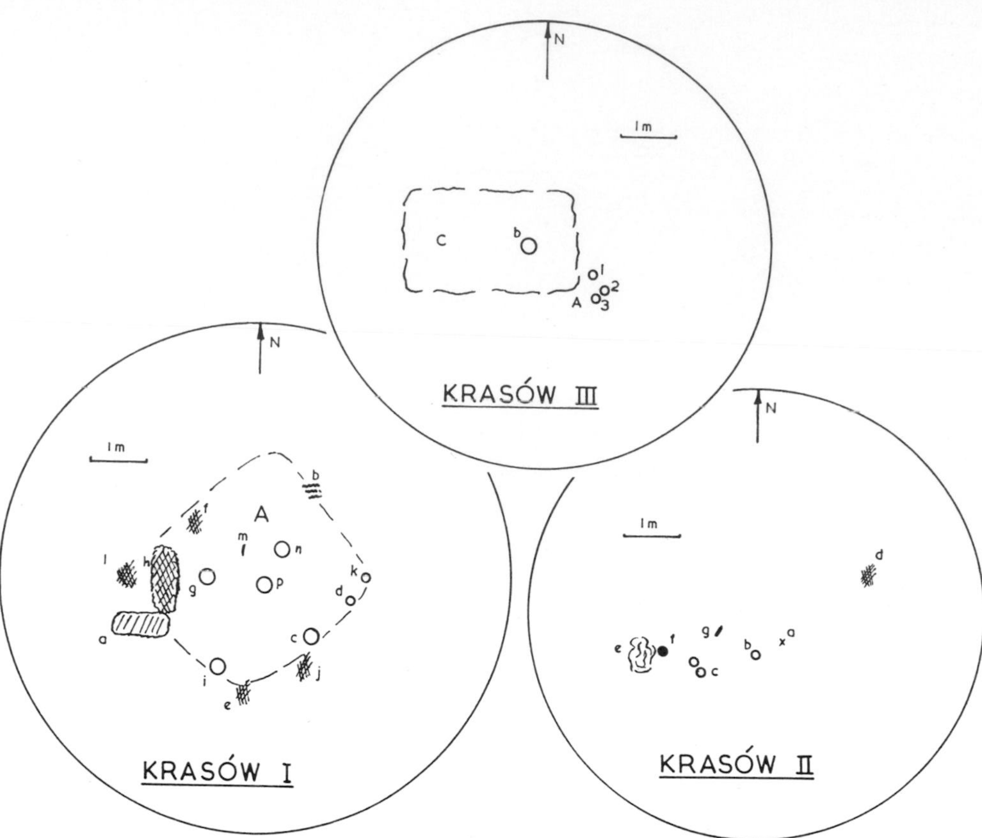

PLAN 33. Three barrow-graves at Krasów (no. 67).

1. Barrow-grave III.
A, two bowls and a cup (Plate 20:8, 10; Plate 19:9); C, shallow grave-shaft; b, small handled cup (Plate 19:11).

2. Barrow-grave I.
A, shallow shaft; a, sandstone slab, its surface fired; b, calcined bones; c, d, g, k, scattered sherds of the Thuringian amphora (Fig. 9:1), its largest part being found in the centre 'n'; e, f, j, l, accumulations of charcoal; h, layer of charcoal; i, small entirely crushed cup; m, axe made of siliceous slate (Fig. 9:4); p, ribbed beaker (Fig. 9:3).

3. Barrow-grave II.
a, flint flake; b, odd potsherd, found with 'a' near the top of the mound; d, lump of charcoal; c, e, broken Thuringian amphora, its fragments scattered; f, flint axe (Fig. 16:22); g, flint knife (Fig. 17:9).

PLAN 34. Two barrow-graves at Krasów (no. 67) and one at Stratyn (no. 87).

1. Krasów V.
a-1, lugged jug (Fig. 30:8); a-2, small cup; b, scattered sherds of a bowl; c, handled cup in a small hole; d, area littered with small pieces and lumps of charcoal.

2. Krasów IV.
a, b, single sherd and accumulation of fragments of an amphora of Roman period found under the humus; c, odd potsherds; d, two small shafts with remains of wooden vertical posts; e, central area littered with charcoal; f, small shaft with calcined human bones on the bottom, covered with decayed timber logs; g, shallow, oval hole in which stood two vessels, a small one, entirely crushed (bowl?), and a larger bowl (Plate 19:13) on which lay a bronze pin, and nearby (3) was a small stone, probably an unperforated shaft-hole axe (Fig. 35:16).

3. Stratyn 2.
a, grave-shaft; b, Thuringian amphora (Plate 5:1).

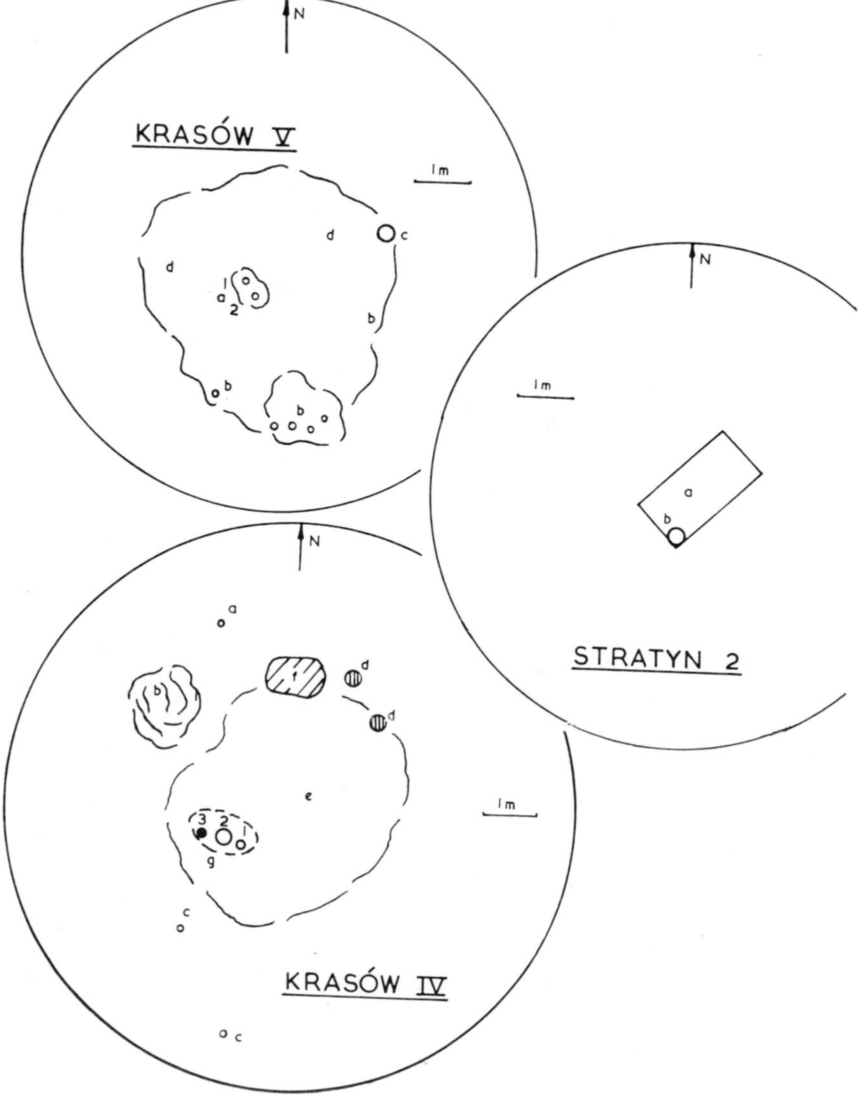

PLAN 35. Three barrow-graves at Rokitno (no. 82) and two at Wolica (no. 91).

1. Rokitno 2.
a, flint burin; b, flint arrow-head; c-1, 2, irregular lumps of sandstone; d, Thuringian amphora (Plate 5:8); e, flint axe; f, amber pendant (Fig. 19:21); g, stone battle-axe (Fig. 15:2); h, stag tooth; i, flint knife; j, flint flake; k, small pebble; A, grave-shaft.

2. Wolica 4.
a, b, two decorated bowls; c, beaker (Plate 19:8); d, tulip-shaped pot (Plate 20:4); e, small entirely crushed cup; f, larger cup (Plate 19:12); g, handled bowl (Plate 19:7); h, i, handled cups (Fig. 30:4, Plate 19:6); k, layer of charcoal (charred log).

3. Wolica 1.
i, large bowl (Plate 20:13); j, tulip-shaped beaker (Plate 20:3); k, small heap of calcined bones; l, handled cup (Plate 19:5); z, small bowl (Fig. 28:6).

4. Rokitno 6.
a, grave-shaft; b, two flint axes (Fig. 15:10, 11), and butt of a third one, nearby three points made of horn (daggers?) (Plate 11:13, 14); c, d, flint knives; e, Thuringian amphora (Plate 5:9); f, bones of a loose human left leg over the skeleton; g, large stone; h, charcoal.

5. Rokitno 3.
a, shaft (modern?); b, female skeleton; c, layer of charcoal over the skeleton; d, jawbone of a lamb; e, large sherd of a cord-decorated beaker; f, grave-shaft with a male skeleton

5a. Profile of shaft 'f' in barrow-grave above.

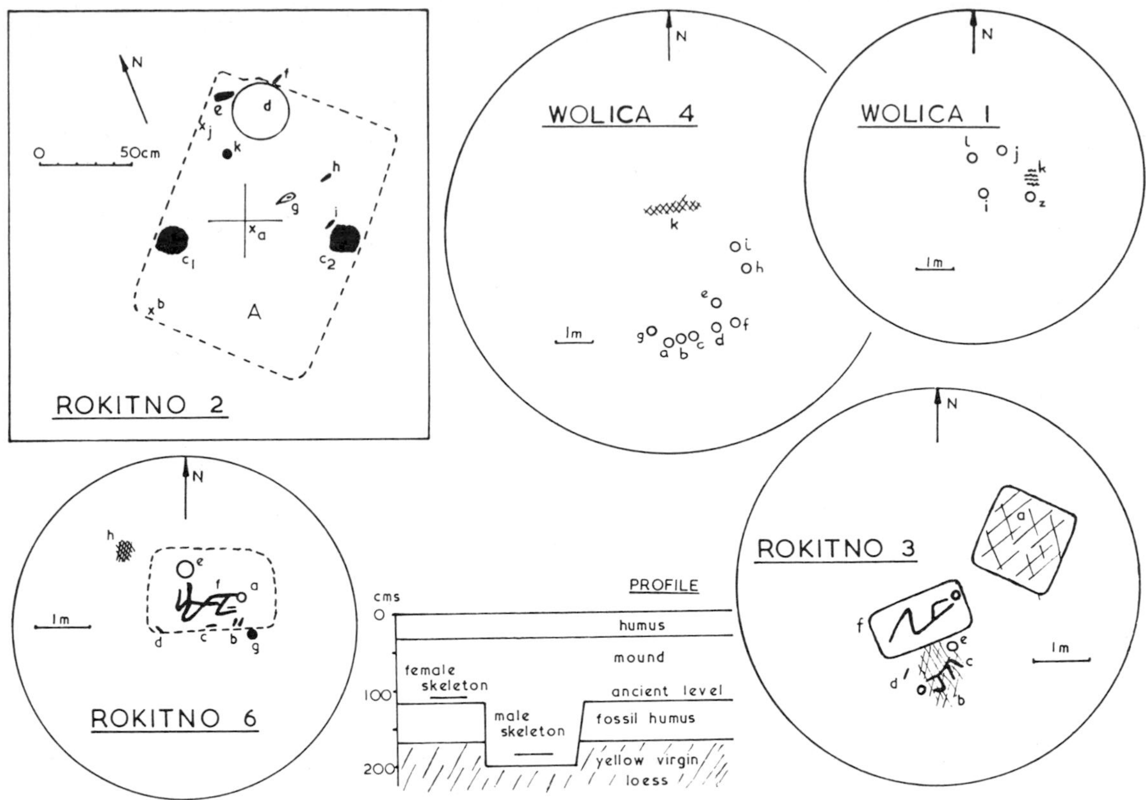

PLAN 36. Three barrow-graves at Sarniki (no. 86).

1. Barrow-grave I.
a, stone battle-axe, bronze dagger (Fig. 19:23) and flint scraper; b, grave-shaft.

2. Barrow-grave III.
a, d, potsherds; b, lump of charcoal; c, flint knife (Fig. 17:10); e, scattered dust and lumps of charcoal; f, flint scraper (Fig. 17:15); g, h, calcined sandstones.

3, 3a. Barrow-grave IV.
A, grave-shaft; f, k, flint flakes; g, lump of charcoal; h, beaker (Plate 18:1); i, smaller bowl (Plate 17:6); j, larger bowl (Plate 17:3); m, a few potsherds; n, beaker (Plate 18:11); *circles:* odd potsherds.

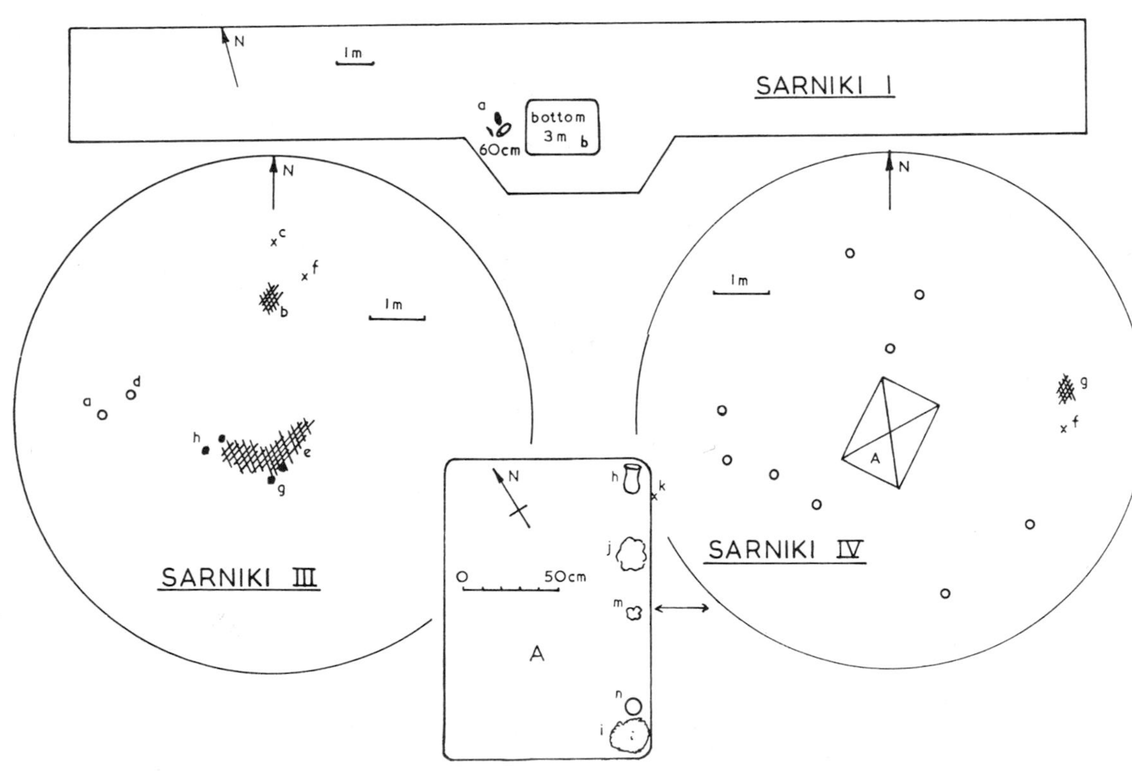

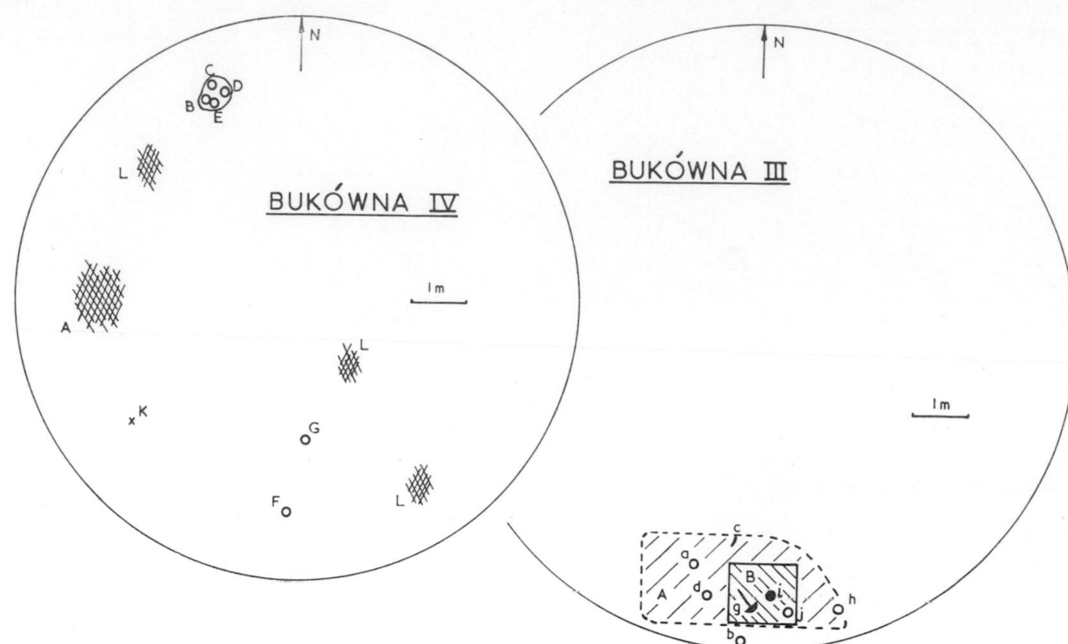

PLAN 37. Two barrow-graves at Bukówna (no. 97).

1. Barrow-grave IV.
A, layer consisting of fired clay and charcoal; B, tulip-shaped pot; C, cup (Plate 20:7); D, bowl (Plate 20:11); E, small bowl or saucer (Fig. 30:6); F, G, two bowls (Plate 19:14, Plate 20:5); K, flint scraper; L, lumps of charcoal.

2. Barrow-grave III.
A, shallow hole; B, deeper part of the hole in which were found ash and calcined human bones; a, crushed vessel; b, potsherds; c, spiral-headed bronze pin; d, bowl (Plate 17:2); g, bronze pin (Fig. 26:12); h, entirely crushed vessel; i, spiral bronze armband (Fig. 26:13); j, cup (Plate 18:12).

PLAN 38. Two barrow-graves at Okniany (no. 106), and one at Bukówna (no. 97).

1. Okniany II.
a, b, tulip-shaped pots one on top of another (Fig. 28:3, Plate 18:6); c, bowl with two lugs (Plate 16:16); d, bowl (Plate 16:15 or Plate 18:15); e, potsherds; f, tulip-shaped pot (Plate 18:4); g, probably a tulip-shaped pot; h, double-handled vase (Plate 17:11); i, handled cup (Plate 17:9); l, double-handled vase (Fig. 28:1); v, bowl (Plate 16:15 or Plate 18:15); x, cup (Plate 18:17).

2. Okniany I.
A, grave-shaft; a, single-lugged mug (Plate 9:14); b, entirely crushed smaller vessel; d, stone battle-axe (Fig. 13:7) found on the top of the mound; c, j-1, 2, three stone battle-axes (Fig. 13:4); e, few flint flakes; f, flint arrow-head; g, three limestones; h, pebbles; k, flint point.

3. Bukówna VI.
a, undecorated tulip-shaped beaker (Plate 20:2); b, c, d, vessels of unknown shape, one of these a decorated handled cup (Plate 19:1); e, two vessels, one of these a large undecorated vase with four perforated lugs on the shoulder (Fig. 28:4).

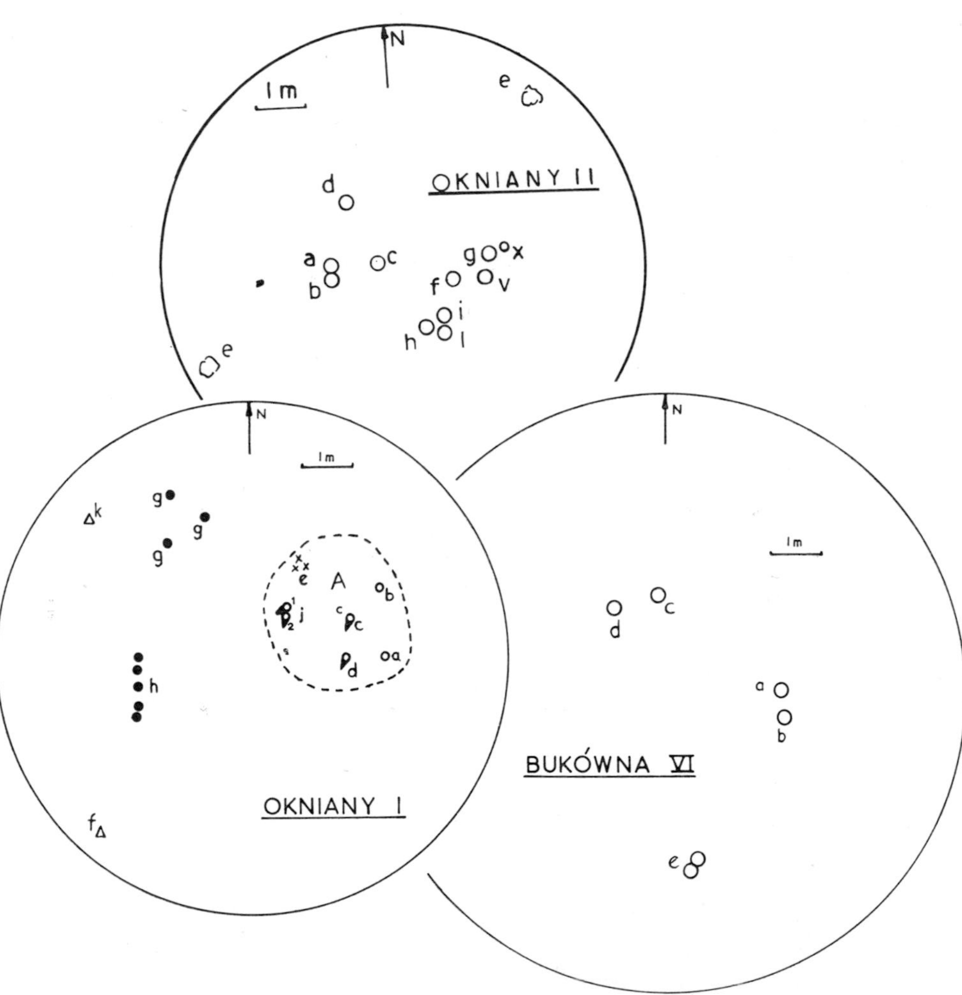

PLAN 39. Plan and cross-section of barrow-grave I at Gwoździec Stary (no. 101).

1. Plan.
A–H, main points of the profiles; K, layer of yellow clay, presumably site of a secondary burial of a later period; L, central area covered with timber logs; M, burial platform on which lay a lump of ochre and charcoal dust and lumps; P, the original base of the mound; a, blade of a broken battle-axe (Plate 10:4); b, flint flakes; c, odd potsherds; d, iron chisel; e, iron nail; f, fragments of broken flint implements; g, red fired clay; h, charcoal; m, accumulations of charcoal and a fragment of a broken flint implement (Fig. 17:12).

2, 3. Profiles of the above barrow along the points marked on the plan.
Lettering corresponds with that of the plan.

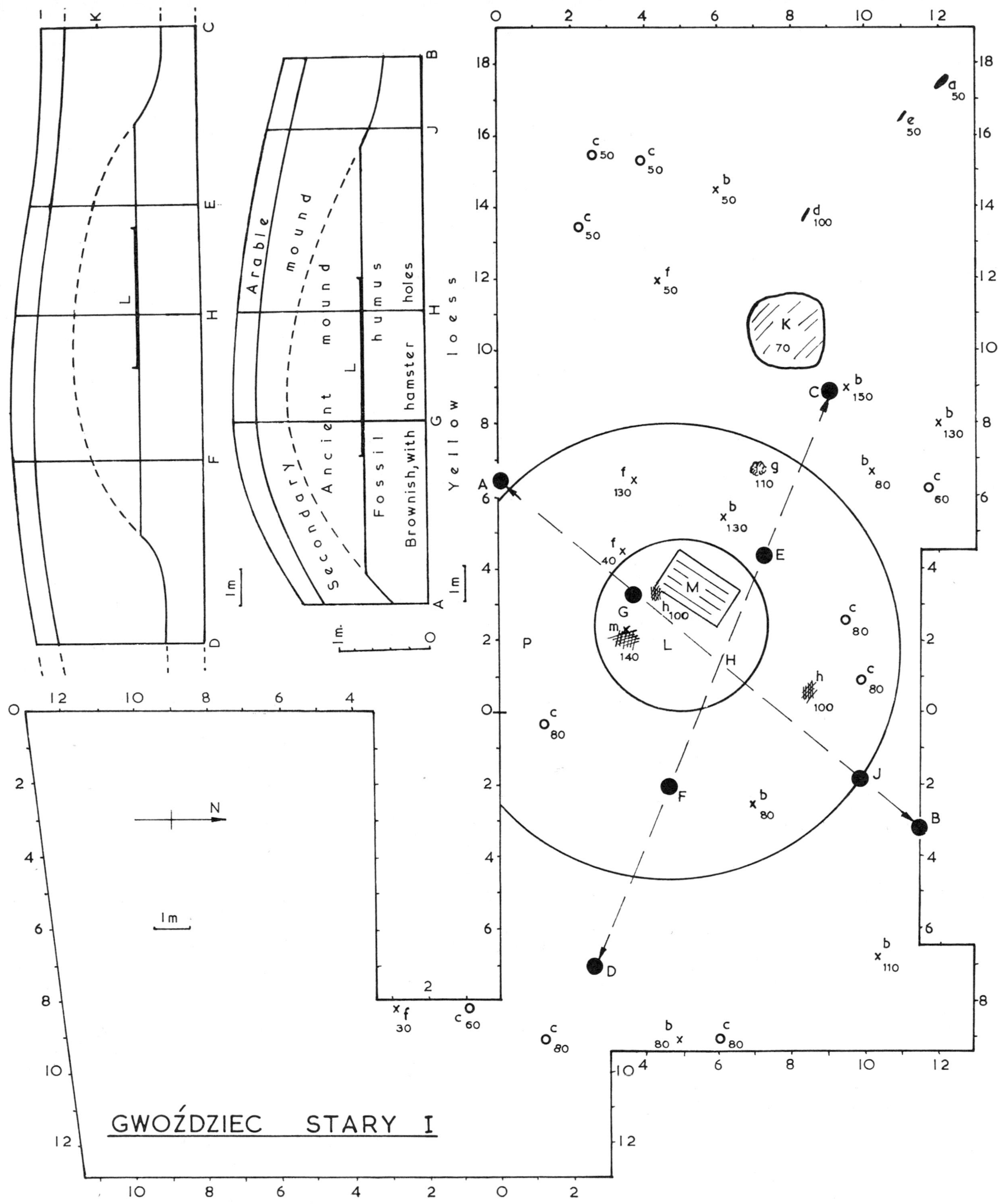

Arable
mound
Secondary
Ancient mound
Fossil humus
Brownish, with hamster holes
Yellow loess
1m
K
70
M
P
L
GWOŹDZIEC STARY I
N

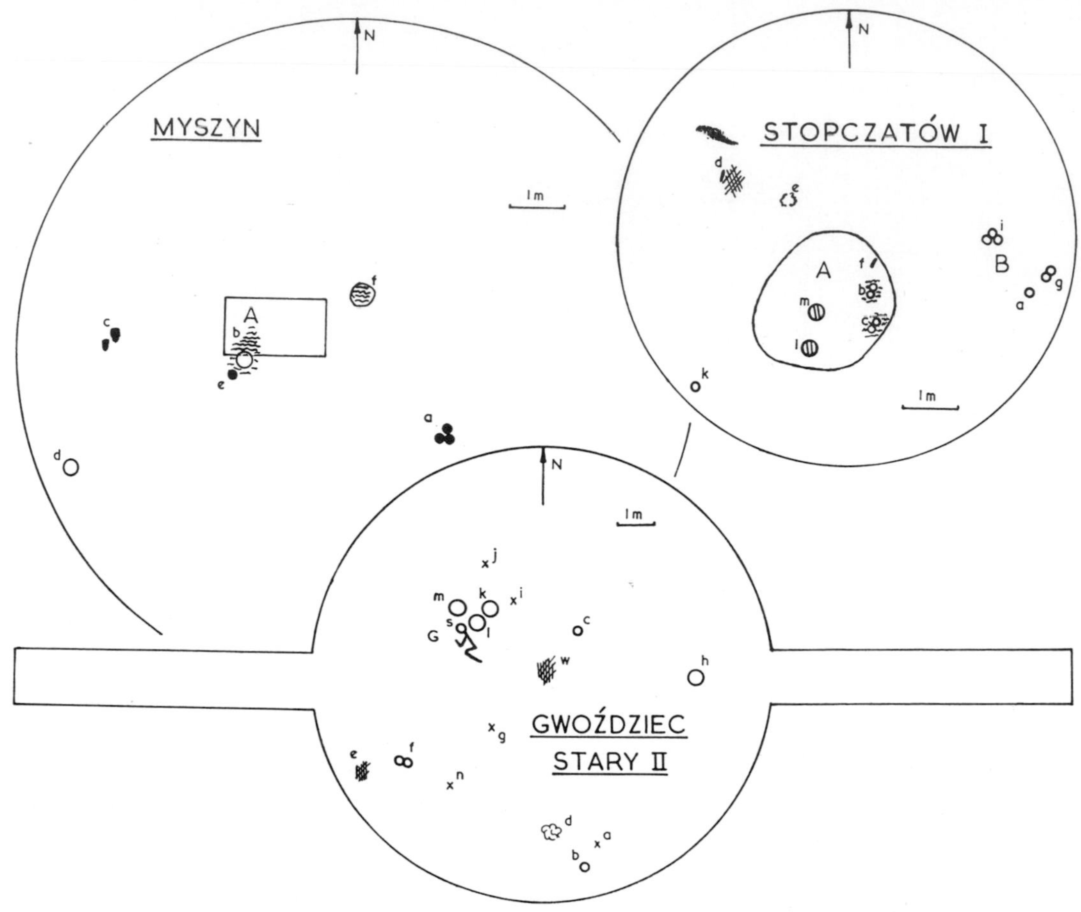

PLAN 40. Three Sub-Carpathian barrow-graves.

1. Myszyn (no. 104).

A, shallow grave-shaft; a, three pebbles; b, heaped calcined human bones; c, butts of two stone battle-axes (Plate 10:6); d, fragments of a vase of the beginning of the Christian era; e, small beaker (Fig. 10:5) and a damaged battle-axe under it (Plate 10:7); f, small hole filled in with calcined human bones.

2. Stopczatów (no. 111).

A, secondary burial of the Roman period; B, the original grave of the Komarów culture; a, tulip-shaped vessel (Plate 20:1); b, c, heaps of calcined human bones, charcoal and a few potsherds; d, heap of charcoal and fired clay, and a part of a bronze horse bit; e, accumulation of burned clay and charcoal; f, damaged bronze clasp; g, small bowl and small cup (Plate 20:6, 9); i, three vessels, small bowl, handled bowl and handled cup (Plate 20:12, Plate 19:2, 3); k, potsherd; l, m, small pits filled in with remains of pyre.

3. Gwoździec Stary II (no. 101).

G, site of the grave; a, trimmed flint blade; b, c, f, potsherds; d, larger dark potsherd; e, w, lumps of charcoal; g, n, flint flakes; h, dark vessel (Plate 9:9); i, flint blade; j, flint burin; k, single-lugged mug (Plate 9:5); l, handled jug (Fig. 10:6); m, small entirely crushed vessel; s, bronze ear-pendant lying on the skull (Plate 9:4).

PLAN 41. Barrow-grave cemetery at Zaborol-Biczal and of five barrow-graves at Biczal (no. 166).

1. Plan of the cemetery Zaborol-Biczal. *crossed:* barrow-graves investigated.

2. Zaborol-Biczal 8.
a, grave-shaft with a few lumps of charcoal in it; *circles:* potsherds; *cross:* flint chip (Fig. 18:1).

3. Zaborol-Biczal 9.
A, B, crushed vessel; b, crushed vessel and charcoal; c, large flint flake and charcoal; *circle:* potsherd; *crosses:* flints; *hatched:* accumulation of charcoal.

4. Zaborol-Izydorówka 1.
a, tulip-shaped pot; i, j, large flint blade (Fig. 18:3, 8, 9); l, decorated vessel, probably tulip-shaped pot; *circles:* potsherds; *crosses:* flints; *black spots:* stones.

5. Zaborol-Izydorówka 4.
A, bowl (Plate 24:3); B, decorated beaker (Plate 24:5) and undecorated cup (Plate 24:4); C (or E), deep bowl (Plate 24:2); D, tulip-shaped pot (Plate 24:1); E (or C), F, two vessels of unknown shape; *circles:* odd potsherds; *crosses:* flints.

6. Zaborol-Biczal 10.
A, pouch-shaped vessel, crushed; w, area strewn with charcoal; *circles:* odd potsherds.

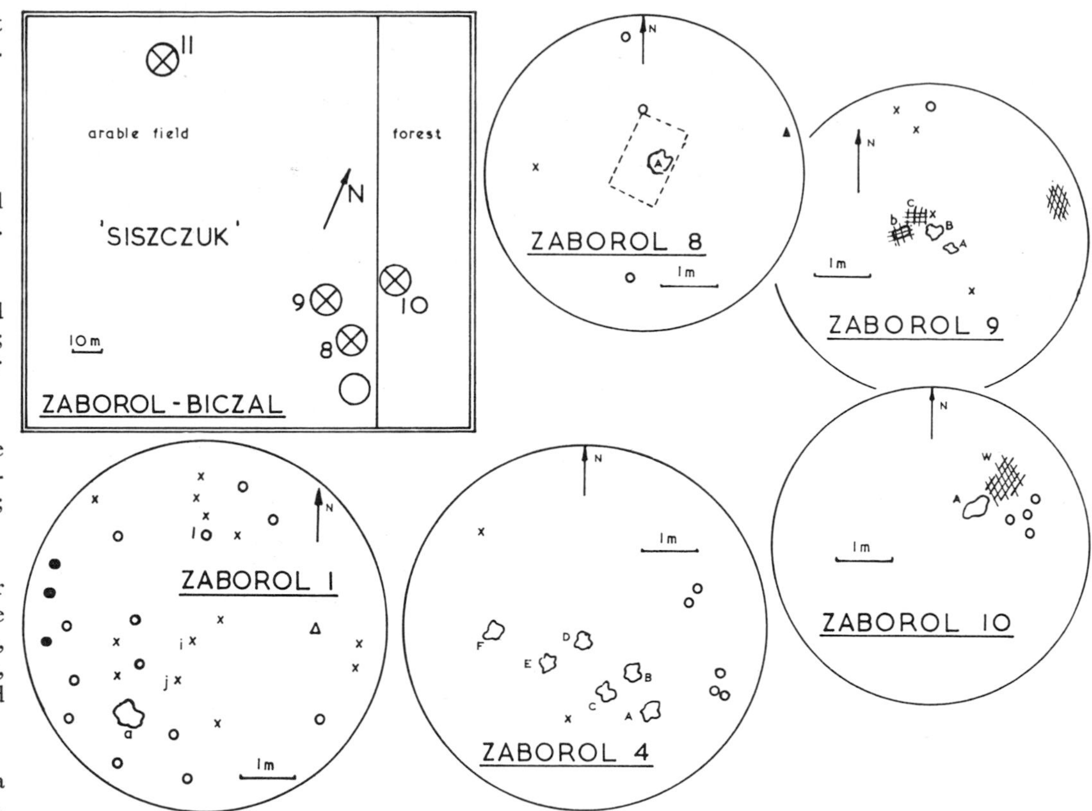

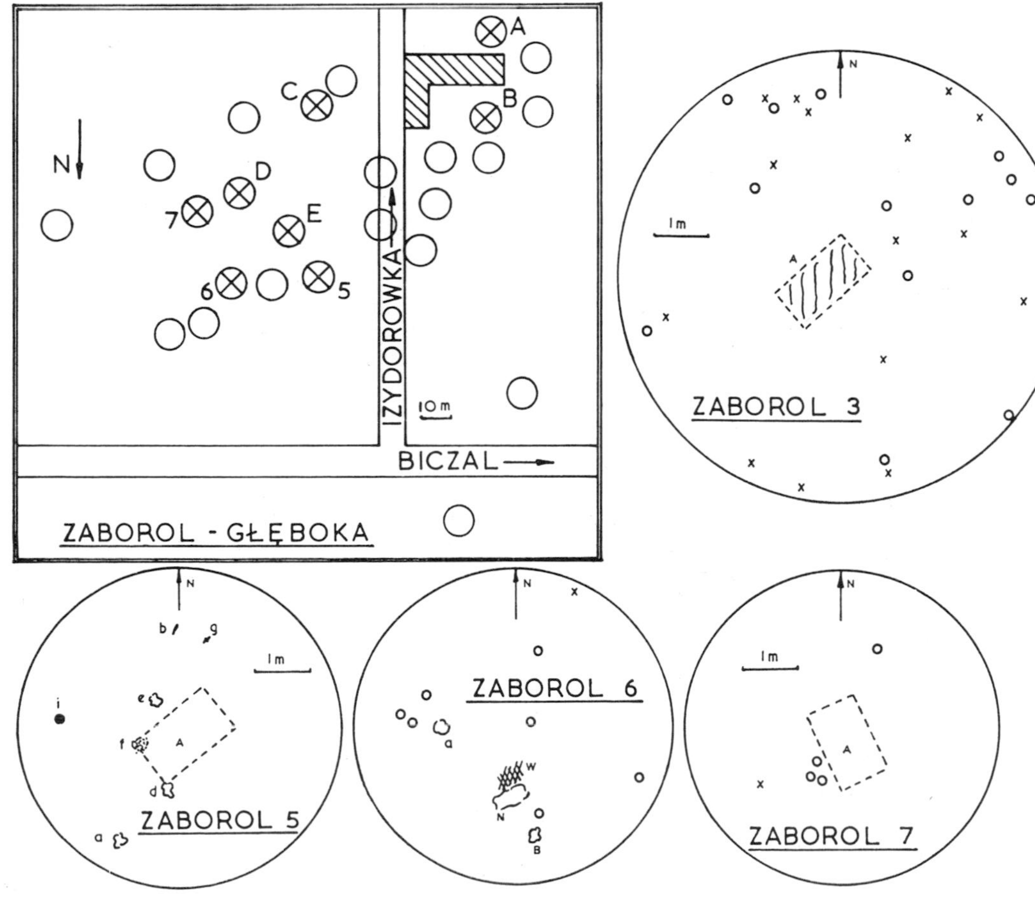

PLAN 42. Barrow-grave cemetery Zaborol-Głęboka and plans of four barrow-graves at Zaborol (no. 166).

1. Plan of the cemetery Zaborol-Głęboka. *crossed:* investigated barrow-graves; *shaded:* site of a house.

2. Zaborol-Izydorówka 3.
A, grave-shaft; *circles:* odd potsherds (Fig. 29:3); *crosses:* flints.

3. Zaborol-Głęboka 5.
A, grave-shaft; a, d, e, crushed pouch-shaped vessels (Plate 23:7); b, iron spear-head; f, handful of charcoal dust; g, fragment of an iron object; i, stone wedge.

4. Zaborol-Głęboka 6.
B, N, large pouch-shaped vessel; a, crushed vessel; w, site of a small hearth; *circles:* odd potsherds; *crosses:* flint flakes (Fig. 17:14, Fig. 18:2, 4–6).

5. Zaborol-Głęboka 7.
A, grave shaft; *circles:* potsherds; *cross:* larger flint.

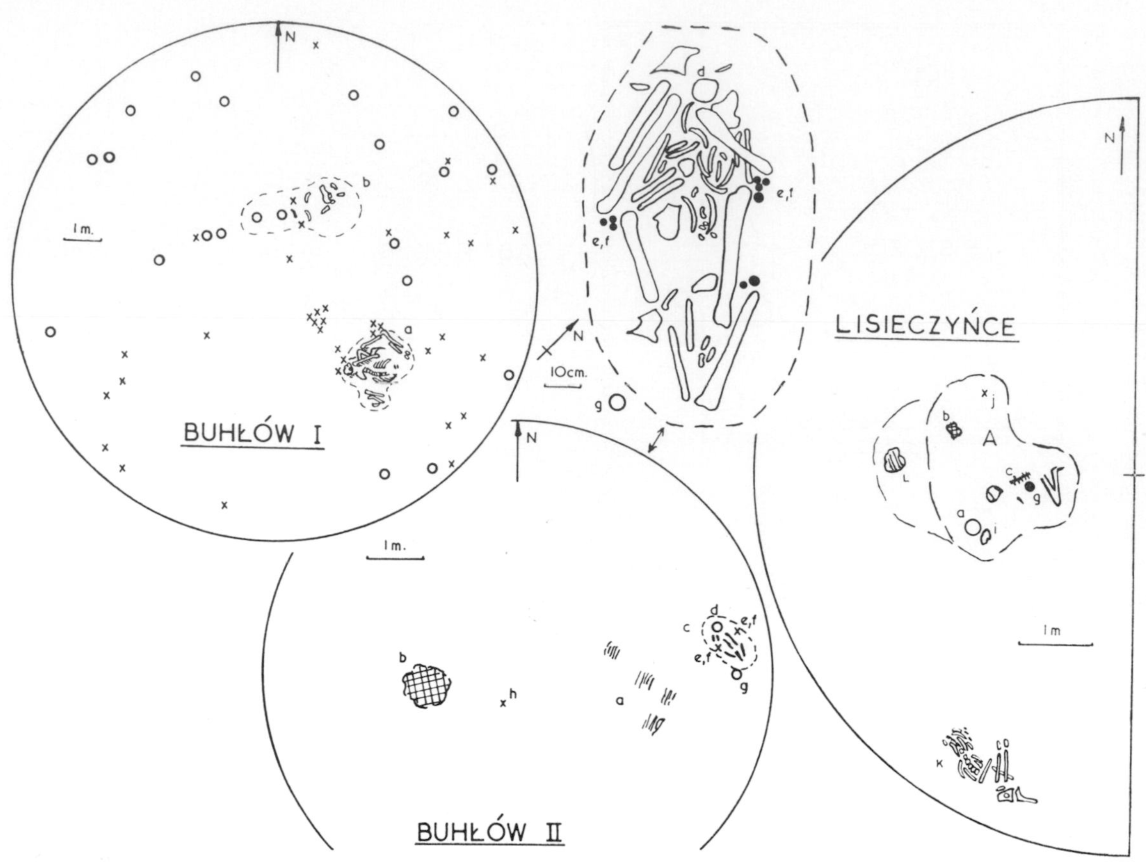

PLAN 43. Two barrow-graves at Buhłów (no. 194), and at Lisieczyńce (no. 203).

1. Buhłów I (Plate 2:3).
a, burial 1 (Plate 2:3); b, burial 2; *circles:* fragments of animal bones; *crosses:* flints.

2, 2a. Buhłów II (Plate 2:1, 2).
a, traces of the decayed skeleton of burial 1; b, traces of a hearth; c, mutilated female skeleton of burial 2 (Plate 2:1, 2); d, single-lugged mug (Plate 9:6); e, f, two silver spiral rings and seven bone beads (Plate 9:10–11); g, the skull; h, flint scraper.

3. Lisieczyńce.
A, patch of very dark earth littered with lumps of charcoal; K, skeleton of a lamb or sheep; L, a few unidentified bones; a, Thuringian amphora (Plate 4:4); b, larger lump of charred wood; c, human skeleton; g, large stone; i, lump of lime; j, flint knife.

PLAN 44. Three barrow-graves in West Podolia.

1. Klimkowce (no. 199).
a, site of grave 1; a-1, 2, two battle-axes (Fig. 13:3; 14:6); a-3, 5, three flint arrow-heads; a-6, single-lugged mug (Fig. 10:4); b, site of grave 2; b-1, stone battle-axe; b-2, 3–5, four flint arrow-heads; b-6, boar tusk and flint scraper; c, calcined animal bones; d, large hearth; e, large pieces of charred wood; f, decayed human bones (grave 3) and accumulations of charcoal; g, a few human bones and charcoal (grave 4?).

2. Łuczka II (no. 204).
A, area littered with charcoal; a, accumulation of calcined human bones; b, large fragment of a large bowl (Fig. 32:2); c, accumulation of charcoal and small lumps of fired clay; d, sherds of vessel 'b' and of two other vessels, deep dish and undecorated pot (Fig. 32:1, 7).

3. Uście Biskupie (no. 219).
a, grave-shaft under a cairn, covered with timber logs, on its bottom scattered lumps of charcoal; b, large sherd of a large vase (Fig. 32:6) found on the layer of logs; c, iron knife (Fig. 32:5) on the bottom of the shaft; *checked:* accumulation of charcoal.

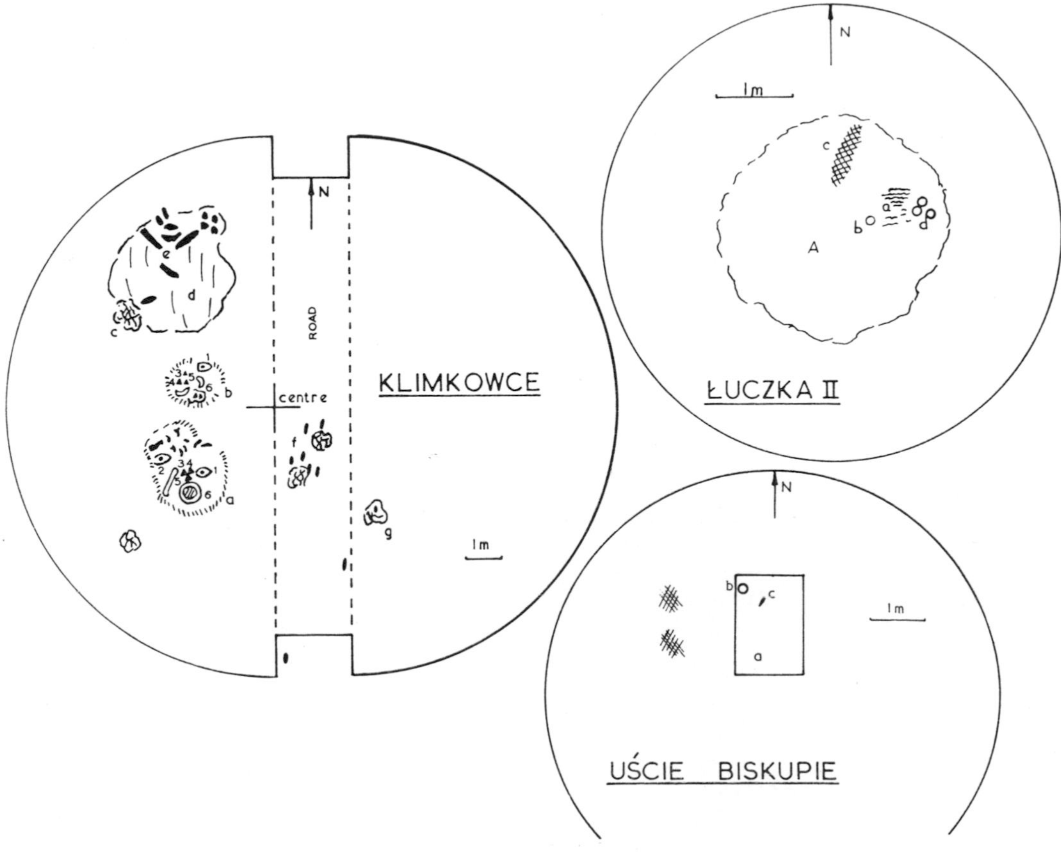

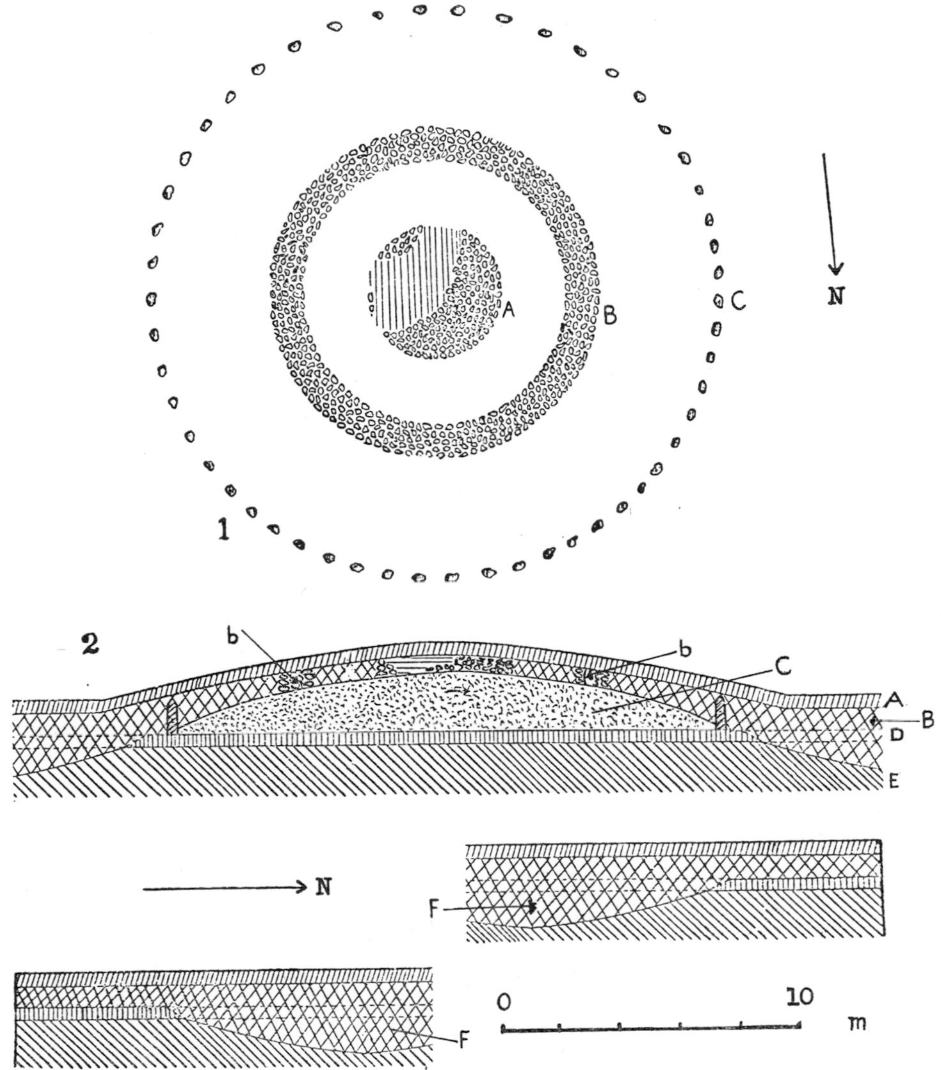

PLAN 45. Plan and cross-section of barrow-grave II at Nowosiółka Jaruzelskich (no. 212) (after J. Bryk).

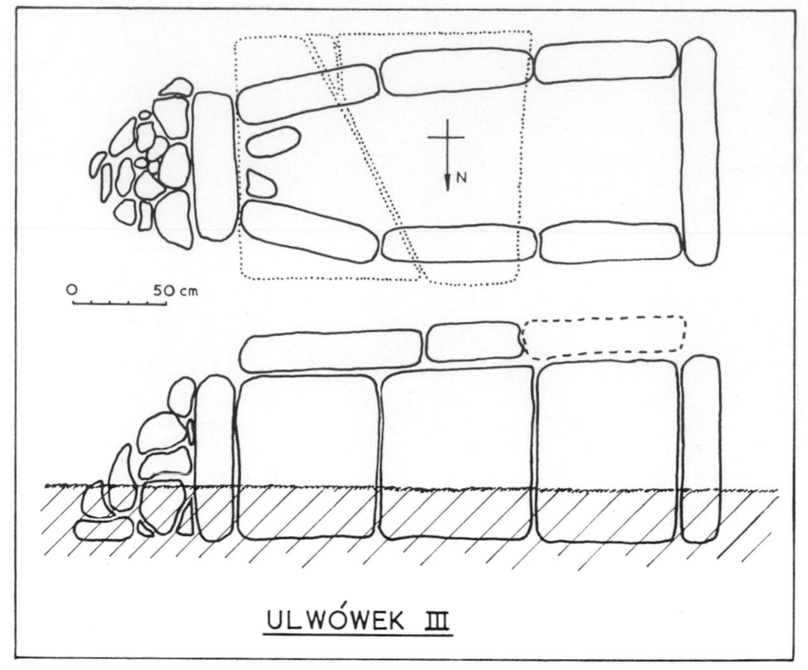

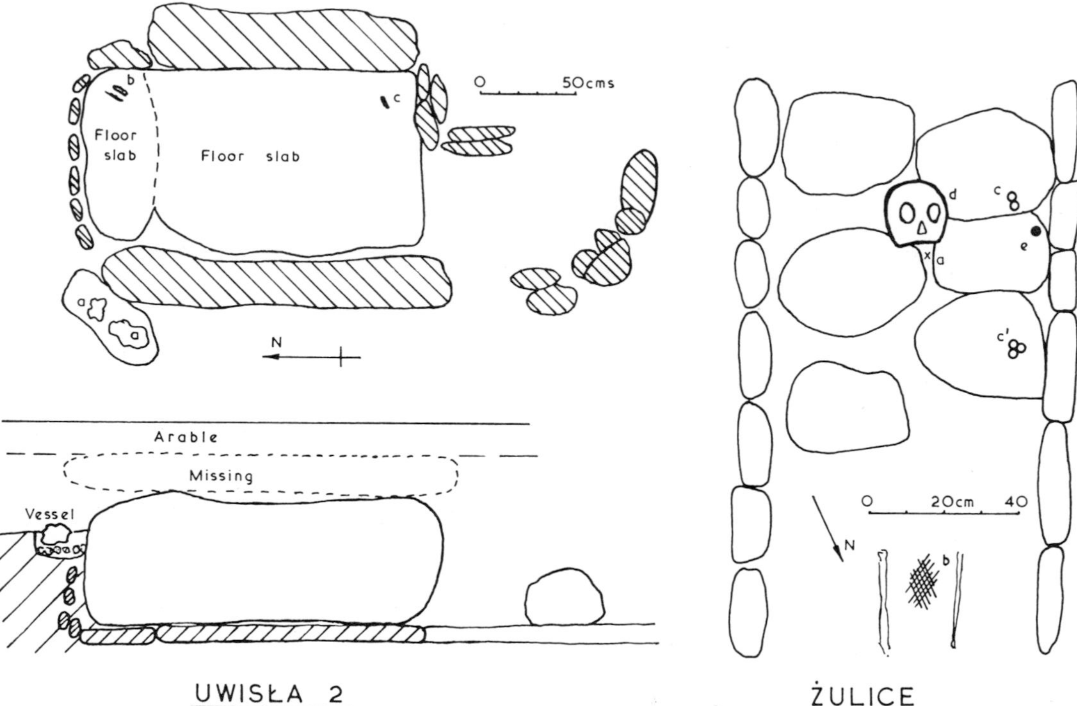

PLAN 46. Three slab-cist graves.

1. Ulwówek III (no. 398) (Plate 12:1, 2).

2. Uwisła 2 (no. 518), plan and cross-section.

a, crushed vessel in a cobbled hole (Plate 22:6); b, pieces of feet bones; c, human tooth.

3. Żulice (no. 426).

a, small flint; b, leg bones; c, sherds of a large vase found on the floor; c¹, sherds of the same vessel found on the covering slab; d, skull; e, small polished stone; *checked:* handful of charcoal on the floor, between the legs.

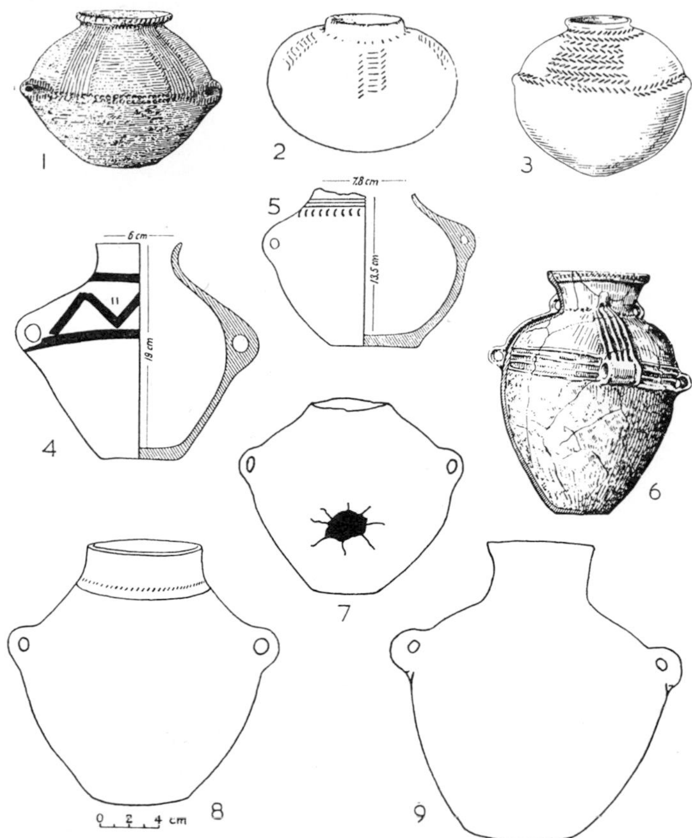

Fig. 1. Thuringian amphorae and their derivative, from various sites in Eastern Europe.

1 – Griščintsy (no. 242) (after V. G. Childe); 2 – Fatyanovo culture (after V. Gorodtsov); 3 – barrow-grave cemetery of Balanovo on the Volga (after O. N. Bader); 4, 5, 8 – Vykhvatyntsi (no. 371) (after A. E. Alikhova and T. S. Passek); 6 – barrow-grave at Valea Lupului, Moldavia (after M. Dinu); 7 – urn of the cremation cemetery at Černyn near Kiev (after V. I. Kanivets); 9 – urn of the cremation cemetery at Červonyi Khutir (Archaeological Institute of the Ukrainian Academy, Kiev).

Fig. 2. Vessels characteristic of the Strzyżów culture from Raciborowice (no. 615) (after Z. Ślusarski): double-lugged amphora, handled cup, double-lugged basin (lugs vertically perforated), beaker.

Fig. 3. Three decorated bowls typical of the Middle Dnieper culture, found in the Crimea (Archaeological Museum, Cracow).

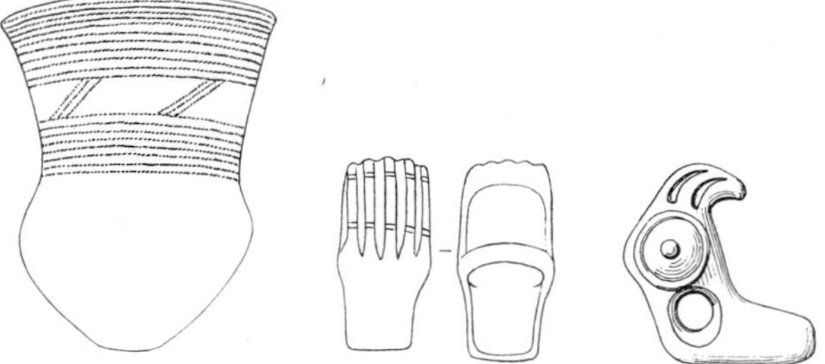

Fig. 4. Cord-decorated beaker from barrow-grave 48 at Jackowica (no. 244) (after A. Bydłowski), and two bronze amulets from barrow-grave 26 at Nowosiółka (no. 253) (after E. Majewski). The third amulet from this grave was identical with the centre one above.

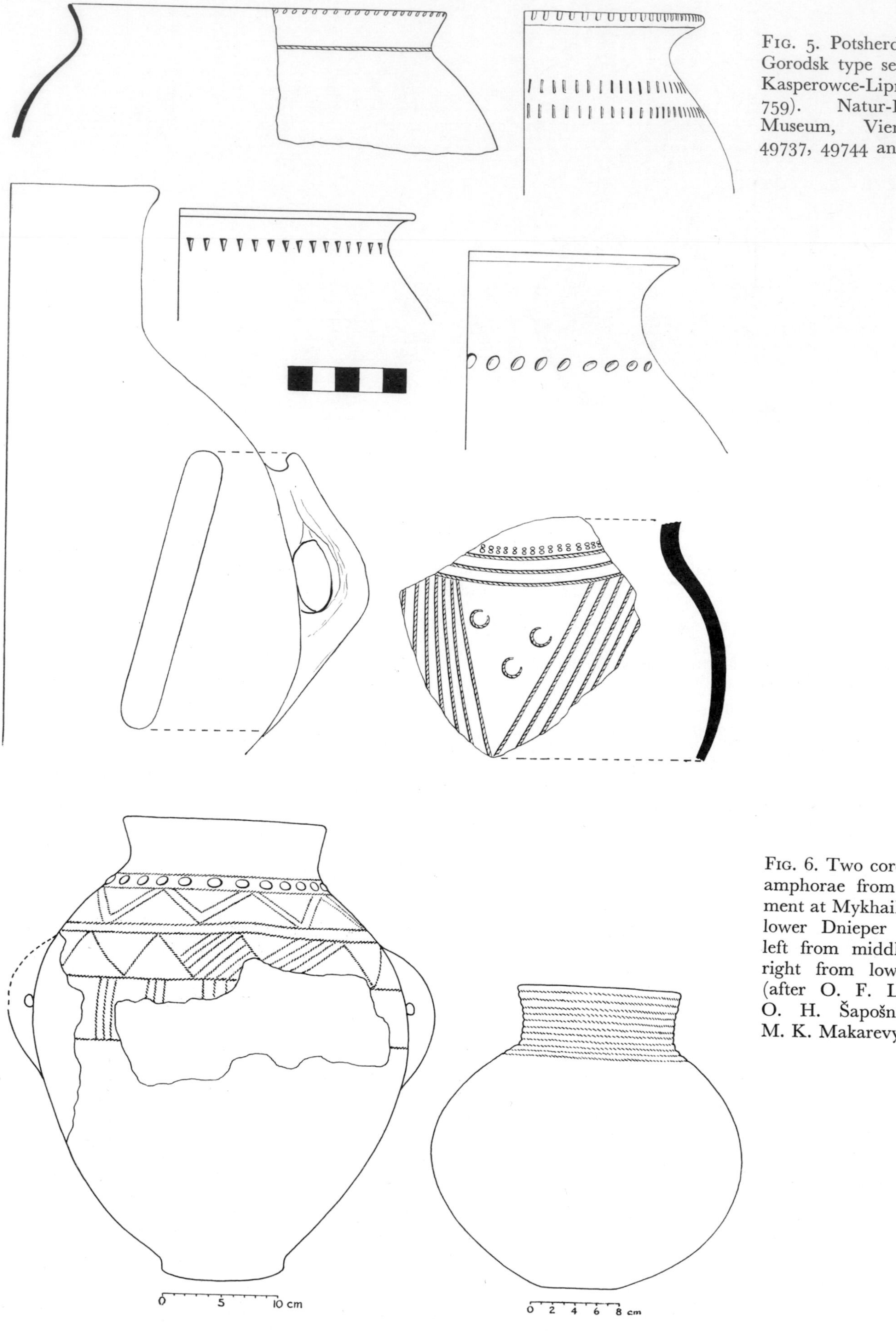

Fig. 5. Potsherds from the Gorodsk type settlement at Kasperowce-Lipniki (no. 759). Natur-Historisches Museum, Vienna, nos. 49737, 49744 and 49763.

Fig. 6. Two cord-decorated amphorae from the settlement at Mykhailivka on the lower Dnieper (no. 333): left from middle layer III right from lower layer I (after O. F. Lahodovska, O. H. Šapošnikova and M. K. Makarevyč).

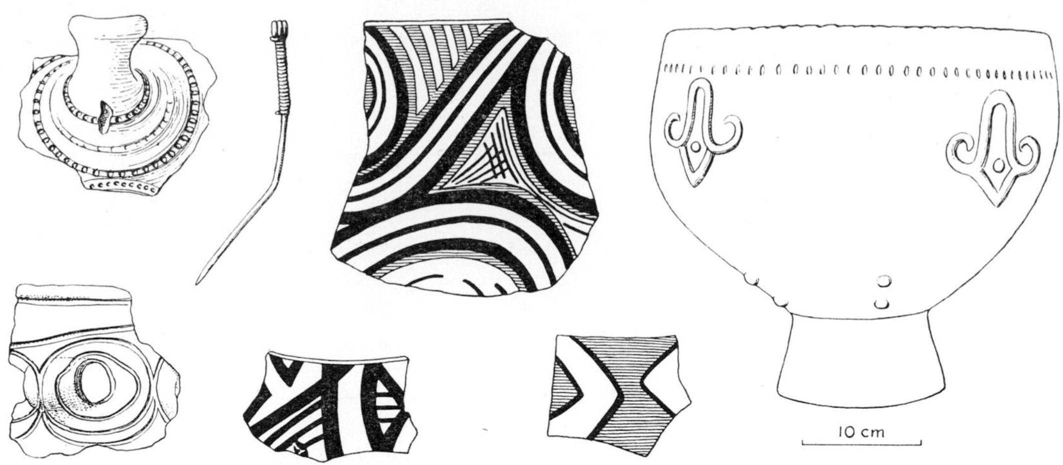

Fig. 8. Potsherds with painted or incised decoration, 'Cypriot' bronze pin and clay cauldron, all excavated in layer 'A' of the Tripolyan settlement at Sabatynivka 1 on the Boh (after A. V. Dobrovolskii).

Fig. 7. Vessels with a pointed base from barrow-graves near Smiela (nos. 289, 300): from left to right barrow-graves nos. 362, 251 and 56 (Historical Museum, Kiev).

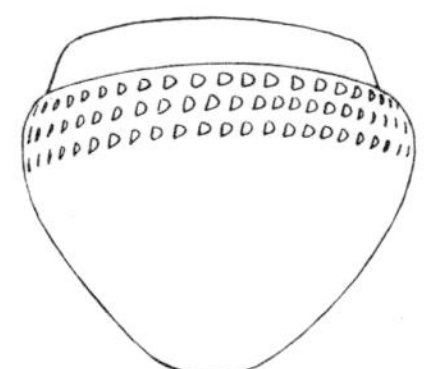

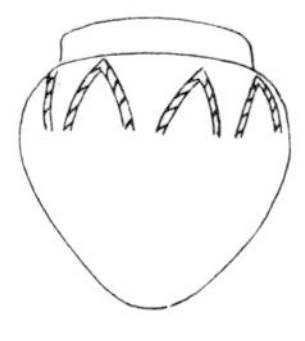

0 5 cm

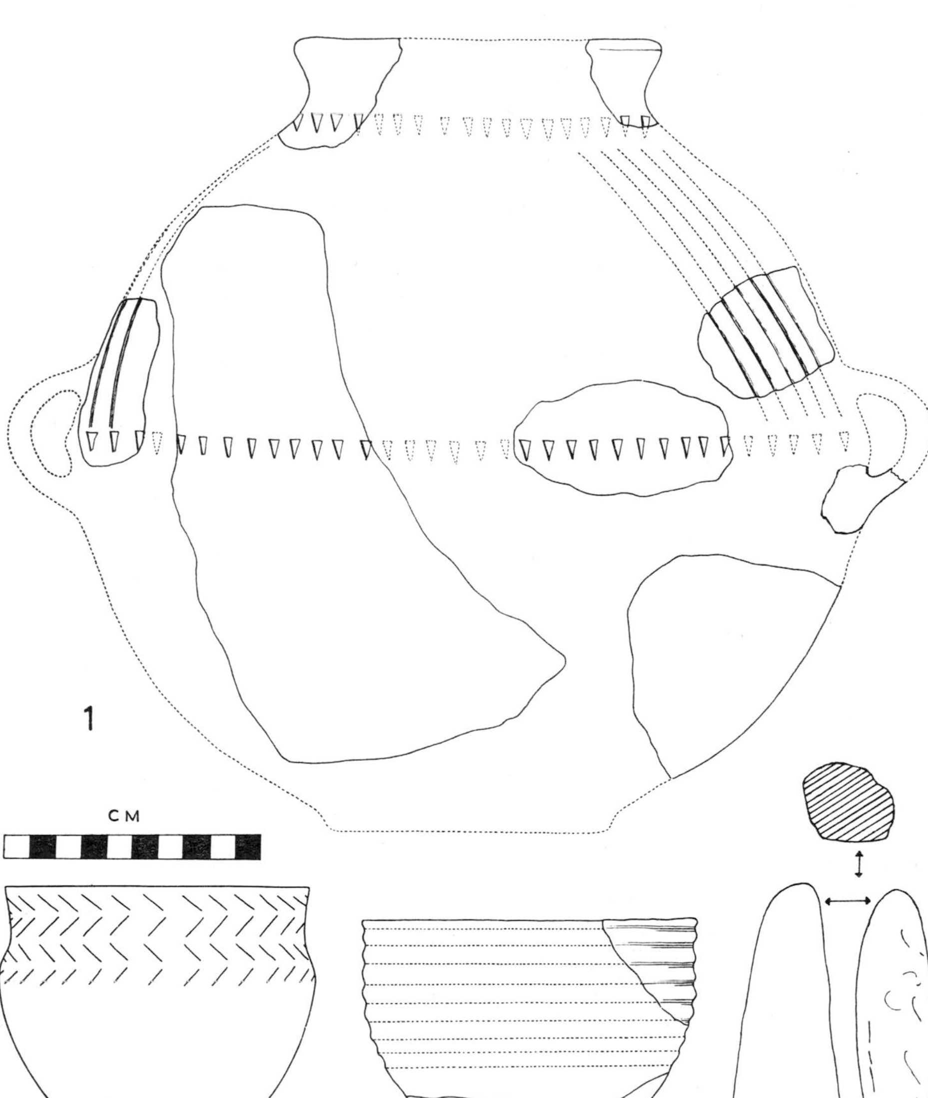

Fig. 9. Various vessels of the Sub-Carpathian barrow-graves.

1, 3, 4. Krasów 1 (no. 67) – Thuringian amphora of type 1; ribbed beaker and axe made of siliceous slate.

2. Komarów 31 (no. 47) – beaker (a-2).

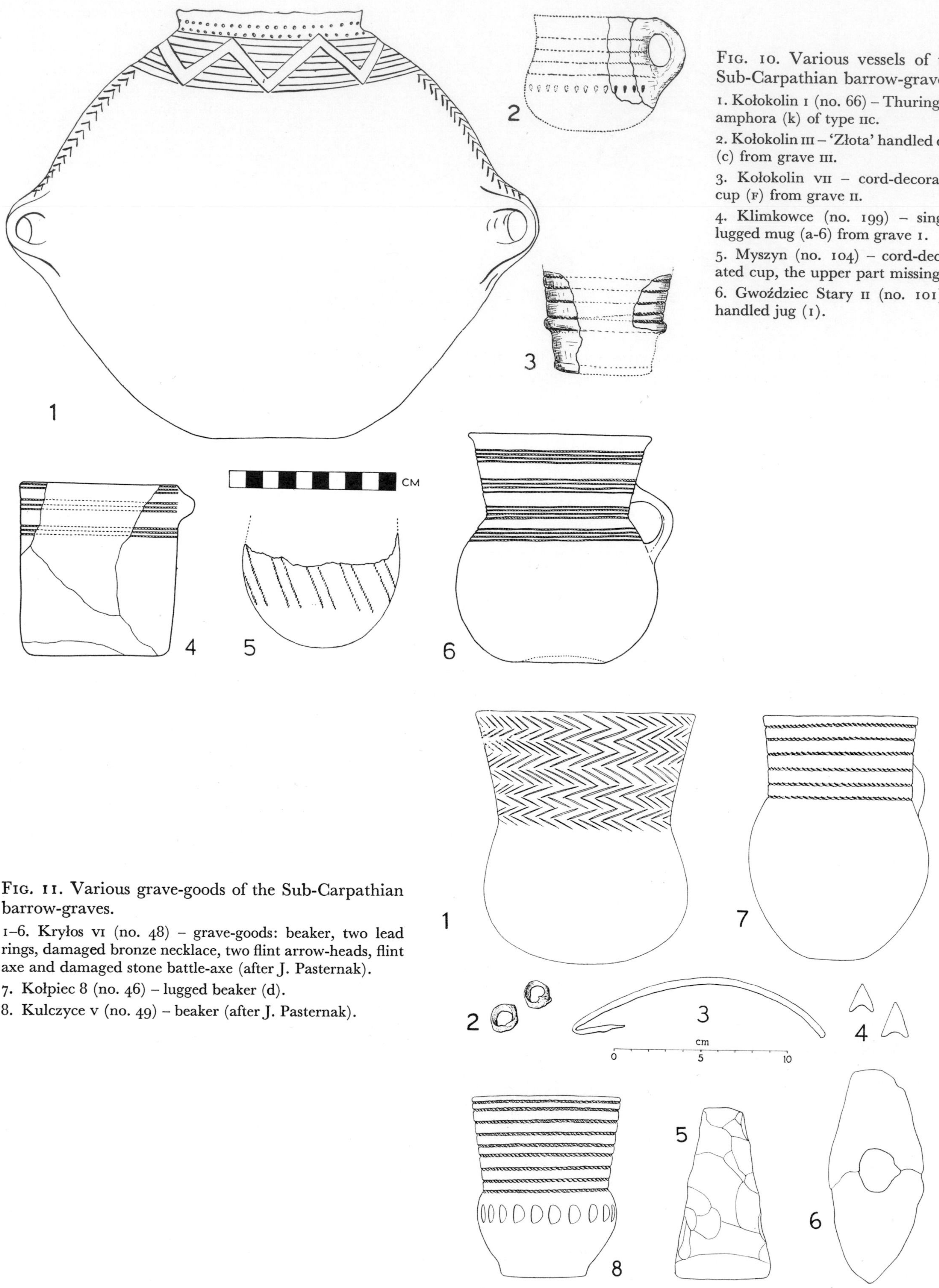

FIG. 10. Various vessels of the Sub-Carpathian barrow-graves.

1. Kołokolin I (no. 66) – Thuringian amphora (k) of type IIc.

2. Kołokolin III – 'Złota' handled cup (c) from grave III.

3. Kołokolin VII – cord-decorated cup (F) from grave II.

4. Klimkowce (no. 199) – single-lugged mug (a-6) from grave I.

5. Myszyn (no. 104) – cord-decorated cup, the upper part missing.

6. Gwoździec Stary II (no. 101) – handled jug (I).

FIG. 11. Various grave-goods of the Sub-Carpathian barrow-graves.

1–6. Kryłos VI (no. 48) – grave-goods: beaker, two lead rings, damaged bronze necklace, two flint arrow-heads, flint axe and damaged stone battle-axe (after J. Pasternak).

7. Kołpiec 8 (no. 46) – lugged beaker (d).

8. Kulczyce V (no. 49) – beaker (after J. Pasternak).

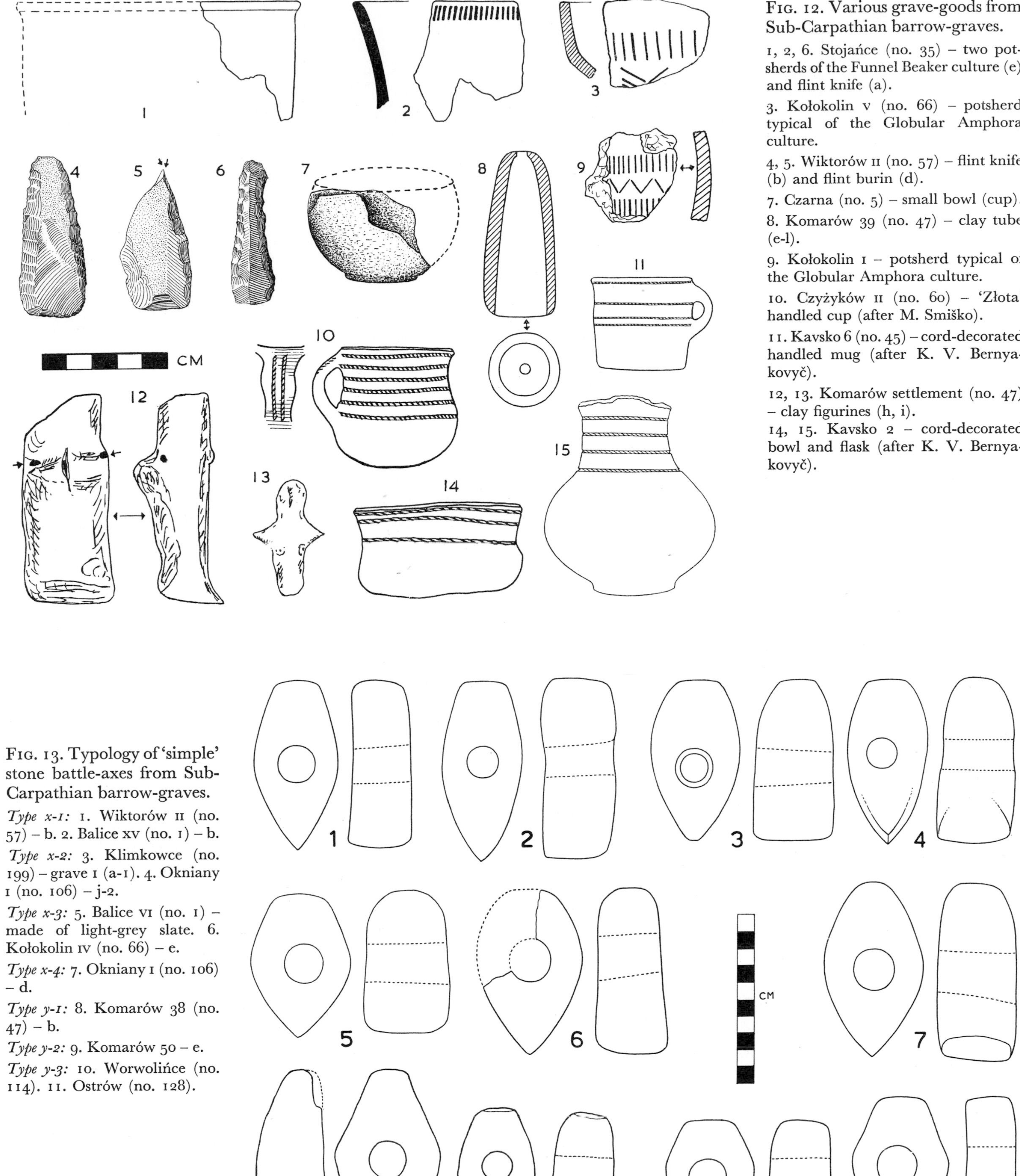

FIG. 12. Various grave-goods from Sub-Carpathian barrow-graves.

1, 2, 6. Stojańce (no. 35) – two potsherds of the Funnel Beaker culture (e) and flint knife (a).

3. Kołokolin V (no. 66) – potsherd typical of the Globular Amphora culture.

4, 5. Wiktorów II (no. 57) – flint knife (b) and flint burin (d).

7. Czarna (no. 5) – small bowl (cup).

8. Komarów 39 (no. 47) – clay tube (e-l).

9. Kołokolin I – potsherd typical of the Globular Amphora culture.

10. Czyżyków II (no. 60) – 'Złota' handled cup (after M. Smiško).

11. Kavsko 6 (no. 45) – cord-decorated handled mug (after K. V. Bernyakovyč).

12, 13. Komarów settlement (no. 47) – clay figurines (h, i).

14, 15. Kavsko 2 – cord-decorated bowl and flask (after K. V. Bernyakovyč).

FIG. 13. Typology of 'simple' stone battle-axes from Sub-Carpathian barrow-graves.

Type x-1: 1. Wiktorów II (no. 57) – b. 2. Balice XV (no. 1) – b.

Type x-2: 3. Klimkowce (no. 199) – grave I (a-1). 4. Okniany I (no. 106) – j-2.

Type x-3: 5. Balice VI (no. 1) – made of light-grey slate. 6. Kołokolin IV (no. 66) – e.

Type x-4: 7. Okniany I (no. 106) – d.

Type y-1: 8. Komarów 38 (no. 47) – b.

Type y-2: 9. Komarów 50 – e.

Type y-3: 10. Worwolińce (no. 114). 11. Ostrów (no. 128).

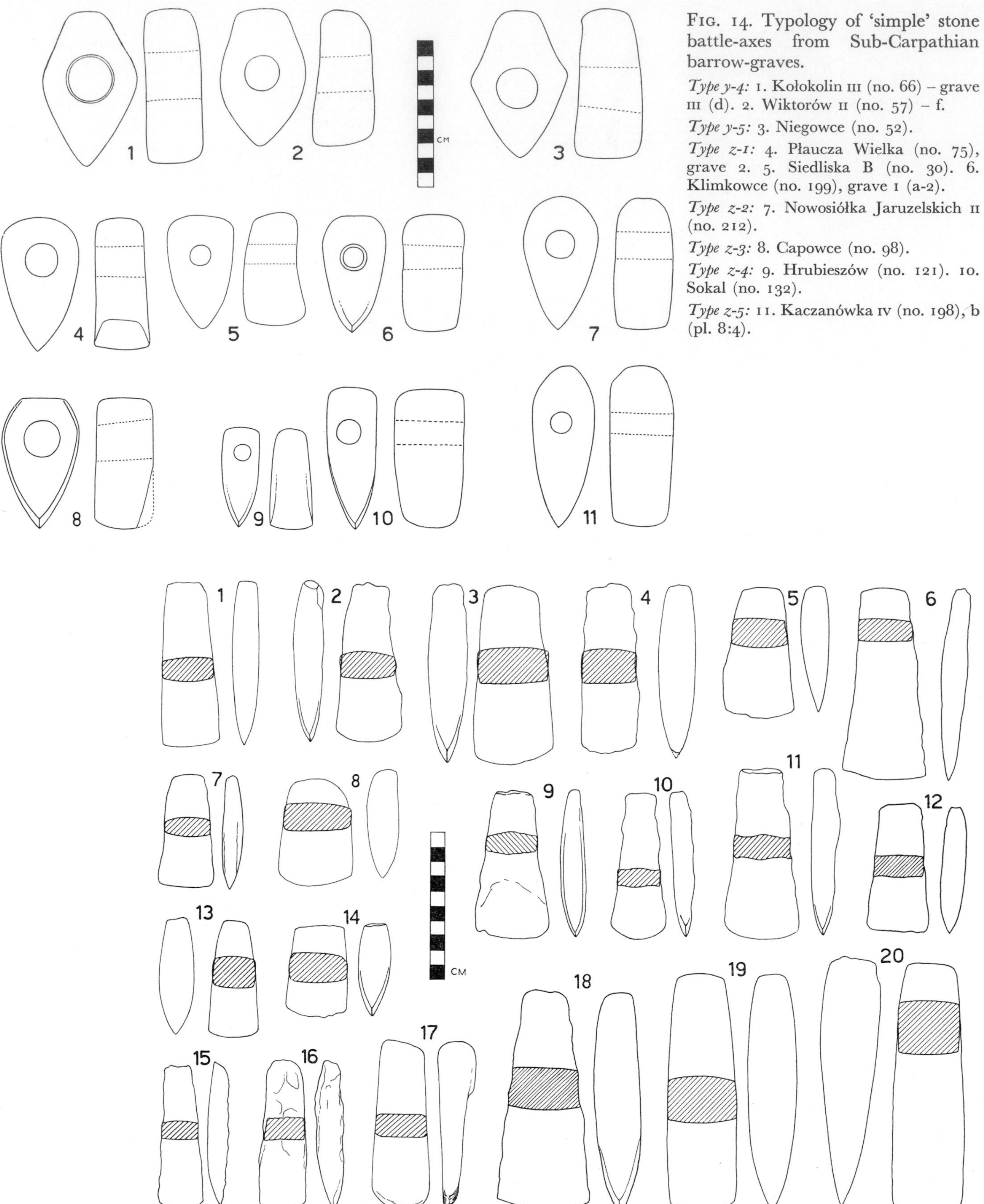

FIG. 14. Typology of 'simple' stone battle-axes from Sub-Carpathian barrow-graves.

Type y-4: 1. Kołokolin III (no. 66) – grave III (d). 2. Wiktorów II (no. 57) – f.
Type y-5: 3. Niegowce (no. 52).
Type z-1: 4. Płaucza Wielka (no. 75), grave 2. 5. Siedliska B (no. 30). 6. Klimkowce (no. 199), grave I (a-2).
Type z-2: 7. Nowosiółka Jaruzelskich II (no. 212).
Type z-3: 8. Capowce (no. 98).
Type z-4: 9. Hrubieszów (no. 121). 10. Sokal (no. 132).
Type z-5: 11. Kaczanówka IV (no. 198), b (pl. 8:4).

FIG. 15. Flint axes, quadrangular in section, from Sub-Carpathian barrow-graves.

1. Kołokolin IV (no. 66) – c, 'Bundsø type'. 2. Rokitno 2 (no. 82) – 'Bundsø type' (?). 3. Rokitno 1 – larger specimen, 'Bundsø type'. 4. Brusno (no. 2) – 'Bundsø type'. 5. Kałusz (no. 44). 6. Sokal (no. 132), smaller specimen, 'Bundsø type'. 7. Komarów 24. 8. Siedliska B (no. 30) – d, made of siliceous slate. 9. Kołokolin II – d. 10, 11. Rokitno 6 (no. 82) – b. 12. Komarów 38 – d. 13. Olszanica (no. 74). 14. Kulczyce Szlacheckie I (no. 49). 15. Podlipce (no. 424) – probably from a slab-cist grave. 16. Komarów 40 – 's' – of Lindø type. 17. Kulczyce Szlacheckie II (no. 49), 'C', made of sandstone. 18. Stare Sioło (no. 34) – Valby type. 19. Beremiany I (no. 96) – Valby type. 20. Sokal (no. 132) – larger specimen, Valby type.

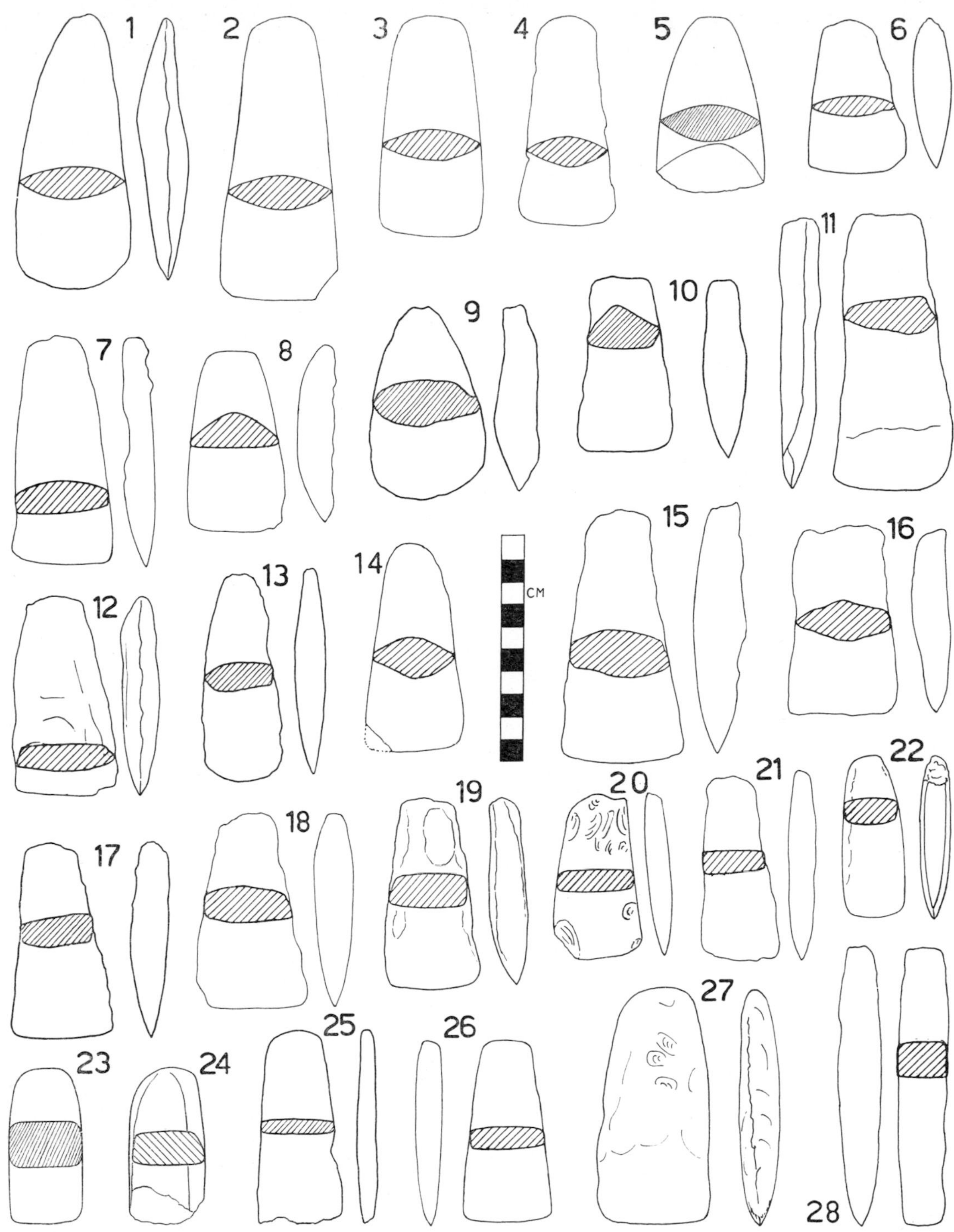

FIG. 16. Flint axes lenticular in cross-section, hybrid forms and special forms, found in Sub-Carpathian barrow-graves.

1. Zagórzyce (no. 37), lenticular. 2. Kołpiec 4 (no. 46), 'b', lenticular. 3. Łotatniki 2 (no. 50), 'e', lenticular. 4. Kołpiec 2 (no. 46), 'c', lenticular. 5. Piatyhorce (Ukraine) (no. 254), lenticular. 6. Wacowice I (no. 56), lenticular. 7. Łotatniki I (no. 50), 'a'. 8. Siedliska B (no. 30), hybrid form. 9. Chocimierz (no. 99), oval, irregular, made of siliceous slate. 10. Komarów 38, 'c', oval, irregular. 11. Komarów 5, hybrid form. 12. Kołokolin V (no. 66), 'a', hybrid form. 13. Komarów 44, 'd', irregular, hybrid form. 14. Kulczyce Szlacheckie III (no. 49), 's', nearly lenticular. 15. Wiktorów I (no. 57), hybrid form. 16. Wiktorów II, hybrid form. 17. Komarów 50, 'd'. 18. Wiktorów VIII, irregular. 19. Komarów 42, 'd', nearly rectangular, edges rounded. 20. Kuźmińczyk II (no. 201), Globular Amphora type. 21. Siedliska B (no. 30), nearly rectangular, edges rounded. 22. Krasów II (no. 67), 'f', small, edges well polished. 23. Piatyhorce (no. 254), diorite hammer. 24. Komarów 32, 'b', upper part of a hammer made of siliceous slate. 25. Siedliska A (no. 30), 'a', Globular Amphora type. 26. Rokitno I (no. 82), Globular Amphora type. 27. Komarów 37, 'a', irregular, oval. 28. Rokitno I, chisel, typical of the Globular Amphora culture.

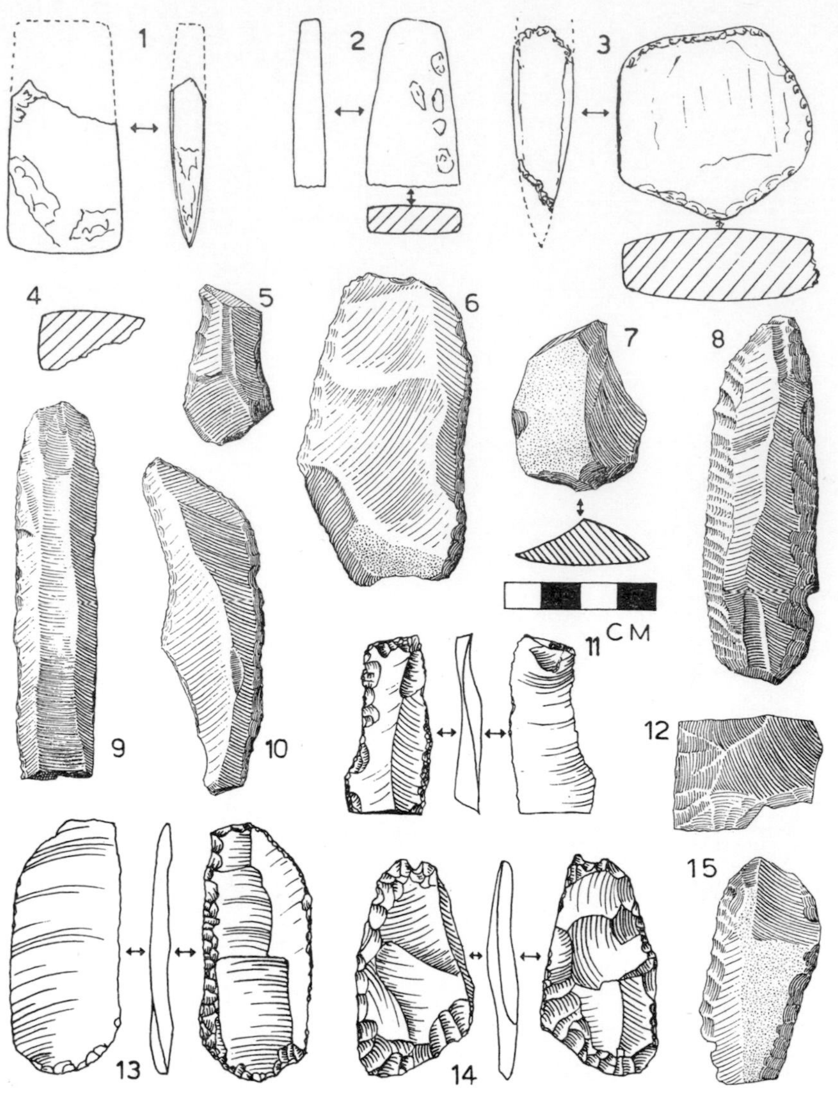

FIG. 17. Various flint implements found in Sub-Carpathian barrow-graves.

1–5. Kołokolin IV (no. 66) – objects from the ruined part of the mound: two small damaged flint axes (g, i), battered fragment of a flint axe used as a hammer (h), fragment of an axe made of banded flint (d), burin made of the 'chocolate' variety of flint.

6. Kołokolin III – wide flint flake from grave I (k-2).

7, 8. Kołokolin II – flint burin and knife (e).

9. Krasów II (no. 67) – flint knife (g).

10, 15. Sarniki III (no. 86) – flint knife (c) and scraper (f).

11, 13. Klimkowce (no. 199) – two flint scrapers.

12. Gwoździec Stary I (no. 101) – fragment of a flint implement (m).

14. Zaborol 6 (no. 166) – flint scraper.

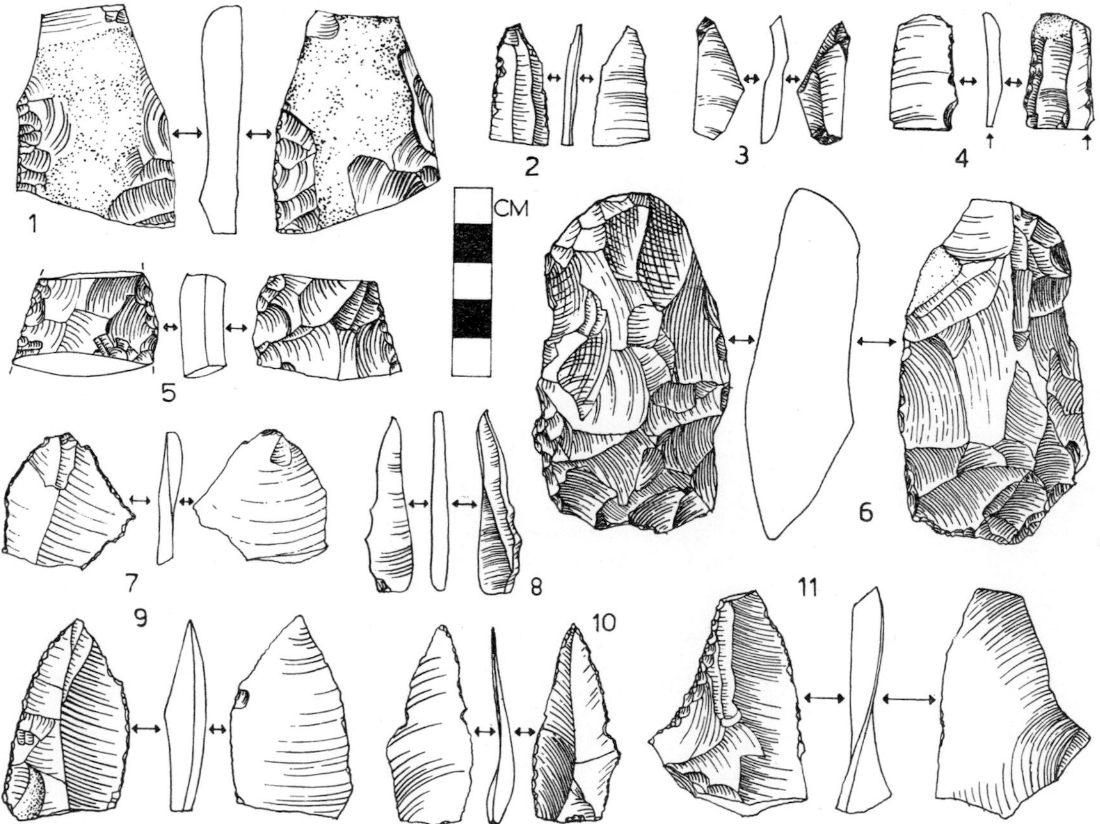

FIG. 18. Various flint implements mainly from West Volhynian barrow-graves.

1. Zaborol 8 (no. 166).

2, 4–6. Zaborol 6 – smaller implements and an unpolished axe.

3, 8, 9. Zaborol I – small implements.

7, 10, 11. Klimkowce (no. 199) – various implements.

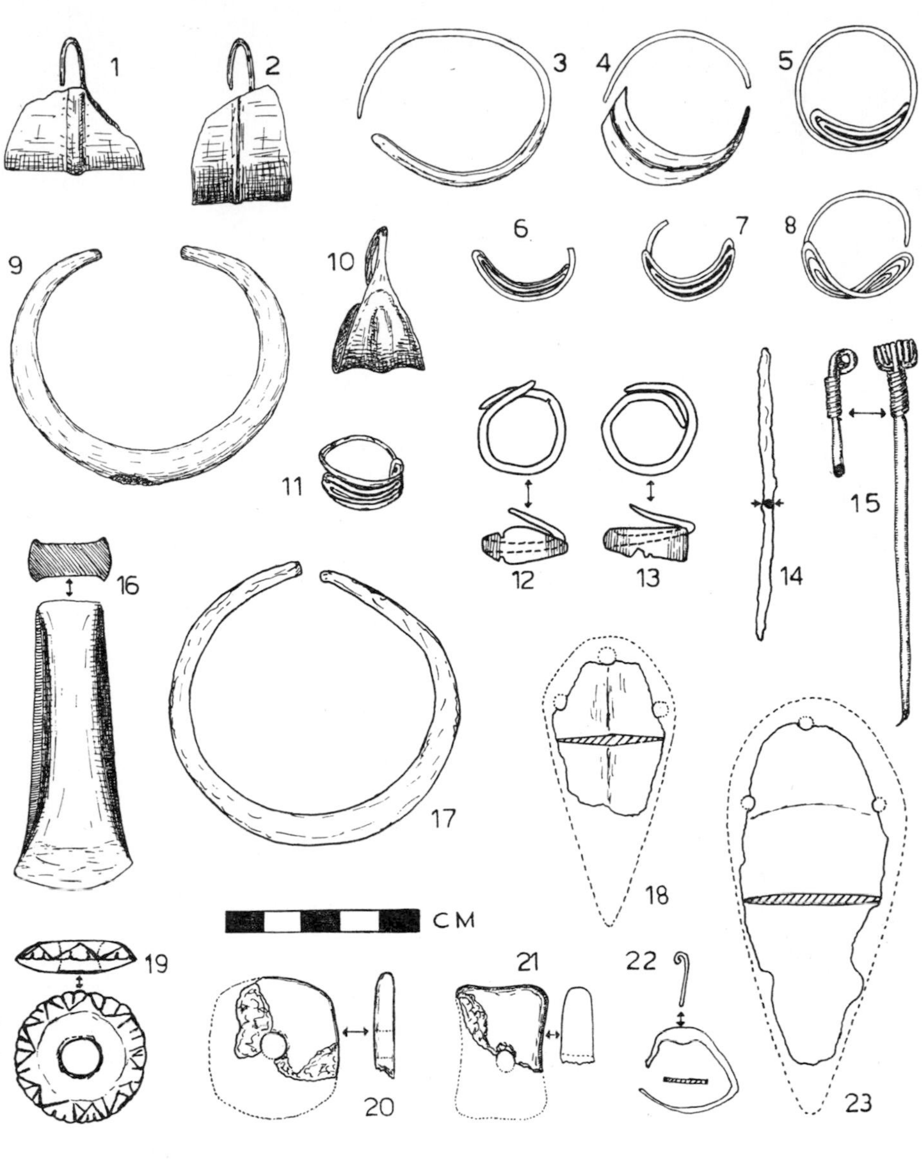

FIG. 19. Ornaments, mainly of bronze, and other objects from Sub-Carpathian barrow-graves.

1–8. Perediwanie (no. 109) – bronze ear-pendants of Stubło type and naprings.

9. Załukiew (no. 58) – bronze bracelet.

10. Chłopy, district of Rudki (no. 737) – bronze ear-pendant of Stubło type found in a peat-bog with a second specimen of the same type.

11. Jaktorów I (no. 63) – bronze napring (after J. Pasternak).

12, 13. Czyżyków II (no. 60) – two bronze ear-rings (after M. Smiško).

14, 17, 18, 22. Balice VII (no. 1) – damaged bronze pin, bronze bracelet, bronze dagger and lead ring.

15. Putiatyńce (no. 79) – 'Cypriot' bronze pin.

16. Chilczyce, district of Złoczów (no. 736) – flanged bronze axe found on a sand-dune.

19. Koropuż (no. 17) – perforated bone disc found in the hut (h).

20. Kołokolin VII (no. 66) – perforated disc-pendant made of baked clay (A-2).

21. Rokitno 2 (no. 82) – perforated amber pendant (f).

23. Sarniki I (no. 86) – bronze dagger (a).

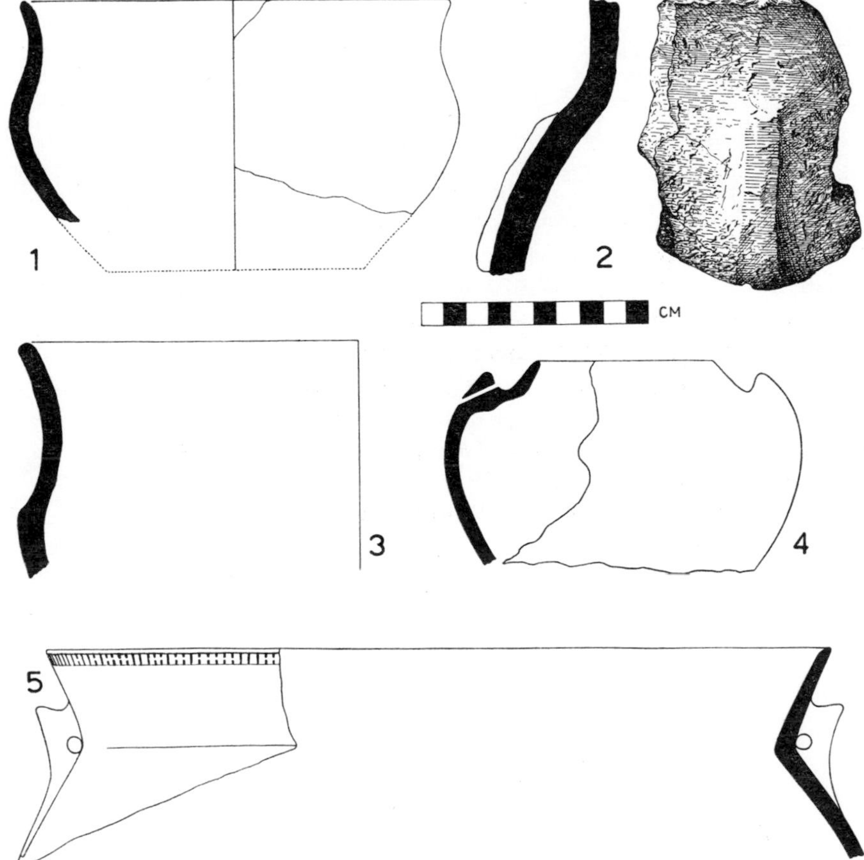

FIG. 20. Pottery from settlements.

1–3. Komarów (no. 47) – fragment of a bowl typical of the Komarów culture; fragment of a vase, the surface black polished, with a vertical rib; fragment of a 'late Tripolyan' vessel (D-ware).

4, 5. Staryj Mylsk (no. 663) – large part of a 'Tripolyan' vase with two perforated lugs on the shoulder; fragment of a large vessel typical of the Funnel Beaker culture.

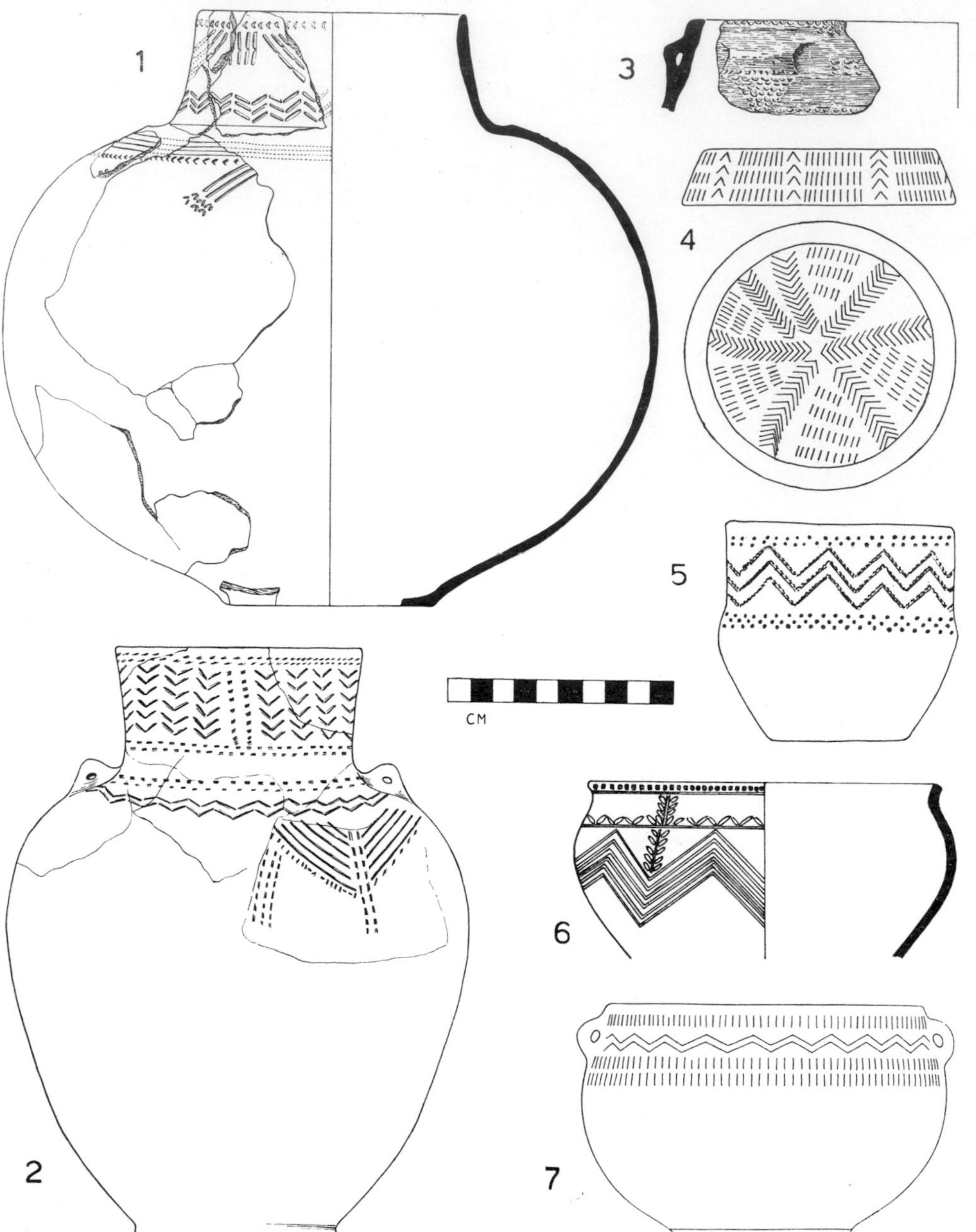

FIG. 21. Various vessels of the Eastern Globular Amphora culture.

1. Kryłów (no. 387) – Kuyavian amphora.
2. Mikołajów (no. 423) – double-lugged amphora with a flat base.
3. Koszyłowce (no. 552) – sherd of the Globular Amphora type found in the Tripolyan settlement 'Obóz'.
4. Suyemtsi 2 (no. 459) – lid of an amphora.
5. Staryi Miropil (no. 458) – beaker.
6. Staryj Mylsk (no. 558, 663) – reconstructed vessel found in the settlement.
7. Skolobiv (no. 475) – decorated double-lugged bowl.

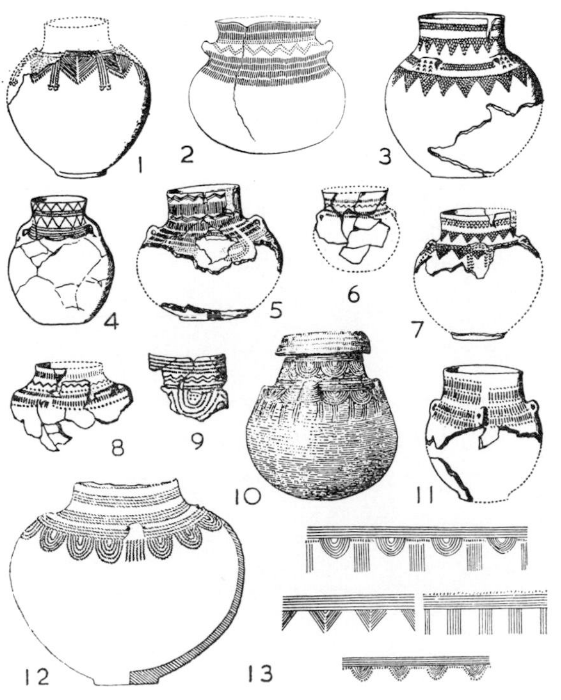

FIG. 22. Amphorae mainly of the eastern groups of the Eastern Globular Amphora culture (after I. Lewyckyj, if not stated otherwise).

1. Varkovytsia (no. 448) – Kuyavian type.
2. Nowa Sieniawa (no. 462) – debased globular type (after G. Ossowski).
3, 7. Lepesivka (no. 433) – two Kuyavian types.
4, 8. Kykova (no. 455) – globular and Kuyavian types.
5, 6. Skolobiv (no. 475) – Kuyavian and globular types.
9. Vysoke (no. 478) – part of the neck of an amphora.
10. Mininy (no. 473) – debased Kuyavian type with a lid (after A. Äyräpää).
11. Suyemtsi 1 (no. 459) – Kuyavian type.
12. Piatra Neamţ (no. 530) – debased Kuyavian type (after C. Mătăsa).
13. Zeiden (no. 545) – decorative motifs typical of the Globular Amphora culture met on vessels of the Bronze Age slab-cist graves of the Schneckenberg culture, Transilvania (after A. Prox).

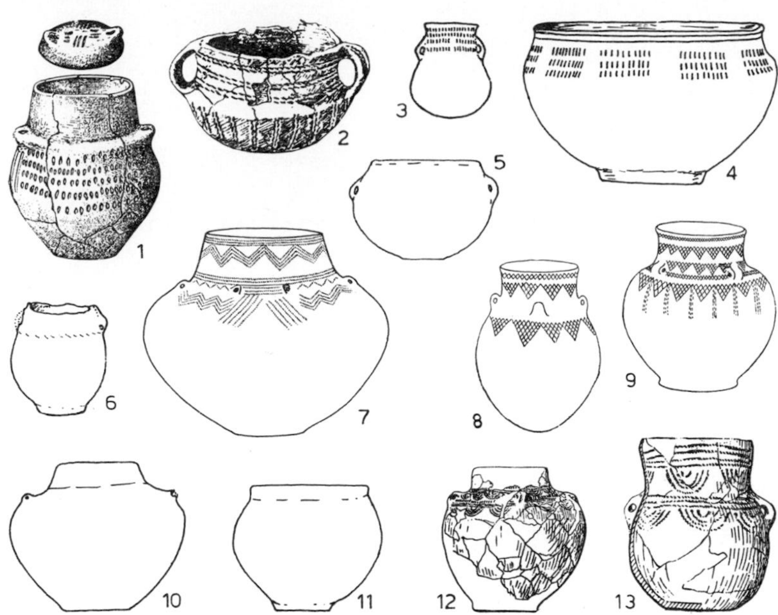

Fig. 23. Various vessels of the Eastern Globular Amphora culture.

1. Pekliuk (no. 546) – debased double-lugged globular amphora, with a lid (after N. Petkov).

2. Popovtsy I (no. 509) – cord-decorated double-handled vase (after I. N. Zakharuk).

3–5, 10–11. Lachów (no. 432) – small double-lugged globular amphora, decorated bowl, double-lugged bowl, large double-lugged debased Kuyavian amphora and a vase (after I. K. Sviešnikov).

6. Kolubaivtsi (no. 500) – small undecorated debased double-lugged amphora.

7. Miedniki (no. 389) – Kuyavian amphora (after S. Nosek).

8, 9. Kociubińce (no. 499) – ovoid four-lugged amphora, and Kuyavian amphora (after L. Kozłowski).

12, 13. Dolheşti Mari (no. 527) – debased Kuyavian amphora and small globular amphora (after M. Dinu).

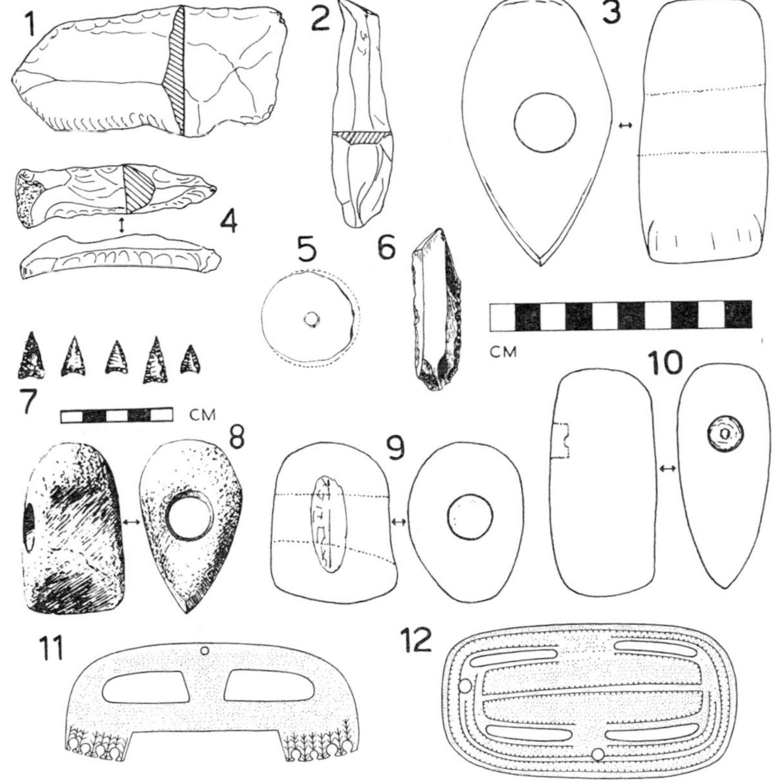

Fig. 24. Weapons and other objects from slab-cist graves of the Eastern Globular Amphora culture.

1–4. Latacz (no. 503) – large worked flint flake, two flint burins and stone battle-axe.

5. Kociubińce (no. 499) – perforated amber disc (after L. Kozłowski).

6. Beremiany 2 (no. 484) – flint implement.

7, 8. Popovtsy II (no. 509) – flint arrow-heads and stone battle-axe (after I. N. Zakharuk).

9. Koszyłowce I (no. 501) – small battle-axe or mace-head.

10. Suyemtsi I (no. 459) – unperforated stone battle-axe.

11, 12. Uwisła I (no. 518) – two bone belt-buckles.

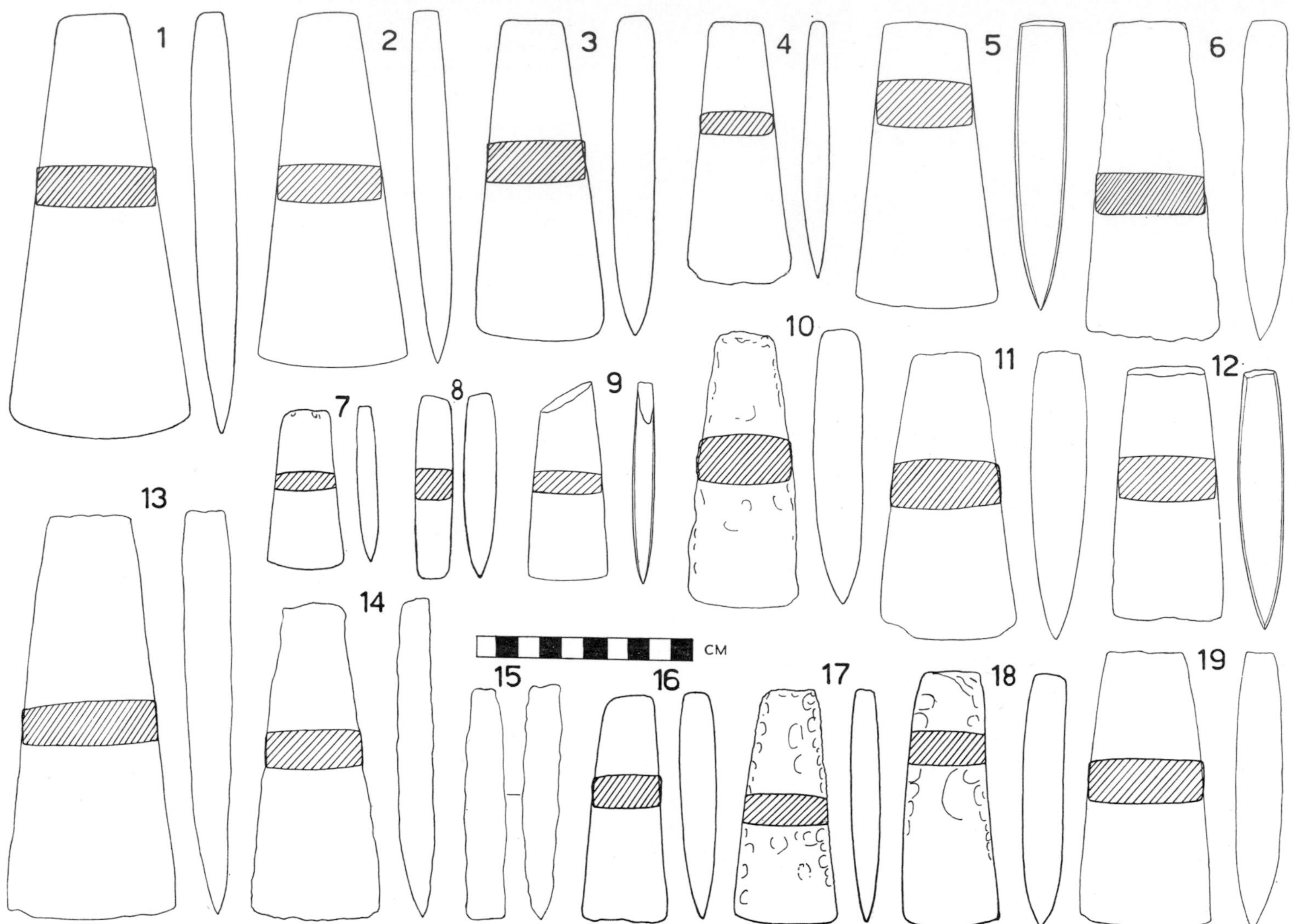

FIG. 25. Flint axes mainly from Podolian slab-cist graves of the Eastern Globular Amphora culture.

1, 3, 16. Velyka Mukša (no. 519) – three well-polished specimens made of 'milky' flint.

2. Bratyszów 2 (no. 486).

4. Uścieczko (no. 517).

5, 9. Zarwanica (no. 521).

6, 12, 15. Chorostków (no. 487) – two axes and chisel.

7. Czarnokońce (no. 489).

8. Tuta Dmitrovskaya (no. 596).

10. Kolubaivtsi (no. 500).

11. Duliby (no. 491).

13, 14, 19. Międzyrzec (no. 435).

17. Suyemtsi 2 (no. 459).

18. Ułaszkowce (no. 516).

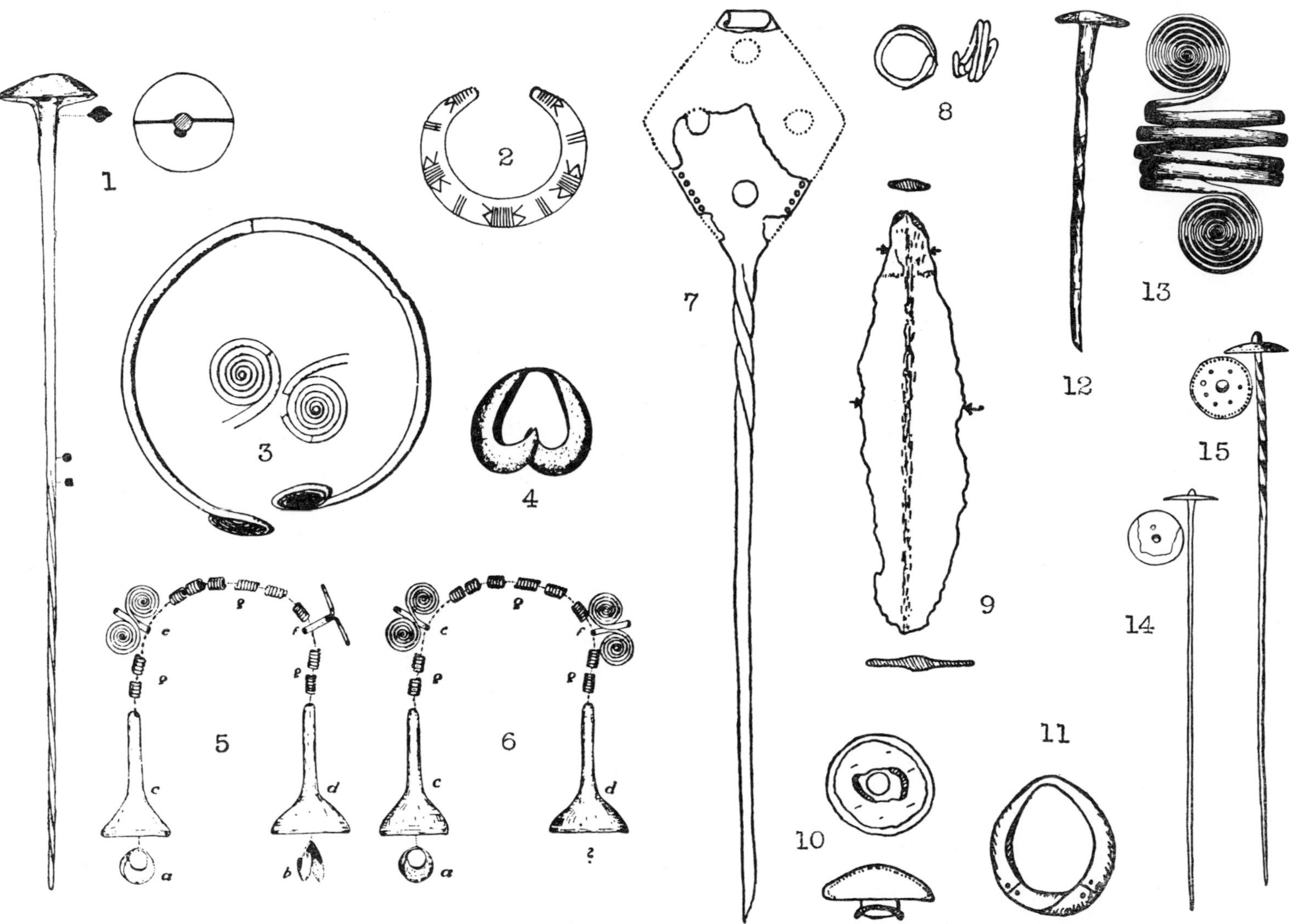

Fig. 26. Bronze ornaments from Sub-Carpathian barrow-graves of the Komarów culture.

1–6. Komarów 8 (no. 47) – bronze pin, bracelet, necklace, gold ear-pendant and two combined hair or ear ornaments (f-1–10).

7–9. Komarów 6 – bronze pin (h), gold ear-ring (g) and bronze dagger (b).

10. Czyżyków I (no. 60) – bone button with thin bronze sheet cover.

11. Komarów 28 – gold ear-pendant (g-2).

12, 13. Bukówna III (no. 97) – bronze pin (g) and spiral armband (i).

14, 15. Putiatyńce (no. 79) – two bronze pins.

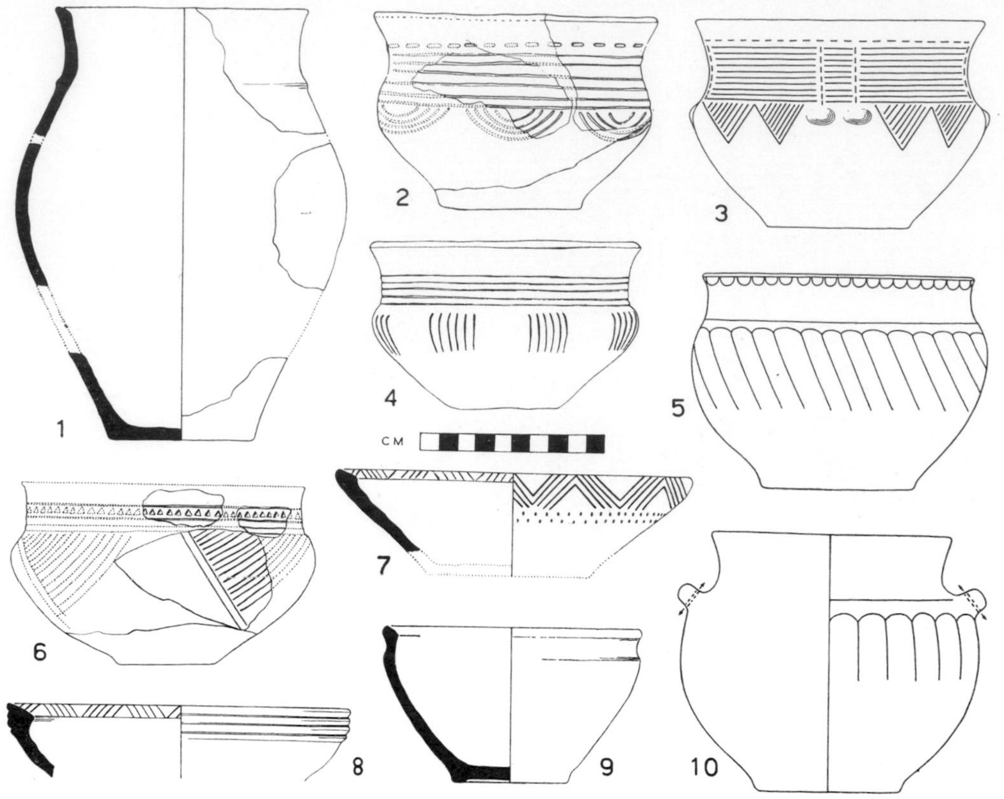

FIG. 27. Vessels of period II of the Komarów culture.

1–4, 9. Komarów 46 – tulip-shaped pot (k) and four bowls (c, I, A, i).

5, 10. Komarów 11 – two bowls (d-k-m, e-f).

6. Radzimin IV–1878 (no. 155) – decorated bowl.

7. Komarów 55 – decorated deep dish (c).

8. Komarów – decorated deep dish.

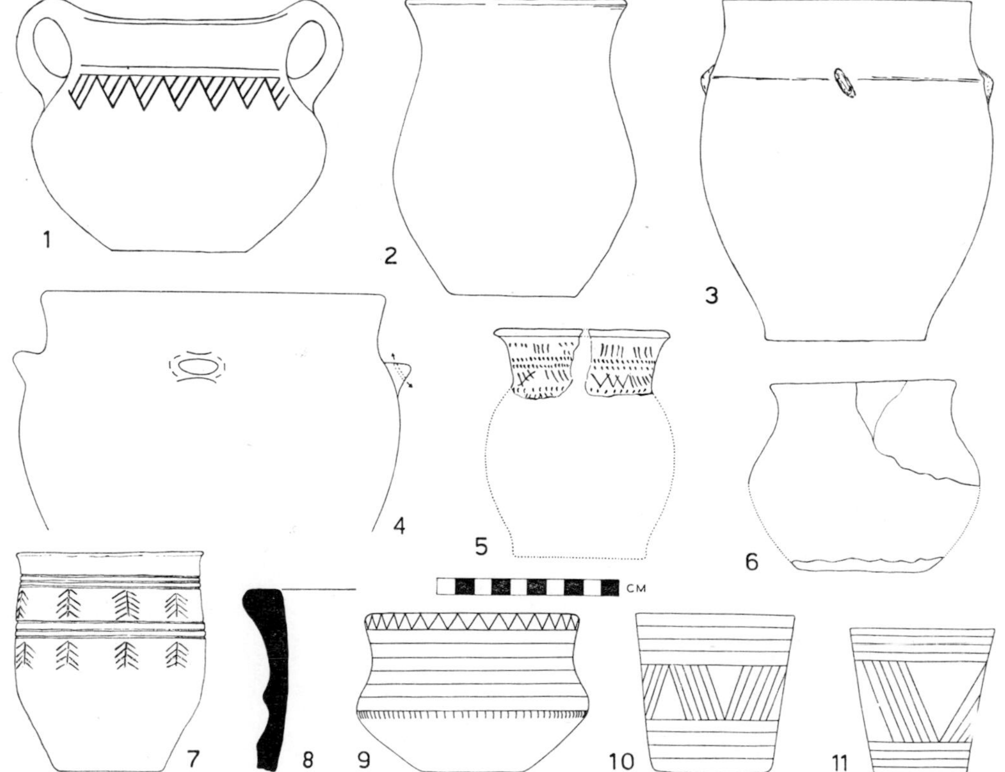

FIG. 28. Vessels of period II of the Komarów culture.

1, 3. Okniany II (no. 106) – double-handled vase (l) and tulip-shaped pot (a).

2. Komarów 11 – tulip-shaped pot (d-k-m).

4. Bukówna VI (no. 97) – large pot (e).

5. Komarów 10 – beaker (e).

6. Wolica I (no. 91) – large cup (z).

7. Komarów 9 – beaker (e) of period I of the Komarów culture.

8–11. Komarów 28 – sherd of a large vase (b), small decorated bowl (e-l) and two cups (i, d).

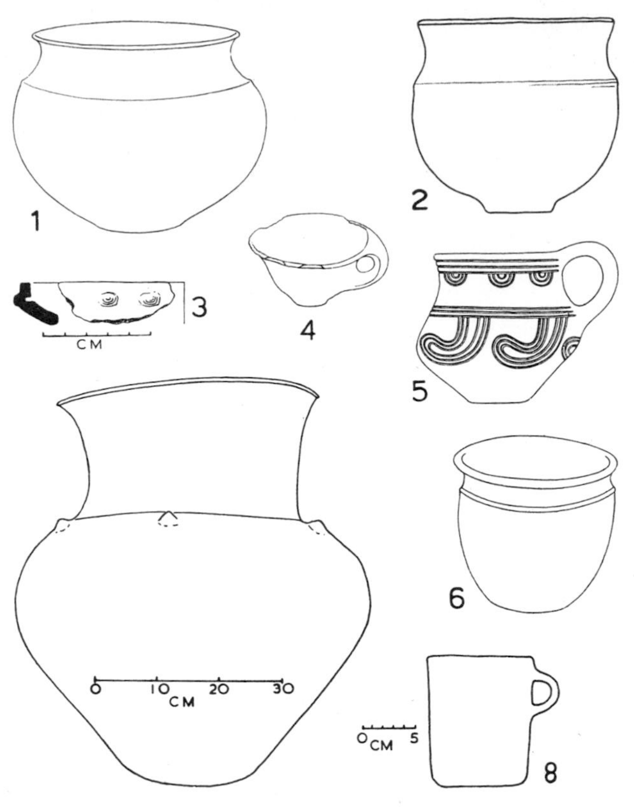

Fig. 29. Vessels of various periods of the Komarów culture.

1, 4. Kavsko 4 (no. 45) – bowl and handled cup.

2, 5, 6. Kavsko 5 – bowl, handled cup and beaker.

3. Zaborol 3 (no. 166) – fragment of a deep dish.

7, 8. Komarów 20 – large vase (j) and handled tankard (f-2).

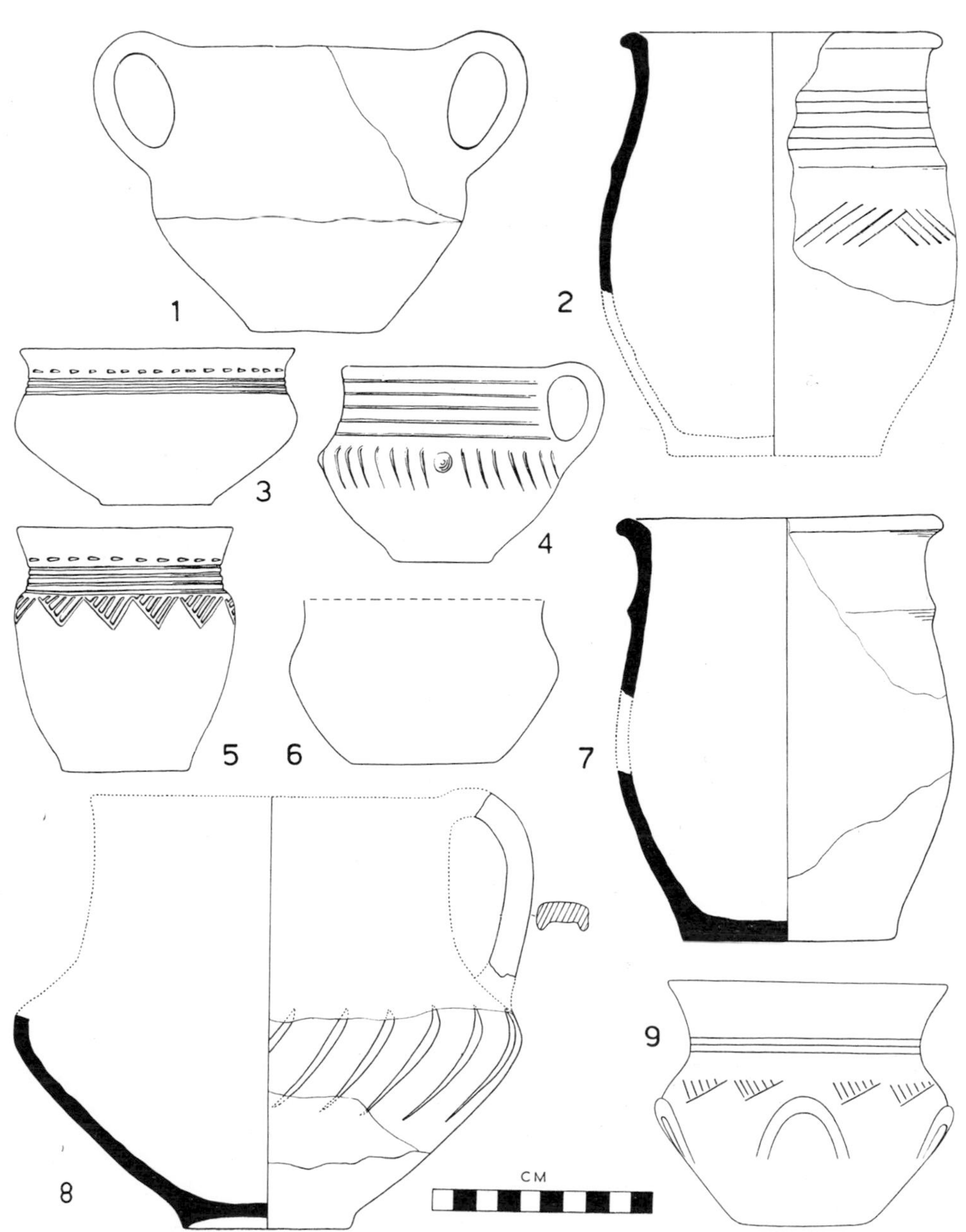

Fig. 30. Vessels of period III of the Komarów culture.

1, 2, 7, 9. Komarów 48 – double-handled vase (3), two tulip-shaped pots (4a, 4) and decorated bowl (b-2).

3, 5. Komarów 45 – bowl (g-5) and beaker (d).

4. Wolica 4 (no. 91) – handled cup (h).

6. Bukówna IV (no. 97) – small bowl (E).

8. Krasów V (no. 67) – handled jug (a-1).

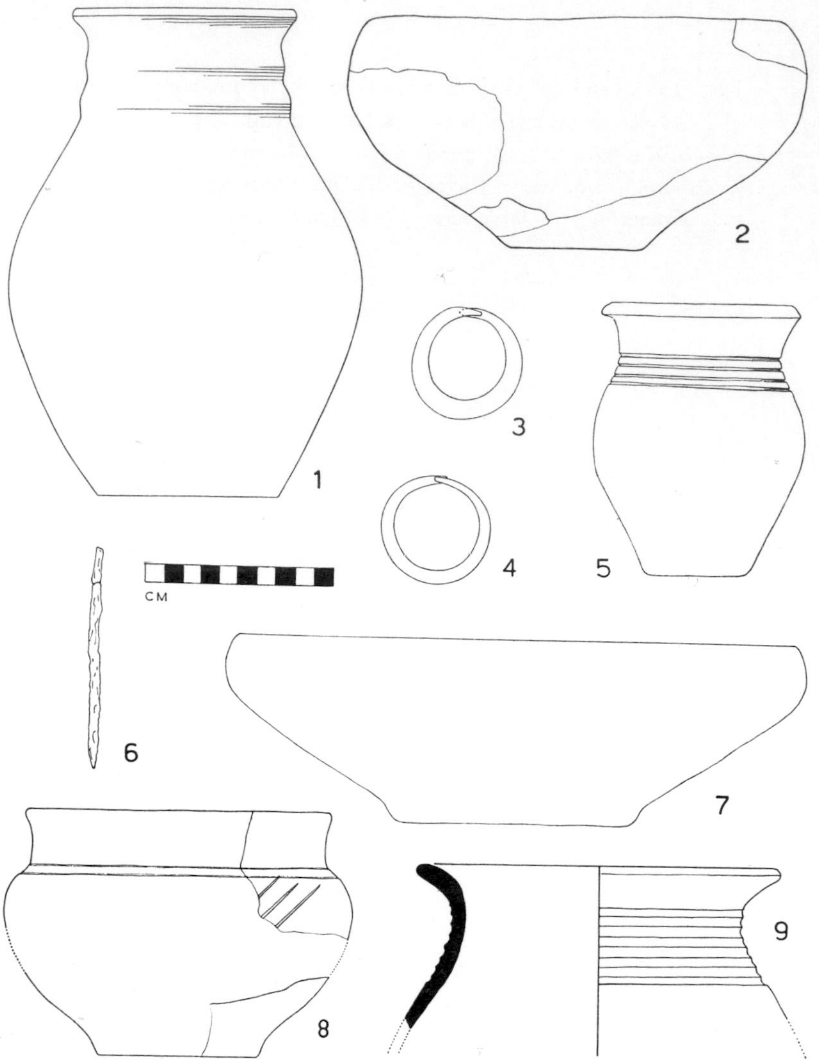

FIG. 31. Vessels and other grave-goods of period IV of the Komarów culture, except no. 2.

1, 3–6. Horodyszcze I (no. 43) – large pot, two bronze bracelets, tulip-shaped beaker and iron pin.

2. Komarów 50 – large bowl (i).

7, 9. Komarów 47 - large dish (c) and upper part of a large vessel (f).

8. Komarów 34 – bowl (II–III).

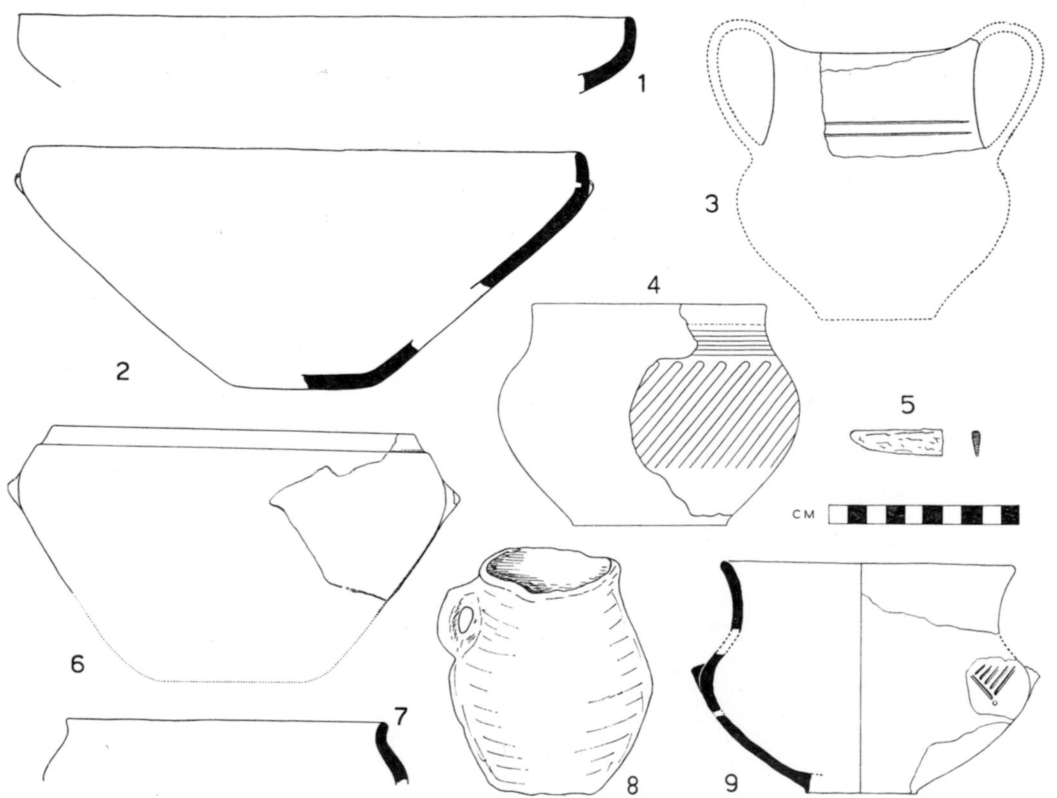

FIG. 32. Vessels from barrow-graves and slab-cists of the Biały-Potok group.

1, 2, 7. Łuczka II (no. 204) – deep dish (d), bowl (b) and upper part of a pot (b).

3. Beremiany 3 (no. 484) – double-handled vase.

4. Trembowla (no. 515) – bowl from a destroyed cemetery.

5, 6. Uście Biskupie (no. 219) – iron knife (c) and vase (b).

8. Grzymałów (no. 196) – handled jug (after I. Skarbowski).

9. Horodnica on the Dniester (no. 493) – vase from slab-cist grave AD.

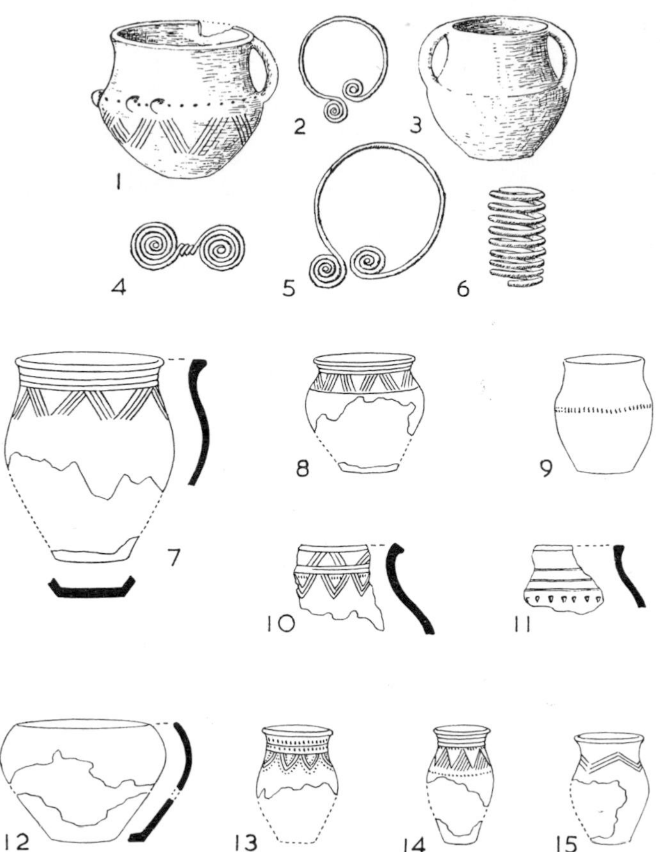

Fig. 33. Grave-goods from East-Volhynian barrow-graves of the Bronze Age.

A. Kustowce (no. 228) – two vases, bronze bracelet, necklace, armlet and a double spiral, from a barrow-grave (after J. Kostrzewski).

B. Narodyči (no. 229) – decorated tulip-shaped pots and a bowl, from barrow-graves of the cemetery I (after I. Levyckyj).

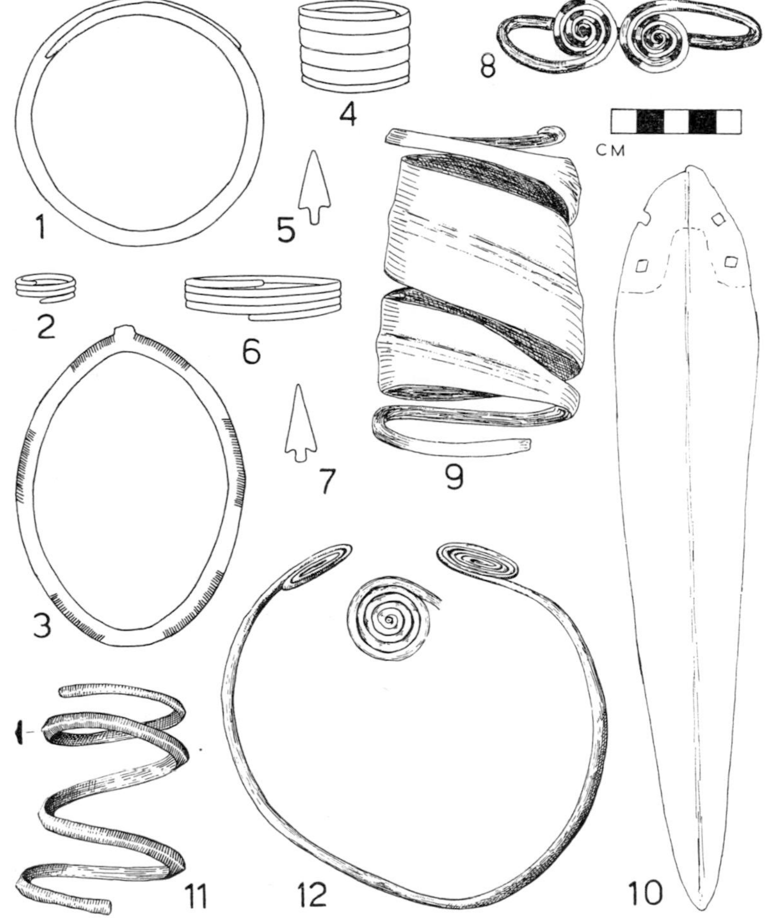

Fig. 34. Bronze ornaments found in barrow-graves of the Middle Bronze Age.

1–7. Skurcze (no. 158) – bronze armlet with overlapping terminals, small spiral ring, oval armlet, two spiral bracelets and two flint arrow-heads.

8. Unijew-Werników (no. 187) – bracelet with spiral terminals from a flat grave.

9, 10. Kamionka Strumiłowa – spiral bronze armlet and bronze dagger with four rivet holes, found together (hoard or grave ?).

11, 12. Barh (no. 192) – spiral bronze armlet and bronze necklace with spiral terminals, from a barrow-grave.

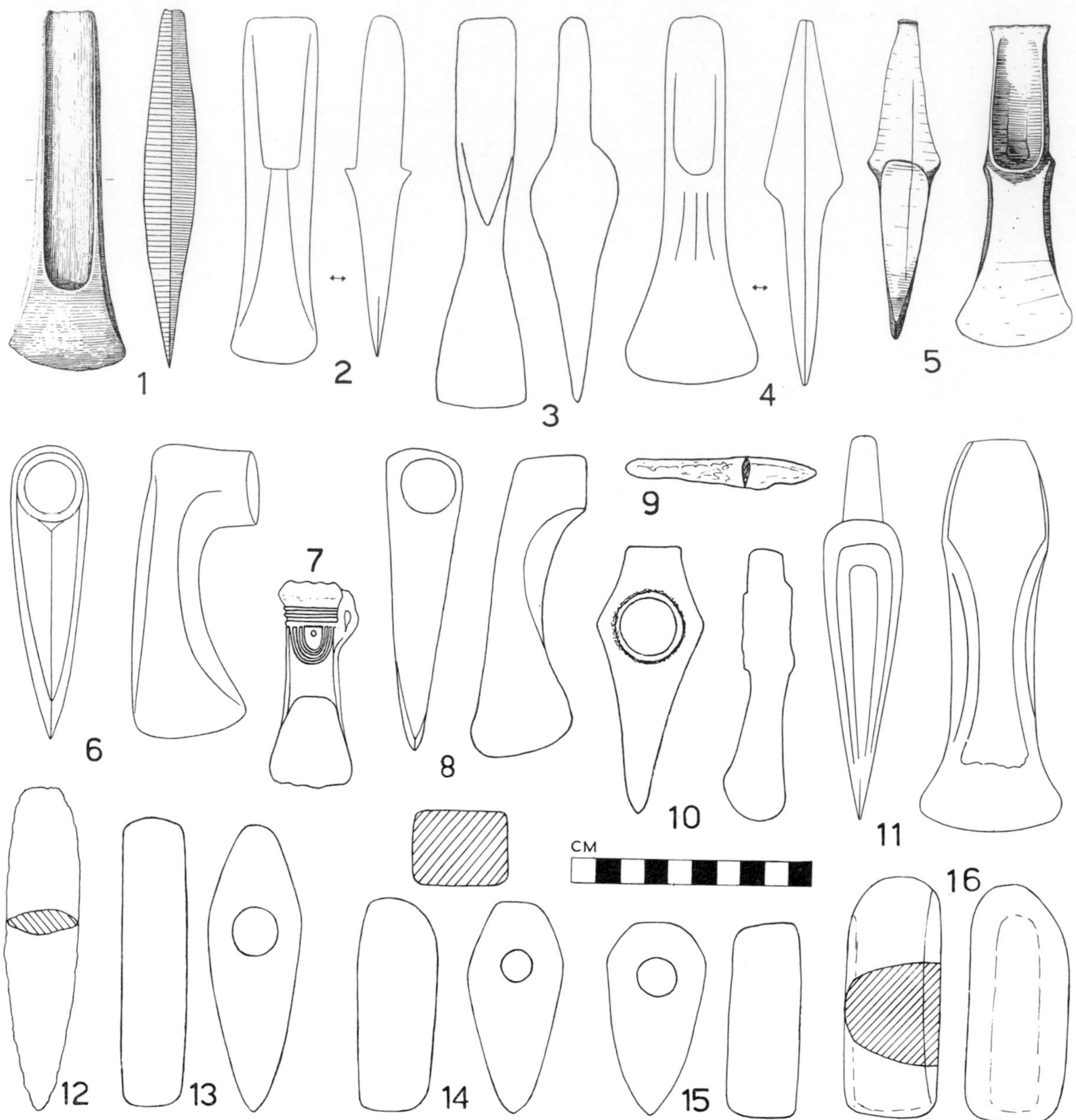

Fig. 35. Various stone and metal weapons or implements of the Bronze Age.

1. Kiev – flanged bronze axe (Czartoryski Museum, Cracow).
2. Ukraine – palstave of North-West European type (Choynowski collection of the Polish Army Museum in Warsaw, no. 32531–18805).
3. Ukraine – winged celt of Bohemian type (Choynowski collection, as above, no. 32876).
4. Ukraine – palstave of Lusatian type (Choynowski collection, as above, no. 32530–18804).
5. Przewodów, district of Sokal – palstave of North-West European type (before the War at the Dzieduszycki Museum, Lwów).
6. Darabani, Bessarabia – copper (or bronze) shaft-hole axe found in the Tripolyan settlement on the Dniester (before the War in the possession of Mr. M. Abrojevici, Cernauţi).
7, 12. Horodenka (no. 102) – bronze socketed axe and flint dagger of type II, found in a barrow-grave (before the War at the Dzieduszycki Museum, Lwów).
8, 9. Komarów – copper shaft-hole axe and copper (or bronze ?) knife, found in the nineteenth century on the site of the settlement investigated subsequently in 1935 (at the Historical Museum, Lviv, no. 1639).
10. Sapohów, district of Stanisławów – copper shaft-hole axe (State Archaeological Museum, Warsaw).
11. Avramovka near Dniepropetrovsk – winged bronze celt of Lusatian type (before the War at the Archaeological Museum, Dniepropetrovsk, no. 9).
13. Komarów 48 – stone battle-axe (b-6).
14. Radzimin IV–1878 (no. 155) – small diorite battle-axe.
15. Komarów 20 – small stone battle-axe (f–3).
16. Krasów IV (no. 67) – whetstone or unperforated hammer (g-3).

Plates

PLATE 1. Views of a few burials in barrow-graves.

1. Ozimina II (no. 53). The almost completely decayed skeleton.
2. Płaucza Wielka (no. 75). Skeleton of grave 1, with legs contracted (Plate 6:22).
3. Balice XVI (no. 1). Skeleton in an extended position, a flint dagger in its right hand (Plate 11: 2), stone battle-axe in the left hand (Plate 10:10) and mace-head near its right shoulder (Plate 10:9) (after A. Chizzola).
4. Rusiłów (no. 84). Crouched skeleton on its right side, a stone slab behind it (Plate 8:1) (after J. Bryk).
5. Rokitno 3 (no. 82). Crouched skeleton on its left side.

1 

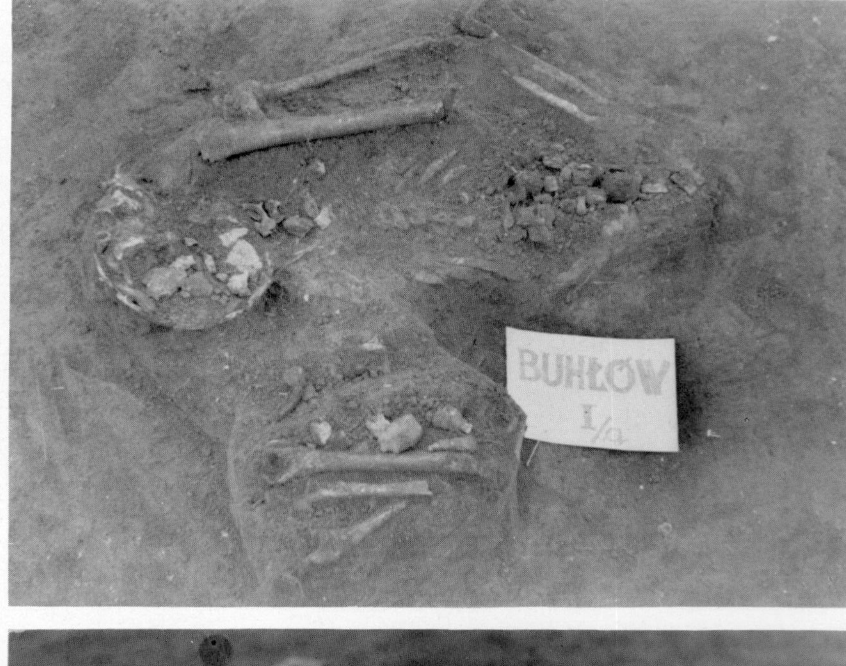

3

2 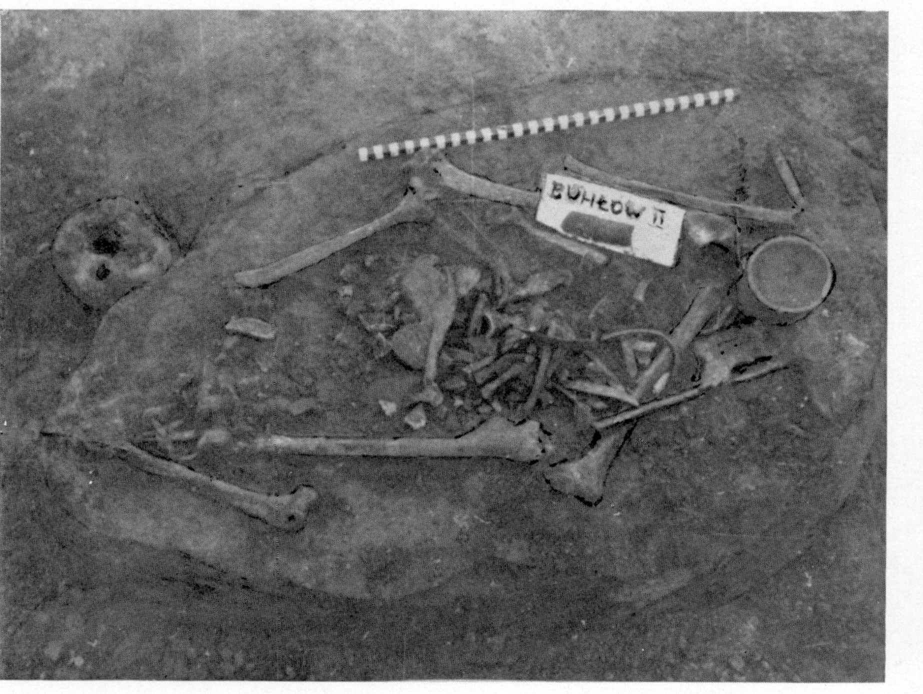

4

PLATE 2. A few burials with mutilated skeletons in barrow-graves.

1, 2. Buhłow II (no. 194). Two views of the dismembered skeleton in grave 2, the skull displaced, the single-lugged mug among the bones (Plate 9: 6, 10, 11).

3. Buhłow I. Dismembered skeleton of grave 'a'.

4. Komarów 38 (no. 47). Grave-goods indicating the site of the burial (Fig. 13:8, Fig. 15:12, Fig. 16:10).

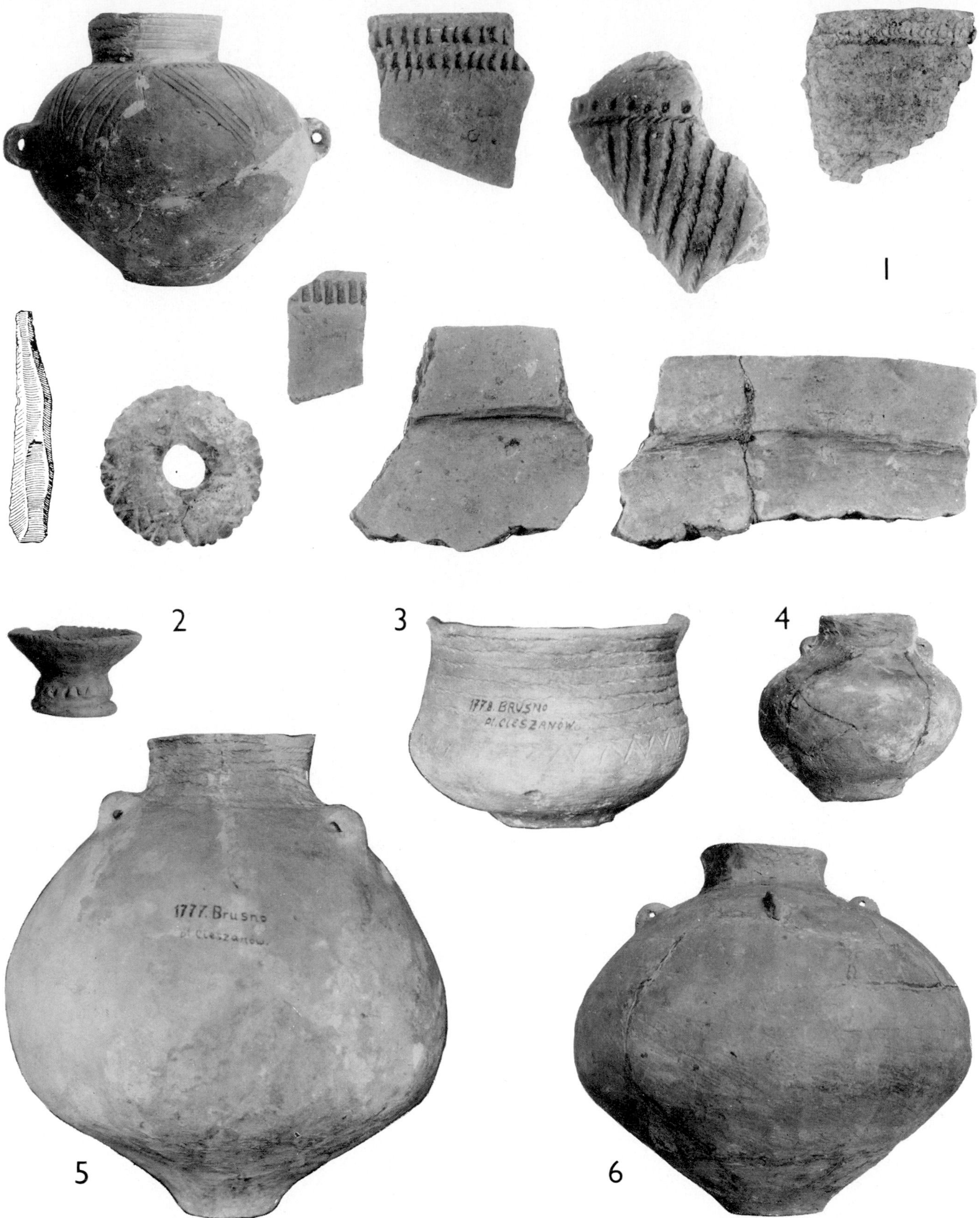

PLATE 3. Pottery of the Przemyśl group of barrow-graves.

1. Koropuż (no. 17). Grave-goods: Thuringian amphora (a) of type I; flint knife (b); bone disc (g); cord-decorated potsherd (d); a few sherds typical of the Funnel Beaker ware (c, e, f, h).

2, 6. Balice VII (no. 1). Small pedestalled dish and a Miechów amphora.

3–5. Brusno (no. 2). Bowl, small amphora and Miechów amphora.

PLATE 4. Thuringian amphorae and a few other vessels from Sub-Carpathian barrow-graves.

1. Kołokolin IV (no. 66) – 'a', type I.
2. Balice XV (no. 1) – type IIC.
3. Załuże (no. 167) – dark double-handled vessel.
4. Lisieczyńce (no. 203) – type I.
5. Krasów II (no. 67) – type I.
6. Ostapie 3 (no. 213) – double-handled vase.
7. Zaborol (no. 188) – a variety of Miechów amphora.
8. Nowosiółka Jaruzelskich III (no. 212) – debased Thuringian amphora of type IIA.
9. Nowosiółka Jaruzelskich II – debased Thuringian amphora of type IIA.

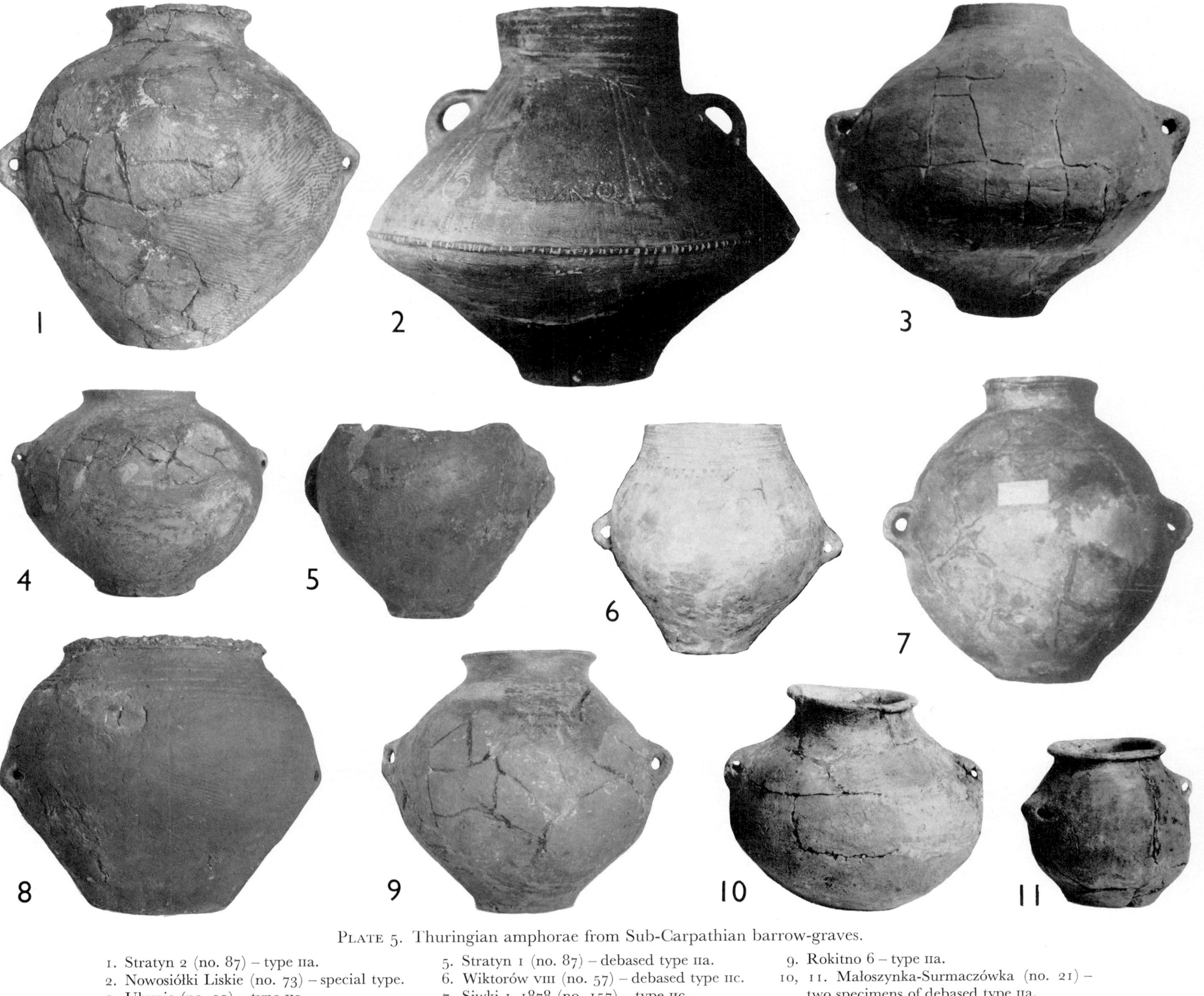

PLATE 5. Thuringian amphorae from Sub-Carpathian barrow-graves.

1. Stratyn 2 (no. 87) – type IIa.
2. Nowosiółki Liskie (no. 73) – special type.
3. Ubynie (no. 90) – type IIa.
4. Kulczyce Szlacheckie II (no. 49) – type IIa.
5. Stratyn I (no. 87) – debased type IIa.
6. Wiktorów VIII (no. 57) – debased type IIc.
7. Siwki I–1878 (no. 157) – type IIc.
8. Rokitno 2 (no. 82) – debased type IIc.
9. Rokitno 6 – type IIa.
10, 11. Małoszynka-Surmaczówka (no. 21) – two specimens of debased type IIa.

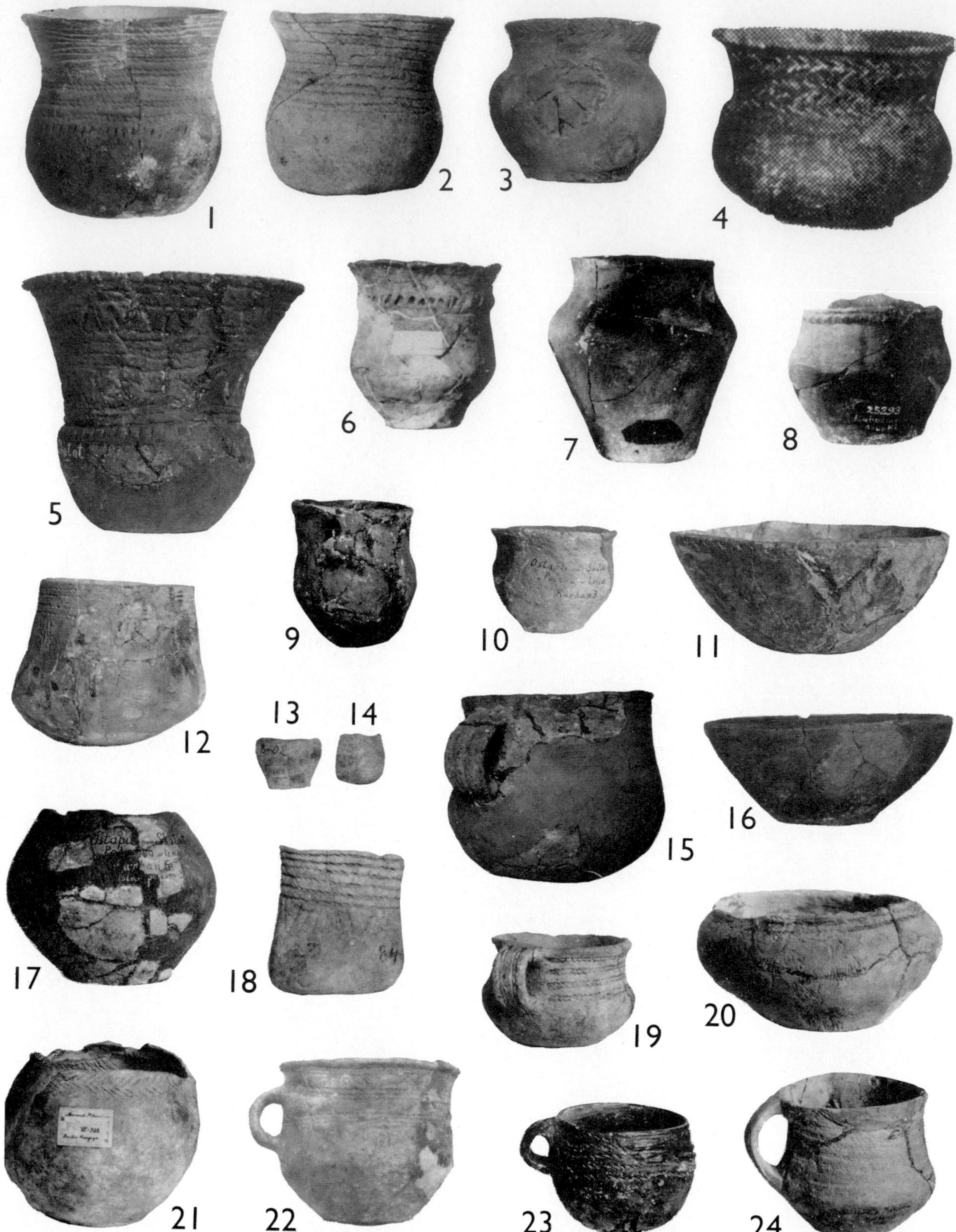

Plate 6. Beakers, bowls and cups from the Sub-Carpathian barrow-graves.

1, 9, 20. Kołokolin I (no. 66) – cord-decorated beaker (M), undecorated beaker (N), and damaged bowl (L).
2. Nowosiółki (Przemyśl) (no. 25) – cord-decorated beaker.
3, 15, 16. Łotatniki 2 (no. 50) – beaker (b), handled bowl (a), wide deep bowl (c).
4. Komarów 39 (no. 47) – wide beaker or bowl (a).
5. Ostapie 5 (no. 213) – beaker.
6. Siwki I–1878 (no. 157) – beaker.
7, 8. Nowosiółki Liskie (no. 73) – pot and beaker.
10. Ostapie 3 – undecorated cup.
11. Balice XVI (no. 1) – wide bowl.
12. Kulczyce Szlacheckie III (no. 49) – beaker (H).
13, 14, 18. Siedliska B (no. 30) – two small cups and beaker.
17. Ostapie 6 (no. 213) – vessel from grave 2.
19. Kołokolin III (no. 66) – 'Złota' cup (k–1) from grave 1.
21. Morawsko (no. 24) – large beaker.
22. Płaucza Wielka (no. 75) – handled jug from grave 1.
23. Dziedziłów (no. 62) – cord-decorated 'Złota' handled cup.
24. Balice IV – cord-decorated 'Złota' handled cup.

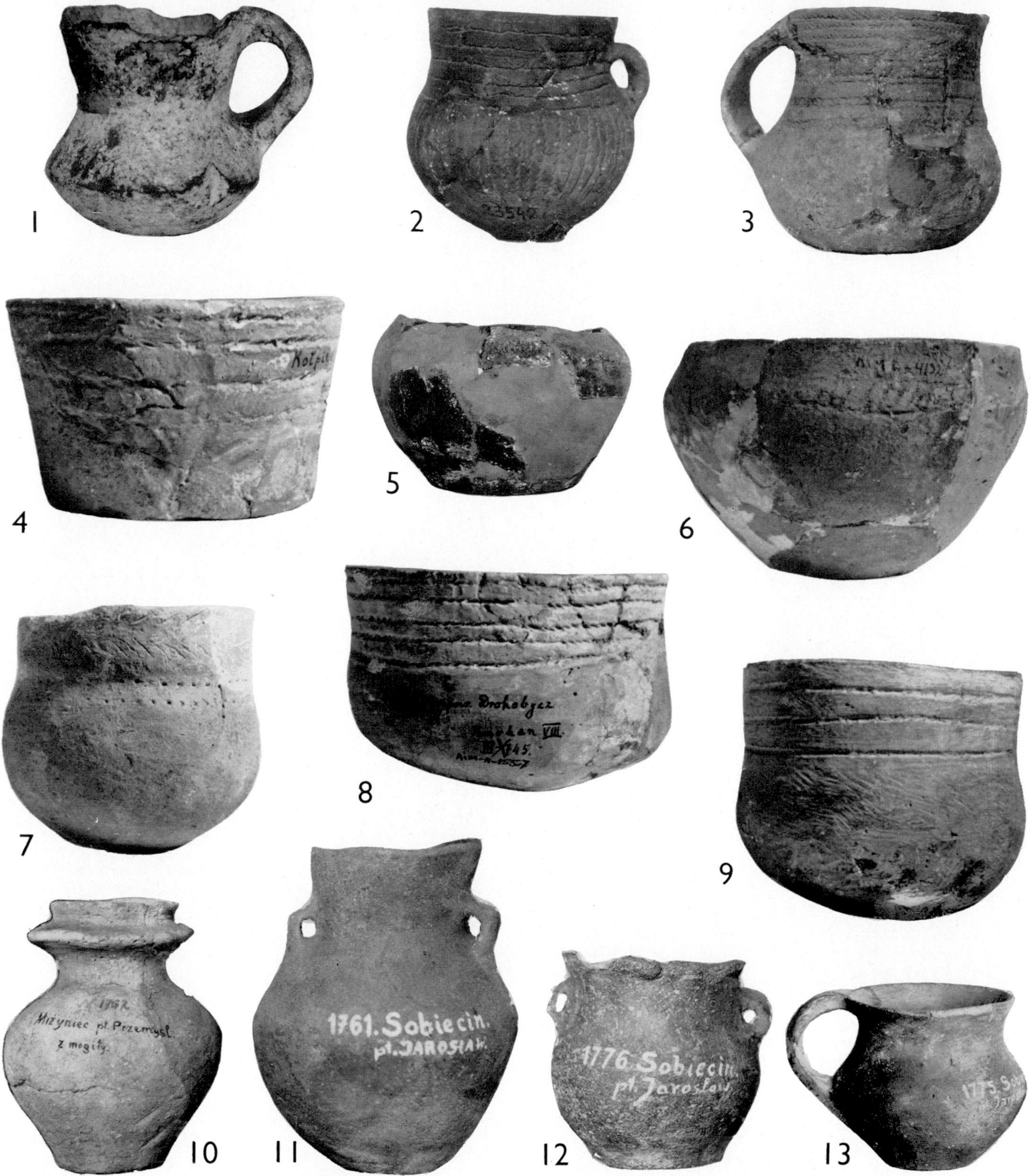

PLATE 7. Various vessels from Sub-Carpathian barrow-graves.

1 Rohatyn (no. 81) – handled cup of Mad'arovce type.
2. Jaktorów II (no. 63) – cord-decorated handled cup (after J. Pasternak).
3. Jaktorów IV – cord-decorated handled cup (after J. Pasternak).
4. Kołpiec 9 (no. 46) – cord-decorated basin.
5. Kołokolin III (no. 66) – damaged bowl (b) from grave 2.
6, 7. Kołokolin II – bowl (c) and beaker (a).
8. Kołpiec 8 – bowl (c-1).
9. Kołpiec 10 – bowl.
10. Miżyniec (no. 22) – collared flask.
11–13. Sobiecin (no. 33) – amphora, handled beaker and handled vase.

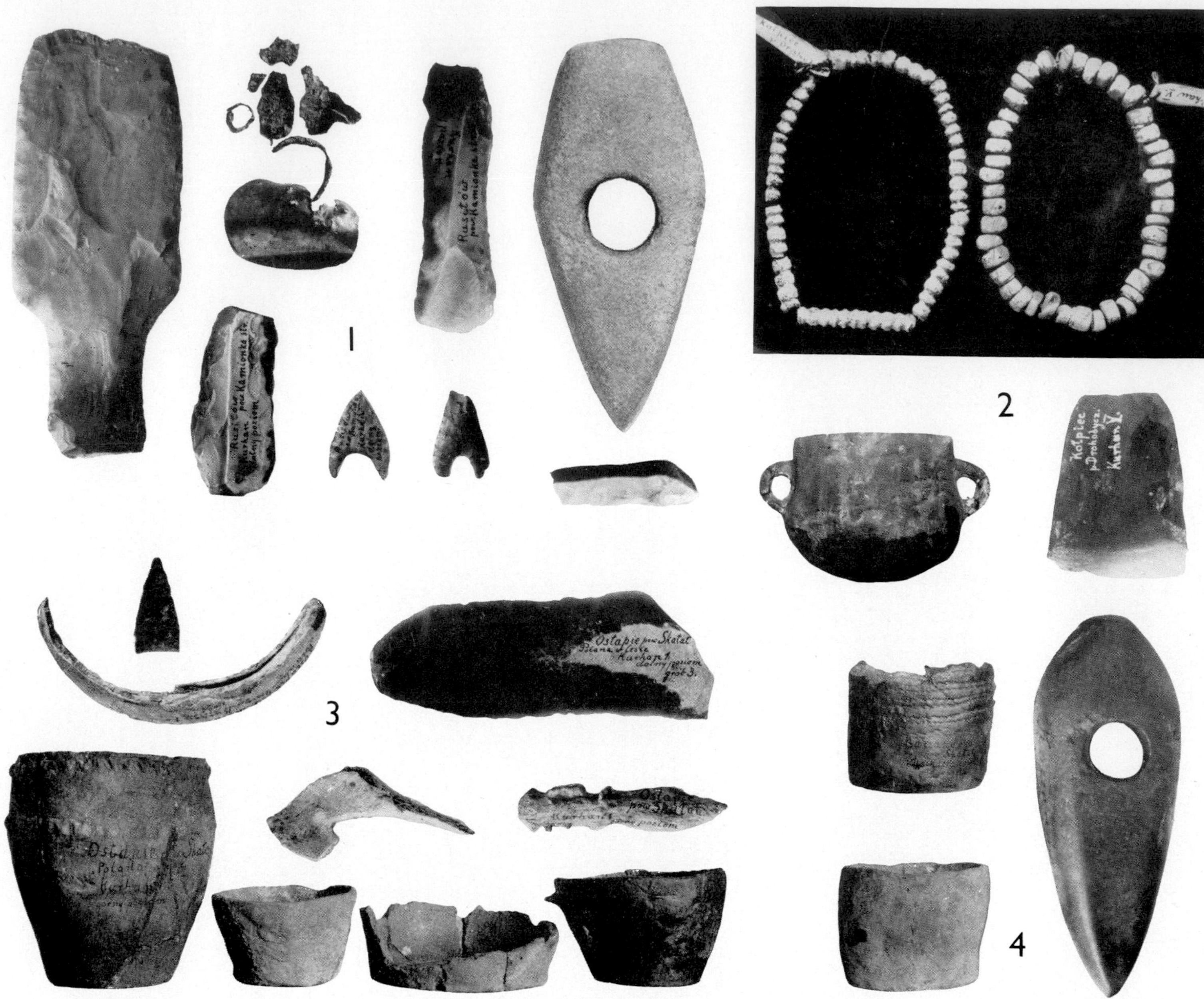

PLATE 8. Grave-goods of a few Sub-Carpathian barrow-graves.

1. Rusiłów (no. 84) – broken dagger, 'Irish' gold ear-pendant repaired and provided with a bronze ring, flint knives, stone battle-axe and flint arrow-heads.
2. Kołpiec 5 (no. 46) – faience beads, some segmented, double handled cup and flint axe.
3. Ostapie I (no. 213) – objects from grave 3: flint arrow-head and flint blade; from grave 2: boar tusk; from secondary grave I: decorated pot, cup, base of a larger vessel, single-lugged mug and two points made of roe antler.
4. Kaczanówka IV (no. 198) – two cups and stone battle-axe.

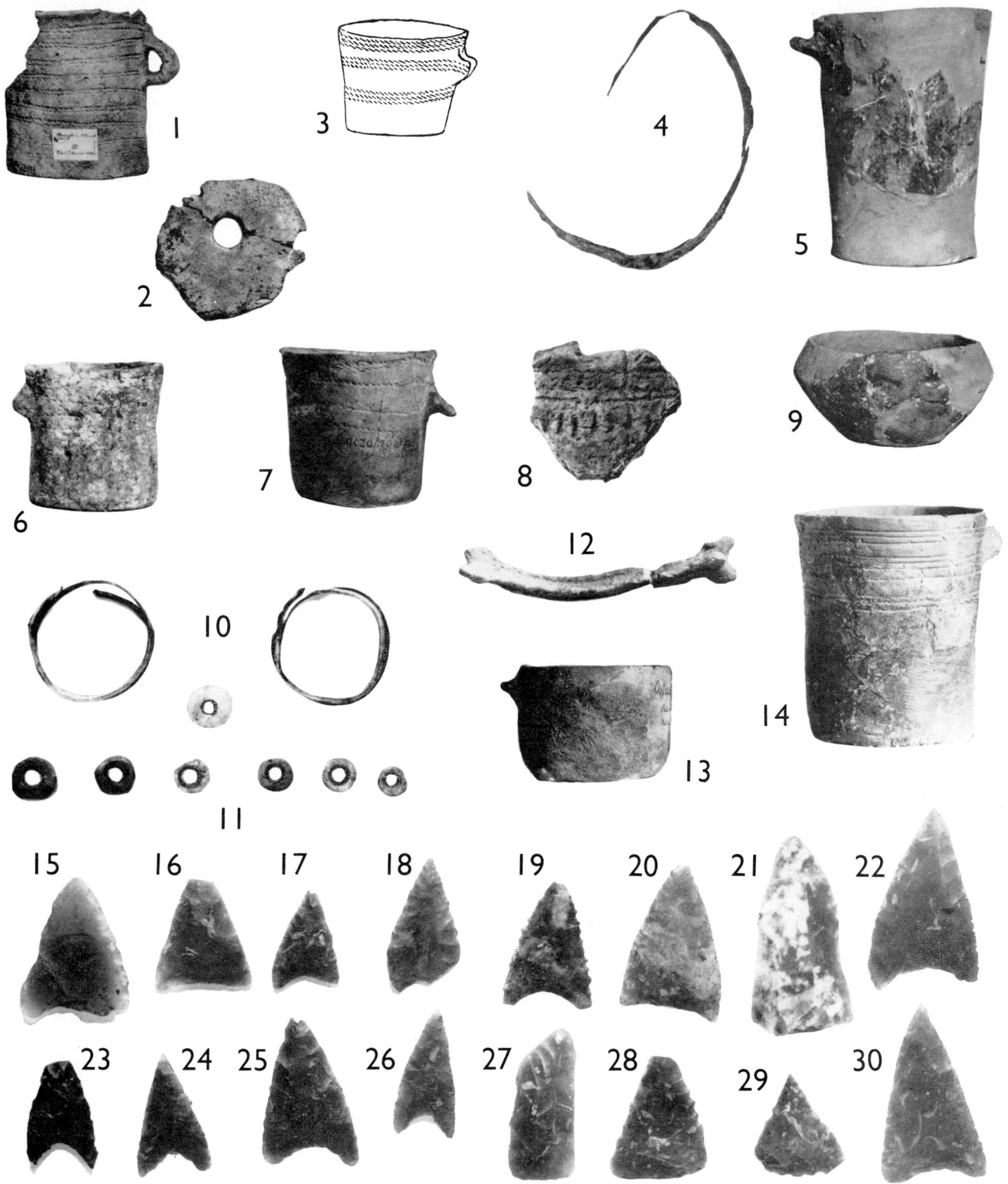

Plate 9. Various grave-goods from Sub-Carpathian barrow-graves.

1, 2. Chorostków I (no. 195) – handled mug and amber disc.
3. Nowa Sieniawa (no. 592) – single-lugged mug.
4–5, 9. Gwoździec Stary II (no. 101) – bronze ear-pendant (s), single-lugged mug (k), dark coloured vessel (h).
7, 8. Kaczanówka III (no. 198) – single-lugged mug and pot-sherd.
6, 10, 11. Buhłow II (no. 194) – single-lugged mug (d), two silver rings and seven bone beads (e, f), all from grave 2.
12, 13. Ostapie 4 (no. 213) – bronze ornament and single-lugged mug.
14. Okniany I (no. 106) – single-lugged mug (a).

Flint arrow-heads from:

15. Komarów 20 (no. 47) – f-1.
16. Komarów 34 – s.
17, 23, 24, 26. Komarów 39 – f.
18. Komarów 21 – b.
19, 22. Kołokolin VII (no. 66) – B,C.
20, 21, 30. Okniany II (no. 106).
25. Kołokolin I – g.
27. Komarów 37 – g. 28, 29. Komarów settlement – g.

PLATE 10. 'Showy' stone battle-axes from Sub-Carpathian barrow-graves.

1. Kołokolin IV (no. 66) – 'Baltic type' (b).
2. Morawsko (no. 24) – type 'A'.
3. Kołokolin III, grave 1 – knob-shaped butt, blade reconstructed (i).
4. Gwoździec Stary I (no. 101) – (a).
5. Kołokolin V – 'Baltic type' (d).
6, 7. Myszyn (no. 104) – type 'B-1' (c), and type 'H–E3' (e).
8. Łotatniki II (no. 50) – 'shoe-last type' (d) made of yellow slate.
9, 10. Balice XVI (no. 1) – mace head, and axe of 'Fatyanovo type'.
11. Zdołbunów (no. 168) – 'Sofiivka type' (after Отчет Арх. комм. 1918).

PLATE 11. Daggers found in western barrow-graves.

1. Ostrożec (no. 150) – flint, type III.
2. Balice XVI (no. 1) – flint, type I.
3. Balice VI – flint, type I.
4. Kavsko 3 (no. 45) – flint, type II.
5. Kołpiec 4 (no. 46) – flint, (c), type II.
6. Załuże (no. 167) – flint, type II.
7. Ostapie 2 (no. 213) – flint knife or dagger of type II.
8. Korytne (no. 146) – flint, type II.
9. Zdołbunów (no. 168) – flint, type III.
10. Balice XIX (no. 1) – flint, type I.

11, 12. Ostapie 5 (no. 213) – two bone points, or daggers.

13, 14. Rokitno 6 (no. 82) – two horn points.

15, 16. Ostapie 6 – bone point found in the halved female skull, and a point made of antler found near the male skeleton.

17. Ostrów (no. 128) – flint, type II.

PLATE 12. Amphorae of the Eastern Globular Amphora culture, of the earliest stage.

1, 2. Ulwówek III (no. 398) – Kuyavian type.
3. Międzyrzec (no. 435) – globular type.
4, 5. Horodnica on the Zbrucz (no. 494) – Kuyavian type, and a bone object.
6. Uwisła I (no. 518) – Kuyavian type with fish-scale decoration.
7. Hlubičok (no. 492) – globular type.

PLATE 13. Vessels mainly of the western groups of the Eastern Globular Amphora culture.

1–4, 6. Mikołajów (no. 423) – two undecorated amphorae, decorated Kuyavian type and two small amphorae and a bowl.

5. Wola Gródecka (no. 399) – bowl decorated in 'Złota' style.

7. Białokrynica (no. 427) – cord-decorated small globular type.

8–10. Tworyczów (no. 397) – Kuyavian type; undecorated amphora; decorated bowl (after S. Nosek).

11. Kykova (no. 455) – spheric, double-lugged bowl, decorated.

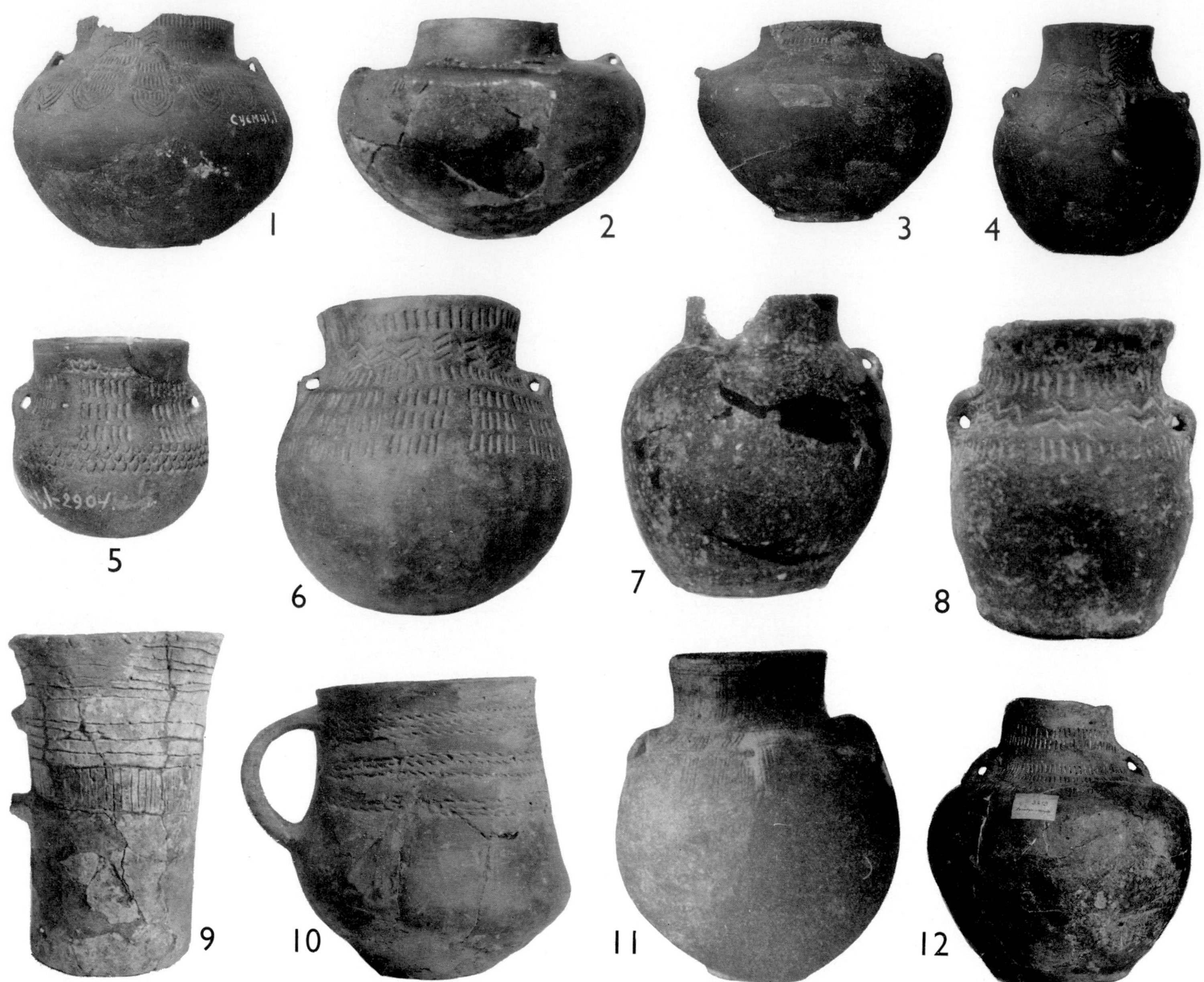

PLATE 14. Vessels mainly of the eastern groups of the Eastern Globular Amphora culture.

1, 5–7. Suyemtsi 1 (no. 459) – Kuyavian amphora, two globular amphorae and a double-lugged undecorated flat-based amphora.
2. Suyemtsi 2 – amphora.
3. Aneta (no. 452) – debased Kuyavian amphora.
4. Skolobiv (no. 475) – four-lugged decorated amphora with a high neck.
8. Vinnitsa (environments) (no. 465) – double-lugged, decorated beaker (a debased globular amphora).
9. Koszyłowce 2 (no. 501) – handled mug.
10. Beremiany 2 (no. 484) – handled jar, cord-decorated.
11. Tartaki (no. 464) – debased Kuyavian amphora.
12. Łosiatyn (no. 250–564) – double-lugged globular amphora with a flat base from a barrow-grave of the Middle Dnieper culture.

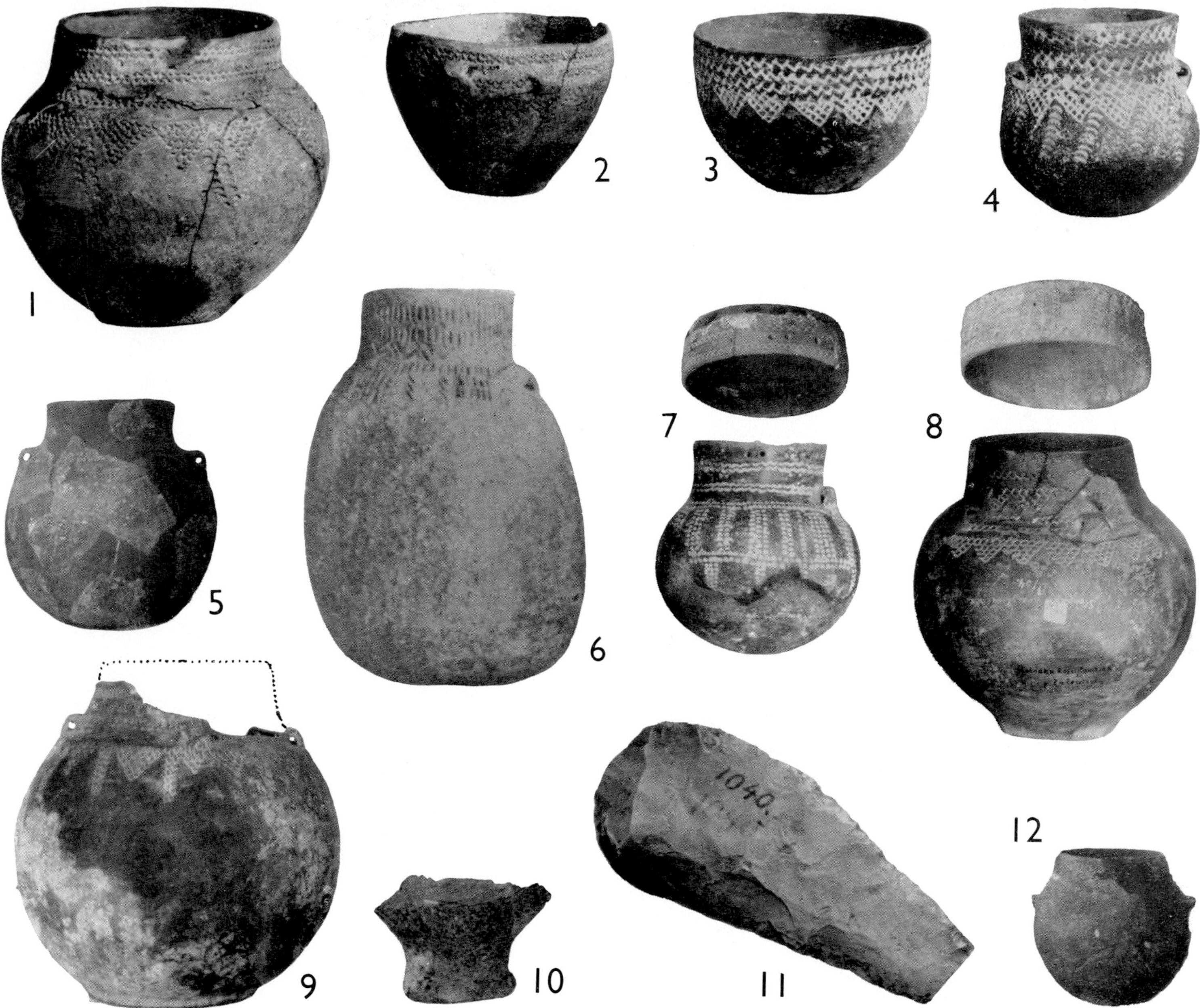

Plate 15. Vessels mainly of the Podolian group of the Eastern Globular Amphora culture.

1–4. Ułaszkowce (no. 516) – Kuyavian amphora, two bowls and globular amphora.
5. Kykova (455) – small double-lugged globular amphora.
6. Voytsekhivka I (no. 460) – debased globular amphora, decorated (after I. Lewyckyj).
7, 8. Słobódka Koszyłowiecka (no. 513) – small globular amphora, and a Kuyavian amphora, both richly decorated and provided with a lid.
9, 10. Velyka Mukš a (no. 519) – Kuyavian amphora and the lower part of a pedestalled vessel.
11. Dublany (no. 419) – flint dagger of type II with the tip broken off.
12. Skolobiv (no. 475) – small double-lugged globular amphora.

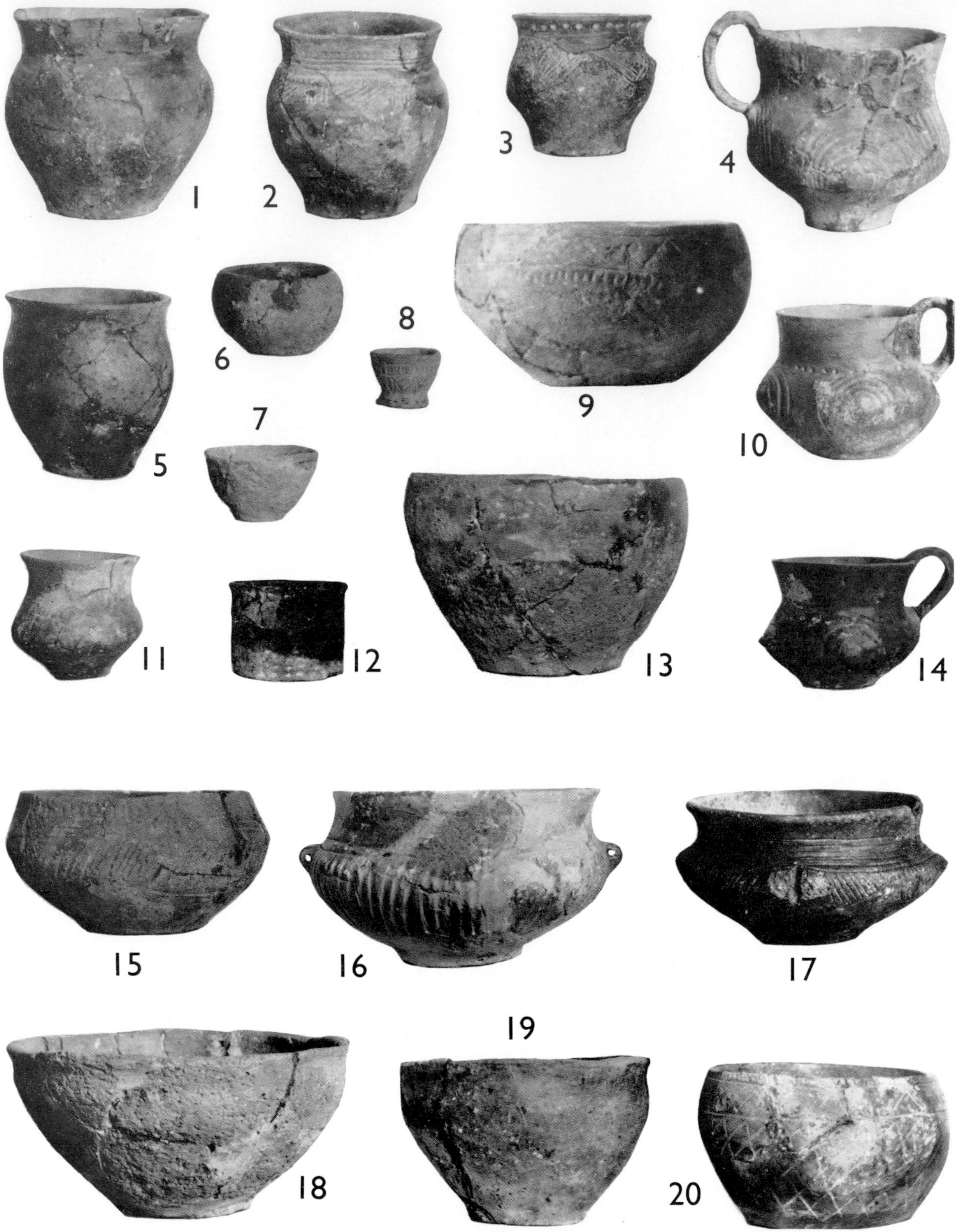

Plate 16. Vessels of periods i and ii of the Komarów culture.

Period I:

1, 7, 8, 10. Komarów 8 (no. 47) – tulip-shaped beaker (b), small cup or bowl (c-3), goblet (c-1), handled cup (e).

2, 6. Komarów 6 – tulip-shaped beaker, decorated (e), and small cup (i-1).

3, 12. Komarów 34 – beaker (iv) and cylindrical cup (vi) from grave B.

4, 11, 14. Komarów 21 – handled cup (1-a), undecorated cup (a-4), and another handled cup (a-2).

5, 9, 13. Komarów 9 – tulip-shaped cup (a-2), decorated (a-3) and undecorated bowls (a-1).

Period II:

15, 16. Okniany ii (no. 106) – decorated bowl (d or v), and another one provided with two perforated lugs (e).

17. Putiatyńce (no. 79) – bowl with vertically perforated protuberance.

18, 20. Komarów 10 – bowls, undecorated (c-2) and decorated (d-2).

19. Czyżyków i (no. 60) – deep bowl (n).

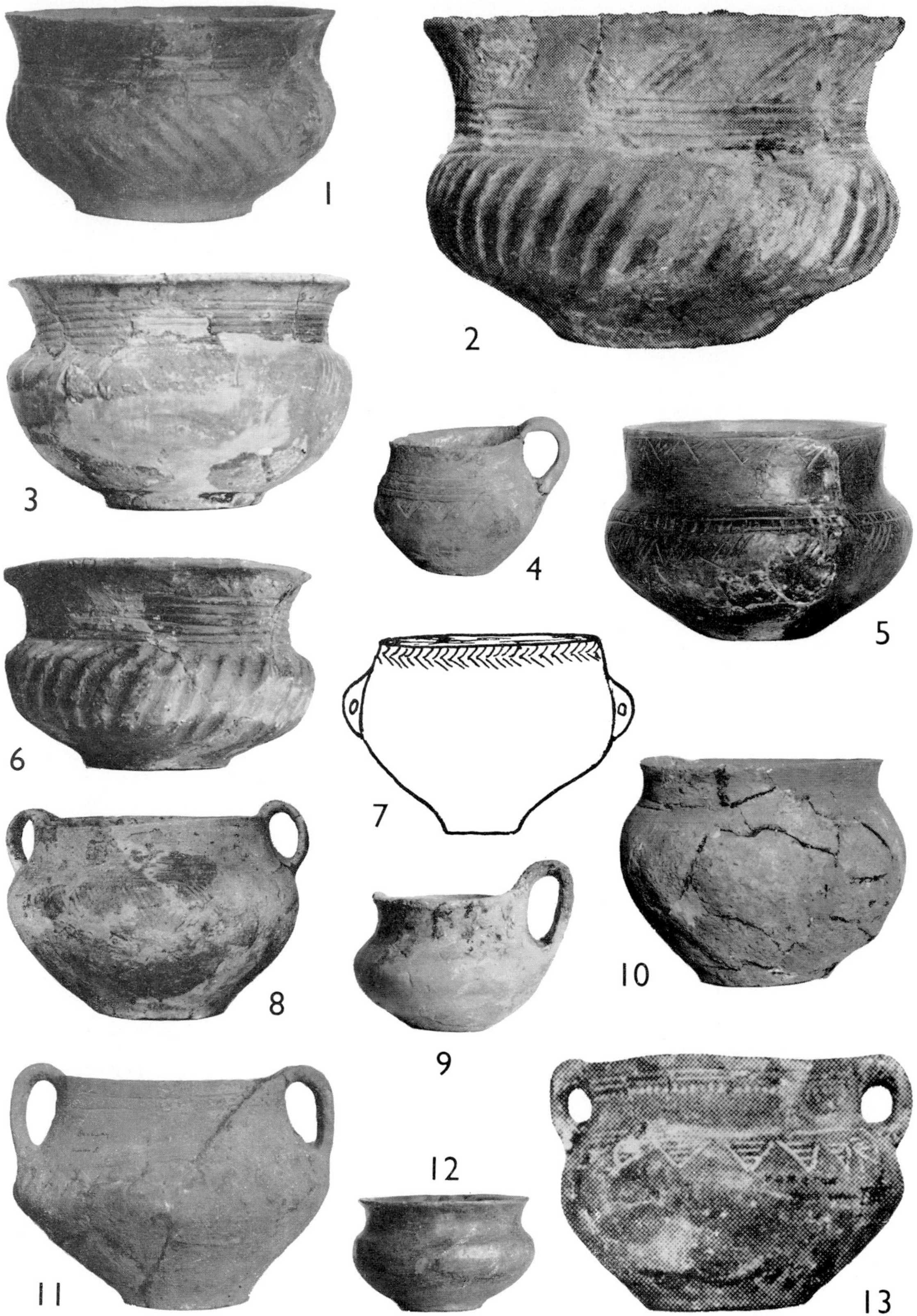

PLATE 17. Vessels of period II of the Komarów culture.

1, 4, 10. Komarów 11 – decorated bowl (a-1), handled cup (p-3) and another decorated bowl (a-2).
2. Bukówna III (no. 97) – decorated bowl (d).
3, 6. Sarniki IV (no. 86) – two bowls (j, i).
5. Komarów 36 – decorated bowl (b).
7. Daszawa II (no. 42) – double-lugged bowl.
8. Komarów 46 – decorated bowl (F).
9, 11. Okniany II (no. 106) – handled cup (i), double-handled vase (h).
12. Czyżyków I (no. 60) – undecorated bowl.
13. Komarów 28 – double-handled vase (j).

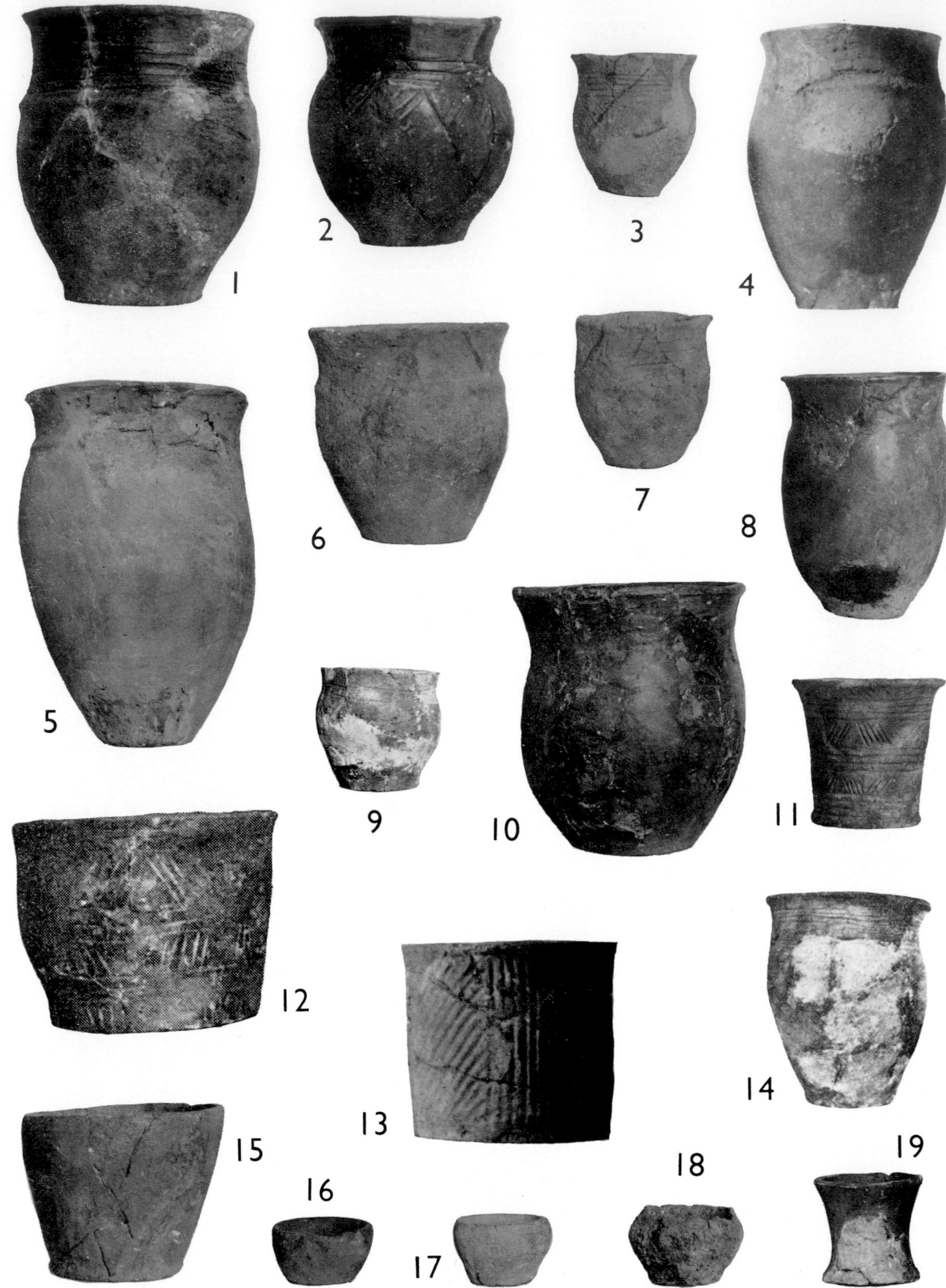

PLATE 18. Vessels of period II of the Komarów culture.

1, 11. Sarniki IV (no. 86) tulip-shaped pot (h) and beaker (n).
2. Czyżków I (no. 60) – decorated tulip-shaped beaker.
3, 5, 7, 8, 16. Komarów 10 – tulip-shaped pots and beakers (d-1-bis, a-1, c-1, f) and small cup (a-2).
4, 6, 15, 17. Okniany II (no. 106) – two tulip-shaped pots (f, b), deep bowl (d or v) and a small cup (x).
9, 13. Komarów 46 – tulip-shaped cup (g) and flowerpot-shaped cup (E).
10. Komarów 23 – tulip-shaped pot (c-1).
12. Bukówna III (no. 97) – decorated cup (j).
14. Komarów 27 – tulip-shaped pot (c).
18. Komarów 11 – small cup (p-1).
19. Komarów 36 – clepsydra-shaped cup (a).

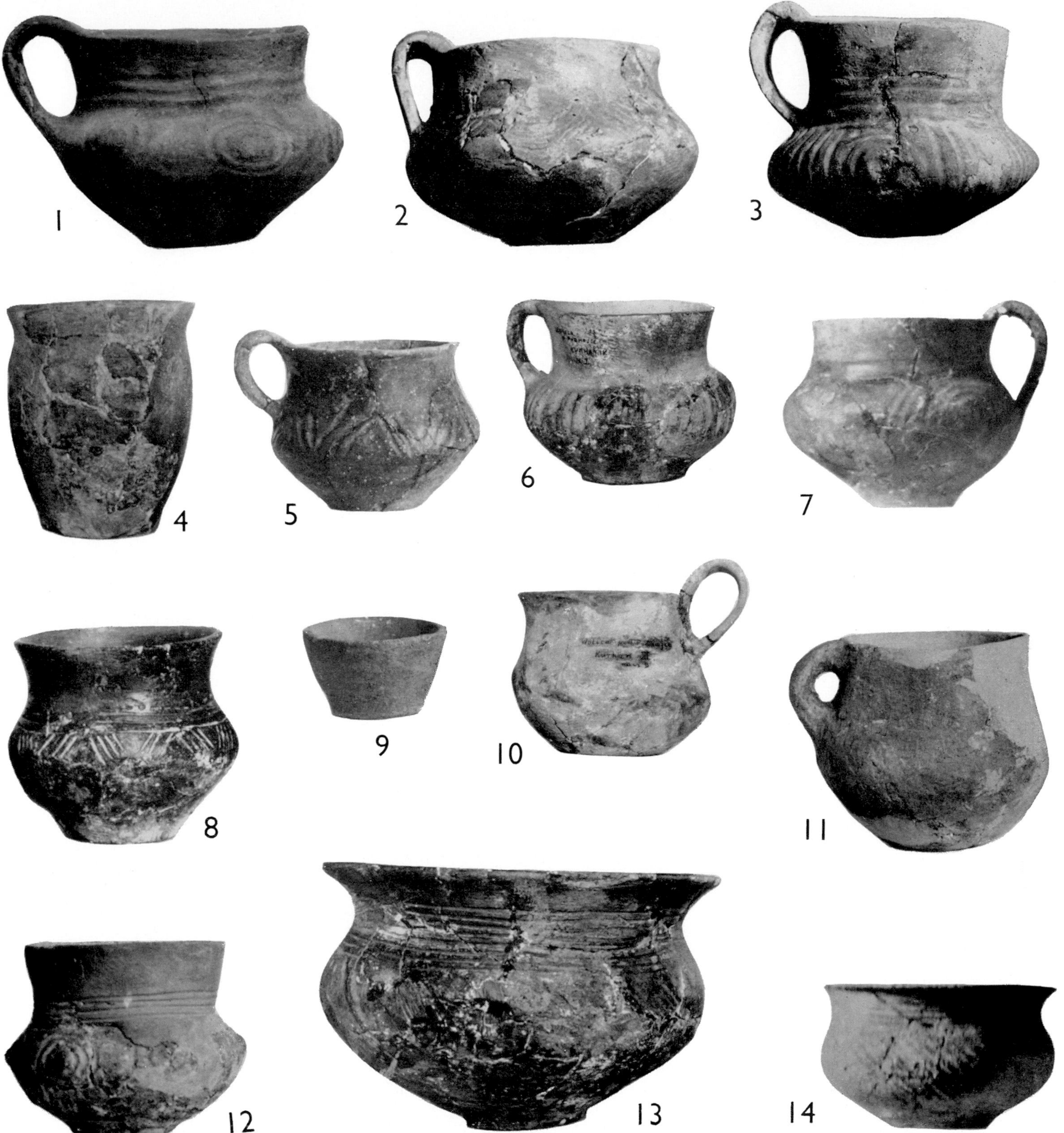

PLATE 19. Vessels of period III of the Komarów culture.

1. Bukówna VI (no. 97) – handled cup.
2, 3. Stopczatów (no. 111) – handled bowl and handled cup (i), from grave A.
4. Komarów 48 – tulip-shaped pot (b-5).
5. Wolica I (no. 91) – handled cup (I).
6–8, 12. Wolica 4 – handled cup (j), handled bowl (g), decorated beaker (c), and decorated cup (f).
9, 11. Krasów III (no. 67) – small cup (A-3) and handled cup (b).
10. Wolica 3 – handled jug (D).
13. Krasów IV – bowl (g-2).
14. Bukówna IV (no. 97) – bowl (F).

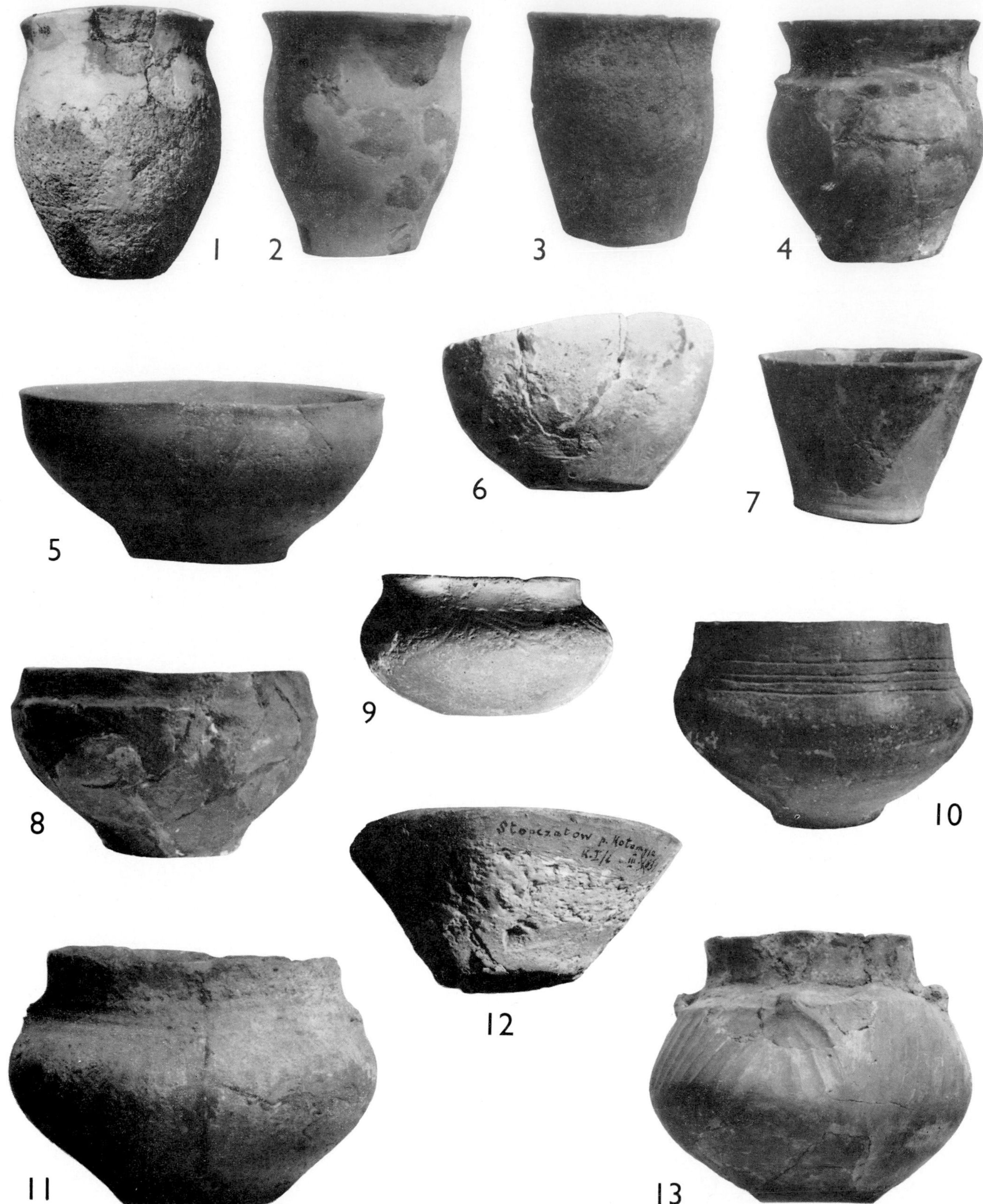

Plate 20. Vessels of period III of the Komarów culture.

1, 6, 9, 12. Stopczatów (no. 111) – tulip-shaped pot (a), small bowl (g-1), cup (g-2) and another small bowl (i-4).

2. Bukówna VI (no. 97) – tulip-shaped beaker (a).

3, 13. Wolica I (no. 91) – tulip-shaped beaker (j) and four-lugged bowl (i).

4. Wolica 4 – tulip-shaped pot (d).

5, 7, 11. Bukówna IV – bowl (G), cup (C) and decorated bowl (D).

8, 10. Krasów III (no. 67) – two bowls (A-2, A-1).

PLATE 21. Vessels of periods III and IV of the Komarów culture.

Period III:

1–7. Komarów 45 – two bowls (g-3, g-7), handled cup (g-4), single-lugged mug (g-4), tulip-shaped pot (g-8), handled bowl (g-1) and deep dish or bowl (g-2).

8–11. Komarów 13 – handled cup (b), small bowl (a), and a cup with a lid (e, d).

Period IV:

12–16. Komarów 33 – tulip-shaped pot (I) *in situ*, three amber beads and two glass beads (a), handled cup (III), small bowl (XI) and another handled cup (II).

PLATE 22. Vessels mainly of period IV of the Komarów-Biały Potok culture.

1, 2. Dubno (no. 170) – beaker and double-handled vase of Noua type.
3, 4. Kulczyce Szlacheckie (no. 49) – wide bowl (dish) and handled cup from the settlement.
5. Semenów (no. 216) – bowl from a barrow-grave.
6. Uwisla 2 (no. 518) – large vase.
7, 8. Podgórzany (no. 594) – tulip-shaped pot and double-handled vase of Noua type (after W. Demetrykiewicz).

PLATE 23. Pottery from Volhynian Bronze Age barrow-graves, except no. 6.

1. Siwki III–1878 (no. 157) – decorated bowl.
2. Korytne II (no. 146) – double-handled vase.
3–5. Staryki (Sternia?) (no. 160) – beaker, stone battle-axe and handled cup.
6. Rakowa I (no. 28) – tulip-shaped pot (I-I, 2).
7. Zaborol 5 (no. 166) – pouch-shaped vessel.
8. Zaborol-Głęboka – pouch-shaped vessel from a destroyed barrow-grave.

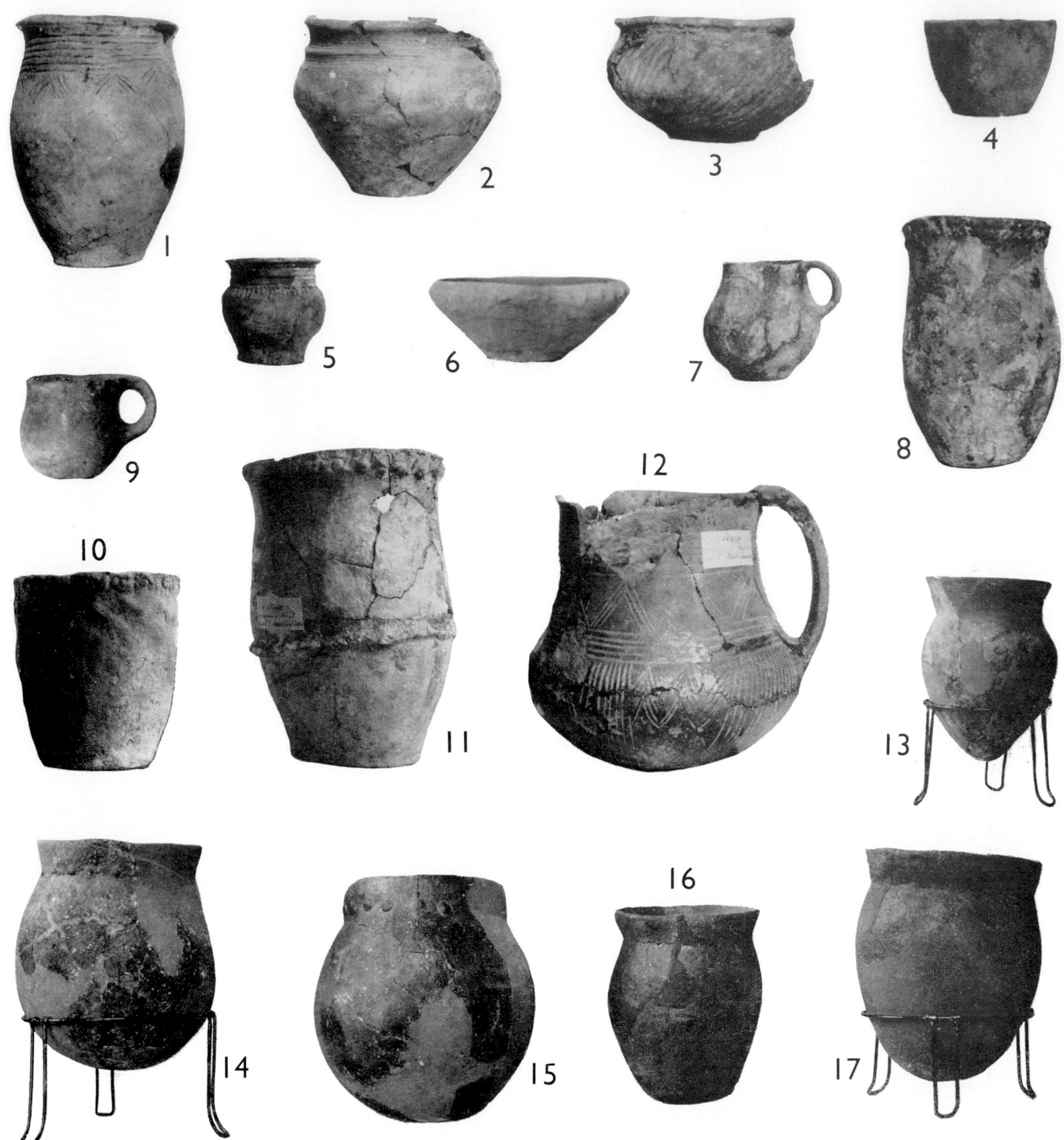

PLATE 24. Pottery from Volhynian Bronze-Age barrow-graves.

1–5. Zaborol 4 (no. 166) – tulip-shaped pot (D), vase (C or E), decorated bowl (A), undecorated cup (B-2), beaker (B-1).
6. Siekierzyńce C (no. 156) – deep dish.
7. Zaborol G – handled cup.
8. Zaborol F – tulip-shaped pot with a row of bosses under the rim.
9. Radzimin II–1876 (no. 155) – undecorated handled cup.
10–12. Radzimin I–1878 – cup, pot and handled jug.
13. Kupyšce (no. 225) – beaker with a pointed base.
14. Narodyči (no. 229) – pouch-shaped vessel from a grave.
15. Selets (no. 233) – pouch-shaped vessel from a barrow-grave.
16, 17. Kurbativka (no. 226) – beaker and pouch-shaped vessel, from barrow-graves at site 'Hremyače'.